1.50

DEVELOPMENTAL RESEARCH METHODS

Scott A. Miller
University of Florida

PRENTICE-HALL, INC.
Englewood Cliffs, New Jersey 07632

Library of Congress Cataloging-in-Publication Data

MILLER, SCOTT A. (date)
   Developmental research methods.

   Includes index and bibliography.
   1. Developmental psychology—Research—Methodology.
I. Title. [DNLM: 1. Human Development. 2. Psychology—
methods. 3. Research—methods. BF 713 M651r]
BF713.M56 1987   155'.0724   86-4979
ISBN 0-13-208133-4

Editorial/production supervision and
   interior design: Mary Bardoni
Cover design: Lundgren Graphics, Ltd.
Manufacturing buyer: Barbara Kelly Kittle

© **1987 by Prentice-Hall, Inc.**
A Division of Simon & Schuster
Englewood Cliffs, New Jersey 07632

Printed in the United States of America

10   9   8   7   6   5   4   3   2

ISBN   0-13-208133-4   01

PRENTICE-HALL INTERNATIONAL (UK) LIMITED, *London*
PRENTICE-HALL OF AUSTRALIA PTY. LIMITED, *Sydney*
PRENTICE-HALL CANADA INC., *Toronto*
PRENTICE-HALL HISPANOAMERICANA, S. A., *Mexico*
PRENTICE-HALL OF INDIA PRIVATE LIMITED, *New Delhi*
PRENTICE-HALL OF JAPAN, INC., *Tokyo*
PRENTICE-HALL OF SOUTHEAST ASIA PTE. LTD., *Singapore*
EDITORA PRENTICE-HALL DO BRASIL, LTDA., *Rio de Janeiro*
WHITEHALL BOOKS LIMITED, *Wellington, New Zealand*

To
Pat, Erica,
and Kevin

CONTENTS

PREFACE

This book is intended for anyone who wants to learn more about how to do research in developmental psychology. It does not teach everything about how to do research—no book could. But it does, I hope, provide a helpful basis, a set of guidelines and principles that can aid in both the execution of one's own research and the evaluation of the research of others.

I have tried to strike a balance between the general and the specific. This balance is reflected in the book's organization: an initial four and final three chapters that discuss general matters, with four (somewhat lengthier) chapters in between devoted to specific research topics in developmental psychology. The balance is also reflected in the approach that is taken to discussing research. This book is neither an abstract "design and analysis" treatise on the one hand, nor a cookbook of hands-on experiences on the other. It is written instead to reflect the way that I believe most of us actually go about doing research—to convey the issues that must be addressed, the decisions that must be made, and the obstacles that must be overcome at every phase in a research project. I hope that the book captures something of both the excitement and the challenge of doing good research on topics that really do matter.

The primary audience for this book will doubtless come from laboratory or research methods courses in developmental or child psychology. I have assumed that any student in such courses will have had at least one prior course in developmental or child psychology. Other kinds of course work (e.g., statistics, psychological research methods) would be helpful but are not necessary. With suitable adjustments by the instructor (e.g., in supplementary readings, lecture and discussion material, hands-on research experiences), the book should be appropriate for both advanced undergraduates and beginning graduate students.

I am grateful to many people for various kinds of help during the writing of the book.

General support was provided by the Department of Psychology, University of Florida. When typing demands exceeded departmental resources, the University's Division of Sponsored Research provided special assistance.

John Isley was the Psychology Editor at Prentice-Hall during the first two-thirds of the book's unexpectedly long gestational period. John was invariably helpful, responsive, and—above all—patient. Susan Willig assumed the editor's role during the last phase of the book's development, and she proved to have exactly the same qualities. My thanks to both.

Among the good services performed by the Prentice-Hall editorial staff was the recruitment of an outstanding group of reviewers. I am happy to thank the following reviewers who read and commented upon various parts of the book: Daniel B. Kaye of the University of California at Los Angeles, Marsha Liss of California State University at San Bernardino, Marion Perlmutter of the University of Michigan at Ann Arbor, Michael Pressley of the University of Western Ontario, and Patricia Worden of California State University at Fullerton. I would like to add a special thanks to James Algina, a colleague at the University of Florida, for his comments on the Statistics chapter.

Although he had no direct involvement with this book, I also owe a debt of gratitude to John Flavell. John was a formative influence during my graduate training, and he is still my (and many people's) model of what a developmental psychologist should be.

My deepest thanks are to my wife Pat, not only for her comments on every chapter of the book but for many other things as well.

chapter 1

INTRODUCTION

A topic of much recent research in developmental psychology has been young children's egocentrism. Egocentrism refers to an inability to break away from one's own perspective to take into account the perspectives of others. That others do not experience the world in exactly the same way that we do—see what we see, know what we know, wish what we wish—seems obvious to older children or adults. This fact is not always obvious to young children, however. Instead, young children often seem to operate as though they assume that everyone shares their own particular point of view upon the world—hence the label "egocentric."

Consider how the young child responds to an experimental task in which he is asked to imagine that he is buying a birthday present for his mother (Flavell, Botkin, Fry, Wright, & Jarvis, 1968). An array of gifts, selected to vary in both age-appropriateness and sex-appropriateness, is laid out before the child. Does the child head immediately for the silk stockings or grown-up

books? While such a response is possible, it is not very common among 3- or 4-year-olds. A more likely response is selection of one of the shiny new toy trucks. The young child knows what he wants; how could mother not want the same?

Textbook writers are in some respects similar to the young child standing before the array of gifts. To them, the interest and importance, even the beauty, of their subject are self-evident. If asked to justify why anyone else should care about the topic, the response may be one of bewilderment or frustration; how could anyone *not* see that this is a fascinating and vitally important subject? One might as well question the value of a shiny new truck!

Nevertheless (and here comes the egocentrism), it is difficult to see that any justification is needed for an interest in research in developmental psychology. What could be more obvious than the need to study how people develop? If some further justification *is* re-

1

quested, it is easy to provide. Certainly no branch of psychology is broader in scope than developmental. And certainly no branch of psychology addresses more fundamental scientific issues than does developmental. For developmental psychology simultaneously encompasses all the other areas of the field (perception, thinking, personality, etc.) and adds to them a single basic question: How do people get to be the way they are? How is it, for example, that virtually all people come to understand and use an incredibly complex language system? Where do individual differences in intelligence or personality come from? What are the effects of early childrearing practices on later development? Questions such as these cut to the heart of what psychology as a science can potentially tell us.

Such questions are not only of scientific interest. More obviously than any other branch of the field, developmental psychology speaks to issues that make a difference in the lives of everyone. Consider again some of the questions posed in the preceding paragraph. The issue of early experience and later development may be a fascinating scientific problem for the researcher, but it is a matter of urgent practical importance for any parent concerned with the optimal development of his or her child. That people differ in intelligence may raise a number of intriguing theoretical questions, but this fact also has enormous interpersonal and societal consequences. One of the exciting things about being a developmental psychologist is this feeling that one is dealing with questions that really matter.

Answers to such questions do not come easily, however. Indeed, it often seems that the most basic and important questions are the hardest to resolve. The difficulty of doing good research is a continuing theme throughout our discussions, and hence need not be documented here. But let us briefly consider one example to introduce some general points. It is a problem that we have already touched on twice: drawing a relation between parental childrearing practices and child development. How might this problem be studied scientifically?

To anyone with even a rudimentary background in scientific methods, the general answer to this question is obvious: through controlled experimental study (if this answer is *not* obvious, it should become so in chapter 2). What might be done, for example, is to randomly assign infants at birth to families of different backgrounds and different childrearing philosophies. Effects of childrearing practice could then be determined apart from the contributions of the parents' genes to the children's development. Or the researcher might decide to assign different childrearing practices on a random basis to different families. This procedure would avoid the confounding factor of parental choice in childrearing and allow a clear focus on the childrearing methods themselves. The researcher might even decide, for purposes of comparison, to include a group of parents who rear their own children in whatever way they wish. In any case, the children would be studied as they grew, and extensive measures would be taken of their development. If such research could be carried out for even a few years, we would know much more about the consequences of different methods of childrearing than we do now.

Needless to say, the research program just outlined is the stuff of science fiction (or of methods textbooks), not fact. We do not have experiments of this sort, and it is to be hoped that we never will.[1] In this case the ethical problems are clearly sufficient to prohibit the research. If they were not, the practical difficulties

---

[1]There *are* accounts, perhaps apocryphal, of ancient rulers who carried out quite systematic experiments in childrearing. One story concerns a 13th century king named Frederick II whose experiment, like many a contemporary study, produced some interesting data but not of the sort that Frederick intended:

> He bade foster mothers and nurses to suckle the children, to bathe and wash them, but in no way to prattle with them, or to speak to them, for he wanted to learn whether they would speak the Hebrew language, which was the oldest, or Greek, or Latin, or Arabic, or perhaps the language of their parents, of whom they had been born. But he laboured in vain because the children all died. For they could not live without the petting and joyful faces and loving words of their foster mothers. (Ross & McLaughlin, 1949, p. 366)

in actually carrying out such studies would be staggering. These two factors—ethical limitations and practical constraints—act to rule out many well-designed, "textbook-like" experiments that any developmental psychologist could easily dream up. The result is that we have to fall back upon less scientifically satisfactory methods of gathering the desired information. That such methods *do* exist, and that they lead to genuine gains in knowledge, is another one of our continuing themes. But the appropriate methods and the resulting knowledge often do not come easily.

The main points of our discussion thus far are easy to summarize. Developmental psychology addresses questions that are of both great scientific and great practical importance. Studying such questions is often very difficult, and these difficulties place serious constraints on what can be known. Nevertheless, methods of study do exist, and gains in knowledge are being made literally every day. What we have, then, is a field of study in which the potential benefits of research are great, the challenges to successful study formidable, and the progress in knowledge slow but meaningful—in short, an ideal place for an ambitious researcher.

GOALS OF THE BOOK

This book has three general goals. The first and most obvious is to help promote the skills necessary to do good research in developmental psychology. To this end, principles and precepts of various sorts are presented. Some of these principles are specific to issues of development; others are more general to the field of psychology. Some, indeed, are not even specific to psychology but reflect applications of the general scientific method. Whenever possible, however, we embed the discussion within the context of developmental issues. And, as already suggested, developmental psychology presents enough methodological problems of its own to challenge any researcher.

A second goal is to provide exposure to important research areas within the field. No one, after all, does "research in development"; studies are always directed to some particular content area, and every content area presents its own set of methodological challenges. It is impossible in one book to cover every interesting topic in the field, or to convey everything that should be conveyed about any given topic. But a start can be made on some of the most interesting and well-studied topics.

The third goal is to foster skills necessary for critically evaluating research and the conclusions that can be drawn from research. Such skills, of course, are not separate from those needed to carry out studies, but for most of us they are likely to be used far more often. Not everyone is going to do research in developmental psychology, but everyone is a consumer of the results of such research. Consider again some of the practical issues for which research in developmental psychology is relevant. Is physical punishment ever justified when disciplining children, or should such techniques be avoided altogether? Does violence on TV promote aggression in children? Should early enrichment programs be provided for so-called "culturally disadvantaged" children? Should children in school be "tracked" according to ability levels, or is such tracking detrimental to some children's development? And what sort of research programs, if any, should the federal government support? Questions such as these are of interest to every parent, taxpayer, or voter. Intelligent answers to the questions are most likely if one knows the conclusions that have been drawn from relevant research. Intelligent answers are even more likely if one knows the methodology behind the research and can sensibly weigh the various strengths, weaknesses, and uncertainties when evaluating the conclusions.

STEPS IN A RESEARCH PROGRAM

What are the things that must go right in the course of a study if the final product is to be an increment in knowledge? The answer is quite a number of things, most of which are discussed at length in later sections. The purpose of the present section is simply to provide an introductory orientation to the skills that are needed to do good research. In so doing we move in order from the start of a study through to its completion.

The starting point for any successful program of research is *good ideas*. This is at once the most obvious and the least teachable of the various requirements. Because it is both obvious and difficult to teach, the criterion of good ideas tends to be neglected in discussions of how to do research, the focus instead being on the skills necessary to implement whatever ideas one may have. This neglect holds true in our later discussions as well. It is important to remember, however, that all the technical skill in the world will not save a study if the ideas behind it are not any good. It is important to realize too that the really important differences among researchers—the factors that separate the average researcher from the one whose research shakes the field—lie less in the technical skill with which they execute studies than in their abilities to think in truly original and penetrating ways about an issue.

A second criterion is *knowledge of past work.* Anyone embarking on a program of research must have a thorough knowledge of what has already been done on the topic in question. Indeed, this step might logically be listed as the first, because really good ideas probably cannot be generated without knowledge of what has gone before. In any case, knowledge of the literature is essential when the researcher comes to evaluate just how testworthy his or her ideas are. There is little point in executing a brilliant idea for a study if someone else has already done exactly the same thing. More common perhaps is the case in which certain important points of procedure would be decided differently if the researcher only knew about similar work by others. Few things can be more depressing to an investigator than to go to all the effort of carrying out a study and only then learn that the findings of some earlier study render the effort pointless.

Keeping abreast of the literature is no easy task at a time when professional journals publish thousands of articles in developmental psychology annually. Luckily, helpful sources do exist. The contents of some books and journals consist solely of review articles on major topics; other journals provide cross-referenced abstracts of articles published elsewhere. Some of the most helpful of these sources are listed and briefly described in Table 1-1. Also described in the table are some of the major empirical journals in which research in developmental psychology is published. It is good practice to scan the most recent volumes of these journals for relevant material before making a final decision about procedures. Finally, the best guide to past work may often come not from written

TABLE 1-1   Useful Sources for Background
Research in Developmental Psychology

Journals of Abstracts
Child Development Abstracts and Bibliography
PsycSCAN: Developmental Psychology
Psychological Abstracts
Psychological Reader's Guide

Books with Literature Reviews
Advances in Child Development and Behavior (Volume 1 published in 1963, new volumes at an almost annual rate since)
Advances in Developmental Psychology (Volume 1 published in 1981)
Annual Review of Psychology (published annually since 1950)
Minnesota Symposia on Child Psychology (published annually since 1967)
Mussen, P. H. (Ed.) *Handbook of Child Psychology*, 4th edition, 1983
New Directions for Child Development (multiple volumes each year, the first appearing in 1978)
Review of Child Development Research (seven volumes published to date, the first appearing in 1963)
Wolman, B. B. (Ed.) *Handbook of Developmental Psychology*, 1982

Major Journals in Developmental Psychology
Child Development
Developmental Psychology
Developmental Review
Genetic Psychology Monographs
Human Development
International Journal of Behavioural Development
Journal of Applied Developmental Psychology
Journal of Experimental Child Psychology
Journal of Genetic Psychology
Merrill-Palmer Quarterly
Monographs of the Society for Research in Child Development

sources but from consultations with an experienced researcher in the field. And bibliographic assistance aside, discussing one's ideas with others is generally a helpful part of the problem-solving process.

Once the ideas for the study have been generated, the next step is to translate them into an *adequate experimental design*. It was suggested earlier that a technically perfect design is of little value if the ideas being tested do not merit study. We must now add the converse point: that a brilliant idea may come to nothing if it cannot be embodied in a scientifically testable form. Matters of experimental design are a central topic in the coming chapters. For now, two points can be made. The first is a reiteration of a point made earlier. Very often in developmental psychology, ethical or practical constraints rule out research designs that, from a purely scientific point of view, would be ideal for studying an issue. The challenge then becomes to devise alternative procedures that can lead to valid conclusions. The second point is that designs in developmental psychology are often complicated by the fact that age is included as a variable of primary interest. As we see later, age is in some ways an especially difficult variable with which to work. But, of course, changes with age are of great interest for most developmental psychologists.

We have now brought our hypothetical researcher to the point at which he or she has an idea for a study, has surveyed the relevant literature, and has decided (at least tentatively) on an experimental design. The next step is to carry out a *pilot study*—that is, to do some preliminary testing and practicing before beginning the experiment proper. There are two general reasons for pilot testing. One is to give the tester practice in working with the particular procedures and subject groups, the goal being to minimize experimenter error once the real study starts. The second is to test out any uncertain aspects of the procedure to make certain that they work more or less as intended. Such testing out may often be especially necessary in work with children, because their reactions to particular procedures can be difficult to predict. In addition, it is sometimes neces-

sary in studies with children to make sure that the sample being tested is at the desired developmental level. Suppose, for example, that the experimenter is interested in comparing two different methods of assessing some cognitive ability in children. There would be no point in doing the study if all the children tested were either so immature that they failed both versions of the problem (a so-called "floor effect") or so mature that they passed both versions (a "ceiling effect"). Pilot work can save the experimenter from such problems by identifying samples that are at the desired transitional level.

Our researcher is now ready to begin the actual study. The next step is again an obvious one: *obtaining subjects*. Obvious though this step may seem, it is not discussed in many textbooks on methodology, in which experimental designs somehow magically eventuate in data without the messy intermediate step of finding people on whom to try them. In fact, many researchers spend a good portion of their professional careers, not in the interesting business of thinking up research, but in the much more tedious business of finding subjects with whom to do the research. This is especially true for developmental psychologists, who do not have readily available populations such as college sophomores or laboratory rats with which to work. The researcher of infancy cannot post sign-up sheets on which babies can volunteer for experiments; he or she must somehow locate parents with infants and induce them to bring their babies in for testing. The reseacher who wishes to study large samples of 5-, 7-, and 9-year-olds will almost certainly need to work through a school system in order to find sufficient numbers to test. The investigator of possible changes in functioning with old age will need to locate and recruit elderly subjects, possibly through contacts with various organizations that serve the elderly. All of these subject groups can present special problems of access.

It is difficult to offer specific guidelines with respect to obtaining subjects, because procedures may vary from one locality to another. A few pieces of very general advice can be offered, however. One is to allow plenty of time. Research almost always takes longer than the beginning researcher expects it to, and one common contributor to the delays is difficulty in obtaining subjects. A second piece of advice is to be as persuasive as possible when presenting one's proposed research to those (principals, teachers, parents, subjects themselves) who must decide about participation. As is stressed in chapter 11 on Ethics, the primary consideration when presenting research to prospective subjects is to be honest and informative, so that decisions about participation can be fairly made. It is also important, however, to be clear about the value of the research, or else no one may decide to participate. Finally, perhaps the most helpful course, once again, is to find an experienced investigator of the subject group in question and solicit his or her advice about how to obtain subjects.

Note that the primary problem posed by difficulties in obtaining subjects is not the inconvenience or loss of time suffered by the experimenter. The problem, rather, is that one aspect of proper experimental design is selection of appropriate subject groups. As we see later, an otherwise well-conducted experiment may be of little value if the experimenter has failed to obtain the right kind of subjects.

Once subjects are in hand, the testing can begin. At this point the experimenter's *testing skills* become important. The phrase "testing skills" is used here to refer to all of the abilities needed in actually working with subjects, whether in face-to-face interactions or in observing and measuring behavior. At issue, then, are questions of the following sort: Have the instructions conveyed clearly to the subjects what is required? Has the tester biased performance through facial cues or inadvertent reinforcement? Have the subjects' responses been accurately recorded? The issue, in short, is whether the on-paper study that has been worked out in advance can be adequately realized in the actual experimental setting. Again, it is clear that a successful passage through the earlier steps of the research program will be of no avail if the present step is not also negotiated successfully. A researcher, for example, may have devised a beautiful plan for studying problem solving in 5-year-olds, but the results are

not likely to mean much if he or she has no conception of how to talk to children and consequently leaves the young subjects either frightened or bewildered.

Discussions of testing skills occur at various places in the coming chapters. As noted, some of the points made are general ones that apply to psychology as a whole, and others are specific to developmental psychology. Although any kind of research can be difficult, the researcher in developmental is often faced with special problems that stem from the special nature of the subject groups tested. Skills that are sufficient when testing a college student may not be sufficient when working with a crying infant, a shy preschooler, or a suspicious octogenarian. The challenge is even greater if several distinct age groups must be accommodated within the same study.

No aspect of research methodology can be conveyed in a totally adequate fashion through a textbook alone. For none, however, is a textbook treatment less adequate than for the question of how to work with subjects. Although various guidelines can be given verbally, the only real way to become skilled in working with infants, preschoolers, or elderly people is to spend considerable amounts of time actually working with infants, preschoolers, or the elderly.

The conclusion of the testing does not mean that the researcher's job is done. The next step is the *statistical analysis* of the data. The question that must be answered now is whether the various factors under study have or have not produced a consistent and meaningful pattern of results. For the great majority of studies, the accepted way to answer this question is through application of certain well-developed statistical procedures to the data. This statistical analysis will not, in itself, answer deeper questions about the theoretical or practical significance of the results. But it does set constraints within which such interpretations must operate.

Statistical analysis is a large topic, the subject of separate courses and books. It is not covered at any length in this book. Chapter 10, however, does provide a summary of certain general principles of statistics.

One point about statistics can be made here. The fact that the discussion of statistics has been left until late in the research program does not mean that the researcher can safely disregard statistical questions until all the data are in. It can be quite hazardous, in fact, to complete all the testing for a study and only then begin to wonder whether there are appropriate statistical procedures for the data. This warning does *not* mean that the researcher must decide on every statistical procedure in advance, or even that he or she must anticipate all the comparisons and contrasts that will prove to be of interest. But it is best to be as clear as possible about statistics before beginning testing.

The final phase of a research program is the *communication* of what has been done and found. Science is a matter of shared information, and a research finding is simply not a finding until it has been communicated to others. The usual way to communicate findings in developmental psychology is through publication in a professional journal. Such publication requires that the researcher prepare a clear, accurate, and concise written report of the study. Advice about how to prepare such reports is given in chapter 12.

PLAN OF THE BOOK

The next four chapters deal with general principals of design and procedure. Chapter 2 is, in fact, entitled "General Principles of Research"; it considers such basic concepts as experimental control, measurement, and validity. Chapter 3 is entitled "Subjects and Designs"; its concern is ways of selecting and comparing subjects, with a special focus on methods of comparing different age groups. In chapter 4, "Working with Subjects," the focus shifts from matters of design to matters of procedure, with an emphasis on problems that can arise when testing subjects, as well as ways to minimize the problems. Finally, chapter 5, "Settings and Control," is concerned with the kinds of settings (e.g., structured lab environment, natural "field" setting) in which developmental research occurs, with a consideration of the advantages and disadvantages of each of the various possibilities. The chapter also includes sections on correlational research and observational research.

The middle section of the book is devoted to specific research areas in developmental psychology. Chapter 6 is concerned with methods of studying development in infancy. The next two chapters are topically defined. In chapter 7 the focus is on ways to study cognitive development, especially during early and middle childhood; in chapter 8 the concern is with the study of social development. Finally, in chapter 9 the focus is again chronological, with a discussion of methods of studying development in old age.

The last three chapters of the book return the discussion to more general matters. Chapter 10 presents some general principles of statistical tests and statistical reasoning. Chapter 11 discusses ethical issues in research in developmental psychology. And chapter 12 presents guidelines for writing papers in psychology.

CONTENT ANALYSIS

One additional feature of the book should be mentioned here. Throughout our discussions we consider a number of dimensions along which research projects and research reports can vary. Is the study conducted in the natural setting or a lab setting, for example, and what kind of design is used for comparing different age groups? Much is said about both what is possible to do and what is desirable to do in regard to these various procedural decisions. But in addition to possibilities and desirabilities it is also important to know something about actualities—what in fact *is* done. What kinds of methodological decisions are developmental psychologists currently making with respect to issues that we identify as important? Some consideration of actual research practice can help to flesh out what otherwise might be a rather abstract presentation of general points.

For this purpose, a content analysis was carried out on two of the leading research journals in the field, *Child Development* and *Developmental*

TABLE 1-2 Dimensions Sampled in Content Analysis of Developmental Psychology Publications

Dimension	Description
Number of age groups	Number of different age groups sampled and compared
Information about the sample	Information about characteristics such as age, sex, race, and social class
Information about the experimenter	Information about the number of experimenters and their characteristics (e.g., age, sex)
Selection of subjects	Manner in which subjects were recruited, and proportion of the initial pool who agreed to participate
Rejection of subjects	Number of subjects rejected in the course of the research, and the reasons for the rejections
Design for comparing ages	Method by which different age groups were compared (e.g., cross-sectional or longitudinal)
Setting	Setting (e.g., natural environment, laboratory) in which variables are manipulated and measured
Reliability	Whether agreement among raters or observers was calculated when appropriate
Blinding	Whether testers or observers were naive when appropriate regarding subjects or hypotheses

Psychology. The survey was based on a random sampling of research reports published in these two journals during 1983—a total of 100 articles and 123 studies. The particular dimensions sampled are listed and briefly described in Table 1-2. The meanings of some of the terms may not be immediately apparent; they should become apparent, however, once we discuss the concepts in the text. As the issues arise for which it is relevant, the results of our content analysis will be brought in.

SUMMARY

The chapter begins with a discussion of both the importance of research in developmental psychology and the challenges in doing such research well. This discussion leads to an overview of the three general goals of the book: to foster the skills necessary to carry out research in developmental psychology, to provide an introduction to interesting and important research topics in the field, and to promote the critical-evaluative skills that will allow readers to become intelligent consumers of research in developmental.

The middle section of the chapter provides

an introductory orientation to the steps that must be successfully negotiated if a research project is to be informative. The starting point is both the most important and the least teachable of the steps: generating *good ideas* that are worthy of empirical study. A closely related and perhaps even prior step is *knowledge of past work*, for research always grows out of what has gone before. Good ideas must be translated into an *adequate experimental design*, from which clear and valid conclusions can be drawn. Before research can begin, it is often necessary to engage in a *pilot study*, both to refine uncertain aspects of the procedure and to sharpen testing skills. Another important and often difficult preliminary to research is *obtaining subjects:* identifying the appropriate subject group and then securing its cooperation. Once the study begins, the experimenter's *testing skills* become important— that is, all the skills needed to interact with subjects and observe behavior in nonbiasing ways. The conclusion of the data collection is followed by *statistical analysis* to determine what reliable and potentially informative patterns are identifiable in the results. The final step is the *communication* of one's research to others, usually in the form of publication in a professional journal.

The runthrough of steps in a research program serves to introduce topics that are considered at various points throughout the book. Further introduction is provided by the concluding section of the chapter, in which each of the remaining chapters is briefly previewed. Also introduced is a content analysis of leading developmental psychology journals, the results of which are interspersed throughout the book.

chapter 2

GENERAL PRINCIPLES OF RESEARCH

Having some specific studies to refer to will help clarify the discussion that follows. Described next, therefore, are two examples of research in developmental psychology. Both studies have been simplified somewhat in order to make the points to be drawn from them easier to follow.

Miller, Weinstein, and Karniol (1978) were interested in the determinants of children's ability to delay gratification. The subjects for their study were kindergarten and third-grade children. After a brief warm-up period, each child in the study was asked to indicate a preference between two possible rewards, either two marshmallows or two pretzels. The experimenter then explained that she had to leave for a while and set forth the following condition: If the child would wait until she returned, then he or she would receive the preferred reward; if the child could not wait and summoned her back, then he or she would receive the nonpreferred reward. This kind of choice—between an attractive but delayed reward and a less attractive but immediate reward—is common in so-called "delay of gratification" research.

Until this point in the procedure all the children were treated the same. Once the basic choice had been explained, however, a difference in treatment was introduced. Some of the children were shown a red light and were told that whenever the light came on they should tell themselves "I'm waiting for the [preferred reward—for example, marshmallows]." Other children were told that the light would come on but were not given any instructions about verbalizing. All children were then left alone for a period of up to 20 minutes, during which they could either wait for their desired rewards or call the experimenter by ringing a bell.

The results of the study are shown in Table 2-1. The third graders, on the average, were better able to delay gratification than were the kindergarteners. In addition, verbalizing about the coming reward increased the length of time that the children were willing to wait for it. Fi-

TABLE 2-1 Mean Number of Seconds before Summoning Experimenter

	No Verbalization	*Verbalization*	*Combined*
Kindergarten	385	744	565
Third Grade	685	933	809
Combined	535	839	

Note: Adapted from ''Effects of Age and Self-Verbalization on Children's Ability to Delay Gratification'' by D. T. Miller, S. M. Weinstein, and R. Karniol, 1978, *Developmental Psychology, 14,* 569–570.

nally, a comparison of the various means suggests that the effects of the verbalization, though present at both ages, were somewhat greater for the kindergarteners than for the third graders.

The second study was concerned with possible memory problems in the elderly. Schonfield and Robertson (1966) presented both young adults (ages 20 to 29) and elderly adults (ages 60 to 75) with two lists of 24 words to remember. The initial instructions about memory were deliberately general (''Try to remember as many words as you can.''). Memory was subsequently tested, however, in two different ways. Following one of the lists the subject was asked to say aloud all the words that he or she could remember. Following the other list the subject was presented with five alternatives for each word and was asked to circle the one that had been shown. The contrast examined, therefore, was between the ability to *recall* words and the ability to *recognize* words.

Schonfield and Robertson's results are presented in Table 2-2. Note that recognition was easier than recall. This is a common and certainly quite expectable finding from memory research. More noteworthy is the fact that the

TABLE 2-2 Mean Recall and Recognition Scores for Young Adults and Elderly Adults

Age Range	*Recall*	*Recognition*
20–29	13.78	20.01
60–75	7.50	20.09
Combined	10.64	20.05

Note: Adapted from ''Memory Storage and Aging'' by D. Schonfield and E. A. Robertson, 1966, *Canadian Journal of Psychology, 20,* 228–236.

recognition-recall difference was much more marked for elderly than for young-adult subjects. Indeed, on the recognition measure there were no differences at all between the two age groups. Only on recall was the performance of the elderly subjects inferior to that of the young adults.

SOME BASIC TERMS AND CONCEPTS

Variables

We begin our discussion of general principles with some terminology. Research in psychology involves variables and the relations that hold among variables. The variables are of two sorts: dependent and independent. *Dependent variables* are outcome variables—those measures whose values constitute the results of a study. In our first example the dependent variable was the number of seconds that the child waited before summoning the experimenter; in the second example the dependent variable was the number of words that the subject was able to remember. Such variables are dependent in the sense that variation in them follows from or depends on other factors. A central job for the researcher is to determine what these other factors are. They are variable necessarily: If there were no possibility of variation in the dependent measure, there would be no point in doing the study.

The dependent variable is something that the researcher measures but does not directly control. *Independent variables,* in contrast, are variables that are under the control of the researcher. The object of the study is to determine whether the particular independent variables chosen do in fact relate to variations in the dependent variable. The independent variables in the Miller et al. study were the age of the child and the verbalization–no verbalization contrast, and in the Schonfield and Robertson study, age and recognition versus recall instructions. Such variables are independent in the sense that their values are decided upon in advance rather than following out as results of the study. The "variable" part is again necessary: If there were no variation in the independent variable, there would be no possibility of determining whether that factor has an effect. Variation and comparison are intrinsic parts of all research.

The description of research as divisible into independent and dependent variables is valid for many but not all studies. Suppose, for example, that we wish to know whether there is a relation between a child's IQ and how well that child does in school. We might test a sample of grade-school children and collect two measures: performance on an IQ test and grades in school. Our interest would be in whether variations on one measure relate to variations on the other—for example, do children with high IQs tend to do well in school? A study like this does not have an independent variable whose values are under the experimenter's control; rather, IQ, grades, and the relation between them are all outcome variables in the study. "Correlational" research of this sort is discussed at length later. The point for now is simply that not all studies fit the independent variable–dependent variable mold.

We still need a bit more terminology before proceeding. Independent variables are also referred to as *factors*, and the particular values that the variables take are referred to as *levels*. Both of our illustrative studies, therefore, can be described as "2 × 2 factorial studies"—that is, as experiments with two factors, each of which has two levels.[1]

Our discussion in this section has touched on two important concepts: measurement and control. Both of these concepts require fuller consideration.

Measurement

Consider two different ways of summarizing one of the findings of the Miller et al. study: "Children are better able to delay gratification if they produce relevant self-verbalizations." "Children who have been promised a preferred reward of two marshmallows rather than a less preferred reward of two pretzels if they will wait alone in a small room for an adult experimenter to return wait longer before summoning the experimenter if, while waiting, they say 'I'm waiting for the marshmallows' every time a red light comes on than if they remain silent when the light comes on." Clearly, the first statement has a more interesting and generalizable (not to mention grammatical) sound to it. But the second statement is more certainly accurate, for it describes exactly what was done and found, whereas the first statement involves various inferences that go beyond the actual data.

The two methods of summarizing Miller et al.'s data raise the important distinction between the conclusions that a researcher wishes to draw from a study and the actual manipulations and measurements of the study. "Delay of gratification" is an interesting construct that is clearly worth knowing about; so is "relevant self-instruction." And so too are any number of other things that developmental psychologists study—intelligence, creativity, self-concept, sex typing. The problem is that attributes like intelligence or creativity are not in fact "things" that are immediately and automati-

---

[1]As noted, our description of the two studies was somewhat simplified. The Miller et al. study in fact contained four experimental conditions, making it a 2(age) × 4(condition) design, and the Schonfield and Robertson study contained five ages, making it a 5(age) × 2(condition) design. Furthermore, describing the two studies as having the same design ignores an important distinction between them: Miller et al. tested different subjects in their experimental conditions, whereas Schonfield and Robertson tested the same subjects in their two conditions. The distinction between within-subject and between-subject designs is discussed in chapter 3.

cally observable; rather, if they are to be studied they must somehow be *operationalized*—that is, translated into a specific and measurable form. All research requires measurement, and all measurement requires that some more general notion be made specific.

The verb operationalize has a noun form: *operational definition*. The notion of operational definition derives from work in physics in the 1920s by P. W. Bridgman. An operational definition defines a variable in terms of the operations needed to produce or measure that variable. Thus, temperature might be defined as the displacement of mercury within a certain kind of container. Intelligence might be defined as performance on the Stanford-Binet IQ test. Or, to return to the Miller et al. study, delay of gratification might be defined along the rather cumbersome lines of our second summary statement. Somewhat more generally, but still within the spirit of the operational approach, delay might be defined as choice of an attractive but delayed reward over a less attractive but immediate reward (with "choice" and "attractiveness" in turn receiving their own operational definitions). In any case, there would be a clear tie to the measurement operations actually used.

A strict interpretation of the operational approach is that researchers are not allowed to make statements about their variables that go beyond the operations used to produce or measure those variables. In fact, few researchers today adhere to such a strict conception of what it means to be operational. Nevertheless, the operational movement has had a lasting and beneficial impact on research in psychology. What it has done is to set a generally accepted framework within which the task of measurement proceeds. The hallmark of this approach is the insistence that measurement operations be clearly specified, objective, and repeatable by any investigator in any appropriately equipped laboratory.

Let us consider how the business of translating theoretical construct into specific measurement might proceed for both the researcher and the reader of a research report. Imagine an observational study of aggression in nursery

school children. The researcher is interested in the possibility that social reinforcement promotes aggression in the nursery school setting. Her first task is to decide on an operational definition for each of these rather global constructs. Because there are a large number of ways in which either construct could be operationalized, this decision will involve selecting particular indices from a larger pool of possibilities. Our researcher might decide, for example, to define social reinforcement as consisting of certain verbalizations (e.g., "good," "OK"), certain facial expressions (e.g., a smile directed toward the child), and certain nonverbal behaviors (e.g., pats or hugs). Aggression might be defined as consisting of various physical actions (e.g., hits, kicks, pinches) whose intent seems to be to injure another. Whatever the specific indices selected, it is then the researcher's job to carry out the measurements as accurately as possible and to convey to the reader exactly what was done.

The eventual reader of such a study has a job to do as well. The reader must begin by recognizing the point just made: that constructs like social reinforcement and aggression have many possible operational definitions, and that any one study will necessarily include only a subset of these possibilities. This means that the particular operational definitions used may not correspond to the reader's own preconceptions about the meanings of social reinforcement and aggression, and they may not correspond to the definitions that he has encountered in other studies of these constructs. What the reader must do, therefore, is to set aside, at least temporarily, whatever preexisting notions he may have and focus instead on what was actually done in the study under consideration. In this case he may decide that the operational definitions are sensible and sufficient, or he may decide that they are in some way inadequate. Perhaps, for example, social reinforcement should include simply attending to the child and not only more obviously positive behaviors such as smiling and praising. Perhaps aggression should include name calling and not just physical actions. Probably the most important skill that the reader of psychology reports must cultivate is the ability to move beyond the nice-sounding summaries found in Abstracts and Discussions (e.g., "social reinforcement promotes aggression") to evaluate research in terms of the specific operations actually used. If the specific operations are not satisfactory, then the general conclusions can hardly be compelling.

Our discussion thus far has stressed the need for choice when translating general construct into specific measurement. This need does not necessarily vanish once the researcher has picked the specific behaviors to measure. Consider the case of hits as a measure of aggression. The researcher who has recorded hitting behavior must still decide exactly which aspect of the behavior to focus on and analyze. She might decide, for example, to work with the *frequency* of the behavior—that is, how many hits a particular child delivers. Such a direct frequency count is probably the most obvious index of what we normally mean by "level of aggression." An alternative possibility, however, is to work not with the frequency of the behavior but with its *intensity*—that is, not how many hits a child delivers but how hard each hit is. Intensity also has an obvious tie to what we normally mean by "aggression." Still another possibility is to focus not on frequency or intensity but on the timing of the behavior. The researcher might decide, for example, to concentrate on the *latency* or quickness with which hits are elicited, or perhaps the total *duration* of the hitting episode. It may well be, of course, that these various measures are related; the child who is quick to hit may also be the child who hits frequently and hits hard. It may be, too, that the researcher will be able to include all of the various indices in her study; indeed, only if she can include several measures will she be able to verify that they *are* related. Often, however, some choice among measures is necessary, and in at least some cases the choice may affect the conclusions. It might be, for example (to return to our hypothetical nursery school study), that social reinforcement in the nursery school affects the frequency of hitting but not the intensity or duration of a hitting episode.

Our introduction to the notion of measurement has barely skimmed the surface of this complex topic. We return to issues of measurement at various points. The important question of reliability of measurement is considered for the first time later in this chapter and then taken up again at several points in subsequent chapters. The concept of levels of measurement, and the relation between such levels and statistical tests, are discussed in chapter 10. And, of course, the coverage of various research areas in chapters 6 through 9 involves much discussion of how constructs of interest to developmental psychologists are in fact measured.

Control

Exact specification and accurate measurement are criteria that apply to both the independent and the dependent variables. There is a third criterion that the independent variable alone must meet—namely, experimental control. Recall, in fact, that the definition of the independent variable is that it is a variable that is under the control of the researcher.

There are three sorts of control that are important in experimental studies. These forms of control are summarized in Table 2-3. Also shown in the table are examples of how each type of control applies or might apply to the illustrative studies that we have been discussing. Both the forms of control and the examples are elaborated and should become clearer as we go. The table is intended simply as a guide to help keep track of the distinctions to be made.

One type of control concerns the exact form of the independent variable. If the interest, for example, is in the effects of a certain kind of reinforcement, then the researcher must be able to deliver exactly this kind of reinforcement to the subjects. If any unintended deviations occur—in form, timing, consistency, or whatever—the researcher can no longer be certain what the independent variable is. Or consider again the Miller et al. study of delay of gratification. Because the researchers' interest was in possible effects of a certain kind of verbalization, it was critical that they induce exactly this verbalization in their subjects. The point being made about this form of control is hardly

TABLE 2-3 Forms of Control in Experimental Research

Type of Control	Methods of Achieving	Examples from Illustrative Studies
Over the independent variable	Make the critical elements of the experimental manipulation the same for all subjects.	In Miller et al., instill exactly the same verbalization in all subjects in a given condition.
Over other potentially important factors in the experimental condition	Hold the other factors constant for all subjects.	In Schonfield and Roberston, use the same quiet testing room for all subjects.
	Disperse variations in the other factors randomly across subjects.	In Miller et al., vary the time since lunch randomly across subjects and conditions.
Over preexisting differences among the subjects	Randomly assign subjects to experimental conditions.	In Miller et al., randomly assign half of the children at each age to the verbalization condition and half to the no-verbalization condition.
	Match subjects on potentially important attributes prior to experimental assignment.	In Miller et al., measure the children's IQs and assign equal-IQ children to the different conditions (not actually done).
	Test each subject under every experimental condition.	In Schonfield and Robertson, test every subject under both the recall and the recognition instructions.

an esoteric one. The point is simply that if one wants to study the possible effects of something one must first be able to produce that something.

The second form of control has to do with factors in the experimental setting other than the independent variable. Independent variables do not occur in a vacuum; there must always be a context for them, and it is the job of the researcher to determine exactly what this context will be. In giving a memory test, for example (as in the Schonfield and Robertson study), the researcher must decide not only what test to use but what the immediate environment for the testing will be like. One easy decision in this particular case is to make the environment as quiet as possible, in order to minimize distractions. Once the experimenter has made this decision, it is then his or her job to ensure that each subject receives the same quiet environment.

Let us introduce some further terminology at this point. Differences in scores on the dependent variable are referred to as the *variance* of the study. Those differences that can be attributed to the independent variable are called *primary variance*; those that result from other factors are called *secondary variance* or *error variance* (the difference between the latter two concepts is not important for our purposes). By controlling the level of other potential variables, the experimenter attempts to maximize the proportion of primary variance in the study. Perhaps even more important, he or she attempts to make sure that other sources of variance are not systematically associated with any of the independent variables. Suppose, for example, that Schonfield and Robertson had tested all of their young adult subjects in a quiet laboratory on campus and all of their elderly subjects in a noisy room at a senior citizens center. Clearly, in this case there would have been two independent variables—age and testing environment—when only one had been intended. Any such unintended conjunction of two potentially important variables is referred to as *confounding*. A major goal of good research design is to rule out confounding.

As Table 2-3 indicates, control of unwanted variables can take a couple of forms. Often it is possible to control the variable by making it the same for all subjects. This is the case in our memory example, in which the noise level of the testing environment is held constant for all subjects. Sometimes, however, such literal equating is not practical. We can return to the Miller et al. study for our example. In work on delay of gratification, a plausible determinant of the child's ability to wait for the desired food is the length of time since he or she last ate. Clearly, Miller et al. would have introduced an important confounding if they had tested all of their third graders immediately after lunch and all of their kindergarteners near the end of the school day. One way to avoid this problem would be to test all of the children at the same point in the day, say 2 hours after lunch. If all the children ate lunch at the same time, however, this procedure would limit the experimenter to a single subject each day. A sensible alternative would be to let the postlunch interval vary across subjects but to make sure that the variations were the same for the different groups being compared—that is, kindergarteners and third graders and verbalization and no-verbalization subjects. In this case the control of the time-since-lunch variable would lie not in its equation but in its randomization—that is, by dispersing differences in it equally across the groups of interest.

Shorn of certain specifics, our discussion thus far should have a familiar sound to it. For what has been presented here is simply the classic scientific method: to determine the effects of some factor, systematically vary that factor (our first form of control) while holding other potentially important factors constant (our second form of control).

There is still a third form of control that is essential. Thus far the "other potentially important factors" that we have discussed have been factors within the experimental setting—for example, the noise level of the testing room. Another important source of variance in any experiment stems from individual differences among the subjects. Subjects are not identical at the start of an experiment, and differences among them contribute error variance to the final results. Because there is no way to rule out such differences, the method of control must again be through dispersion rather than equation. What the experimenter must ensure is that differences among the subjects are spread

equally across the different treatment groups—or, to make the same point in different words, that the groups are equivalent prior to the application of the treatment. Doing so requires that the experimenter have control not only over the form of the treatment but also over who gets what treatment.

How can the experimenter assign subjects to groups in a way that will ensure that the groups are initially equivalent? The answer is that there is no way to literally ensure equivalence, but that there are ways to come as close as can reasonably be expected. The most common method is through *random assignment* of subjects to the different groups. As the term implies, random assignment means that each subject has an equal chance of being assigned to each group. If each subject has an equal chance of being assigned to each group, then the characteristics associated with each subject (IQ, sex, relevant past experience—whatever might affect the results) have an equal chance of falling in each group. It follows that the most probable outcome of the assignment process is that these characteristics will end up equally distributed in the different groups, which, of course, is the researcher's goal. Note, however, that the probability of obtaining the desired distribution varies directly with the sample size. One could not randomly divide eight subjects into two groups and conclude with any confidence that the randomization had produced equivalent groups. With 80 subjects the odds are much better.

In practice, researchers in developmental psychology seldom use totally random asssignment to form their groups. Instead, they use *random assignment within constraints*. Usually, for example, the researcher wishes to work with equal-sized experimental groups. No matter how large the sample, random assignment cannot guarantee that the groups will end up with exactly the same number. It is easy enough, however, to set a constraint that the final group sizes be equal, while still maintaining the randomness of any particular subject's assignment. Similarly, even if the researcher is not interested in sex differences, it is good practice to ensure that any groups being compared have equal proportions of boys and girls. Or in a grade-school setting, it is good practice to make sure that the different classrooms at a grade level contribute equally to the different groups. All of these desired outcomes can be guaranteed by setting certain constraints on the randomness of the assignment.

Our discussion of the need for constraints on randomness raises a natural question: Why use random assignment at all? The researcher's goal, after all, is to ensure that the groups are initially equivalent, yet we have seen that randomness cannot ensure this equivalence. If we can match subjects on sex and classroom, why not go ahead and match them on *all* characteristics of interest, thus *ensuring* that our groups are equivalent? The general answer to this question is that such matching is more difficult than might at first appear, and that the attempt to achieve it can sometimes create more problems than it solves. A more specific answer is given in chapter 3, when we return to the issue of selecting and assigning subjects. Also discussed in chapter 3 is the third general technique for achieving equivalence: testing every subject under each experimental condition.

SUBJECT VARIABLES

Manipulable versus Nonmanipulable Variables

Thus far our discussion of experimental control has focused on the ideal situation for research: the case in which the researcher can systematically manipulate the independent variables of interest while holding all other variables constant, and can assign subjects to the different treatment groups either randomly or randomly within certain desired constraints. With many variables such control is not only desirable but quite feasible. We saw examples of this kind of control in both of our cited studies: the verbalization–no verbalization variable in the Miller et al. study, and the recall–recognition contrast in the Schonfield and Robertson study.

The developmental psychologist's life is

complicated, however, by the fact that not all variables of interest lend themselves to the kind of manipulation that good research design demands. Again, both of our cited studies provide examples, and in this case it is the same example: chronological age. Clearly, age is not something that the researcher randomly assigns to subjects; rather it is a characteristic that subjects bring to the experimental setting. Age is just one example of what are called *subject* (or *classification*) *variables*: intrinsic properties of individuals that cannot be experimentally manipulated but must be taken as they naturally are. Other common examples are race and (recent advances in surgery notwithstanding) sex. The researcher who wishes to work with such characteristics as independent variables foregoes the possibility of control through manipulation. The only control possible in such cases is control through selection of people who already possess the characteristic.

A number of other variables of interest, although not literally nonmanipulable, are never in fact the subject of controlled experiments with human subjects. From a theoretical perspective, for example, it would be very interesting to know whether infants deprived of mothers develop in the same way as infants who have mothers. Despite the early work of Frederick II (noted in chapter 1), we do not have manipulative studies of this issue. Yet there has long been a literature on "maternal deprivation" and its effects on the child. What researchers have done is to identify situations in which infants have already been left motherless (usually in orphanages) and then taken advantage of these "natural experiments" by studying how the infants develop. And there are numerous similar examples of psychologists' ability to capitalize upon naturally occurring events—studies of malnutrition in infancy, of father absence during childhood, of social isolation in old age, and so forth. In each case the independent variable is created through selection rather than experimental manipulation.

Research with nonmanipulable variables does not attain the status of the "true experiment," because the controlled manipulation that constitutes the heart of an experiment is not possible. For this reason such research is labeled as *preexperimental* in Campbell and Stanley's (1966) influential discussion of experimental design. Another term for such studies is *correlational*, not in the sense that correlation statistics are necessarily calculated, but in the sense that the best that the researcher can hope to demonstrate is a correlation between two factors—for example, malnutrition and depressed development. Such studies can never establish cause-and-effect conclusions with the certainty that is possible in a manipulative experiment.

What exactly are the limitations of research with nonmanipulative variables? The problems are of two main sorts. First, it is impossible to assign subjects randomly to groups. Because random assignment is impossible, there is no way to be sure that the groups under study are equivalent except for the variable of interest (e.g., presence or absence of mother), and therefore no way to be sure that any differences between the groups are caused by that variable. This, in fact, was one criticism of the early maternal-deprivation studies. Perhaps babies who grow up in orphanages are a nonrandom subset of the general population of babies, a subset that includes an unusually high proportion of genetic or organic problems. If so, then differences between orphanage babies and other babies could not be attributed with any confidence to the effects of the orphanage rearing. In a well-designed experiment, such confounding would be ruled out by random assignment.

The other problem concerns the broad-scale and long-standing nature of most subject variables. Orphanage rearing, father absence, social isolation, growing up black (or white), and growing up male (or female) all encompass a host of factors that can affect an individual's development. Thus, even if we find a significant effect associated with a particular subject variable, we still do not know what the specific causal factors are. This, too, has been a problem in research on maternal deprivation. Although the deleterious effects of certain kinds of orphanage rearing are not in dispute, there has long been debate about whether the effects result from lack of normal mothering (as claimed, for example, by Bowlby, 1952) or from

more general cognitive-perceptual deprivation (as claimed, for example, by Casler, 1961). Even if we could conclude that mothering per se is important, we still would not know which of the many things that mothers normally do with infants are critical to the effect. Again, there is a confounding of factors that a well-designed experiment would keep separate. A researcher with control over variables is unlikely to set up an independent variable that is so global that its effects cannot be interpreted.

This discussion is not meant to suggest that there is no value in demonstrating that a variable like maternal deprivation or sex or age is associated with important outcomes in the child. But it should be realized that such a demonstration is merely the first step in a research program.

Age as a Variable

Because of its importance in developmental research, the variable of chronological age deserves a somewhat fuller consideration. Much research in developmental psychology has as one of its points a demonstration that subjects of different ages either are or are not similar on the dependent variables being studied. Our survey of the journals *Child Development* and *Developmental Psychology* (see Table 1-2) indicates that 66% of the studies included at least two different age groups; 31% included three or more different ages. And these figures are certainly an underestimation of the extent to which age comparisons enter into developmental research, for often the age comparison is implicit rather than explicit. A researcher of neonates, for example, may not include a comparison group of older children in the study, but findings about how neonates function can nevertheless be interpreted in light of a large body of information about the functioning of older children. To take a very simple example, one would hardly do research to determine whether young infants have color vision (e.g., Bornstein, 1978) unless one already knew that color vision is eventually part of the human competence.

Developmental psychologists are sometimes apologetic about the "merely age differences" nature of much research in developmental psychology. But the identification of genuine changes with age is clearly a valid part of a science of development. Not only is description a legitimate part of any science, but accurate description provides the phenomena to which explanatory models must speak. It is only when we know, for example, that young children do not understand conservation (Piaget & Szeminska, 1952) that we can begin to build a model of why this is and of where eventual understanding comes from.

Although we may agree that the study of age changes is legitimate, it is important to be clear about exactly what is meant by a "genuine change with age." What is *not* meant, certainly, is that chronological age in any direct sense causes the change. What *is* meant is that variables that are regularly and naturally associated with age produce the change. It is then the job of the researcher to determine which of the potentially important variables are in fact important.

Our earlier discussion stressed that a primary goal of experimental control is the creation of groups that are equivalent in every way except for the independent variable being examined. This goal takes on special meaning in the case of a broad subject variable like age. Let us imagine that we are interested in comparing 7-year-olds and 12-year-olds. If we wish to make our groups equivalent in every way except age, then we will have to find 7- and 12-year-olds whose levels of biological maturation are the same, who have been going to school for the same number of years, whose general experiences in the world are equivalent, and so forth. Clearly, such a goal is not only impossible but quite misguided. Variables like biological maturation, years of schooling, and general experience are among the variables that are "regularly and naturally associated with age." As such, they are factors to be studied, not ruled out through experimental control.

On the other hand, there are other potentially important factors that must not be allowed to confound the age comparison. A very obvious kind of confounding would occur if all of the 7-year-olds were boys and all of the 12-

year-olds girls. Maleness is not an intrinsic part of being 7, nor is femaleness an intrinsic part of being 12; hence this factor must not be allowed to covary with age. A somewhat less obvious confounding might occur if all of the 7-year-olds were drawn from one school and all of the 12-year-olds from another school. The mere fact of attending different schools is probably not important, and in any case this difference may be unavoidable for the particular age range studied. Nevertheless, it will be important for the researcher to select schools that are as comparable as possible on dimensions such as educational philosophy, geographical location, and socioeconomic status of the population served. If this criterion is not met, then an apparent age change may not in fact be genuine.

As our examples suggest, decisions about what to match and what not to match when comparing different ages are generally straightforward. As we will see, however, such decisions are not always straightforward, nor is it always easy to achieve whatever matching one has decided on. We return to the issue of age comparisons in chapter 3.

INTERACTION

There is one further point to be made about subject variables. This point will lead, in turn, to a more general point concerning possible outcomes in research. Often, subject variables are of interest not only for the effects associated directly with them but also for their possible influence on other independent variables being studied. Or, to adopt the standard statistical terminology, subject variables may be of interest not just as *main effects* but as components of *interaction*. An interaction occurs whenever the effect of one independent variable varies with the level of another independent variable.

Examples of interactions can be found in both of the studies described at the beginning of the chapter. The Schonfield and Robertson study provides the simpler case. In this study, the differences between recall and recognition were greater for older subjects, and it was only

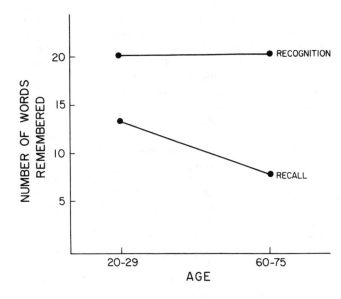

FIGURE 2-1. Interaction of age and experimental condition in the Schonfield and Robertson study. Adapted from "Memory Storage and Aging" by D. Schonfield and E. A. Robertson, 1966, *Canadian Journal of Psychology, 20,* 228–236.

on recall that an age difference emerged. This two-way interaction ("two-way" because two independent variables are involved) is graphed in Figure 2-1. The data are the same as those presented in Table 2-1; the figural presentation, however, makes the nature of the interaction more visible.

The interaction in the Miller et al. study is a bit more complicated. Explaining it requires that we fill in some details of their study that were omitted in our initial description. As noted in Footnote 1, the study actually contained four experimental conditions. Two of the conditions were described earlier: a *no-verbalization* condition and a verbalization condition that the authors labeled the *task-oriented* condition (the "I'm waiting for the marshmallows" manipulation). There were two additional verbalization conditions: a *reward oriented* condition, in which the verbalization focused on the desirability of the reward (e.g., "The marshmallows are yummy."), and an *irrelevant* verbalization condition, in which the child simply counted to three when the light came on. The results for all four conditions are pictured in Figure 2-2. As the flat lines suggest, kindergarteners and third graders did not differ under either the reward-oriented or the irrelevant condition. Despite the apparent trend, they also did not differ significantly under the task-oriented condition. It was only under the no-verbalization condition that third graders showed significantly greater delay than kindergarteners. There was, then, an interaction of age and condition: The effects of the age variable depended on the particular experimental condition that was examined. As with any interaction, the results can also be stated with the opposite emphasis: The effects of the experimental condition depended on the particular age group being studied.

Although interactions between subject variables and manipulable variables may often be of special interest, interactions can occur between independent variables of any sort. They are possible, therefore, in any multiple-factor experiment. Figure 2-3 shows an interaction between two experimentally manipulated variables, and Figure 2-4 shows an interaction between two subject variables. The main finding of the Patterson and Carter (1979) study, pictured in Figure 2-3, was that the presence of a desired reward lessened children's self-control in a standard delay-of-gratification paradigm but enhanced self-control in a situation in which the child was working to complete a task rather than simply waiting for the reward. One find-

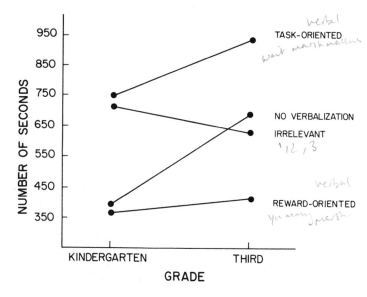

FIGURE 2–2. Interaction of age and experimental condition in the Miller, Weinstein, and Karniol study. Adapted from "Effects of Age and Self-Verbalization on Children's Ability to Delay Gratification" by D. T. Miller, S. M. Weinstein, and R. Karniol, 1978, *Developmental Psychology, 14,* 569–570.

ing from the Stein and Smithells (1969) study, pictured in Figure 2–4, was that children's ratings of athletic activities as masculine or feminine varied as a function of both the age and the sex of the child. At the younger ages there was a clear sex difference, with boys assigning more masculine ratings than girls; by 12th grade this sex difference had disappeared.

As a comparison of Figures 2–1 through 2–4 suggests, interactions can take a variety of forms. They can also become exceedingly complicated when more than two independent variables are involved. Although some researchers try, it is seldom possible to make sense of a four- or five-way interaction.

Interpreting any sort of interaction can be a

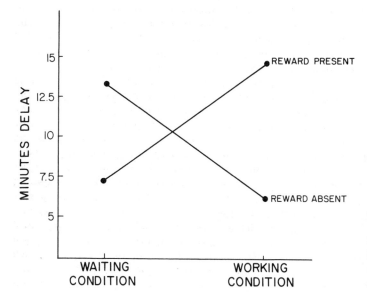

FIGURE 2–3. Interaction of experimental conditions in the Patterson and Carter study. Adapted from "Attentional Determinants of Children's Self-Control in Waiting and Working Situations" by C. J. Patterson and D. B. Carter, 1979, *Child Development, 50,* 272–275.

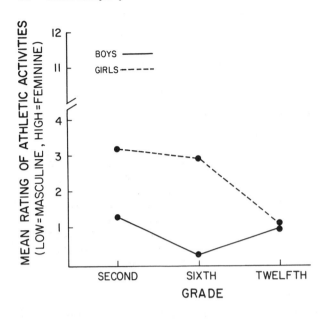

FIGURE 2-4. Interaction of age and sex in the Stein and Smithells study. Adapted from "Age and Sex Differences in Children's Sex-Role Standards about Achievement" by A. H. Stein and J. Smithells, 1969, *Developmental Psychology, 1,* 252–259. Copyright 1969 by the American Psychological Association. Adapted by permission.

complex matter, both statistically and theoretically. Two points can be made here. First, the most general implication of a significant interaction between two variables is that interpretations of main effects involving those variables must be made with caution. In the Stein and Smithells study, for example, there were significant main effects of both age and sex; as Figure 2-4 reveals, however, the age effect was limited to the girls and the sex effect was limited to the younger subjects. In the Patterson and Carter study, in contrast, the main effect of the reward-present–reward absent manipulation was *not* significant, a finding that would suggest that this variable had no effect. Such a conclusion, however, is clearly contradicted by a separate analysis of the working and waiting conditions. An interaction, then, is a signal that the world is more complicated than we might have expected. Studying an independent variable in isolation cannot give us a full picture of the way that that variable operates.

The second point concerns the relevance of interactions to an understanding of subject variables. We have seen that the global and nonmanipulable nature of subject variables makes the isolation of causal factors very difficult. We may be quite certain that boys differ

from girls or young subjects from older subjects on some measure, but determining where the differences come from can be very difficult. Often, however, useful clues may be provided by a demonstration that the subject variable interacts with some experimentally manipulated variable. This, in fact, may be the case in the Miller et al. study. A possible explanation for the different effects of verbalization at the different ages is that kindergarteners are less likely to produce self-guiding verbalizations spontaneously than are third graders. Because kindergarteners do not generate such mediators on their own, their performance is aided by any sort of helpful verbalization and is unaffected by the potentially disruptive reward-oriented verbalization. Many third graders, in contrast, are already producing appropriate self-directions; thus they gain less than do younger children from the induction of such mediators but are hampered when required to focus on the reward. The interaction, then, suggests an explanation for the general developmental increase in delay of gratification: As children develop they are more likely to use appropriate self-verbalization to help mediate delay. Once this explanation has been suggested by the interaction, it can then be subjected to further test.

The general point being made here again has to do with manipulation and control. A subject variable like age is not manipulable, but then age is not in itself a causal factor. Potential causal factors associated with age often *are* manipulable, and it is consequently to these variables that the researcher may wish to direct his or her attention. (For a fuller discussion of the utility of subject variable by experimental variable interactions, see Underwood and Shaughnessy, 1975. Discussion of some of the statistical complexities involved in interpreting interactions can be found in Stanovich, 1976, and Baron and Treiman, 1980.)

VALIDITY AND RELIABILITY

Validity

It is time to make explicit a concept that has been hovering around our discussions throughout this chapter. The central question that can be asked of any study is whether the study has in fact unequivocally demonstrated what it claims to demonstrate. All the issues of measurement and control come down to this basic question of how accurate the conclusions of the study are. This is the question of *validity*.

There are two forms of validity: *internal validity* and *external validity*. Internal validity applies within the context of the study itself. The issue in question is whether the data have really come about for the reasons hypothesized—or, to return to our usual terminology, whether the independent variables really relate to the dependent variables in the manner claimed. This is the form of validity that has been the concern of most of our discussions so far. If we now apply the concept explicitly to the Miller et al. study, we can say that their conclusions are internally valid if the third graders they studied really were better able to delay gratification than the kindergarteners, if the various verbalizations really did have differential effects on the ability to wait, and if the effects of the verbalizations really did vary across age in the manner described. If there is a plausible alternative explanation for any of these findings, then the internal validity of the study is thrown in doubt.

The question of external validity is the question of generalizability. It applies, therefore, once we move outside the immediate context of the study. The question now is whether the findings of the study can be generalized to other samples, situations, and behaviors—not just any samples, situations, and behaviors, of course, but those for which we wish the study to be predictive. Let us take the Schonfield and Robertson study as our example of this concept. Their findings would have external validity if recognition tasks really are in general easier than recall tasks, if young adults really do in general recall better than elderly adults, and if young adults and elderly adults really are in general equal in recognition ability. In each case the "in general" refers to what is found across a variety of samples of young and old and a variety of recall and recognition measures. If any of the findings fails to generalize to other samples or other measures, then that finding lacks external validity.

A satisfactory study must have both internal validity and external validity. As Campbell and Stanley (1966) observe, "internal validity is the basic minimum without which any experiment is uninterpretable" (p. 5). Logically the internal validity question is the primary one, because findings can hardly be generalized if there are no valid findings in the first place. External validity is also critical, however. Internally valid conclusions do not mean much if they cannot be generalized beyond the study in which they occur.

The task of achieving both internal and external validity is complicated by the fact that there is often a trade-off between the two goals. In general, the more tightly controlled an experiment, the greater its internal validity—that is, the more certain the experimenter can be that the variables really do relate in the manner hypothesized. At the same time, the artificiality of a tightly controlled experiment may make generalization to the nonlaboratory world hazardous. Conversely, research conducted in natural settings with naturally occurring behaviors may pose little problem of generalizability, because the situations to which the researcher wishes to generalize are precisely those under study. The lack of experimental control, however, may make the establishment of valid relationships very difficult. We return to this issue of the trade-off between internal and external validity in chapter 5.

Reliability

As noted, our earlier discussion of measurement deferred consideration of several important concepts. It is time now to deal with one of these, the problem of *reliability*.

Reliability refers to the consistency or repeatability of a measurement. The issue is whether repeated applications of a measuring technique will yield identical or at least highly similar values. The repeated applications may consist of readministrations of the same measurement at different times (e.g., a child taking the same IQ test twice on consecutive days), or they may consist of values obtained from two or more measuring instruments at the same time (e.g., two observers rating the same behavior). In either case, the higher the degree of agreement between the independently obtained values, the higher the reliability of the measurement. Clearly, one goal of good measurement is to maximize reliablity.

It is important to distinguish reliability from certain other constructs that also deal with the consistency of independently obtained measurements. Suppose that our administrations of the IQ test are separated not by 1 day but by 2 years. If we find that the two scores differ substantially, should we conclude that the IQ test is unreliable or should we conclude that the child's IQ has really changed in 2 years? Suppose that instead of intelligence we decided to measure weight. If our measurements show that the child weighs 15 pounds more at age 9 than at age 7, should we conclude that our scale is unreliable? A much more likely conclusion, of course, is that the child's weight has really changed in 2 years—that is, that the *stability* of weight is less than perfect as children grow. Many aspects of the child's functioning (including performance on IQ tests) are less than

perfectly stable as the child develops. It is important, therefore, to distinguish between the reliability of a measurement and the stability of a behavior.

It is important, too, to distinguish between the reliability of a measurement and the extent to which a behavior generalizes. The issue of generalization is the issue of consistency in behavior across different situations. Suppose that our interest now is in aggression in preschool children. We go into a nursery school and make extensive recordings of the many acts of aggression there on display. From these we derive a level-of-aggressiveness measure for each child. We then go into the children's homes and measure aggressiveness there. We find that our measure of nursery-school aggression is only weakly related to our measure of home aggression—that, in short, there is a good deal of inconsistency between the two scores. Do we conclude that one or both of the measures are unreliable? Although this is a possible conclusion, it may be more reasonable to conclude that aggressive behavior is simply not very consistent from one environmental setting to another quite different environmental setting. If so, our finding has to do with generalization, not reliability.

It may be helpful to summarize the distinctions just made. Reliability is a property of a measurement; stability and generalization are properties of behavior. Reliability is something that the researcher always seeks to maximize. Stability and generalization, however, are phenomena to be studied, not maximized. Finally, these phenomena *can* be studied only if we have first achieved a satisfactory degree of reliability. It is only if we can be sure that our measures are reliable for a particular time and situation that we can hope to study consistency in behavior over time (the stability question) or situations (the generalization question).

Validity and Reliability of Tests

Thus far we have discussed validity and reliability with respect to studies and the conclusions that can be drawn from studies. Not all encounters of psychologist and subject are in the context of studies, however. Often the psychologist's purpose in working with a child is not to test a hypothesis but to test the child—that is, to obtain information about important attributes of that particular child. The number of attributes that might be studied in this way is very large; a few were mentioned earlier (intelligence, creativity, self-concept, sex typing), and many more could be added. The number of standardized tests that purport to measure such attributes is larger still. How can a researcher interested in some attribute evaluate and choose among the many possible tests?

Like studies, standardized tests must satisfy the twin criteria of validity and reliability. The issue of *validity* as applied to tests is quite straightforward: Does the test in fact measure what it claims to measure? If the test is an IQ test, for example, does it really measure individual differences in intelligence, or do differences in people's scores have some other basis? Clearly, the mere fact that the test is labeled "IQ" cannot decide this issue; we need other criteria. In general, three main sorts of validity criteria are possible.

A first possibility is that the test has *content validity*. The term content validity refers to the adequacy with which the test items represent the conceptual domain of interest. Does the test include all of the important aspects of the target that we wish to measure, and are the various aspects properly weighted? Suppose that our test is designed to tap knowledge of fourth-grade arithmetic. A test that consisted solely of addition problems would have poor content validity. A test composed of a representative sampling of addition, subtraction, multiplication, and division problems would have much better content validity.

Content validity is usually desirable, but it is not always easy to achieve. Even with a target as circumscribed as elementary arithmetic, disagreements about the adequacy of the sampling may arise. How many two-digit and how many three-digit problems should there be, for example, and in what context or contexts should the problems be embedded? When the target is more complex than elementary arithmetic, content validity may be virtually impossible to demonstrate. Consider a very global construct like intelligence. No matter how wide ranging the sampling of items, it is doubtful that any test could ever be shown, through content analysis alone, to comprise a complete and representative sampling of every possible aspect of "intelligence." In such cases other indices of validity are necessary.

A second form of validity is *criterion validity* (also sometimes labeled *predictive validity*). The issue in criterion validity is whether a subject's performance on the test relates to some measure of the attribute in question—to some external criterion. In the case of a knowledge-of-arithmetic test a reasonable criterion might be grades in arithmetic across the school year. A test that correlated highly with such grades would have good criterion validity. In the case of intelligence a common criterion has been the ability of IQ tests to predict performance in school or on standardized achievement tests; indeed, historically it was the need to predict school performance that led to the development of the first IQ test (that of Binet and Simon in 1905). More generally, criterion validity is the main form of validity for any test whose primary function is prediction for pragmatic purposes. Thus, it is criterion validity that underlies the use of SATs or GREs to predict success in college, the use of times in the 40-yard dash to predict success as a professional football player, and so forth.

The final form of validity that we consider is *construct validity*. Among psychometricians, construct validity is generally regarded as the most important form of test validity. Unfortunately, it is also the most difficult form for the researcher to achieve, as well as the most difficult form for the textbook author to convey. We will have to settle for a brief introduction to this complex notion. Fuller discussions can be found in many sources, including Kerlinger (1986) and Nunnally (1978).

The distinguishing aspect of construct validity is its theoretical grounding. As Kerlinger (1986) notes, "It is not simply a question of validating a test. One must try to validate the theory behind the test" (p. 420). The starting point, therefore, is some theory of the construct (intelligence, creativity, self-concept, anxiety, etc.) that we wish to measure. From this theory various predictions can be drawn. These predictions typically include hypotheses about which measures of the construct should correlate with which other measures. If we were seeking to devise a test of anxiety, for example, we might predict that self-report measures of anxiety would correlate with physiological changes thought to indicate anxiety (e.g., increased heart rate). The predictions might also include hypotheses about which measures should *not* correlate. In our study of anxiety, for example, it might be important to demonstrate that some kinds of physiological changes do not relate to self-reported anxiety, thus ruling out generalized arousal as an explanation for the results. Finally, the predictions may include hypotheses about the effects of certain kinds of experimental manipulations. We might predict, for example, that heightening the demand pressures of a testing situation would lead to increased scores on our measures of anxiety. All of these predictions, once generated by theory, must be empirically tested. To the extent that the predictions are confirmed, the construct validity of our measures is increased. Any disconfirmations would indicate a need to revise either the measures or the theory or both.

As the preceding discussion indicates, construct validity, like criterion validity, is established largely through the demonstration of expected correlations among measures. There are, however, important differences between the two kinds of validity. With criterion validity there is usually a single external target, such as performance in school, to which we wish to predict; with construct validity there is a whole network of hypothesized interrelations. With criterion validity the goal is generally prediction for pragmatic purposes; with construct validity the goal is validation of an underlying theory.

In addition to validity, standardized tests must possess satisfactory reliability. The issue of *reliability* as applied to tests is also straightforward: Does the test consistently measure whatever it is that it does measure? One of our earlier examples of reliability was in fact a problem in test reliability: Does an IQ test given to the same child on consecutive days yield similar or different scores? Highly similar scores would indicate good reliability; markedly different scores would indicate poor reliability.

The IQ example illustrates one common form of reliability: *test-retest* reliability. There are two ways to assess test-retest reliability. One is to give literally the same test on two separate occasions. Clearly, however, if the tests are identical the child may remember many of his or her responses, and this fact could artificially inflate the reliability (it could also *deflate* the reliability, if the child perceives the readministration of the test as a signal that he or she should change the answers). To avoid this problem, retest reliability is sometimes assessed via an *alternative-forms* procedure. As the name implies, the alternative-forms approach requires two different but equivalent versions of the test, with one version given at time 1 and the other version at time 2. Again, high agreement in response would indicate high reliability.

The second main type of test reliability is labeled *split-half* reliability. The question at issue now is the consistency of response across the different items of a single test given at a single time. A common procedure is to divide the test into the odd-numbered items and the even-numbered items (thus the "split-half") and to compare response between these two categories. Once again, high reliability would be indicated by a high agreement in response. Clearly, what the split-half approach measures is the internal consistency of the test, or the extent to which the different items evoke similar responses. Indeed, the label *internal consistency* is sometimes used for this form of reliability.

We have discussed both test validity and test reliability. The relation between these two concepts should be easy to discern. Reliability is a necessary but not sufficient condition for validity. If the scores on a test have little or no consistency, then the test can hardly provide a valid measure of the attribute in question. Consistency alone, however, is no guarantee that a test is valid. We might design an "intelligence" test that consists of the ability to hop on one foot. Scores on this test might be perfectly consistent across items (the two feet) and across time; this perfect reliability, however, would not mean that we had succeeded in measuring intelligence.

Regression

Let us return for a moment to test-retest reliability. Less-than-perfect reliability means that scores on the second administration of a test will tend to differ from those on the first administration. Is it possible to go beyond this general statement to say something about the *direction* of the difference—that is, whether scores are likely to go up or down on the second test? In the case of any individual subject it is impossible to predict with certainty whether the score will be higher or lower the second time around than the first. At the level of group averages, however, a prediction *can* be made: On the average, subjects with low scores on the first test will have higher scores on the second test, and subjects with high scores on the first test will have lower scores on the second test. This tendency for initially extreme scores to move toward the group mean upon retesting is referred to as *regression toward the mean*.

Let us try a concrete example of this phenomenon before considering why it occurs. Suppose we give an IQ test to a sample of children and obtain the distribution of scores shown in Figure 2-5. Some children (the open circles) score distinctly below average, some (the closed circles) score distinctly above average, and some (the crossed circles) score within a range of average performance. Now suppose we administer the same test to the same sample a week later and obtain the distribution of scores shown in Figure 2-6. The figure shows that the initially low-scoring children have, on the average, moved up, and the initially high-scoring children have, on the average, moved down. Thus, both groups have "regressed toward the mean." Because some of the initially average scorers have gone up or down, however, the overall range and mean remain about what they were originally.

Why does regression occur? Any subject's score on a test can be thought of as consisting

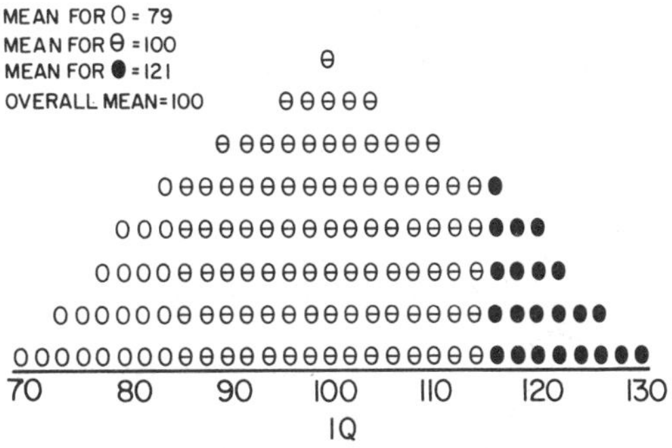

MEAN FOR ○ = 79
MEAN FOR ⊖ = 100
MEAN FOR ● = 121
OVERALL MEAN = 100

FIGURE 2-5. Hypothetical distribution of scores upon initial administration of an IQ test.

of two components: the "true score," or the subject's actual value on the dimension being measured, and error stemming from imperfect measurement. Clearly, "error" is just another way to talk about reliability: Perfect reliability means an absence of error; conversely, the greater the error the lower the reliability. Two assumptions are generally valid concerning error. One is that errors are normally distributed about the true score. This means that small errors are more likely than large errors; it also means that errors are equally likely to inflate or to deflate a particular subject's score. The second assumption is that errors occur randomly across subjects and across testing occasions. This means that the errors for a particular subject are uncorrelated from one test to the next; the error on the first test has no implications for the error on the second test.

FIGURE 2-6. Hypothetical distribution of scores upon readministration of the IQ test.

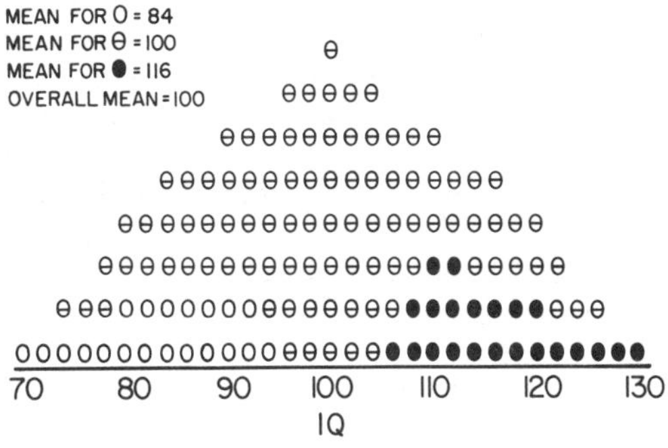

MEAN FOR ○ = 84
MEAN FOR ⊖ = 100
MEAN FOR ● = 116
OVERALL MEAN = 100

Consider now the scores in Figure 2–5. How have errors of measurement affected these scores? In particular, how have the relatively extreme errors, those that substantially inflate or deflate a score, affected the obtained distribution? It is reasonable to assume that the low-scoring (open circle) children, on the average, have suffered from a disproportionate number of negative errors; this is one reason that their scores are low. Similarly, it is reasonable to assume that the high-scoring children, on the average, have benefited from a disproportionate number of positive errors; this is one reason that their scores are high. But what happens when we retest the children? Recall that errors are uncorrelated from one test to the next. It is quite unlikely, therefore, that the extreme errors will affect the same children in the same way. The most probable outcome for any subject, rather, is a relatively small error that is equally likely to inflate or deflate the true score. This "evening out" of errors over tests ensures that low scores will tend to move up and high scores tend to move down—ensures, in short, that we will find regression toward the mean.

The basic problem posed by regression should be obvious. Like poor reliability in general, regression is a threat to the validity of research. Furthermore, because regression is a systematic phenomenon it can produce systematically incorrect conclusions. Suppose, for example, that in the IQ study described earlier we had not simply retested the children but had introduced a new educational program between the first and second tests. Given the results in Figures 2–5 and 2–6, we might then have concluded that the effects of our program depend on the initial level of ability: The program enhances IQ for low-ability children but actually depresses IQ for high-ability children. Clearly, in such a case regression could produce a spurious impression of change where no change had occurred. Alternatively, regression might mask a true change; perhaps the program actually does benefit high-ability children, but the gains in true score are offset by the losses via regression.

We will return to regression, and to possible solutions to the problems posed by regression, at various later points. For now, one further point can be made. It is a rather complex point that we will settle for simply stating; a helpful further discussion can be found in Furby (1973). Thus far we have been discussing regression as an artifact stemming from imperfect reliability. Regression is actually a much more general phenomenon, however, because it can occur even with perfectly reliable measurements—can occur, therefore, with true scores as well as with errors. In general, whenever there is a less-than-perfect correlation between two measures there will be a tendency for relatively extreme values on the first measure to become less extreme on the second measure. This regression in true scores comes about for essentially the same reason as regression in errors: a tendency for the factors producing extreme values (e.g., an especially favorable environment) to even out over time.

THREATS TO VALIDITY

As noted, regression constitutes a threat to validity. It is just one of many possible threats to validity; some others were touched on earlier (e.g., biased assignment of subjects to experimental groups), and many more are discussed in the coming chapters. It will be helpful for this coming discussion to have a brief overview of the factors to be considered—an overall list and set of definitions to which we can refer back as needed. This is the purpose of Table 2–4.

Table 2–4 is derived from Campbell and Stanley (1966; see also Cook & Campbell, 1979). Their monograph includes an extended discussion of various threats to both internal and external validity. The factors in Table 2–4 are not an exhaustive list of things that can go wrong; they do, however, include most of the problems that we consider later. Again, there is no expectation that the table is completely self-explanatory; its purpose, rather, is as a preliminary guide to concepts that are discussed more fully in the text.

TABLE 2-4 Threats to Validity

Source	Description
Selection bias	Assignment of initially nonequivalent subjects to the groups being compared
Selective drop-out	Nonrandom, systematically biased loss of subjects in the course of the study
History	Potentially important events occurring between early and later measurements in addition to the independent variables being studied
Maturation	Naturally occurring changes in the subjects as a function of the passage of time during the study
Testing	Effects of taking a test upon performance on a later test
Reactivity	Unintended effects of the experimental arrangements upon subjects' responses
Instrumentation	Unintended changes in experimenters, observers, or measuring instruments in the course of the study
Statistical regression	Tendency of initially extreme scores to move toward the group mean upon retesting

SUMMARY

This chapter begins with some basic terms and concepts. All research involves variables. *Dependent variables* are the outcome variables in research—for example, the number of aggressive acts in a study of aggression. *Independent variables* are potential causal factors that are controlled by the researcher—for example, reinforcement for aggression. The goal of most research is to determine whether variations in the independent variable relate to variations in the dependent variable—for example, does aggression increase following reinforcement?

Determining the causal relation between variables requires both measurement and control. Variables are defined (*operationally*) by the way in which they are measured. Measurement always involves translation of some global construct (such as aggression or reinforcement) into some more specific, objective, and quantifiable form. This translation always involves choice of particular measures from a larger pool of possibilities. A central task for the researcher is to select measuring instruments that are appropriate for the problem under study and to convey these choices clearly to others.

Control applies to the independent variable. Three kinds of control are important if clear cause-and-effect conclusions are to be drawn. A first is over the exact form of the independent variable. A second is over other potentially important factors in the situation. Two methods

of achieving this second form of control are discussed: holding the other factors constant and randomly dispersing variations in them across subjects. The third kind of control is over preexisting differences among subjects. One method of achieving this form of control, *random assignment*, is discussed in the present chapter; two others (matching and within-subject testing) are deferred for later consideration.

The discussion turns next to situations in which the degree of control is limited by the nature of the variables. The term *subject variable* refers to preexisting differences among people that are not experimentally manipulable; examples include age, sex, and race. The only control possible with such variables is through selection, a point that applies also to situations (e.g., maternal deprivation) whose experimental induction would be unethical. Although nonmanipulable variables are often of great interest to the developmental psychologist, cause-and-effect conclusions are difficult to establish in the absence of experimental manipulation. Specifying the exact basis for an effect can be a problem with a broad and multifaceted variable; ruling out other possible causal factors can also be difficult.

Subject variables are often of special interest when they enter into interactions. An *interaction* occurs whenever the effects of one independent variable depend on the level of another variable. Age by condition interactions can be especially informative, for they may suggest a causal basis for changes with age. Interactions can occur with independent variables of any sort, and they can take a variety of forms. Their most general message is that relations are complicated, and that conclusions about any one variable must be made with caution.

The final section of the chapter discusses the concepts of validity and reliability. *Validity* refers to the accuracy with which conclusions can be drawn from research. There are two forms: *internal validity*, which concerns the accuracy of cause-and-effect conclusions within the context of the study, and *external validity*, which concerns generalizability beyond the study. *Reliability* refers to consistency or repeatability of measurement, the extent to which a measuring instrument yields similar values over different occasions or different users. One goal of measurement is always to maximize reliability.

Validity and reliability apply to standardized tests as well as to the outcomes of research. As applied to a test or measuring instrument, the validity question is whether the test really measures what it is intended to measure. Three forms of test validity are discussed: *content validity*, *criterion validity*, (sometimes labeled *predictive validity*), and *construct validity*. The reliability question is whether the test consistently measures whatever it is that it does measure. Two forms of reliability are considered: *test-retest* and *split-half* or internal consistency.

The discussion of reliability leads to examination of a particular problem that can arise in the absence of perfect reliability. Whenever a measure is less than perfectly reliable, there will be a tendency for extreme scores on one occasion to become less extreme, or *regress toward the mean*, on another occasion. Such regression effects may lead to incorrect conclusions. Regression is just one of a number of threats to the validity of research. The chapter concludes with an overview of various threats that are considered throughout the book.

chapter 3
SUBJECTS AND DESIGNS

We noted in chapter 2 that all research involves comparison. In most cases the comparison is between different levels of an independent variable. If the independent variable is a nonmanipulable subject characteristic such as age, then the researcher must select subjects who already possess different levels of the characteristic. If the independent variable is an experimentally manipulable factor, then the researcher must assign subjects to conditions that embody the desired levels of the factor. In either case, the researcher must do the selecting and assigning in a way that will allow a clear, nonconfounded comparison of the different levels being studied (the internal validity question), as well as permit generalization to other samples of interest (the external validity question). It is to the issue of how to select, assign, and compare subjects that the present chapter is directed.

We deal with three sorts of questions. The most general of these concerns the identification and sampling of subjects. In what kind of population is the researcher interested, and how can he or she select subjects in a way that will allow generalization to this population? The other two questions are the somewhat more specific ones sketched in the preceding paragraph: What are the best ways to make comparisons between different levels of a nonmanipulable subject variable? And what are the best ways to make comparisons between different tasks or experimental conditions? Given our developmental focus, the subject variable on which we concentrate is chronological age.

Once again, we can use the sample studies described at the beginning of chapter 2 to illustrate some general points and standard terminology. Both the Miller et al. and the Schonfield and Robertson studies included two levels of an experimentally manipulated variable: verbalization versus no-verbalization in Miller et al., recall versus recognition in Schonfield and Robertson. Miller et al. assigned separate subjects to their two experimental conditions; hence their approach can be labeled a *between-subject design*. Schonfield and Robertson tested all of their subjects in both the recall and the recognition conditions; hence their approach can be labeled a *within-subject design*. One very basic decision that a researcher must make is whether to use the same or different subjects when comparing the effects of two or more experimental treatments. Strengths and weaknesses of both possible approaches are discussed later in the chapter.

Both of the sample studies also included the nonmanipulable variable of chronological age. In this case the methodological decision was the same: Both sets of researchers tested separate subjects at the different ages. The strategy of testing different groups of subjects at different ages is referred to as a *cross-sectional design*. It is not the only possible approach to studying differences with age. Miller et al., for example, might have tested a sample of 5-year-olds, waited 3 years, and then retested the same children as 8-year-olds. The strategy of repeatedly testing the same sample of subjects as that sample develops is referred to as a *longitudinal design*. It should be clear that there is a basic similarity between the between versus within contrast and the cross-sectional versus longitudinal contrast. In both cases the central issue is whether to examine effects within the same subjects or across different subjects. The relative merits of cross-sectional and longitudinal approaches are also discussed shortly.

Because our focus is on the subject variable of age, it may be worth noting an important difference between age and most other subject variables. The researcher of a variable like sex or race does not have the option of waiting for his or her subjects to change from one level of the variable to another; rather studies of these variables must necessarily involve separate groups of subjects. In the case of age, however, today's 6-year-old is tomorrow's 8-, 10-, or 20-year old. It is because of this natural change along the age dimension that the researcher of age differences has the option of adopting either a same-subjects or a different-subjects approach.

There is a further point here as well. If we do a study to compare boys and girls, then our interest clearly is in differences (or, of course, lack of differences) between boys and girls. If we do a study to compare 6- and 10-year olds, our interest may be partly in differences between 6- and 10-year olds, but it is likely to go deeper as well. What we may really be interested in is the possibility that the 6-year-old *will become like* the 10-year-old, or, equivalently, that the 10-year-old *was once like* the 6-year old. Our interest, in short, may be not just in age *differences* but in age *changes*. As we will see, one of the thorny problems for developmental research is to determine when differences between age groups really reflect natural changes with age as people develop.

SAMPLING

With very rare exceptions, psychologists do not study all of the members of the populations in which they are interested. The researcher of infancy, for example, is not going to test all of the world's babies, nor even all those within the United States, nor (probably) even all those within one specific geographical community. Instead, what researchers do is to test *samples,* from which they hope to generalize to the larger *population* of interest. The generalization is legitimate if the sample is *representative* of the larger population. This, clearly, is an issue of external validity.

How can the researcher ensure that a sample is representative of the population to which he or she wishes to generalize? A logical first step is to define what the population of interest is. It need not be as broad as all the world's infants; more likely, perhaps, is something like "all full-term, healthy, 3-month-olds growing up in the United States." Once the desired population has been defined, the next step is *random sampling* from that population. The logic of the random-sampling approach is the same as that for the random-assignment approach discussed earlier: If all members of the population have an equal chance of being sampled, then the most probable outcome of the sampling process is that the characteristics of the sample will mirror those of the total population. Again, the likelihood that the desired outcome will in fact be achieved varies directly with the size of the sample. A random sample of 100 is much more likely to be representative than a random sample of three.

How often do psychologists in fact proceed in the textbook-perfect fashion just described? The answer is: almost never. Most researchers, certainly, start with at least an implicit notion of the population to which they wish to generalize, and most would certainly avoid selecting a sample that is clearly nonrepresentative of this population. Actual random sampling from the target population, however, is very rare. The most obvious and frequent deviation from randomness is geographical. Researchers tend to draw samples from the communities in which they themselves live and work. Often, moreover, they may sample from only one or a few of the available hospitals, day-care centers, or grade schools within that community. The resulting sample may not be representative of the broader population with respect to variables like social class and race, and it *cannot* be completely representative of the broader population with respect to variables like region of the country or size of the community.

Some information about the nature of samples in developmental research is provided by White and Duker (1973). These authors collated information about subject samples from articles published in four developmental psychology journals; issues surveyed ranged from 1964 to 1970. One clear finding was that many of the articles provided very little information about the nature of their samples, a deficiency that, of course, makes it difficult to evaluate how representative the samples were. Thus, only 67% reported the sex of their subjects, only 31% reported social class (with only 2% indicating how social class was calculated), and only 17% reported race. The question of what sort of information authors should provide their readers is an issue of scientific communication, and as such is discussed more fully in chapter 12.

Some information that *was* obtained in White and Duker's survey is presented in Table 3–1.

TABLE 3–1 Types of Schools Sampled in Research with Children

Type	Number
University affiliated	16
Labeled middle-class	10
Near the university or in a university community	8
Project-related schools	7
Religious-affiliated schools	5
Working class	3
Urban	3
Central city	3
Lower-class	2
Children of graduate students	2
Upper-middle-class setting	1
Suburban	1
Total	61

Note. From "Suggested Standards for Children's Samples," by M. A. White and J. Duker, 1973, *American Psychologist, 28,* p. 702. Copyright 1973 by the American Psychological Association. Reprinted by permission.

The table shows the kinds of schools from which child-research subjects tend to be drawn. Note that there is a definite bias toward middle-class or university-affiliated schools. A reasonable conclusion is that researchers seeking a school for research are often guided less by considerations of representativeness than by factors of convenience or cooperation. In White and Duker's (1973) words, "Psychology professors practice research on the most readily available bodies: their graduate students, their colleagues' children, their graduate students' children, and those children that live near the university" (p. 703).

Our survey of the journals *Child Development* and *Developmental Psychology* provides some further information about the samples used by developmental researchers. We can ask first about the information that we are given concerning these samples. In the articles surveyed we are always told the number of subjects and their ages, and in 75% of the cases we are told their distribution by sex (although the latter often takes the form of a phrase such as "approximately equal numbers" rather than exact information). We learn something about the social class of the subjects in 52% of the cases, and something about their race in 24%. Here in particular, however, vagueness rather than specificity is the rule. Thus, phrases like "predominantly white" and "predominantly middle-class" are common; exact numbers and methods of calculation are less common. In partial defense of such vagueness, we can note that developmental researchers seldom have access to the data (e.g., parents' income or educational level) from which social class is determined; thus, "predominantly middle-class" may be as specific as the researcher can be. Nevertheless, there is an unfortunate blurriness about matters that may be of some importance.

Less defensible is the frequent failure to say anything about how the sample was recruited. As we noted in chapter 1, subjects do not magically appear to be tested; rather, the researcher must always make various decisions about whom to approach and how. Three questions are of importance. First, what was the initial pool from which subjects were solicited? In infancy research, for example, has the researcher worked from birth announcements in the local newspaper, from the rolls of a well-baby clinic, or from names provided by pediatricians? The populations that can be identified from these various sources may well differ. A second question concerns the percentage of potential participants who did in fact agree to participate. If 100 recent mothers have been contacted, for example, how many actually end up bringing their babies in for testing? Or in a study with grade-school children, what percentage of parents return the parental consent forms that are almost always required these days in research with children? The final question concerns the percentage of subjects who begin the research who are still present at the end—or, to put it differently, how many must be rejected in the course of the study. In some kinds of research, most notably almost anything with infants, loss of subjects may be a real problem. In contrast to data about social class, information about selection of subjects *is* available to the researcher. Yet, our survey indicates that such information is seldom reported. In only 12% of the articles are we told with any exactness how the sample

was recruited and what proportion of those contacted agreed to participate. In only 36% are we told how many subjects were rejected in the course of the study.

Given these gaps in reporting, what can be said about samples in developmental research? Such samples appear to be generally of sufficient size, and they typically include both males and females. Although both sexes may be studied, however, in only 57% of the cases is sex included as a variable in the analyses; thus, we often do not learn whether boys and girls were similar or different in response. The samples are clearly predominantly white, with substantial numbers of black children appearing only when possible group differences are a specific focus of the research. The samples are also mostly middle class, and they appear to be drawn primarily from towns or cities in which universities, and thus researchers, are located. Inner-city and rural children are especially underrepresented. Finally, we can note that in those studies that compare children's performance with that of adults the adult samples are invariably college students—hardly a random or representative sample of the general adult population.

What are the implications of this survey? Clearly, the samples studied by developmental psychologists often depart from perfect representativeness in a variety of ways. But how serious are the effects of these departures? Do they really throw into question the external validity of much of what is done in developmental psychology? For various reasons, the answer to this question is probably no. Because virtually any sample is going to deviate from perfect representativeness in some way, the question becomes whether it is at all plausible that the particular deviations have any effect on the generalizability of the results. Often it is not plausible that they do. Generalization always involves going beyond what can be logically guaranteed by the data, and in many cases it simply makes more sense to generalize than not to generalize.

This optimistic appraisal concerning external validity requires some qualifications. First, the confidence with which we can generalize from an admittedly less-than-perfect sample varies with the particular behavior being studied. If our interest, for example, is in infant heart rate change to repeated stimulation, then any sample of healthy, normally reared babies is likely to be predictive of any other such sample. If we wish to study the development of political beliefs, however, then a single limited sample may be a quite shaky basis for generalization. Generalizability may also vary with the particular aspect of a behavioral system that we are studying. In Piagetian testing, for example (see chapter 7), the age at which a particular conservation problem is mastered may vary markedly from sample to sample. On the other hand, the general movement from nonconservation to conservation, or the relative ordering of different conservation concepts, may be quite invariant across a wide variety of samples. Again, what we can generalize depends on what we are studying.

The argument just offered raises a natural question: How can we know which phenomena are readily generalizable and which are more sample-specific? In some cases (e.g., the heart rate–political belief contrast) the answer may seem intuitively obvious, and in some cases (e.g., the different Piagetian phenomena) it may be predicted from theory. The only way ever to be sure, however, is to study the same phenomenon in a variety of samples. Such *replication* efforts, in fact, should extend not just to different samples but to different investigators, different laboratories, and different specific (but presumably irrelevant) aspects of procedure. It is only if the result is replicable across such variations that we can really have confidence in its external validity.

We are ready now to move from the general question of what samples are like to more specific questions of how to make comparisons between various groups within a sample. As noted, we consider comparisons of two sorts: between different ages and between different experimental conditions. Because the former is the more specifically developmental question, we begin with it, and with one of the two main approaches for making age comparisons: the longitudinal approach.

AGE COMPARISONS

Longitudinal Designs

A *longitudinal study* tests the same sample at least twice across some period of time. Although there are no clear-cut rules for deciding when a study with repeated testing becomes "longitudinal," at least two rough criteria seem to govern use of the label. First, the reference is usually to the study of naturally occurring rather than experimentally induced changes. Thus, the use of delayed follow-up tests in intervention or training research is not usually classified as longitudinal, even though the same children may be tested several times. Second, the reference is typically to repeated tests that span an appreciable period of time. Thus, simply testing the same people several times at 1-week intervals is not likely to earn a study the designation "longitudinal." Note, however, that what constitutes "an appreciable period of time" will vary with the developmental level of the sample. A series of 1-week retests probably *would* be considered longitudinal if the subjects were only a few days old at the time of the initial testing.

As noted in Table 1-2, our journal search included a tabulation of the proportion of longitudinal and cross-sectional studies in the articles surveyed. As might be expected, the cross-sectional approach is by far the dominant method of studying age differences, accounting for some 81% of the studies, as compared to 14% for longitudinal and 5% for mixed designs.[1] A little thought will immediately suggest

---

[1]Our survey's focus on the journals *Child Development* and *Developmental Psychology* may result in a slight underestimation of the frequency of longitudinal research. Because of the quantity of information obtained, longitudinal studies may often be published in monograph or book form. During the years 1981 to 1983, for example, 47% of the articles published in the *Monographs of the Society for Research in Child Development* included longitudinal testing.

one set of reasons for this disparity: Longitudinal studies are more time-consuming, more expensive, and more difficult to bring to successful completion than are cross-sectional studies. Consider as examples our two illustrative studies from chapter 2. The Miller et al. delay-of-gratification experiment probably took a few weeks to complete. Had they opted for longitudinal rather than cross-sectional testing, the minimum time period for the study would have been 3 years. The contrast is, of course, even clearer for the Schonfield and Robertson study. If these authors had decided on a longitudinal approach, they would have had to wait 40 or 50 years for their young adults to turn into elderly adults.

In itself, the extended time frame of the longitudinal approach is simply a practical problem—bothersome certainly, but not a threat to the validity of the conclusions. There are other problems associated with the extended time, however, that do threaten validity. One is the possible obsolescence of the tests and instruments being used. Because the essence of the longitudinal design is the earlier time–later time comparison, the researcher is committed to continued use of whatever measures were selected at the beginning of the project. Often, however, a test may become outmoded or lose its theoretical interest in the course of a long study; conversely, new tests and new issues will almost certainly arise. Thus, what one wants to know in 1970 may not be what one wished to know in 1940. This problem of test obsolescence is especially great in really long-term studies, such as some of the life-span studies begun in the 1920s (Kagan, 1964). It need not be a problem in more short-term longitudinal efforts.

Other problems relate to the nature of the sample in longitudinal research. Any at all long-term longitudinal study requires a substantial commitment of time and effort on the part of its subjects (and, in the case of child samples, the parents of the subjects as well). Samples may be selected, therefore, at least partly on the basis of factors such as belief in the value of research or probable geographical stability. If so, they may not be representative of the population to which the researcher wishes to generalize. Furthermore, any single longitudinal sample, all born at about the same time, constitutes but a single generation or *cohort,* and any findings may be at least somewhat specific to this one generation. We may be interested, for example, in how people change across the first 30 years of life. If all of our sample were born in 1940, however, then all we know with any certainty is how people born in 1940 changed as they encountered the changing world of the 1940s, 1950s, and 1960s. Had our sample been born either earlier or later, we might have obtained somewhat different results.

Although longitudinal samples may be nonrepresentative in various ways, they do at least avoid Campbell and Stanley's (1966) problem of *selection bias*—that is, the selection of initially nonequivalent groups for comparison. There can be no problem of selection bias when each subject is being compared with him- or herself. There can, however, be *selective drop-out* (also labeled *attrition* or *mortality*), and such drop-out does in fact occur. Subjects can be lost from longitudinal samples for a variety of reasons—change of residence, unwillingness to continue to participate, or (especially in elderly samples) mortality in its literal sense. If such drop-outs were random, then the only problems would be the reduction in sample size and the waste of effort in collecting early measures for which there turns out to be no later counterpart. Often, however, the drop-out is not random but selective—that is, subjects who are lost from the study are systematically different from those who remain. In longitudinal studies of IQ, for example, subjects who drop out tend to have lower scores on the initial tests than do subjects who continue (e.g., Schaie, Labouvie, & Barrett, 1973). Because the lower-competence drop-outs contribute scores at the younger but not the older ages, the result is a "positive bias" in favor of the older groups. It is possible, of course, to limit the younger-older comparison to subjects who remain in the study and thus contribute scores at all ages. In this case, however, the initially nonrepresentative sample becomes even more nonrepresentative.

There is still one further way in which the

subjects of a longitudinal study differ from the broader population to which the researcher wishes to generalize. The difference is an obvious one: The subjects in a longitudinal study undergo repeated psychological testing of a kind that most of the population escapes. Two of Campbell and Stanley's (1966) threats to validity are therefore potentially relevant. One is *testing*: the effects upon later test performance of having taken the same or a similar test earlier. It seems likely, for example, that taking the same IQ test repeatedly at fairly close intervals could eventually begin to affect a subject's responses, and indeed research demonstrates that practice effects do occur (e.g., Nesselroade & Baltes, 1974). The second problem is the more general one of *reactivity*. Knowledge that one is the subject of research can affect any subject's responses, and such knowledge is probably especially salient for the subjects of long-term, frequent-measurement longitudinal studies. Responses obtained from such subjects, therefore, may not be representative of the typical course of development.

Note that the problems just discussed need not apply to all longitudinal studies. They are probably most likely in studies that involve frequent and explicit testing of developmentally mature samples. At the other extreme, the researcher who carries out an observational study of infant development probably does not need to worry much about either testing or reactivity.

The final problem to be noted is an elaboration of our earlier point about the one-generational nature of many longitudinal samples. In longitudinal research there is an inevitable confounding between the age of the subjects and the historical time of testing. This confounding follows from the fact that the age comparisons are all within subject; if we want different ages, therefore, we must test at different times. Suppose, for example, that we wish to examine possible changes between age 15 and age 20. We select a sample born in 1965 whom we test at age 15 and again at age 20. Should the second measure differ from the first, we would have two possible explanations for the difference: the fact that the subjects are 5 years older, or the fact that one test was given in 1980 and the other in 1985. Age can never be disentangled from time in a longitudinal design.

Once again, the likelihood that the potential problem is in reality a problem depends on the particular phenomena being studied. Let us move to the elderly years for our example of this point. Imagine that our interest is in changes in visual acuity as people age. We test a sample of 60-year-olds in 1970 and the same people at age 70 in 1980. Although historical time is a logically possible explanation for any changes we find, it is not a very plausible explanation in the case of a dependent variable like acuity. What is more likely, should we find differences, is that the visual system really undergoes natural changes between age 60 and age 70. Imagine, however, that instead of visual acuity we had tested attitudes toward political leaders. We find that such attitudes are more negative at age 70 than at age 60. A clear case of political alienation with increasing age? Hardly, given the political events of the early 1970s. In this case the historical-cultural explanation seems the more plausible one. In both cases, however, the standard longitudinal design permits conclusions that are at best plausible, not certain. The confounding of age and time can never be removed.

Our catalogue of the woes that can beset the longitudinal researcher raises the question of why anyone other than a confirmed masochist would ever attempt a longitudinal study. The answer, as might be expected, is that the longitudinal approach has a number of compensating virtues. It is to the more positive side of longitudinal studies that we turn next.

We noted earlier the distinction between age changes and age differences. As long as different samples are studied at different ages, the only direct measure a study can provide is of age differences; it is a further inference that any differences found reflect changes from the earlier to the later age. In longitudinal studies, however, the measure of age changes is direct rather than inferred. As we have seen, there can be questions about why the changes occur or how generalizable they are. But at least the focus is squarely on the central question of developmental psychology: that of intraindividual development over time.

The focus on intraindividual development makes the longitudinal approach uniquely suited to questions of individual consistency or individual change. Suppose that we wish to know whether a child's IQ tends to remain the same or to go up or down as the child develops. Clearly, we cannot answer this question by testing different children at different ages; rather, we must follow the same child as he or she develops. The issue of "constancy of IQ" has in fact been the subject of a number of longitudinal studies, both of historic vintage (e.g., Thorndike, 1933) and more recent (e.g., Rubin & Balow, 1979). Whenever our interest is in individual consistency or change, then the longitudinal approach is not merely a nicety; it is a must.

The value of the longitudinal approach is not limited to tracing the course of a single trait or a single behavioral system over time. The value, rather, is much broader, for potentially *any* interesting cross-age patterning can be examined if we only obtain the measures of interest. In some cases the focus may be on the relation between one aspect of the child's development early in life and some other aspect later in life. We might seek to determine, for example, whether speed of skeletal maturation in the first two years relates to age of onset of puberty at adolescence. In other cases the interest may be in the relation between some aspect of the environment early in life and some aspect of development later in life. Thus, we might try to determine whether the parents' childrearing practices during the child's first two years relate to measures of the child's personality at middle childhood or adolescence. Whenever our interest is in the relation between something early and something later, then the longitudinal approach is again a must.

Longitudinal research is also especially suited for tracing the continuous and progressive transformations that certain very general behavioral systems undergo as the child develops. This rather murky statement needs to be clarified by examples, and two examples will in fact readily occur to anyone familiar with research in developmental psychology. One is Piaget's research on the development of intelligence in infancy (Piaget, 1952). Piaget studied each of his three children longitudinally from birth to about 2½, painstakingly charting the sequences within and relations among various domains of intelligent behavior. The result was a conception of infant intelligence that in scope and insight surpassed anything that had come before and has served as a model for much that has been done since. It is possible that at least some of the same insights might have been derived from a judicious cross-sectional study of different babies at different ages; it is doubtful, however, that the full picture of infant intelligence and how it develops could ever have emerged without the intensive, almost day-to-day study of changes within a single child over time.

A similar argument can be made for research on early language development (e.g., Brown, 1973). In much the same way as Piaget, researchers of child language have used the longitudinal approach to trace gradual changes in language across the early years of language learning. What, for example, is the earliest form that negation takes in the child's speech, and how does this rudimentary form eventually turn into the complex rule system of the older child or adult? Again, the intensive longitudinal study, in which changes can be charted within a single child, has made possible a view of early language and how it evolves that probably could not have been gleaned from cross-sectional study alone.

Clearly, longitudinal research of the sort just described involves more than simply testing the same child at least twice; such research becomes, rather, an extended case history of individual development. When is such intensive longitudinal study likely to prove most fruitful? We can note first that it is likely to be most feasible with young subjects whose behavior is least likely to be affected by the frequent observations. This practical point aside, certainly a prime rationale for the kind of longitudinal research just discussed lies in its application to new research terrain in which many of the basic phenomena still remain to be discovered. "New terrain" was certainly an accurate description of the field of infant intelligence when Piaget began his work. Once some idea of the general form and salient landmarks of development has emerged, more focused cross-sectional studies can be profitably applied. Longitudinal study is also especially suited to tracing the gradual construction of new abilities, the slow evolution of initially primitive forms through various intermediate steps to full maturity. How, for example (to add a Piagetian instance to the earlier example of negation), does the neonate's primitive grasping reflex eventually become the skilled, visually directed reaching of the older infant? Finally, the intensive study of the same children over time may be especially helpful when it comes to *interpreting* behavior—that is, attempting to move beyond the surface behavior itself to some conception of the underlying basis for it (a cognitive structure? linguistic rule? individually learned response? or what?). In most research the investigator sees the subjects for the first and only time when they appear for testing, and his or her ability to make sense of their behavior is dependent on this very brief interaction. Piaget, however, had been studying the same children literally since birth, and his extensive knowledge of each child's background gave him an excellent basis for interpreting any particular behavior from the child.[2]

Our last argument in support of the longitudinal approach is of a more negative sort. The main alternative to the longitudinal design is the cross-sectional design, yet the cross-sectional design is also subject to a number of serious criticisms. Possible problems with cross-sectional studies are the subject of our next section.

Cross-Sectional Designs

A *cross-sectional study* tests different people at different ages. For this reason, the cross-sectional approach cannot measure age changes

directly, nor can it answer questions about individual stability over time. As we saw, these limitations of the cross-sectional approach provide a primary motivation for longitudinal study.

There are other possible problems. Because cross-sectional studies test different samples at different ages, the possibility of *selection bias* arises. Perhaps the groups being compared differ not just on the independent variable of interest (in this case age) but in other ways as well, and it is these other differences that produce differences on the dependent measures. This issue was discussed briefly in chapter 2 when we considered the special nature of age as an independent variable. As noted there, the goal is not to rule out *all* differences between groups other than chronological age, but just those differences that are not naturally associated with age. We noted too that in most cases the decision about what to match is fairly obvious—for example, sex, race, social class, IQ. What must be added now, however, is that actually achieving the desired matching may not always be easy. Developmental researchers typically draw samples of different ages from quite different sources—newborns from a hospital nursery, infants from parents who respond to solicitations to participate, preschoolers from nursery schools or day-care centers, children between 5 and 11 from elementary schools, adolescents from junior high schools or high schools, adults from college classes. The populations served by these different settings may differ in a number of ways. Thus, even though the researcher may realize the importance of matching, selecting groups that are in fact comparable may prove difficult.

Bias can also occur in the form of *selective drop-out* from the study. An initial equivalence between groups may quickly vanish if some subjects drop out before testing is completed. The problem is not simply that there may be more drop-outs at one age than another. The problem, rather, is the same one identified for longitudinal studies: Subjects who drop out may be different from those who remain in. Thus, once again it is the "selective" part of selective drop-out that threatens validity.

---

[2]Ginsburg and Opper (1979) provide a good discussion of both this point and other virtues of Piaget's approach.

It is not hard to imagine situations in which selective drop-out might bias comparisons between different ages. Suppose that we are doing a study of nursery-school children. We divide our sample into younger (2½ to 4) and older (4 to 5½) children, thus giving us two groups to compare. Our procedure is a fairly demanding one, requiring the child to process a variety of instructions and to continue to respond appropriately for a lengthy period. Not all nursery-school children are capable of such responding, and some are therefore lost from the study. The odds are strong that more children will be lost from the younger group than from the older group. The odds are strong also that those children who are lost will be, on the average, the less competent members of the sample. If so, we will end up with two noncomparable groups: a fairly representative sample of older children, and a distinctly nonrepresentative, biased-toward-superior sample of younger children. Clearly, any such differential drop-out would decrease the chances of finding an improvement in performance with age.

In general, selective drop-out in cross-sectional studies with children probably works in the manner just suggested and has the effect just suggested—that is, creation of a positive bias in favor of the younger group. The result would be some underestimation of the extent to which performance improves with age. Because the researcher generally expects to find improvement with age, the bias would work against one of the hypotheses of the study. If there must be bias in a study, then it is best to have it work against the investigator's hypothesis. Clearly, however, it is better to have no bias at all.

Let us return to the issue of initial selection of subjects. We have twice stated that decisions about what to match when comparing different age groups are generally straightforward. It is time now to consider the exceptions implied by the qualifier "generally." Uncertainties about what should be matched are most likely when there is a wide separation between the ages being compared and thus many ways in which the groups potentially differ. They loom largest, therefore, in research comparing elderly adults with younger samples. Baltes, Reese, and

Nesselroade (1977) provide a nice example. They note that the average amount of schooling completed is considerably greater now than it was in the early part of the century. Suppose, then, that we wish to do a study comparing 25-year-olds and 75-year-olds. If we sample randomly at each age, our younger sample will be more highly educated than our older sample. We would have, then, a confounding of age and educational level. If we restrict our older sample to the more highly educated individuals, we will achieve comparability in educational level, but at the cost of selecting a nonrepresentative, positively biased older group. Neither solution is very satisfactory; perhaps the best course, if the researcher has the resources, is to incorporate both approaches (see Green, 1969, for an example). The main point, however, is that age and educational level, at this point in history, are unavoidably confounded in any attempt to compare adults of different ages.

The point just made about matching is actually part of a larger point concerning cross-sectional designs. We noted earlier that the longitudinal approach to studying age differences involves an inevitable confounding of age and time of testing. We can note now that the cross-sectional approach involves an inevitable confounding of age and generation or cohort. The samples in a cross-sectional study, being different ages, must necessarily be born at different times and grow up under at least somewhat different sets of circumstances. The disparity in educational opportunities between today's 25-year-old and today's 75-year-old is just one example of such generational differences. Many other examples could easily be cited. Today's 75-year-olds encountered one world war during childhood and another during adulthood, coped with the Great Depression during their early years of employment, somehow survived until well into adulthood without TV and many other commonplaces of modern life, and so forth. Suppose, then, that we find that 25-year-olds and 75-year-olds differ on our dependent measure. Should we attribute the difference to differences in age or differences in generation?

As with the other threats to validity discussed in this chapter, the extent to which the age-cohort confound is in fact a problem depends on the particular kind of study being done. Two factors are important in assessing the likelihood of cohort effects. One is the dependent variable under study. We can return again to some of our earlier examples to illustrate this point. If our focus is on political attitudes or IQ test performance, then cohort effects may be quite important; indeed, such effects have been clearly demonstrated in the study of IQ (e.g., Schaie & Labouvie-Vief, 1974). If our focus is on heart-rate change or visual acuity, then cohort effects are much less likely to be important. In general, the more "basic" and "biological" a dependent variable appears, the less likely it is to vary across cohorts. Note, however, that there can almost always be dispute about how "basic" and cohort-general a particular variable is. Perhaps, for example, visual acuity actually *does* vary across generations as a function of changes in factors such as adequacy of artificial lighting or presence of TV during the formative years.

The other factor to consider is the age spread of the sample. Cohort effects are most obviously a problem in studies with widely separated age groups. Indeed, the issue of cohort differences first arose in research comparing young adult and old adult samples, and it is still most often discussed in that context. At the other extreme, the child psychologist who compares 3- and 4-year-olds probably does not need to worry about the fact that one group was born in 1979 and the other in 1980. Samples within the span of childhood can usually be assumed to belong to the same generation. Even here, however, doubts may arise. What about a comparison between a pre-Sesame Street 14-year-old and a post-Sesame Street 8-year-old? What about a comparison between a "new math" 11-year-old and a "back-to-basics" 7-year-old? We live in a time of rapid cultural and educational change, and these changes may affect at least some between-age comparisons even among child samples.

The final problem to be noted is that of *measurement equivalence*. If we wish to compare the level of a particular behavior or particular ability in different age groups, then we need a procedure that can accurately tap the behavior or ability at each of the ages being studied. Often, however, a test that is appropriate for one age may not be appropriate for another age. A test of classification skills, for example, may be a fine indicator of such skills among 7-year-olds but may be too verbally demanding for many 4-year-olds. If so, the test may measure different things at the two ages: classification at age 7 and vocabulary at age 4. Note that the test would still reveal a genuine and perhaps important difference between the two ages: 7-year-olds really do perform better on this measure than do 4-year-olds. But the basis for the difference might not be the one that the investigator is seeking to study.

The problem of measurement equivalence is not limited to cross-sectional studies. The issue arises in any comparison of different ages; thus it applies with equal force to the longitudinal approach. The particular form of the equivalence problem, however, is likely to be different in longitudinal than in cross-sectional studies. Consider the longitudinal study of aggression (e.g., Kagan & Moss, 1962). The investigator who studies aggression in a group of children at age 2 and again at age 12 is unlikely to be interested simply in comparing levels of aggression at the two ages. If levels of aggression *were* the focus, then serious problems would arise from the fact that the forms that aggression takes and the circumstances under which it occurs are quite different at age 12 than at age 2. The fact that the same children are being studied over time, however, probably means that the real interest of the longitudinal investigator is in the *stability of individual differences* in aggression as children develop. The question, in other words, is whether children who are relatively high or low in aggression at age 2 are also relatively high or low in aggression at age 12. A child may be high in aggression at both 2 and 12 even though the frequency and forms of the behavior have changed greatly. This focus on relative standing within a group, rather than absolute level of response, provides a partial solution to the measurement-equivalence problem. Note, however, that it is still necessary to have valid measures of aggression at both ages.

More Complicated Designs

A clear message from the preceding discussion is that both the longitudinal and the cross-sectional approach suffer from various limitations. Table 3–2 summarizes the problems that we have discussed. Some of these problems are at least in principle avoidable—for example, the possibility of selection bias in cross-sectional research. Some of the problems, however, are intrinsic to the longitudinal and cross-sectional designs and hence can never be ruled out. Specifically, it is impossible ever to avoid the confounding of age with generation in the cross-sectional approach or the confounding of age with time of measurement in the longitudinal approach.

These limitations of the traditional longitudinal and cross-sectional designs have been much discussed in recent years, and they have motivated the development of several new procedures for studying changes with age. Because these new procedures have thus far been applied most often in studies of old age, we defer our main discussion of them until the chapter on aging (chapter 9). A brief introduction is possible here, however.

Figure 3–1 provides a schematic summary of the two designs that we have discussed thus far. The body of the figure shows the ages that would be obtained from the various combinations of date of birth and year of measurement. A longitudinal design would be represented by any of the rows in the figure. In this case, a sample of subjects born at the same time is

TABLE 3–2 Problems with Longitudinal and Cross-Sectional Designs

Longitudinal	Cross-Sectional
Practical difficulties (expensive, time-consuming)	No direct measure of age changes
Possible obsolescence of measures	Inapplicable to issues of individual stability
Possible nonrepresentative samples	Possible selection bias
Limitation to a single cohort	Possible selective drop-out
Possible selective drop-out	Difficulty in establishing equivalent measures
Effects of repeated testing	Confounding of age and time of birth (cohort)
Difficulty in establishing equivalent measures	
Confounding of age and time of measurement	

studied repeatedly across a span of ages. A cross-sectional design would be represented by any of the columns in the figure. In this case, separate samples born in different years are studied at the same time.

Figure 3–1 also includes a third design that we have not yet discussed: the *time-lag design*. A time-lag design would be represented by any of the diagonals in the figure. Thus, we might study a sample of 40-year-olds in 1980, another sample of 40-year-olds in 1990, another sample of 40-year-olds in 2000, and another sample in 2010. Clearly, the time-lag design cannot give us direct information about age changes or age differences, because only one age group is studied. What it can do, however, is provide information about factors that may confound the age

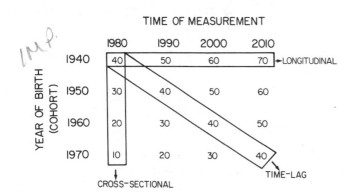

FIGURE 3–1. Examples of longitudinal, cross-sectional, and time-lag designs (numbers in the body of the figure indicate ages).

comparisons in longitudinal or cross-sectional designs. Specifically, if we find differences among our samples of 40-year-olds, then we know that these differences must reflect either generational factors (the main confound in the cross-sectional design) or time-of-measurement factors (the main confound in the longitudinal design) or, of course, some combination of the two factors. The fact that we cannot be certain which factor is important indicates that the time-lag design suffers from its own brand of confounding: a confound between generation and time of measurement.

Figure 3-2 pictures two more complicated designs. The *longitudinal-sequential design* selects samples from different cohorts (i.e., years of birth) and tests them repeatedly across the same span of time. In the example shown in the figure, groups born in 1960 and 1970 are tested repeatedly from 1980 to 2010.[3] Such a design offers three advantages over a standard longitudinal approach: (1) Because samples are drawn from different years of birth, the longitudinal comparisons are not limited to a single generation or cohort. (2) Because different age groups are tested at each time of measurement, there is a cross-sectional as well as a longitudinal dimension to the study. (3) Because the same age group is represented at different times of measurement, there is also a time-lag dimension to the study. There is, in short, more information than in a standard longitudinal study, and thus more chance to disentangle the contributions of age, generation, and time of measurement.

Also shown in Figure 3-2 is the *cross-sectional–sequential design*. A cross-sectional–sequential study tests separate cross-sectional samples at two or more times of measurement. In the example shown, a standard cross-sectional study is first performed with subjects from four different cohorts, all of whom are tested in 1980. Ten years later, a second cross-sectional comparison is made with *different* members of the same four cohorts. Because different people are studied at the two times, this design does not provide the direct measure of intraindividual change that is the core of the longitudinal approach. At the same time, the design avoids some of the problems found with longitudinal designs, such as the effects of repeated testing on the subject's behavior. In comparison to a standard cross-sectional design, the sequential approach has the advantage of at least partially unconfounding age and year of birth (because we have at least two different cohorts for each age tested); it also provides a time-lag comparison through the appearance of the same age group at different times of testing. Again, there is simply more information to work with than in the standard design.

As noted, we consider these designs more fully in chapter 9. Two points can be made

---

[3]It should be clear that the entire figure could also be considered a longitudinal-sequential design—that is, if we filled all the cells in the figure, selecting samples from all four cohorts and testing them at all four times of measurement, what we would have is a (quite complex) longitudinal-sequential study.

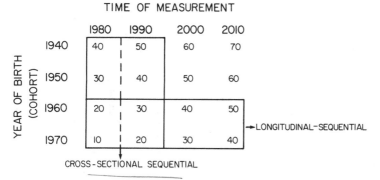

TIME OF MEASUREMENT

FIGURE 3-2. Examples of longitudinal-sequential and cross-sectional–sequential designs (numbers in the body of the figure indicate ages).

here, however. First, it is obvious that sequential designs, though more informative, are also considerably more costly—in time, effort, and money—than the simpler cross-sectional and longitudinal designs. At the extreme, consider the challenge that would face a researcher who actually attempted the task described in Footnote 3—that is, to fill all the cells in Figure 3–2! In any research project there are a large number of things that would be desirable to do, only a subset of which it is actually possible to do. The best designs are always those that can actually be carried out.

The second point concerns recent criticisms that have been directed to the traditional longitudinal and cross-sectional designs. In some cases these criticisms have been quite severe. Baltes et al. (1977), for example, write that "both the simple cross-sectional and longitudinal methods show such a lack of necessary control that data collected by application of either of them are for the most part of little validity and little use to the developmental researcher" (p. 124). This is a serious indictment, given the fact that (at a conservative estimate) 99% of the data we have concerning changes with age come from either cross-sectional or longitudinal studies. Is most of what developmental psychologists have done really worthless?

Many developmentalists would dispute such a pessimistic verdict. It is true that the goal of good research design is always to minimize threats to validity, and that the ideal design would be one that removes all such threats. Unfortunately, it is never possible to rule out every conceivable alternative explanation for one's findings. The question then becomes how plausible the alternative explanations are. As argued earlier, often such explanations are not at all plausible. Especially when we are dealing with samples within the span of childhood, and especially when we are studying basic sorts of development (physical maturation, perceptual constancy, Piagetian concepts, linguistic rules—the list could be made quite long), the traditional longitudinal and cross-sectional methods may be perfectly adequate. Suppose, for example, that we are studying the Piagetian con-

cept of conservation of number—that is, the realization that number is invariant in the face of an irrelevant perceptual change. We find that 6-year-olds can conserve number whereas 4-year-olds cannot. It is wildly unlikely that such a finding results either from the fact that one group was born in 1978 and one group in 1980 (as might be true in a cross-sectional study) or from the fact that one group was tested in 1982 and one group in 1984 (as might be true in a longitudinal study). It is much more plausible, rather (and indeed, given our current knowledge, quite without dispute), that such a finding reflects a genuine change with age. In such cases, cross-sectional or longitudinal methods may produce data about age changes that are of considerable validity and considerable use. (For another defense of the traditional methods, oriented especially to the value of longitudinal study, see McCall, 1977.)

CONDITION COMPARISONS

Within-Subject versus Between-Subject Designs

We turn now to the question of how to make comparisons between two or more tests or experimental conditions. We noted earlier that two general approaches are possible: administering all tasks or conditions to the same subjects or assigning different subjects to different experimental groups. The former is labeled a *within-subject design*; the latter, a *between-subject design*. Because our discussion of these two approaches involves much back-and-forth comparison, it is simplest to consider them together rather than separately.

How does an investigator decide whether to make comparisons within or between subjects? Just as in the longitudinal versus cross-sectional decision, matters of convenience may often play an important role. Usually (with a qualifier to be noted shortly), a within-subject approach means that fewer subjects are needed. Suppose, for example, that we have three tasks whose difficulty we wish to compare, and we know that we will need at least 20 respondents on each task to determine whether any differences in difficulty are present. If we opt for a between-subject approach we will need at least 60 subjects to complete the study; with a within-subject approach, however, a mere 20 may suffice. Whenever the pool of possible subjects is limited, the economy of a within-subject design may be quite attractive.

Considerations of convenience do not always fall on the side of the within-subject approach, however. The smaller sample size in a within-subject study is bought at an obvious price— namely, more time spent with each subject, either in longer experimental sessions or in a greater number of sessions. Especially in work with young children, lengthy or repeated sessions may tax the subject's motivation or endurance. Even if the investigator is not concerned about such demands on the subject, the parents or school authorities may be. In such situations, a between-subject design, in which the demands on any one child are minimized, may be the most sensible approach.

Statistical considerations may also affect the within versus between decision. The statistical tests appropriate for within-subject comparisons are somewhat different from those appropriate for between-subject comparisons. Furthermore, within-subject tests are often more powerful than between-subject tests—that is, more likely to reveal a significant difference if a difference does in fact exist. This greater power stems from the reduction in unwanted variance afforded by the within-subject design. Recall our earlier discussion of primary variance compared to secondary or error variance. As we noted then, a goal of good experimental design is to maximize primary variance, or variance associated with the independent variable, and to minimize unwanted variance from other sources. We noted too that the inevitable differences that exist among different subjects are one source of unwanted variance. Use of the same subjects for all experimental conditions reduces such variance and hence enhances the power of any comparisons made. The result is a greater likelihood that a difference of a given magnitude will achieve statistical significance.

Both between-subject and within-subject designs are subject to their own particular forms of bias. The obvious threat in between-subject designs is selection bias. Because different subjects are assigned to different conditions, the possibility will always exist that any differences that are found between conditions reflect preexisting differences among the subjects and not a true effect of the experimental manipulations. This possibility does not arise in a within-subject design, in which each subject responds under each condition. Note that this advantage of within-subject over between-subject designs parallels an advantage discussed earlier for longitudinal compared to cross-sectional approaches.

There are two ways to try to rule out possible selection biases in a between-subject design (recall Table 2–3). One is to match subjects on variables of potential importance. We consider the pros and cons of matching shortly. The other is the approach discussed in chapter 2: random assignment of subjects to different groups. If the sample size is sufficiently large, and if the assignment of subjects to conditions is truly random, then preexisting differences among subjects should be controlled and confounding of subject and condition avoided. As argued in chapter 2, the logic of the random-assignment approach is impeccable; the challenge is to ensure that the two "if" questions really do receive positive answers.

The most obvious threat to the validity of within-subject designs concerns the possible effects of repeated testing. Consider a study in which the researcher wishes to compare the relative difficulty of several cognitive tasks. He or she decides to use a within-subject design, in which every child receives every task. Because presenting several tasks takes time, the children may well become increasingly tired or bored as they move through the series of problems. If so, performance may be poorer on later tasks than on earlier ones. Alternatively, the children may be somewhat timid or confused at the start of the study but become increasingly relaxed and confident as the testing proceeds. In this case, performance may be better on later tasks than on earlier ones. In either case, the effects stemming from the repeated testing would cloud the intertask comparison that is the researcher's real interest.

"Warm-up" or "fatigue" effects of the sort just described fall under the general heading of order effects. The term *order effect* refers to any general tendency for response to change in a systematic fashion from early in a session to later in a session. Usually, the systematic change is either a general improvement or a general decrement in performance. Another potential problem in within-subject designs is the possibility of carry-over effects. A *carry-over effect* occurs whenever response to one task or condition varies as a function of whether another task or condition precedes or follows it. Let us try a simple example to clarify this rather forbidding-sounding definition. Imagine that we wish to compare the relative difficulty of two tasks: A and B. We will suppose that either task, presented in isolation, elicits 50% correct responding from our sample. It turns out, however, that when task A is presented first it suggests a helpful means of attacking task B; correct responses to B consequently rise to 70%. In contrast, when task B is presented first it suggests a means of solution that is maladaptive for task A; correct responses to A consequently fall to 30%. Note that in this case there is no general improvement or decline across the experimen-

tal session; rather, the finding is that response to one task depends on whether it is presented before or after the other task. Although the specific mechanism may differ, however, the general import of order effects and carry-over effects is the same: complications in the interpretation of task or condition comparisons.

Problems created by order effects are most likely when the experimenter adopts a constant order of presentation for the different tasks or conditions. An obvious prescription follows: Whenever comparisons among tasks or conditions are of interest, a single order of presentation should be avoided. Two alternatives to constant order exist. One is to *randomize* the order of tasks or conditions. In certain cases, perhaps especially when the number of tasks is large, randomization may be the most sensible approach. Generally, however, a better alternative than randomization is to *counterbalance* the order of presentation. Counterbalancing is conveyed more easily through example than through definition; a simple example is given in the upper left portion of Table 3-3. As can be seen, counterbalancing is a method for distributing a particular task or condition equivalently across the various possible ordinal positions. Thus, in the example task A occurs equally often in the first, second, and third po-

TABLE 3-3 Examples of Complete and Partial Counterbalancing

Complete Balancing	Three Tasks	Four Tasks			
	A B C	A B C D	B A C D	C A B D	D A B C
	A C B	A B D C	B A D C	C A D B	D A C B
	B A C	A C B D	B C A D	C B A D	D B A C
	B C A	A C D B	B C D A	C B D A	D B C A
	C A B	A D B C	B D A C	C D A B	D C A B
	C B A	A D C B	B D C A	C D B A	D C B A

Partial Balancing	Four Tasks	Five Tasks
	A B C D	A B C D E
	B D A C	B E D A C
	C A D B	C A E B D
	D C B A	D C B E A
		E D A C B

sitions; furthermore, it precedes and follows tasks B and C equally often in each position. The counterbalancing in this case is complete— that is, all possible permutations of the three tasks are used. Clearly, with more tasks the number of possible permutations increases; with four tasks there are 24 permutations (these are shown in the upper right part of Table 3–3), and with five tasks there are 120 permutations. In such cases complete counterbalancing may not be feasible; it is still possible, however, to select a subset of orders that will provide a reasonable degree of balancing. Examples of such orders for four-task and five-task studies are shown in the bottom part of Table 3–3.

Counterbalancing has two advantages over randomization. First, it *ensures* that there is no confounding of task and order of presentation, an outcome that cannot be ensured by randomization alone. Second, because confounding has been ruled out, it permits the researcher to compare the different orders of presentation and tease out any order effects or carry-over effects that may be present in the data. Note, however, that such effects are likely to be identifiable only if the sample size is reasonably large and each order is represented sufficiently often. This point provides the qualifier for our earlier statement that within-subject designs require fewer subjects than between-subject designs: Whenever possible effects of order are of interest, then the N necessary for a within-subject study may increase substantially.

Thus far we have discussed a number of factors that a researcher can weigh in deciding between a within-subject and a between-subject design. In some cases, however, there is no decision to make; the nature of the research question dictates the design to be used. Specifically, whenever the interest is in within-subject patterning of performance, then a within-subject design is necessary. Whenever the interest is in definite and persistent change as a result of the experimental manipulation, then a between-subject design is necessary. We now elaborate on both of these points.

The argument with respect to within-subject patterning parallels an argument made earlier in support of longitudinal designs. There, we saw that questions concerning individual consistency or individual change over time require a longitudinal approach in which the same people are studied as they develop. Similarly, questions concerning the relation between two or more measures at any given time require a within-subject approach in which the same people are studied across the different measures. Suppose, for example, that we wish to know whether a child's role-taking skills relate to his or her ability to communicate information to others (e.g., Shantz, 1975). Clearly, we cannot assess role taking in one group of children and communication in another group; rather we must have both measures for all children. Suppose (to return to an earlier example) that we wish to know whether children's IQs relate to their grades in school. We cannot assess IQ in one sample and grades in another sample; again, we must have both measures for all children. Or suppose (to preview an example discussed more fully in chapter 7) that we wish to know the order in which various cognitive concepts are acquired. Is it the case, for example, as Piaget has claimed, that all children master conservation of mass before conservation of weight and conservation of weight before conservation of volume? The only way to find out is to study all three concepts in the same group of children. All of these examples illustrate a prime rationale for within-subject study: to identify interrelations and patterning in development.

The argument with respect to manipulations that produce change is in some respects similar to points made earlier concerning testing effects in longitudinal designs and carry-over effects in within-subject designs. The essential point is that administering one task or experimental condition may change the subject in a way that makes him or her unusable for other tasks or conditions. Suppose that we wish to compare the effectiveness of several different methods of training conservation concepts (e.g., Smith, 1968). We select a group of nonconservers and administer training condition A. We can hardly then take the same children and administer condition B, for if condition A is at all effective many of the children will no longer be nonconservers! The same argument applies to any research whose goal is to bring about lasting change in its subjects—intervention programs for so-called disadvantaged children, therapy programs for disturbed children, parent-education programs for new parents, and so forth. In each case, if we wish to compare the effectiveness of different programs we need a between-subject design that assigns different subjects to the different approaches. Note too that the argument is not limited to attempts to produce sweeping changes à la intervention or therapy; it may apply to more focused, short-term changes as well. Suppose, for example, that we wish to know whether inducing children to use verbal rehearsal helps them on a short-term memory task (e.g., Ferguson & Bray, 1976). We cannot expect that children who have been taught such a strategy will necessarily abandon it once we remove the instruction to verbalize; rather, if we want a rehearsal–no rehearsal comparison we need to test separate groups of subjects.

There is a possible objection to our last example and the conclusion drawn from it. In the verbal-rehearsal case our interest is not in the relative effectiveness of several different treatments; the interest, rather, is in whether a *single* treatment will lead to improvement over a no-treatment baseline. It is true that we cannot apply the treatment and later expect to get a measure of performance in its absence. But why not proceed in the opposite order—that is, first measure the children's natural level of memory performance, then apply the treatment, and then measure memory performance again? Doing so would give us an example of what Campbell and Stanley (1966) label a One-Group Pretest–Posttest Design. The rationale would be that any improvement in performance from the pretest to the posttest would reflect the effects of the intervening treatment. If this rationale is valid, then there is no need to set up separate groups of subjects.

In certain simple situations this kind of One-Group design may be sufficient for the researcher's purposes. Generally, however, it is not. The weakness of such a design should be evident from our earlier discussion of experimental control: It permits a confounding of the experimental treatment with a number of other factors that might produce a pretest to posttest change. Let us take intervention programs as our example to make this point. Imagine that we find a group of disadvantaged 4-year-olds, give them a test of "academic readiness," subject them to a one-year intervention program designed to enhance academic skills, readminister the academic-readiness test at the end of the program, and find that scores have improved significantly. Evidence for the effectiveness of our program? Not necessarily. It may be that the improvement results from natural biological-maturational changes as the children age from 4 to 5—Campbell and Stanley's *maturation* variable. It may be that the improvement results from other events in the children's lives during the course of the program—Campbell and Stanley's *history* variable. It may be that the improvement results from practice effects gained from taking the initial pretest—Campbell and Stanley's *testing* variable. Or it may be that the improvement results from the natural upward movement of initially low scores upon retesting—Campbell and Stanley's *regression* variable. None of these rival hypotheses can be ruled out with a One-Group design; all could be ruled out if we included a separate, no-treatment control group.

Our comparison of within-subject and between-subject approaches could use some summarizing. Listed in Table 3–4 are the various pros and cons that we have discussed as relevant to the within-subject versus between-subject decision.

Matching

A clear comparison of different experimental conditions requires that the subjects assigned to the different conditions be equivalent at the start of the study. We have discussed two methods for creating such equivalence: random assignment of different subjects to different conditions, and repeated testing of the same subjects across all conditions. We turn now to a third possibility: *matching* subjects prior to their assignment to conditions.

TABLE 3–4 Relative Merits of Within-Subject and Between-Subject Designs

Factor	Comparison of Designs
Convenience	Fewer subjects with within; less time per subject with between
Statistical tests	Generally more powerful with within
Effects of repeated testing	A problem with within; not a problem with between
Possible selection bias	A problem with between; not a problem with within
Focus on within-subject patterning	Must have within; impossible with between
Focus on procedures that produce lasting change	Must have between; impossible with within

As we noted in chapter 2, virtually any between-subject study includes a limited degree of matching for obvious variables like age and sex. The question was posed then: Why limit ourselves to the obvious variables; why not go ahead and match on *all* variables of potential importance? A little thought will suggest an answer: We can never identify all potentially important variables, and even if we could we could never get the necessary data and achieve the necessary matching. Matching is always necessarily partial matching. Still, partial matching is presumably better than none; why not utilize it? It turns out that doing so has both advantages and disadvantages.

Probably the most often matched-for variable in research with children is IQ; we consequently take it as our example. If we wish to match children on IQ, we must first administer IQ tests to all of our potential subjects (or, perhaps, go to the school files and obtain already-collected IQ data). We then group together children with identical or close-to-identical IQ scores. The number of children in a group will depend on the number of experimental conditions—pairs of children if there are two conditions, trios if there are three conditions, and so forth. Working within these same-IQ groups, we then randomly assign different children to the different experimental conditions. Note, therefore, that random assignment remains important even in a matched-group design. Note also, however, that the initial matching on IQ ensures what randomization alone cannot ensure: that the experimental groups end up with equal IQs.

The great strength of the matching approach is that it does provide such exact and certain control for variables that might otherwise bias results. If IQ really does relate to performance on our dependent variable, then it is critical that there be no confounding of IQ and experimental condition. Matching also has certain statistical advantages. In much the same way as within-subject designs, a matched-group design reduces unwanted variance and hence increases the power of the statistical tests.

The main disadvantages of matching revolve around the question: Is it worth it? Matching typically requires a substantial investment of effort on the investigator's part, especially if he or she must pretest all of the potential subjects (as opposed to relying on already-existing data). If the matched-for variable is not in fact related to performance on the dependent variable, then the matching will have added nothing. If the sample size is large and random assignment is used, the groups will probably end up equivalent anyway, and again matching will add nothing. The point here has to do with efficiency of effort. We noted earlier that any research project involves selection of a relatively few specific procedures from a much larger pool of potentially informative procedures. To devote a portion of one's limited time and effort to procedures that do not enhance the study is simply bad research practice.

In addition to the possible waste of effort, matching can sometimes create particular problems. In some cases administering the matching pretest may bias the subjects' responses to the later test of interest (Campbell and Stanley's *reactivity* variable). Perhaps, for example, being taken out of their classroom and given an IQ test is anxiety arousing for some children, and makes them suspicious of the friendly tester who later invites them to "come play a game." The tester's attempt to create a game-like atmosphere for his or her measures may therefore come to naught, and the validity of the study may be affected. Matching can also sometimes result in loss of subjects. If subjects are matched in the manner described earlier, then the unit becomes the matched group rather than the individual child—for example, the trios of matched-for-IQ children in a study with three experimental conditions. If any member of a trio is lost from the study for any reason, then the other two must be eliminated as well. Whenever attrition of subjects seems likely, matching may turn out to be a costly decision.

There is one situation in which matching is a tempting but usually unsound procedure. It is the case in which the investigator wishes to bring about equality in initially unequal groups of subjects. We saw an earlier example in the discussion of the differing educational levels of young adult and elderly adult samples. Another example can be drawn from the domain of early-intervention programs. Imagine that we have designed a program intended to raise young children's scores on tests of academic readiness. We wish to know whether the program is equally effective for children from lower-class homes and children from middle-class homes. We run into a problem, however: On the average, pretest scores on our measures are higher for middle-class children than they are for lower-class children. This initial inequality creates problems in trying to determine whether the two groups benefit equally from the intervention. Suppose that the mean for the lower-class children rises from 40 to 60 and that for the middle-class children rises from 60 to 80. Are these equivalent gains (both, after all, are 20 points), or is the first a greater gain than the second (a 50% improvement versus a 33% improvement)? One way around this problem would be to select our samples initially so that both groups begin with mean scores of 50. In this case the gain scores could presumably be directly compared.

The major problem with such a procedure should be clear from our earlier discussion of statistical regression. In our attempt to begin

with equivalent groups we have selected the opposite extremes from our two initial populations: unusually high scoring lower-class children, and unusually low scoring middle-class children. This concentration on the extreme groups guarantees that regression will occur. Quite apart from the effects of our experimental treatment, we can be certain that on the average the scores for lower-class children will drop and those for middle-class children will rise. These regression effects will impede the identification of genuine treatment effects; they may even lead to the erroneous impression that the intervention is more effective for middle-class than for lower-class children.

Statistical regression is not the only problem that can arise from the attempt to match nonequivalent groups. Neale and Liebert (1980) provide a good discussion of some of the other difficulties that inappropriate matching can create. Whatever the specific problem, however, the general point is the same: Matching cannot be used to make two groups equivalent when the groups are in fact not equivalent.

SUMMARY

This chapter addresses three issues: sampling of subjects, comparison of different age groups, and comparison of different experimental conditions.

The goal in sampling subjects is to obtain a sample that is representative of the larger population to which the researcher wishes to generalize. The common prescription for achieving representativeness is to do *random sampling* from the target population. If sampling is truly random, the most likely outcome is a sample whose characteristics reflect those of the parent population. In fact, most research in developmental psychology employs sampling procedures that are less than totally random, and most samples in developmental psychology depart from perfect representativeness in various ways. How important such departures are depends on the topic being studied. For many basic topics in the field the typical samples are probably quite adequate. Nevertheless, representativeness and external validity remain important questions to examine for any study.

The discussion turns next to designs for comparing different age groups. Two designs have been most common in developmental research: the longitudinal and the cross-sectional. In a *longitudinal study* the same subjects are studied across some span of time. Such an approach provides the only direct measure of age changes as opposed to age differences. It also provides the only way to study individual stability or individual change over time. On the negative side, longitudinal research is costly and time-consuming, factors that undoubtedly contribute to its relative infrequency. Longitudinal research is also subject to a number of biases. These biases include *selective drop-out* of subjects in the course of the project, *testing* effects stemming from repeated exposure to the same measures, and the inevitable confounding between the age of the subject and the time of measurement.

In a *cross-sectional study* different subjects are studied at different ages. The cross-sectional approach is generally more economical than the longitudinal approach, it avoids many of the problems of longitudinal study, and for many research questions it is perfectly adequate. Cross-sectional designs also have their limitations, however. Because each subject is studied just once, a cross-sectional study cannot provide direct evidence of changes with age. *Selection bias* in the formation of the different age groups may hamper the age comparisons, as may *selective drop-out* of subjects across age groups. A further problem, which applies to both cross-sectional and longitudinal designs, is that of *measurement equivalence*: selecting measuring instruments that are equally appropriate for the age groups being compared. Finally, cross-sectional designs also contain an inevitable confounding: between the age of the subject and the generation or cohort to which the subject belongs.

Limitations of the classic longitudinal and cross-sectional approaches have led in recent years to the development of alternative designs. In a *time-lag design* age is held constant while generation and time of measurement are varied. Such designs provide an estimate of the importance of factors that are confounded with age in the traditional designs. More ambitious are the various *sequential designs,* which involve combinations of the simpler longitudinal, cross-sectional, and time-lag approaches. Sequential designs are unquestionably more informative than the simpler approaches; they are also more costly, however, and they still do not remove all possible sources of confounding.

The final section of the chapter is devoted to designs for comparing different tasks or experimental conditions. Two main approaches exist: *within-subject designs,* in which every subject responds to every task or condition, and *between-subject designs,* in which different subjects are assigned to the different tasks or conditions. The within-subject approach is sometimes more economical, often affords greater statistical power, and is free of some of the problems (such as selection bias) that can affect between-subject designs. A within-subject approach is also essential when the interest is in within-subject patterning of performance. A between-subject approach, in turn, avoids many of the problems of within-subject testing—in particular, *order* or *carry-over effects* stemming from the repeated testing. A between-subject approach is also essential when the experimental manipulation is intended to produce definite and lasting change.

The chapter concludes with a consideration of a particular form of between-subject research, that in which subjects are *matched* prior to assignment to experimental conditions. The advantage of matching is that it ensures that groups are equivalent on variables (such as IQ) that might affect performance. Possible disadvantages include the increased time and effort, the potentially biasing effects of taking a matching pretest, and the increased subject attrition if any matched-for subject is lost from the study. In addition, the possibility of regression effects means that matching is a dubious procedure for equating initially unequal groups.

chapter 4

WORKING WITH SUBJECTS

Thus far most of our discussion has concerned matters that are normally grouped under the heading of "experimental design." How should we go about selecting subjects and assigning them to conditions? What are the best ways to compare different ages or experimental treatments? How, in short, can we set up a well-designed study that will yield valid results?

Matters of experimental design are obviously crucial to good research; as indicated in chapter 1, however, they are not sufficient. Working out a satisfactory design brings us to the brink of research; the design must then be implemented by actually testing or observing subjects. In this implementation a host of problems may arise. It is to these problems—things that can go wrong in the course of carrying out a study—that the present chapter is devoted. Or, more positively stated, this chapter deals with the skills needed to avoid the problems and arrive at valid outcomes.

A point noted in chapter 1 should be reiter-ated here. General prescriptions about how to carry out research can take us only so far. Eventually, such prescriptions must be supplemented by actually doing research, and thus by direct experience with the subject groups and experimental procedures of interest.

STANDARDIZATION

We begin with something that is a clearly desirable goal in most research: standardization. *Standardization* refers to the attempt to keep all aspects of the experimental procedure the same for all subjects. To achieve standardization, the researcher must decide in advance exactly how each aspect of the procedure is to be handled—what the wording of the instructions will be, how and when stimuli will be presented, and so forth. Once these decisions have been made, the researcher must then make sure that the standardized procedure is in fact followed.

The basic reason for standardization was discussed in chapter 2: the need for experimental control. Anyone carrying out a study must be able to control a number of aspects of the experimental setting: the exact form of the independent variables, the way in which the dependent variables are measured, other factors in the situation. If such control is not exerted, then there is simply no way of knowing exactly what it is that the study is doing—and no way of interpreting any results that are found.

Let us briefly consider some examples of problems that might arise in the absence of adequate standardization. In the Schonfield and Robertson memory study that was first described in chapter 2, adult subjects of various ages were given two lists of 24 words to remember. On one trial memory was assessed via recognition of the words; on one trial it was assessed via recall. Table 4–1 shows various ways in which a tester in such a study might deviate from standardization and thus bias the results (presumably, none of these problems actually occurred in Schonfield and Robertson).

The tester might, for example, inadvertently vary the exposure time for different words or different subjects. Or the tester might forget to tell some of the subjects that the words can be reported in any order, a fairly important matter when one is trying to recall a long list of items. Or the tester might probe more on the recall trials for some subjects than for others, thus eliciting better overall performance.

As Table 4–1 indicates, such lapses from standardization can create problems of various sorts. At the least, imperfect standardization means uncertainty: It is no longer clear exactly what a given condition consists of, and therefore no longer clear how to interpret the results. This uncertainty may cloud the descriptive information that the study would otherwise yield: How impressive is a particular level of recall, for example, if we do not know what the exposure time was or how much probing was used? It may also affect the external validity of the results. If what is found depends on some particular (unintended and unknown) mixture of procedures, then findings may not be gen-

TABLE 4–1 Examples of Possible Deviations from Standardization and their Effects in a Developmental Study of Memory

Aspect of Procedure	Intended Procedure	Deviation from Standardization	Possible Effects
Wording of instructions	Tell all subjects that the items can be recalled in any order.	Only some subjects are given the instructions regarding the unimportance of order.	General: Unintended variance is introduced, and results may no longer be clearly interpretable. Specific and biasing: If the wording varies across age groups, age differences may be either obscured or artifactually produced.
Exposure time	Expose all words for the same length of time for all subjects.	Exposure time varies across words or across subjects.	General: same as preceding Specific and biasing: If exposure times vary across either age or condition, then false conclusions may be drawn about differences between groups.
Degree of probing	Include the same predetermined amount of probing for all subjects.	Some subjects receive more probing than do others.	General: same as preceding Specific and biasing: If the probing varies across age groups, age differences may be either obscured or artifactually produced.

eralizable to the contexts that the researcher hopes to generalize to.

Imperfect standardization may also threaten the internal validity of a study. Problems of internal validity arise whenever the deviations from standardization vary systematically across the groups being compared. Suppose, for example, that the tester probes more on the recall trials for young adults than for elderly adults (perhaps out of a belief that the correct answer is more likely to be "really in there" for younger subjects). In such a case an apparent age difference may actually reflect a difference in procedure. We would have an incorrect conclusion concerning a cause-and-effect relation, and hence a lack of internal validity.

Standardization, then, is important. But achieving standardization might seem easy enough—all that is necessary is to make procedural decisions in advance and then act upon them. In fact, as anyone who has done much research knows, things are not always so easy. It can be difficult to anticipate all the procedural issues that can arise in the course of a study; it can also be difficult to stick faithfully to a long and complicated procedure when actually face to face with a subject. These difficulties are compounded by the fact that subjects do not always respond in the way that the researcher expects; children, in particular, are notorious for doing things for which even the most experienced tester is unprepared. The difficulties are compounded too by the fact that in most kinds of research with children it is desirable to interact with the child in a natural, spontaneous-seeming manner, the better to keep the child at ease and attentive. Reading from a script—the easiest way to achieve standardization—may undercut the naturalness that is needed to keep the child happy and responsive.

Probably the best route to satisfactory standardization is experience, both general experience in doing research and specific experience with the age groups and procedures under study. Although general experience comes only with time, the needed specific experience can be gained, at least in part, through *pilot testing*: experimenting with and practicing one's pro-

spective procedures before beginning the actual study. Careful pilot testing can enable the researcher to iron out kinks and uncertainties in advance, thereby arriving at a well-standardized procedure before the first real subject appears for testing. Pilot testing can also help the researcher to become smooth and assured in delivering instructions and interacting with subjects, thus avoiding the kind of stilted, nose-in-a-script behavior that may upset young children. And pilot testing can help the researcher to anticipate, and be ready to respond to, at least some of the problematic subject behaviors that can force departures from a standardized script. Often in research with children, the most important attribute that a tester must have is not simply the ability to follow a standardized script but the skill to adapt to the vicissitudes of the individual child in a way that neither biases the experiment nor alienates the child.

Departures from Standardization

Standardization is desirable, but it is not an unquestionable goal. Frequently, it makes sense to settle for less-than-perfect standardization. We have just seen one such case: the situation in which the subject's behavior forces a departure from the standardized procedure. In this section we consider several others.

We begin by recalling a point made in chapter 2: Total standardization, in the sense of making everything literally the same for all subjects, is never possible. If we are doing individual testing, for example, we are not going to be able to test all of our subjects at 10 in the morning on September 30; time of testing will necessarily vary across subjects. Nor are we likely to be able to hold constant such factors as the ongoing school activities, the outside weather, the attractiveness of the day's lunch, or a number of other things that may affect the child's performance. As we saw in chapter 2, the important point is not to make everything the same for all subjects; it is to ensure that any potentially biasing factors are equally distributed across the groups being compared. If we disperse such factors equally across groups, then we can avoid confounding any particular factor with the independent variables of interest.

Further departures from standardization may be forced by the attempt in developmental research to accommodate distinct age groups within the same study. Consider a study of problem solving that spans the age period from kindergarten through college (e.g., Zelnicker, Oppenheimer, & Renan, 1975). Age is one of the independent variables in such research; by the prescription just given, therefore, we should make sure that there are no systematic differences in procedure for subjects of different ages. It is quite unlikely, however, that any researcher will treat 5-year-olds and 20-year-olds in exactly the same way. The immediate testing environment is likely to differ; children are typically tested in an unused room at their school, adults in a laboratory on a university campus. The wording for at least part of the procedure will probably differ; one does not recruit a 20-year-old for an experiment by inviting him to "come play a game." Even if the wording is kept the same for different ages, the pacing and tone of voice will probably not be; natural conversational style is simply not the same for 5-year-olds and 20-year-olds. Finally, there may also be more substantive-looking changes in procedure; young children may sometimes need help that is unnecessary for older subjects. The Zelnicker et al. study, for example, included some pretraining for the youngest children that was omitted for the older subjects.

The preceding is not meant to suggest that standardization and control must fall by the wayside in studies with widely separated age groups. Standardization remains important within an age group. Furthermore, any obviously critical elements of the procedure, such as the content of the problems to be solved in a study such as Zelnicker et al.'s, must be kept the same for all subjects; otherwise there is no point in making the age comparison. For other aspects of the procedure, however, what the researcher of different ages may opt for is a kind of functional rather than literal equivalence of procedure. The goal, in other words, may be to make sure that the procedure is *equally age-appropriate* for all of the age groups tested. A grade-school library and a university laboratory are obviously different rooms; they may, however, be equally natural and familiar settings for the groups being studied. What is equated in this case is not the room itself but the familiarity of the testing environment. A similar argument can be offered in support of age-appropriate adjustments in wording, tone of voice, feedback and praise, and so forth. In each case, what the researcher attempts to do is to devise a procedure that is appropriate within age and as comparable as possible across ages. The challenge in this attempt is to ensure that the cross-age procedural adjustments do not bias the age comparisons of interest.

A final instance of departure from strict standardization is found in exploratory research. As the name suggests, *exploratory research* refers to research whose goal is to explore—to break new research ground, to attack some little-studied problem in some new and mostly nonpredetermined ways. The essence of such research lies in the possibility for creativity on the part of the researcher—the possibility for following up unexpected findings, trying out various methods of study, and in general experimenting with and modifying one's procedure as one goes. A classic example of exploratory research is found in much of Piaget's work (e.g., Piaget, 1926; Piaget & Szeminska, 1952). As we will see more fully in later chapters, an important element in Piaget's success was his ability to uncover and to probe new phenomena, utilizing a flexible style of questioning and posing problems that was guided as much by the child's responses as by any preset procedure. It is precisely this sort of experimentation and change that is ruled out in a strictly standardized study.

We will see another point in our later discussions of Piaget. Testing the validity of Piaget's claims has required a large number of more tightly controlled and standardized follow-up studies. Exploratory research is uniquely suited for discovering new phenomena and generating interesting ideas; verification of these phenomena and ideas, however, may depend on the rigor and control that only a more standardized approach can bring.

Overstandardization

As we have just seen, standardization is always less than perfect. Total standardization is not literally possible; certain things will always vary across subjects. No matter how standardized the researcher may intend to be, the subject's responses may force deviations from the preset procedure. The researcher of different age groups may deliberately vary certain procedural features across ages. The researcher of a new content area may deliberately forego standardization for the possibility of exploration and discovery.

But suppose that we are dealing with a case that does not fit any of the just-named exceptions. Suppose that we have a study with a single age group, a well-worked-out procedure, good control over the situation, and an interest not in open-ended exploration but in determining as precisely as possible how certain specific variables relate. Is there any reason in this case not to aim for the highest degree of standardization possible? Or can there be such a thing, even here, as too much standardization?

Campbell and Stanley (1966) suggest that there can in fact be overstandardization. Their example concerns a study of persuasion designed to compare the effectiveness of a rational appeal and an emotional appeal. To maximize standardization, the researcher decides to tape record a single version of each appeal, thus ensuring that all subjects in a given condition receive exactly the same stimulus. Such control might seem desirable, because we presumably will then know exactly what a given experimental condition consists of. In fact, however, the decision to hold everything constant means that we may not be able to determine exactly which aspects of a particular condition are responsible for any effects we find. Perhaps the important factor is the one that we set out to study: the emotional versus rational content of the message. Or perhaps the important factor is the sex of the speaker, or distinctive voice qualities of the particular individual who serves as speaker, or the tone or pacing with which the message is delivered. Perhaps the important factor is the *combination* of these particular qual-

ities—for example, an emotional appeal delivered by a male speaker with a distinctive voice. The point is that anything that is kept the same for all subjects becomes potentially part of the independent variable. A better approach might be to let these extraneous factors (sex, voice qualities, etc.) vary across subjects, while holding constant the one factor in which we are really interested: the content of the message. Any effects could then be more confidently attributed to content per se.

It should be clear that the kind of overstandardization just described is a threat to the external validity of research. In a study such as that just sketched, the goal is to derive at least somewhat general conclusions about the persuasive effects of an emotional or a rational message. What we do not want are effects that are dependent on idiosyncratic features of a particular speaker or particular delivery, and therefore not generalizable beyond the bounds of our study.

The dangers posed by overstandardization provide another argument for the importance of replication in scientific research. A replication, by definition, holds constant those features that are the intended focus of the research, such as the emotional or rational content of the message in our study of persuasion. At the same time, other features of the procedure will almost certainly vary, especially if the replication is carried out by a different researcher in a different laboratory. Thus, the particular individual who delivers the persuasive appeal will probably differ, as will the tester who interacts with the subjects, the room in which the testing is done, the time of year at which the study occurs, and so forth. If we find the same effects of an emotional or rational appeal despite these changes, then we can be more certain that message content really does determine the outcome. Conversely, a failure to replicate our original results would suggest that supposedly irrelevant features of the procedure, such as the particular speaker, may not be so irrelevant after all.

When is overstandardization likely to be a problem in developmental research? Probably the most common instance is a variant of

Campbell and Stanley's example: the case in which a single tester collects all the data for a study. Our survey of developmental journals (Table 1-2) indicates that use of one or at most a few testers is quite typical in developmental research. In 43% of the articles surveyed we find but a single tester; in only 24% are as many as four testers used. Note that fully 83% of the articles had to be omitted from these calculations because they provided no information about the number of testers; indeed, 68% provided no information at all about their testers.

It is not surprising that one-tester studies are so common. Using a single tester is less expensive than using many, requires less training time on the part of the researcher, and avoids complicated problems of scheduling and balancing different testers. Attractive though this option may be, however, it must be remembered that the one tester then becomes a constant element in the experimental procedure, an element that may affect what is found. Obtaining the same results across a variety of different testers would provide more impressive evidence for the external validity of the research.

SOME SOURCES OF BIAS

We have seen that either too little or too much standardization can cause problems in research. In this section we consider some further, somewhat more specific threats to validity. In doing so we draw from the discussion by Campbell and Stanley (1966) that was summarized in Table 2-3. We discuss four specific threats: instrumentation, selection bias, history, and reactivity.

Instrumentation refers to changes in either physical instruments or human testers or observers across the course of a study. It falls under the general heading, therefore, of imperfect standardization: Some aspect of the procedure that was meant to be constant in fact changes from early to late in the study. Although the change may in some cases involve instruments in the literal sense (e.g., a stopwatch that begins to malfunction as the weather turns humid), a more common problem in most developmental

research is a change in the human instrument who serves as tester or observer. Perhaps the tester becomes more skilled and assured in delivering instructions across the course of the study. Alternatively, perhaps the tester becomes bored or discouraged as the study progresses and begins to behave in an increasingly perfunctory manner. In either case, the procedure would be different for subjects tested early in the project than for subjects tested late.

The major threat posed by problems of instrumentation occurs when the cross-study changes are confounded with one of the independent variables being examined. Consider a study one of whose purposes is to compare the responses of kindergarteners and second graders to some experimental task. The researcher decides to test most or all of the kindergarteners before starting with the second graders. There are a number of possible reasons for such a decision: only one teacher, classroom, and set of permission slips must be dealt with at a time; the eagerness of the children within a class to "come play the game" may be less likely to dissipate; the teachers may prefer that the testing within their room be completed quickly; and so forth. The researcher who gives in to such factors of convenience, however, is allowing a potentially important source of confounding into the study. If there is any possibility of change in the tester over time, then differences between kindergarteners and second graders will not be clearly interpretable.

The instrumentation issue applies not just to age comparisons but to comparisons between two or more experimental conditions. Often it is simplest in studies with multiple conditions to do all the data collecting for one condition before beginning another, because then only one set of materials and procedures need be mastered at a time. Again, however, the convenience is bought at the price of possible confounding. Better practice would be to distribute the testing times for each experimental condition at least roughly equally over the course of the study.

There is another possible source of bias when one experimental condition is completed before another is begun. It is a bias that is made possible by the ubiquitous parental permission slips that are required for almost all research with children these days. Imagine that a researcher sends home 30 permission slips with children from a grade-school classroom. Fifteen slips are returned promptly, and these 15 children are tested under Condition 1. A week later the other 15 slips have been returned, and these children are tested under Condition 2. In this case the threat to validity (in addition to instrumentation) is *selection bias*. Parents who are prompt to return permission slips may well differ from those who are less prompt. If so, the children of the two groups of parents may also differ in ways quite apart from the Condition 1-Condition 2 manipulation.

Still one more argument can be offered in support of not confounding age or condition with time of testing. No matter how constant testers or instruments may remain, other potentially important factors may change across the course of a study. Any developmental researcher who has ever tried to test school children the day before a holiday, or even simply on a Friday afternoon, is well aware of this phenomenon. Research occurs in the midst of numerous other events in the subjects' lives, and care must be taken to ensure that these other events do not confound any comparisons being made.

The point just made provides a bridge to Campbell and Stanley's *history* variable. As Campbell and Stanley use the term, history has to do with the issue that we have just been discussing: the effect of outside-the-study events on the outcome of research. The specific reference, however, is to pretest-posttest designs in which some intervening event provides an alternative explanation, in addition to that offered by the independent variable, for any changes that occur. Suppose that we are studying delay of gratification in a manner similar to that of the Miller et al. (1978) study described in chapter 2. After assessing the children's initial ability to delay gratification, we introduce an experimental treatment that is intended to enhance the ability to delay. Our treatment extends through the last part of October, and we test for possible effects in early November. We

find that the children are better able to resist the immediately available sweet after our treatment than they were at the start of the study. Evidence for the effectiveness of our manipulation? Not necessarily, given the intervention of Halloween, and thus of massive quantities of sweets for most children, between our first and second measurements. There is a confounding of treatment and history, and thus no clear interpretation of the results.

The history variable was briefly discussed in chapter 3. In that case the example concerned the effects of an educational intervention program on disadvantaged children's academic skills. We saw there the obvious solution to problems posed by history: include a no-treatment control group—that is, a group that experiences the same historical events as the experimental group but does not undergo any experimental treatment. In the case of our delay-of-gratification study, we could simply test a group of children before and after the onslaught of Halloween treats.[1] Note, however, that such a no-treatment control group does not solve all the problems posed by the impact of some extraexperimental event upon research. In some cases an historical event may interact with an experimental treatment. Perhaps both the natural experiences of Halloween and the contrived experiences of our treatment are effective only when they occur in combination with each other; neither treats nor treatment alone, however, has any effect on children's ability to delay gratification. In such a case a no-treatment control could not make clear what is happening. And in such a case we would have a severe constraint upon the generalizability of our results.

REACTIVITY AND RELATED PROBLEMS

The next threat to validity is important enough to merit a section of its own. As noted in Table 2-3, the term *reactivity* refers to unintended ef-

---

[1] A simpler solution still, of course, would be to do the study at some time other than Halloween.

fects of the experimental arrangements upon the subject's behavior—or, more simply, the fact that people may behave differently when they are being studied than when they are not being studied. In research with adults such effects typically stem from the subjects' explicit awareness that they are taking part in a psychology experiment. In research with children such explicit knowledge is less likely; indeed, in very young children or infants it is obviously impossible. Nevertheless, the fact of being studied may alter anyone's behavior, and thus reactivity may be a problem at any age.

Research with adult subjects has identified a number of specific problems that fall under the general heading of reactivity (see Silverman, 1977, for a review). Two problems in particular deserve mention. The first is best introduced through example. Some 20 years ago Martin Orne (1962) set out to find a task that could be used in his studies of hypnotic control. What he wanted was a task that was so boring that eventually any nonhypnotized subject would refuse to work further on it. One task that was tried required the subject to carry out repeated additions of pairs of random digits. A single sheet contained 224 problems, and the subject was given a stack of 5,000 sheets. Five and one-half hours later a number of subjects were still working! Orne then added a further stipulation: After completing each sheet the subject was required to tear the sheet into no fewer than 32 pieces. Despite the patentedly ridiculous nature of the task, some subjects continued to work until the experimenter finally told them to stop.

What this study and other studies by Orne revealed was that people who are taking part in an experiment will often go to great lengths to do whatever it is that they perceive the experimenter as wanting. Such "good-subject" behavior can include both a general willingness to follow directives and specific attempts to validate whatever hypothesis the subject believes underlies the research. In Orne's terms the subject responds to the *demand characteristics* of the experiment—that is, "the totality of cues which convey an experimental hypothesis to the subject" (Orne, 1962, p. 779). Assuming that the subject has accurately perceived what the ex-

perimenter expects, the result will be confirmation of the hypothesis. The problem, of course, is that the subject's behavior may be systematically different from what it would be in any nonexperimental setting, and any findings obtained may lack both internal and external validity.

A second source of bias has been labeled the "evaluation apprehension" effect (Rosenberg, 1965); another term, to contrast with the "good subject," is the "prideful subject" (Silverman, 1977). The reference here is to the fact that people taking part in an experiment often behave in ways that will maximize the experimenter's positive evaluation of them. They try, in short, to look good. Looking good may, of course, be compatible with doing what the experimenter apparently wants, in which case the demand factor and the evaluation factor converge on the same effect. The two are not always synonymous, however; for example, the subject may try to give "sophisticated-sounding" answers that are beyond those that he or she believes the experimenter expects. Silverman (1977), in fact, cites evidence indicating that when the demand factor and the evaluation factor conflict it is usually the latter that wins out.

Although they are not limited to such research, problems of evaluation apprehension are probably greatest in studies using *self-report measures*. As the term suggests, with self-report measures the data consist of peoples' verbal reports about themselves—their own characteristics, past experiences, typical behaviors, or whatever. It may be both tempting and easy in such research for subjects to tilt their answers toward what sounds best rather than what actually is. In a study of childrearing practices, for example, a mother may report that she never spanks her child even though in fact she does occasionally resort to spanking.

We noted that the effects discussed in this section have been studied most often with adult subjects. How applicable are they in developmental research? The childrearing example just given suggests one application, an application to which we return in chapter 8 when we discuss ways to study childrearing. More generally, because "developmental research" may encompass any part of the life span, such effects must be of concern to anyone who considers him- or herself a developmental rather than merely a child psychologist. Indeed, the "adult" subjects in most of the studies summarized in this section were in fact 19-year-old college sophomores barely beyond the adolescent period that everyone agrees to be the province of the developmental psychologist.

But what about children? It seems clear that if we go young enough we do not need to worry about either demand effects or evaluation effects in anything like the sense identified in the adult literature. Indeed, the researcher of infants or toddlers may bemoan the fact that his or her young subjects show so little regard for the goals of the research and the desires of the researcher! The cooperative attitude that is part of the demand effect can be a very welcome, albeit dangerous, part of the research process. Even with very young children, however, the strangeness or artificiality of an experimental situation may have reactive effects. As would be expected, infants are more likely to show anxiety or upset when tested in a laboratory than when tested in a familiar home environment. Preschoolers may clam up or generally withdraw when questioned by a strange adult; alternatively, they may become so fascinated by the stimulus materials or the adult attention that they talk about or do almost anything except what the researcher wishes. And by grade-school age children begin to show quite clearly some of the classic reactivity effects demonstrated in the adult literature. Anyone who has tested grade-school children is familiar with the child who continually reads the adult's face for clues as to what is expected, who answers each question with an am-I-right rise in intonation at the end, and who in general seems to be most concerned with pleasing the adult, being well thought of, or both.

How can reactivity effects be minimized? Because reactivity stems from an awareness of being studied, an obvious approach is to disguise the fact that a study is occurring. Various degrees of disguise are possible. At a very simple level it is common for researchers of young children to introduce their experimental tasks

as "games" rather than "tests" or "experiments." Such a description is often reasonably accurate, may convey more to a child than would the more complicated terminology, and presumably is less likely to arouse anxiety than is reference to tests. It is also common for researchers of preschoolers to spend some time playing with their young subjects in an attempt to build *rapport* prior to the start of testing. It should be clear, of course, that such reassuring wording and reassuring behavior do not guarantee an absence of anxiety or resistance; the child is still aware that something out of the ordinary is happening. Futhermore, the researcher must guard against the helpful teacher who undermines his or her efforts by telling the child to "go take some tests with Dr. So-and-So."

Reactivity should be least likely in research that most closely approximates the natural setting. Consider a study of nursery-school children's preferences for different toys. The researcher might study this issue by taking children individually to an experimental room and there administering a toy questionnaire or test (labeled, however, as a "game" rather than "test"). In this case the measure is direct and efficient, but the possibility of reactivity (anxiety about being questioned, saying what the adult apparently wants, etc.) is maximal. Another possibility would also involve bringing the children to some special experimental room, but in this case the researcher would simply observe with which of various toys placed around the room the child chooses to play. Especially if the opportunity to play is offered in a casual and natural way (e.g., "You can play with these toys while I finish working on these papers."), reactive effects may be unlikely. A third possibility is to observe children in the natural nursery-school setting; playing with toys is, after all, a major part of a preschooler's day. If the researcher can observe without being observed (through a one-way mirror, for example), then reactivity should not be an issue at all. Finally, in some cases behaviors may be inferred from their physical effects, without the subjects themselves ever being observed. The popularity of different toys might be studied, for example, by charting which toys are still untouched on the shelves at the end of the school day and which are strewn about the room. Across a longer period, toy popularity might be studied by tracing physical wear and tear; which toys are still bright and shiny at the end of the school year and which are scruffy and broken? Here, obviously, there is no possibility of reactivity. A book by Webb, Campbell, Schwartz, and Sechrest (1966) provides a detailed discussion of the use of such "unobtrusive measures" to infer behavior patterns.

Response Sets

We turn from reactivity to another, closely related problem. The term *response set* refers to a subject's tendency to respond to a question or task in a predetermined, biased fashion that is independent of task content. By this definition, the "good-subject" behavior discussed under reactivity can be considered a kind of response set: The subject attempts to say or do what the experimenter apparently wants, rather than responding to the task itself. In this section we consider response sets that are more clearly brought to the study by the subject rather than elicited by the demands of the experimental setting. There is, however, an admittedly thin and rather arbitrary dividing line between the problems of reactivity just discussed and the response sets considered next. In both cases we are talking about biased responses that may lead to invalid conclusions.

A concrete example can help clarify the points made in this section. Figure 4–1 shows

a task that we consider more fully in chapter 7: the Piagetian conservation-of-number problem (Piaget & Szeminska, 1952). As applied to number, conservation refers to the knowledge that the number of objects in a set does not change just because its perceptual appearance changes. Figure 4–1 shows several perceptual transformations that might be used to tap this knowledge. It also shows various ways in which the conservation question might be worded.

What kinds of response set might children bring to the conservation task? One common form of response set is *yes saying:* the tendency to say yes whatever the question asked. Clearly, such yes saying is a potential problem whenever a one-directional question is used, as in the first two examples in Figure 4–1. Children who are always asked "Same?" and always respond "Yes." will appear to be conservers, even though their answers may be quite unrelated to the task in front of them.

Simple yes saying can be precluded through use of a two-directional question, as in the third example in the figure. Other problems may still arise, however. Some children have a tendency to *choose the last-named alternative*—that is, to agree with whatever happens to come last in the adult's question. If the wording of the question is always that given in the third example, the result will be consistent (but perhaps pseudo) nonconservation. Other children have a tendency to *alternate answers,* to change from one answer to another simply as a function of repeated questioning. In conservation research such alternation may apply across trials or within a trial, since the question about number

	Possible Arrays	Possible Questions
Initial	• • • • •	
	• • • • •	Do the two rows have the same number
Final	• • • • • • •	of chips?
Initial	• • • • •	Does one row have more chips than the
	• • • • •	other?
Final	• • • • •	
Initial	• • • • •	Do the two rows have the same number
	• • • • •	of chips or does one row have more chips
Final	• • • • •	than the other?
	• •	

FIGURE 4–1. Possible perceptual arrays and conservation questions in a study of conservation of number.

preferred way of wording

is typically posed both before and after the perceptual change. Finally, with some kinds of tasks, including conservation, *positional preferences* may be a problem. A young child, for example, might always pick the row that happens to be closer to him or her as the one that has more.

Several general points should be made concerning response sets. First, although we have drawn our examples from the conservation task, such problems are by no means limited to conservation, or, for that matter, to school-aged children. Whenever verbal responses are elicited, biases such as yes saying may enter in. And as we see in chapter 6, certain kinds of positional preference may be present even in neonates.

The second point concerns the interpretation of response sets. What does it mean if a child always answers "yes" to the conservation question no matter how the question is worded? Such a response might well be taken as evidence of an inability to conserve—the child who falls back upon such a simple response bias could hardly understand much about the phenomenon of conservation. And indeed, this interpretation may often be justified. The problem is that there is no way to know for sure. If a child consistently picks the longer row as having more then he has given a clear-cut wrong answer that is in response to the task manipulation. But the child who always says "yes" is simply not responding to the task—perhaps because he does not understand the phenomenon being measured, perhaps because he is confused by the wording, perhaps because he is not motivated to think carefully, or perhaps for any of a number of other reasons. Response sets lead to no clear conclusion—except that the child has a response set.

This brings us to the final point: Response sets are clearly something that the researcher wishes to minimize. Various approaches are possible. In the case of conservation the researcher might work with maximally simple language, provide some verbal pretraining before the test itself, use incentives to try to ensure careful response, and so forth. No matter how skilled the procedure, however, response sets may in some cases be unavoidable. In such cases it is critical that the researcher at least be able to *identify* the fact that a response set has occurred, lest the subject's behavior be misinterpreted. A researcher who tests conservation by presenting a single trial can never know for certain what the child's judgment means. Presenting a number of trials of varied form provides a much firmer basis for deciding whether the child really understands conservation, really believes in nonconservation, or is showing some irrelevant response bias.

Intersubject Communication

An experiment by Horka and Farrow (1970) demonstrated a rather odd-looking response bias, one not fitting any of the patterns discussed in the previous section. In their study the subjects (fifth- and sixth-grade children in a public school) were required to identify a set of letters embedded as the white ground within a group of black nonsense figures. The stimuli used are shown in Figure 4-2. Half of the subjects, tested in the morning of a single day, were presented with the stimulus shown at the bottom of the figure; half, tested that same afternoon, were presented with the stimulus shown at the top of the figure. The children were given 4 minutes to look at the figure and say what they saw, and they received a reward of 50¢ if they were able to name the correct pattern.

The response bias was shown by the afternoon subjects. A substantial number of children tested in the afternoon indicated that they saw the word LEFT—that is, they gave the response that had been correct in the morning. This answer was approximately twice as likely as was the actual correct answer for the afternoon. Responses of LEFT were also twice as frequent in the afternoon as they had been in the morning, when LEFT was in fact the stimulus shown!

What had happened, clearly, was that some of the afternoon subjects had been talking to some of the morning subjects. The children tested in the morning were all told the correct

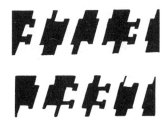

FIGURE 4-2. Stimuli used in the Horka and Farrow study of intersubject communication. From "A Methodological Note on Intersubject Communication as a Contaminating Factor in Psychological Experiments" by S. Horka and B. Farrow, 1970, *Journal of Experimental Child Psychology, 10*, p. 364.

answer once they had finished, and were all reminded that they could have won 50¢ for simply saying the word "left." They were also asked not to tell anyone about the study. Apparently, however, this admonition was not very effective in the face of a chance to help a friend or, perhaps, simply to appear knowledgeable about an unusual event.

The Horka and Farrow study demonstrates that another kind of response bias that subjects can bring to an experiment stems from whatever it is that other subjects have told them about the study. Such *intersubject communication* can have various effects. Subjects may sometimes perform better than they otherwise would have, perhaps because other subjects have told them the right answers, or have alerted them to some aspect of the procedure that was meant to be secret. They may sometimes perform worse, perhaps because the procedure differs for different subjects (as in Horka and Farrow), or because the account they have received is too jumbled to be helpful. Certainly anyone who has ever listened to young children recount their research experiences knows that there can be a sizable gap between what happens in an experiment and the later retelling of it. Or the effects of the communication may be more general, with later subjects made more or less eager, more or less apprehensive, or whatever, as a function of what they have heard. Whatever the

specific effect, the general import is the same: bias that may invalidate the results.

How general a problem is intersubject communication? Clearly, there are some studies in which communication is not an issue—research with babies, for example (but watch the parents!), or studies in which the subjects either are unacquainted or have no opportunity for contact during the study. At the other extreme, the Horka and Farrow study includes a number of features that seem likely to maximize communication. Among these is the simple, easily verbalized, and lucrative right answer, a feature that is by no means present in every study. For these reasons, it is wise to be cautious about generalizing from Horka and Farrow's findings to research in general. Still, as Horka and Farrow argue, their procedure does bear some similarity to many learning or problem-solving studies with children, in which right answers exist and can be fairly easily transmitted from one child to another. Furthermore, the more general aspects of the study—testing in a public-school setting, with subjects who know each other and have ample opportunity to communicate—are quite common in research with children. Indeed, of all the research areas in psychology, it may well be research with school-aged children in which intersubject communication is most likely to be a problem.

At a hypothetical level, it is not difficult to think of ways to reduce the probability of communication among subjects. Children can be drawn from different schools, for example, or the critical task can be embedded within a number of "filler" items—that is, items whose only purpose is to draw attention away from the critical items and thus make their later communication less likely. Brooks and Kendall (1982) provide a fuller discussion of various possibilities. The real difficulty, of course, comes in implementing such safeguards, since doing so may often be beyond the resources of the experimenter. The most general advice is to be aware of the possibility of intersubject communication, to include whatever safeguards are feasible, and to build in checks to determine whether communication has in fact occurred. As with any form of bias, prevention is the first goal; detection, the second.

EXPERIMENTER BIAS

We have discussed a variety of kinds of bias, including those that the researcher brings upon him- or herself through procedural miscalculations. With the possible exception of the demand effect, however, the biases that we have been considering are all essentially nondirectional, in the sense that they are equally likely to work for or against the researcher's hypothesis. We turn now to what is perhaps the most insidious form of bias: the possibility that researchers may systematically bias their research to obtain the results that they desire. Such systematic bias yields what is known as the *experimenter bias effect;* another often-used label is the *researcher expectancy effect.*

The pioneering work on experimenter bias was carried out by Robert Rosenthal (1976). In a typical Rosenthal study a number of individuals, often undergraduate students, are recruited to serve as testers. These testers are randomly divided into two groups. As part of its training, each group is given a clear expectancy regarding the probable outcome of the experiment to be run—that is, they are told what the principal investigator expects (and perhaps hopes) to find. The groups differ, however, in that the expectancies they receive are directly opposed. One group, for example, might be told to expect good performance from their subjects, whereas the other group might be told to expect poor performance. Apart from this difference in expectancy, the two groups are trained equivalently and are presumably following exactly the same experimental procedure. Despite this equivalence, the results obtained for the two groups often diverge, and the divergence is in the direction of the induced expectancies. In short, testers find what they expect to find.

Let us consider a specific example before turning to possible mechanisms and possible solutions. We draw our example not from Rosenthal's original work but from a similar study with children by Hunt (1975). Hunt's study was

directed to the Piagetian conservation-of-number concept discussed in the section on response sets. The particular focus was on a procedure devised by Mehler and Bever (1967) for assessing conservation in very young children. The Mehler and Bever procedure involves allowing the child to choose between two perceptually discrepant rows of candy, with choice of the shorter but more numerous row taken as evidence of conservation. (This general approach is considered more fully in chapter 7.) Research using Mehler and Bever's paradigm has produced conflicting results about young children's abilities. The Hunt study probed the possibility that these conflicting results might stem, at least in part, from the different expectancies that different testers bring to the research. A Rosenthal-type study was devised with two groups of testers: one group led to expect a high proportion of correct answers, the other group led to expect a low proportion. The results provided clear support for the experimenter bias hypothesis. Children tested by researchers with positive expectancies averaged 2.65 correct responses across the 4 trials; those tested by researchers with negative expectancies averaged 1.93 correct responses.

How do the researcher's expectancies exert their effects? Barber and Silver (1968) identified 11 ways in which a tester might bias the outcomes of a study. These sources of bias are listed in Table 4–2. Of greatest interest typically are the first five: those in which the bias is mediated through unintentional, and presumably often rather subtle, means. There is some evidence, across both Rosenthal's work and that of others, that each of the 11 kinds of bias can indeed play a role. It should be noted, however, that determining the exact locus for experimenter bias effects has often proved difficult. A study like Hunt's, for example, demonstrates that the effect occurs, but provides no clear indication of how.

There are other criticisms that have been leveled against the Rosenthal research (see Barber, 1976; Barber and Silver, 1968; and Rosenthal, 1968, for discussions). Perhaps the most important concerns the issue of external validity. In much of the research demonstrating

TABLE 4-2 Possible Bases for an Experimenter Bias Effect

Unintentional Bases

---

1. The experimenter may influence the subjects' behavior through unintentional paralinguistic cues—for example, variations in tone of voice.
2. The experimenter may influence the subjects' behavior through unintentional kinesic cues—for example, changes in posture or facial expression.
3. The experimenter may influence the subjects' behavior through unintentional verbal reinforcement.
4. The experimenter may unintentionally misjudge the subjects' behavior.
5. The experimenter may unintentionally misrecord the subjects' behavior.

Intentional Bases

6-10. The experimenter may *intentionally* engage in each of the preceding practices.
11. The experimenter may fabricate all of his or her data.

Source: Adapted from T. X. Barber and M. J. Silver, "Fact, Fiction, and the Experimenter Bias Effect," *Psychological Bulletin Monograph Supplement,* 1968, *70,* 1-29.

bias effects the testers are quite inexperienced, consisting of undergraduate students recruited solely for the purposes of the research. Each tester is given a very clear expectancy regarding the likely outcomes of the study. In some cases (including the Hunt study) the testers are also promised larger payments for their services if their results support the investigator's hypothesis than if they fail to support it. Everything, in short, is geared toward maximizing the likelihood of an expectancy effect. What the studies may simply show, however, is that it is possible to do bad research. They have more general relevance—that is, they possess external validity—only to the extent that research in general embodies the flaws that are built into the expectancy studies.

Some obvious ways to minimize experimenter bias follow from the possible sources just discussed. If inexperienced testers must be used, then they clearly should be trained as carefully as possible before data collection begins. This training should emphasize standardization, since deviations from standardization provide

one obvious opening for the introduction of bias. If possible, testers should not only be trained in a standardized procedure but also periodically *monitored* as they test, to ensure that an initial rigor is not lost in the course of the study. The use of extra payment for desired results is, needless to say, to be avoided. In addition, investigators should guard against differential use of *non*monetary rewards—for example, responding with obvious pleasure when a tester brings in desired results and obvious displeasure when he or she does not. Since the bias effect depends on expectancy, it is clearly desirable to prevent testers from forming clearcut expectancies. To this end, testers are sometimes kept uninformed about the hypotheses behind a study or the status (e.g., experimental or control condition) of a particular subject. Such deliberate withholding of potentially biasing information is referred to as *blinding* the tester.[2]

Although it is easy enough to state safeguards against experimenter bias, actually implementing these safeguards is, once again, not always so easy. In particular, blinding of testers or observers may sometimes be difficult. In some studies the principal investigator (i.e., the person who designs the study) also tests the subjects, in which case blinding with regard to the study's hypotheses is obviously impossible. In other cases it may be unrealistic to think that a tester, no matter how initially naive, will not form hypotheses concerning the study's purposes and probable results. In research like Mehler and Bever's (1967), for example, the only conceivable reason for contrasting the pick-the-candies procedure with a standard verbal procedure is the possibility that the two will yield different results; furthermore, it does not take much of an intuitive leap to guess that young children might find the former procedure easier. In some cases it may be impossible to blind the tester with regard to the subject's

---

[2] A distinction is sometimes made between a "blind" tester and a "naive" tester. A blind tester is aware of the purposes of the research but is not aware of the status (e.g., experimental or control) of a particular subject. A naive tester is not even aware of the purposes of the research.

status. A tester will know, for example, when he or she is working with a 3-year-old and when with a 5-year-old, or when with a boy and when with a girl, and this knowledge of the subject's age or sex may bias behavior. Indeed, it is worth noting that developmental researchers are almost never blind with respect to one of their principal independent variables: the age of the subject. Finally, even in those cases when blinding *is* possible it may not be employed. Included in our journal survey (Table 1–2) was an indication of whether blinding of tester or observer was used in cases in which it seemed clearly appropriate. Only 49% of the authors reported the use of blinding.

Questions were raised earlier about the external validity of experimenter bias research. The gist of the preceding paragraph is that such research cannot be too readily dismissed as the limited product of a contrived experimental situation. There seems little doubt that experimenter bias effects do occur in developmental research. How often they occur, and how many false conclusions they produce, remain debatable. One goal of any researcher should be to forestall any debate in his or her case—that is, to design, execute, and report research in a way that minimizes the possibility of experimenter bias.

LOSS OF SUBJECTS

Much of this chapter has been concerned with problems that can arise when working with subjects. In some cases the problems may be so severe—and also so readily apparent—that there is no possibility of keeping the subject's data. Loss of subjects (also labeled drop-out, attrition, or mortality) may occur for any of a number of reasons discussed in this chapter—a critical deviation from standardization on the experimenter's part, an especially strong reactive response to the experimental arrangements on the subject's part, a persistent response set that the subject refuses to break away from. In addition, some subject groups or kinds of research may present special problems that can lead to subject loss in even the best executed of

studies. Babies may fall asleep or begin to cry uncontrollably part way through a study. Preschoolers may need to go to the bathroom at a critical point in the experimental procedure. In longitudinal research, subjects may move away or die before the testing can be completed.

The most basic point concerning subject loss is that such loss should be minimized. Drop-out from research can cause various problems. There is the practical problem of waste of time, on both the experimenter's and the subject's part. If the drop-out is substantial, the researcher may end up with too small a sample to draw any conclusions. Finally—and most critically—if the drop-out is at all selective, then the validity of the study may be threatened. This is the issue that was discussed at various points in chapter 3. Drop-out from research often *is* selective, involving those subjects who are least competent, least motivated, least willing to comply with the requests of a stranger, or whatever. As we saw in chapter 3, such drop-out can affect the external validity or the generalizability of the results: The experimenter may no longer be studying the population to whom he or she wishes to generalize. If the drop-out is differential for particular ages or conditions, then it may also affect the internal validity of the conclusions.

Methods useful for minimizing subject loss can be inferred from the various problems and corresponding prescriptions discussed throughout this chapter. Two general pieces of advice are worth reiterating here. One is to build *rapport* before attempting to test children, especially toddlers or preschoolers. The second is to *pilot test* the procedures as extensively as needed before beginning the actual study. A researcher who ends up with procedures that simply do not work for a substantial proportion of his or her subjects has probably neglected the pilot-test phase of the study.

In addition to minimizing the number of subjects who are lost, a researcher has two further responsibilities. One is to decide, as far as possible, on objective, in-advance criteria for rejection of subjects. The researcher should know at the start of the study exactly what it is that a subject can do that will make his or her data unusable. The particular criteria will vary from study to study; they might include going to sleep or crying uncontrollably in infants, failure to pass a verbal pretest in preschoolers, or a clear recognition of some attempted experimental deception in older children or adults. The point is that it can be dangerous to collect all the data for a subject, see whether those data agree or disagree with one's hypothesis, and only then begin to worry about criteria for deciding whether the subject is keepable. The danger is that the researcher may be too easily tempted to keep results that fit with his or her expectations and discard those that do not.

The second responsibility is the one noted in chapter 3: to report clearly the criteria for rejecting subjects and the number of subjects rejected. As we saw in chapter 3, this responsibility is not always met; only 36% of the articles in our journal survey included such information. What do we learn from these articles? At least in these particular studies, loss of subjects does not seem to be a terribly pervasive problem. In 45% of the cases the reported subject loss is less than 10%; in 70% of the cases it is less than 25%. If we assume, as seems reasonable, that subject loss is generally low in studies that do not report such information, then the picture becomes more positive still. On the other hand, it is clear that there are some kinds of research, including kinds that may be underrepresented in our survey, in which subject loss can be quite severe. Drop-out is clearly more likely in longitudinal studies than in cross-sectional studies. It is also more likely with infants than with older subjects. We return to the issue of loss of subjects in infant research in chapter 6.

There is one more point to be made. We have been stressing the desirability of keeping as high a proportion of one's subjects as possible. Clearly, however, this advice does not mean that a screaming infant or a terrified preschooler should be forced to continue in an experiment. Two arguments can be advanced against such a practice. First, as we have seen throughout this chapter, data collected from such subjects are not likely to mean very much. Second and more basically, as we will see in

chapter 11, a primary ethical principal in research with human subjects is that the subject has the right to withdraw from an experiment at any time. This right applies at least as strongly to the nonverbal infant or toddler as to any other subject. And the rights of the subject always take precedence over the preferences of the experimenter.

SUMMARY

This chapter discusses the translation of abstract design into experimental procedure. It concerns problems that can arise in working with subjects, as well as ways to minimize the problems.

A central concept is that of *standardization:* keeping important elements of an experimental procedure the same for all subjects. Standardization is the procedural counterpart to the notion of control in experimental design. If standardization is not maintained, procedures may vary from subject to subject, biases can arise, and results may no longer be clearly interpretable. Probably the best route to standardization is to practice one's procedures thoroughly by *pilot testing* them before beginning the actual study. The best tester is one who can combine standardization with naturalness, and who is flexible enough to adapt as necessary to the individual subject.

Although standardization is desirable, some departure from standardization is both inevitable and often quite sensible. Total standardization is never possible, for some aspects of the procedure (e.g., the exact time of testing) will necessarily vary across subjects. In developmental research with different age groups alterations may be necessary to make the procedure *equally age-appropriate* for the different groups. In *exploratory research* the goal is to uncover the interesting phenomena in some new research domain, and flexibility may therefore be more important than standardization. Finally, any aspect of the procedure that is held constant (such as the tester who collects the data) becomes potentially part of the independent variable, and such *overstandardization* may result in findings of limited generality. Allowing supposedly irrelevant features to vary across subjects may enhance the validity of the study.

The discussion turns next to some specific threats to validity. *Instrumentation* refers to unintended changes in either physical instruments or human testers or observers across the course of a study. Such changes are of greatest concern when they are confounded with age or experimental condition, as can happen if all or most of the subjects from one group are tested before the subjects from other groups. Another reason to avoid confounding of condition and order of testing is the possibility of *selection bias:* Subjects who are quick to volunteer (or whose parents are quick to return permission slips) may differ in various ways from those who are slower to respond. Possible effects of outside-the-study events, such as the excitement surrounding a holiday, provide a third reason to balance order of testing across groups. In pretest-posttest designs such outside-the-study events may give rise to the threat to validity labeled *history:* change produced by uncontrolled events occurring during the course of the study.

A very general threat to validity is *reactivity:* unintended and biasing effects of being studied upon the subject's behavior. Two much-studied forms of reactivity are ''good-subject'' behavior, in which the subject attempts to respond in ways desired by the experimenter, and ''prideful-subject'' behavior, in which the subject attempts to look good. Although its specific form may vary, reactivity can be a problem with subjects of any age. The most general way to reduce its likelihood is to use procedures that minimize the obviousness of the experimental manipulations and measurements. A closely related problem is that of *response sets:* subjects' tendency to respond in a predetermined, biased fashion that is independent of task content. Among the response sets that are found in childhood are *yes saying, choice of the last-named alternative, alternation of response,* and *positional preferences.* Researchers must also guard against *intersubject communication,* in which the subject's response is biased by what other subjects have said about the study.

A particularly insidious form of bias occurs when the researcher's hopes and expectations affect what is found. Such *experimenter bias effects* can come about in a variety of ways. Although the generality of the phenomenon has been disputed, experimenter bias remains an issue to consider and guard against in any research project. When possible, testers or observers should be blinded to minimize potentially biasing expectations. Training and monitoring of testers to ensure standardization are also important.

In some cases the problems discussed throughout the chapter are so severe that the subject must be rejected. Several points are made concerning subject loss. One is that such loss should be minimized, since it can affect both the internal validity and the external validity of the study. A second is that the researcher should decide in advance what the criteria are for rejection of subjects, and should convey clearly in the final report how many subjects were rejected and for what reasons. A final point is that subjects must not be coerced to remain in a study against their will.

chapter 5

SETTINGS AND CONTROL

In this chapter we consider three general topics. The first concerns the settings in which research occurs. Research in psychology, unlike that in some sciences, is carried out in a variety of settings, ranging from highly controlled and artificial laboratory environments to the everyday, naturalistic world of the preschool, playground, or supermarket. Each setting has its pros and cons and its particular appropriateness for particular research questions—which, of course, is why different settings are used. These pros and cons will be our first topic.

A consistent theme in the early chapters concerned the importance of experimental control in research. Indeed, the key construct of an independent variable was defined as a variable that is under the control of the researcher. The ease with which a variable can be controlled, however, can vary greatly as a function of both the nature of the variable and the setting in which the research takes place. We consider such variations as part of our discussion of different settings. In addition, a second main section of the chapter focuses on cases in which variables are *not* experimentally controlled but simply measured and then related—that is, *correlational research*.

Just as would-be independent variables may vary in how readily they can be controlled, so dependent variables can' vary in how readily they can be measured. The setting is again an important determinant of what is possible, and such variations are accordingly discussed in the first part of the chapter. Again, however, there is a particular form of research that deserves special attention because it presents special challenges: the case in which measurement is dependent on the observations of a human observer. The final section of the chapter therefore focuses on *observational research*.

SETTINGS FOR RESEARCH

There are various ways in which research settings can be classified. The system that we use for our initial classification is adopted from an article by Ross Parke (1979) and is summarized in Table 5–1. Parke begins with the familiar distinction between "field" settings and "lab" settings. Field research is carried out in the natural environment of the subject—for example, the playground or supermarket settings mentioned earlier. Lab research occurs in a setting specifically designed for research, a setting that may be quite different from the subject's natural environment and to which the subject is brought solely for the purpose of the research. A mobile laboratory research trailer within which heart-rate responses are recorded as tones are presented through earphones and would fit anyone's description of a laboratory setting.

In examples like those just given the field-lab distinction seems clear-cut. Often, however, the distinction is a good deal murkier. "Lab" settings can vary greatly in the extent to which they approximate a natural environment. "Field" settings may rapidly lose their naturalness as experimental controls and measurement procedures are imposed. For these reasons, the field-lab distinction is best thought of as a continuum rather than a dichotomy. In addition, "naturalness" is not a unitary construct; rather there are several dimensions along which the naturalness of a setting can vary.

TABLE 5–1   Classification of Research Settings

		LOCUS OF DEPENDENT VARIABLE	
		Laboratory	*Field*
Locus of	*Laboratory*	1	2
Independent	*Field*	3	4
Variable			

Note: Adapted from "Interactional Designs" by R. D. Parke. In R. B. Cairns (Ed.), *The Analysis of Social Interactions: Methods, Issues, and Illustrations* (pp. 15–35), 1979, Hillsdale, NJ: Lawrence Erlbaum Associates. Copyright 1979 by Lawrence Erlbaum Associates. Adapted by permission.

Parke discusses three such dimensions: the general physical environment, the immediate stimulus field, and the social agents present in the situation.[1] Because of these complexities, the use of "field" and "lab" in the discussion that follows should be recognized as a simplification, useful for making methodological points but nevertheless a distortion of a more complex reality.

The second factor in Parke's classification scheme concerns the independent variable–dependent variable distinction. The independent variables in a study can be manipulated in either a laboratory or a field setting. The dependent variables can be measured in either a laboratory or a field setting. The conjunction of lab and field and independent and dependent yields the four cells shown in Table 5–1.

Using a specific research example can help clarify our discussion. The example that we use concerns the issue of TV violence and aggression. Does exposure to violence on TV make children more aggressive? This is an interesting, much-studied, and much-debated question. It is a question that can be—and has been—examined via each of the four approaches shown in Table 5–1, which makes it a good example for our purposes. As we go, however, we also consider other examples, both in this chapter and in chapters to come. Indeed, a central issue we evaluate is which research questions *can* be examined through each of the four approaches.

Design 1: Lab-Lab Studies

Research under this heading probably best fits most people's conceptions of an "experiment in psychology." An experimental manipulation is administered in a controlled laboratory setting, and the effects of this manipulation are assessed in the same laboratory environment. In the case of TV violence and

---

[1]Bronfenbrenner (1979) provides a more complex, and theoretically oriented, analysis of different social systems and environmental settings.

aggression, a typical sequence might be the following. Subjects are first randomly divided into two conditions, an experimental group that is to be exposed to violent TV and a control group that will receive nonviolent fare. Children from both groups are taken individually to the experimental room and there shown the particular TV segment designated for their group. Some time shortly afterward the child is given a chance, in the same laboratory setting, to engage in aggressive behavior. Greater aggression in the experimental than the control group would be taken as evidence of the impact of TV modeling.

Within this basic paradigm a number of variations are possible. A pair of studies by Bandura, Ross, and Ross (1963a) and Liebert and Baron (1972) can serve to illustrate some of the possibilities. The TV segments presented to the children may be more or less similar to actual TV material. In some cases films have been constructed especially for the purposes of the research (Bandura et al.); in other cases episodes from commercial television have been shown (Liebert & Baron). The aggressive responses may also vary in their similarity to real-life aggression. In some cases the target of the aggression has been an inanimate object (a Bobo doll in Bandura et al.); in other cases it has been another child (Liebert & Baron). In some cases the aggressive behaviors have been physically identical to real-life aggression (hitting and kicking in Bandura et al.); in other cases they have been physically quite different (a button press in Liebert & Baron).[2] Finally, the aggressive behaviors may vary in the ease with which they can be measured. The button-press response in the Liebert and Baron study

could be automatically recorded; hits and kicks, however, typically require a human observer to make decisions about the occurrence and meaning of the behavior.

Research in a controlled laboratory setting offers two great advantages. One is the degree of control over the independent variable. In studying effects of TV on aggression, the researcher can decide exactly what sort of films will be shown to the subjects, exactly which subjects will be shown which films, and exactly what the general context will be within which the films are viewed. As we saw, it is precisely these kinds of control that are necessary if clear cause-and-effect conclusions are to be drawn. On balance, research under the lab-lab heading is most likely to maximize internal validity.

The second advantage of laboratory research lies at the dependent-variable end. By definition, the dependent variable is free to vary and therefore is never under the control of the researcher. Dependent variables must, however, be measured, and such measurement is generally easiest in a structured laboratory environment. It might be possible in a lab, for example, to videotape the aggressive behavior for later replaying and analysis—a luxury that is unlikely to be available on a nursery-school playground or within a home. It may also be possible to forego the human observer altogether and to work with recordings that are either literally or essentially automatic. The button press in Liebert and Baron's study is one example of such automatic recording of aggression; an automated Bobo doll that registers every hit that it receives (Deur & Parke, 1970) is another. Finally, as we see shortly, some dependent variables simply cannot be measured except in controlled laboratory settings.

The strengths of the laboratory approach are balanced by some weaknesses. Just as the strengths can be summarized by the word "control," so can the weaknesses be summarized by a single word: "artificiality." Laboratory environments may vary in the degree to which they resemble the real-life settings of interest; they are always somewhat different from these settings, however, and often they are very

---

[2]A fuller description of Liebert and Baron's procedure may be in order. Subjects in their study were told that a child in another room was playing a game that involved turning a handle. The subjects could help the other child by pushing a button labeled "help," which would make the handle easier to turn, or they could hurt the other child by pushing a button labeled "hurt," which would make the handle hot and painful. Selections of the hurt button then served as the primary measure of aggression.

different. The question thus arises: Can results obtained in the laboratory be generalized to more natural settings? This is the issue of the trade-off between internal validity and external validity that we discussed in chapter 2. As we saw then, the same factors that maximize internal validity may often operate to reduce external validity.

Consider the issue of TV violence and aggression. No matter how naturally the opportunity to watch TV is presented, the viewing situation in the lab is necessarily somewhat different from that in the child's home. For one thing, the child is not in the home, where he has watched most TV to this point in his life. Not only the physical setting but the social setting may differ. The child may usually watch TV in the company of siblings or peers; now he is watching alone. The fact that an adult has explicitly directed him to this particular TV segment is a further difference. The adult's presentation of the TV material may impart a kind of sanction to the content, and to the child's subsequent imitation of it, that is not found in the home. Finally, the exposure to TV in the lab is necessarily fairly brief; any generalization to the effects of long-term, hours-a-day viewing must therefore be tentative.

Limitations also exist with respect to the dependent variable. Hitting a Bobo doll is not the same thing as hitting another child; delivering a purportedly painful stimulus to an unseen child in another room is also not the same thing. At least partly for ethical reasons, laboratory measures of aggression have often involved a kind of pseudoaggression—less clearly interpersonal than real-life aggression, and less likely to elicit negative reactions from an adult. Whether such responses are predictive of genuinely aggressive behaviors in less permissive contexts is debatable. Even when ethical factors are not an issue, capturing complex social behaviors in a laboratory setting can be difficult. As we see repeatedly in later chapters, the laboratory analogues for behaviors of interest to the developmental psychologist are often quite distant from their real-life counterparts. In some cases the very nature of the research question may preclude laboratory study. If our specific

interest, for example, is in aggression toward familiar peers on the nursery-school playground, then research in a laboratory setting is simply not one of our options.

Laboratory studies are also especially subject to the problems of reactivity and response set discussed in the last chapter. The child in a lab environment may become anxious and nonresponsive, may attempt to do whatever it is that the adult apparently wants, may become distracted by all the fancy equipment, and so forth. It is true, as we saw in chapter 4, that experimental arrangements can sometimes be disguised and reactivity minimized. It is worth noting, in fact, that the "lab" settings used in most studies with preschool and grade-school children are unused rooms in the children's own school—hardly the alien, apparatus-loaded environment conveyed by the word "laboratory." Nevertheless, the fact remains that the children *are* being brought to an unusual setting by an unfamiliar adult and there subjected to experiences that they would not otherwise encounter, and all of these departures from the ordinary can introduce various kinds of bias.

Rather than working through Table 5–1 in order, we turn next to the cell that is most distinct from the one just considered: field-field studies. Once we have discussed both the lab and field approaches, it will be easy to fill in the two combination cells in the table.

Design 4: Field-Field Studies

Our concern now is with research in which the independent variable is manipulated in the natural setting and the dependent variable is measured in the natural setting. It is true, as noted earlier, that the experimental manipulation and measurement necessarily change the "natural" setting to some extent. Still, in this case, in distinction to laboratory research, the starting point is the natural environment, and the setting remains toward the natural end of the lab-field continuum.

An example for the problem of TV and aggression is provided by a study by Feshbach and Singer (1971). The subjects for their study were preadolescent and adolescent boys living in various residential centers. For a period of 6 weeks Feshbach and Singer were able to control the TV "diets" experienced by the subjects. Half of the boys were randomly assigned to a diet of violent TV shows across the 6 weeks and half were assigned to a diet of nonviolent shows. In this case, therefore, the manipulation of TV viewing was carried out in the subjects' natural environments. Effects of the TV viewing were determined from counselors' and supervisors' ratings of the boys' naturally occurring aggression across the 6-week span. Thus the locus of the dependent variable was also in the natural setting.

The great advantage of field research is conveyed by the word "natural." What we are principally interested in with respect to TV and aggression is whether the TV that children watch at home affects the aggression that they produce at home, at school, on the playground—wherever children naturally find themselves. As we saw, laboratory research can provide only an indirect answer to this question, because laboratory research neither manipulates home TV viewing nor measures aggression in the natural setting. With field research, however, the focus is directly on the situations and behaviors of interest. This means that the external validity is likely to be higher than in a comparable laboratory study. If we really can exert the necessary control over the independent variable, and if we really can accurately measure the dependent variable, then the internal validity should also be high.

The disadvantages of field research are suggested by the "ifs" in the preceding sentence. Some manipulations and some measurements are difficult, if not impossible, to carry out in the natural setting. Think for a moment about the problems involved in controlling, for an extended period of time, the kinds of TV shows that large numbers of children watch. It is no surprise to learn that there are only a handful of field studies like Feshbach and Singer's, or that such studies tend to be carried out with "captive" populations—for example, adolescents in boarding schools. Whether results obtained with such populations and in such settings are generalizable to the more normal

home situation is debatable. Furthermore, the introduction of experimental control is in itself a major and very noticeable change in the natural environment. Few children have their TV viewing totally controlled by an adult, and the sudden imposition of such control opens the way for various reactive or confounding effects. In Feshbach and Singer's study, for example, there was some evidence that the boys subjected to the nonviolent TV diet became frustrated, and thus more aggressive, as a function of having lost their favorite shows.

It should be noted that the importance of the problems just discussed does vary to some extent across different kinds of independent variables. Some variables lend themselves more readily to natural, nonreactive manipulation in a field setting than does TV viewing. It is fairly easy, for instance, to hang mobiles over babies' cribs in a study of visual attention (e.g., Weizmann, Cohen, & Pratt, 1971), or to vary the situational supports for cheating in the classroom in a study of moral development (e.g., Hartshorne & May, 1928). On the other hand, some variables are even harder to manipulate in the field than is TV. Sometimes practical and ethical contraints combine to make experimental manipulation essentially impossible; parental childrearing practices are a common and very important example. In other cases the interest of the researcher lies in the effects of quite specific and tightly controlled stimuli that by their very nature are somewhat artificial—for example, repeated tones in a study of auditory habituation, tachistoscopic flashes in a study of visual detection, lists of words in a study of short-term memory. It might sometimes be possible to embed such stimuli in the subject's natural environment, but there would be little point in doing so: The environment would quickly become far from "natural," and the other factors present in the situation could well bias performance and confound the differences among subjects. In such cases laboratory study is the most sensible option for the researcher's purpose.

The second general problem in field research concerns the second of the two "ifs" cited earlier: accurate measurement of the dependent variable. Consider the example of auditory habituation. The term habituation refers to a lessening or dropping out of an initial attentional response to a stimulus as the stimulus is repeated. Such "getting used to it" is commonly indexed by changes in heart rate as the stimulus is presented repeatedly. Clearly, heart rate is not a dependent variable that can be measured in a field setting. Even if the investigator does succeed in importing the EKG equipment into the subject's home, all the wires, electrodes, and such constitute a very obvious departure from the natural environment. The same argument applies whenever physiological responses are the dependent variable.

Nor is the argument limited to physiological measures. A number of responses of interest to the developmental psychologist are simply very difficult to elicit and measure in the natural environment. Many of the concepts studied by Piaget fall in this category. The conservation concept may well be the important component of children's thinking that Piaget believes it to be. Conservation, however, is rarely directly and clearly expressed in the child's naturally occurring behavior; rather, determining its presence or absence requires a test explicitly designed for this purpose, such as the test shown in Figure 4-1. It is true, as will be argued in chapter 7, that there is still some point in making this test as close to real life, and perhaps as nontest-like, as possible. But some explicit elicitation of the concept is required, and this elicitation necessarily shifts the study in the direction of the laboratory end of the lab-field continuum.

The point of the preceding is that some behaviors are either literally (e.g., heart rate) or figuratively (e.g., understanding of conservation) beneath the surface, and thus are hard to measure in a natural setting. But what about aggression? Aggression, after all, is a frequent, overt, observable, and inherently social behavior, and as such would seem a good candidate for measurement in a field setting. And indeed, measuring aggression in the field, as we saw, has some definite advantages over attempts to measure aggression in the laboratory. But major problems of feasibility and accuracy still

remain. Two general approaches to field measurement of social behaviors can be identified: ratings of the behavior by someone who knows the child (as in Feshbach and Singer's study), and direct observations of the behavior as it occurs. Observational techniques are the subject of the last part of this chapter, and both ratings and observations are considered with respect to particular aspects of social development in chapter 8. The complexities involved in both sorts of measurement should become evident then. For now, we settle for simply reiterating the general point: Whatever the behavior, accurate measurement in a field setting can be very difficult.

Design 2: Lab-Field Studies

In this case the independent variable is manipulated in the laboratory and the dependent variable is measured in the field. A study by Ellis and Sekyra (1972) provides an example with respect to TV and aggression. First-grade children were assigned to one of three experimental conditions: exposure to an aggressive cartoon, shown in a small, unused room at their school; exposure to a nonaggressive cartoon, shown in the same room; or no cartoon exposure at all. The independent variable was thus manipulated in a laboratory setting. The children were subsequently observed in their regular classroom, and all acts of aggression were recorded. The dependent variable was thus measured in a field setting.

The strengths of a study like Ellis and Sekyra's are the particular strengths of lab manipulation and field measurement discussed previously. Such research affords both good control over the independent variable and ecologically valid measurement of the dependent variable. The confidence with which effects can be attributed to the experimental manipulation is thus enhanced, as is the likelihood that the effects tell us something about real-life aggression. Furthermore, the combination of lab manipulation and field measurement makes possible both a spatial and a temporal separation of independent variable and dependent variable that may be less likely in lab-lab or field-field studies. This separation may in itself increase the generalizability of the results, as well as reduce the probability of reactivity or response bias. In Ellis and Sekrya's study, for example, the fact that aggression was measured at a time and place different from the TV viewing may have reduced the chances that children would imitate simply because the immediate situational cues supported aggression or the adult seemed to expect imitation of the film.

The weaknesses of lab-field studies are also derivable from our discussion of lab approaches and field approaches separately. The laboratory locus of the independent variable raises the possibility of artificiality and nongeneralizability; the field locus of the dependent variable increases the problems of accurate measurement. In addition, there can sometimes be practical obstacles to combining a lab component and a field component within the same study. As we see shortly, lab-field studies in fact constitute a rather small proportion of research in developmental psychology.

Design 3: Field-Lab Studies

The final possibility involves manipulation of the independent variable in a field setting and measurement of the dependent variable in a lab setting. Our example in this case is a study by Parke, Berkowitz, Leyens, West, and Sebastian (1977). Parke et al.'s study was in part similar to the Feshbach and Singer (1971) study discussed earlier. Their subjects were adolescent boys, half of whom were shown violent films in their dormitories across a 5-day period, and half of whom were shown nonviolent films. In this case, however, one measure of the effects of the film viewing was a later laboratory test in which the subject was given a chance to deliver shocks to an unseen peer (a measure similar to that in the Liebert and Baron, 1972, study). Thus a lab setting was used to assess the effects of manipulating TV viewing in the natural environment.

Once again, the strengths and weaknesses of the approach follow from the general points made with respect to lab and field studies. The natural setting for the independent variable is a virtue, as is the rigor with which the dependent variable can be measured. On the negative side, the attempt to impose experimental control in a natural setting may result in some loss of both naturalness and control. The measurement of the dependent variable in a lab setting may result in a precise but artificial index that has an uncertain relation to real-life aggression. And again, special difficulties may be involved in attempting to do both lab research and field research within the same study.

Overview and Evaluation

Two general themes emerge from our discussion of different settings for research. One concerns the trade-off among the various goals that the researcher would like to achieve. What we would like to be able to do is to carry out studies that yield clear cause-and-effect conclusions that are generalizable across a wide range of real-life situations. Doing so requires that we have exact control over our independent variables, precise measurement of our dependent variables, and a general context for the research that is similar enough to naturally occurring situations to permit generalization. It is this conjunction of goals that is difficult to achieve, because methodological decisions that work in favor of one goal often work against one of the other goals.

The second theme follows from the first. Because no single approach to studying an issue is perfect, there is no justification for adopting but a single approach. Much more informative is the use, either within a study or across studies, of a variety of different methods of attacking any particular issue. Such a multipronged research strategy is often referred to as the method of *converging operations*. The idea behind converging operations is that the weaknesses of any one method of study can be to at least some extent compensated for by the strengths of another, and that conclusions based upon a convergence of evidence from different methods can be held with greater certainty than conclusions based on one approach alone.

Let us apply the argument to the problem of TV and aggression. We saw that any single method of studying this issue is subject to various criticisms. If we find, however (as in fact we do), that all four of the approaches described in the preceding pages lead to the same conclusion—namely, that TV violence promotes aggression—then we can have considerably more confidence that this conclusion really is valid.

Our discussion of research settings has been oriented thus far to possibilities. We turn next to actualities, and some data about the extent to which the different approaches we have been discussing are actually used in developmental psychology. Before we can do so, however, it is necessary to note some complications in the simple classification scheme that we have been using to this point, for many studies do not fall clearly or exclusively into one of the four cells in Table 5–1.

Let us begin at the independent variable end. We have been talking about the setting in which independent variables are manipulated. In some cases, however, independent variables are not manipulated, because the nature of the variable precludes experimental manipulation. This is the case of *subject variables* discussed in chapter 2: variables such as age, sex, or race that are controlled and examined through selection of subjects rather than experimental manipulation. Such studies may still vary in whether the dependent variable is assessed in the lab or in the field. But the lab-field distinction no longer applies to the independent variable.

Consider next a complication with regard to the dependent variable. If a researcher's measure of aggression consists of attacks on a Bobo doll in some special experimental room, then the study falls clearly in the category of laboratory research. If the measure of aggression is derived from observing the child's attacks on other children on the nursery-school playground, then the study falls clearly in the category of field research. But what about the case in which the measure of aggression comes from *asking* someone who knows the child about the child's typical behavior—that is, some sort of interview or rating approach? In our discussion of the Feshbach and Singer (1971) study such

research was classified under the heading of "field," the rationale being that the focus is on behavior in the natural setting rather than in a structured lab. Clearly, however, any such verbal-report measure lacks the immediacy and naturalness that the term "field research" usually conveys. It seems, in fact, to fall part way between field and lab: toward the field end in the sense that the focus *is* on naturally occurring behavior; toward the lab end in the sense that the measurement operation is both obvious and fairly far removed from the actual behavior.

A final complication concerns the independent variable–dependent variable distinction. In some studies there is no distinction, since the study includes neither manipulation of an experimental variable nor selection of a subject variable. The goal of the research may be essentially descriptive, an attempt to uncover interesting phenomena that might later be the subject of experimental study. Or the goal may be to assess how subjects stand on two or more variables and then draw relations among the measures. We consider such "correlational" research shortly. In either case, there must be measurement, and this measurement can be carried out in the lab, in the field, or with some combination of lab and field approaches.

Our journal survey (Table 1–2) included a tabulation of research settings along dimensions such as lab versus field and the degree of control exerted over variables. Because of the complexities of classification just discussed, as well as the limited sampling of studies, not too much should be made of the numbers from this survey. Still, some suggestive findings do emerge.

Of the studies surveyed, 70% included some manipulation of an independent variable. In 78% of these studies some subject variable was also included; age was the most popular subject variable, followed by sex. In 25% of the studies surveyed subject variables constituted the only independent variables. Completely correlational studies—that is, studies with neither manipulation of an experimental variable nor selection of a subject variable—accounted for 5% of the articles. And 33% of the studies with independent variables included a correlational component as well.

What about the lab-field distinction? Consider first studies with some manipulation of an independent variable. In 92% of these cases the experimental manipulation occurred in a laboratory setting, leaving only a minute 8% for field manipulation of independent variables. Consider next the issue of the setting in which outcome variables are measured. In 69% of the studies surveyed all measurement occurred in a laboratory setting, in 7% all measurement occurred in a field setting, in 11% all measurement occurred via interviews or questionnaires, and in 13% a combination of approaches was used. Finally, with reference to Table 5–1, it can be noted that Design 1, the lab-lab approach, was indeed the most common, accounting for 91% of the studies in which an independent variable was experimentally manipulated. Design 4, the field-field approach, accounted for 7%; the two mixed designs made up the other 2%.

What can be concluded from these numbers? Our survey confirms the common perception that research in developmental psychology has been tilted toward manipulative designs and laboratory contexts. It is true that subject variables, especially age, appear frequently, and that correlational designs, or at least correlational components within larger studies, are also prominent. But research that truly merits the designation "naturalistic" is not very common. Controlled experiments with a grounding in field settings are rare, and completely naturalistic studies with no experimental control are rarer still.

Is this situation to be deplored? Recently several prominent developmental psychologists have suggested that developmental psychology has been overly dependent on controlled studies in laboratory settings. McCall (1977) has written that "we rarely take the time to keep our experimental hands off a behavior long enough to make systematic descriptive observations in naturalistic settings" (p. 336). Bronfenbrenner (1977) has charged that "much of contemporary developmental psychology is *the science of the strange behavior of children in strange situations with*

strange adults for the briefest possible periods of time" (p. 513; italics in original).

That laboratory studies have their limitations should be clear from much of what has been said in this chapter. The point of critiques like those just quoted, however, is not to question the value of controlled laboratory research, but to question an overreliance on this strategy to the neglect of other ways of learning about children. The point again has to do with the value of converging operations. Because any single method of study is imperfect, it is important to attack research questions through as many different methods as possible.

The quotation from McCall suggests a further point as well, one having to do with ordering within a research program. Often it makes sense to defer controlled experimental study until a phase of naturalistic observation has made clear what the interesting variables are that are worthy of further study. This is a similar point to that made in chapter 4 regarding the value of exploratory research prior to the onset of standardization and control. Furthermore, at whatever phase of the research program it occurs, naturalistic observation may be essential for answering questions that cannot be answered through controlled experimental studies alone. As McCall points out, experimental studies are geared to questions of "can": *Can* a change in variable X produce a corresponding effect in variable Y? Such studies cannot answer the questions of "does": *Does* X in fact vary in children's environments, *does* Y in fact show interesting individual differences among children, and *does* X in fact cause at least some differences in Y? Answering questions of "does" requires study in the natural, nonmanipulated environment.

CORRELATIONAL RESEARCH

In our discussion of research settings we described four different approaches to studying the issue of TV violence and aggression. Consider now a fifth approach. McLeod, Atkin, and Chaffee (1972) collected various measures of aggression in a sample of sixth- through tenth-graders. They also measured (via self-reports) how much violent TV each child in the sample typically watched. Their interest was in whether there was a relation between watching violent TV and being aggressive—that is, did the children who watched the most violence on TV also tend to be the most aggressive? In their study there *was* such a relationship, an outcome compatible with the hypothesis that watching violent television promotes aggression.

McLeod et al.'s study is an example of *correlational research*. It is correlational because there was no manipulation of an independent variable. McLeod et al. did not experimentally control the type of TV that their sample watched, nor did they control the level of aggression that the children showed. Instead, both TV viewing and aggression were *measured* as they naturally occurred, the intent being to see whether scores on one index covaried with scores on the other. Such a relation might be positive, with high scores on one measure tending to go with high scores on the other. This was the case in McLeod et al.'s study. Or the relation might be negative, with high scores on one measure tending to go with low scores on the other.

Outcomes in correlational research are often assessed through use of a *correlational statistic*. Correlation statistics will be discussed more fully in chapter 10. For now, we note that a correlation statistic is a measure of the degree of relation between two variables; it ranges from −1 (a perfect negative relation) through 0 (no relation) to +1 (a perfect positive relation). In McLeod et al.'s study the correlations varied to some extent depending on the age and sex of the sample and the particular measure of aggression used; most, however, fell in the range of .2 to .3. Such correlations indicate a modest positive relation between TV violence and aggression.

Although correlation statistics are typically associated with correlational research designs, it is important to note that the statistic and the design are separable. Statistics other than correlations can be used to examine the results of correlational research. McLeod et al., for example, might have divided their sample into high, medium, and low TV watchers and then used *t* tests or analysis of variance to compare levels of aggression across the three groups. In this case the statistic would be different, but the design would remain correlational. For our purposes the design, not the statistic, is important, and the defining aspect of a correlational design is that variables are simply measured, not experimentally controlled. It is in this respect that the McLeod et al. study differs from the other studies of TV and aggression described earlier in the chapter.

Correlation and Causation

One of the truisms of research is that correlation does not demonstrate causation. That is, simply from knowing that two variables are correlated, we cannot establish what causal relation, if any, holds between them. Thus, the results of the McLeod et al. study are compatible with the hypothesis that TV violence causes aggression, but they cannot prove that this hypothesis is true.

This basic limitation in correlational research stems from the absence of experimental control. As we have stressed repeatedly, it is control—control over the nature of the independent variable, control over the assignment of subjects to conditions, control over other potentially important variables—that makes internally valid conclusions about cause and effect possible. Because correlational research lacks all these forms of control, the best that such studies can do is to demonstrate that two or more measures covary. They cannot tell us why.

Consider the McLeod et al. study. There are in this study, as in most correlational studies, three possible explanations for the correlation. One possibility is that watching violent TV causes children to be more aggressive. Had McLeod et al. experimentally manipulated TV viewing, as was done in the other studies described in this chapter, they might have established this conclusion with some confidence. But because there was no experimental manipulation, there is a second possibility: Perhaps children who are already aggressive seek out violent TV. In this case it is the aggressive tendency that causes the TV viewing, not the reverse. Finally, there is still a third possibility: Perhaps TV viewing and aggression are both caused by some third factor but are not themselves causally related. It may be, for example, that certain parents' childrearing practices promote both aggressive behavior and a liking for violent TV; the two measures thus covary, but neither one has any causal effect on the other.

This argument can be put in more general terms. Whenever there is a correlation between variable A and variable B three possible explanations must be considered: A causes B, B causes A, or some third factor C causes both A and B.

The inability to establish causal relations is obviously a critical limitation to correlational designs. Why, then, are such designs used? The reasons should be apparent from the discussion in the first part of the chapter. Many variables cannot be experimentally manipulated for ethical or practical reasons—parental childrearing practices, for example, or exposure to drugs during the prenatal period. In such cases the only approach possible is a correlational one. In other cases experimental manipulation is possible but difficult, especially if the goal is to combine experimental control with a natural setting. As we saw, TV viewing falls in this hard-to-control category, and each of the various methods of creating control is subject to a number of criticisms. In a study like McLeod et al.'s, however, the focus is squarely on the two variables of interest: naturally occcurring TV viewing and naturally occurring aggression. In addition, the correlational approach may allow us to sample a wider range of variation than is possible with an experimental design. In an experimental study of TV and aggression we would probably have to limit ourselves to presenting two or three different types of TV experience. With a correlational approach, however, we can encompass the whole range of naturally occurring experiences, from 2 or 3 hours per week viewing on the one end to perhaps 40 or 50 hours on the other.

The contrast between experimental designs and correlational designs raises again the concept of converging operations. Correlational designs avoid many of the pitfalls of manipulative studies but are intrinsically limited in what they can tell us about cause and effect. Experimental designs are uniquely suited for studying cause and effect, but may suffer from all of the various problems (artificiality, reactivity, etc.) that we have been discussing. Often, however, the experimental approach and the correlational approach complement each other and thus bring us closer to a satisfactory resolution of an issue. In the case of TV and aggression, for example, the correlational data from studies like McLeod et al.'s give us more confidence that experimental demonstrations of the impact of TV violence really do have some real-life generalizability. Correspondingly, the fact that experimental manipulations of TV violence affect aggression gives us a basis for arguing that TV viewing is really the causal factor in the TV-aggression correlation.

Let us consider more generally the question of how to get closer to causality in correlational research. One way is by combining the correlational approach with an experimental manipulation, as in the TV and aggression example just discussed. At least three other ways can be identified.

The first strategy is quite commonsensical but still worth noting. In some cases one of the A-B causal directions is ruled out by the nature of the variables. Suppose that we find a positive correlation between body size and level of aggression. It is plausible that body size in some way affects aggression (although we would still need to specify exactly how). It is not plausible, however, that level of aggression has any causal effect on body size. In cases such as this we need to entertain just two hypotheses: A causes B, or C causes A and B. The B to A link, however, is not a concern.

A second method is especially appropriate for eliminating third-factor explanations. It makes use of a statistical technique called *partial correlation*. Partial correlation is a procedure for statistically removing, or "partialling out," the contribution of one variable from a correlation between two other variables. Essentially, what the partial-correlation technique does is to hold the potentially troublesome third variable constant while examining the relation between the two variables of interest. It is equivalent to asking how A and B relate in a sample all of whom have the same score on variable C. The issue, of course, is whether the A-B correlation remains significant even when we control for C.

Suppose that we find a positive correlation between TV viewing and aggression but suspect that the correlation is actually produced by some third factor, such as methods of childrearing. Assuming that we can obtain acceptable measures of childrearing, we could then use the partial-correlation technique to eliminate the contribution of childrearing from the TV-aggression correlation. If we find that the correlation remains as large or about as large as it was originally, we could conclude that childrearing was not an important confounding factor. Conversely, a substantial drop in the size of the correlation would indicate that childrearing does make an important contribution to the TV-aggression correlation.

Although the specific procedures differ, the goal behind the partial-correlation technique is the same as that for the matching technique discussed in chapter 3. In both cases the researcher seeks to eliminate confounding factors by equalizing them across the groups being compared. With matching the equalization comes before the fact, in the assignment of subjects to groups; with partial correlation it comes after the fact, in the statistical removal of the confounding factors. Partial correlation also shares

the same basic limitation that we saw in the case of matching: It is impossible through such techniques ever to remove *all* possible confounding factors. There are, in other words, lots of variable Cs, and no researcher is ever able to measure and control for them all.

A final set of procedures for extracting causality from correlational data revolves around the temporal relation between variables. Such procedures make use of the fact that causes must come before their effects. Thus, by charting variations in the relation between A and B over time, we can come closer to determining whether it is A that leads to B or the reverse.

The most ambitious form of temporal analysis comes in a procedure called *cross-lagged panel correlation* (Campbell & Stanley, 1966). The cross-lagged technique requires a longitudinal approach, in which at least two variables are measured at two or more points in time. Such a study yields a number of correlations, both within a particular time and across time periods. Figure 5–1 shows the possible correlations for a study with two variables and two times of measurement (the symbol *r* stands for correlation). We can look at the correlation between A and B at both time 1 and time 2. We can look at the cross-time stability correlations for both A and B separately. And, most critically, we can look at the cross-time correlations between A and B—that is, the correlations shown on the two diagonals. It is the information on the diagonals that is essential for deter-

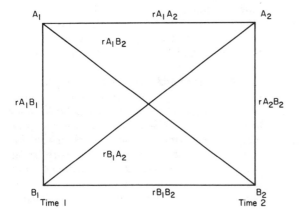

FIGURE 5–1. Correlations between variables in a cross-lagged panel design.

mining the causal direction between A and B. If A is the causal factor, then we would expect a significant correlation between A at time 1 and B at time 2—variations in the cause should lead to later variations in the effect. The correlation between B at time 1 and A at time 2 should be substantially lower. Conversely, if B is the causal factor we would expect just the reverse: a higher correlation for B_1 and A_2 than for A_1 and B_2.

This argument may be easier to follow in the context of an actual example. Lefkowitz, Eron, Walder, and Huesmann (1972) applied the cross-lagged technique to the issue that we have been considering throughout this chapter: the relation between TV violence and aggression (see also Huesmann, Lagerspetz, & Eron, 1984). They collected measures of both TV viewing and aggression at the third-grade level and then again (for the subset of the sample that was still available) 10 years later. Their results for the male half of their sample are shown in Figure 5–2. Note that there was no support for the hypothesis that aggressive tendencies lead to a preference for violent TV; the correlation

between aggression at time 1 and TV viewing at time 2 was essentially 0. There *was* support, however, for the opposite hypothesis, because TV viewing at time 1 did relate significantly to aggression at time 2.

It should be noted that the Lefkowitz et al. study has been included simply as an illustration of the cross-lagged approach. There are in fact a number of criticisms that can be directed against this study and its conclusions (Freedman, 1984). More generally, the cross-lagged approach, though fairly straightforward at the level at which we have presented it, has a number of complexities and statistical assumptions built into it. It is questionable just how often these assumptions are met, and therefore just how generally applicable the approach is. Rogosa (1980) provides a detailed critique of the attempt to derive causal inferences from cross-lagged analyses. Good introductions to the general topic can be found in Campbell and Stanley (1966) and Kenny (1975).

Correlations and Patterning

Thus far our focus has been on the use of correlational designs to examine questions of cause and effect—for example, does exposure to violent TV lead to an increase in aggressive behavior? In this section we consider a somewhat different use of the correlational approach. We begin with an example. Rubin (1978) was interested in the Piagetian concept of role taking—that is, the child's ability to take the perspective of someone whose point of view is different from his or her own. There are a variety of kinds of role taking (perceptual, cognitive, affective, etc.), as well as a variety of ways to measure each of the different kinds. A reasonable, and theoretically interesting, question concerns the extent to which these different measures relate to each other. The usual assumption, following Piaget, has been that the measures *should* relate—that different forms of role taking are reflections of a general underlying role-taking ability, and thus should correlate fairly strongly. Rubin tested this assumption by administering six different role-taking tasks to a sample of 5- to 10-year-old

FIGURE 5–2. Correlations between TV preference and aggression in a cross-lagged study of TV and aggression. Adapted from "Television Violence and Child Aggression: A Follow-up Study" by M. M. Lefkowitz, L. D. Eron, L. O. Walder, and L. R. Huesmann, 1972. In *Television and Social Behavior. Vol. 3: Television and Adolescent Aggressiveness* by G. A. Comstock and E. A. Rubinstein, Washington, DC: United States Government Printing Office. Copyright 1972 by the United States Government Printing Office. Adapted by permission.

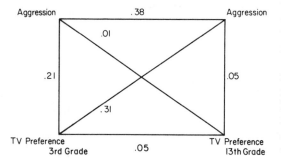

children. He found only very low correlations among the different measures, and thus little support for the usual assumption.

Note the differences in orientation between a study like Rubin's and a study like that of McLeod et al. (1972). In Rubin's study there is not a single variable, such as TV viewing, that is thought to play a causal role with respect to other variables. The hypothesis, rather, is that each of the different variables has a common underlying core—hence, the expected correlation among them. The focus, in short, is on patterning or interrelations in development.

Suppose that Rubin *had* found substantial correlations among the different measures. Would such an outcome have validated the construct of a general role-taking ability? The answer is that such positive correlations are necessary but not sufficient for concluding that different measures have a common underlying basis. What is also necessary is to rule out other, competing explanations for the correlations. Various such competitors must be considered.

One obvious possibility in the case of a cognitive measure like role taking is that the correlations come about simply because of differences in general ability level. Perhaps the especially competent children in the sample do well whatever the task, and the less competent children do poorly whatever the task. If so, the different measures will correlate, but not because of anything specific to role-taking ability. What we need to do is to show that other, theoretically less related measures of cognitive functioning do *not* correlate with the role-taking tasks. In his study, for example, Rubin included tests of IQ and cognitive style. Validation of a general construct of role taking would require that the correlations be higher among the role-taking measures than between role taking and the other cognitive tests.

The point here is the same as a point made in the discussion of test validity in chapter 2. As we saw then, the notion of construct validity is built upon patterns of expected correlations. It is important in validating a test for some construct that measures that are expected to correlate do in fact correlate. Such correlations give a test what is called *convergent validity.* It is also

important, however, that measures that are thought to be independent of the construct do *not* correlate. A finding that theoretically unrelated measures do not correlate with the target measures gives a test what is called *divergent* (or *discriminant*) validity.

A related problem in developmental research concerns general changes in performance with age. Suppose that Rubin had calculated correlations for his entire 5- to 10-year-old sample. Such a procedure would guarantee some correlation among the measures simply because older children, on the average, perform better than younger children whatever the task. There are two ways to avoid this problem, both of which were in fact used by Rubin. One is to calculate the correlations within rather than across age. The other is to use the partial-correlation technique to remove the contribution of age from the role-taking correlations.

There is one more potential problem. Sometimes artificially high correlations can come about because of methodological similarity across the tasks being correlated. Perhaps the role-taking tasks are all highly verbal, require sustained compliance with an adult tester, depend upon ability to avoid distractions, and so forth. If so, correlations in performance might result simply from these general methodological similarities, quite apart from the particular content (i.e., role taking) that the tests are supposed to tap. Correlations that result from the methodological overlap among tasks are said to reflect *shared methods variance.* The obvious way to guard against this problem is to reduce the overlap—to devise methodologically diverse ways to tap the construct under study. Positive correlations could then be more confidently attributed to the common content elicited by the tests.

Our focus so far has been on various factors that may lead to misleadingly high correlations, and thus to an impression of more consistency or patterning than actually exists. It is important to add that there are also factors that can lead to misleadingly *low* correlations. This issue is explored in a recent paper by Rushton, Brainerd, and Pressley (1983). As these authors note, the chief villain is lack of perfect reliability. Whenever a measure is less than perfectly reliable, correlations involving that measure will reflect random error as well as differences in true score. The lower the reliability, the more serious the effect on the correlations. Single measures or tests of a particular construct (e.g., specific measures of different kinds of role taking) tend to be of rather low reliability. What happens, then, if we correlate a single measure of, say, cognitive role taking with a single measure of affective role taking? What we will be correlating (in part) is one set of errors of measurement with another set of errors of measurement, a procedure that guarantees a far from perfect correlation.

There are two possible solutions to this problem. One is to correct statistically for the low reliability. If the reliabilities for the two measures are known, then standard procedures exist for adjusting the correlation upward to reflect the relation between true scores shorn of errors of measurement (see, for example, Kenny, 1979). The other, which is the approach discussed by Rushton et al., is to work with aggregate scores rather than single measures. The term *aggregate* refers to a score based on an adding together or aggregation of related measures—for example, an overall cognitive role-taking score based on the sum of three separate role-taking measures. Such aggregate scores have higher reliability than the individual measures that go into them, and hence are more likely to reveal genuine relations between constructs.

OBSERVATIONAL METHODS

In this final section we turn from questions of design to questions of measurement. As suggested earlier, the use of observational techniques to measure behavior raises some special questions that the researcher must resolve. We conclude the chapter, therefore, with a discussion of some of the complexities involved in observing behavior.

Some definition is in order at the start. In a sense, all research involves observation of behavior; how else would we get our dependent variables? In some cases, however, the recording of behavior is essentially, if not literally, automatic. Heart-rate responses may be recorded via an electrocardiogram. Judgments on a problem-solving task may be indicated by pushing a button. Questionnaires may be used to elicit a variety of responses from developmentally mature subjects. Whatever the other problems in such research, the accuracy of the behavioral recording is not usually an issue.

In observational research the accuracy of the recording definitely *is* an issue. In observational studies the focus is generally on fairly large chunks of natural, ongoing behavior. Such behavior is not automatically recordable; rather, a human observer is required to make judgments about the occurrence and meaning of the behavior. The central question then is how accurately the observer can make these decisions.

We divide our discussion of observational methods into three general issues: deciding what to observe, deciding how to observe it, and determining the accuracy of the observations. Useful further sources include Irwin and Bushnell (1980), Kent and Foster (1977), Sackett (1978), and Yarrow and Waxler (1979).

Deciding What to Observe

At one level, answers to the "what" question are straightforward. Clearly, the researcher's general interests provide an initial delimiting of the behaviors that might be observed. The nature of the behavior then determines whether observational assessment is a reasonable option or not. Some behaviors lend themselves more readily to observation than do others. Aggression, for example, is a natural candidate for observational assessment: a frequent, overt, readily "see-able" behavior. Other techniques of measurement (e.g., rating scales, contrived experimental tests) do exist, but may often be less satisfactory for the researcher's purpose. Conversely, heart-rate changes, or physiological responses in general, are poor candidates for observational assessment. Such responses are difficult and in some cases impossible to see, and alternative methods of assessment are both available and, in most cases, far more sensible.

Things become more complicated once the researcher moves beyond the initial decision to use observational techniques and attempts to determine exactly which aspects of the behavior to record. Suppose that we are studying mothers' styles of interacting with their infants (perhaps *the* most common arena for observational techniques in developmental research today). We know to start with that we cannot record *everything;* observation always involves some abstraction from the moment-to-moment specifics of the behavior. But at what level of specificity should we abstract? Should we record the fact that the mother raised her eyebrows, opened her eyes wider, turned up the corners of her mouth, and emitted a vocalization? Or should we work at a more global and interpretive level and record the fact that the mother smiled at and talked to her baby? Should we become more global and interpretive still and indicate that the mother seemed to encourage the behavior just produced by the baby? Or should we move to an even more global level and record that the mother acted in a warm, positive manner toward her child?

The distinctions just raised are often discussed under the heading of *molecular* as opposed to *molar* approaches to observation (Sackett, Ruppenthal, & Gluck, 1978). Another pair of terms with essentially the same meaning is *microanalytic* and *macroanalytic* approaches (Lamb, Thompson, & Frodi, 1982). A molecular or microanalytic approach focuses on relatively fine-grained details of behavior, staying close to the actual behavior and to an essentially neutral depicting of exactly what occurs. There is, of course, still some loss of detail and some interpretation involved; even so, the attempt is to be relatively complete, specific, and nonevaluative. A molar or macroanalytic approach, in contrast, involves some stepping back from the actual behavior, some summing together of molecular units to arrive at a more evaluative overall category. "Smiles" or "hugs" would be examples of molar categories at a relatively specific level; "encourages" or

"distracts" would be examples at a more global and interpretive level.

As the preceding may suggest, molecular versus molar is another contrast that is really more a continuum than a dichotomy. Observational systems may embody various degrees of specificity and interpetation. Tables 5-2 and 5-3 give examples of systems for the study of mother-infant interaction that fall fairly clearly into the molecular and molar categories. In the Als, Tronick, and Brazelton (1979) research, described in Table 5-2, the interest was in very basic forms of organization and adaptation shown by young infants in interaction with their mothers. In the Lamb (1976) research, described in Table 5-3, the interest was in infants' methods of maintaining contact with their parents in a strange situation, including possible differences in response to mothers and to fathers. The main contrast drawn concerned the two global and clearly molar categories, distal/affiliative and proximal/attachment.

Two general factors determine just where on the molecular-molar continuum a researcher is likely to work. One is the purpose behind the research. If the interest is in the topography of facial movements in various affective states (e.g., Izard, 1979), then a molecular observational system is clearly necessary. If the interest is in the social determinants of smiling or laughing (e.g., Sroufe, Waters, & Matas, 1974), then a more molar system is probably more sensible. It may be possible, of course, to combine molecular and molar analyses in the same study, especially if the behavior can be filmed or videotaped. Note, however, the constraints on direction of movement when on-the-spot recording is used. It is often possible to work with a molecular system and later extract molar information from it—for example, to score details of facial movements and later determine the frequency of smiling. It is not possible, however, to record at a molar level and later extract molecular detail.

The second general determinant of level of observation falls under the heading of feasibility. Whatever the researcher may *wish* to observe, the ultimate determinant of the obser-

TABLE 5–2 An Example of a Molecular Observational System for Recording Infant Behavior during Mother-Infant Interaction

---

I. Type of Vocalization:

1. none; 2. isolated sound; 3. grunt; 4. coo; 5. cry; 6. fuss; 7. laugh.

II. Direction of Visual Attention:

1. Direction of Gaze: 1. towards mother's face; 2. away from mother's face; 3. following mother's face; 4. part side, nose level; 5. part side, nose down; 6. part side, nose up; 7. complete side, nose level; 8. complete side, nose down; 9. complete side, nose up.
2. Head Orientation: 1. towards, nose level; 2. towards, nose down; 3. towards, nose up; 4. part side, nose level; 5. part side, nose down; 6. part side, nose up; 7. complete side, nose level; 8. complete side, nose down; 9. complete side, nose up.
3. Left/Right Modifier of Head Position: 1. infant's left; 2. infant's right.
4. Blinks and Specific Eye Movements: 1. blink; 2. eyes crossed; 3. away and focused on specifiable object (such as chair side) which is not used by mother as part of interaction; 4. eyes shifted markedly to side relative to axis of nose.

III. Facial Expression:

1. Position of Infant's Cheeks (examples only): 1. neutral, relaxed position; 2. elongated, hollow; 3. raised upward and puffed.
2. Eyebrow Position (examples only): 1. neutral resting position; 2. rounded with elevation in center; 3. flashing—rapid up and down.
3. Mouth Position (examples only): 1. neutral resting position; 2. slightly opened without tension; 3. broad smile; 4. yawn—open.
4. Eye Width: 1. neutral; 2. wide; 3. narrow; 4. closed.
5. Tongue Placement: 1. not exposed; 2. tongue exposed but not extended beyond lips; 3. tongue exposed and extended beyond lips.
6. Specific Facial Expressions: 1. cry face; 2. grimace; 3. pout; 4 wary/sober; 5. lidding; 6. yawn; 7. neutral; 8. sneeze; 9. softening; 10. brightening; 11. simple smile; 12. coo face; 13 broad smile.

IV. Body Position and Movement:

1. leaning forward and doubled over; 2. body turned off to one side; 3. arching; 4. leaning back; 5. slumped to one side; 6. neutral; 7. position being changed by mother; 8. moving up in vertical plane; 9. upright with head raised off cushion or neck extended and trunk elongated; 10. leaning forward with back straight.

V. Limb Movements

1. Size of Limb Movement: 1. none; 2. small; 3. medium; 4. large.
2. Number of Limbs in Movement: 1. none; 2. 1 limb; 3. 2 limbs; 4. 3 limbs; 5. 4 limbs; 6. only arms seen because of maternal position – 1 moving; 7. as in 6. – 2 moving.
3. Place of Movement: 1. none; 2. midline; 3. between midline and shoulders; 4. side.
4. Specific Arm and Hand Gestures: 1. eye rubbing; 2. hand to mouth; 3. swiping; 4. digit fidgits; 5. hands held together at midline; 6. all four limbs extended forward.
5. Specific Leg Gestures: 1. kicking; 2. startle.

Note: From "Analysis of Face-to-Face Interaction in Infant-Adult Dyads" (pp. 43–44) by H. Als, E. Tronick, and T. Berry Brazelton. In M. E. Lamb, S. J. Suomi, and G. R. Stephenson (Eds.), *Social Interaction Analysis* (pp. 33–76), Copyright 1979, Madison, WI: The University of Wisconsin Press. Reprinted by permission.

vational system is what *can* be observed. Recording of molecular detail, for example, may be possible only in environments in which the observer can remain very close to the subject, or in which the behavior can be filmed or video-taped. Researchers working in other environments (which would include, of course, most natural settings) may have to settle for a more molar observational system. A further consideration, which is elaborated on shortly, con-

TABLE 5-3 An Example of a Molar Observational System for Recording Infant Behavior during Parent-Infant Interaction

	Distal/Affiliative Behaviors
Behavior	*Definition*
Smiling	A facial expression in which the brows were not drawn together, but the corners of the mouth were retracted and raised.
Looking	Direction of gaze toward the person concerned.
Vocalizing	Includes all directed nondistress vocalizations except giggling or laughing, which were tabulated as instances of laughing.
Proffering	Occasions on which the infant either offered, showed, or pointed out an object or toy to an adult.

	Proximal/Attachment Behaviors
Behavior	*Definition*
Proximity	Coded once in each 15-second unit that the infant was within 3 feet of the adult concerned.
Approach	A move from beyond to within 3 feet—that is, a move into proximity—of a person.
Fussing	Any distress-type vocalization directed toward an adult.
Touching	Coded when the infant made physical contact with the body or clothing of an adult.
Reaching	The child gestures to the adult by raising and moving a hand in the direction of the person.
Seeking to be picked up	Manifested by one or more of the following: fussing, reaching to, vocalizing, or clinging to the legs of the person.

Note: Adapted from ''Twelve-Month-Olds and their Parents: Interaction in a Laboratory Playroom'' by M. E. Lamb, 1976, *Developmental Psychology, 12,* pp. 237–244.

cerns the *reliability* of the observations. Observations do not mean very much if two independent observers cannot agree on what is being observed. Sometimes the fine detail required in a molecular system may exceed the observers' capacities, forcing the researcher to move to somewhat grosser scoring categories. Sometimes the interpretations required in a molar system (Was that maternal behavior really rejection, or simply an attempt to redirect the child?) may frustrate agreement, forcing the researcher to stay closer to the level of the actual behavior (e.g., turns away from child). Whatever the specific problem, the general point is the one just made: The level of detail and interpretation in an observational system is always determined not only by what is desirable but also by what is possible.

Deciding How to Observe

The ''how'' question involves a number of complexities that are beyond our scope. Nevertheless, a few points can be made.

Suppose that a researcher has arrived at a nursery school, pen and clipboard in hand and ready to observe the interesting behaviors of preschool children. How might he or she go about recording the data of interest?

One possibility is simply to write down, in narrative form, a description of the behavior as it occurs. Such a technique is called a *running narrative record;* other often-used terms are *specimen records* and (from the pioneering work of Barker and Wright, 1951) the *stream of behavior* approach. Of course, some selectivity is necessarily involved in even the fullest narrative record. The focus is typically on only one child at a time, with other children brought in only as they interact with the target child. In observing the target child decisions must continually be made about which behaviors are significant enough to record and which behaviors (e.g., blinks, swallows) can be ignored. Decisions must also be made about the level at which behaviors should be described—for example, did Johnny close his fingers together, make a fist, or threaten some other child? With a narrative record approach the observer functions to some extent like a combination camera-tape recorder. He or she is, however, a camera-recorder with a strong decision-making editor built in.

Despite the constraints just noted, a major strength of the narrative record approach is its relative completeness. More of the information about behavior is preserved than in any other method of observation. This relative completeness makes the narrative record especially useful for practitioners who require detailed information about a particular child. Narrative records are thus commonly used by teachers working in educational settings, or by clinicians compiling case studies of individual children. Such records can also be used as starting points for research programs, suggesting phenomena that can then be followed up with more systematic and focused methods of study. Recall that this was one use of naturalistic observation suggested by McCall (1977). Finally, narrative records need not always be just the preliminary to research; if the recording is carried out in a sufficiently skillful and systematic manner, the narrative record may serve as the basic data for a study. In such cases the narrative record provides the raw data; further coding and analysis are then necessary to winnow the behavior stream down to the units and phenomena of interest.

On the debit side, compiling narrative records can be a very costly and time-consuming process. The demands on the observer may be especially great, as may be the possiblities for various forms of subjectivity and bias. The researcher may end up with a huge mass of information, only a small portion of which turns out to be of interest. Or the researcher may have clear-cut goals and hypotheses before beginning the observation, in which case the narrative record may be a very uneconomical form of data collection. In such cases other, more focused forms of observation may make more sense.

A second general approach to observation is labeled *time sampling*. Two features distinguish time sampling from narrative record. First, with time sampling the focus is on a relatively few specific and well-defined behaviors, not on the entire stream of ongoing behavior. The examples of molecular and molar approaches shown in Tables 5–2 and 5–3 were, as actually applied, also examples of time sampling. Here, a specific set of behaviors is precisely defined in advance, and *only* these behaviors are recorded. Because precise definitions already exist, there is no need to write a narrative description of the behavior; rather, some sort of checklist or coding system can be used. The second distinguishing feature is the division of the observation period into exact and usually rather brief units of time. The observer might observe for 15 seconds, turn away and record for 15 seconds, observe for another 15 seconds, record for 15 seconds, and so forth. The "sampling" part of time sampling is thus two-fold: Only a few of the ongoing behaviors are examined, and only some segments of the total observation period are included.

There is still a third general approach to observation, one that we introduce by example. In what is often referred to as one of the "classic" studies of child psychology, Dawe (1934) set out to study nursery-school children's quarrels. Although the perceptions of many nursery-school teachers might differ, quarrels turned out to be fairly infrequent, occurring at an average of 3.4 per hour. Given the infrequency of the behavior, both narrative record and time sampling would have been inefficient methods of study. Time sampling might also have been misleading; it would be quite possible for the observer to miss a quarrel if it happened to occur during one of the nonobservation periods, or to see only a portion of the quarrel if it cut across periods. The method Dawe adopted instead is labeled *event sampling*. In event sampling the target behavior itself, and not time, serves as the unit of analysis. As in time sampling, the observer begins by carefully defining the behaviors of interest. With event sampling, however, the observer simply waits until the behavior occurs and begins recording only then. The recording can take a variety of forms, ranging from a narrative description to a precoded checklist. Dawe employed a combination of predetermined categories and supplementary running notes in her research;

among the categories scored were "passive behavior," "retaliative behavior," and "undirected energy." Whatever the form of recording, the focus on the target behavior as the basic unit may allow the observer to capture information (e.g., average duration of the behavior, antecedents and consequences) that might be missed with a time-sampling approach.

In general, the factors that influence choice of a recording system are the same as those that influence the molecular-molar decision: goals and feasibility. In some observational studies (e.g., clinical case reports) a narrative record is essential; in others the more focused approach of time or event sampling is more appropriate. Whatever the goals of the study, the researcher must select a system that can be applied within the available environmental setting, does not place impossible demands on either the time or the abilities of the observers, and yields a reasonable ratio of usable data to time and effort expended.

Determining the Accuracy of Observations

This section is a counterpart to the whole of chapter 4, the focus now being on problems that can arise in observing behavior rather than in testing subjects. We begin by considering two specific threats to the accuracy of observations. We then conclude with a discussion of the thorny problem of reliability.

The behaviors recorded in an observational study may be a function of any number of antecedent or contemporary factors. One factor that we do *not* wish to have influence the behavior, however, is the mere presence of the observer. Yet the presence of the observer, and the concomitant knowledge that one is being observed, may alter behavior in various ways. Such effects fall under the general heading of *reactivity:* unintended effects of the experimental arrangements upon the subject's behavior. When the context is observational research, reactive effects are often referred to as the problem of *observer influence.*

Just how important reactivity is in observational studies has long been a matter of dispute (see Kent and Foster, 1977, for a discussion). There is evidence that both adults and children may behave differently when they know that they are being observed; there is also evidence that under some circumstances behavior is not at all affected by observation. Two general techniques exist for reducing the possibility of observer influence. One is to *habituate* the subjects to the presence of the observer—that is, to introduce the observer into the setting some time before the onset of observation, and to begin recording only once subjects have become accustomed to the observer and their behavior has returned to normal. This technique is sometimes referred to as "fading into the woodwork." A variant of it, which is sometimes but by no means always possible, is to have the observations made by someone who is already a natural and familiar part of the setting, such as a parent or teacher.

The second strategy is to disguise the fact that observations are being made. It may be possible, for example, to film the behavior with a hidden camera, or to observe subjects through a one-way mirror. Of course, it may also *not* be possible to—such techniques tend to be feasible only in certain special environments. In addition, there may be ethical as well as logistical constraints on the possibility of surreptitious observation. As we see in chapter 11, observing subjects without their knowledge raises a number of ethical questions.

A second general problem in observational research is *observer bias.* Here too, the threat to observational study is merely a specific instance of a more general problem. As Rosenthal's (1976) work makes clear, the expectations of the researcher may bias results, moving outcomes in the direction of what was expected or desired. In observational study the danger is that the observer may see and record what he or she expects to occur, rather than what actually happens.

A study by Kent, O'Leary, Diament, and Dietz (1974) provides an example. The observers in this study viewed videotapes that supposedly showed the baseline and treatment phases of a program intended to reduce disruptive behavior in a classroom setting. Half of the observers were told that a decrease in disruptive behavior from baseline to treatment was predicted; half were told that no change was predicted. In fact, all the observers viewed the same videotape, in which no change occurred for any of the behavioral categories. When later asked to make a global rating of the effectiveness of the program, however, 9 of the 10 observers who had been led to expect a decrease in disruptive behavior reported that a decrease had in fact occurred. In contrast, 7 of the 10 observers led to expect no change reported no change. It is interesting to note that there were *no* differences between the two groups in the actual behavioral recordings made while watching the tape. Only on the overall global rating did the expectancy manipulation have an effect.

The findings of the Kent et al. study suggest one way to reduce the probability of observer bias: Make the scoring categories as specific and objective as possible. The greater the leeway for interpretation in scoring, the greater the opportunity for the observer to inject his or her own biases. The other general way to reduce observer bias is to keep the observer uninformed about the hypotheses of the study or the group to which the subject belongs. This is the technique of *blinding* discussed in chapter 4. The rationale is straightforward: If no expectancies exist, then there is no danger of a researcher expectancy effect. As we saw in chapter 4, however, blinding may be difficult and in some cases impossible to achieve. Furthermore, even when blinding *is* possible, it is by no means always used.

A final set of problems revolves around the concept of *reliability*. As noted in chapter 2, reliability refers to consistency of measurement. In the case of observational methods, the key issue is that of *interobserver agreement:* Can two or more independent observers arrive at the same interpretation of a behavior? Such agreement is a necessary basis for concluding that the observations are accurate. It is not a sufficient basis, however, because it is possible for two observers to arrive at the same wrong interpretation of the behavior. Two wrongs may not make a

right, but they can lead to high agreement. This, too, is a specific instance of a general point: Reliability is necessary but not sufficient for validity.

There are various ways to calculate reliability. For some kinds of data the *correlation statistic* is appropriate. The higher the correlation between the recordings of two observers, the more satisfactory the reliability. Another commonly used index is *percentage of agreement.* Suppose that there are 20 opportunities to score the occurrence of some behavior. Agreement by two observers on 19 of the 20 instances would yield a percentage of agreement of 95%, a satisfactorily high reliability. Agreement on only 13 of the 20 instances would yield a percentage of agreement of 65%, which is not likely to be considered satisfactory. Other methods of calculating reliability, as well as the complexities associated with each of the different methods, are discussed in Hollenbeck (1978) and Mitchell (1979).

Questions about how to calculate reliability apply only once the researcher has realized that reliability is in fact necessary for his or her study. Our journal survey (Table 1–2) included a tabulation of whether reliability was calculated in cases in which doing so seemed appropriate. The survey suggests a high but not perfect awareness of the need for reliability: Data concerning reliability were reported in 88% of the relevant instances.

Procedures useful for maximizing reliability are easy enough to state, if not always to apply. Observers should be carefully trained before the start of actual data collection. The scoring system should be as clear and as specific as possible. Pilot testing can be used both to train observers and to refine the system, with categories that prove infrequent or unscorable either dropped or transformed into more usable categories. Finally, when possible, filming or videotaping can be used to produce a permanent, replayable record of the behavior.

As the preceding suggests, it is desirable to achieve reliability as early as possible in the process of data collection. It may also be desirable, however, to continue to monitor for reliability throughout the course of a study.

Research by Reid (1970; Taplin & Reid, 1973) makes this point. In the Taplin and Reid study observers were first trained to an acceptable level of reliability. Subsequently, one group of observers was told that reliability would no longer be assessed, whereas a second group was told that periodic and unpredictable reliability checks would be made. In fact, every observer's recordings continued to be checked against predetermined criterion ratings. The results were clear: The observers who expected to have their ratings checked maintained better reliability than those who did not expect a reliability assessment. This tendency for initially reliable observers to drop in reliability when they are no longer being monitored has been labeled *observer drift*. Observer drift falls under the general heading of Campbell and Stanley's (1966) *instrumentation:* an unintended change in a measuring instrument across the course of a study.

Thus far we have been discussing reliability as though there were a single overall index of reliability that a study either achieves or fails to achieve. In fact, in the typical case there are a number of potential reliabilities—for particular behaviors, particular aspects of a behavior, particular time periods, particular subgroups of subjects, and so forth. The essential point with respect to these various possibilities is that reliability must be demonstrated *at the level at which the data are to be analyzed.* If, for example, the researcher wishes to examine posttest differences following some treatment, then it is necessary to demonstrate that the posttest data can be scored reliably; reliability achieved during the pretest phase is not sufficient. Similarly, if the analyses involve total number of aggressive acts, then reliability for global ratings of aggression is not sufficient; the researcher must also show that observers can agree on specific instances of aggressive behavior.

Yarrow and Waxler (1979) provide an interesting, and somewhat less obvious, example of this same point. These authors report various observational studies in which reliability was calculated separately for boys and girls. In some cases a behavior turned out to be more reliably scored for one sex than for the other. At least in these studies, for example, aggression could be scored more reliably for boys than for girls. Furthermore, individual differences in aggression showed sensible relations to other measures for boys, not, however, for girls. As Yarrow and Waxler note, this finding could reflect a genuine sex difference, or it might come about simply because the measures of aggression were not sufficiently reliable for girls. Again, reliability is necessary at the level at which the data are to be used.

Yarrow and Waxler (1979) also provide a good overview of the pros and cons of using a human observer as a measuring instrument. Their overview can serve as summary for our discussion of observational methods:

Though exceedingly practiced, the human observer, by many criteria, is a poor scientific instrument: nonstandard, not readily calibrated, and often inconsistent or unreliable. Counterbalancing these failures are the human capabilities of extraordinary sensitivity, flexibility, and precision. The challenge is to discover how to conduct disciplined observing while making full use of the discriminations of which the human observer is capable. (p. 37)

SUMMARY

The first section of this chapter considers the settings within which research in developmental psychology occurs. It is organized in terms of the distinction between structured laboratory settings and natural field settings. Independent variables can be manipulated and dependent variables measured in either setting, yielding four general designs.

Research under the lab-lab heading tends to maximize both control of the independent variable and accurate measurement of the dependent variable. Such research, therefore, is often high in internal validity. Furthermore, some topics in developmental psychology (e.g., many issues in perceptual development) can be clearly studied only within the controlled environment of the laboratory. On the negative side, laboratory manipulations and measures are often quite different from the real-life situations of interest, and this artificiality raises questions of external validity. Laboratory research may also be especially subject to problems of reactivity and response bias.

The strengths and weaknesses of field research tend to be the converse of those of laboratory research. The great advantage of research under the field-field heading is the locus of both the independent variable and the dependent variable in the natural setting. Problems of artificiality and consequent lack of external validity are therefore reduced. The major limitation concerns feasibility: Control of the independent variable and measurement of the dependent variable are more difficult in the natural setting than in the laboratory, and with some variables such control and measurement are impossible.

The advantages and disadvantages of the two combined approaches (lab-field and field-lab) follow from the general points made concerning laboratory research and field research. A further advantage is the temporal and spatial separation of the independent and dependent variables, a feature that may sometimes increase validity. A further disadvantage lies in the practical obstacles to combining laboratory and field components within the same study.

Following the runthrough of designs the discussion turns to an overview and evaluation. Some further complications in the classification of research approaches are introduced, prior to discussion of a journal survey that tabulates the frequency of different approaches. The survey provides some support for the common criticism that developmental research has been oriented too exclusively to laboratory settings. Valuable though the laboratory approach is, it is limited to answering questions of "can" rather than "does," and it may be most informative after an initial phase of research in the natural setting. Most generally, the section stresses the value of *converging operations:* studying a topic in as many different ways as possible so that the inevitable limitations of any one approach are compensated for by the strengths of other approaches.

The middle section of the chapter deals with *correlational research.* In a correlational study there is no control of an independent variable; rather, two or more variables are measured, and the interest is in whether scores on the different measures covary. Correlational designs may be the only research option available for variables whose experimental manipulation is either impossible or very difficult. Furthermore, correlational research has the advantage of encompassing more levels of a variable than is usually possible in a controlled experimental study. On the negative side, the absence of experimental control means that correlational designs are intrinsically limited in what they can tell us about cause and effect. Methods useful for reducing the uncertainty and moving closer to the determination of causality include experimental manipulation of one of the variables; logical analysis of which causal directions are possible; *partial correlation,* in which the contribution of third-factor variables is statistically removed; and *cross-lagged panel correlation,* in which the pattern of correlations is studied over time.

In addition to issues of causality, correlational research can also be used to examine patterning or interrelations in development. The hypothesis of interest is generally that some set of measures has a common underlying core, and hence that performance on the measures should correlate. Validation of this hypothesis requires that other possible explanations for positive correlations be ruled out. Among the competing explanations that may be relevant are general improvement with age in performance on any measure, shared methods variance among the tasks being compared, and general differences in competence that guarantee some degree of correlation across any set of cognitive measures. The last of these possibilities illustrates the need for research to demonstrate not only *convergent validity*—that is, positive correlations among measures that are expected to relate—but also *divergent validity*—that is, absence of correlations for theoretically unrelated measures.

The final section of the chapter discusses observational research. Three general issues are considered. A first concerns the level of specificity at which behavior is recorded. A *molecular* or *microanalytic* observational system attempts to capture relatively fine-grained details of behavior; a *molar* or *macroanalytic* observational system consists of more global and interpretive categories. The goals of the research are one determinant of where on the molecular to molar continuum a researcher will work. Another is feasibility: A particular observational system is usable only if the required observations can be made accurately. Goals and feasibility are also relevant to the second general issue discussed: the method of recording observations. The *running narrative record* provides the fullest account of ongoing behavior. More focused methods of observation are either *time sampling* or *event sampling*. In both cases specific recording categories are decided on in advance; observations are then made within the framework of either units of time (time sampling) or behaviors of interest (event sampling).

The last issue discussed concerns problems that can arise in observational research. *Observer influence* is a particular form of *reactivity;* it refers to the fact that subjects' behavior may be altered by the knowledge that they are being observed. Various techniques for reducing such bias are discussed. The expectancies of the observer are another possible source of bias, for observers may sometimes slant their observations toward what they expect to find. The best way to guard against this form of bias is to minimize the expectancies. Finally, the utility of observations is dependent on the demonstration of *interobserver reliability*, that is, agreement by two or more independent observers about how behavior is to be classified. Reliability should be monitored throughout the study, to guard against the phenomenon of *observer drift*. It should also be demonstrated at the level at which the data are analyzed.

chapter 6

INFANCY

In the next four chapters we turn from general principles of research to specific research topics in developmental psychology. Our organization is partly chronological and partly topical. The section begins with a chapter on infancy and concludes with a chapter on aging. In between are chapters devoted to cognitive development and social development. Untidy though this chronological-topical division may seem, it is in fact typical of the field. Some developmental psychologists identify themselves primarily in terms of age group studied and others identify themselves primarily in terms of topic. Similarly, some methodological issues are peculiar to the study of particular age groups and others are most closely linked to particular topics.

The discussion of infancy is divided into two broad sections. We begin by considering some of the general issues involved in doing research with babies. For the most part these issues consist of specific applications of points discussed in the preceding chapters, especially chapter 4.

As we will see, however, some methodological challenges are especially acute for the researcher who decides to study infants.

The second, and longer, section is devoted to particular kinds of infancy research. It is here, for the first time, that we get into some of the specific research techniques used by developmental psychologists. Our coverage of topics is necessarily selective, as indeed it is throughout the next four chapters. It should be possible, however, to highlight some of the most important, and methodologically interesting, kinds of infant study.

GENERAL ISSUES

Getting and Keeping Subjects

We begin with one of the basic steps in research identified in chapter 1: getting subjects. It was suggested in chapter 1 that this problem tends to be especially great for developmental psychologists. We can add now that the researcher of infancy can probably lay claim to the greatest woes with respect to subject recruitment. Infants cannot volunteer for experiments, as can older children or adults. Nor can they be readily recruited from some institutional setting, such as a grade school, introductory psychology class, or nursing home. How, then, do researchers find babies to study?

The answer is: in a variety of ways, with the particular way dependent on both the age of the infant and the resources of the researcher. When newborns are the subjects an institutional source may be available, if the babies can be tested before being taken home from the hospital. Note, however, that such early hospital testing has become less feasible than it used to be, given the steady decline in length of hospital stay for both newborn and mother. When older babies are the target group, recruitment may be possible through the rolls of pediatricians or well-baby clinics. In such cases the name list provides a starting point; the researcher must still induce the parent to allow the baby's participation. Babies of any age may be solicited through newspaper advertisements describing the research and inviting interested parents to call. Or the direction of contact may be reversed: Some researchers keep track of birth announcements and then call parents as the baby reaches the appropriate age for the study. Whatever the initial approach, the willingness of the parent to allow the baby to be studied remains the sine qua non.

As the preceding suggests, finding infants to study may be a time-consuming and expensive process. The real issue, however, is the representativeness of the sample obtained. We noted in chapter 3 that truly random sampling from a target population is a desirable but rarely attained goal. Some deviation from randomness is the norm in research. At least within the span of childhood, however, such deviations are probably greater for infancy than for any other age group. Babies who are brought to well-baby clinics are a particular subset of the population of babies as a whole; babies who are brought to pediatricians are a different subset. Parents who

respond positively to phone calls soliciting participation are a particular subset of parents; those who respond to newspaper ads are another, undoubtedly smaller, subset. In general, it seems likely that parents who volunteer their babies for research are better educated than parents as a whole; in some cases they may also be poorer, and thus more susceptible to whatever financial inducements accompany the research (note that student parents fit both categories!). For all of these reasons, babies who find their way into research are often a distinctly nonrandom sample of the larger population in which the researcher is interested.

A second issue concerns how many babies make it through to the end of the study. Drop-out in infant research is substantial. Indeed, the drop-out rate is almost certainly greater in studies of infancy than in any other sort of research with human subjects, figures of up to 50% to 60% being not uncommon. The most frequently cited reason for loss of infant subjects is fussiness (a term that may often be a euphemism); drowsiness or going to sleep is also a common problem. To the extent that babies who drop out of research differ from those who remain in, then an initially nonrandom sample will become even more nonrandom.

The sampling problems just discussed have not received much explicit attention among infancy researchers. There are probably two reasons for this apparent lack of concern. First, there is often little that can be done: A researcher can work only with those subjects who are available, and no researcher can force a baby to stay happy or awake through an experimental session. It is the nature of the infant to be a difficult experimental subject. Second, the fact that a sample is nonrandom does not necessarily mean that findings obtained with it cannot be generalized to some larger group. This is the point that was made in chapter 3 in our general discussion of sampling. As noted then, the issue in selecting a sample is not randomness per se; it is whether any deviations from randomness are at all likely to bias the results. With many kinds of research it is simply not plausible that the nonrandom nature of the sample could make any difference. This argument is probably more applicable to infancy and to the kinds of issues studied with infants than it is to older, more diversified age groups. And it can be applied not only to initial sampling but also to the problem of drop-out. All babies are at times fussy and sleepy. Some babies happen to be fussy or sleepy during the experiment and therefore drop out; other babies happen not to be and therefore remain in. But there is no reason to think that the two groups are systematically different.

Although this kind of plausibility argument may be generally valid, its application to particular cases still requires scrutiny. Particularly when the initial selection is unusual or the drop-out substantial, questions of external validity may be quite legitimate. In addition, there are some data to question the assumption that drop-out in infant research is random and therefore nonbiasing. Lewis and Johnson (1971) tested 3- and 6-month-old infants on a series of measures of visual and auditory attention. They compared responses on a subset of the visual measures for two groups of babies: 22 infants who completed the entire series of tests, and 15 infants who provided data on the target measures but dropped out before the testing was completed. Infants who remained available for the entire series showed greater ability to distinguish between simple and complex stimuli than did infants who eventually dropped out; this finding held for both visual fixation and changes in heart rate. Lewis and Johnson (1971) concluded from these results that "our implicit assumption about the composition of those infants who are excluded from data analysis may be wrong. . . . The elimination of infants, especially in the large numbers, may result in serious biasing of the obtained data" (p. 1055). (See also Richardson and McCluskey, 1983.)

The Importance of State

We noted in the previous section that the infant is a difficult experimental subject, often too fussy or too sleepy to make it through an experiment. This observation has general significance, for it highlights the importance of *state* in attempting to make sense of infant behavior.

How a baby responds to the environment depends very much on his or her immediate state of arousal. Is the baby awake and alert? Drowsy and about to drift off to sleep? Hungry and therefore irritable? Screaming with rage? Or perhaps deep in peaceful sleep?

As this runthrough of possibilities suggests, the categories of "fussy" and "sleepy" that we have been using thus far are rather gross indices of state. Psychologists have in fact devised more refined classification schemes. One common scheme, adapted from the work of Peter Wolff (1966), is shown in Table 6–1.

The importance of state is not limited to infants, of course. Any of us is more likely to be responsive to an environmental stimulus when wide awake than when sound asleep, and any of us may behave differently when hunger pangs are gnawing than when they are not. For various reasons, however, state looms larger in the study of infants than it does in the study of older children or adults. States tend to be more labile in infancy, and shifts are frequent from one state to another. As this lability suggests, infants are less able to control their state than are older children or adults. One can assume that a 10-year-old who is awake and alert at the start of an experiment will still be reasonably awake and alert 20 minutes later. No such assumption can be made for the infant. Finally, the proportion of time spent in the various states changes with development. Most obviously (although not only), the proportion of time awake and alert increases dramatically with age. The newborn sleeps an average of 16 to 17 hours a day, with much of the waking period devoted to feeding (Parmelee, Wenner, & Schultz, 1964). Only about 10% of the newborn's time is spent in the state of alert inactivity (Berg, Adkinson, & Strock, 1973).

The most general implication of state is the one noted earlier: Understanding infant behavior requires knowledge of the infant's state. In some studies state is included as one of the variables whose effects are being determined. Researchers have looked, for example, for differences in response to tactile stimuli during quiet and active sleep (e.g., Rose, Schmidt, & Bridger, 1978), or at heart-rate responses to au-

TABLE 6-1 States of Arousal in Infants

State	Description
Regular Sleep	During regular sleep babies lie quite still with their eyes closed and unmoving. Their respiration is even, and their skin is pale.
Irregular Sleep	During irregular sleep babies' muscular response to pressure is stronger than in regular sleep. Babies jerk, startle, and grimace spontaneously. The eyes are clearly closed but sometimes they move. The skin may be flushed, and breathing is irregular.
Periodic Sleep	Periodic sleep is a combination of regular and irregular sleep: it consists of bursts of rapid breathing, jerks, and startles, followed by spells of quiet.
Drowsiness	During drowsy states babies are moderately active. Their eyes open and close intermittently, and they look glazed. Respiration is regular but more rapid than in regular sleep.
Alert Inactivity	Alert, inactive babies are awake. Their eyes are open and shining, and they look at their surroundings with interest. Babies' bodies are relatively still, and their respiration is rather fast and irregular.
Waking Activity	During waking activity babies are awake but their eyes focus less often, and they have spurts of vigorous activity. During these random spurts they move their legs and arms and twist their torsos. The length and intensity of these activity spurts vary.
Crying	During crying states infants engage in vigorous activity. Their skin is flushed and they cry (although without tears yet).

Note: From *Understanding Infancy* (pp. 38, 40) by E. Willemsen, 1979, San Francisco: W. H. Freeman & Co. Copyright 1979 by W. H. Freeman & Co. Reprinted by permission. Willemsen's descriptions are adapted from Wolff (1966).

ditory stimuli in sleeping and awake infants (e.g., Berg, Berg, & Graham, 1971). In some studies state has served as a dependent variable, the goal being to identify factors that affect state. There are studies, for example, of the effects of experimental alteration of sleep cycles on the baby's subsequent state (e.g., Anders & Roffwarg, 1973) or the role that caretaking practices play in mediating state (e.g., Korner & Thoman, 1972). Most commonly in infant research, however, the goal has not been to study state but to *control* for it. What the researcher seeks, in other words, is to test all subjects in the same state, whatever state is deemed most appropriate for the issue being examined. In most cases the goal has been to work with babies while they are quiet and alert, for this is the state most conducive to perceptual and cognitive functioning.

Researchers of infancy resort to various stratagems in the attempt to get babies while they are in the desired quiet and alert state. It is common practice to ask parents to bring babies in for testing at a time of day when the babies are usually awake and happy. Nap times are obviously to be avoided; there is some dispute, however, about how close to feeding time

is optimal (Field, 1982). Various manipulations are also possible in the experimental setting. The position of the infant can have an effect on state. It has been found, for example, that very young infants are typically more alert when upright than when lying down (Korner & Thoman, 1970). It has long been known that change in position can serve to wake up a drowsy baby or quiet a fussy one. Pacifiers have also been used to calm fussy babies; recent evidence indicates, however, that pacifiers may also affect other aspects of the baby's response, and their use in research has therefore become less common (Field, 1982).

However ingenious the researcher, he or she still remains at the mercy of the infant. This dependence on the whims of the subject has some definite methodological implications. Testing sessions must be kept fairly short, lest the infants move out of the desired state. Multiple experimental sessions may therefore be necessary, or perhaps adoption of a between-subject rather than within-subject design. If within-subject testing *is* used, counterbalancing of tasks or conditions is even more important than usual. An assumption that order is irrelevant is dubious at any age; with the rapidly changing infant, however, such an assumption is out of the question.

The most serious methodological implication concerns the selectivity involved in research on infancy. This selectivity operates at two levels. As we have already seen, there is selectivity with respect to who stays in the study and who drops out. Only babies who can maintain the desired state end up as subjects in research. There is also selectivity with regard to which aspects of these eventual subjects' behavior are considered. Studies tend to take the baby at his or her very best—at those times when the baby is happy, awake, and alert. Especially for young infants, such times do not occupy a very large proportion of the baby's day. The focus in research is typically on the infant's *optimal* performance, a quite legitimate and important question. It is important to remember, however, that the infant's *typical* performance may fall well short of this optimum.

Response Measures

Coping with state is one of the two great challenges of infant research. The other is finding responses from which the baby's capacities can be inferred.

Consider the most challenging case of all: the newborn infant. The newborn is not totally helpless; rather he or she comes into the world equipped with various adaptive reflexes—that is, wired-in, automatic responses to particular kinds of stimuli. The newborn does not come equipped, however, with much in the way of skilled, voluntary motoric behavior. Nor, of course, does the newborn possess language. The latter deficiency persists throughout infancy; indeed, the term ''infant'' means ''without language.'' It is worth reflecting for a moment about the extent to which our assessments of older children and adults depend upon the use of language. With infants, however, all of the verbally based techniques that we routinely use to study older subjects are ruled out. How, then, can we figure out what a baby is thinking or experiencing?

To a good extent, the history of research on infancy is a history of the gradual discovery of more and more responses from which the infant's experience of the world can be inferred. Much of the remainder of this chapter discusses what these responses are. The present section is intended simply as a preview of some of the most informative and generally applicable response measures in infancy. Although the responses that we consider might at first seem diverse, they do share several features: All place minimal motoric demands on the infant, all can therefore be emitted by even a very young infant, all can be accurately measured, and all lend themselves (at least sometimes) to clear interpretation.

One common measure is *visual fixation*. Even a newborn can, and does, look at objects. Furthermore, even a newborn can exercise some selectivity in what he or she looks at. As we will see shortly, the fact that infants tend to look more at some stimuli than at others has proved invaluable in the study of perceptual abilities and perceptual preferences. Looking responses also play a role in the study of the other two domains that we consider in this chapter: early cognitive development and early social development.

A second frequently utilized response is *sucking*. Sucking, too, is a response that is available to the infant from birth, and it too is a response in which all infants engage. Most infants, in fact, spend more time in nonnutritive sucking than they do in sucking for food. What is commonly examined in studies that measure sucking are changes in sucking in response to environmental change around the baby. For example, does the baby stop sucking if a novel stimulus suddenly appears in his or her field of vision?

Physiological responses constitute a third important class of dependent measures in research on infancy. Here, obviously, the motoric demands on the infant disappear completely. With modern technology a wide range of physiological responses can be assessed. The most popular measure in research on infancy has been *heart rate*. Heart rate has several desirable qualities from the point of view of a researcher. Unlike some physiological responses, heart rate can be recorded in response to any sort of stimulus in any modality. The physiological system that mediates heart rate is relatively mature at birth, making heart rate a usable measure even in a newborn. Finally, changes in heart rate are directional—that is, the rate either speeds up or slows down. As we will see, considerable evidence indicates that heart-rate deceleration has a different meaning than does heart-rate acceleration. Changes in heart rate can thus provide information that may not be available when a unidirectional response is measured.

The three responses just considered by no means exhaust the infant behaviors that are of interest to developmental researchers. Nor, of course, does this brief introduction make clear how fixation, sucking, or heart rate is actually used in research. We consider response measures more fully when we discuss various kinds of infancy research.

Age Comparisons

The general issue of age comparisons was discussed at length in chapter 3. Our focus now is on age comparisons that involve infants. Drawing valid age comparisons is in some ways easier and in some ways more difficult when infants are the subjects. The ease or difficulty depends on both the particular ages and the particular response measures examined.

Consider first a comparison of different ages within the span of infancy. Such studies tend to be primarily cross-sectional rather than longitudinal, just as does developmental research in general. In research with infants, however, some of the problem of cross-sectional designs discussed in chapter 3 are greatly reduced. In particular, the possibility of cohort effects—that is, effects stemming from differences in generation rather than differences in age—is much less than when older samples are compared. With rare exceptions, researchers can assume that 4-, 8-, and 12-month-old babies belong to the same generation, and that any age differences that may be found are therefore not confounded with differences in cohort. It is, of course, still important to determine why the age

differences appear; one major class of explanations, however, can be ruled out.

Longitudinal research also tends to be more clearly interpretable when the time span is confined to infancy. Recall that a major problem in longitudinal designs is the confounding of age and time of measurement. This confounding holds whatever the age of the sample, but it is much less likely to be a factor in studies of infants. It is implausible, for example, that a baby will behave differently at 12 than at 6 months simply because one assessment is made in March, 1985, and the other in September, 1984. Both the short time span and the nature of the infant make it unlikely that historical-cultural change can account for a change in behavior. Other possible problems in longitudinal research may also be reduced when the focus is on infants. Awareness of being repeatedly studied, for example, is less likely to be a biasing factor for infants than for older children or adults. Finally, interpretive issues aside, longitudinal research is simply more feasible with infants than with older samples. As we saw, a major obstacle to longitudinal study is the fact that the researcher must wait for the subjects to age across some developmentally interesting span—for 10-year-olds to turn into 18-year-olds, 50-year-olds into 70-year-olds, and so forth. The researcher of infancy, however, can chart dramatic developmental changes within the span of a few months.

We have focused so far on studies of infants. Consider now a developmental study that does not stop with infancy but rather attempts to compare infants with older subjects. Here, clearly, problems are more likely to arise. The kinds of confounding just discussed increase in importance as the span of ages increases. The practical difficulties of matching subjects in cross-sectional research or retaining subjects in longitudinal research also increase as the age range increases. Perhaps most important, however, is another of the problems discussed in chapter 3: *measurement equivalence*. Comparing different age groups requires that we have psychologically equivalent measures at the different ages. Only if our measures are tapping the same construct for different groups can we make sense of similarities or differences in performance, or of individual stability or individual change over time.

A little thought about the differences between infants and older children should clarify the magnitude of the measurement-equivalence problem. Imagine a comparison between an 8-month-old and an 8-year-old. Behaviors typical at the two ages, as well as the situations under which the behaviors occur, are quite different. To take an obvious example, much of an 8-year-old's problem solving and social interaction is mediated through language, something that is not true for an infant. Even when the same behavior can be assessed at different ages, its meaning may be quite different. Smiling, for example, may have different origins and different significance at 8 months than at 8 years. Crying is even more likely to have different meaning at the two ages.

Even within infancy, the marked developmental changes from one age to another can give rise to problems of measurement equivalence. The heart-rate response discussed earlier provides an example. There is ample evidence to indicate that newborns tend to respond to a new stimulus with heart-rate acceleration, whereas older infants tend to respond with heart-rate deceleration (Berg & Berg, 1979). In older subjects, heart-rate acceleration is associated with fear or defense, and heart-rate deceleration is associated with attention. Some investigators, therefore, have interpreted this change in infancy as evidence of a shift from a primarily defensive to a primarily attentive response to new stimuli. Others have argued, however, that the shift may be unrelated to defense-attention, but may result instead from further maturation of the physiological system that controls heart rate (Porges, 1979). Thus, the fact that the same response can be measured at different ages does not guarantee that the response has the same meaning.

We turn next from general issues to particular kinds of infancy research. We discuss three topics that have been very popular foci for research in infancy: infant perception, infant cognitive development, and infant social development.

INFANT PERCEPTION

Two general issues have been of interest in studies of infant perception. One is the question of *perceptual ability*. How well developed are the baby's perceptual abilities at birth, and what are the developmental changes in these abilities across the first 2 years? Numerous specific questions fall within this broad domain. How clearly can a newborn see an object, and what kinds of visual discriminations can a newborn make or not make? What is the newborn's threshold for detecting a sound, and what differences in sound are or are not discriminable? Does a newborn or young infant possess perceptual constancy, and if not, when does constancy develop? Any question that can be asked of perception in general can be asked from the developmental point of view, starting with infancy.

The second general issue is that of *perceptual preference*. Given the abilities that an infant has, toward what sorts of stimuli does he or she direct attention? What do babies find interesting to look at, listen to, or touch? And why do babies show the preferences that they do?

Several general points about research on perception are worth making before we turn to specific methods of study. First, the great majority of studies of infant perception are cross-sectional rather than longitudinal. Although this emphasis is potentially biasing, it seems doubtful, for reasons discussed in the previous section, that the cross-sectional focus has led to incorrect conclusions about changes with age. Furthermore, most studies of infant perception have been concerned with commonalities of development rather than individual differences among children. An ability like depth perception, for example, is eventually present in all children, and the typical research interest has been in when and how it develops, not in individual differences in the speed or quality of development. As we saw in chapter 3, a prime motivation for longitudinal research is to examine the consistency of individual differences over time. Because individual differences are seldom a concern in work on infant perception, a longitudinal design may add little.

A second point has to do with the lab-field continuum discussed in chapter 5. The great majority of studies of infant perception are carried out in laboratory rather than field settings. Furthermore, the settings that are used are definitely toward the lab end of the continuum—artificial, highly controlled, distinct from "real life" in various ways. This is not, of course, because perception does not occur in the natural environment; perception is the most pervasive of psychological processes. Studying perception, however, typically requires exact knowledge of what the stimulus is and precise measurement of rather subtle responses to it, and these criteria can usually be met only in the laboratory.

A final point concerns the two obstacles to infancy research discussed earlier: the baby's shifting state and limited response repertoire. There is no aspect of infancy research for which these problems are more pressing than the study of perception. Researchers of perception typically attempt to work with babies in the quiet and alert state that is optimal for most kinds of perceptual functioning. This attempt embodies all of the practical difficulties and selectivity discussed earlier. The problem of response measures arises not only because of the infant's limited repertoire but also because of the nature of perception: an internal, experiential phenomenon that is not necessarily linked to overt, measurable behavior. Finding response measures from which the baby's perceptual experience can be inferred is thus especially challenging.

Preference Method

The preference method is a technique devised by Robert Fantz (1961) to study visual perception in infancy. The specific question that it is designed to answer is the question of visual discrimination: Given any two visual stimuli, can a baby tell them apart? This question,

clearly, is central to any assessment of babies' visual capacities.

An early version of Fantz's apparatus is shown in Figure 6-1. The infant is positioned in the looking chamber so that he or she can look at either of two stimuli suspended above. The stimuli are just far enough apart so that they cannot be fixated simultaneously; rather, a slight head turn is necessary to direct the eyes to one or the other. This head turn is a response that even a newborn can make. Apart from the head turn, the only behavior required of the infant is fixation—that is, looking at one or the other stimulus. The dependent measure is how long the infant looks at each stimulus. As Figure 6-1 shows, fixation can be easily measured by an observer stationed above the chamber who notes which stimulus is reflected in the infant's eyes.

In a typical study with the Fantz procedure the two stimuli that are being compared are presented for a number of trials. A particular stimulus appears on the left half the time and on the right half the time. The question of interest is whether, over trials, the infant looks significantly longer at one stimulus than at the other. If the infant does look longer at one stimulus, he or she is said to show a preference for that stimulus. And if the infant shows a preference, the conclusion drawn is that he or she must be able to discriminate between the stimuli. The reasoning is straightforward: Only if the infant can see a difference could a preference possibly emerge. If the stimuli look the same, then there is no basis for looking systematically longer at one stimulus than at the other.

The preference method has been applied to a wide range of visual stimuli. It has been used, for example, to determine whether infants can discriminate between a patterned stimulus and a comparable nonpatterned stimulus (e.g., a bull's eye and a plain circle), between a colored stimulus and a comparable noncolored one, between two-dimensional and three-dimensional versions of an object, between a novel stimulus and a familiar one, and between their mothers' faces and those of strangers. Note that the method provides information not only about discrimination but also about the second gen-

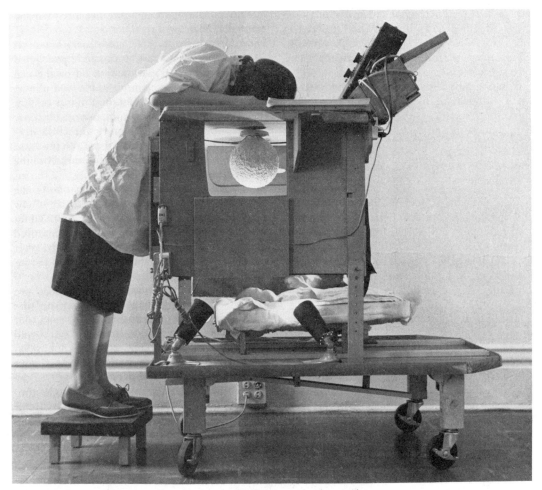

FIGURE 6–1. Apparatus used in the Fantz preference method to study infants' visual abilities. From "The Origin of Form Perception" by R. L. Fantz, 1961, *Scientific American, 204,* p. 66. Copyright 1961 by Scientific American, Inc. Reprinted by permission. Photograph by David Linton.

eral question introduced earlier: perceptual preference. Suppose we find (as we do) that a newborn looks longer at a patterned stimulus than at a nonpatterned one. This finding tells us something about the baby's ability to discriminate patterning in stimulation. It also tells us something about the baby's preferences: Not only can the baby see patterning, but the baby *prefers* patterning.

The strengths of the preference method lie in its minimal response demands and wide scope of application. The method also has some limitations. Specifying the exact basis for a discrimination can sometimes be difficult. If the baby shows a preference, we know that he or she can see *some* difference between the stimuli, but we do not necessarily know what information was used to make the discrimination. One way around this problem is to attempt to design stimuli that differ in only one critical respect, such as a two-dimensional circle and an otherwise identical three-dimensional sphere. If only a single difference exists, then presumably infants must be using this difference if they show a preference.

Another possibility is to record not only at which stimulus the infant looks but also exactly where on the stimulus the infant's eyes fixate. With modern infrared photography it is possible to obtain very exact records of eye movements and eye fixations, and this information can help to pin down the basis for a discrimination. Such *eye-movement recording* constitutes, in fact, a valuable tool in its own right for studying early visual development, quite apart from its application to the preference method. Figure 6–2 shows a schematic representation of a typical system for recording eye movements. Comparing this figure with Figure 6–1 gives some idea of the extent of technological advances in the last 20 years!

The main limitation of the preference method is that negative results cannot be interpreted. Suppose that the infant does not show a preference. This result could come about for various reasons. In the simplest case, the infant shows a *response bias*—that is, looks only or mainly to one of the two sides. Many young infants do show such positional preferences, generally favoring the right side (Acredelo & Hake, 1982). Because the stimuli are balanced for position across trials, a consistent positional bias will result in equal fixation on each stimulus, and thus no preference. This case is simple in the sense that the response bias is readily detectable and no false conclusions need be drawn about the infant's ability or lack of ability. Because of the bias, however, the question of whether the baby can discriminate remains completely unresolved.

In a more complicated case, the infant does not show a response bias yet distributes attention equally to the two stimuli. This result could occur because the infant cannot discriminate between the stimuli; as argued previously, preference is possible only if there is discrimination. Such a negative conclusion cannot be drawn with certainty, however, because there is another possibility: Perhaps the infant can discriminate perfectly well but simply does not care which stimulus he or she looks at. As Flavell (1985) puts it, "preference logically implies discrimination but discrimination certainly does not logically imply preference" (p. 170). And this is the basic ambiguity in the preference method: Negative results may mean absence of

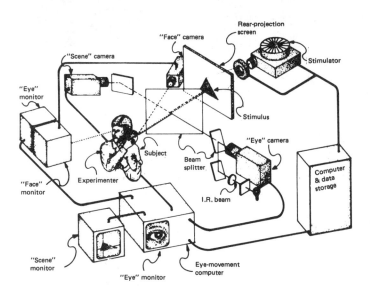

FIGURE 6–2. A schematic representation of an eye-movement recording system for use with infants. From "Infants' Scanning of Geometric Forms Varying in Size" by L. Hainline and E. Lemerise, 1982, *Journal of Experimental Child Psychology, 33,* p. 241. Copyright 1982 by Academic Press. Reprinted by permission.

discrimination, or they may simply mean absence of preference.

Habituation-Dishabituation

Imagine the following sequence of events. You enter a new room and are at first very aware of a loudly ticking clock. You sit and read for a few minutes and soon no longer notice the clock at all. The clock then stops ticking, and you immediately react to the change.

This sequence illustrates three related and very important psychological processes. When a new stimulus appears, many organisms, including humans, show what is called an *orienting response*. The orienting response is actually a complex of related responses whose purpose is to maximize attention to a new event. These responses typically include a momentary cessation of any ongoing behavior, orienting of receptors toward the new stimulus, and a number of characteristic physiological changes (e.g., heart-rate deceleration). This set of behaviors is simple but very adaptive, for it represents an automatic way to pay attention to what is new in the environment.

Consider next what happens when a stimulus that elicits the orienting response continues to occur, as does the ticking of the clock in our example. Eventually, the orienting response will diminish and perhaps drop out altogether. This dropping out of the orienting response to a repeated stimulus is referred to as *habituation*. Habituation, too, is a very adaptive process: Once a stimulus has become familiar, there is no longer need to pay close attention to it.

Consider finally what happens when there is a change in a stimulus to which the organism has habituated, such as the disappearance of the ticking in our example. This change in the accustomed stimulation will evoke a new response of attention from the organism. The renewal of attention when an habituated stimulus changes is referred to as *dishabituation*. Dishabituation is also adaptive: When a stimulus changes, there is again need to orient to what is new.

As might be guessed from their inclusion in this chapter, all three of the phenomena just described are found in infancy. How early they

can be found has been a subject of dispute, but it now seems clear that even newborns will orient, habituate, and dishabituate, given optimal conditions for eliciting the behaviors (Berg & Berg, 1979). Probably the most common dependent variable in infant research has been change in heart rate: Cardiac deceleration has been considered as an index of orienting, and reduced change or no change as an index of habituation. The other two response measures introduced earlier have also been used. When sucking is measured, the baby sucks on a specially wired pacifier; interruption of sucking is considered as evidence of orienting, and continued, uninterrupted sucking is considered as evidence of habituation. When visual fixation is measured, the interest is in total fixation time on the stimulus; initial high attention indicates orienting, and a drop-off in fixation indicates habituation.

How can these processes be used to study infant perception? At the simplest level, the orienting response can be used to answer the question of detection: Can the infant detect the stimulus at all? Clearly, if the stimulus is below the threshold for a particular perceptual modality, there is no possibility of orienting to it. Although this point is obvious, the behaviors that can be elicited as signs of detection are often rather subtle. In particular, physiological responses may tell us that an infant has detected a stimulus when there is no overt response to the stimulus at all. The heart-rate change measured in studies of orienting is one example, and a number of other physiological changes can be elicited in response to particular kinds of stimulation. Berg and Berg (1979) discuss more fully the use of physiological change to measure detection thresholds.

Suppose that we are interested not just in detection of a single stimulus but in discrimination between two stimuli. Here the habituation-dishabituation part of the sequence becomes relevant. Let us say that we wish to know whether the infant can discriminate between two auditory stimuli, say the speech sounds "pa" and "ba." What we could do is present the "pa" sound repeatedly until the infant habituates to it. At the time that the next "pa" would normally appear we then substitute a "ba." If the infant dishabituates to the "ba" we know that he or she can discriminate between the sounds.

This example suggests an obvious strength of the habituation approach in comparison to the preference method: its wider scope of applicability. The preference method cannot really be applied to auditory perception; it is difficult to present two sounds simultaneously and see which one the infant prefers to listen to. It is easy, however, to present a single sound until response to it disappears and then a second sound that differs in some critical way from the first. Indeed, habituation has been the most popular method for studying auditory perception in infancy. The method has also been applied to olfactory perception—that is, the infant's ability to discriminate between different smells (e.g., Engen, Lipsitt, & Kaye, 1963). And it has been used to study visual discrimination as well.

Conditioning

Habituation can be regarded as a kind of learning—learning not to respond to a stimulus that is already familiar. In this section we turn to another basic form of learning: learning to repeat a response that pays off in reinforcement. Learning which is supported by the fact that it results in reinforcement is referred to as *instrumental* (or *operant*) *conditioning*.

Instrumental conditioning has been used in several different ways to study infant perception. The simplest way is similar to the habituation-dishabituation paradigm just discussed. Consider an application to the issue of speech perception. We begin by reinforcing the infant for sucking on a pacifier, with the rate of reinforcement tied to the rate of sucking. The faster the infant sucks, the more frequent the reinforcement. Such an arrangement is referred to as "conjugate reinforcement." The reinforcement consists of a speech sound, say the sound "ba." At first this reinforcement is quite effective, and the infant sucks rapidly. Eventually, however, the "ba" begins to lose its fascination, and the rate of sucking drops off. This

drop-off is a reflection of *satiation:* the decrement in a reinforcer's value as a function of repetition of the reinforcer. When the sucking response has reached a low level, we change reinforcers, substituting a "pa" for the "ba." If the rate of sucking increases significantly, we know the infant can discriminate between "pa" and "ba."

As noted, the satiation approach is quite similar to the habituation-dishabituation paradigm. Indeed, in some accounts no distinction is made between the two, and a study like the one just described is referred to as an instance of habituation. There is, however, a difference: Habituation refers to a drop-off in the orienting response as a function of stimulus repetition, whereas satiation refers to a drop-off in reinforcer effectiveness as a function of reinforcer repetition. Despite this difference, the logic behind the two approaches is the same: Look for a change in response as evidence that the infant has detected a change in the stimulus.

A second sort of conditioning approach, labeled *conditioned head turning,* makes use of the fact that infants can learn to attach a response to a particular stimulus. Suppose that we sound a tone to the baby's right. At first the baby is likely to orient toward the sound; if the tone is presented repeatedly, however, the orienting response will eventually diminish. But what happens if we add a reinforcer? Suppose that every time the infant turns in response to the tone an interesting visual stimulus appears, perhaps an array of flashing lights or an animated toy. In this case the head-turn response will remain strong. And in this case the tone will become a signal, or *discriminative stimulus,* for the response: As soon as the infant hears the tone he or she will turn to the right in anticipation of the reinforcement. Once this contingency has been established, the discriminative stimulus can be altered in various ways to probe the baby's auditory capacities. We might change the intensity or frequency of the tone to test for the baby's auditory threshold (e.g., Schneider, Trehub, & Bull, 1980). Or we might present two different stimuli, only one of which is associated with the reinforcement. Head turns in response to one but not the other stimulus would be evidence that the baby can discriminate between the stimuli.

A final conditioning-based approach is similar to the procedure just described but adds to it a focus on generalization. *Generalization* refers to the tendency for a response that has been learned to one stimulus to be emitted also to other, similar stimuli. Because the degree of generalization depends on the similarity between the original stimulus and the new stimulus, we can use generalization to draw inferences about how similar two stimuli look or sound.

Undoubtedly the best-known example of the use of generalization to study infant perception is an experiment by Bower (1966). Bower's research was directed to one of the classic issues of perceptual theory: perceptual constancy. Constancy *is* an issue for perceptual theory because our perception seems to be better than it ought to be given the retinal image that we receive. Thus, we somehow perceive things as maintaining a constant size despite continual changes in the size of the retinal image, as maintaining a constant shape despite continual changes in the orientation of the image, and so forth. The specific question that Bower addressed concerned the infant and the issue of size constancy. Does the infant experience the same constant-sized world that we do, or do the objects of the infant's world seem to grow or shrink as the retinal image grows or shrinks?

Bower began by conditioning his subjects (infants 60 to 80 days old) to make a simple head-turn response to obtain reinforcement. As in the studies just discussed, the conditioning

was established in response to a discriminative stimulus. In Bower's study the discriminative stimulus was a 30 cm cube presented 1 m in front of the infant. Head turns were reinforced whenever the cube was present; they were not reinforced when the cube was absent. Thus, in the first phase of the study the infants learned to turn their heads whenever the cube was placed at the proper distance in front of them.

The second phase of the study tested for generalization. Four stimuli, balanced for order, were presented to each infant. The four stimuli, and the rationale for them, are shown in Table 6–2. Stimulus 1 was identical to the original training stimulus, stimulus 2 matched the original in size but differed in distance, stimulus 3 matched the original in distance but differed in size, and stimulus 4 differed from the original in both size and distance but, being both three times larger and three times further away, projected the same-sized retinal image. If infants lack size constancy and are dependent on the retinal image, they should respond to stimulus 4 in the same way as they do to stimulus 1. In fact, as the table shows, stimulus 4 was treated quite differently from stimulus 1, eliciting by far the lowest level of responding. Stimulus 2, however, elicited an appreciable degree of responding, even though it was a different distance and therefore a different retinal image. It is on this basis that Bower concluded that infants as young as 2 months old are capable of a fairly good degree of size constancy.

Summaries of Bower's research almost always end by raising the issue of replication. Our summary is no exception. Bower's ingenious

TABLE 6–2 Stimuli and Results in the Generalization Phase of Bower's Study of Size Constancy

STIMULUS		Relation to Discriminative Stimulus	Mean Number of Responses
Size	*Distance*		
1. 30 cm	1 m	Identical	98
2. 30 cm	3 m	Same size	58
3. 90 cm	1 m	Same distance	54
4. 90 cm	3 m	Same retinal image	22

Note: Adapted from "The Visual World of Infants" by T. G. R. Bower, 1966, *Scientific American, 215,* 90–92.

study has proved difficult to replicate, and the issue of exactly when infants possess size constancy is therefore still in dispute. For our purposes, an understanding of the methodology is more important than the substantive claim about constancy. Like habituation, generalization constitutes a simple but powerful technique for inferring which things look similar and which things look different to infants. And like habituation, the generalization approach can be applied to a number of different perceptual issues.

Visual Cliff

The final procedure that we consider is more limited in scope than the techniques that we have been discussing so far. The visual cliff (developed originally by Walk and Gibson, 1961) is directed to a single question: Can babies perceive depth? The particular form of depth perception at issue is perception of a drop-off or "cliff." For example, if the baby leans over the edge of a bed to peer down at the floor, does he or she perceive the drop-off? This is a question of both theoretical and practical importance.

The visual cliff is pictured in Figure 6–3. As the figure illustrates, the cliff consists of a large glass-covered table divided by a center board. In the typical method of testing, a checkerboard pattern is placed under the glass on each side of the center board. On one side the pattern is directly under the glass, thus creating the perception of a solid surface emanating from the center board. This side is referred to as the "shallow side." On the other side the checkerboard pattern is several feet below the glass, thus creating the perception of a drop-off or cliff. This side is referred to as the "deep side." Testing typically begins with the infant placed

FIGURE 6–3. Visual-cliff apparatus for testing depth perception. From "A Comparative and Analytic Study of Visual Depth Perception" by R. D. Walk and E. J. Gibson, 1961, *Psychological Monographs, 75* (No. 15, Whole No. 519), p. 8. Copyright 1961 by the American Psychological Association. Reprinted by permission.

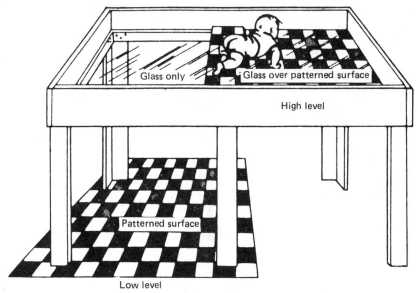

Glass only

Glass over patterned surface

High level

Patterned surface

Low level

in crawling position on the center board. The mother then goes to each side and attempts to coax the infant to crawl across the glass to her. An alternative method is to use a center board that gets progressively narrower at one end. The mother is stationed at this end, and, in crawling to her, the infant is forced eventually to go off the board onto the glass. In either case, the question is the same: Will the infant crawl across the shallow side but refuse to venture onto the deep side? If so, the inference drawn is that the infant can perceive the depth.

Tests of this sort have revealed that infants as young as 6 months old will avoid the deep side, thus demonstrating some ability to perceive depth (Walk, 1981). Infants younger than 6 months cannot be tested with the methods described, because these methods depend on ability to crawl. Thus, the classic visual-cliff test cannot tell us how early depth perception is present. An alternative testing method developed for younger infants consists of simply placing an infant face down on each side of the cliff and measuring his or her reaction. Crying and changes in heart rate are the variables usually measured. Researchers using this approach have found that infants as young as 2 months old do respond differentially to the two sides, thus showing some ability to discriminate between the deep and shallow surfaces. They do not show a clear-cut fear reaction to the deep side, however, and thus their ability to perceive depth remains uncertain (Campos, Langer, & Krowitz, 1970).

The visual cliff is not the only procedure that has been devised to test depth perception in infants. Among the other measures that have been utilized are the baby's reaching behaviors in response to objects of different distances (e.g., Field, 1977) and avoidant behaviors in response to rapidly approaching, or "looming," objects (e.g., Yonas et al., 1977). More generally, our survey of methods for studying infant perception has barely skimmed the surface of this large and rapidly expanding literature. Fuller discussions can be found in Aslin, Pisoni, and Jusczyk (1983), Banks and Salapatek (1983), and Gottlieb and Krasnegor (1984).

INFANT COGNITIVE DEVELOPMENT

By far the dominant approach to the study of infant cognition has been Piaget's. We therefore concentrate in this section on Piaget's work (Piaget, 1951, 1952, 1954) and some of the follow-up research that it has inspired. We touch on some other approaches to the study of cognition in infancy in the next chapter, when we deal with cognitive development in general.

Piaget's studies of infancy are far too extensive to be exhaustively summarized here. What we aim for instead are two goals. One is to convey some of the general aspects of the Piagetian approach to studying the infant. The other is to describe the procedures used to study one of the most important achievements of infancy—the object concept.

Piaget's conclusions about infant development are based on his study of his own three infants during the first 2½ to 3 years of their lives. His approach is an extension of one of the historically earliest methods in child psychology, the *baby biography*. In a baby biography, a scientist-parent makes extensive observations of the development of his or her own child, observations that then serve as the data base for drawing some more general conclusions about human development. Such studies became fairly popular enterprises during the last half of the nineteenth century. Prior to Piaget's work, the most famous such effort was Charles Darwin's (1877) study of his infant son.

In Piaget's case the studies of infancy went well beyond a simple compilation of interesting-looking behaviors. From the start the work was theoretically guided, with a consistent attempt to answer basic philosophical questions, such as the origins of concepts of space, time, and causality. We consider one such concept, object permanence, shortly. The work also included more than simple observation of naturally occurring behavior. Naturalistic observation *was* used—many hundreds of hours, in fact, of quite painstaking observation. But such observations were continually supplemented by small-scale experimentation. If, for example, Piaget was interested one day in his daughter's response to obstacles, he would not necessarily wait until an obstacle happened to come along in her path. Instead, he might interpose a pillow between daughter and favorite toy, and then record how she responded to this challenge.

Piaget's observations are summarized in hundreds of "protocols" of infant behavior, and it is impossible to convey the flavor of the work without quoting some of these protocols. Box 6-1 includes a sampling of protocols dealing with the infant's gradual mastery of principles of causality. Note the interweaving of naturally occurring and experimentally elicited behavior. Note also the interweaving of straight description and more interpretive commentary.

In trying to abstract general features of the Piagetian approach, it is helpful to contrast Piaget's studies with the work on infant perception discussed in the previous section. There are a number of differences. Piaget's studies were carried out in the child's natural environment; research on perception, as we saw, has been almost totally confined to laboratory settings. Piaget's studies made essentially no use of special

apparatus; the child interacted with the objects and people of the everyday environment, and the only recording instrument was the father. Studies of perception, in contrast, have relied heavily on complicated apparatus such as eye-movement cameras and EKG machines. Piaget's conclusions depended on observations by a human observer; in perception research automatic recording has been the norm. Finally, Piaget's work was longitudinal, whereas studies of infant perception have been primarily cross-sectional.

Why so many differences in approach? The differences are probably partly a function of the content being studied and partly a result of certain idiosyncrasies in Piaget's style of research. As we saw in the previous section, the issues of interest in the study of infant perception do not lend themselves to observational assessment in the natural environment. Through what naturally occurring and observable behaviors could we determine whether infants perceive a receding object as constant or changing in size? Behaviors indicative of cognitive development, in contrast, often *are* discernible in the child's nat-

---

BOX 6-1 Examples of Piagetian protocols concerned with the infant's understanding of causality

---

Obs. 128

At 0;3 (12) that is to say, several days after he revealed his capacity to grasp objects seen, Laurent is confronted by a rattle hanging from his bassinet top; a watch chain hangs from the rattle. . . . From the point of view of the relationships between the chain and the rattle the result of the experiment is wholly negative: Laurent does not pull the chain by himself and when I place it in his hands and he happens to shake it and hears the noise, he waves his

hand but drops the chain. On the other hand, he seems immediately to establish a connection between the movements of his hand and those of the rattle, for having shaken his hand by chance and heard the sound of the rattle he waves his empty hand again, while looking at the rattle, and even waves it harder and harder. . . .

Observing that the rattle no longer moves—and this is what we wanted to come to—or rather, no longer seeing anything of interest in it, Laurent looks again at his hands, which he is still waving. He then examines most attentively his right hand, which he is swinging, meanwhile retaining exactly the same facial expression

Note. From *The Construction of Reality in the Child* (pp. 261–262, 276–277, 309–310, 334–335), by J. Piaget, 1954, New York: Basic Books. Copyright 1954 by Basic Books, Inc. Reprinted by permission.

he had when watching the rattle. It is as though he were studying his own power over it (just as he has already seen his power over the rattle).

Obs. 134

At 0;7 (7) Laurent looks at me very attentively when I drum with my finger tips on a tin box of 15 × 20 centimeters. The box lies on a cushion before him and is just two centimeters beyond his reach. On the other hand, as soon as I pause in my game I place my hand five centimeters from his, while he watches, and leave it there motionless. So long as I drum Laurent smiles delightedly but when I pause he looks for a moment at my hand, then proceeds very rapidly to examine the box and then, while looking at it, claps his hands, waves goodbye with both hands, shakes his head, arches upward, etc. In short, he uses the whole collection of his usual magico-phenomenalistic procedures. With regard to my hand, placed before his eyes, he grasps it for a moment twice in succession, shakes it, strikes it, etc. But he does not lead it back to the box, although that would be easy, nor does he try to discover a specific procedure to set its activity in motion.

Obs. 149

At 1;0 (29) for the first time Jacqueline is in the presence of the well-known toy consisting of chickens set in motion by a weight. A certain number of chickens are arranged in a circle on a wooden ring and the front of each chicken is connected by a string to a heavy ball placed on a lower plane than the ring: thus the slightest movement of the ball sets the chickens in motion, and they knock with their beaks against the edge of the ring.

Jacqueline, after examining for a moment the toy which I put into action by displacing it gently, first touches the ball and notes the concomitant movement of the chickens. She then systematically moves the ball as she watches the chickens. Thus

convinced of the existence of a relationship which she obviously does not understand in detail, she pushes the ball very delicately with her right index finger each time the swinging stops completely.

In this example Jacqueline therefore does not attribute spontaneous movements to the ball (as she did in the preceding example of the ball or the plush toy), but she definitely conceives the activity of the ball as causing that of the chickens. Therefore from this point of view there is objectification of causality. Moreover the ball is not, to her, a mere extension of her manual action (like the strings hanging from the bassinet hood, etc.); she makes it active simply by releasing it.

Obs. 157

At 1;6 (8) Jacqueline sits on a bed beside her mother. I am at the foot of the bed on the side opposite Jacqueline, and she neither sees me nor knows I am in the room. I bandish over the bed a cane to which a brush is attached at one end and I swing the whole thing. Jacqueline is very much interested in this sight: she says "cane, cane" and examines the swinging most attentively. At a certain moment she stops looking at the end of the cane and obviously tries to understand. Then she tries to perceive the other end of the cane and to do so, leans in front of her mother, then behind her, until she has seen me. She expresses no surprise, as though she knew I was the cause of the sight.

A moment later, while Jacqueline is hidden under the covers to distract her attention, I go to the foot of the bed and resume my game. Jacqueline laughs, says "Papa," looks for me in the place where she saw me the first time, then tries to find me in the room, while the cane is still moving. She does not think of finding me at the foot of the bed (I am hidden by the footboard), but she has no doubt that I am the cause of the phenomenon.

ural dealings with the environment, especially during infancy. The infant's explorations of causality described in the protocols of Box 6–1 are one example. The work on object concept that we discuss shortly is another. Although the distinction is an admittedly shaky one (as is the "perception"-"cognition" contrast in general), it can be argued that cognitive functioning, especially in infancy, is more readily visible than is perceptual functioning.

The second basis for the difference lies in Piaget's preferred approach to research. As we see more fully in the next chapter, many of the characteristics of Piaget's infancy research are also found in his studies of older children. These include a preference for flexible probing over tight standardization, for simple and familiar materials over complicated apparatus, and for interpretive analyses of individual protocols over standard statistical tests. There are also some characteristics of Piaget's infancy research that follow necessarily from the circumstances under which he was working. With a sample of three there hardly *could* be much in the way of standard statistical tests. In-the-home recording sets definite constraints on the apparatus that can be used, and in any case many of the technological tools that are mainstays of modern research had not been invented when Piaget began his work 55 years ago.

Piaget's approach to studying the infant has both strengths and weaknesses. The weaknesses are perhaps more obvious. The sample is both very small and distinctly nonrandom. Despite the total reliance on observational data, Piaget made no attempt to demonstrate any sort of interobserver reliability. Even with a sample of three, there are opportunities for standardization and control that are missed. The method of presenting the results often blurs the distinction between data and conclusions. And Piaget's emphasis on overt motor behavior in diagnosing infant development may lead to an underestimation of the infant's ability. We return to this criticism shortly.

Many of the strengths of Piaget's studies were noted earlier. The discussion of exploratory research in chapter 4 cited Piaget's work as a prime example of the value of a flexible, discovery-oriented approach to studying the child. The discussion of longitudinal research in chapter 3 cited the Piaget infancy studies as an example of the value of an intensive, case-study approach to the development of individual children. There is probably no better example in the field of the value of naturalistic observation in the hands of a skilled observer. Most generally, the fact that Piaget's work continues to dominate the study of infant cognition more than 40 years after its original publication is ample testimony to its viability.

Let us turn now to the work on the object concept. The term *object concept* refers to the knowledge that objects have a permanent existence that is independent of our perceptual contact with them. It is the knowledge, thus, that an object does not cease to exist simply because at the moment we cannot see it, hear it, feel it, or whatever. It is hard to imagine a more basic piece of knowledge than this. Yet Piaget's work indicates that the object concept is not present at birth, that it develops only gradually across the first 2 years, and that there is a definite sequence of stages through which the infant passes in mastering the concept. This set of findings is of considerable theoretical and empirical importance, which accounts for the attention that the concept has received in follow-up research. For our purposes it is the methodological challenge that is of interest. How does Piaget—or anyone—determine what an infant knows or does not know about objects?

As noted, Piaget's observations are reported in the form of protocols—some 66 protocols, many of them with multiple observations, in the case of the object concept. A small sampling of these protocols is quoted in Box 6–2. These sample protocols illustrate some of the points made across the next several paragraphs.

Piaget's studies of the object concept are centered on the infant's response to the disappearance of objects. Such disappearances are, of course, a common occurrence in the baby's natural interactions with objects. A toy falls from the high chair or crib. Mother or father walks out of the room. The baby turns around and can no longer see bottle or mother. In ad-

BOX 6–2   Examples of Piagetian protocols concerned with the infant's understanding of object concept

Obs. 2

. . . . Jacqueline, as early as 0;2 (27) follows her mother with her eyes, and when her mother leaves the visual field, continues to look in the same direction until the picture reappears.

Same observation with Laurent at 0;2 (1). I look at him through the hood of his bassinet and from time to time I appear at a more or less constant point; Laurent then watches that point when I am out of his sight and obviously expects to see me reappear.

Obs. 28

At 0;7 (28) Jacqueline tries to grasp a celluloid duck on top of her quilt. She almost catches it, shakes herself, and the duck slides down beside her. It falls very close to her hand but behind a fold in the sheet. Jacqueline's eyes have followed the movement, she has even followed it with her outstretched hand. But as soon as the duck has disappeared—nothing more! It does not occur to her to search behind the fold of the sheet, which would be very easy to do (she twists it mechanically without searching at all). But, curiously, she again begins to stir about as she did when trying to get the duck and again glances at the top of the quilt.

I then take the duck from its hiding-place and place it near her hand three times. All three times she tries to grasp it, but when she is about to touch it I replace it very obviously under the sheet. Jacqueline immediately withdraws her hand and gives up. The second and third times I make her grasp the duck through the sheet and she

shakes it for a brief moment but it does not occur to her to raise the cloth.

Obs. 40

At 0;10 (18) Jacqueline is seated on a mattress without anything to disturb or distract her (no coverlets, etc.). I take her parrot from her hands and hide it twice in succession under the mattress, on her left, in A. Both times Jacqueline looks for the object immediately and grabs it. Then I take it from her hands and move it very slowly before her eyes to the corresponding place on her right, under the mattress, in B. Jacqueline watches this movement very attentively, but at the moment when the parrot disappears in B she turns to her left and looks where it was before, in A.

During the next four attempts I hide the parrot in B every time without having first placed it in A. Every time Jacqueline watches me attentively. Nevertheless each time she immediately tries to rediscover the object in A; she turns the mattress over and examines it conscientiously. During the last two attempts, however, the search tapers off.

Obs. 55

At 1;8 (8) Jacqueline is sitting on a green rug and playing with a potato which interests her very much (it is a new object for her). She says ''po-terre'' and amuses herself by putting it into an empty box and taking it out again. For several days she has been enthusiastic about this game.

I. I then take the potato and put it in the box while Jacqueline watches. Then I place the box under the rug and turn it upside down thus leaving the object hidden by the rug without letting the child see my maneuver, and I bring out the empty box. I say to Jacqueline, who has not stopped

(Continued)

BOX 6-2 *(Continued)*

looking at the rug and who has realized that I was doing something under it: "Give papa the potato." She searches for the object in the box, looks at me, again looks at the box minutely, looks at the rug, etc., but it does not occur to her to raise the rug in order to find the potato underneath.

During the five subsequent attempts the reaction is uniformly negative. I begin again, however, each time putting the object in the box as the child watches, putting the box under the rug, and bringing it out empty. Each time Jacqueline looks in the box, then looks at everything around her including the rug, but does not search under it.

---

dition to such naturally occurring events, it is quite easy for an experimenter to contrive particular kinds of disappearance. Papa Piaget, for example, can drop a handkerchief over a toy, or hide a small toy in his hand and move it from one hiding place to another. We can see here one of the general characteristics of Piaget's approach noted earlier: the mixture of naturally occurring and experimentally elicited observations.

The basic question when the object disappears is whether the infant realizes that it still exists. Because a baby cannot tell us in words, we must select some observable behavior from which we can infer the infant's knowledge. Piaget looks primarily at various kinds of search behavior. Does the baby attempt to track the object with her eyes as it moves outside her field of vision? Does she lean over and gaze at the floor when a toy drops? Does she reach out and remove a cover that has been dropped over a toy? Does she turn immediately to the spot where some plaything was left, even though she has not looked at it for several minutes? There are many behaviors by which the infant can demonstrate that she knows, or does not know, that an object still exists. It is characteristic of Piaget's approach that he looks at a wide range of relevant behaviors. It is also characteristic that many of the behaviors that are stressed, especially at the more advanced levels, involve some active motoric response on the baby's part.

Just as search can occur in many ways, so can an object disappear in many ways. Did the infant's own actions make the object disappear,

or was some external source responsible? Is the object completely gone, or are parts of it still visible? If the object has vanished completely, are there nevertheless auditory or tactual cues to its presence? Is more than one hiding place involved, and, if so, can the child keep track not only of the fact that the object still exists but of *where* it exists? We can see in these diverse questions another characteristic of Piaget's approach: the emphasis on the use of many different kinds of problems in studying the development of any concept. This methodological emphasis has a theoretical corollary: the belief that important cognitive acquisitions, such as the object concept, do not emerge full-blown but rather are gradually mastered through a sequence of stages. It is to chart these stages that Piaget looks at many problems and many behaviors.

Piaget's ingenious studies have left no shortage of issues for later researchers to explore. Follow-up studies have taken various forms, but they do share several characteristics. The more recent work (almost necessarily) has looked at larger and more representative samples than did Piaget. Along with the larger samples has come an emphasis on standardization and experimental control that is seldom found in Piaget's studies. Laboratory settings have become the norm for research on infant cognition; in-the-home study has become rare, and truly naturalistic study rarer still. The laboratory locus has made possible the use of various technological tools (e.g., videotaping) that were not available to Piaget. In general, more modern research has attempted to shed many of the idiosyncracies of Piaget's original work while still maintaining the focus on basic and developmentally interesting forms of knowledge. This attempt has involved some changes that are clearly positive (e.g., the greater control and representativeness) and others (e.g., the shift from natural environment to lab) whose value is more mixed.

At a more specific level, follow-up studies of Piaget's infancy work have taken several directions. We will settle here for discussing one important line of research. A common, and very basic, concern has been with the adequacy of Piaget's assessment techniques. Do Piaget's observations and simple experiments really give an accurate picture of what the infant understands or does not understand about the world? Or are there instances in which Piaget may be miscalculating the baby's true abilities? In particular, are there instances in which Piaget is underestimating the baby's ability, perhaps especially because of the emphasis that he places on overt motoric behaviors? It seems possible, for example, that an infant knows perfectly well that an object still exists, but is simply unable to engage in the kind of active search behaviors that Piaget often requires.

Some research by Bower (summarized in Bower, 1982) can serve as an example of the kinds of diagnostic follow-ups that the object concept work has inspired. Across a series of studies Bower has varied both the manner in which the object disappears and the response required of the infant. Objects have been made to vanish instantaneously or to fade away more gradually. They have passed behind a screen or have had a screen pass in front of them. They have disappeared completely or they have reappeared in altered form—for example, different in shape or color. The infant's comprehension of these events has been gauged not only through active search behaviors but also through less motorically demanding responses. Tracking of the object via eye movements has been used much more systematically than in Piaget's studies, with a methodological sophistication (videotape recording) that was unavailable to Piaget. Surprise reactions (assessed via heart-rate change) have also been measured in response to various sorts of object disappearance or reappearance. The reasoning behind the use of surprise is straightforward: If the infant believes in the continued existence of a covered object, then he or she should be surprised if uncovering reveals that the object has vanished or otherwise magically changed.

Although methods rather than findings are our concern here, we can note two general conclusions from Bower's research. These studies—and those of other post-Piaget researchers as well—have indicated that various phases in the mastery of object permanence are achieved somewhat earlier than Piaget thought. They have also indicated that object permanence is an even more complex, multifaceted concept than Piaget believed. In addition to these substantive conclusions, it is worth noting that the technological refinements of recent years have hardly solved all of the problems involved in assessing object concept. Surprise, in particular, has proved difficult to measure in infancy. It is questionable whether Bower's equation of surprise with heart-rate change is justified, and attempts to utilize facial expressions to measure surprise (e.g., Charlesworth, 1966) have encountered formidable difficulties in establishing reliability.

INFANT SOCIAL DEVELOPMENT

Like perception and cognition, social development in infancy is a large topic. Our coverage is divided into two parts. We begin with some general points about how the infant's social world is typically studied. We then focus on what has been the most popular topic for research on infant social development: the concept of *attachment*.

It is again instructive to do some contrasting of our new topic with topics already covered in this chapter. There are both similarities and differences. On the one hand, the researcher of infant social development faces many of the same problems as does the researcher of infant perception or cognition. In particular, the infant remains a nonverbal, often recalcitrant subject, difficult to recruit for research in the first place and difficult to keep in a study once things are under way. On the other hand, many of the "problem behaviors" that bedevil the researcher of perception or cognition are no longer problems, for they constitute the responses of interest. Does the infant start to cry when the mother attempts to separate from him or her in the experimental setting? Does the infant direct attention only to the mother, refusing to respond to stimuli proffered by a strange adult? These behaviors, so vexing in some studies, may be precisely what the researcher of social development seeks to discover.

There are other differences as well. As we saw, studies of infant perception, as well as most post-Piaget studies of infant cognition, have been conducted primarily in laboratory settings. Research on social development includes a much higher proportion of studies carried out in the natural setting—that is, the infant's home. Even when a laboratory setting *is* used, the lab environment tends to approximate the natural setting much more closely than is true in other kinds of infant research. Toys and picture books are more likely to populate the experimental environment than are t-scopes or EKG machines. It is true, of course, that the testing environment is still a strange room rather than the familiar home, and many infants are clearly aware of this. Indeed, one well-established finding from research on infant social development is that various distress reactions of interest—for example, crying upon separation from the mother, upset upon being confronted by a stranger—are more marked in the lab than in the home. We return to this point shortly.

Two other differences between work on social development and work on perception and cognition can be noted. The first is implied by the term "social." What we are interested in now is not the infant in isolation but the infant in interaction with other people. The most commonly studied other person has been the infant's mother. In some cases the mother's behavior is controlled by instructions from the experimenter; in other cases her behavior is left free to vary and is in fact one of the things being studied. Although the mother has been the tra-

ditional focus for study, in recent years the father has also been accorded a prominent role in some research programs. Interactions with other children are sometimes studied, especially once the infant has achieved the status of "toddler" (at about 18 to 24 months). And response to such familiar people is often contrasted with response to "strangers"—that is, anyone whom the infant has not encountered before.

The second difference concerns measuring instruments. Work on perception has relied mainly on automatic recording of responses. Although Piaget's studies were observational, more recent research on infant cognition has also moved in the direction of automatic recording—for example, Bower's (1982) eye-movement and heart-rate measures. Studies of social development have relied heavily on observational assessment by a human observer. Such assessments are often aided by sophisticated technological tools, such as videotape cameras and event recorders; nevertheless, what gets recorded and analyzed is ultimately dependent on the decision of a human observer. This reliance on observational assessment follows necessarily from the concern in research on social development: to identify naturally occurring, socially meaningful units of response—"smiles," "cries," "seeks contact," "resists." Technology can be, and often is, an enormous help in this endeavor (see Lamb, Suomi, & Stephenson, 1979, and Sackett, 1978, for extended discussions of technological aids to observational assessment). The human observer, however, remains a necessary component.

We turn now to research on attachment. Attachment is a broad construct that encompasses many phenomena in the social development of the infant. The core reference is to what is sometimes called "the first love relationship": the strong emotional bond that forms between the infant and his or her parents. What we are interested in is how this bond comes about, and also why some babies develop less satisfactory attachments than do others. There is probably no more important issue in developmental psychology than this.

From a methodological point of view the study of attachment presents several challenges.

A first question concerns the behaviors from which we can determine the presence or absence of attachment. "Attachment," like "object concept," "depth perception," or any other developmental outcome of interest, is not an immediate behavioral given; rather it is a higher-level construct that must be inferred from a variety of relevant behaviors. Across the last 20 years there has been a steady expansion in the range of behaviors that are considered relevant to the assessment of attachment. The earliest systematic studies of the construct (e.g., Schaffer & Emerson, 1964) focused primarily on *separation distress*—that is, the infant's tendency to be upset when separated from the attachment object. Does the baby cry, for example, when the mother walks out of the room or when he or she is left alone in the crib at night? Separation distress has a good deal of intuitive appeal as a measure of attachment; we would expect a baby who has formed an emotional bond to another person to be more likely to protest separation than a baby who has not yet formed an attachment. Furthermore, separation distress shows the developmental course that we would expect of a measure of attachment: It is absent in the early months of life but typically emerges, often in quite strong form, some time between 6 and 12 months.

More recent research retains separation distress as one useful measure but adds a number of other behaviors as well. These additional behaviors include several more positive ways by which an infant can convey that he or she is forming an attachment to the parent. Does the baby smile or babble more readily to the mother than to other people? Such *differential responsiveness* is not a full-blown attachment, but it is usually considered as a phase in the movement toward full attachment. Is the baby more secure in the mother's presence, better able to venture out and explore new things or to interact with new people? The ability to use the mother as a *secure base* was first emphasized in Harlow's (1958) work with infant monkeys; it turns out to be important in human infants also. Does the baby brighten when the mother enters the room and engage in *greeting or contact-eliciting behaviors*? In general, does the baby seem to enjoy the

mother's presence and do various things either to keep her near when she is already present or to bring her back when she is gone? There are a variety of attachment behaviors, and they vary across situations, developmental levels, and individual children; all, however, have this general quality of pleasure and security in the presence of the attachment object.

Deciding which behaviors to study is just one step in the research process. Another important step is deciding how to get evidence with respect to these behaviors. How can we find out whether a baby protests separation from the mother, reacts more positively to familiar people than to strangers, uses the mother as a secure base, or does whatever else it is that we have decided is relevant to attachment? Three general approaches can be taken. We consider these approaches more fully in chapter 8, when we discuss social development in general. Here we settle for a brief overview of the application of each approach to infant attachment, followed by a concentration on a particular method that has proved especially informative in recent years.

One possibility is to obtain the data through *parental interview*. In this case the parent (usually the mother) is the source for information about the child's behavior. This was the primary approach taken in the Schaffer and Emerson (1964) study referred to earlier. These authors asked the mothers in their sample various questions about their babies' typical responses in attachment-relevant situations. As noted, a particular interest of their study was in the baby's response to separation from the mother. The seven situations that were asked about, as well as the information that was elicited for each situation, are shown in Table 6–3.

In skilled hands the interview approach has a number of strengths. A major strength is the broad scope of application: We can ask about literally anything that a mother might know about her child's development. We can thus sample across a wide range of situations, ages, and behaviors in a way that is impossible in any study that is based on direct obervation of behavior. A major weakness, however, is precisely that we are *not* obtaining direct observations of

TABLE 6–3 Summary of the Schaffer and Emerson Interview Approach to the Assessment of Attachment

Situations Asked About	*Information Elicited*
1. The infant is left alone in a room.	a. Does the infant show any form of protest under the defined circumstances?
2. The infant is left with other people.	
3. The infant is left in his pram outside the house.	b. If protest occurs, does it invariably appear in this situation or only under certain conditions or at certain times?
4. The infant is left in his pram outside the shop.	
5. The infant is left in his cot at night.	c. If protest occurs, how intense is it (a "full-blooded" cry, for instance, or only a whimper, a moan, etc.)?
6. The infant is put down after being held in the adult's arms or lap.	
7. The infant is passed by while in his cot or chair.	d. If protest occurs, at whom is it directed, i.e., whose departure elicits it?

Note: From "The Development of Social Attachments in Infancy" by H. R. Schaffer and P. Emerson, 1964, *Monographs of the Society for Research in Child Development, 29* (3, Serial No. 94), pp. 14–15. Copyright 1964 by the Society for Research in Child Development. Reprinted by permission.

behavior; what we are obtaining, rather, are verbal reports about behavior. Our data are accurate only to the extent that parents' descriptions of their children's behavior are accurate. As we will see in chapter 8, evidence indicates that parents are by no means always accurate in describing their children's (or for that matter their own) behavior.

A second possibility is to obtain the data through *naturalistic observation*. In this case we would go into the natural setting and directly observe the behaviors of interest. Another of the pioneering studies of attachment, that of Mary Ainsworth (1967) in Uganda, was based largely on naturalistic observation (though interviews were also used). Ainsworth lived among the 28 Ugandan families that she was studying for a period of 9 months, during which time she made frequent visits to the homes of each of her subjects. These home visits were the context for both interviews with the mothers about infant development and direct observations of infant behavior and interactions between infants and mothers. These observations provided direct evidence with respect to a wide range of attachment-relevant behaviors (separation distress, differential responsiveness, use of the mother as a secure base, etc.). Box 6–3 contains some sample observations for one of Ainsworth's subjects.

Naturalistic observation has the virtue of measuring behavior directly rather than relying on verbal report. Furthermore, the measure is of naturally occurring behavior in the natural setting—precisely what we are interested in. As we saw in chapter 5, this method also has its problems. Compared to other methods of gathering data, naturalistic observation may be quite uneconomical; the researcher may observe several hours in order to record a few minutes of interesting behavior. The observations are useful only if reliability can be ascertained, which may be difficult in the natural setting. And there is always the possibility that the presence of the observer may affect the behavior. This possibility is especially worrisome in the case of attachment, for here it is the infant's response to people that is the focus of the study. Introducing a stranger into the home may well alter the baby's social behaviors; indeed, one finding from research on attachment is that strangers *do* alter how babies behave. And, of course, there is the chance that the mother may behave differently as well.

The third approach to measuring attachment consists of a *structured laboratory assessment*. Again the work of Ainsworth provides an example. Ainsworth and her associates (Ainsworth, Blehar, Waters, & Wall, 1978) have devised a procedure for measuring attachment that they call the *strange situation*. The physical setting for the strange situation is pictured in Figure 6–4. As the figure illustrates, there are three participants: mother, stranger (an adult female), and baby. The room is located in a university building and is unfamiliar to both baby and mother; hence it qualifies as "lab" rather than natural setting. The environment is designed, however, to have a comfortable, even playroom-like quality to it. Thus, there are chairs and magazines for the adults, bright pic-

BOX 6–3 Example of observations from Ainsworth's observational study of attachment

Paulo [age 29 weeks] was asleep under a crocheted coverlet when we arrived for our first visit. After a while his mother wakened him and held him on her lap. He sat quietly at first but gradually became more active. His mother gave him to me to hold. He did not protest, but he was very active on my lap, occasionally throwing himself back in my arms and arching his back. He seemed very strong. Since he was restless and oriented toward his mother, I gave him back to her. . . . A week later when Paulo was thirty weeks old, he spent most of the time playing actively on the floor, playing with the lid of a biscuit box, interested in looking at his reflection in the shiny metal inside the lid, manipulating an empty roller for adhesive tape, putting it in and out of its container, and also banging the roller against the lid very noisily. He looked fat and healthy and was naked except for strings of beads around his waist and ankles. For a while he was given to Mrs. Kibuka [the translator] to hold. He seemed content on her lap until his mother left the room for a minute. Paulo immediately let out a yell that continued until his mother returned. . . . During the brief visit when Paulo was forty-one weeks old, he wanted to stay close to his mother, either on her lap or on the floor beside her. His mother tried to hand him to me to hold, but he protested vigorously, and she did not force the issue. He did not cry, however, when his mother went out for a few moments to cut some sugar cane for us. While she was away, the maternal uncle came into the house. Paulo scuttled quickly across the room to meet him and crowed with glee as his uncle picked him up. A little later he squealed in protest when his uncle began to put him down, so the uncle came out into the yard with Paulo in his arms as we said our farewells. His mother told us later that he was very fond of his uncle but would not let any other person pick him up. . . . At forty-six weeks Paulo began the visit on his mother's lap and kept throwing himself back against her. Presently he began to creep about the floor exploring; occasionally he stopped in a squatting position. Later, he played in the doorway, making several short excursions outside. Each time his mother called him back, and if he did not come, she went out to get him. She said that she liked to keep him in sight always. Back in the house he played intently with two bottle caps. After a while his mother picked him up, intending to give him to Mrs. Kibuka to hold. Seeming to anticipate her intention, Paulo began to struggle and scream, hitting at his mother, but since she was holding him face out he could not reach her with his blows. Resisting his protest, the mother placed him on Mrs. Kibuka's lap where he continued to scream until he was put down. . . . Our next visit occurred when Paulo was thirteen months old. He was outside by himself when we arrived. He became quite excited when he saw us and ran to get his mother—literally ran. I could not judge from the distance whether he was frightened or merely excited. During the visit he sat near his mother and played on the floor. Once his mother got up and went outside to get us a gift. Paulo began to scream. His uncle picked him up, but Paulo continued to scream until his mother returned and took him on her lap.

Note. From *Infancy in Uganda* (pp. 289–292, 295) by M. D. S. Ainsworth, 1967, Baltimore: The Johns Hopkins Press. Copyright 1967 by the Johns Hopkins Press. Reprinted by permission.

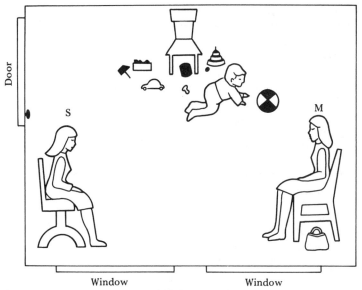

FIGURE 6–4. Physical arrangement of the strange situation for assessing attachment. From *Patterns of Attachment* (p. 34) by M. D. S. Ainsworth, M. C. Blehar, E. Waters, and N. J. Wall, 1978, Hillsdale, NJ: Lawrence Erlbaum Associates. Copyright 1978 by Lawrence Erlbaum Associates. Reprinted by permission.

tures on the wall, and toys aplenty for the baby to play with. Although the figure does not show it, there is another feature as well: a one-way mirror through which the room can be viewed surreptitiously. The mother is aware of the mirror and the observer behind it; the baby, however, is not. The baby's behavior, therefore, should be unaffected by the presence of an observer.

The strange stituation test consists of eight ordered episodes, summarized in Table 6–4. Throughout the eight episodes the mother's behavior is largely (although not totally) controlled. The baby's behavior, however, is not controlled, and it is the baby who is the focus of the study. As the descriptions in the table suggest, the eight episodes are designed to elicit a variety of attachment behaviors. Thus, the baby is observed in interaction with the mother, both before and after being separated from her and both alone and with a stranger present. The baby is also observed with a stranger, and similarities and differences in response to mother

and stranger can be noted. The sequence includes both separation episodes and reunion episodes; when the mother departs, the baby is sometimes left alone and sometimes left with the stranger. In general, the procedure is an attempt to capsulize, within a span of about 20 minutes, a high proportion of the situations and behaviors that have been used to study attachment.

Ainsworth et al.'s measurements come from direct observations of the infant's behavior. Three different levels of scoring are used. At the most molecular level, specific, discrete behaviors are recorded. Examples of categories at this level include crying, smiling, vocalization, and locomotion; in each case the overall category subsumes several more specific labels (e.g., screaming and fussing within the category of crying). The second level concerns interactive behavior. There are six categories of interactive behavior, each of which contains a number of more specific subcategories: proximity and contact seeking, contact maintaining, resis-

TABLE 6–4 Summary of Episodes of the Strange Situation

Number of Episode	Persons Present	Duration	Brief Descripton of Action
1	Mother, baby, & observer	30 secs.	Observer introduces mother and baby to experimental room, then leaves.
2	Mother & baby	3 min.	Mother is nonparticipant while baby explores; if necessary, play is stimulated after 2 minutes.
3	Stranger, mother, & baby	3 min.	Stranger enters. First minute: stranger silent. Second minute: Stranger converses with mother. Third minute: Stranger approaches baby. After 3 minutes mother leaves unobtrusively.
4	Stranger & baby	3 min or less[a]	First separation episode. Stranger's behavior is geared to that of baby.
5	Mother & baby	3 min or more[b]	First reunion episode. Mother greets and/or comforts baby, then tries to settle him again in play. Mother then leaves, saying "bye-bye."
6	Baby alone	3 min or less[a]	Second separation episode.
7	Stranger & baby	3 min or less[a]	Continuation of second separation episode. Stranger enters and gears her behavior to that of baby.
8	Mother & baby	3 min	Second reunion episode. Mother enters, greets baby, then picks him up. Meanwhile stranger leaves unobtrusively.

Note: From *Patterns of Attachment* (p. 37) by M. D. S. Ainsworth, M. C. Blehar, E. Waters, & S. Wall, 1978, Hillsdale, NJ: Lawrence Erlbaum Associates. Copyright 1978 by Lawrence Erlbaum Associates. Reprinted by permission.

[a]Episode is curtailed if the baby is unduly distressed.

[b]Episode is prolonged if more time is required for the baby to become reinvolved in play.

tance, avoidance, search, and distance interaction. Scoring at this second level requires more interpretation than does scoring at the first (e.g., "resistance" versus "crying"); a further difference is that the categories at the second level are explicitly social in nature. Finally, the third level of scoring involves a qualitative classification of the overall attachment relation between infant and mother. Three general categories are used, again with specific subcategories within each. Of these three attachment patterns the most adaptive is Type B, which is the label used for a secure, satisfactory form of attachment. The Type B infant is clearly happiest in the mother's presence and is upset when she leaves; he or she is not devastated by the mother's absence, however, and is in general able to adapt well to the cumulative stresses of a strange environment, a strange person, and various comings and goings of the mother. The other two forms of attachment are less secure and satisfactory. The Type A infant shows little distress at separation from the mother and little joy at reunion with her; this infant also demonstrates relatively little differentation among behaviors directed to the mother and those directed to the stranger. The Type C infant has a more upset and angry look. This baby may be strongly distressed during the separation, and may either actively resist the mother during reunion or else respond in an ambivalent fashion, perhaps both clinging to her and pushing her away.

As this description should suggest, the strange situation elicits a wealth of behaviors relevant to attachment. A major strength of structured laboratory assessment is this rich behavioral yield; the approach is both more economical than naturalistic observation and more direct than an interview. On the negative side, the focus on behavior in the natural setting, a strength of the other two approaches, is lost with the strange situation. Despite the lab locus and the adjective "strange," however, the experiences sampled are clearly quite typical ones in the lives of most infants. Babies *are* taken to new rooms by their mothers, do encounter strangers, are sometimes left alone by their mothers, and so forth. What the strange situation does is to compress a variety of such experiences into a brief period of time. This compression, coupled with the novelty of the environment, is admittedly stressful for the infant, and babies are in fact more likely to show distress in the strange situation than they are at home. Ainsworth et al. (1978) argue, however, that the accumulation of stresses is informative, for it permits a highlighting of attachment behaviors. In their words:

Just because the procedure provides increasingly strong instigation to attachment behavior through its cumulative nature, one may observe in a relatively short span of time attachment behavior under conditions of activation from relatively weak to very strong. In the familiar home environment, occasions for strong activation of attachment behavior are infrequent, so that it requires many hours of observation to encompass a similar range. . . . (p. xi)

Let us turn now to some of the issues that can be examined with the strange situation procedure. The thrust of the Ainsworth group's research has been toward individual differences in attachment among samples of 12-month-olds. A major accomplishment of the research has been the demonstration that there are in fact interesting and important individual differences. Findings from the strange situation have allowed researchers to go beyond general statements that the child is "attached" or "not attached" to focus on the *quality* of the attachment. Most 12-month-olds are attached to their mothers; the quality and security of the attachments, however, can vary greatly across children.

Once we know that individual differences exist, what else might we seek to discover? There are at least three further questions that can be asked with regard to individual differences. One concerns the *origins* of such differences. Why do some infants develop secure, satisfactory attachments whereas other infants form avoidant or ambivalent relations with their mothers? The most common approach to answering this question has been to attempt to identify maternal childrearing practices that underlie the different attachment patterns. Ain-

sworth et al. have included measures of maternal behavior in some of their research, and have reported evidence of systematic differences among mothers of Type A, B, and C infants (Ainsworth, Bell, & Stayton, 1974; Ainsworth et al., 1978). They have found, for example, that mothers of Type B infants tend to be more sensitive and responsive to signals from their infants than do mothers from the other two groups. Others researchers (e.g., Clarke-Stewart, 1973; Grossmann & Grossmann, 1982) have also searched for maternal behaviors that might contribute to differences in attachment. Such efforts fall under the general heading of childrearing research, an important and methodologically challenging topic to which we return in chapter 8.

The two remaining questions both have to do with the consistency of the individual differences that are identified in the strange situation. One question concerns consistency across different situations. Suppose that we study the same sample of infants at home; will we observe the same individual differences in attachment patterns that we found in the lab? If, for example, the infant was diagnosed as a secure Type B in the lab, will the infant also look like a secure Type B at home? This question is important, for much of the interest in the strange situation rests on the assumption that it is tapping differences that have some generality. The answer to the question appears to be a qualified "yes." Although the similarity is by no means perfect, there is a significant relation between attachment behavior in the lab and attachment behavior in the home (Ainsworth et al., 1978).

The other sort is consistency over time. Suppose that we study the same children 2, 3, or 4 years later; will the different attachment patterns identified in infancy prove predictive of later differences in development? Note that to answer this question we need a longitudinal design. Note also that we need to solve one of the major problems of longitudinal research: measurement equivalence. The situations in which children find themselves and the behaviors they emit are somewhat different at age 5 than at age 1; what, then, might a secure attachment at age 1 predict to at age 5? Researchers who have searched for predictability over time have reported that there is in fact some predictability—not perfect by any means, but some consistent links between early attachment and later personality. It has been found, for example, that children who were securely attached in infancy are on the average more socially competent in nursery school than children who were less securely attached (Waters, Wippman, & Sroufe, 1979). Similarly, problem-solving behavior in kindergarten can be partly predicted from knowledge of the kind of attachment relation that the child formed in infancy (Matas, Arend, & Sroufe, 1978).

Two further points about the research on consistency are worth making. A first is that the extent to which early attachment is predictive of later development depends not only on what happens in infancy but on the later environment as well. Early attachment is most likely to be predictive when the quality of the environment remains relatively constant as the child develops. Conversely, a marked change in the environment, either for better or for worse, can lead to definite changes in the child's social functioning (e.g., Thompson, Lamb, & Estes, 1982). The child's future, then, is not totally determined by what happens during infancy; it is merely started in a particular direction.

The second point applies to both situational and temporal consistency. The extent to which consistency is found can depend on exactly what level of measurement and analysis is used. If the focus is on specific, discrete behaviors—for example, smiling, crying, vocalization—then consistency, across either situations or time, is generally modest at best. Knowing how much the child cries in the strange situation does not give much basis for predicting how much the child will cry at home, or how much he or she will later cry in nursery school. On the other hand, if the focus is on more global, qualitative categories—such as Ainsworth's Types A, B, and C—then some degree of consistency generally *is* found.

Because the emphasis in this section has been on the Ainsworth strange situation, it should be pointed out that criticisms of this approach and some of the conclusions drawn from it do exist.

A review article by Campos, Barrett, Lamb, Goldsmith, and Stenberg (1983) provides a good summary of the criticisms and related evidence.

SUMMARY

This chapter begins with a discussion of some of the problems involved in doing research with infants. Three general difficulties are discussed. The first is finding and retaining subjects. Infants can be difficult to recruit for research, and infants have the highest drop-out rate of any group of human subjects. The result is that infant samples are often distinctly nonrandom. The second difficulty is related to the high drop-out rate; it concerns the influence of state on the infant's behavior. The infant's state of arousal is a very important determinant of the way that he or she responds to the environment; furthermore, infants are often in states (e.g., sleepy, distressed) that preclude optimal responsiveness. The final difficulty concerns response measures. Infants are nonverbal, and young infants in particular have limited motoric skills; the result is that considerable ingenuity is necessary to find responses from which the infant's experience of the world can be inferred. Three response systems that have proved especially informative are introduced: *visual fixation, sucking,* and *physiological responses.*

The discussion turns next to the issue of age comparisons. The ease of making valid age comparisons depends in part on the age range of the sample. We can therefore reduce some of the problems of cross-sectional and longitudinal designs (e.g., the confounding of age with other dimensions) if we confine ourselves to the span of infancy. On the other hand, these problems are a definite concern if we attempt to compare infants with older children. A particularly important problem, which can apply whatever the ages being compared, is that of *measurement equivalence:* finding responses that are psychologically equivalent at the different ages.

The first specific topic that the chapter considers is infant perception. The problem of response measures is especially challenging in the study of perception, for perception is an experiential phenomenon that is not always clearly expressed in overt behavior. Research on infant perception has concentrated on responses that can be precisely, often automatically, recorded in laboratory settings; a further virtue of the laboratory locus is that it allows precise control of the stimulus. Four methods of studying perception are discussed. The preference method is directed to the question of visual discrimination; two visual stimuli are presented, and differential fixation on the stimuli is taken as evidence that the infant can discriminate between them. The habituation-dishabituation technique is broader in scope, for it can be applied to any perceptual modality. Response is first habituated to one stimulus; reemergence of the response to a second stimulus constitutes evidence of discrimination. Conditioning has been used in various ways to study infant perception, including satiation, in which the recovery of reinforcer effectiveness signals discrimination, and generalization, in which perceptual similarity is inferred from the degree to which a response generalizes from one stimulus to another. Finally, the visual cliff is used to study a single issue of considerable theoretical interest: depth perception in infancy.

Research on infant cognition has been dominated by the work of Piaget. Piaget's studies differ from studies of infant perception in several ways, most notably in the Piagetian emphases on naturalistic observation and on flexible, discovery-oriented probing of the child's abilities. Among the many basic forms of knowledge studied by Piaget is the *object con-cept:* the knowledge that objects have a permanent existence that is independent of immediate perceptual contact. Piaget's methods of studying the object concept center on the infant's search for vanished objects; a variety of forms of search and a variety of kinds of disappearance are examined. The object concept has also been the most popular topic for post-Piaget studies of infant cognition. This more recent work is more tightly controlled and standardized than were Piaget's studies, with more use of laboratory settings and automated recordings of response. A question of particular interest has concerned the effects of less motorically demanding methods of assessment on the child's performance.

Research on social development has been less bound to laboratory settings than has most work on perception or cognition. The interest now is in the infant's interactions with other people, most commonly the mother. Of particular interest has been the development of *attachment,* an emotional bond with the caregiver that is expressed through a variety of behaviors. Information about attachment can be obtained through *parental interview, naturalistic observation,* or *structured laboratory assessment.* A particularly informative example of the last category is a procedure called the *strange situation.* Studies using the strange situation have revealed important individual differences in the quality of children's attachments. Further studies have examined the childrearing origins of such differences and their consistency across situations and across time.

chapter 7

COGNITIVE DEVELOPMENT

The topics into which the field of developmental psychology can be divided are as many and as diverse as the topical divisions for psychology as a whole. The organizational scheme that we follow in the next two chapters—a division into "cognitive" and "social"—is perhaps the broadest and most general cut that can be made. This scheme does not encompass every possible topic in the field, nor is the borderline between cognitive and social always clear. Nevertheless, the division is a typical and generally useful one.

In the present chapter we will consider four major approaches to the study of cognitive development: the Piagetian approach, the intelligence test or IQ approach, the information-processing approach, and studies of memory. As we will see, there is no single dimension along which these approaches can be neatly compared; rather, contrasts can be found in the kinds of abilities that are examined, the theoretical issues that are of interest, and the specific methods of study that are used. What the

various approaches have in common is the reason for their selection here: All represent informative and contemporaneously influential ways to study cognition and the ways in which it changes with development.

The age period for most of the research considered in this chapter is from 2 to 16—that is, postinfancy childhood. We discussed the Piagetian approach to the study of infant cognition in chapter 6; we briefly consider applications of some of the other approaches to infancy at various points in this chapter. We also return to several of the approaches in chapter 9 when we discuss research on aging.

THE PIAGETIAN APPROACH

Piaget's Studies

We saw in chapter 6 that Piaget's work has dominated the study of infant cognition. The Piagetian approach to later childhood has been equally influential. It also constitutes a much larger literature than the infancy studies—some 25 books by Piaget and associates, as well as literally thousands of related studies by others. The goal of this section is to highlight some central themes and important research examples. Fuller discussions can be found in Flavell (1963), Ginsburg and Opper (1979), Voyat (1982), and Miller (1982).

We begin with an example. Box 7-1 presents two protocols from Piaget and Szeminska's (1952) *The Child's Conception of Number*. The concept under examination is *conservation*: the realization that the quantitative properties of an object or collection of objects are not changed by a change in perceptual appearance. The specific form of conservation at issue is conservation of number: the realization that number is invariant in the face of an irrelevant perceptual change. As the protocols reveal, young children do not at first understand conservation; rather, they tend to judge quantities in terms of immediate perceptual appearance. Thus, to 4-year-old Boq it is obvious that the longer of two rows must contain more sweets.

We can see immediately several similarities between Piaget's studies of infancy and his approach to later periods of development. He again focuses on basic, epistemologically central kinds of knowledge. Just as the object concept represents a major achievement in the infant's mastery of the sensorimotor world, so are principles of conservation central to the older child's capacity for more advanced forms of thought. Object concept and conservation show a more specific similarity as well. Both represent important *invariants*: aspects of the world that stay the same even though other, more obvious aspects are changing. Throughout his research career Piaget was interested in the invariants that the child comes to understand at different points in development. The phrase "comes to understand" reflects still another similarity: Both object concept and conservation, basic though they seem, are not always present; rather they must be developed in the course of childhood. Certainly one of the reasons for interest in Piaget's work has always lain in his ability to surprise us with respect to what children, at least for a while, do *not* know.

BOX 7-1   Examples of responses to Piaget's conservation of number task

---

Hoc (4; 3):

'Look, imagine that these are bottles in a cafe. You are the waiter, and you have to take some glasses out of the cupboard. Each bottle must have a glass.' He put one glass opposite each bottle and ignored the other glasses. 'Is there the same number?—*Yes.*—(The bottles were then grouped together.) Is there the same number of glasses and bottles?—*No.*—Where are there more?—*There are more glasses.*' The bottles were put back, one opposite each glass, and the glasses were then grouped together. 'Is there the same number of

Note. From *The Child's Conception of Number* (pp. 44, 75) by J. Piaget and A. Szeminska, 1952, New York: Humanities. Copyright 1952 by Humanities Press. Reprinted by permission.

glasses and bottles?—*No.*—Where are there more?—*More bottles.*—Why are there more bottles?—*Just because.*'

Boq (4; 7):

'Put as many sweets here as there are there. Those (6) are for Roger. You are to take as many as he has.—(He made a compact row of about ten, which was shorter than the model.)—Are they the same?—*Not yet* (adding some).—And now?—*Yes.*—Why?—*Because they're like that* (indicating the length).—(The 6 in the model were then spread out.) Who has more?—*Roger.*—Why?—*Because they go right up to there.*—What can we do to make them the same?—*Put some more* (adding 1).—(The 6 were then closed up and his were spread out.)—*Now I've got more.*'

In addition to these similarities in content, the comparison of object concept and conservation reveals some more general similarities in approach to research. Once again Piaget eschews a highly standardized approach in favor of a flexible, discovery-oriented method of probing the child's knowledge. And once again Piaget reports his results mainly in terms of individual protocols rather than group means and statistical tests.

There are also some important differences between the studies of infancy and the studies of later childhood. One obvious difference concerns sample size. As we saw, the sample for the infancy work was limited to Piaget's own three children. The samples for the work on later childhood are considerably larger and more representative. Beyond this rather general statement it is difficult to say much, for Piaget seldom provides precise information about sample size or composition (although one book, *The Early Growth of Logic in the Child,* does report a total sample of 2,159!). Piaget's failure to describe the samples that he studies is just one of the sins of scientific reporting that he routinely commits. Nevertheless, it is safe to say that his samples for later childhood are much larger than those for infancy.

Some further differences follow from this difference in samples. Piaget's studies of infancy were longitudinal. With the exception of some work on long-term memory (Piaget & Inhelder, 1973), the research on later childhood is all cross-sectional. Similarly, the studies of infancy were within-subject, in the sense that the phenomena of interest were examined in all three babies and interrelations in development were probed for each child. The work on later childhood is, apparently, just about all between-subject. The "apparently" stems from the fact that Piaget often fails to make clear whether a particular conclusion is based on within-subject or between-subject comparisons. Generally, however, the latter appears to be the case. We return to the absence of within-subject analyses shortly when we discuss issues and follow-up work.

A final difference concerns the locus for the observations. The studies of infancy were carried out in the home and focused largely on naturally occurring situations and naturally occurring behaviors. The studies of older children have concentrated mainly on elicited responses to tasks presented in some laboratory context. As the protocols from the *Number* book suggest, the procedure may still be more game-like than test-like, and the interchanges between adult and child may resemble spontaneous conversations more than school-like inquisitions. The fact remains, however, that the measurement is of task-elicited behavior in experimentally contrived situations, and not of spontaneously occurring cognitive activities. We return later to this issue also.

It is time to add some more illustrations of Piagetian tasks to the conservation-of-number example. We can note first that Piaget studies conservation in many quantitative domains in addition to number. Indeed, most of the books devoted to cognition in early and middle childhood include tests of conservation. There are studies of conservation of mass, weight, and volume, of length, area, and distance, of time, speed, and movement. All embody the same general approach: Two stimuli are shown to be equal on some quantitative dimension, one of the stimuli is then perceptually transformed so that the quantities no longer *look* equal, and the child is asked whether the quantities are now the same or different. All also show the same developmental progression from perceptually based nonconservation to logically based conservation. The protocols in Box 7–2 illustrate this progression with respect to conservation of weight.

Conservation is just one of dozens of basic logical or physical concepts that Piaget and his many coworkers have studied. We settle here for briefly describing two other important examples. One is *class inclusion*: the principle that a subclass cannot be larger than the superordinate class that contains it. Class inclusion is the knowledge, for example, that there can never be more poppies than flowers, or more ducks than birds. Both of these problems were in fact included in Piaget's studies of classification (Inhelder & Piaget, 1964; Piaget & Szeminska, 1952). Box 7–3 presents a third ex-

BOX 7–2 Examples of responses to Piaget's conservation of weight task

SUZ (6; 6) examines the two balls: *'Oh sure, they weigh the same.—And if I pull this one out into a thread will they still weigh the same?—We'll have to see.'* One of the two balls is pulled out: *'No, the ball is quite heavy but that one weighs a little more, you've pulled it out so it's bound to weigh more.—Can we turn it back into a ball?—Yes.—Will it get bigger or smaller?—*

Note. From *The Child's Construction of Quantities* (pp. 24, 43) by J. Piaget and B. Inhelder, 1974, New York: Basic Books. Copyright 1974 by Basic Books, Inc. Reprinted by permission.

I don't know; oh, it'll be the same because it was a ball before.—Do the two have as much clay as each other now?—Yes.—And the same weight?—No.'

FOG (9; 9) *'They're the same weight. They're the same balls, you've just pulled this one out.—Didn't the weight change when I pulled it out?—First it was round and now it's long, but it's the same clay; you didn't take any away.—Can I turn it back into a ball that weighs the same as before?—Of course you can, there's no extra clay.'*

ample. The stimuli for the task are a set of wooden beads, most of which are brown but two of which are white. The response of 6-year-old Bis indicates that class inclusion, like conservation, is another basic concept that is not at first present but rather must develop.

In addition to classes, Piaget's research includes a focus on the child's understanding of relations. Of particular interest is the relational concept of *transitivity*. Transitivity is embodied

in reasoning of the following sort: If A is equal to B and B equal to C on some quantitative dimension, then A must be equal to C. Or if A is greater than B and B is greater than C, then A must be greater than C. Such reasoning has been studied most often with respect to length and weight, the usual stimuli being sticks of different length or clay balls of different weight. Whatever the specific quantity involved, the approach is the same: demonstration of the A–

BOX 7–3 Example of response to Piaget's class inclusion task

Bis (6; 8):

'Are there more wooden beads or more brown beads?—*More brown ones, because there are two white ones.—Are the white ones made of wood?—Yes.—And the brown ones?—Yes.—Then are there more brown ones or more wooden ones?—More brown ones.—What colour would a necklace made of the wooden beads be?—Brown and white* (thus showing that Bis clearly understood the problem).—And what col-

Note. From *The Child's Conception of Number* (p. 164) by J. Piaget and A. Szeminska, 1952, New York: Humanities. Copyright 1952 by Humanities Press. Reprinted by permission.

our would a necklace made with the brown beads be?—*Brown.*—Then which would be longer, the one made with the wooden beads or the one made with the brown beads?—*The one with the brown beads.*—Draw the necklace for me. (Bis drew a series of black rings for the necklace of brown beads, and a series of black rings plus two white rings for the necklace of wooden beads.)—Good. Now which will be longer, the one with the brown beads or the one with the wooden beads?—*The one with the brown beads.*' Thus, in spite of having clearly understood, and having correctly drawn the data of the problem, Bis was unable to solve it by including the class of brown beads in the class of wooden beads!

B and B–C relations, followed by a request to judge A and C. Note that the quantitative relation between A and C is not perceptually apparent; hence the child must use the information in the initial two comparisons to deduce the correct answer. According to Piaget's studies it is not until about age 8 or 9 that children are capable of such logical reasoning.

The tasks that we have described thus far are directed to thought in middle childhood, or what is labeled the concrete-operational period in Piaget's theory. In a book entitled *The Growth of Logical Thinking from Childhood to Adolescence,* Inhelder and Piaget (1958) examined a more advanced form of thinking, which they found to emerge only around adolescence. This final period in Piaget's theory is the period of *formal operations.* The essence of formal operations is the capacity for hypothetical-deductive reasoning, the ability to go beyond immediate reality to work systematically and logically within the

realm of the possible. The prototype of such reasoning is scientific problem solving; Inhelder and Piaget's tasks for studying formal operations in fact consisted mainly of problems drawn from the physical sciences. One of these problems, the pendulum task, is the source for the protocols reprinted in Box 7–4. The child's job is to determine what factor or factors influence the frequency of oscillation of a simple pendulum. Solution requires identifying each of the potentially important variables (weight, length of string, force of push, etc.), systematically testing out each variable while holding the other variables constant, and finally drawing logical conclusions from the overall pattern of results. Box 7–4 presents examples of both the failure of the younger child and the success of the older child on such problems.

We consider one final example of a Piagetian task. Not all of the studies fit the logical or physical mold of the work described so far. Piaget's first book, *The Language and Thought of the*

BOX 7–4   Examples of responses to the Inhelder and Piaget formal-operational pendulum task

---

PER (10; 7) is a remarkable case of a failure to separate variables: he varies simultaneously the weight and the impetus; then the weight, the impetus, and the length; then the impetus, the weight, and the elevation, etc., and first concludes: *"It's by changing the weight and the push, certainly not the string."*—"How do you know that the string has nothing to do with it?"—*Because it's the same string."*—He has not varied its length in the last several trials; previously he had varied it simultaneously with the impetus, thus complicating the account of the experiment.—"But does the rate of speed change?"—*"That depends, sometimes it's the same . . . . Yes, not much . . . .It also depends on the height that you*

Note. From *The Growth of Logical Thinking from Childhood to Adolescence* (pp. 71, 75) by B. Inhelder and J. Piaget, 1958, New York: Basic Books. Copyright 1958 by Basic Books, Inc. Reprinted by permission.

put it at [the string]. *When you let go low down, there isn't much speed."* He then draws the conclusion that all four factors operate: *"It's in changing the weight, the push, etc. With the short string, it goes faster,"* but also *"by changing the weight, by giving a stronger push,"* and *"for height, you can put it higher or lower."*—"How can you prove that?"—*"You have to try to give it a push, to lower or raise the string, to change the height and the weight."* He wants to vary all factors simultaneously.

EME (15; 1), after having selected 100 grams with a long string and a medium length string, then 20 grams with a long and a short string, and finally 200 grams with a long and a short, concludes: *"It's the length of the string that makes it go faster or slower; the weight doesn't play any role."* She discounts likewise the height of the drop and the force of her push.

Child (1926), was directed to an important component in the child's understanding of the social world: the ability to take someone else's point of view. Can the child figure out what someone else sees at the moment, or thinks, or feels, or wishes? In particular, can the child make such judgments when the other's perspective is different from his or her own? Such *role taking* is critical to social understanding and social interaction. Role taking has a converse in *egocentrism*: the inability to break away from one's own perspective to take the perspective of others. It should come as no surprise, in light of the cognitive deficits that we have discussed so far, to learn that Piaget finds that young children are often egocentric.

As the preceding paragraph suggests, role taking can occur in many contexts and can take many forms. In Piaget's original studies role taking was examined in two main contexts. One concerned children's attempts to communicate. In communication there is an obvious need to break away from one's own perspective so that messages can be tailored to the informational needs of the listener. Piaget studied such communicative role taking both in children's spontaneous conversations and in experimental tasks which required one child to transmit some body of information to another (for example, to retell a story that he or she had just been told). The second context concerned spatial perspective taking, or the ability to figure out what someone else sees. The main apparatus for studying spatial perspective taking was the "three-mountains" model shown in Figure 7–1. After walking around the display, the child was seated on one side of the model; his or her task then was to describe what would be seen by a doll placed at various locations around the display.

We return to several of the tasks that we have just described shortly when we discuss follow-up work. Before doing so, however, let us note a few more points about the general Piagetian approach to research. The interview procedure illustrated in the various protocols in this chapter is referred to as the *clinical method* of testing. Piaget (1929) adopted the term "clinical method" because of the similarity of his approach to that of a skilled clinician attempting to diagnose and treat emotional problems. In both cases the essence of the approach is flexibility: the freedom for the investigator to deviate from preset procedure to probe the individual subject's response in a variety of nonpredetermined ways. In skilled hands the clinical method can be a discovery procedure par excellence for uncovering the phenomena of interest in a new research area. It can also be an excellent diagnostic technique for determining exactly what it is that a young child really believes, a determination that may be difficult with a highly standardized procedure that cannot bend to the needs (vocabulary problems, momentary distractions, idiosyncratic interpretations, etc.) of the individual child.

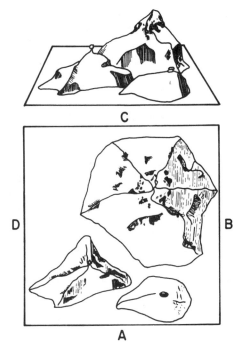

FIGURE 7–1. Three-mountains task for assessing visual perspective taking. From *The Child's Conception of Space* (p. 211) by J. Piaget and B. Inhelder, 1956, London: Routledge & Kegan Paul. Copyright 1956 by Routledge & Kegan Paul. Reprinted by permission.

Piaget's fullest discussion of the clinical method is found in one of his early books, *The Child's Conception of the World*. The following passage is worth quoting in full:

It is our opinion that in child psychology as in pathological psychology, at least a year of daily practice is necessary before passing beyond the inevitable fumbling stage of the beginner. It is so hard not to talk too much when questioning a child, expecially for a pedagogue! It is so hard not to be suggestive! And above all, it is so hard to find the middle course between systematisation due to preconceived ideas and incoherence due to the absence of any directing hypothesis! The good experimenter must, in fact, unite two often incompatible qualities; he must know how to observe, that is to say, to let the child talk freely, without ever checking or side-tracking his utterance, and at the same time he must constantly be alert for something definitive, at every moment he must have some working hypothesis, some theory, true or false, which he is seeking to check. To appreciate the real difficulty of the clinical method one must have taught it. When students begin they either suggest to the child all they hope to find, or they suggest nothing at all, because they are not on the look-out for anything, in which case, to be sure, they will never find anything. (Piaget, 1929, pp. 7–8)

The clinical method is an important component in Piaget's research, but it would not mean very much unless there were interesting concepts to which it could be applied. And here we have reached perhaps the greatest strength of Piagetian research: the incredible range of interesting forms of knowledge and insightful procedures for probing this knowledge. This richness can be only hinted at in the brief sampling of tasks and findings included here. Book after Piagetian book is full of novel and informative methods for studying how children think—methods that have set the mold for a substantial proportion of later research on cognitive development. We noted in chapter 1 that technical skill in executing research must always be joined with good ideas about what is interesting to study and how to go about studying it. It is doubtful that anyone else in the history of developmental psychology has had as many good ideas as Piaget.

Issues and Follow-up Studies

We turn immediately from praise to problems. Piaget's studies have elicited an enormous amount of follow-up research, much of it motivated by perceived deficiencies in the original Piagetian research. We discuss this follow-up work under three headings: assessment, patterning, and cognitive change.

The *assessment* question is the same basic issue that we considered with respect to Piaget's infancy work: Do Piaget's procedures really give an accurate picture of the child's abilities? As with the infancy studies, the main concern has been that Piaget may underestimate what the young child really knows. Although various possible sources of misdiagnosis have been identified, probably the most common criticism concerns the heavy verbal emphasis in many Piagetian tasks. This emphasis should be clear from the protocols quoted earlier in the chapter. Consider the conservation task. The purpose of this task is to assess the child's understanding of the logic underlying conservation. This logic, however, is not directly observable; rather its discovery depends on the use of language, both in the questions that are asked of the child and in the responses that the child must make. It seems quite possible that a young "nonconserver" does not really believe in nonconservation but is simply confused by the use of words like "same," "more," "less," and "number." Perhaps, for example, the child thinks that "more" refers to length of row rather than number of objects.

Various approaches have been taken in response to this possibility. Some investigators have used verbal pretests in an attempt to ensure that the child understands the words that are used on the conservation test (e.g., Miller, 1977). Others have gone beyond pretesting to attempt verbal pretraining—that is, teaching the relevant words to the child prior to the test (e.g., Gruen, 1965). And some have attempted to do away with the potentially confusing language altogether by devising "nonverbal" procedures for assessing Piagetian concepts. Such procedures are seldom literally nonverbal; they are simplified linguistically, however, and they do avoid such potentially troublesome words as "same" or "more." One strategy has been to engineer a violation of the concept (e.g., an apparent instance of nonconservation) and then measure the child's response, the rationale being that a reaction of surprise is evidence for some understanding of the concept (e.g., Gelman, 1972a). Recall that this same sort of violation-of-expectancy approach has been used to study the infant's understanding of object permanence. Another common technique has been to assess the child's understanding of relative quantity by allowing him or her to choose between two collections of candies, one of which might appear greater (the developmentally immature response) but the other of which is in fact greater (the developmentally mature response). Figure 7–2 illustrates the application of this approach to three concepts: conservation of number, conservation of discontinuous quantity, and class inclusion.

Not all diagnostic revisions have been directed to language. A recent interest has been in the general context within which conservation is typically assessed. This context is in fact a rather strange one, and it includes a number of features that may bias the child toward a nonconservation answer. Among these features are the explicit focus on quantity, the seemingly arbitrary nature of the transformation (*why* is the adult spreading out the candies?), and the presentation of the identical conservation question twice within a short period, a repetition that may suggest to young children that they should change their answers. Perhaps if the context

could be made more natural and familiar the child would be less likely to look like a nonconserver.

This possibility has been tested in various ways. Rose and Blank (1974) examined the effects of the usual two-questions format by simply omitting the initial pretransformation question for half their subjects and asking only the final conservation question. McGarrigle and Donaldson (1974) replaced the intentional transformation by an adult experimenter with an apparently accidental transformation by a "naughty" teddy bear, the expectation being that children might find the latter more familiar and less imbued with magical quantity-changing properties. Light, Buckingham, and Robbins (1979) performed a similar manipulation but with an *incidental* rather than accidental change—that is, a transformation that was not directed solely to the issue of conservation but occurred naturally in the course of an ongoing game.

So far nothing has been said about results from such modified-assessment studies. Although the interpretation of this research is somewhat controversial, three general conclusions seem tenable (see Donaldson, 1982; Miller, 1976b; Miller, 1982; and Siegel, 1978, for further discussion). The first is that Piaget's methods do in fact result in some underestimation of the young child's abilities, for children often perform better on modified tests than on standard Piagetian tests. The second is that the underestimation is probably not great, and that phenomena such as nonconservation are by no means totally explicable on the basis of

FIGURE 7–2.   Examples of nonverbal tests of Piagetian concepts.

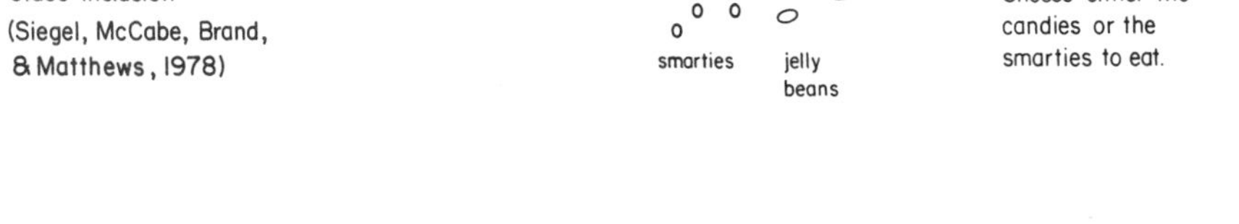

Concept	Initial State	Final State	Response
Conservation of Number (Miller, 1976a)	o o o o o o o o o / o o o o o o o o	o o o o o o o o o / o o o o o o o o	Choose a row of candies to eat.
Conservation of Quantity (Silverman & Schneider, 1968)			Choose one of the collections of candies to eat.
Class Inclusion (Siegel, McCabe, Brand, & Matthews, 1978)		smarties jelly beans	Choose either the candies or the smarties to eat.

verbal confusions or contextual biases. The third is that the development of concepts such as conservation and role taking is more extended and multifaceted than Piaget imagined, with a number of earlier levels and precursor skills not tapped by Piaget's own procedures. This conclusion comes not only from the studies discussed but also from programs of research whose explicit focus has been on simpler and developmentally earlier skills than those examined in Piaget's research. Notable in this regard is the work of John Flavell on role taking (e.g., Flavell, 1974, 1978) and Rochel Gelman on concepts of number (e.g., Gelman, 1972b; Gelman & Gallistel, 1978).

One final point can be made about the modified-assessment studies. The major goal of such research has been to identify the child's optimal level of performance, a goal stemming from the belief that Piaget's techniques often fail to capture the child's true abilities. The work on context effects, however, is also relevant to another important question: that of the child's *typical* level of performance. As we saw, Piaget's post-infancy studies have focused mainly on test-elicited behaviors in laboratory settings. The studies of different contexts are a beginning, albeit a very limited one, toward an examination of more spontaneous cognitive activities in settings that more closely approximate those in which children usually express their abilities. As such, they constitute an important step toward extending the external validity of Piagetian assessment.

The second general issue that we consider concerns *patterning* in development. The issue of patterning is the issue of how different cognitive abilities fit together. Piaget's theory claims that there are two important kinds of patterning in the development of cognitive skills. One is invariant sequence: the emergence of two or more abilities in the same developmental order in all children. The theoretical interest of invariant sequence lies in the possibility that the developmentally earlier ability serves as a necessary mediator or building block in the mastery of the developmentally later ability. The other kind of pattern is concurrence: the emergence of two or more abilities at the same time in development. The theoretical claim at issue here is that of a common underlying basis for the different abilities.

From a methodological standpoint, the study of sequences or concurrences requires two things. One is within-subject testing. This point was made in chapter 3 in the general discussion of between-subject and within-subject designs. Identification of interrelations or patterns in development is possible only if each subject contributes data on all of the tasks being compared. Given such within-subject testing, sequences or concurrences can be inferred from the pattern of successes and failures. Table 7-1 shows the patterns that would be necessary to verify the hypotheses of invariant sequence or concurrence in the emergence of two abilities. The same logic that applies in the two-concept case can be extended to comparisons of three or more abilities. For example, if the hypothesis is that abilities A, B, and C emerge in sequence, then four outcomes would be compatible: failure on all tasks, success on A only, success on A and B only, or success on all three tasks.

The second requirement for research on patterning is the equation of task sensitivity for the

TABLE 7–1 Patterns of Success and Failure and their Relation to Sequences and Concurrences

Hypothesized Relationship	Congruent Patterns	Incongruent Patterns
A-B sequence	A+ B+, A+ B−, A− B−	A − B+
A-B concurrence	A+ B+, A− B−	A+ B−, A− B+

Note: + denotes success, − denotes failure.

different concepts being compared. Determining the relative difficulty of concepts A and B is possible only if the tests that are used to measure A and B are equally sensitive—that is, equally likely to elicit whatever genuine understanding the child may have. If the tests are not equally sensitive, then false conclusions about developmental ordering may well emerge. Suppose, for example, that the test that we select to measure concept A is a highly simplified one that is likely to reveal the very earliest glimmers of understanding. Suppose that our test for concept B is considerably less sensitive, loaded, perhaps, with verbal complexities or memory demands that are absent in the assessment of A. We may well find that task A is mastered before task B, perhaps even in what appears to be an invariant sequence. But the actual developmental relation between abilities A and B may be something quite other than what these particular measures suggest.

As sketched here, the sensitivity problem seems easy enough to solve—simply avoid selecting tasks that are obviously different in their extraneous response demands. Like many methodological prescriptions, however, this piece of advice is easier to state than to follow. Deciding what is "extraneous" may be difficult; any concept, after all, is always embedded in some context, with particular stimuli, words, memory requirements, and so forth. If we are assessing conservation, for example, we will have to decide, among other things, what materials to use as stimuli, how to establish the initial equality, what kinds of perceptual transformations to perform, how to word the conservation question, and whether to require an explanation as well as a correct judgment. It is an illusion to think that a concept like conservation can ever be measured in a "pure" form in the absence of such context. It is also an illusion to think that the concepts of interest in developmental psychology are single, homogeneous entities—*the* ability of conservation or transitivity or role taking, just waiting to be revealed by the one "right" test. Rather, as our discussion of the assessment issue stressed, any construct of interest embodies a number of different levels and component skills, levels and

skills whose expression may vary across different contexts. All of these considerations complicate greatly the task of identifying interrelations in development.

How well does Piaget's research solve the problems just discussed? A brief but fair answer is: not very well. Piaget is certainly aware of the issue of task sensitivity; indeed, his book on number contains an eloquent discussion of the problem (Piaget & Szeminska, 1952, p. 149). His own studies, however, show only sporadic and often unconvincing attempts at equating task sensitivity when comparing different concepts. Perhaps even more serious is another problem mentioned earlier: the absence of within-subject comparisons. With rare exceptions, Piaget's conclusions about patterning in postinfancy development are based on mean ages of mastery for different samples of children responding to different tasks. If, for example, one group of children masters task A at about age 6 whereas a second group masters task B at about 8, then an A-B sequence may be claimed; if both groups show success at about 8, then the conclusion may be one of concurrence. Such an approach, it should be clear, can provide only shaky and inconclusive evidence with regard to patterning in development.

Research since Piaget's has adopted a within-subject approach to the issue of patterning, often with multiple tasks and sophisticated statistical techniques for analyzing the resulting interrelations (e.g., Kofsky, 1966; Toussaint, 1974). Such studies have also made more serious attempts to equate task sensitivity than is evident in Piaget's work. That there is no easy or perfect answer to the task-sensitivity issue, however, should be clear from the preceding discussion. Differences in approach in fact abound, with resulting controversies about exactly what patterns the development of cognition shows. A very general conclusion from this research is that many of the sequences claimed by Piaget hold up well; concurrences in development, however, have proved much harder to find (see Flavell, 1982, and Miller, 1982, for further discussion).

The final issue that we consider is that of *cognitive change*. How does the child acquire all of the various abilities that Piaget's work has shown must somehow be acquired? How, for example, does a belief in nonconservation give way to an understanding of conservation, or an initial egocentric perspective turn into skilled role taking? How, more generally, does a child move from one Piagetian stage of development to the next? And, of course, the specific question that is of interest in a text on methodology: How can we study this issue of cognitive change?

Piaget has often been criticized for telling us more about the stages through which the child moves than the processes by which this movement occurs. This criticism is probably justified. The problem is not that Piaget fails to address the issue of cognitive change; the topic is a prominent one in his theorizing. The problem is that there often seems to be a sizable gap between theory and relevant evidence. Often, in fact, it is not even clear what evidence might be relevant, or through what methodological techniques it might be gathered.

One of the differences noted earlier between the infancy studies and the studies of later childhood is relevant here. The infancy research was both naturalistic and longitudinal, a combination that allowed Piaget to observe the child in the process of coping with new problems and moving, often very gradually, to new levels of understanding. It seems probable, in fact, that many of Piaget's ideas about cognitive change were shaped by what he saw occur in his own infants. The work on later childhood, however, is neither naturalistic nor longitudinal, and it contains few direct observations of children in the process of mastering something new. Instead, the studies of later childhood (and the protocols that we have cited should make this point) are essentially all *diagnostic*—that is, concerned with identifying cognitive skills that the child already possesses.

We turn, therefore, to work by others on the issue of cognitive change. By far the most popular paradigm for studying cognitive change has been the *training study*. As the name suggests, the goal of a training study is to teach a concept to children who do not yet understand it. The most commonly studied concept has been con-

servation, and we therefore take conservation as our example. The first phase of a training study consists of a conservation pretest to determine which children already understand conservation and which children do not, and are therefore candidates for training. The nonconservers so identified then participate in the second, or training, phase of the study. During this phase the children are subjected to experiences whose purpose is to induce in them an understanding of conservation. The particular experiences may vary greatly depending on the theoretical predilections of the researcher; the common hope, however, is that the experimentally provided experiences have some relation to the real-life situations or processes through which children acquire conservation. The final phase is then a conservation posttest to determine whether the training has been successful. If the training *is* successful, then its success may tell us something about the real-life routes to conservation.

A large number of training studies exist. Not all have produced gains; indeed, the first such studies to appear, in the late 1950s and early 1960s, were mostly unsuccessful (see Flavell, 1963, for a review of this early work). More recently, however, the trend has shifted, and by now there is no doubt that conservation *can* be successfully trained—not in all children, certainly, but in at least some. It is clear, moreover, that a wide variety of seemingly disparate training procedures can produce success. Table 7–2 summarizes some of the training methods that have been shown, in laboratory settings, to result in the acquisition of conservation.

What factors should be taken into account in evaluating training research? At least three questions must be asked.

One concerns the accuracy of the diagnosis. Were the children really nonconservers prior to the training? And, most critically, have they really become conservers by the end of training? Getting the child to answer "same" to a string of conservation problems is not particularly difficult; the real issue is whether the training has instilled a genuine understanding of the concept, an understanding that is comparable to that of normal, nontrained devel-

TABLE 7-2   Examples of Piagetian Training Studies

Study	Concepts Trained	Type of Training	Procedure
Beilin (1965)	Conservation of number, conservation of length	Verbal rule instruction	Provision of a verbal rule explaining the conservation principle following each incorrect answer—e.g., "Now I am moving them. See, they are standing in a different place, but there are just as many dots as before. They only look different. See, I can put them back just the way they were, so you see, there are still the same number as before because I did not add any dots or take away any dots. I only moved them."
Wallach, Wall, & Anderson (1967)	Conservation of number	Reversibility	Demonstration that the conservation transformation can be reversed and the numbers remain equal. Stimuli were dolls and toy beds; training trials showed that one doll could still be placed in each bed regardless of the spreading or bunching of one or the other collection.
Gelman (1969)	Conservation of number, conservation of length	Attention to quantity	Learning set training designed to direct attention to the relevant quantitative attribute (number or length) and away from irrelevant attributes. Training consisted of a series of trials on which the child had to pick the two stimuli out of three that were the "same"; reinforcement was for choices based on quantity (e.g., number) rather than perceptual features (e.g., spreading or bunching).
Bucher & Schneider (1973)	Conservation of number, conservation of mass, conservation of liquid	Operant conditioning	Reinforcement (with praise and a token) of correct answers across a graded series of training trials. Trials varied in form and progressed from relatively simple to more complex.
Zimmerman & Rosenthal (1974)	Conservation of number, conservation of length, conservation of area	Modeling	Demonstration of the correct response by an adult model on a series of conservation trials similar to those administered to the child. Modeling included both the correct judgment and an adequate explanation (e.g., "because they both had the same amount in the first place").

opment. Piagetian-oriented psychologists have typically insisted on rigorous criteria before acknowledging the genuineness of training. These criteria include the presence of a logical explanation for the answer as well as a correct judgment, generalization of the correct response to other, related problems, and persistence of the correct response over time (for example, on a delayed posttest).

A second question concerns the basis for the training's success. All investigators, of course, have some theoretical or empirical reason for the training that they design, some set of putatively important situations or processes that the training is meant to capture. Table 7-2 indicates the theoretical constructs (reversibility, attention, etc.) that underlay the training efforts summarized in the table. The problem is that there is never a direct, unquestionable link between construct (e.g., reversibility) and experimental manipulation (e.g., reestablishing an initial equality by matching dolls with beds after one or the other array has been perceptually transformed). There is, rather, always an inferential leap in moving from manipulation to explanation, which means that there are always alternative explanations for the success of any training procedure. A carefully designed study can delimit these alternative explanations, but it can never rule them out entirely. Thus, we often know that training has been successful, but we do not know for certain why.

The final issue is that of external validity. What training studies demonstrate, at best, is that certain experiences are sufficient to induce cognitive progress; they do not demonstrate that such experiences are either necessary or typical contributors to real-life cognitive change. The problem is that all training manipulations involve situations and experiences that are different from those in the child's natural environment. Often the situations and experiences are very different from those that children naturally encounter. There is, of course, a reason for this deliberate nonnaturalness, and it is the general reason for experimental-laboratory study: the possibility for precise control and measurement of variables, and thus for a high degree of internal validity in determining cause and effect relations. Training researchers are not attempting an exact mirror of real life; they are attempting to condense relevant experiences and abstract and highlight critical processes. Nevertheless, the "can" versus "does" distinction that was raised in chapter 5 remains relevant here. Training studies have identified a variety of experiences that *can* induce cognitive change. It is still unclear which of these experiences actually *do* contribute to normal, nontrained cognitive development.

THE INTELLIGENCE TEST APPROACH

The Nature of IQ Tests

The intelligence test, or IQ, approach to intelligence is in many ways quite different from the Piagetian approach. Because our emphasis so far has been on Piaget, we begin by noting what some of the differences are.

Piaget's interest was always in commonalities of development—that is, ways in which all children are alike as they grow. A concept like conservation of number, for example, is eventually mastered by all normal children. More broadly, a stage like concrete operations is eventually attained by virtually every child. What individual differences there are seem to lie in the rate of development, and such differences were never of interest to Piaget. In contrast, the whole point of IQ tests is to identify individual differences among children. Such tests, moreover, measure not only differences but *ordered* differences—we say that one child is "higher" or "lower" in intelligence than another, or that a particular child is "above" or "below" average in intelligence. There is an evaluative component that is impossible to escape from in using IQ tests. The fact that such tests force us to make value judgments about children is one reason that their use has always been so controversial.

From the start Piaget's work was theoretically guided, the goal being to answer basic epistemological questions about the child's understanding of domains such as number, space, time, and causality. Whatever practical applications the work has had (e.g., influences on school curriculum) have come later, and Piaget himself was never a major contributor to such applications. IQ tests, in contrast, have been pragmatically oriented from the start. The first successful IQ test, an instrument designed by Binet and Simon in Paris in 1905, was constructed for the very pragmatic purpose of predicting how well children would do in school. Indeed, the ability to predict school performance was an explicit criterion in the selection of items for the test. IQ tests ever since have had similar practical groundings and practical applications. Binet, it is true, did have some conception of intelligence behind his generation of items, and there did eventually emerge a number of elaborate theories of just what it is that such tests measure. For the most part, however, the theories came after the instrument. The sequence was thus the reverse of that with Piaget: practical applications first, theory only later.

A final difference concerns the quantitative

emphasis in IQ tests. IQ tests are directed to questions of how much and not to questions of how. What the tests yield is a number that tells how much intelligence a particular child has. Some tests yield several numbers, corresponding to different kinds of intelligence; the approach, however, remains basically quantitative. All that is of concern in scoring an IQ test is how many right answers the child gives, and all that is done with the right answers is to add them together to get an overall point total. The focus is thus on the products of cognitive activity, and not the underlying processes from which these products came. For Piagetians, in contrast, the interest is always more in processes than in products. The attempt in Piagetian research is to move beyond the child's right or wrong answer to identify the qualitative nature of the underlying thought system and the qualitative changes that the system undergoes as the child develops. The Piagetian focus is thus more on the how than the how much.

What has been said so far about IQ tests has a rather negative sound to it. Such tests are more quantitative than qualitative, more concerned with products than underlying processes, more pragmatic than theoretical in their origins and construction. Nor are these the only criticisms that can be lodged against IQ tests; we have not even mentioned the common complaint that such tests are biased against certain groups. Given these various problems, the obvious question becomes: Why should anyone take IQ tests seriously? What is the evidence that such tests are really measuring intelligence? What, in short, is the evidence for the *validity* of the tests?

The general issue of test validity was discussed in chapter 2. Recall that the validity of a test is generally established through demonstrating that the test correlates with other measures to which it ought to relate, "ought to" either for purposes of pragmatic prediction or for reasons of theoretical cogency. The validation of IQ tests has always rested upon such correlational power. The first such test, that of Binet and Simon, was deemed successful because it was able to differentiate among children who were likely to do well in school and

those who were likely to do poorly in school. Ever since the original Binet and Simon test, correlations with school performance or academic achievement tests have been a major validity index for IQ tests designed for children. Typically, such correlations are in the neighborhood of .5, a figure that indicates a moderately strong but certainly far from perfect relation. The correlational power of IQ is not limited to academic contexts, however. IQ also correlates with occupational status in adulthood and with performance on a wide range of learning and cognitive measures (Jensen, 1981). It is this ability to predict (albeit imperfectly) to so many contexts that clearly require intelligence that constitutes the validity argument for IQ tests as measures of intelligence.[1]

Recall also from chapter 2 that standardized tests must demonstrate *reliability* as well as validity. The form of reliability of greatest concern is test-retest: If we administer the same test twice within a short period of time will we obtain highly similar scores? The answer to this question with regard to IQ should already be evident from our discussion of validity. Reliability is necessary for validity, and hence a demonstration that a test is valid implies that it is also reliable. In fact, the test-retest reliability for the major tests of childhood IQ is quite high, correlations between first and second test typically falling around .9.

A Sampling of Tests

A number of tests purport to measure intelligence, and they vary along several dimensions. Some provide a single overall score as a measure of global or general intelligence. Probably the best-known test of general intelligence is the Stanford-Binet (Terman & Merrill, 1973), the direct historical descendant of the original Binet and Simon test. Other tests provide more

---

[1]Actually, one of the most common validity indices is correlation with *other* intelligence tests. A new test, for example, is likely to be taken seriously only if it correlates fairly substantially with a well-established test like the Stanford-Binet or WISC. Similarly, a new version of an established test is justified largely on the basis of its correlation with the preceding version of the test.

specific or differentiated information. An often-used test with children, for example, is the Peabody Picture Vocabulary Test (Dunn & Dunn, 1981), which furnishes a measure of receptive oral vocabulary. The various Wechsler tests (Wechsler, 1967, 1974, 1981) all provide measures of both verbal IQ and performance IQ; summed together, the Verbal and Performance scales yield an overall IQ.

Tests also vary in the age group for whom they are intended. The three Wechsler tests are designed for three different age groups: the Wechsler Preschool and Primary Scale of Intelligence, or WPPSI, is intended for ages 4 to 6½; the Wechsler Intelligence Scale for Children, or WISC, is intended for ages 6 to 16; and the Wechsler Adult Intelligence Scale, or WAIS, is intended for adults. The age placement for items in the Stanford-Binet (i.e., the average age at which the item can be passed) ranges from 2 to 14. Since several different levels of adult items are also included, the test can actually be given to subjects of any age from about 2 on. Finally, although infancy is the only age group excluded from the Wechsler and Stanford-Binet, there *are* tests that are specifically designed to measure development in infancy (e.g., the Bayley Scales of Infant Development).

A final contrast concerns the method of administration. Some tests are designed for individual administration—that is, one tester and one subject at a time. This is true of all of the tests of childhood or adult IQ that have been mentioned so far: the Stanford-Binet, the Wechsler, and the Peabody. It is also true, necessarily, of all tests of infant intelligence. Other tests are designed for group administration, which means that many subjects can be tested at one time. Group tests of intelligence first came to prominence during World War I when they were used to screen Army recruits. Since that time group tests for children have also become common in school settings. Such tests have the obvious advantages of ease of administration and efficiency—30 or 40 subjects can be tested in the time that would be required for one subject with the Stanford-Binet. Group tests also have some obvious disadvantages: They are

limited to subjects who are mature enough to respond to the paper-and-pencil format, and they may be less likely than individual tests to elicit the subject's optimal performance.

So far we have said little about the content of IQ tests. Tables 7–3 and 7–4 show examples of the types of items that appear on two of the major tests of childhood IQ: the Stanford-Binet and the WISC. As the tables suggest, there are two principal differences in the way in which these two tests are constructed. The first difference was noted earlier: The WISC has a division into Verbal and Performance scales that is not found in the Stanford-Binet. There are 10 subtests in the WISC, five for the Verbal scale and five for the Performance. The second difference is that items in the Stanford-Binet are age-graded on the basis of the average age at which children succeed on them. There are 2-year-old items, 2½-year-old items, and so forth—six items per age level, going up in half-year chunks from 2 to 5 and at one-year intervals from age 5 on. The WISC does not contain any age grouping; rather, the same 10 tests apply whatever the developmental level of the subject. What *does* change with development in the WISC is how far the subject can go with each test and thus how much credit is earned. An average 7-year-old, for example, can solve 7 or 8 of the Arithmetic items and define 19 or 20 of the Vocabulary words. An average 12-year-old can handle 14 Arithmetic items and define 35 to 40 words.

Despite these differences, the Stanford-Binet and the WISC are certainly more alike than they are different. A basic similarity concerns the kinds of cognitive abilities that are stressed. Verbal skills are important in both tests. Even items that are not explicitly verbal (e.g., the WISC Performance tests) typically depend on the subject's understanding of verbal instructions. This verbal loading tends to increase with the age of the subject. Memory is also important, both memory for meaningful material and rote memory for unrelated items (both tests, for example, include measures of digit span). Arithmetical ability is the focus of a number of subtests—for example, Block Counting at age 10 in the Stanford-Binet or the entire Arith-

TABLE 7-3 Examples of Items from the Stanford-Binet Intelligence Scale

Age Level	Item	Materials	Task	Criterion for Passing
4	Picture vocabulary	Pictures of 18 common objects 1. Airplane 2. Telephone .. .. 10. Ship 11. Umbrella .. .. 17. Pitcher 18. Leaf	Name the object	14 correct
	Naming objects from memory	Automobile, dog, shoe, cat, spoon, engine, doll, scissors, thimble	Three objects are presented; they are then screened, one object is hidden, and the screen is removed. Task is to name the hidden object.	Correct on 2 of 3 trials
	Discrimination of Forms	2 sets of 10 geometrical forms	Match a form from one set with the corresponding form in the other set.	8 of 10 correct
	Comprehension II		"Why do we have houses?" "Why do we have books?"	2 correct
8	Vocabulary		"What is a _____ " or "What does _____ mean?" 1. Orange 2. Envelope 3. Straw 4. Puddle .. .. 16. Haste 17. Peculiarity 18. Priceless .. .. 44. Sudorific 45. Parterre	8 correct
	Memory for Stories	Card with story; child follows along as story is read.	"The Wet Fall" "Once there was a little girl named Betty. She lived on a farm with her brother Dick. One day their father gave them a Shetland pony. They had lots of fun with it. One day, when Dick was riding on it, the pony became frightened and ran away. Poor Dick fell into a ditch. How Betty laughed when she saw him! He was covered with mud from head to foot." 1. "What is the name of this story?" 2. "What was Betty's brother's name?"	5 correct

TABLE 7–3 *Continued*

Age Level	Item	Materials	Task	Criterion for Passing
			3. "Where did they live?"	
			4. "Who gave the pony to them?"	
			5. "What did the pony do?"	
			6. "What happened?"	
	Similarities and Differences		"In what way are _____ and _____ alike, and how are they different?"	3 correct
			1. Baseball and orange	
			2. Airplane and kite	
			3. Ocean and river	
			4. Penny and quarter	
	Comprehension IV	1. "What should you do if you found on the streets of a city a three-year-old baby that was lost from its parents?"		4 correct
		2. "What's the thing for you to do when you have broken something that belongs to someone else?"		
		3. "What's the thing for you to do when you are on your way to school and see that you are in danger of being late?"		
		4. "What makes a sailboat move?"		
		5. "What's the thing for you to do if another boy [or girl] hits you without meaning to do it?"		
		6. "What should you say when you are in a strange city and someone asks you how to find a certain address?"		

Note: The *Stanford-Binet Intelligence Scale* (pp. 76, 77, 78, 88, 89, 90, 91) is from Form L-M of the Stanford-Binet Copyright © 1973, and is reproduced with the permission of The Riverside Publishing Company, 8420 Bryn Mawr Avenue, Chicago, IL 60631.

TABLE 7-4 Types of Items Included on the Wechsler Intelligence Scale for Children (WISC)

Subtest	Verbal Scale
Information	How many wings does a bird have? How many nickels make a dime? What is pepper?
Arithmetic	Sam had three pieces of candy and Joe gave him four more. How many pieces of candy did Sam have altogether? If two apples cost $.15, what will be the cost of a dozen apples?
Vocabulary	What is a ————— ? or What does ————— mean? Hammer Protect Epidemic

Subtest	Performance Scale
Object Assembly	Put the pieces together to make a familiar object.

Note: Adapted from *Wechsler Intelligence Scale for Children—Revised* by D. Wechsler, 1974, New York: The Psychological Corporation. Copyright 1974 by the Psychological Corporation. Adapted by permission.

metic subtest of the WISC. Reasoning ability clearly enters into solution of many items—for example, the Comprehension items on the Stanford-Binet. So too does the subject's store of real-world factual knowledge, a store that is tapped most explicitly by the Information subtest of the WISC. In general, IQ tests for children are oriented to the kinds of skills that are needed for success in school—vocabulary, memory, arithmetic, problem solving. It is not surprising, therefore, that performance on such tests correlates with performance in school.

The Stanford-Binet and the WISC share other similarities as well. In both tests, a child's IQ is a function of how fast the child is developing in comparison to other children of the same age. The original formula for calculating Stanford-Binet IQs expressed this conception directly: Intelligence Quotient equals Mental Age (as determined by the age placement of the items that the subject passes) divided by Chronological Age times 100. For various reasons this formula is no longer used; instead, IQ is based on the deviation between the child's score and the average score for his or her age group. The logic, however, remains the same: Children who are developing faster than average have above-average IQs; children who are developing more slowly than average have below-average IQs. Childhood IQ is thus a measure of rate of development. It is also an inherently *relative* measure. There is no absolute metric for measuring a child's intelligence, as there is, for example, for measuring physical characteristics such as height or weight. Instead, IQ is always a matter of how the child compares to other children.

A final set of similarities between the Stanford-Binet and the WISC concerns the method of administration. There are two central emphases in the administration of any IQ test. One is the need for *standardization*. As was just stressed, IQ tests are relative measures, a child's IQ being a function of how his or her performance compares to that of other children. The only way that a score is interpretable is if the test is administered and scored in exactly the same way for all children. It is critical, therefore, that the tester know and follow the standardized instructions. The second emphasis is on the need to establish and maintain *rapport*. An IQ score is supposed to be a measure of the child's optimal performance, and this optimum can be achieved only if the child remains at ease and motivated to respond carefully. The best tester is the one who can successfully combine these two goals, maintaining the necessary standardization while at the same time using his or her clinical skills to elicit the best performance that the child can give.

The examples in Tables 7–3 and 7–4 give an idea of the nature of IQ tests during the preschool and school-aged years. Tables 7–5 and 7–6 round off the developmental picture by providing examples of tests from the other parts of the life span. Table 7–5 shows a sampling of items from the Bayley Scales of Infant Development (Bayley, 1969), a major test of development during infancy. It should come as no surprise to learn that infant tests are considerably less verbal and less academically oriented than are tests given during later childhood. Table 7–6 shows a sampling of the types of items that appear on the most advanced Wechsler test, the Wechsler Adult Intelligence Scale (Wechsler, 1981). This test is the source for much of the research on aging that we discuss in chapter 9.

Issues and Research Paradigms

Many of the issues that have always surrounded IQ tests have concerned their pragmatic uses—for example, tracking children in school based upon IQ scores. Our concentration here is on more theoretically oriented questions about the development of intelligence. Two such questions have provoked much re-

TABLE 7–5 Examples of Items from the Bayley Scales of Infant Development

Item Number	Age Placement (in months)	Ability Measured	Procedure	Credit
1	.1	Responds to sound of bell	Ring bell about 12 inches from child's ear.	Any definite response to the sound
14	1.0	Vertical eye coordination	Move red ring slowly back and forth in vertical plane before child.	If child's eyes follow the ring for several excursions
75	6.0	Looks for fallen spoon	Attract child's attention to a spoon and then drop spoon to floor.	If child definitely looks for the fallen spoon
102	12.0	Uncovers blue box	Place a toy in blue box and close lid. Open box and remove toy, then return toy to box and replace cover. Hand box to child and say, "Baby get the . . ."	If child is able to remove the cover at least twice
146	24.0	Names 3 objects	Show child ball, watch, pencil, scissors, and cup. Ask "What is this?"	If child names at least 3 objects

Note: From *Bayley Scales of Infant Development* (pp. 40, 43, 57, 63, 75) by N. Bayley, 1969, New York: The Psychological Corporation. Copyright 1969 by The Psychological Corporation. Reprinted by permission.

TABLE 7-6 Types of Items Included on the Wechsler Adult Intelligence Scale (WAIS)

Subtest	Verbal Scale
Information	What is steam made of?
	Who wrote "Tom Sawyer"?
Arithmetic	Three women divided 18 golf balls equally among themselves. How many golf balls did each person receive?
	If 10 men can build a house in 12 days, how long would it take 4 men to build the house?

Subtest	Performance Scale
Picture Completion	Indicate the missing part.

Note: Adapted from *Wechsler Adult Intelligence Scale—Revised* by D. Wechsler, 1981, New York: The Psychological Corporation. Copyright 1955, 1980 by The Psychological Corporation. Adapted by permission.

search and much controversy: the issue of the stability of IQ and the issue of the determinants of differences in IQ.

Our consideration of the stability issue can be brief, for most of the relevant points were made in chapter 3 in the discussion of longitudinal designs. Studying stability in fact requires a longitudinal approach, because our interest is in the relation between a child's performance early in life and that same child's performance later in life. The specific form of stability at issue is the stability of individual differences. Do children maintain their relative standing on IQ tests as they develop, those who are high remaining high and those who are low remaining low, or can changes occur? Typically, this question has been examined through correlations between first test and second; the higher the correlation, the greater the stability. Because IQ tests for children are designed to

yield the same mean IQ at each age, it is also possible to look at the constancy of the IQ value itself. IQ, after all, *is* relative standing, and thus constancy of relative standing implies constancy of IQ. We can ask, for example, whether a child with an IQ of 90 at age 4 will still have an IQ of 90 at age 6 or 10 or 20.

IQ has been a popular topic for longitudinal study for close to 60 years now. Such studies can and often do encounter all of the problems of longitudinal research that we discussed in chapter 3. Subjects who are both able and willing to be repeatedly tested may not be a representative sample of the population as a whole, a bias that limits the generalizability of the results. Drop-out in the course of the study may be selective, and, if so, the sample will become even more biased. Repeated administrations of the same test can result in practice effects, thus inflating later scores relative to early ones. And questions of measurement equivalence may arise if the study spans distinct age groups that require different IQ tests (e.g., infants and older children).

Several conclusions from the stability studies can be noted (Bayley, 1970; Jencks, 1972). Except for extremely low scores, performance on infant tests is not predictive of later IQ; correlations between infant scores and later scores typically hover around zero. Beyond infancy, scores do begin to correlate significantly from one age period to another; the stability, however, is far from perfect. In general, correlations—and thus similarity in IQ—are higher the closer together the ages being compared; they are also higher the older the child is at the time of initial testing. The latter statement is equivalent to saying that there is increased stability of IQ with increasing age.

The question of where differences in IQ come from has been hotly debated ever since the first IQ tests were developed. Part of the reason for the debate lies in the difficulty of getting clear evidence on the question. There are two possible sources for differences in IQ: the different genes with which people are born, or the different environments in which they grow up. It is easy enough to imagine a well-designed scientific study that would disentangle these two factors: All that need be done is to hold one factor constant while systematically varying the other. It is equally easy to see that such studies are impossible to do. The result is that we must fall back upon less satisfactory sorts of evidence. Two kinds of evidence have been prominent in the heredity-environment debate: studies of twins and studies of adopted children.

The twin studies capitalize on the fact that there are two kinds of twins. Monozygotic or identical twins come from the same egg and are thus genetically identical; dizygotic or fraternal twins come from different eggs and thus have only a 50% average genetic overlap—the same as ordinary siblings. We have, then, a naturally occurring experiment with variation in the genetic variable. If genes are important for IQ, identical twins should be more similar in IQ than are fraternal twins. And this, in fact, is the finding. Reported correlations in IQ for iden-

tical twin pairs are in the .80s; correlations for fraternal twin pairs are typically in the .50s or .60s (Herrnstein, 1973; Nichols, 1976).

There is an obvious criticism of this genetic interpretation of the twin data. Perhaps environments are on the average more similar for identical twins than for fraternal twins. Identical twins, after all, look and in some ways act more alike than fraternal twins, and they may elicit a more similar treatment from their environments. There is an obvious answer to this obvious criticism: Study identical twins who have been separated early in life and brought up in different environments. Such twins are not easy to come by—there are only a handful of such studies, and none has a very large sample size. Furthermore, no one separates twins for the purposes of scientific study; separations occur for a variety of reasons under a variety of circumstances, and this lack of control hampers clear interpretation. Nevertheless, the data from such studies appear strongly supportive of a genetic model. Reported correlations in IQ for identical twins reared apart average around .75—only slightly lower than those for nonseparated identical twins, and higher than those for fraternal twins brought up in the same home (Herrnstein, 1973).

Impressive though these results appear, there are a number of criticisms of the studies of identical twins reared apart. A basic criticism is that twins who are separated early in life constitute a small and quite possibly atypical sample, and we should be cautious about generalizing to human development in general from such a sample. To this general limitation Leon Kamin (1974) has added a number of specific criticisms of specific studies. In some cases the "separate" environments in which the twins are reared are in fact not very distinct; they may go to different branches of the same family, for example. In one study the IQ correlations are higher when members of a twin pair are tested by the same tester than when they are tested by different testers, a finding that suggests the operation of tester bias. And in some studies the IQ data come not from well-established tests like the Stanford-Binet or WISC but from little-known tests whose validity is doubtful and whose poor standardization ensures some correlation for purely artifactual reasons.[2] (See also Farber, 1981, for a further discussion of twins reared apart.)

Studies of adopted children constitute a larger literature than studies of twins. The starting point for such studies is the finding that parents and children typically correlate about .5 in IQ. Children tend, therefore, to resemble their parents; the problem is to figure out why. Each parent contributes 50% of the child's genes; thus there is a genetic basis for the correlation. But each parent also contributes a major part of the child's environment; thus there is also an environmental basis. Studies of adopted children offer the possibility of pulling apart these two contributors. What we can look at are two sets of correlations. One is the correlation between an adopted child's IQ and the IQs of the adoptive parents. In this case the environmental basis remains; the genetic contribution, however, is ruled out. The other is the correlation between an adopted child's IQ and the IQ of the biological mother (data on fathers are seldom available). In this case the environmental contribution (apart from the prenatal and perhaps early postbirth environment) is ruled out; the genetic basis, however, remains.

Two main findings emerge from the studies of adopted children (Scarr, 1977; Willerman, 1979). One is that the child's IQ correlates more highly with that of the biological mother (correlations of about .5) than with those of the adoptive parents (correlations in the range of .2 to .3). This is evidence in support of the importance of genetic factors. The second finding is that the mean IQ for samples of adopted children is typically about 20 points higher than the mean IQ for their biological mothers. Because correlation is a measure of relative standing, a mean difference of this sort can come about even though the two sets of scores are fairly highly correlated. Part of the mother-child difference can be attributed to regression to the mean, a phenomenon that also applies to cross-generation comparisons (i.e., parents with below-average IQs tend to have children whose IQs are higher than their own). Part of it, however, is almost certainly a reflection of the above-average nature of adoptive homes. Such homes tend to be privileged in various ways, and they apparently boost the IQs of children who grow up in them. Thus, the studies of adopted children provide evidence for both genetic and environmental effects.

It should be noted that the adopted child studies, like the twin studies, do have some limitations. The kinds of correlations described in the preceding paragraph are possible only if we have IQ scores for the various groups. In some studies some IQs have been unavailable and it has been necessary to estimate them from educational level, a dubious and potentially biasing procedure. Another concern is the possibility of selective placement—that is, the tendency of adoption agencies to do some matching of the adoptive home with characteristics of the biological parents. To the extent that such selective placement occurs, interpretation of the parent-child correlations becomes very difficult. Still another problem is the restricted range of variation among adoptive homes. As the preceding paragraph noted, such homes are not a random subset of the population of homes in general; rather they tend to be above average in various ways. This also means, however, that they tend to be fairly homogeneous, and such homogeneity is a problem in a correlational study. The lower the variation in a variable (in this case, characteristics of adoptive homes, including adoptive parents' IQs), the less likely it is that that variable will correlate significantly with other variables. This factor sets an important qualification on the low correlation between adopted child and adoptive parents.[3]

---

[2]Another quite serious criticism is specific to the work of Cyril Burt (e.g., 1966, 1972): Kamin presents evidence that Burt almost certainly fabricated part of his data. Others have reached the same conclusion (e.g., Wade, 1976).

---

[3]No attempt has been made to deal with a controversial offshoot of the genetics-environment debate: the issue of social class or racial differences in IQ (Loehlin, Lindzey, & Spuhler, 1975; Scarr, 1981). It is worth noting, however, that the methodological obstacles to gaining clear evidence are multiplied in the case of group differences, especially black-white differences in IQ. It is also worth noting that

THE INFORMATION-PROCESSING APPROACH

The Nature of the Approach

In part, both the Piagetian approach and the intelligence test approach can be characterized by the tasks that are used. If we want to convey quickly what Piaget studies, we can simply point to tasks such as object concept, conservation, and class inclusion. Similarly, to give an idea of what "IQ" means we can simply list the contents of a test such as the Stanford-Binet or WISC.

The information-processing approach is not so easily capsulized. "Information-processing" is not a single theory; rather, it is a general framework that encompasses a number of specific theories and programs of research. These programs of research, moreover, span a wide range of different abilities and corresponding experimental tasks. Piagetian concepts fall within the scope of some information-processing researchers; indeed, Piagetian tasks have been a popular focus for applications of information processing to children (e.g., Klahr & Wallace, 1976). The kinds of academic-verbal skills that are stressed in IQ tests have also been targets of information-processing research; reading (e.g., Wilkinson, 1980) and arithmetic (e.g., Woods, Resnick, & Groen, 1975) are two major examples. Finally, the memory tasks that are the subject of our next section have also been examined from an information-processing perspective; indeed, it could be argued that this perspective is the dominant one for the contemporary study of memory.

If pointing at tasks does not do the job, how *can* the information-processing approach be characterized? Researchers who classify themselves as information-processing psychologists tend to share a number of assumptions, both about how theories should be built and about how research should be carried out. Although

the latter set of assumptions concerns us most here, a brief consideration of theory is also relevant, for the methodological emphases that we discuss follow closely from the theoretical emphases.

The distinctive characteristics of information-processing theories can be conveyed either through verbal summary or through example. We will try both strategies here. The following passage from P. Miller (1983) captures themes that are found to some extent in every information-processing theory:

These investigators study the flow of information through the cognitive system. This flow begins with an *input*, usually a stimulus, into the human information-processing system. The flow ends with an *output*, which could be information stored in long-term memory, physical behavior, speech, or a decision. Between input and output, the information may be attended to, transformed into some type of mental representation, compared with information already in long-term memory, assigned meaning, used to formulate a response, and so on. These mental processes are similar in some ways to the workings of a computer as it takes information, performs certain operations on it, and stores it. More generally, both humans and computers manipulate symbols and transform input into output. (pp. 248–249)

Let us try some examples. Figures 7–3 and 7–4 provide schematic summaries of theories that everyone would agree fall under the heading of information processing. These particular theories are, of course, much more detailed and complicated than any graphic summary can convey. The figures do serve to give some idea of the flavor of such theorizing, however, and this general orientation is what is important here. The kind of "flow chart" approach illustrated in the figures is in fact quite typical of information-processing theories. Such charts express the central goal of the information-processing theorist: to specify all of the psychologically relevant processes that intervene between the presentation of some input to the cognitive system and the eventual output from the system.

Several emphases are embedded in the attempt to develop the kind of theory that is il-

---

the existence of a genetic contribution within a racial group (the apparent finding in the twin and adopted child studies) tells us nothing for certain about a genetic contribution to between-race differences.

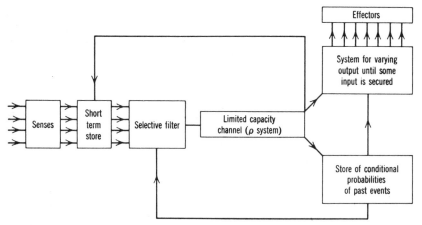

FIGURE 7–3. An example of an information-processing model of perception. From *Perception and Communication* (p. 299) by D. E. Broadbent, 1958, London: Pergamon Press. Copyright 1958 by Donald Broadbent. Reprinted by permission.

lustrated in the figures. One concerns the process-product distinction that was raised with regard to Piaget and IQ. The focus of the information-processing approach, even more than of the Piagetian approach, is on the *processes* rather than the products of cognitive activity. The final response, or "output," is often of relatively little interest; the question, rather, is *how* the subject arrives at this response. The goal of the theory is to explain all of the psychological processes that go into this how. The corresponding methodological goal, of course, is to devise procedures through which these processes can be studied.

We have twice referred to the attempt to capture "all" of the relevant psychological processes. This wording reflects another distingushing characteristic of the information-processing approach: the attempt to develop a relatively *complete* theory of cognition. Consider a Piagetian concept such as transitivity. The Piagetian explanation for transitivity stresses the underlying logical structure that makes correct response possible—specifically, a cognitive structure known as the logical addition of relations. An information-processing researcher would not necessarily deny that this logical structure is part of the basis for correct answers.

Such a researcher would insist, however, that the logical core is at best only part of what needs to be explained. How does the subject make the necessary perceptual discriminations among the stimuli? How is the information from the initial quantitative comparisons entered into memory? In what form is this information stored over time? How is it activated at the time of solution? All of these questions must be answered in a full model of transitive inference.

Information-processing theories are also relatively *specific*. The attempt is to spell out each step in the problem-solving process in as precise and unambiguous a fashion as possible. The implication, of course, is that other theories, including Piaget's, often fall short of the desired level of precision. The ultimate in specificity comes in the attempt, engaged in by some but not all information-processing researchers, to write computer programs that simulate the cognitive behaviors of interest. In a computer program every step in the solution to a problem must be spelled out exactly, for if the steps are not adequately specified, the program will not run. Even information-processing researchers who do not produce simulations themselves find the computer a useful metaphor for the kind of theory building that they are attempting.

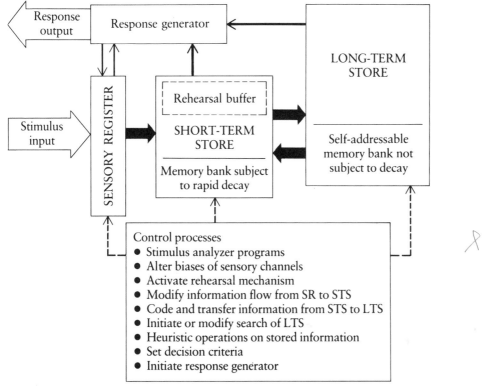

FIGURE 7–4. An example of an information-processing model of memory. From "Storage and Retrieval Processes in Long-Term Memory" by R. M. Shiffrin and R. C. Atkinson, 1969, *Psychological Review, 76*, p. 180. Copyright 1969 by the American Psychological Association. Reprinted by permission.

A final characteristic is that information-processing theories are relatively *testable*. This characteristic is closely related to the preceding one: If a theory is not specific, then clear empirical tests may be impossible. Information-processing theorists would argue that lack of sufficient precision has always hampered the attempt to get clear tests of Piaget's theory. An information-processing theory, in contrast, is designed to yield specific—and therefore *disconfirmable*—predictions. Again, the ultimate comes in a computer simulation. The attempt in a computer simulation is to write a program that can reproduce the problem-solving behavior of a human subject. A program that can generate the same behaviors as a human con-stitutes a theory of the rules and processes that the human uses. Running the program is then a test of the theory, and failure of the program to simulate the behavior is a clear disconfirmation of the theory.

Specific Methods

We turn next to some of the specific methods of study used by information processing researchers. Three methods have been especially important: computer simulation, rule assessment, and response time.

The rationale for the *computer simulation* approach was introduced in the preceding section. The goal of a simulation is to generate some segment of behavior in the same way that the human does. The phrase "in the same way" deserves comment. Clearly, the correspondence between human and computer is only partial; computer hardware, for example, is quite different from human physiology. The correspondence is thus at the "software" level—a match in terms of processes and rules and not physical mechanisms. It is important to add, however, that the whole point of the approach is that there *is* correspondence at the level of process. Computers can be programmed to perform a variety of intelligent behaviors in ways different from, and often more powerful than, humans; mathematical calculations are a familiar example. A program that performs a thousand calculations per second, however, is not a simulation of human mathematical abilities. It is important to distinguish such "artificial intelligence" endeavors from the simulations that are of interest here.

How does a researcher go about creating a simulation? A first step is to obtain *protocols* of the behaviors of interest. A protocol is essentially as complete a record as possible of the processes that the subject engages in while carrying out some task. Such protocols may include verbalizations; a common technique, in fact, is to ask subjects to say aloud what they are thinking as they work on a problem. The point of the saying-aloud technique is to translate processes that are normally covert into an at least somewhat observable form. The protocol may also include nonverbal behavior; indeed, with young children the protocol may *have* to be primarily nonverbal. The example that we will see shortly relies on nonverbal behaviors.

Once an initial protocol has been generated there is typically a back-and-forth movement between protocol and program. Shortcomings in the data base may become evident when an attempt is made to write a program based upon the protocol, and if so further data will have to be collected. Even if a program *can* be written that reproduces the original data, this initial simulation is just the starting point. Can the program not only reproduce the original behavior but also predict how the child will per-

form on other, related tasks? Can the program predict how *other* children will perform on the same task? To the extent that individual or developmental differences exist, can programs be written that account for them? All of these questions require the collection of further protocols, from which modified or new programs can be constructed. The existence of a program, in turn, may suggest new issues or hypotheses and thus lead to further experimental work.

It is time for an example. Ideally, what we would like is a brief and simple example that clearly illustrates the virtues of the simulation approach. Unfortunately, there *are* no brief and simple examples of computer simulations. Simply mastering the language in which a simulation is written can be a very time-consuming process. Simulations of even simple behaviors may require lengthy and complex programs. At the extreme, Newell and Simon (1972) took over 200 pages to model the behaviors of one subject solving a single crytarithmetic problem!

What we will settle for is a *relatively* simple example. Baylor, Gascon, Lemoyne, and Pothier (1973) applied the computer simulation approach to the Piagetian concept of seriation of weight. The issue in seriation of weight is whether the child can systematically and successfully order identical-looking objects in terms of weight. Baylor et al. used seven identical-looking blocks that varied in weight from 100.2 to 106.5 grams, differences too small to be detected by feel alone. They also used a 2-pan balance scale that permitted a determination of the relative weights of any pair of blocks. The child was allowed to carry out as many pairwise weighings as he or she wished in an attempt to discover the overall order of weights. Each child was filmed while performing the task, and the protocol was derived from this filmed record.

Table 7–7 shows the protocol for 6-year-old Nathalie. (Actually, what the figure shows is Kail and Bisanz's, 1982, simplification of the original Baylor et al. protocol.) Note that Nathalie's approach to the task is quite systematic. What she does at each step is to weigh the two rightmost blocks in the unordered array and then place them, one at a time, in their correct

TABLE 7-7 Nathalie's Solution of the Baylor et al. Seriation of Weight Task

	Unordered Array	Balance	Weighing	Ordered Array
Initial position	3 6 4 1 7 2 5			
Step 1	3 6 4 1 7	2 5	5 > 2	
Step 2	3 6 4 1 7	2		5
Step 3	3 6 4 1 7			5 2
Step 4	3 6 4	1 7	7 > 1	5 2
Step 5	3 6 4	1		5 2 7
Step 6	3 6 4			5 2 7 1
Step 7	3	6 4	6 > 4	5 2 7 1
Step 8	3	4		5 2 7 1 6
Step 9	3			5 2 7 1 6 4
Step 10				5 2 7 1 6 4 3

Note: From "Cognitive Development: An Information-Processing Perspective" (p. 232) by R. Kail and J. Bisanz, 1982. In R. Vasta (Ed.), *Strategies and Techniques of Child Study,* New York: Academic Press. Copyright 1982 by Academic Press, Inc. Reprinted by permission. Kail and Bisanz's table is adapted from Baylor et al. (1973).

relative positions in the final array. Unfortunately, this is *all* that she does. Nathalie makes no attempt to carry out any of the additional weighings (e.g., block 5 with block 7) that would be necessary to determine the complete ordering. The result is that she ends up with what Baylor et al. label "juxtaposition of uncoordinated couples"—that is, groups of independent pairs, rather than an ordered series. This sort of pattern is in fact a typical preoperational response to the seriation task.

The kind of computer program that Baylor et al. use to simulate seriation is called a "production system." Table 7-8 shows its application to Nathalie. A production system consists of a set of rules—four rules in Nathalie's case. Each rule has a left side and a right side. The left side gives the conditions that must obtain if

the rule is to be applied. In the case of rule 1, for example, the conditions are that there must be more than one block in the initial position and no blocks on the scale. The right side gives the actions to be applied when the conditions are met. For rule 1 the action is to move the two rightmost blocks from the initial position to the scale. This action in turn creates the condition for rule 2, which is that there be two blocks on the scale. The rule 2 actions are then to weigh the two blocks, followed by moves of the heavier block and then the lighter block to the final position. These actions in turn create the conditions for either rule 1 (if at least two blocks are left in the initial position), rule 3 (if one block is left), or rule 4 (if no blocks are left). When rule 4 is reached, the program terminates.

TABLE 7-8 Production System for Nathalie

Rule	Conditions[a]	Actions[a]
P1	<PO> 1> • <PB = O>	MOVE (block • block, PO (end position • next end position); PB)
P2	<PB = 2>	WEIGH (block • block) (= = > heavier block; lighter block); MOVE (heavier block, PB; PF (right end)); MOVE (lighter block, PB; PF (right end))
P3	<PO = 1> • <PB = 0>	MOVE (block, PO; PF (right end))
P4	<PO = 0>	STOP

Note: From "An Information Processing Model of Some Seriation Tasks" by G. W. Baylor, J. Gascon, G. Lemoyne, and N. Pothier, 1973, *The Canadian Psychologist, 14,* p. 173. Copyright 1973 by the Canadian Psychological Association. Reprinted by permission.

[a]PO refers to the unordered array; PB refers to the balance; PF refers to the final ordered array.

The program in Table 7–8 provides a perfect simulation of Nathalie's approach to seriation. As noted before, however, such an achievement is just the starting point. If a simulation is to be informative it must have some generality beyond the data from which it was derived in the first place. Suppose, for example, that we vary the task, perhaps by using eight blocks instead of seven, or by presenting an additional block once the child has completed a seven-block series. The computer program will generate a response to these variations, and we can then see whether Nathalie responds in the same way. Any discrepancies between computer and child would indicate a need to modify the program. We can also test other children to determine whether Nathalie's response pattern is at all general. Once individual or developmental differences are found, we can write new programs that attempt to explain these differences. Baylor et al., for example, were able to construct more complicated production systems to account for the seriation behavior of more advanced subjects. (One of these systems, designed for an intermediate-level child, contains nine rules and requires two full pages to present!)

The virtues of the computer simulation approach are the general virtues of information-processing research noted earlier. In particular, the attempt to produce simulations ensures a very high level of specificity and testability. There are also some limitations of the approach, at least as it has been developed to date. One concerns the goal of completeness. Computer simulations tend to be mixed with regard to the criterion of completeness. Such theories are quite complete for the segment of behavior being modeled, often, however, at the expense of other parts of the problem-solving process. Baylor et al., for example, made no attempt to simulate either the child's perception of the blocks or the motoric responses through which the blocks were moved. According to Siegler (1983), this neglect of the perceptual and motoric aspects of cognitive behavior is a general one in computer simulations to date.

Consider next the goal of specificity. The high level of specificity in simulations is an undeniable virtue. In practice, however, achieving this level has meant a serious restriction in another important dimension: breadth of application. Researchers who produce simulations have tended to concentrate their efforts on fairly narrow domains of behavior. In Kail and Bisanz's (1982) words, "the result of this policy is that a number of highly precise 'minitheories' are generated that account for a small and specifically defined set of behaviors, but little effort is made to integrate these theories" (p. 238). It is probably true, as Kail and Bisanz go on to argue, that this narrowness of scope is a characteristic of particular research programs and not intrinsic to the information-processing approach per se. Nevertheless, it *is* a characteristic of research to date.

A final issue concerns the verification of theory. As noted earlier, failure of a program to simulate the target behavior is a clear indication that something is wrong with the theory. *Success* of a simulation, however, is not proof that the theory is correct. It is not proof because there are always multiple models that are sufficient to generate any string of behaviors. It is quite possible, therefore, that the child generates the behaviors through one set of processes and the computer generates the same behaviors through a quite different set of processes. Information-processing researchers are, of course, aware of this point; indeed, it is a frequent topic in their writings. Simon (1972) has suggested a number of criteria that could help to pare the number of sufficient theories down to those that are most plausible as models of human behavior. Among these criteria are consistency with what is known about the physiology of the nervous system and consistency with what is known about behavior in other situations.

The second methodology that we consider is labeled the *rule assessment* approach. Like a computer simulation, the rule assessment approach begins with a careful "task analysis" of the cognitive domain of interest. This analysis is intended to identify the various aspects or steps in the task and to suggest the psychological processes that might be involved in solution. In the case of rule assessment the analysis leads to the postulation of various "rules" through which the task might be solved. These rules typically differ in complexity, and they lead to different predictions about the pattern of successes and failures that a subject might show across various versions of the task. Subjects are in fact tested on these different versions, and the actual patterns of response are compared with the predicted ones. A good fit between predicted and actual would be evidence for the psychological reality of the hypothesized rules.

The best-known application of the rule assessment approach is Robert Siegler's balance-scale task (Siegler, 1978). The apparatus for this task consists of a simple balance with eight pegs, four on each side of the fulcrum, on which weights can be placed. The child's task is to predict, for various configurations of weight, whether the balance will remain even or go down on one or the other side.

Siegler hypothesized that children's knowledge of the balance could be expressed in terms of one of four developmentally ordered rules.

At the simplest level of Rule 1, the child judges solely in terms of the number of weights on each side, ignoring distance from the fulcrum. The child using Rule 2 also judges solely in terms of weight if the weights on the two sides are different; if the weights are equal, however, the Rule 2 child can also take into account the distance from the fulcrum. With Rule 3 the child begins to consider both weight and distance in every case and is correct whenever one or both are equal; if the two are in conflict, however (i.e., greater weight on one side and greater distance on the other), then the child is confused and has no certain basis for response. Finally, the Rule 4 child has mastered the weight times distance rule and can thus handle any version of the task.

Siegler devised six balance-scale problems through which to probe these hypothesized rules. These problems are shown in Table 7–9. Also shown are the predicted response patterns for subjects using any of the four rules. Note

TABLE 7–9 Types of Problems and Predicted Responses on the Siegler Balance-Scale Task

PROBLEM TYPE	RULE			
	I	II	III	IV
Balance	100	100	100	100
Weight	100	100	100	100
Distance	0 (Should say "Balance")	100	100	100
Conflict-Weight	100	100	33 (Chance Responding)	100
Conflict-Distance	0 (Should say "Right Down")	0 (Should say "Right Down")	33 (Chance Responding)	100
Conflict-Balance	0 (Should say "Right Down")	0 (Should say "Right Down")	33 (Chance Responding)	100

Note: From "The Origins of Scientific Reasoning" (p. 115) by R. S. Siegler. In R. S. Siegler (Ed.), *Children's Thinking: What Develops?* (pp. 109–149), 1978, Hillsdale, NJ: Lawrence Erlbaum Associates. Copyright 1978 by Lawrence Erlbaum Associates. Reprinted by permission.

that one interesting aspect of this approach is that performance is not invariably better with more advanced rules; in some situations, for example, Rule 1 leads to better performance than Rule 3.

Siegler tested his model by administering the six problem types to subjects ranging in age from 5 to 17. Each subject received 30 problems equally distributed across the six types. Two main findings emerged. One was that the hypothesized rules did in fact characterize the performance of the great majority of subjects. Using a criterion of fit between performance and rule on at least 26 of the 30 trials, Siegler found that 89% of the subjects showed consistent use of one of the four rules. The second finding concerned developmental changes. As expected, 5-year-olds were most likely to use Rule 1; by age 17 rules 3 and 4 were much more common. As also expected, these developmental changes in rule usage resulted in occasional decrements in correct performance with increased age. On conflict-weight problems, for example, the percentage of correct answers declined from 93% at age 5 to 46% at age 17 (which reflects the fact that even at 17 Rule 3 was more common than Rule 4).

Some obvious similarities exist between the rule assessment approach and the computer simulation approach. Both involve the postulation of rules that lead to precise predictions about performance on particular tasks. Both involve a continuous process of testing and revising in the back-and-forth movement between hypothesized rules and actual performance. Both provide an excellent framework for characterizing and explaining individual and developmental differences in cognitive abilities. And both embody to the extreme the virtues of specificity and testability that are so important to information-processing researchers.

The rule assessment approach is also subject to some of the same criticisms as computer simulations. Again, the fact that a rule system can mimic human behavior does not guarantee that the rules are the ones actually used by humans. It is possible (perhaps especially with more complex tasks than the balance) that the same overt pattern of results might be generated in

two at least somewhat different ways. The issue of specificity versus generality also arises again. The rule assessment approach provides a very specific account of how the balance-scale problem is solved. But do the rules identified for this task have any relation to how the child performs on other tasks? Is the rule assessment approach itself applicable to tasks that do not fit the neat two-variable, additive-factors format of the balance? It should be noted with regard to these questions that Siegler (1981) has provided evidence both for the applicability of the general approach and for some generality of particular rules across 10 different cognitive tasks. He has also argued that the approach should be adaptable to a number of tasks and formats in addition to those that have been examined so far (see also Kail and Bisanz, 1982, and Strauss and Levin, 1981).

The final approach that we consider, measuring *response time*, is based upon a simple assumption: Cognitive processes take time. A further assumption is that the times required, although perhaps very brief, are measurable. It follows that we may be able to learn something about underlying processes by measuring the time required to perform a task. A solution based upon three component processes should take longer than one based upon two. Adding steps to a problem should result in regular increments in the time necessary for solution. Again, precise and testable predictions can be drawn, in this case predictions having to do with time.

The example that we use comes from work by Trabasso and his associates on the Piagetian concept of transitivity of length (e.g., Trabasso, 1975; Trabasso, Riley, & Wilson, 1975). Recall that transitivity involves reasoning of the form A greater than B plus B greater than C implies A greater than C. Normally, transitivity has been studied with exactly this kind of format— that is, three sticks that differ in length, with two of the possible pairwise comparisons presented as premises and the third left to be inferred. One of Trabasso et al.'s innovations was to work not with three but with *six* sticks. As we see shortly, this change permitted a number of interesting analyses that are not possible with

TABLE 7–10 Examples of Mnemonic Strategies

General Strategy	Experimental Task	Subject's Procedure
Verbal rehearsal	Ten pictures of familiar but unrelated objects are presented one at a time and then removed. The child's task is to recall as many of the pictures as possible.	Single-item rehearsal: Label each picture repeatedly as it is presented—e.g., "apple, apple, apple, flag, flag, flag . . . ." Cumulative rehearsal: Label each picture as it is presented and then rehearse all of the labels to that point—e.g., "apple, apple-flag, apple-flag-moon . . . ."
Elaboration	Twenty pairs of familiar but unrelated words are presented (e.g., "cow-tie," "car-tree"). Subsequently one member of each pair is presented; the child's task is to recall the other member of the pair.	Pictorial elaboration: Create a mental image that relates the members of a pair in some way—e.g., picture to oneself a cow wearing a tie, a car driving up a tree . . . . Verbal elaboration: Create a sentence or phrase that relates the members of a pair in some way—e.g., "the cow wore a tie," "the car drove up the tree . . . ."
Organization	Twenty pictures of familiar objects are presented, drawn from four conceptual categories: animals, vehicles, clothing, furniture. The pictures are not grouped by category during presentation. The child's task is to recall as many of the pictures as possible.	Clustering: Organize the pictures in terms of the four categories and recall members from the same category together—e.g., "dog, horse, camel, bear, squirrel, car, truck, plane . . . ."

rehearse the items during the delay period, whereas the younger children do not. Such an inference becomes more certain if we can identify developmental changes not only in the level but in the *pattern* of performance. For example, a classic finding from the adult memory literature concerns the so-called "primacy effect": the tendency for the first items in a stimulus list to be remembered better than later items. This effect is typically attributed to verbal rehearsal of the early items. When comparable studies are done developmentally the finding is that older children show the primacy effect; younger children, however, usually do not (e.g., Cole, Frankel, & Sharp, 1971). Such a pattern is consistent with the hypothesis of a developmental increase in verbal rehearsal.

A second general approach is to *induce* the use of the strategy. In this case we do not guess at the presence of the strategy; rather we instruct subjects in its use and then observe the effects. We might, for example, tell half of our subjects to rehearse the items during the delay period, but give no such instructions to the other, control half. Several findings emerge from studies of induced strategy use. A basic finding is that such instruction is beneficial; subjects who are helped to use a strategy generally perform better than subjects who are not. Note that we have here the kind of convergence of evidence that was discussed in chapter 5: Studies of inferred strategy use suggest that some helpful mnemonic strategy is being used; studies of induced strategy use confirm that the strategy is in fact helpful. A second finding concerns type of strategy. It is possible in such studies to move beyond a simple strategy versus no strategy comparison to examine the effects of different sorts of strategy. Ferguson and Bray (1976), for example, showed that cumulative rehearsal (saying the names of all of the items that had been presented) was more effective than noncumulative rehearsal (saying over and over again the name of the most recently presented item). Finally, a common finding in such research is that experimental condition interacts with age of subject, induced strategies being helpful for younger subjects but having little or no effect for older subjects (e.g., Hagen & Kingsley, 1968). This finding is compatible with the hypothesis that older children, but not younger, are already spontaneously producing strategies themselves. We can see again the value of age by condition interactions.

A study by Ornstein, Naus, and Liberty (1975) provides an interesting extension of the research just discussed. These investigators instructed their subjects (third through ninth graders) to rehearse aloud when each item on the stimulus list was presented. In contrast to the studies of the preceding paragraph, however, subjects were not told *how* to rehearse. It was possible, therefore, to look for naturally occurring (as opposed to experimentally induced) differences in type of rehearsal. In fact such differences did occur, and they showed a sensible pattern: Older children used more complex forms of rehearsal than younger children (e.g., cumulative rather than single-item rehearsal), and memory performance was related to complexity and appropriateness of strategy. This study is just one example of a general and important conclusion from the strategy literature: Developmental changes occur not only in the tendency to use strategies but also in the complexity of the strategies that are available and the ability to match strategy to task demands.

Although the studies that we have been discussing are informative, they do have their limitations. Studies that infer strategy use have the obvious limitation that the use *is* inferred; we do not know for certain what the subject is doing. Studies that induce strategy use avoid this problem but run into another: Because we have forced the subjects to use a strategy, we do not know what they would have done on their own.

A breakthrough in the study of children's memory occurred in the 1960s with the discovery of experimental situations in which children would spontaneously produce strategies that were at least somewhat overt, and therefore measurable. This discovery made it possible to combine the best elements of the other two approaches: to study strategies that were both spontaneous and observable. John Flavell was a pioneering researcher in this area, and we will consequently use two of his studies as examples.

Flavell, Beach, and Chinsky (1966) presented pictures of seven common objects to kindergarten, second-, and fifth-grade children. On each trial the experimenter pointed in a particular order to a subset of the pictures; the child's task was to recall the designated pictures in the correct order. A delay of 15 seconds intervened between pointing and recall test. The child wore a toy space helmet throughout the study, and during the delay period the visor of the helmet was pulled down, thus ensuring that the child could not see the pictures. The visor had a second purpose as well: It allowed one of the experimenters to stare at the child's mouth during the delay. This experimenter's job was to record any verbalizations by the subject, both overt verbalizations and semiovert ones (the experimenter had been trained to lipread prior to the study). Of particular interest, of course, were instances of apparent rehearsal. Subjects did rehearse, but the probability of rehearsal was strongly tied to age: 17 of 20 fifth-graders showed detectable rehearsal, whereas only 2 of 20 kindergarteners did. A subsequent study with a similar procedure (Keeney, Cannizzo, & Flavell, 1967) demonstrated that individual differences in rehearsal within an age group (first grade) correlated with recall performance—that is, children who spontaneously rehearsed showed better recall than children who did not.

Our second example is of a strategy other than rehearsal. Moely, Olson, Hawles, and Flavell (1969), like Flavell et al. (1966), used pictures of familiar objects as their stimuli. In this case, however, the pictures were drawn from four categories: animals, vehicles, furniture, and clothing. Such "clusterable" items are commonly used to study the mnemonic strategy of organization. The question is whether the subject organizes by categories during recall (e.g., names all of the animals together), even though the stimuli were not grouped by category in the original presentation. Moely et al. included this standard measure but also went beyond it to measure clustering in a more direct and literal fashion. The pictures were originally arranged in a circle on the table, and during the delay period the child was allowed to move them around in any way that he or she liked. It was possible,

infant can show dishabituation to a new stimulus is if he or she remembers the original stimulus and realizes that the new stimulus is in some way different.

Memory is not an intrinsic part of the preference method, but it can easily be built into the procedure. All that need be done is to make familiarity the critical dimension along which the two stimuli differ. Suppose, for example, that we run a series of trials on which one of the two stimuli is always a triangle; the other stimulus, however, changes from trial to trial. The question is whether, over trials, the infant begins to look longer at the relatively novel or the relatively familiar stimulus. Infants older than about 2 months in fact show a preference for novelty; infants younger than 2 months may prefer familiarity (e.g., Weizmann, Cohen, & Pratt, 1971; Wetherford & Cohen, 1973). The point for now is that either kind of preference— for the novel or for the familiar—implies the operation of memory.

We noted in chapter 6 that habituation and dishabituation can be demonstrated in the newborn. We know, then, that some memory capacity is present from birth. The natural next questions are how strong this capacity is and what kinds of developmental changes it undergoes.

One obvious dimension about which we can ask concerns the duration of the memory. In most habituation studies the interval between one stimulus and the next is quite brief, perhaps a matter of a few seconds. In most studies with the preference method intertrial intervals are similarly brief. What these studies demonstrate, therefore, is very short-term memory. Can babies remember things across longer time periods?

In a sense, this question is easy to study: All we need do is increase the time between initial exposure and test for memory. In another sense, such research can be very difficult to do, because the general problems of infant research that were discussed in chapter 6 may be present in acute form (e.g., controlling the baby's state across an extended period or inducing the mother to bring the baby in on two or three different occasions). Despite these obstacles, a number of studies of long-term memory in infants do exist, and they provide impressive testimony to babies' abilities. Fagan (1973), for example, using a variant of the preference method, showed that 5-month-old infants could recognize a photograph of a human face 2 weeks after an initial 2-minute presentation. Other researchers have shown that 6-week-olds can remember stimuli across at least 24 hours (Weizmann et al., 1971).

In addition to duration, another important question concerns the specific information that the infant retains. If the infant does distinguish between familiar and novel, then we know that *something* is being remembered. But what exactly is this something? The entire stimulus in all its detail? Or perhaps just one or a few salient aspects, such as the color or outer configuration?

The way to answer this question is through systematic variation of the test stimuli. If we can present stimuli that vary along all of the potentially important dimensions—color, configuration, and so forth—then we should be able to determine what information is retained and what information is lost. An experiment by Strauss and Cohen (1980) provides a good example. These researchers habituated their 5-month-old subjects to a 3-dimensional Styrofoam figure and then tested for recognition immediately, after a 10-minute delay, and after a 24-hour delay. Five test stimuli were used: the original figure and figures that differed in shape, color, size, or orientation. On the immediate test infants demonstrated recognition on all four dimensions—that is, they attended more to any of the changed stimuli than to the original stimulus. This finding tells us that the information about the different stimulus dimensions *was* processed; thus any decrements on the later tests can be attributed to memory rather than to initial attention. There were in fact decrements. On the 10-minute test only the color and form were still recognized, and on the 24-hour test only the form was still retained. This study thus demonstrates an interaction between the two variables that we have been considering: the length of the delay period and the nature of the stimulus information.

The kind of memory that is demonstrated in all of the examples that we have discussed is what is called *recognition memory*. Psychology's definition of "recognition" is the same as the everyday, dictionary definition: realizing that something new is the same as something encountered before. An infant who habituates is thus showing recognition, as is an infant who responds to the familiarity of his or her mother's face. Recognition can be contrasted with another basic form of memory: *recall memory*. Recall refers to the active retrieval of some memory material that is not immediately present. A child who relates what happened at his or her birthday party of a week before is demonstrating recall; so too is a child who draws a picture of the party.

Little is known about recall in infancy, beyond a general consensus that such memory is probably absent at birth and is certainly present by the end of infancy. Recall is difficult to study in infants, for the methods that are used with older children, such as verbal reports or drawings, are unavailable with babies. There is, in fact, no clear agreement on just what it is that a young infant might do that would unequivocally indicate recall. It is for this reason that our focus in this section has been on the much more often studied topic of recognition memory. (See Sophian, 1980, for a critique of the dependence on habituation paradigms in the study of infant memory, as well as Ashmead and Perlmutter, 1980, and DeLoache, 1980, for some interesting work on what may be early forms of recall.)

As soon as we move to older children, studies of recall become much more common than studies of recognition. It has been clear for a long time that older children, on the average, recall things better than younger children. The question is why they do. We turn next to two kinds of study that have attempted to explain the developmental improvement in recall across the childhood years.

Mnemonic Strategies

The basic idea behind the study of strategies is that developmental improvements in recall do not result solely—or perhaps at all—from a simple quantitative expansion in the size of the memory "store." The improvements, rather, reflect the greater tendency of older children to *do* something—to utilize some mnemonic strategy—to help themselves remember. Such strategies may come at the time of initial exposure to the material, or during the delay period between exposure and memory test, or at the point of attempting to retrieve the material. They may take a variety of forms: some verbal, some nonverbal, some simple, some very complex. Their common property is that they do, at least usually, facilitate memory.

Let us briefly consider what mnemonic strategies look like, before moving on to the question of how to study them. Table 7–10 shows examples of three general classes of mnemonic strategies. The strategies in the table are by no means the only ones that children might use; they are, however, among the ones that have received the most research attention.

How can strategies be studied? Some strategies are by their nature overt and thus relatively easy to study. Note taking, for example, is a common and easily observable mnemonic strategy. So is asking one's parents for help in remembering something. Perhaps because such external strategies seem so obvious, however, they have not received much attention from developmental psychologists. The interest, rather, has been in more internal, in-the-head strategies such as those in the table—in the kinds of strategies that are necessary precisely when external aids like notes or parents are *not* available. And here, clearly, we run into a measurement problem. How can an in-the-head strategy be measured?

One possibility is to *infer* the use of a strategy from the subject's overt memory performance. Suppose, for example, that we have a memory task that is heavily verbal, we study verbally mature older children and verbally immature younger children, and we find that the older children perform better. A reasonable (although of course not certain) inference is that the older children perform better because they are using their verbal skills to help themselves remember. Perhaps, for example, they verbally

the standard format. The sticks differed in both length and color; for ease of communication, the colors have been replaced in Figure 7-5 by letters. During the initial phase the child was carefully trained on each of the adjacent comparisons—A longer than B, B longer than C, and so forth. During the final test phase, however, the child was asked not only about the trained pairs but about *all* of the possible pairwise comparisons.

Let us focus on two comparisons: B versus D and B versus E. Because neither of these pairs had been presented during training, consistently correct responding on the test trials must reflect some capacity for logical inference—that is, some ability to make use of the information that *was* presented (B versus C, C versus D, etc.) to draw the necessary conclusions. One finding from the Trabasso research was that quite young children—6-year olds in Trabasso et al. (1975), 4-year-olds in an earlier study by Bryant and Trabasso (1971)—were capable of above-chance performance on such inferential trials. We have, then, another instance in which Piaget (who places transitivity of length at about 7 or 8 years) seems to underestimate young children's ability. In Bryant and Trabasso's analysis, children may fail the standard Piagetian task because of difficulty in remembering the premises, a difficulty that is removed by the extensive training in the first phase of their procedure. We can see here a characteristic that is

quite typical of information-processing theories: an emphasis on the importance of memory in problem solving.

The second finding from Trabasso et al.'s research concerned response time. By having the child push a window to signal his or her response, Trabasso et al. were able to measure the time between the experimenter's question about relative length and the child's choice of a stick. Consider again the B-D and B-E comparisons. In some theories of transitive inference—including, presumably, Piaget's—the child arrives at the correct answer by logically adding together the premises at the time of solution. According to such theories, solving B versus E should take longer than solving B versus D, since the former involves three premises (B > C, C > D, and D > E) whereas the latter involves only two (B > C and C > D). In fact, Trabasso et al. found that the B versus E comparison was solved faster than B versus D. In general, the further apart two sticks were in the array, the more rapid was the subject's judgment of relative length. This meant, for example, that B versus E was solved more rapidly than B versus C, even though the latter pair had been presented together during training and the former pair had not.

The relation between magnitude of difference and speed of response has been labeled the "distance effect." Trabasso (1975) discusses various models that have been proposed to account for this effect. The core element in the model preferred by Trabasso is the notion that the child does not add together premises at the time of solution; rather he or she integrates the information at the time of training. This integration results in an internal representation of the overall array, a mental picture of the A through E ordering. Once this representation of a linear order has been constructed, the child can solve any problem by simply reading off the relative size of the two sticks from the array. This reading off is easier for distant pairs than for close pairs—hence, the distance effect.

The preceding is, of course, a very sketchy summary of Trabasso's theory. For our purposes the methodological implications of response time are more important than the

FIGURE 7-5. Stimuli for the Trabasso transitivity research.

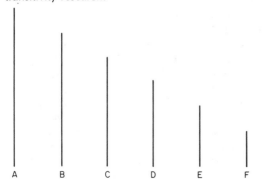

A　B　C　D　E　F

particular theory. In Trabasso et al.'s research it was possible to set up a clear contrast between two models of transitivity: one based on addition of premises and one based on construction of a linear order. These models led to different predictions about speed of response, and the reaction time data then provided a basis for choosing one model over the other. The strategy utilized in this research is typical of the use of response time in information-processing studies: infer underlying process from the time required to produce various overt behaviors. Other examples of this strategy—including applications to non-Piagetian tasks—can be found in Kail and Bisanz (1982) and Siegler (1983).

As with all methods, the use of response time has some limitations. There are definite limits on applicability: Not all theories can be contrasted in terms of predictions about time, and not all situations or behaviors lend themselves to the precise control and measurement that are necessary to record response time. Even when measurement *is* possible, the accuracy of the recordings can be an issue. The times of interest in such studies are often very brief—perhaps a difference of 100 or 200 milliseconds between one experimental condition and another. It is critical, therefore, that accurate and reliable measures be obtained for each child. To this end, various techniques are common in response time studies. Subjects may receive extensive training at the outset of the session, the goal being to stabilize response times prior to the critical test trials. Within-subject designs are often preferred to between-subject designs because of the reduction in error variance that the within-subject approach affords (see chapter 3). Large numbers of trials may be run in an attempt to cancel out the errors of measurement that will occur on any one trial. All of these techniques, though desirable with regard to accuracy, may create unwanted practice, fatigue, or carryover effects. The general concern is that the constraints necessary for measuring response time—both those just noted and others (e.g., use of a motoric response rather than a verbal response)—may result in a style of responding that is different from that in the more normal situations to which we hope to generalize (see Pachella, 1974, and Kail and Bisanz, 1982, for further discussion).

MEMORY

There is an obvious difference between this section and the first three sections of the chapter. Here the focus is not on a general approach to research; rather it is on a specific content domain. The content domain, moreover, is one that is found within each of the approaches that we have considered: Piaget studies memory (Piaget & Inhelder, 1973); memory tasks are prominent in IQ tests; and memory has long been a favorite topic for information-processing psychologists. There is, then, a certain organizational inconsistency in singling out memory as a subject in itself. Nevertheless, memory is such an important—and much-studied—topic that some consideration of paradigms for studying memory is justified.

Memory in Infancy

Memory was not one of the topics in chapter 6's discussion of research on infancy. Nevertheless, many of the procedures that we considered then, whatever their primary focus, necessarily tell us something about infant memory as well. Piaget's work, for example, shows infants remembering things and acting accordingly from very early in life. Similarly, many phenomena in the development of attachment, such as the infant's preference for mother over stranger, clearly imply the operation of memory.

The main procedures for the explicit study of infant memory have come from two other approaches discussed in chapter 6: the habituation-dishabituation paradigm and the Fantz preference method. Memory is an intrinsic part of the habituation-dishabituation procedure. The only way that an infant can habituate to a stimulus is if he or she can store information about the stimulus over time and recognize it as familiar when it is encountered again. If there were no memory for past events there could be no habituation. Similarly, the only way that an

plain the developmental improvement in recall across the childhood years. Two approaches to this issue are discussed. Research on *strategies* attempts to measure the existence and effects of various mnemonic strategies that can be used to aid recall. In some cases it is possible to observe the spontaneous occurrence of the strategy; in other cases it may be necessary either to infer the use of the strategy from overt memory performance or to induce its use experimentally. Research on *constructive memory* examines the effects of the general knowledge system, and of developmental changes in this system, upon memory. Two examples of studies of constructive memory are discussed, one involving memory for sentences and one involving memory for stories.

chapter 8

SOCIAL DEVELOPMENT

Like chapter 7, this chapter concentrates on development during the postinfancy childhood years. Our interest now is in the child's social development, a topic at least as large and as methodologically challenging as the topic of how cognition develops. Our coverage is again selective, the goal being to consider a few important subjects in some depth, rather than many subjects superficially.

The chapter is divided into two major sections. The first is directed to important outcomes of the socialization process. One such outcome, the baby's attachment to the parent, was discussed in chapter 6. In this chapter we will add three others: the development of moral standards and moral behaviors, the development of sex typing and sex differences, and the development of individual differences in temperament and personality.

For any topic that we might consider there are two general methodological issues that must be addressed. One is the question of how to measure the outcomes of interest in the child's development—the various moral behaviors, instances of sex typing, or whatever that the child shows. This question is the focus of the first part of the chapter. Our discussions include both applications of general points made earlier in the book (e.g., the distinction between lab studies and field studies) and the introduction of techniques specific to each content domain.

The second general issue is the question of determinants—where do these outcomes come from? Why are certain behaviors part of the child's social repertoire, and what is the explanation for developmental or individual differences in them? It is this question that occupies the second part of the chapter. Again, our discussion is a mixture of general and more content-specific points.

go to 165

Note the basic difference between the first four questions and the last four. The first four concern specific information that is given directly in the story. The last four, however, can be answered only on the basis of inferences that go beyond the information that is explicitly provided. A basic finding—not only from the Paris study but from other such studies as well—is that even young children do make the kinds of inferences that are required by the second set of questions. The tendency to make inferences, as well as the complexity of the inferences that are possible, increases with development (Paris & Upton, 1976). But from early in life memory—whether for a story, a conversation, an event seen, or whatever—is for meaning and not simply for verbatim detail.

Studies of children's recall for stories can also be constructed to yield memory errors that are similar to those found in the studies of memory for sentences. Brown, Smiley, Day, Townsend, and Lawton (1977) read children a story concerning a young warrior who underwent various hardships while attempting to carry out a brave deed that would prove his manhood. A week prior to the story, half of the children had been told that the warrior belonged to a tribe of Eskimos and half that he belonged to a tribe of desert Indians. When later asked to retell the story, children showed definite effects of this initial context. Those in the Eskimo group, for example, described the weather (referred to only as "bad" with "extreme temperature" in the actual story) as icy and freezing; those in the desert group talked about the heat and drought. Note that in this case the memory errors occurred in recall, in contrast to the recognition measures that have been common in the sentence memory studies.

There are numerous other approaches to the study of constructive memory that we have not had space to include here. One of the most interesting such approaches was initiated by Piaget and Inhelder's (1973) claim that the constructive workings of the cognitive system could in some cases lead to actual improvements in long-term memory. Reviews of the research inspired by this claim can be found in Liben (1977a, 1977b).

SUMMARY

This chapter considers four general approaches to the study of cognitive development in childhood. Piaget's work has long been a dominant force in the study of children's thinking, and the chapter consequently begins with a discussion of Piaget. Just as is true for infancy, Piaget's research on later childhood is distinguished by its ability to identify interesting and developmentally basic forms of knowledge, all studied through the flexible "clinical method" of testing. Among these forms of knowledge, *conservation*—the knowledge that quantities remain invariant in the face of perceptual change—has proved especially intriguing to both Piaget and later researchers. To the discussion of conservation are added descriptions of four other Piagetian concepts: *class inclusion, transitivity, formal-operational reasoning,* and *role taking.*

Piaget's work has spawned a host of follow-up studies intended both to challenge and to extend Piaget. This work is discussed with respect to three important issues in the study of cognitive development. One is the question of *assessment:* How accurately do our experimental procedures assess the child's abilities? Piaget has long been charged with underestimating the child's ability, primarily because of the heavy verbal emphasis in many Piagetian tasks. That there is some validity to this charge is suggested by a discussion of two sorts of studies: those that have simplified the language involved in Piagetian assessment, and those that have increased the naturalness of the assessment situation. A second basic issue is *patterning*: How do different cognitive abilities fit together? Although Piaget's theory stresses both sequences and concurrences in development, his experimental procedures provide only inconclusive evidence with respect to such patterns. Both the general difficulties in studying patterning and the specific problems of Piaget's approach are discussed. A final issue is *cognitive change*: How do new abilities enter the cognitive system? Because the topic of change is relatively understudied in Piaget's own research, the discussion focuses on an approach that has been common in more recent studies: the use of the *training study* to infer the processes through which change occurs.

The intelligence test or IQ approach to children's intelligence is in many ways quite different from the Piagetian approach. A discussion of the differences serves as a lead-in to a sampling of items from two leading IQ tests: the Stanford-Binet and the WISC. These tests are highly standardized instruments whose purpose is to identify individual differences among children. Their content is oriented to the kinds of academic-verbal skills that are important in school, an emphasis that is not surprising in view of the pragmatic origins of IQ testing. Indeed, it is the predictive power of the tests, including correlations with school performance, that has always served as their chief validity index.

The description of IQ tests is followed by a consideration of some of the theoretical issues that have been of interest in the study of IQ. One is the question of stability: Is a child's IQ constant across development, or can the value go up or down? Answering this question requires a longitudinal approach; hence this section of the chapter serves as a reminder of some of the points about longitudinal designs that were made in chapter 3. Another basic question concerns the determinants of differences in IQ—specifically, the extent to which such differences are genetic or environmental in origin. Two approaches to this question are reviewed. Twin studies capitalize on the fact that identical twins are more genetically alike than are fraternal twins; greater similarity in IQ for identicals is then taken as evidence for the importance of genetic factors. Studies of twins reared apart have been considered especially informative in this regard. Adopted child studies offer the opportunity to disentangle the genetic and environmental factors that are confounded in the normal parent-child correlation. The adopted child's IQ can be compared with that of the biological mother (with whom he or she has a genetic relation) and with those of the adoptive parents (with whom he or she has an environmental relation). Influential though the twin and adopted child studies have been, they

do have their limitations, and these limitations are discussed along with the findings.

Unlike the Piagetian or IQ approach, the information-processing approach cannot be easily characterized by the abilities that are studied, for information-processing psychologists study a wide range of abilities. The distinctive aspects of information processing lie in the kinds of theories that are constructed and in the corresponding approach that is taken to doing research. Information-processing psychologists attempt to develop relatively complete theories of cognition that are highly specific and, because specific, empirically testable. Three research strategies are described. In a *computer simulation* study the researcher first collects protocols of the cognitive behaviors of interest and then uses these protocols as a basis for writing a computer program designed to simulate the behaviors. Such a program constitutes a theory of human cognitive processes, and it provides, in conjunction with further empirical work, a vehicle for testing models of individual or developmental differences. Although computers are not used, the *rule assessment* approach shares many features with the simulation approach. Again, a careful task analysis provides a set of processes or "rules" that might be applied to a particular cognitive task. These rules lead to specific predictions about how subjects at different developmental levels will perform, predictions that are then tested and refined in light of developmental data. Finally, measuring *response time* is based upon the assumption that the times required to perform various cognitive tasks can yield evidence about the underlying psychological processes. In the example discussed, response times provided a basis for choosing between two models of transitive inference.

The chapter concludes with a discussion of an important content domain in the study of children's cognition: the development of memory. Memory in infancy seems to consist mainly of *recognition memory*, which has typically been studied through either the habituation-dishabituation paradigm or the Fantz preference method. Studies of older children have concentrated on *recall memory* and on the attempt to ex-

therefore, to measure physical clustering—for example, placing all the animal pictures together. This strategy was rare in the youngest children but became common by about age 10 or 11.

It should be clear that a typical finding from the strategy literature is that children younger than 5 or 6 often fail to generate mnemonic strategies. Lest it be thought that this is an absolute deficit, consider a study by Wellman, Ritter, and Flavell (1975). Their subjects were 3-year-old children, and their experimental procedure is summarized in the following passage:

I want to tell you a story about this dog. See, here he is on the playground [table top]. He loves to play, he runs, he jumps, . . . but he was playing so hard he got very hungry. So he went to look for some food. When he was looking he went by this dog house, and this dog house, and this dog house, and this dog house [dog is walked by all four cups]. And then he went in this dog house to find some food [dog is hidden]. You know what, I have another toy I could get to help us tell the story. I'll go get it because we need it for the story. (p. 781)

At this point instructions diverged for the two experimental conditions. Children in the Wait condition were told simply to wait with the dog. Children in the Remember condition were told to remember where the dog was. The question, of course, was whether the children who were told to remember would behave differently from those who were told simply to wait. The answer is that they did behave differently, and in a very sensible way: Children instructed to remember were much more likely to spend the delay period with their eyes glued to the critical cup and possibly their fingers touching it as well. These are, it is true, very simple mnemonic strategies, but they *are* strategies, and they are available by age 3. We can see here another example of what has become a recurrent theme in developmental psychology: It is dangerous ever to assert that some ability (in this case, mnemonic strategies) is totally lacking in the young child.

We might add that it is also dangerous to assert that some ability is ever totally developed. The development of mnemonic strategies does not cease at age 10 or 11, even though a relatively simple strategy like verbal rehearsal may be quite skillfully executed by that age. In recent years memory researchers have shown increasing interest in complex mnemonic strategies that may not appear until adolescence or even adulthood. Perhaps most noteworthy is the work of Ann Brown and her associates on study strategies that can be applied to school material (Brown, 1982). A general review and discussion of late-emerging mnemonic strategies can be found in Pressley, Levin, and Bryant (1983).

Constructive Memory

Important though they are, strategies do not account for all memory phenomena of interest or for every important developmental change in memory. Consider some of the limitations of the studies of strategic memory. Such studies have typically focused on memory for arbitrary and meaningless material (e.g., lists of unrelated words); clearly, however, much of real-life memory is for meaningful material. Studies of strategic memory have focused on intentional memory; much (perhaps most) of real-life memory, however, is unintentional or incidental, in the sense that we remember things that we never attempted to commit to memory. Finally, studies of strategic memory concern definite and discrete techniques for storing or retrieving the memory material. But not all of the cognitive activities involved in memory can be accounted for in terms of such definite and intentional strategies.

The study of constructive memory concerns the effects of the general knowledge system upon memory. The basic idea behind this approach is that memory is simply a form of applied cognition, that form that has to do with storing information over time and retrieving information from the past. Like any form of cognition, memory involves action and understanding, not merely passive registration of input. And like any form of cognition, memory shows definite developmental changes as the child's understanding of the world changes. In Flavell's (1985) words, ''What the head knows has an enormous effect on what the head learns and remembers. But, of course, what the head knows changes enormously in the course of development, and these changes consequently make for changes in memory behavior" (p. 213).

Let us consider some examples. Paris and Carter (1973) presented 7- and 10-year-old children with a list of 21 sentences to remember. The sentences were grouped into seven unrelated "stories," each of which comprised three sentences. One such story, for example, was the following: "The bird is inside the cage. The cage is under the table. The bird is yellow." All of the story trios followed this same format: two premise statements, one of which established an A-B relation (e.g., between bird and cage) and one of which established a B-C relation (e.g., between cage and table), followed by a filler statement (e.g., "The bird is yellow"). Subjects were subsequently tested for recognition of the sentences. The recognition test was composed of four sentences for each of the seven stories. One sentence was a true premise—for example, "The bird is inside the cage." A second was a slightly altered false premise—for example, "The cage is over the table." A third was a true inference regarding the A-C relation—for example, "The bird is under the table." The fourth was a false inference regarding the A-C relation—for example, "The bird is over the table." Thus, only one of the four sentences had actually appeared in the original list; a second, however, followed logically from the information that had been presented.

The 7- and 10-year-olds showed similar patterns of errors. For both groups, errors were low on three of the four sentence types: the true premise, the false premise, and the false inference. On the true inferences, however, errors occurred on some 60% to 70% of the trials. Thus, children showed a strong tendency to "recognize" sentences that they had never seen before. Such responses are errors, but note what intelligent errors they are. What the child is doing on these trials is integrating information from the two premises to arrive at a logical conclusion. He or she is going beyond the information given in a way that in most contexts

(except laboratory recognition tests) is quite intelligent and adaptive.

Two more points can be made about this finding. First, the phenomenon of memory errors that result from inference is not limited to children; adults also show such responses (e.g., Bransford, Barclay, & Franks, 1972). Indeed, it was the discovery of the phenomenon with adults that led to the research with children. Second, inferences and resulting errors are not limited to verbal stimuli. Paris and Mahoney (1974) demonstrated that the same findings emerge when pictures rather than words are used as the stimuli. (See also Liben and Posnansky, 1977, for a critique and extension of the Paris and Carter study, and Trabasso and Nicholas, 1980, for a general discussion of methodological challenges in such research.)

What do children do when presented with more extended vignettes than the three-sentence "stories" used by Paris and Carter? Paris (1975) read the following story to kindergarten through fifth-grade children:

Linda was playing with her new doll in front of her big red house. Suddenly she heard a strange sound coming from under the porch. It was the flapping of wings. Linda wanted to help so much, but she did not know what to do. She ran inside the house and grabbed a shoe box from the closet. Then Linda looked inside her desk until she found eight sheets of yellow paper. She cut up the paper into little pieces and put them in the bottom of the box. Linda gently picked up the helpless creature and took it with her. Her teacher knew what to do. (p. 233)

Following the story, children were asked eight questions:

1. Was Linda's doll new?
2. Did Linda grab a match box?
3. Was the strange sound coming from under the porch?
4. Was Linda playing behind her house?
5. Did Linda like to take care of animals?
6. Did Linda take what she found to the police station?
7. Did Linda find a frog?
8. Did Linda use a pair of scissors? (p. 233)

MORAL DEVELOPMENT

"Moral development" is potentially a huge topic, encompassing many aspects of the child's development. In fact, as developmental psychologists have studied morality, the topic *is* huge, for many different facets of development are examined under this heading. This first section is consequently the longest one in the chapter.

It is traditional to distinguish three aspects of morality: the behavioral, the emotional, and the cognitive (but see Rest, 1983, for a dissent and alternative approach). Our organization follows this traditional division, with subsections for each of the three aspects. The focus in each section is on the first of the general questions identified previously: how to measure the developmental outcomes of interest. The second general question, how to study the determinants of these outcomes, is addressed in the concluding part of the chapter.

Behavior

The behavioral aspect of morality refers to moral action—to behaving in moral, good, socially acceptable ways. Exactly what the criteria are for defining a "moral" behavior is a complex and long-debated question that is well beyond our scope here. We can note, however, that one component of almost anyone's definition is the notion that the behavior must be at least partly internally generated and not solely in response to immediate external pressures. A child who does not cheat because a teacher is standing over him is not behaving morally (or immorally, for that matter), nor is a child who shares candies with a younger brother because his mother is about to spank him if he refuses to share. On the other hand, a child who is left at least somewhat on his own and *decides* not to cheat or *decides* to share *would* be demonstrating moral behavior.

Note that this definitional point has a methodological corollary. It means that what we need to study are situations, either naturally occurring or experimentally contrived, in which chil-

dren have an opportunity to behave morally but are not forced to do so by the immediate environmental pressures. We describe a number of such situations as we go.

What specific behaviors fall under the heading of the behavioral aspect of morality? There are a large number of behaviors, and they can be roughly divided into two general classes, classes that correspond to the two examples sketched earlier. In some cases the issue is whether the child can avoid doing something wrong. This is the case, for example, with cheating, a common measure of moral behavior in studies of school-aged children. Cheating is actually a particular instance of a more general construct known as *resistance to temptation*. A resistance-to-temptation test sets up a conflict between some behavior in which the child would like to engage (such as cheating to do better on a task) and some sanction or prohibition against the behavior (such as rules against cheating, or the disapproval of a teacher or parent). The question then is whether the child resists or fails to resist the temptation. A common resistance measure geared to younger children, the "forbidden toys test," is described shortly.

For years the study of moral behavior was oriented mainly to resistance situations and to whether the child could avoid misbehaving. In recent years this negative focus has been complemented by a greatly increased interest in the more positive side of morality: whether the child will not only avoid bad behavior but also actively engage in good behavior. Such active production of socially beneficial behaviors is referred to as *prosocial behavior*. Sharing would be an example of prosocial behavior. So too would showing sympathy for someone in distress or offering to help in some way to alleviate the distress. More formally, prosocial behavior has been defined (Mussen & Eisenberg-Berg, 1977) as "actions that are intended to aid or benefit another person or groups of people without the actor's anticipation of external rewards" (pp.3–4). Note again the emphasis on the freedom from external control in moral behavior.

Whatever the specific behavior that we decide to study, there are several approaches that we can take to gathering evidence. We discussed these approaches at a general level in chapter 5; here we consider some specific applications to the measurement of moral development.

One possibility is to go into some naturally occurring "field" setting and collect *naturalistic observations* of the behaviors of interest. A study by Barrett and Yarrow (1977) provides an example. These investigators studied 5- to 8-year-old children who were attending a summer day camp. A time-sampling observational approach was used, with each child observed for a total of eight 15-minute periods, each observation period in turn being divided into three 5-minute blocks. Among the behaviors recorded were instances of prosocial behavior, defined as

attempts to fulfill another person's need for physical or emotional support. They include acts of comforting (physically or verbally expressing sympathy or reassurance), sharing (giving materials or work space that one is using or giving a "turn" to another person), and helping (physically assisting or offering physical assistance). (p. 476)

Also recorded were *opportunities* for prosocial behavior—that is, cues from other children that indicated a need for comfort, sharing, or helping.

The obvious strength of an approach like Barrett and Yarrow's was noted in chapter 5. With naturalistic observation our focus is directly on what we hope to explain: the natural occurrence of behaviors in the natural setting. A further, more specific strength of this particular study is the measurement of opportunities for prosocial behavior as well as actual occurrences of the behavior. A common limitation in naturalistic study is that the eliciting conditions for a behavior may vary across children. Perhaps, for example, a particular child scores low on the comforting measure simply because he or she happened to have few opportunities to offer comfort during the observation period. This problem follows from the lack of control in a naturalistic study: We are unable to set up the same environment for all subjects, but

rather have to take conditions as they happen to occur. One way around this problem is to *measure* these conditions for each child and to adjust the analyses accordingly, which is what Barrett and Yarrow did with their measurement of opportunities to be prosocial. Another way, also utilized by Barrett and Yarrow, is to collect a large sample of each child's behavior. The logic in sampling behavior is the same as that discussed earlier for sampling of subjects: The larger the sample that we are able to obtain, the more likely it is that chance variations will even out and we will end up with a representative picture.

As we saw earlier, the strengths of the naturalistic approach are balanced by some weaknesses. Ensuring the accuracy of the measurements may be difficult, especially when the observations must be carried out in an uncontrolled field setting. The interobserver reliabilities in Barrett and Yarrow's study were in fact modest, most falling in the .7 and .8 range. Another possible problem concerns effects of the observer on the behavior being observed. It is true that in a free-play school situation, such as that studied by Barrett and Yarrow, the presence of various adults may be common and easily adapted to. Nevertheless, it is wise not to become too sanguine about this issue. Reactive effects from being observed may in fact be especially likely with moral behaviors, a domain in which there is a clear "should" for how one behaves while being watched by adults (i.e., one should share, should offer help, etc.). Prosocial behaviors may be less likely when there is no adult around.

We consider one more example of the naturalistic observation approach. It is an unusually ambitious example, and one that may minimize some of the problems just discussed. Zahn-Waxler, Radke-Yarrow, and King (1979) studied responses to distress in others in a sample of 1½- to 2½-year-olds—in itself an ambitious undertaking, for the toddler is a challenging and understudied research subject. Zahn-Waxler et al. were especially interested in prosocial responses to the other's distress, such as expressing sympathy or offering help. Such responses were studied longitudinally across a 9-month period, which is another ambitious aspect of the study. Finally, the observations were made not by the usual research assistant but by the children's own mothers. Prior to the start of the study, the mothers underwent three training sessions, totaling 8 hours, during which they learned to make the kinds of observations that the investigators were interested in. The observational method used was a combination of event sampling and narrative record: Whenever an incident of distress to another occurred, the mother dictated a description into a tape recorder, attempting to capture the incident itself, the events preceding it, and the child's response to the distress. Through this approach Zahn-Waxler et al. were able to document early forms of sympathy and prosocial behavior in an age group that had generally been thought to be incapable of such responses.

It is perhaps unnecessary to point out that there are difficulties aplenty in a study like Zahn-Waxler et al.'s, both practical difficulties in securing the necessary cooperation and more substantive difficulties in verifying the accuracy of the mothers' reports. Their approach also has some definite strengths, however, especially in comparison to the usual observational study. Two such strengths are worth noting. First, there is no worry about biasing effects from introducing an observer, for the mother is a natural part of the child's environment. Even though observations are still limited to events that the mother is present to witness, reactivity in the usual sense is not a concern. Second, the breadth of the observations—and the resulting quantity of information—is enormously greater than in a typical observational study. We can have considerably more confidence, therefore, that we really have obtained a representative sampling of the child's behavior.

The second general approach that we consider is *laboratory elicitation* of the behaviors of interest. In this case the locus for our observations is some structured lab environment, an environment designed to permit the occurrence and measurement of the particular moral behavior that we are interested in studying. We

consider two main examples of this approach, one directed to the negative, avoidance aspect of morality and one directed to the more positive, prosocial aspect.

As mentioned earlier, a common measure of resistance to temptation with young children is the "forbidden toys test." An early study by Parke (1967) provides a typical example of its use. In Parke's study the subjects (first- and second-grade children) were brought individually to a mobile laboratory trailer, where they first spent about 10 minutes drawing. Following the drawing phase, each child was seated at a table containing five toys, and the following instructions were given:

"You can sit here. [The cloth covering the toys is removed by *E*]. Now, these toys have been arranged for someone else, so you'd better not touch them. If you are a good boy (girl) and do not touch the toys, we can play a game together in a little while, but I have forgotten something and have to go into the school and get it. While I am gone, you can look at this book. I'm going to close the door so that no one will bother you. When I come back, I'll knock, so you'll know it's me." Then *E* left through the door leading to the other side of the trailer. (p. 1105)

The child was then left alone for 15 minutes with the toys, during which time his or her behavior was monitored through a one-way mirror. The question, of course, was whether the child would give in and play with the toys, and, if so, how quick and how broad the deviation would be. It turns out that children vary widely in their ability to resist the temptation, and that a number of variables affect resistance. We consider one such variable later in the chapter when we discuss studies of punishment.

Our second example of a laboratory study concerns the prosocial behavior of sharing. A study by Barnett, King, and Howard (1979) illustrates what in recent years has become a popular procedure for studying sharing. Each of the grade-school subjects in their study received 30 prize chips as a reward for answering some questions about what children remember. The chips could be exchanged for prizes at the end of the study once all the children had a chance to participate. Before the child could leave with his or her chips, however, the experimenter pointed to a nearby donation cannister and informed the child that

there are some other children who go to another school a lot like yours who won't have a chance to be in the study and earn prize chips. Later, if you want, you may share with those children by putting some of your prize chips in the donation can. You don't have to share, but you may if you want. (Barnett et al., 1979, p. 165)

The child was subsequently left alone for 1 minute, during which time he or she could donate or not without being observed. The fact that the cannister already contained a number of chips heightened the impression of anonymity. Despite this impression, however, the child's behavior was in fact no freer from scrutiny than that of the subject in the forbidden toys study described earlier. By simply counting the number of chips in the cannister after each subject, the experimenter was able to measure how much each child had donated.

The laboratory approach has a number of virtues. In comparison to naturalistic observation, a lab assessment is an extremely efficient way of gathering information about a behavior. Rather than wait for perhaps hours for the relevant behavior to occur, we can set up a situation that will elicit the behavior (resisting or not resisting, sharing or not sharing, etc.) within a matter of minutes. We can do so, moreover, in a way that is comparable for all subjects. As we saw, lack of comparability in eliciting conditions can be a problem in a purely naturalistic study. And we can do so in a way that permits precise and objective measurement of the behavior. It is quite easy, for example, to record whether and how quickly a child plays with the forbidden toys. It is even easier to record how many chips a child donates.

One further virtue can be noted. Once a basic laboratory paradigm has been developed, such as the forbidden toys or donation measure, it is possible to contrive almost endless variations of it. We can see what happens to resistance, for example, if we vary the attractiveness

of the forbidden toys, or the strength of the prohibition against playing, or the availability of alternative activities. In a study of sharing we can vary the quantity or the attractiveness of the to-be-shared objects, or the familiarity or deservingness of the recipients of the sharing, or the presence or absence of the experimenter at the time of donation. We can, in short, carry out systematic experimental manipulations of a large number of potentially important independent variables.

The limitations of the laboratory approach can be summarized with the same one-word description used in chapter 5: artificiality. Grusec (1982) summarizes the standard criticisms:

Is resisting playing with an arbitrarily forbidden toy akin in any way to resisting the temptation to lie or cheat or steal? Is donating tokens just won in a preceding game to unseen poor children at all related to helping a friend who is in real trouble? (p. 259)

The issue is one of external validity—whether the lab situation is similar enough to real life to permit generalization of findings. It is not hard to find possible problems and biases in any specific laboratory measure. We return to this issue when we discuss laboratory studies of the determinants of moral behavior.

On the other hand, another point made in chapter 5 is also worth reiterating. Lab versus field is a continuum rather than a dichotomy, and experimentally contrived laboratory situations do not have to be radically different from the child's natural experiences. Indeed, a case could be made that moral behavior, more than most topics, lends itself to natural and nonreactive measurement in a laboratory setting. The donation measure is a possible example— a casual and plausible request that is seemingly quite unrelated to the purposes of the experiment. Similarly, help giving has been measured by having the experimenter "accidentally" spill a box of tennis balls and then seeing whether the child helps to pick them up. Sympathy has been measured by having the experimenter pinch her finger in a drawer and then noting the child's reaction (Yarrow & Waxler, 1976).

If skillfully executed (a big "if"), such measures may be quite natural and informative.

We can note finally that it may sometimes be possible to embed the experimental elicitation of a behavior within the natural setting. This was done, for example, in the Zahn-Waxler et al. (1979) study described earlier. In addition to their measures of naturally occurring distress situations, these investigators measured the child's response to simulated distress by the mother—for example, to her apparent pain after banging her ankle. In a similar manner, it has sometimes been possible in cheating research to create opportunities for cheating, and for the detection of that cheating, in the child's natural environment. The best-known example comes in a massive research project by Hartshorne and May (1928). These investigators were able to set up various familiar situations—some academic, some athletic, some game playing—in which children had some task to carry out and also some opportunity to cheat in order to do better. Although the child was apparently free from detection, Hartshorne and May were in fact able, via various clever stratagems, to measure the occurrence of cheating. On one measure, for example, the children had a chance to change their responses after learning the right answers to a test, without realizing that their original response sheets had been duplicated by the experimenters. On another measure the children were allowed to report their own scores, and implausibly high scores were taken as evidence of cheating.

The final general approach that we consider is the *rating* approach. Ratings share several characteristics with naturalistic observations. Our focus is again on naturally occurring behaviors in the natural setting, as opposed to experimentally elicited behaviors in a laboratory setting. Our measurement again requires judgments by a human observer, as opposed to the automatic or essentially automatic recordings that may be made in the lab. Ratings, however, are considerably more global, more evaluative, and more removed from immediate behavior than are observations. With observations the attempt is to capture the specifics of ongoing behavior, generally by means of a precise and objective recording system and highly trained observers. With ratings the attempt is to identify general characteristics of the child—how honest or dishonest, how generous or stingy, and so forth. These characteristics are not direct behavioral measures but are abstracted, usually retrospectively, from a large number of observations made, usually naturally and unsystematically, by someone who knows the child well. This someone is most often a teacher or parent. In studies of older children it may be another child or the subject him- or herself. In any case, our measure is based on what someone who knows the child tells us about the child.

Let us consider a couple of examples. Rutherford and Mussen (1968) used ratings by nursery-school teachers to assess generosity in a sample of preschool boys. Each teacher was given cards with the names of each boy in her class and was asked to sort the cards into five piles. Pile one was for those "who are among the most generous, least selfish nursery school boys I have ever known." At the other extreme, pile five was for those "who are among the most selfish, least generous nursery school boys I have known." In between was pile three: for those "who seem about average in generosity, neither highly generous nor highly selfish in their behavior." This sort of card-sorting procedure is a fairly common method of obtaining ratings. Whether cards are used or not, ratings typically involve placement of the subject along some dimension—that is, some evaluation not just of presence or absence but of *degree* of generosity, degree of honesty, or whatever. Ratings also tend, either explicitly or implicitly, to be relative measures, involving comparison of the child with other children.

As Mussen and Eisenberg-Berg (1977) note, teacher ratings are most likely to be useful with nursery-school children, with whom teachers have frequent and varied experiences in relatively unstructured situations. In more structured grade-school or high-school classrooms, teachers may lack sufficient experience with their pupils to make many kinds of ratings. By this age, however, peers can often be useful informants. Martin Hoffman, in particular, has used such "sociometric" peer ratings in a number of studies to assess aspects of moral development (Hoffman, 1975; Hoffman & Saltzstein, 1967). In one study, for example, Hoffman (1975) measured concern for others by having fifth-grade children nominate the three same-sexed classmates who were most likely to "care about how other kids feel and try not to hurt their feelings" and "to stick up for some kid that the other kids are making fun of or calling names."

Like all measures, ratings have both advantages and disadvantages. On the negative side, the obvious problem with ratings is that they are not direct measures of behavior; rather they are second-order reports about behavior. There are many reasons why ratings may paint an inaccurate picture of what a child is really like—insufficient or biased opportunities for observation, misunderstanding of instructions, forgetting, willful distortion, stereotyping. In addition, ratings, oriented as they are to the abstraction of general characteristics, are poor instruments for the study of the immediate determinants of specific behaviors. On the positive side, if skillfully elicited from a genuinely knowledgeable informant, ratings may provide a scope and depth of information about a child that is unavailable with other methods. Laboratory measures are necessarily limited to very brief and possibly atypical samplings of behavior. Observations in the natural setting, the efforts of Zahn-Waxler et al. (1979) notwithstanding, also tend to be severely limited in the situations and behaviors that can be sampled. With ratings, however, the scope for our conclusions about a child is enormously broader—potentially everything that a parent, teacher, or friend has ever seen the child do. (For further discussion of ratings versus observations, see Cairns and Green, 1979.)

The most general conclusion to be drawn from this section should be familiar from chapter 5. All methods have their limitations. What we need, therefore, is a *convergence* of methods—an attack upon the particular research problem (in this case, the development of moral behaviors) through as many different methods as possible.

Emotion

We turn now to the emotional aspect of morality—to how the child feels in morally relevant situations. Of greatest interest historically has been the negative emotion of guilt—that is, unpleasant, self-punitive feelings that occur when one has done something wrong (or perhaps even *thinks* about doing something wrong). More recently, there has been considerable interest in the more positive emotion of empathy—that is, the tendency to share the emotional reactions of others (for example, to feel sad when someone else feels sad).

Emotions are by definition internal phenomena, and as such present a definite methodological challenge to the researcher. We begin by considering two approaches to measuring guilt in children. We then move on to some work on empathy.

The most common method of measuring guilt has been to present stories in which the central character (who is usually similar to the subject) misbehaves in some way. The story is broken off following the misbehavior, and the subject is asked to provide an ending. Of particular interest are endings that focus on the story character's emotional reactions, including reactions of guilt. The character's subsequent behaviors may also be of interest; for example, does he run off and hide, confess his wrongdoing, attempt to make restitution, or what? Whatever the particular response ascribed to the character, the assumption is that it tells us something about how the child himself would feel and act in a similar situation. The child is assumed to "project" his own emotions onto the character, which is why this kind of measure is called a *projective test*. Examples of two such stories that have been used to assess guilt are shown in Box 8-1.

The story-completion method has several virtues. It is relatively easy to administer and to score, and it allows us to sample reactions across a wide range of kinds and degrees of transgression, certainly a much wider range than we are likely to be able to sample with any other measurement technique. The most basic

BOX 8-1   Examples of projective stories used to assess guilt

1. Early one evening Bob and his friend are hurrying along the street on their way to the biggest basketball game of the season. Bob can't wait to see the game. It starts in five minutes, and they don't want to miss any of it. All the kids will be there. On the way they see a little boy wandering around across the street. He seems to be calling out somebody's name. Bob and his friend are the only ones around. They don't know who he is. Bob turns to his friend and says, 'Gee, that little kid looks lost. Maybe we ought to go over and help him. It will only take a few minutes.' But his friend says, 'Come on, let's mind our own business. We don't want to miss any of the game, do we? Besides, his parents will find him after a while and he'll be all right. Come on, are you my friend or aren't you?' Bob finally says, 'Okay. I suppose you're right. His folks will find him soon.' They get to the game in time and really enjoy it. The next morning Bob goes out to ride his bike. On the way he looks at a newspaper. He notices a picture of the same little boy. The newspaper says that a neighbor lady was taking care of the little boy for the afternoon. She left the four-year-old

boy outside a hairdressing shop while she had her hair fixed. She told the little boy to play outside and wait for her. But the little boy started walking around and got lost. Before the neighbor lady could find him, the little boy ran across the street and got hit by a car. The newspaper says he died on the way to the hospital.

2. Art and his friends are at a school picnic. The picnic includes many contests. Art likes to take part in the contests and wants to win one very badly. Friends of his win the jumping contest, the treasure hunt, and the running race. Art is one of the kids who hasn't come close to winning anything. He even came in last in a few contests. He thinks to himself: 'Maybe I can win the swimming race. That's the main event!' When the swimming race comes up, Art sees a way to win. The contest is to swim underwater to a big white float and back. The total distance is about 25 feet. Art knows no one could see him if he turned around underwater before actually reaching the bottom of the float, because a lot of people have been swimming in the pond and it's a little muddy. So Art swims only part way, turns around, and comes in first. Everyone cheers his victory. When the other swimmers come in, they tell Art what a good swimmer he is. No one saw Art turn around. He is given a ribbon, and no one realizes he is not the best swimmer.

Note. From "Conscience, Personality, and Socialization Techniques" by M. L. Hoffman, 1970, *Human Development, 13,* p. 98. Copyright 1970 by S. Karger. Reprinted by permission.

---

criticism of the method, of course, concerns the central assumption underlying its use: the assumption that the child responds by projecting his own emotions onto the story character (as opposed, for example, to saying what he thinks the adult wants to hear). Research using such measures leaves little doubt that this assumption is *sometimes* justified; how generally valid it is, however, remains debatable. It is worth noting that stories such as those in Box 8-1 can also be used in a more direct, less projective manner by simply asking the child directly how he would think or feel if he were the story protagonist (e.g., Thompson & Hoffman, 1980).

Still, the measure remains a verbal report about emotions and not a direct measurement of emotions.

The second approach to assessing guilt is a structured laboratory test that closely resembles the resistance-to-temptation tests that are used to study behavioral morality. In this case, however, the interest is not in whether the child deviates or not (the behavioral question); rather the situation is contrived so that eventually almost every child *will* deviate. The interest is in the child's emotional reaction following the deviation.

A study by Sears, Rau, and Alpert (1965)

provides an example. The nursery-school subjects in their study were taken from their classrooms to a nearby experimental room that was stocked with all sorts of interesting toys. Also in the room, in a box off in one corner, was a hamster. The experimenter explained that the hamster belonged to him, and that the box was a cage that he was in the process of building. Because the cage was not yet complete, the hamster tended to escape unless watched closely. The child was given the job—a very important job, it was stressed—of watching the hamster while the experimenter left for a while. The experimenter was in fact gone for up to 25 minutes—a very long time for a young child to keep his or her eyes on the hamster and away from the toys. Eventually, almost all of the children turned away at least momentarily from the cage. At this point a trap door in the cage opened, the hamster fell through, and the door shut again, the result being that when the child looked back at the hamster he or she was confronted by an empty cage. The measurement of the child's response included both overt behaviors (e.g., going to search for the experimenter, confession when the experimenter reappeared) and signs of upset or distress.

In comparison to the story-completion technique, a measure like Sears et al.'s has the advantage of looking at actual emotions to an actual transgression, rather than inferring emotions from verbal statements about a hypothetical transgression. It also has the general laboratory virtues of experimental control and comparability across subjects. At the same time, the measure may rank high on the artificiality dimension; the deviation, after all, *is* contrived, and even a 4-year-old may realize that he or she has not really done anything wrong. Despite the lab locus, the problems of accurately measuring emotions remain substantial. And finally (an issue to which we return in chapter 11), there are ethical questions that must be raised about any procedure that induces children to do something wrong in an attempt to arouse negative feelings. (Given this ethical problem, it should be noted that Sears et al. *did* end their procedure by very carefully assuring the child

that the hamster was all right and that the child had not really done anything wrong).

We turn now to empathy. Empathy is defined, both theoretically and operationally, in somewhat different ways by different researchers. Although we have classified it under the emotional aspect of morality, empathy may also involve cognitive elements (a kind of affective role taking to figure out the other's emotions) and behaviors (showing sympathy or attempting to help). The core element, however, is emotional: the vicarious experience of someone else's affect.

Perhaps the most widely used measure of empathy with children is the Feshbach and Roe (1968) Affective Situation Test for Empathy. The Feshbach and Roe test consists of eight slide sequences depicting 6- and 7-year-old children in various affect-arousing situations. Two of the sequences are intended to portray happiness, two sadness, two fear, and two anger. For example, one of the happiness sequences shows a child (either a boy or girl depending on the subject's sex) at a birthday party. One of the sadness sequences concerns a lost dog; the accompanying narration is shown here:

Slide I	Here is a boy and his dog. This boy goes everywhere with his dog, but sometimes the dog tries to run away.
Slide II	Here the dog is running away again.
Slide III	This time the boy cannot find him, and he may be gone and lost forever. (p. 135)

The Feshbach and Roe procedure is quite simple. Following each slide sequence the child is asked "How do you feel?" The interest in the scoring (which, Feshbach and Roe report, can be done quite reliably) is in the fit between the child's reported emotion and that appropriate for the story character. Two scoring systems have been used. To be credited with specific empathy the child must report feeling the same emotion as the story character—thus, happy for the birthday party, sad for the lost dog, and so forth. To be credited with broader empathy the child's emotion need only match that of the story character in positive or negative valence. Thus, for example, any negative emotion, such as "bad" or scared," would be credited in response to the lost dog story.

Drawing upon work with adults by Mehrabian and Epstein (1972), Bryant (1982) has recently developed an alternative method of assessing empathy in children. The Bryant procedure is intended to be simpler to administer and score than the Feshbach and Roe test and to be applicable across a wider range of ages. It consists of 22 questions, which are shown in Table 8-1. The questions sample both positive and negative empathic reactions across a number of different situations. With young children a simple yes/no response is all that is required. With older children or adolescents a 9-point rating scale can be used to indicate more precisely the degree of agreement or disagreement with a particular statement.

The main criticism of tests like Feshbach and Roe's and Bryant's is the same criticism noted earlier for story-completion measures of guilt: Such tests measure verbal reports about emotions and not emotions directly. The challenge, of course, is to come up with any more direct measure of emotional state. Both facial expressions (e.g., Sawin, 1980) and physiological change (e.g., Sawin, 1979) have been explored in recent research. Neither measure has as yet been used much with children, however, and neither is likely to be sufficient without further evidence about what the facial expression or physiological change means. The point here is the same as the point with which we concluded the section on behavioral morality: What is needed in measuring empathy, or emotions in general, is a convergence of evidence from as many different methods as possible. (See Hoffman, 1982, and Sawin, 1979, for further discussion of the measurement of empathy.)

TABLE 8-1 The Bryant Empathy Test for Children and Adolescents

Statement	Response[a]
1. It makes me sad to see a girl who can't find anyone to play with	(+)
2. People who kiss and hug in public are silly	(−)
3. Boys who cry because they are happy are silly	(−)
4. I really like to watch people open presents, even when I don't get a present myself	(+)
5. Seeing a boy who is crying makes me feel like crying	(+)
6. I get upset when I see a girl being hurt	(+)
7. Even when I don't know why someone is laughing, I laugh too	(+)
8. Sometimes I cry when I watch TV	(+)
9. Girls who cry because they are happy are silly	(−)
10. It's hard for me to see why someone else gets upset	(−)
11. I get upset when I see an animal being hurt	(+)
12. It makes me sad to see a boy who can't find anyone to play with	(+)
13. Some songs make me so sad I feel like crying	(+)
14. I get upset when I see a boy being hurt	(+)
15. Grown-ups sometimes cry even when they have nothing to be sad about	(−)
16. It's silly to treat dogs and cats as though they have feelings like people	(−)
17. I get mad when I see a classmate pretending to need help from the teacher all the time	(−)
18. Kids who have no friends probably don't want any	(−)
19. Seeing a girl who is crying makes me feel like crying	(+)
20. I think it is funny that some people cry during a sad movie or while reading a sad book	(−)
21. I am able to eat all my cookies even when I see someone looking at me wanting one	(−)
22. I don't feel upset when I see a classmate being punished by a teacher for not obeying school rules	(−)

Note. From "An Index of Empathy for Children and Adolescents" by B. K. Bryant, 1982, *Child Development, 53*, p. 416. Copyright 1982 by the Society for Research in Child Development. Reprinted by permission.

[a](+) indicates that an affirmative answer is empathic; (−) indicates that a negative answer is empathic.

Cognition

Our final topic for this section is the cognitive aspect of morality. Our interest now is in how the child reasons about moral issues, and in developmental changes in such reasoning as the child's cognitive abilities mature.

There have been two major bodies of research on the cognitive aspect of morality. We begin here with the work carried out by Piaget in the 1920s and since followed up in literally hundreds of studies. We then move on to the other, a more recent program of research by Lawrence Kohlberg and associates.

Piaget's work on morality is reported in a single book, *The Moral Judgment of the Child* (Piaget, 1932). As noted, this work was carried out in the 1920s, which places it among the earliest group of Piagetian studies. This means that it is not clearly integrated with the later work on cognitive development that we discussed in chapter 7. Nevertheless, many of the basic Piagetian ideas are already evident. These ideas include the belief that the child's moral reasoning is not simply a passive mirror of what parents or society has taught him or her but rather reflects the child's own level of cognitive development. They include also the corollary belief that developmental changes in moral reasoning result largely from developmental changes in the child's cognitive abilities. And methodologically, as we will see, they include an emphasis on the flexible "clinical method" of testing as the best way to probe the child's beliefs.

Piaget used two main techniques in his studies of moral reasoning. One was to ask children about the rules for games, especially the game of marbles. In Piaget's view, children's games constitute a kind of microcosm of the social world in general, complete with socially transmitted rules, established interpersonal relations, sanctions for deviating from the rules, and so forth. It is for this reason that the study of games can tell us something about the child's level of moral reasoning. Piaget was interested both in the child's adherence to the rules and in his understanding of the origin and nature

of rules.[1] The questioning, all conducted in the flexible clinical method style, was directed to points such as the following: What are the rules of the game? Have the rules always been what they are now? Who invented the rules? And could the rules ever be changed?

Box 8-2 shows a small sampling of what Piaget found. As can be seen, there are definite developmental changes in children's conceptions of rules. Younger children tend to view the rules for games as sacred and unchangeable—the rules have always been as they are, having been handed down either from God or the child's father, and they can never be changed. Older children are much more aware that the rules for games are at least somewhat arbitrary and changeable. This developmental shift is, in Piaget's view, part of a much more general shift from a "morality of constraint," or "moral realism," to a "morality of cooperation," or "moral relativism." We consider other examples of this shift shortly.

Piaget's second general technique for studying morality has elicited much more follow-up research. The technique consists of presenting stories that pose some sort of moral dilemma and then questioning children about the stories. The best-known example, and the one on which we concentrate, concerns the issue of whether the morality of a harmful action should be judged "objectively," in terms of the material consequences of the act, or "subjectively," in terms of the intentions behind the act. Box 8-3 shows the five stories that Piaget used to study this issue, and Box 8-4 presents examples of children's responses. As can be seen, the developmental change is from an early "objective" focus on consequences to a more mature "subjective" concern with intentions. To give an idea of some of the other issues examined in Piaget's research, Box 8-5 presents two other examples of Piagetian stories and accompanying responses. The first example concerns the

---

[1]The "his" is not sexist in this case. In Switzerland in the 1920s only boys played marbles; hence the subjects for this part of Piaget's research were only boys.

BOX 8–2   Examples of responses to Piaget's questions concerning the rules for games

Fal (5) . . . "Long ago when people were beginning to build the town of Neuchatel, did little children play at marbles the way you showed me?—*Yes.*—Always that way?—*Yes.*—How did you get to know the rules?—*When I was quite little my brother showed me. My Daddy showed my brother.*—And how did your daddy know?—*My Daddy just knew. No one told him.*—How did he know?—*No one showed him!*" . . . —Who invented the game of marbles?—*My Daddy did.*

Stor (7) tells us that children played at marbles before Noah's ark: "How did they play?—*Like we played.*—How did it begin?—*They bought some marbles.*—But how did they learn?—*His daddy taught them.*" Stor invents a new game in the shape of a triangle. He admits that his friends would be glad to play at it, "*but not all of them. Not the big ones, the quite big ones.*—Why?—*Because it isn't a game for*

the big ones.—Is it as fair a game as the one you showed me?—*No.*—Why?—*Because it isn't a square.*—And if everyone played that way, even the big ones, would it be fair?—*No.*—Why not?—*Because it isn't a square.*"

Malb (12) . . . "Does everyone play the way you showed me?—*Yes.*—And did they play like that long ago?—*No.*—Why not?—*They used different words.*—And how about the rules?—*They didn't use them either, because my father told me he didn't play that way.*—But long ago did people play with the same rules?—*Not quite the same.*—How about the rule not hitting for one?—*I think that must have come later.*—Did they play marbles when your grandfather was little?—*Yes.*—Like they do now? —*Oh, no, different kinds of games.*— . . . Could one change the rules?—*Yes.*—Could you?—*Yes, I could make up another game. We were playing at home one evening and we found out a new one* [he shows it to us].—Are these new rules as fair as the others?—*Yes.*—Which is the fairest, the game you showed me first or the one you invented?—*Both the same.*"

Note. From *The Moral Judgment of the Child* (pp. 55, 60, 66–67) by J. Piaget, 1932. New York: Free Press. Copyright 1932 by The Free Press. Reprinted by permission.

issue of why it is wrong to tell a lie; the second concerns the concept of "immanent justice," or the belief in an automatic system of punishments for bad behavior.

Let us focus on the stories in Box 8-3 and the issue of objective versus subjective morality. Later researchers have found much to criticize in the original Piagetian stories, and it may be a useful exercise to think about possible problems before reading further. We have space, in fact, to list only some of the modifications that have been explored in later research. Some researchers have argued that the order of presentation in Piaget's stories, in which information about consequences always comes last, may bias young children to attend more to consequences than to intentions; they have therefore varied

order either within or across subjects (e.g., Nummedal & Bass, 1976). Others have focused on the difficulties that young children may have in understanding and remembering all of the information in pairs of stories that are orally presented. Some have simplified the task by presenting just one story with one kind of information at a time and then comparing judgments of naughtiness across the different stories (e.g., Berg-Cross, 1975). Others have replaced the Piagetian oral-presentation format with videotapes of the behaviors to be judged (e.g., Chandler, Greenspan, & Barenboim, 1973). Some researchers have concentrated on the responses through which the child communicates his or her judgment of morality. In addition to the judgments and explanations elicited by Pi-

BOX 8-3 Stories used by Piaget to study objective versus subjective responsibility

I. A. A little boy who is called John is in his room. He is called to dinner. He goes into the dining room. But behind the door there was a chair, and on the chair there was a tray with fifteen cups on it. John couldn't have known that there was all this behind the door. He goes in, the door knocks against the tray, bang go the fifteen cups and they all get broken!

B. Once there was a little boy whose name was Henry. One day when his mother was out he tried to get some jam out of the cupboard. He climbed up on to a chair and stretched out his arm. But the jam was too high up and he couldn't reach it and have any. But while he was trying to get it he knocked over a cup. The cup fell down and broke.

II. A. There was a little boy called Julian. His father had gone out and Julian thought it would be fun to play with his father's ink-pot. First he played with the pen, and then he made a little blot on the table cloth.

B. A little boy who was called Augustus once noticed that his father's ink-pot was empty. One day that his father was away he thought of filling the ink-pot so as to help his father, and so that he should find it full when he came home. But while he was opening the ink-bottle he made a big blot on the table cloth.

III. A. There was once a little girl who was called Marie. She wanted to give her

mother a nice surprise, and cut out a piece of sewing for her. But she didn't know how to use the scissors properly and cut a big hole in her dress.

B. A little girl called Margaret went and took her mother's scissors one day that her mother was out. She played with them for a bit. Then as she didn't know how to use them properly she made a little hole in her dress.

IV. A. Alfred meets a little friend of his who is very poor. This friend tells him that he has had no dinner that day because there was nothing to eat in his home. Then Alfred goes into a baker's shop, and as he has no money, he waits till the baker's back is turned and steals a roll. Then he runs out and gives the roll to his friend.

B. Henriette goes into a shop. She sees a pretty piece of ribbon on a table and thinks to herself that it would look very nice on her dress. So while the shop lady's back is turned (while the shop lady is not looking), she steals the ribbon and runs away at once.

V. A. Albertine had a little friend who kept a bird in a cage. Albertine thought the bird was very unhappy, and she was always asking her friend to let him out. But the friend wouldn't. So one day when her friend wasn't there, Albertine went and stole the bird. She let it fly away and hid the cage in the attic so that the bird should never be shut up in it again.

B. Juliet stole some sweeties from her mother one day that her mother was not there, and she hid and ate them up.

Note. From *The Moral Judgment of the Child* (pp. 122–123) by J. Piaget, 1932. New York: Free Press. Copyright 1932 by The Free Press. Reprinted by permission.

aget, researchers have used rating scales to measure degree of perceived naughtiness (e.g., Buchanan & Thompson, 1973) and reaction time to measure the speed with which the child reaches a judgment (e.g., Imamoglu, 1975). Finally, probably the most important change in later research has involved an attempt to disen-

tangle factors that are confounded in the original Piagetian stories. Because motive (Was the action for a good or bad purpose?) and degree of damage covary in most Piagetian stories, it is impossible to determine exactly what information the child is capable of using. Furthermore, Piaget's studies do not clearly distinguish

BOX 8–4   Examples of responses to the stories in Box 8–3

Geo (6): "Have you understood these stories?—*Yes.*—What did the first boy do?—*He broke eleven cups.*—And the second one?—*He broke a cup by moving roughly.*—Why did the first one break the cups?—*Because the door knocked them.*—And the second?—*He was clumsy. When he was getting the jam the cup fell down.*—Is one of the boys naughtier than the other?—*The first is because he knocked over twelve cups.*—If you were the daddy, which one would you punish most?—*The one who broke twelve cups.*"

Const (7) . . . repeats correctly the story of the blot of ink: "*A little boy sees that his father's ink-pot is empty. He takes the ink-bottle, but he is clumsy and makes a big blot.*—And the other one?—*There was a boy who was always touching things. He takes the ink and makes a little blot.*—Are they both equally naughty or not?—*No.*—Which is the most naughty?—*The one who made the big blot.*—Why?—*Because it was

big.*—Why did he make a big blot?—*To be helpful.*—And why did the other one make a little blot?—*Because he was always touching things. He made a little blot.*—Then which of them is the naughtiest?—*The one who made a big blot.*"

Gros (9): "What did the first one do?—*He broke fifteen cups as he was opening a door.*—And the second one?—*He broke one cup as he was taking some jam.*—Which of these two silly things was naughtiest, do you think?—*The one where he tried to take hold of a cup was* [the silliest] *because the other didn't see* [that there were some cups behind the door]. *He saw what he was doing.*—How many did he break?—*One cup.*—And the other one?—*Fifteen.*—Then which one would you punish most?—*The one who broke one cup.*—Why?—*He did it on purpose. If he hadn't taken the jam, it wouldn't have happened.*"

Nuss (10): The naughtiest is "*the one who wanted to take the jam.*—Does it make any difference the other one having broken more cups?—*No, because the one who broke fifteen cups didn't do it on purpose.*"

Note: From *The Moral Judgment of the Child* (pp. 124–125, 126, 129–130) by J. Piaget, 1932. New York: Free Press. Copyright 1932 by The Free Press. Reprinted by permission.

---

between motive and intentionality (Was the action intentional or accidental?). Keasey (1978) discusses various approaches to pulling apart these factors.

Three very general conclusions can be drawn from this follow-up research. They parallel conclusions noted in chapter 7 for follow-up studies of Piaget's work on cognitive development. First, Piaget's methods lead to some underestimation of the young child's abilities, for performance is often more mature with the modified procedures of more recent research. Second, the domain of moral reasoning is more complicated and multidetermined than Piaget envisioned, and all sorts of variables may affect the way a child responds (although in fairness to Piaget it should be noted that his

book on moral judgment contains numerous cautions about differences across tasks and children and the consequent looseness of any age norms or "stages" of moral reasoning). Finally, whatever the problems in Piaget's studies, there is little doubt about the overall worth of the enterprise, not only with respect to some of the specific findings but also with respect to its pioneering role in establishing the cognitive aspect of morality as an area of study. We turn next to the major contemporary approach to moral reasoning, that of Lawrence Kohlberg.

Like Piaget, Kohlberg bases his approach upon the subject's response to hypothetical moral dilemmas. Kohlberg is interested in more advanced forms of moral reasoning than was Piaget, however, and the dilemmas that he

BOX 8–5   Examples of Piagetian stories and accompanying responses for the concepts of lying and immanent justice

---

A. "A little boy [or a little girl] goes for a walk in the street and meets a big dog who frightens him very much. So then he goes home and tells his mother he has seen a dog that was a big as a cow."

B. "A child comes home from school and tells his mother that the teacher had given him good marks, but it was not true; the teacher had given him no marks at all, either good or bad. Then his mother was very pleased and rewarded him."

Fel (6) repeats the two stories correctly: "Which of these two children is naughtiest?—*The little girl who said she saw a dog as big as a cow.*—Why is she the naughtiest?—*Because it could never happen.*—Did her mother believe her?—*No because they never are* [dogs as big as cows]. Why did she say that?—*To exaggerate.*—And why did the other one tell a lie?—*Because she wanted to make people believe that she had a good report.*—Did her mother believe her?—*Yes.*—Which would you punish most if you were the mother?—*The one with the dog because she told the worst lies and was the naughtiest.*"

Arl (10): "The naughtiest is the one "*who deceived his mother by saying that the teacher was pleased.*—Why is he the naughtiest?—*Because the mother knows*

quite well that there aren't any dogs as big as cows. But she believed the child who said the teacher was pleased.—Why did the child say the dog was as big as the cow?—*To make them believe it. As a joke.*—And why did the other one say that the teacher was pleased?—*Because he had done his work badly.*—Was that a joke?—*No, it is a lie.*—Is a lie the same thing as a joke?—*No, it is a lie.*—Is a lie the same thing as a joke?—*A lie is worse because it is bigger.*"

Once there were two children who were stealing apples in an orchard. Suddenly a policeman comes along and the two children run away. One of them is caught. The other one, going home by a roundabout way, crosses a river on a rotten bridge and falls into the water. Now what do you think? If he had not stolen the apples and had crossed the river on that rotten bridge all the same, would he also have fallen into the water?

Pail (7) . . . "What do you think of that?—*It's fair. It serves him right.*—Why?—*Because he should not have stolen.*—If he had not stolen, would he have fallen into the water?—*No.*—Why?—*Because he would not have done wrong.*—Why did he fall in?—*To punish him.*"

Fran (13) . . . "And if he had not stolen the apples, would he have fallen into the water?—*Yes. If the bridge was going to give way, it would have given way just the same, since it was in bad repair.*"

Note. From *The Moral Judgment of the Child* (pp. 148, 150–151, 157–158, 252, 253–254, 255) by J. Piaget, 1932. New York: Free Press. Copyright 1932 by The Free Press. Reprinted by permission.

---

poses are correspondingly a good deal more complex. There are nine Kohlberg dilemmas in all. Box 8–6 reproduces three of the dilemmas, including the best-known and most often cited one: the Heinz story.

The first response elicited following presentation of a dilemma is the yes/no judgment concerning the morality of the story character's

behavior (e.g., Should Heinz have stolen the drug? Should the captain order a man to go or go himself?). The real interest, however, is in the reasoning behind this yes/no answer. The "why" question is a first attempt to elicit this reasoning, and the experimenter is then free to follow up on the initial response in a variety of semistandardized ways. In scoring the subject's

BOX 8–6 Examples of Kohlberg's moral dilemmas

Dilemma III: In Europe, a woman was near death from a special kind of cancer. There was one drug that the doctors thought might save her. It was a form of radium that a druggist in the same town had recently discovered. The drug was expensive to make, but the druggist was charging 10 times what the drug cost him to make. He paid $200 for the radium and charged $2,000 for a small dose of the drug. The sick woman's husband, Heinz, went to everyone he knew to borrow the money, but he could only get together about $1,000, which is half of what it cost. He told the druggist that his wife was dying and asked him to sell it cheaper or let him pay later. But the druggist said, "No, I discovered the drug and I'm going to make money from it." So Heinz gets desperate and considers breaking into the man's store to steal the drug for his wife. Should Heinz steal the drug? Why or why not?

Dilemma V: In Korea, a company of Marines was greatly outnumbered and was retreating before the enemy. The company had crossed a bridge over a river, but the enemy were mostly still on the other side. If someone went back to the bridge and

blew it up, with the head start the rest of the men in the company would have, they could probably then escape. But the man who stayed back to blow up the bridge would probably not be able to escape alive; there would be about 4:1 chance he would be killed. The captain himself is the man who knows best how to lead the retreat. He asks for volunteers, but no one will volunteer. If he goes himself, the men will probably not get back safely and he is the only one who knows how to lead the retreat. Should the captain order a man to go on this very dangerous mission or should he go himself? Why?

Dilemma VIII: In a country in Europe, a poor man named Valjean could find no work, nor could his sister and brother. Without money, he stole food and medicine that they needed. He was captured and sentenced to prison for 6 years. After a couple of years, he escaped from the prison and went to live in another part of the country under a new name. He saved money and slowly built up a big factory. He gave his workers the highest wages and used most of his profits to build a hospital for people who couldn't afford good medical care. Twenty years had passed when a tailor recognized the factory owner as being Valjean, the escaped convict whom the police had been looking for back in his home town. Should the tailor report Valjean to the police? Would it be right or wrong to keep it quiet? Why?

Note. From "A Longitudinal Study of Moral Judgment" by A. Colby, L. Kohlberg, J. Gibbs, and M. Lieberman, 1983, *Monographs of the Society for Research in Child Development, 48*, pp. 77, 82, and 83. Copyright 1983 by the Society for Research in Child Development. Reprinted by permission.

responses and assigning a stage level it is the reasoning, and not the yes/no judgment, that is critical.

Most presentations of Kohlberg's theory identify six developmentally ordered stages.[2]

The stages, in turn, can be grouped into three developmental levels. Table 8–2 lists the stages and corresponding levels, along with examples of responses drawn from the Heinz story. As the table illustrates, with development there is

---

[2]In Kohlberg's most recent writings (e.g., Colby, Kohlberg, Gibbs, & Lieberman, 1983) Stages 5 and 6 have been combined, resulting in a five-stage rather than a six-stage model.

TABLE 8-2 Kohlberg's Stages of Moral Reasoning

Levels and Stages	Description	Pro	Con
Preconventional Level			
Stage 1: Punishment-obedience orientation	To obey the rules of others in order to avoid punishment. Obedience for its own sake, and avoiding physical damage to persons and property.	He should steal the drug. It is not really bad to take it. It is not like he did not ask to pay for it first. The drug he would take is only worth $200; he is not really taking a $2000 drug.	Heinz shouldn't steal; he should buy the drug. If he steals the drug, he might get put in jail and have to put the drug back anyway.
Stage 2: Instrumental-exchange orientation	Following rules only when it is to your advantage; acting to meet your own interests and needs and letting others do the same. Right is also what is fair, what is an equal exchange, a deal, an agreement.	Heinz should steal the drug to save his wife's life. He might get sent to jail, but he'd still have his wife.	He should not steal it. The druggist is not wrong or bad; he just wants to make a profit. That is what you are in business for, to make money.
Conventional Level			
Stage 3: Good-boy-nice-girl orientation	Living up to what is expected by people close to you or what people generally expect of people in your role as son, brother, friend, and so on. Being "good" is important and means having good motives, showing concern for others. It also means having mutual relationships based on trust, loyalty, respect, and gratitude.	If I was Heinz, I would have stolen the drug for my wife. You can't put a price on love, no amount of gifts make love. You can't put a price on life either.	He should not steal. If his wife dies, he cannot be blamed. It is not because he is heartless or that he does not love her enough to do everything that he legally can. The druggist is the selfish or heartless one.
Stage 4: System-maintaining orientation	Carrying out the duties that are our obligation. Laws are to uphold except in the extreme case when they conflict with other fixed social duties. Right is also contributing to society, the group, or institution.	When you get married, you take a vow to love and cherish your wife. Marriage is not only love, it's an obligation. Like a legal contract.	It is a natural thing for Heinz to want to save his wife, but it is still always wrong to steal. He still knows he is stealing and taking a valuable drug from the man who made it.

a progressive increase in the complexity of the reasoning, as the child moves from a focus on external rewards and punishments to a concern with society's expectations and rules to the formulation of internal principles of conscience.

Note that the highest stages are unlikely to be found before adolescence and are only moderately common even in adulthood.

Nothing has been said so far about how the subject's answers are scored and assigned to a

TABLE 8–2 *Continued*

Levels and Stages	Description	Pro	Con
Postconventional Level			
Stage 5: Social-contract orientation	Being aware that people hold a variety of values and opinions, that most values and rules are relative to the group. These relative rules should usually be upheld, however, in the interest of impartiality and because they are the social contract. Some values and rights, such as life and liberty, however, must be upheld in any society, regardless of majority opinion.	The law was not set up for these circumstances. Taking the drug in this situation is not really right, but it is justified to do it.	You cannot completely blame someone for stealing, but extreme circumstances do not really justify taking the law in your own hands. You cannot have everyone stealing whenever they get desperate. The end may be good, but the ends do not justify the means.
Stage 6: Universal-ethical-principles orientation	Following the self-chosen ethical principles. Particular laws or social agreements are usually valid because they rest on such principles. When laws violate these principles, you must act in accordance with the principles, which are universal: giving equal rights to all and respecting the dignity of human beings as individual persons.	This is a situation which forces him to choose between stealing and letting his wife die. In a situation where the choices must be made, it is morally right to steal. He has to act in terms of the principle of preserving and respecting life.	Heinz is faced with the decision of whether to consider the other people who need the drug just as badly as his wife. Heinz ought to act not according to his particular feelings toward his wife but considering the value of all the lives involved.

Note. From "Stage and Sequence: The Cognitive-Developmental Approach to Socialization" (pp. 379–380) by L. Kohlberg. In D. A. Goslin (Ed.), *Handbook of Socialization Theory and Research* (pp. 347–480), 1969, Chicago: Rand McNally. Copyright 1969 by Rand McNally. Reprinted by permission.

stage. This issue is difficult to discuss at all briefly, for several reasons. First, the Kohlberg scoring system is extremely complex; indeed, it may be *the* most complex scoring system in the psychological literature. The current "Standard Issue Scoring Manual" (Colby et al., in press), for example, is more than 800 pages long! Second, the Kohlberg scoring system has undergone substantial revision in the 25 years since Kohlberg began his research on moral development. The current "Standard Issue" scoring is the third major version of a scoring system that Kohlberg and associates have used. That the changes have been substantial is shown by the fact that scores obtained with the current

system correlate only .39 with those obtained using the original system.

There are, of course, justifications for both the complexity of the scoring and the changes over time. In general, what the Kohlberg group has attempted in their various revisions has been to bring the scoring system into closer correspondence with Kohlberg's theory of how moral reasoning develops. In particular, over time the scoring has become less dependent on the specific content of the child's answer and more exclusively oriented, as is Kohlberg's theory, to the level and the structure of the reasoning. There are also more psychometric justifications for the changes. The earlier Kohlberg scoring systems were subjective and difficult to apply, and the reliability of the scoring was therefore a major issue (Kurtines & Greif, 1974). The most recent version, though still difficult to learn to use, does show good interrater reliability and moderately good test-retest reliability (Colby, 1978; Colby, Kohlberg, Gibbs, & Lieberman, 1983).

Although the complexity of the Kohlberg scoring system may be justified, this complexity nevertheless presents some definite obstacles to research. An interested researcher cannot simply go out and do a ''Kohlberg study'' in the same way that he or she might do a ''Piaget study.'' Instead, research in the Kohlberg framework requires access to the Kohlberg materials and training, by the Kohlberg group, in how to use them. Indeed, even to *evaluate* such research may require access to the original data and to the system that was used to score the data. The result is that ''Kohlberg studies'' tend to be done mainly by Kohlberg or by people trained by or associated with Kohlberg. This state of affairs makes it difficult to get an outside test of the theory.

Given these problems, it should be noted that two main alternatives to the standard Kohlberg approach have been developed. One alternative is the Sociomoral Reflection Measure, or SRM (Gibbs, Widaman, & Colby, 1982). The SRM presents the same moral dilemmas and is intended to tap the same kinds of moral reasoning as the Kohlberg interview. In the SRM, however, the dilemmas are presented in writing and the subject responds in writing. The SRM is thus suitable for group testing, and it is easier both to administer and to score than the Kohlberg interviews. Gibbs et al. report impressive degrees of similarity in stage assignment between the SRM and the standard Kohlberg measures. They also report a variety of other kinds of evidence in support of both the reliability and the validity of the SRM.

The other main alternative is somewhat more distinct from the traditional Kohlberg approach. It is an instrument called the Defining Issues Test, or DIT, developed by James Rest (1979). The DIT makes use of the same sort of moral dilemmas as does Kohlberg. In the DIT,

however, the presentation of each dilemma is followed by a set of 12 issues that the subject ranks with regard to how important each is in deciding what ought to be done. For the Heinz story, for example, the issues include such questions as ''whether or not a community's laws are going to be upheld'' and ''what values are going to be the basis for governing human interactions.'' It is from the subject's evaluation of the importance of these issues that a stage score is derived. The DIT is thus a multiple-choice comprehension and evaluation measure, in contrast to the more open-ended production measure used by Kohlberg. Scores on the two tests are moderately but not perfectly correlated; typical values fall in the .60s or .70s. Not surprisingly, the stage level credited to the subject tends to be higher with the DIT, which requires only comprehension and evaluation, than with the Kohlberg procedure, which requires active generation of an answer. From a methodological viewpoint the DIT has several virtues: It is less time-consuming than the Kohlberg approach, it places less premium on verbal expressiveness, and it can be objectively scored.

Let us move from the method itself to a brief consideration of some of the issues raised by Kohlberg's work. A number of issues have sparked both research and controversy, including the question of the relation between moral reasoning and moral behavior (e.g., Blasi, 1980) and the possibility of moral education programs based on Kohlberg's theory (e.g., Hersch, Paolitto, & Reimer, 1979). We concentrate here, however, on an issue that is central to the theory: the claim that moral stages develop in an invariant sequence. In Kohlberg's view, later stages are in various ways ''higher'' and ''better'' than earlier ones. These more advanced stages are possible only once the earlier stages have been achieved; correspondingly, any particular stage serves as the building block for the stage that succeeds it. In this view, it should be impossible for a child ever to skip a stage or to reverse the order of the stages.

This claim has been tested in various ways. Kohlberg's own research program contains not only cross-sectional comparisons of subjects of different ages but also longitudinal study of the same group of subjects as they develop. The most recent report of the research (Colby et al., 1983), in fact, presents data from a 20-year longitudinal study; subjects were tested first in the late 1950s when they were between 10 and 16 years old and then five more times at 3- or 4-year intervals across the next 20 years. Colby et al. report no instances of stage skipping in their data and only a small number of cases of apparent backward movement, a finding that they attribute to measurement error rather than genuine regression. It should be noted, however, that apparent regressions in earlier longitudinal data served as one basis for revising the scoring system; that is, the regression was removed by changing the scoring to place the apparently immature response at a higher level. Although this approach is defensible (Colby, 1978; Colby et al., 1983), it does raise doubts in a skeptic's mind about just how empirically testable the claim of invariant sequence is.

A second approach to the issue of sequence involves cross-cultural study. Kohlberg's theory, with its emphasis on the basic cognitive-structural component of morality, predicts a good deal of similarity in moral development across even diverse cultural settings. The theory does allow for differences in the rate of development, or in the final level of development achieved, or in the specific content of some of the answers. What it insists on, however, is that the *order* of the stages be the same in all cultures. Edwards (1980) reviews research from 14 different cultures in which Kohlberg measures have been utilized. The age trends in each culture are compatible with the notion of a progression from lower to higher stages; so too are the data from the only two longitudinal studies in other cultures (one in Turkey and one in the Bahamas). Edwards also reports, however, that Stage 4 appears to be the highest level reached by subjects in non-Western cultures. At present it is unclear whether this finding reflects a genuine cultural difference or a failure of the Kohlberg approach to capture the highest levels of reasoning in cultures that are very different from our own. As Box 8–6 and Table 8–2 should make clear, translating the Kohlberg dilemmas

and scoring criteria into forms that are appropriate for different cultures is an extremely challenging enterprise.

We have limited our coverage in this section to Piaget and Kohlberg and to work directly derived from theirs. It should be noted, however, that recent years have seen the development of a number of other theories and related programs of research that fall within the general Piaget-Kohlberg-cognitive structuralist approach. Within the specific domain of moral reasoning perhaps the most noteworthy work is that of Eisenberg on children's reasoning with regard to prosocial behavior (e.g., Eisenberg, 1982; Eisenberg-Berg, 1979). Like Kohlberg, Eisenberg presents stories and derives stages from response to the stories; in contrast to the prohibition-authority orientation in Kohlberg, however, Eisenberg's stories focus on explanations for prosocial behavior. More generally, the characteristics, both methodological and theoretical, that distinguish the Piaget-Kohlberg approach can be found in a number of recent programs of research directed to the child's understanding of aspects of the social world. Examples include studies of children's conceptions of friendship (Youniss, 1980), of justice (Damon, 1977), and of social institutions (Furth, Baur, & Smith, 1976).

SEX DIFFERENCES

Some General Points

As Maccoby and Jacklin (1974) point out, the topic of sex differences is an unusual one in that the great majority of findings are incidental to the main purpose of the studies from which they come. That is, when someone reports data on depth perception or conservation or aggression it is because he or she set out to study depth perception or conservation or aggression. Data on sex differences, however, may emerge from literally any study on any topic, just as long as the study happens (as do most) to include both sexes.

This incidental nature of most data on sex differences has at least two implications. First, it means that the data base for discussions of sex differences is both huge and extremely heterogeneous. This mass of potentially relevant evidence presents a formidable challenge to anyone attempting to survey the literature and distill conclusions from it. Suppose, for example, that 200 studies of conservation report analyses for sex differences. Of these 200 studies perhaps a dozen had the explicit goal of looking for sex differences; in the others the variable of sex was incidental to the main goals of the research. Some studies have small samples; some large. In some studies the measures are clearly valid and reliable; in others the measures are more dubious. How, then, should this mass of evidence be sifted and evaluated? It is not very satisfactory simply to tally up a "box score" of the number of studies that show or do not show a significant sex difference. But any attempt to weight studies in a more differential manner requires both prodigious effort and considerable expertise, and is likely to lead nonetheless to decision rules that other researchers will disagree with. A graphic example of this point is provided by Block's (1976) critique of the Maccoby and Jacklin (1974) analysis of sex differences.

Our focus so far has been on how to interpret published reports about sex differences. A prior question concerns what information is likely to get published in the first place. Biases can be argued in either direction. According to Maccoby and Jacklin (1974), the finding of a significant difference is newsworthy; the absence of a difference is much less newsworthy. Researchers tend, therefore, to notice, analyze, and report those cases in which the sexes happen to differ, and to ignore those (much more frequent) cases in which no differences emerge. The result is an inflated picture of the extent to which sex differences actually exist. Block (1976), however, has argued that biases may also work in the opposite direction. As she notes, many researchers regard sex differences as nuisances that are to be ruled out whenever possible. Measures may be selected, therefore, in part precisely because they are already known not to show sex differences. In doubtful cases pilot testing may be used to ensure that the sexes

respond equivalently. Even though analyses for sex differences then become trivial, some journals or reviewers require that such analyses be performed and the results reported for any study that includes both sexes. The result, according to Block, is a proliferation of meaningless negative results.

Both kinds of biases just discussed undoubtedly exist; no one, however, knows how widespread they are and which, if either, is more important. The general problem is again the incidental nature of most information about sex differences. This factor makes the literature on sex differences unusually difficult to interpret, and accounts in part for the controversies that have always surrounded the topic.

Let us turn now to some issues that were introduced in earlier chapters. In chapter 4 we discussed the biasing effects that the researcher's expectancies may have on the outcomes of research. As we noted then, the obvious way to guard against such bias is to remove the expectancies—to *blind* the tester or observer with regard to the hypotheses of the study or the group membership of the subject. With many independent variables such blinding is possible. With the variable of sex it generally is not. Sometimes when babies are the subjects the tester or (more probably) the observer may be kept unaware of the subject's sex. When verbal responses are tape recorded for later analysis the person scoring the tapes may not be able to tell whether a boy or girl is talking. If responses are transcribed before scoring, then the sex of subjects of any age can usually be disguised. These cases, however, are exceptions to the general rule: Usually the observer who evaluates a behavior, and almost always the tester who elicits the behavior, are aware of the sex of the subject.

The distinction between observational measures and rating measures is relevant here. As discussed earlier in the chapter, some studies draw their data from direct observations of the child's behavior, whereas in other studies the data come from ratings by someone who knows the child. Which approach is more valid for the study of sex differences has been a subject of much dispute. Observations are more objective, and thus should be less susceptible to biases caused by the researcher's expectancies about how the two sexes *should* behave. There is evidence, in fact, that ratings do sometimes indicate more apparent sex differences than do observations (e.g., Loo & Wenar, 1971). On the other hand, it is not necessarily the case that this finding reflects the stereotyping bias of ratings; as argued earlier, ratings may sometimes pick up genuine differences that are not evident in short-term, situation-specific observations. Furthermore, to the extent that ratings do reflect stereotypes, it is not clear which direction the bias should go. As Maccoby and Jacklin (1974) note:

Ratings are notoriously subject to shifting anchor points. For example, if a parent is asked "How often does your daughter cry?" the parent may answer "Not very often," meaning "Not very often *for a girl*." The same frequency of behavior might have been rated "quite often" for a boy, from whom the behavior was less expected. (p. 356)

In this case, the bias in ratings would work *against* finding the usual stereotypical sex difference. The general point again has to do with expectancies and blinding: Because adults know the sex of the child with whom they are interacting or whose behavior they are judging, their observations may be colored by their preexisting beliefs about how boys and girls differ.

Several recent studies provide a neat confirmation of the argument just made concerning expectancies and bias. What these studies examine is the effects of *experimentally labeling* a child as a boy or a girl. Half of the adult subjects in such studies are told that the baby or toddler with whom they are interacting or whose behavior they are observing is a boy; half are told that the child is a girl. Because the child is in fact the same for all subjects, possible differential cues from boys and girls are ruled out and the effects of the adult's expectancies can be looked at directly. Such studies demonstrate that the gender label can affect the adult's behavior toward the child (e.g., Smith & Lloyd, 1978), a finding of considerable importance for the issue of origins of sex differences and the possibility of differential socialization. More

clearly relevant to the present discussion is the finding that gender labels can also affect an adult's *interpretation* of the child's behavior. Condry and Condry (1976), for example, showed that the same segment of behavior (animated response to a jack-in-the-box) tended to be interpreted as anger when produced (supposedly) by a boy but as fear when produced by a girl.

There is one final point. We have been discussing the effects of the adult's knowledge of the child's sex. But the converse also holds: The child knows the sex of the adult with whom he or she is interacting. In some cases children respond differently to a male tester than to a female tester. The problematic aspect for interpreting sex differences comes when there is not simply a main effect of sex of tester but an interaction between sex of tester and sex of child. Perhaps, for example, boys respond better to a female tester whereas girls respond better to a male tester. At some ages and for some tasks such interactions do exist; for example, studies of children's response to social reinforcement show such a "cross-sex effect," with greater response when the reinforcement is delivered by an adult of the opposite sex (Stevenson, 1965). Note that there *is* a sex difference here; the difference, however (as with all interactions), is more complicated than might at first appear. And it is a difference that might well be misinterpreted by a researcher whose study, as do most, has included only one sex of tester.

The general message of this section can be easily summarized. The determination of which aspects of psychological development show sex differences might seem easy—measures of development already exist, and all that need be done is to apply them to both sexes. For reasons that we have discussed, the determination is not so easy, and sex differences therefore remains one of the most controversial topics in the field.

Measures of Sex Typing and Sex-Role Development

A major point of the preceding section was that one does not need to set out to study sex differences to obtain information about sex differences. But there are, of course, researchers whose primary interest is in the nature and origins of sex differences. There are also a number of measures that have been explicitly designed to provide information about the development of sex differences and sex typing. In this section we consider several such measures.

We begin with the historically earliest measures, so-called tests of sex typing. Sex typing has been defined as "role behavior appropriate to [the child's] ascribed gender . . . the attitudes, feelings, interests, tastes, mannerisms, traits, and habit structures characterizing children of that gender in the particular culture in which the child's rearing occurs" (Sears et al., 1965, p. 171). The starting point, therefore, is the assumption that there *are* characteristic, on-the-average differences between the sexes—ways of thinking, feeling, or behaving that can be labeled as either "masculine" or "feminine." The goal of a test of sex typing is to capture, within a fairly brief testing period, a child's standing on the masculine-feminine dimension. Such tests can be used to chart developmental changes in degree of sex typing across childhood. They can also be used to look for possible sex differences in sex typing itself—that is, to see whether, at particular points in

development, either boys or girls adhere more strongly to their sex-ascribed roles. And they can be used to identify individual differences in degree of sex typing within a sex, differences whose origins can then be explored in further research (e.g., studies of parental childrearing practices).

Let us consider some examples. A popular measure in much of the early research on sex typing was the It Test (Brown, 1956). "It" is a stick figure of a child that is intended to be neutral with regards to sex. The subject is shown It, along with 36 cards depicting objects or figures identified with either the masculine or feminine role. The items for the test are shown in Table 8-3. For each set of pictures the child is asked to pick the items that It would like to play with or to be. The assumption is that "the child will project himself or herself into the It-figure on the basis of his or her own sex-role preference, and will attribute to It the child's own role preference" (Brown, 1956, p. 5). We have, then, another example of a projective test.

One finding from early studies with the It Test was that boys appeared to develop masculine preferences earlier than girls developed feminine preferences. This conclusion was called into question, however, by the possibility

TABLE 8-3 Items for the It Test

Toy Pictures			
Necklace	Train engine	Cradle	Soldiers
Tractor	Purse	Racer	Doll buggy
Doll	Gun	Dishes	Knife
Dump truck	High chair	Earthmover	Baby bath

Paired Pictures	
Indian princess—Indian chief	Mechanical tools—Household objects
Trousers and shirt—Dress	Men's shoes—Women's shoes
Sewing materials—Airplane parts	Girls playing—Boys playing
Cosmetic articles—Shaving articles	Building tools—Baking articles

Child Figures

Girl
Girlish boy (boy dressed as girl)
Boyish girl (girl dressed as boy)
Boy

Note. Adapted from "Sex Role Preference in Young Children" by D. C. Brown, 1956, *Psychological Monographs, 70,* 14 (Whole No. 421).

that the It figure actually looked more like a boy than a girl (Brown, 1962; Thompson & McCandless, 1970). More recent versions of the test, therefore, have done away with the visual clue, either by concealing the figure in an envelope (e.g., Paludi, 1981) or by presenting a blank card and allowing the child to imagine It (e.g., Fling & Manosevitz, 1972). As with the projective measures discussed in the section on guilt, it is also possible to remove the projective element by asking the child directly about his or her own probable response, in this case preferences for either masculine or feminine activities (e.g., Edelbrock & Sugawara, 1978).

Whether projective or not, tests such as those just discussed remain verbal, self-report measures about behavior. As such, they have both the strengths and the weaknesses of verbal measures that we discussed earlier in the chapter. The alternative is to look directly at the behaviors themselves. Such observational measures can be carried out either in the natural setting or in some specially designed laboratory setting. One example of the former is provided by the "area usage score" of Sears et al. (1965). These investigators first mapped a nursery school and playground into 45 play areas and then measured the amount of time spent by boys and girls in each of the areas. Areas that were occupied at least 65% of the time by one sex were designated either "masculine" or "feminine." Each child's sex typing was then determined from the proportion of time that he or she spent in the empirically determined "sex-appropriate" areas. A more recent example of the same approach can be found in Serbin, Connor, and Citron (1981).

Consider next a laboratory analogue to such naturalistic observation. Goldberg and Lewis (1969) observed 13-month-old children and their mothers in a standardized laboratory playroom. The playroom contained a variety of age-appropriate toys, and for most of the session the children were simply allowed to play in any manner that they wished. Measures were taken of toy preference, type of play, and time spent with mother, and possible sex differences were examined for each measure. In addition, after 15 minutes of such free play a "barrier

test" was imposed: A mesh barrier on a wood frame was placed between child and mother, and the child's reaction was observed. Figure 8–1 shows reactions that Goldberg and Lewis found to be typical of the two sexes. It should be noted that a subsequent study with similar procedures (Jacklin, Maccoby, & Dick, 1973) reported less evidence of sex differences, including differences in response to the barrier, than had Lewis and Goldberg.

Several findings from such measures can be noted. There *are* on-the-average sex differences on measures such as toy or game preference. Indeed, it is the fact that such average differences exist that justifies the use of such measures to assess any particular child's degree of sex typing. Differences between the sexes emerge earlier on measures of naturally occurring play behavior than on verbal instruments like the It Test (Fagot, 1982). Sex typing may occur earlier and in stronger form for boys than for girls, but the differences are probably not as marked as was once thought. Finally, there are only very modest correlations between a child's standing on one measure of sex typing and his or her standing on other measures. Thus, children are far from perfectly consistent in the degree to which they exhibit sex-typed behaviors.

One criticism of the kinds of measures just discussed is that they treat "masculine" and "feminine" as opposite ends of a single dimension. That is, a relatively high score on one set of attributes, say those labeled "masculine," automatically guarantees a low score on attributes from the other end of the dimension, in this case so-called "feminine" qualities. It seems possible, however, that some individuals might combine attributes that fall at opposite ends of the traditional scales. Perhaps, for example, a particular individual is both independent and assertive (traditional "masculine" qualities) and compassionate and nurturant (traditional "feminine" qualities).

In recent years several investigators have developed instruments that attempt to overcome the dichotomy of "masculine" and "feminine" to allow for a more androgynous mixture of traits. The best-known such measures are the Bem Sex-Role Inventory (Bem, 1974) and the

FIGURE 8–1. Early sex differences in response to a frustrating barrier.
From "Play Behavior in the Year-Old Infant: Early Sex Differences" by S. Goldberg and M. Lewis, 1969, *Child Development, 40,* p. 27. Copyright 1969 by the Society for Research in Child Development. Reprinted by permission.

Spence and Helmreich Personal Attributes Questionnaire (Spence & Helmreich, 1978). Because the latter has so far had more applications to childhood, we concentrate on it. For a discussion of the applicability of the Bem approach across the life span, see Hyde and Phillis (1979).

The Personal Attributes Questionnaire, or PAQ, was developed on a sample of college students (Spence & Helmreich, 1978). The PAQ consists of three scales: a Masculinity scale, a Femininity scale, and a Masculinity-Femininity scale. Items on the Masculinity scale measure attributes that were judged, by the Spence and Helmreich standardization sample, as socially desirable for both sexes but as more typical of males. Items on the Femininity scale measure attributes that were judged as socially desirable for both sexes but more typical of females. Note that because separate unipolar scales are used, rather than a single bipolar scale (like the It Test, for example), a subject may score high on both the Masculine and the Feminine attributes. Finally, items on the Masculinity-Femininity scale measure attributes that were judged as more socially desirable for one or the other sex.

Hall and Halberstadt (1980) reported a modification of the PAQ for children, labeled the Children's Personal Attributes Questionnaire or CPAQ. Like the PAQ, the CPAQ consists of three scales: Masculine, Feminine, and Feminine-Masculine. Box 8-7 shows examples of items for the three scales. The children (third through sixth graders) responded to each item by selecting a point on a 4-point scale: (1) very true of me, (2) mostly true of me, (3) a little true of me, or (4) not at all true of me. Note that in some cases it is the "very true" response that leads to a high score and in some cases it is the "not at all true" response.

The goal of the Hall and Halberstadt study was to demonstrate the validity of the CPAQ as a measure of masculinity and femininity in children. Their report provides, therefore, a useful illustration of many of the points about test va-

lidity that we discussed in chapter 2. Hall and Halberstadt demonstrated, for example, that their measure possessed satisfactory reliability, both test-retest reliability and internal consistency. Recall that reliability is a necessary condition for validity. Further analyses were directed to the issue of predictive or criterion validity: the ability of their measure to predict scores on other measures. The target used to assess the criterion validity of the child's CPAQ score was the mother's rating of her child on the CPAQ. As predicted, the correlations between the two scores were positive and significant (although also small—values ranged from .25 to .33). Finally, Hall and Halberstadt also examined the more theoretically oriented notion of construct validity. Based on both theory and past research, a number of predictions were generated regarding both measures that should correlate with the CPAQ and measures that should *not* correlate with the CPAQ. Hall and Halberstadt found, for example, that relatively

---

BOX 8–7 Examples of items from the Children's Personal Attributes Questionnaire

---

Masculine Scale

It is hard for me to make up my mind about things.
In most ways, I am better than most of the other kids my age.
I would rather do things for myself than ask grown-ups and other kids for help.
When things get tough, I almost always keep going.
I give up easily.
I am often the leader among my friends.
I almost always stand up for what I believe in.
It is easy for people to make me change my mind.

Note. From "Masculinity and Femininity in Children: Development of the Children's Personal Attributes Questionnaire" by J. A. Hall and A. G. Halberstadt, 1980, *Development Psychology, 16*, pp. 272–273. Copyright 1980 by the American Psychological Association. Reprinted by permission.

Feminine Scale

My artwork and my ideas are creative and original.
I do *not* help other people very much.
I am a very considerate person.
I am kind to other people almost all of the time.
I try to do everything I can for the people I care about.
I am a gentle person.
I like art and music a lot.
I like younger kids and babies a lot.

Feminine-Masculine Scale

It is hard to hurt my feelings.
I am often very pushy with other people.
I am a quiet person.
I cry when things upset me.
I am *not* good at fixing things or working with tools.

high masculine responses on their scales were positively related to measures of self-concept, a finding predicted from past research. They also found that for the most part scores on the CPAQ were *not* related to measures of intellectual ability, a finding supportive of the divergent validity of the test as something other than a measure of intelligence.

The final set of measures that we consider parallels approaches we discussed in the last part of the Moral Development section. There we considered the cognitive side of morality: methods of studying the way that the child reasons about moral issues. Here our focus is on the cognitive side of sex typing: how the child thinks about sex roles and sex differences, as well as how such thinking changes with development.

What sorts of questions fall under the heading of the cognitive aspect of sex typing? The simplest question concerns the child's ability to label the sexes appropriately. At what point in development can a boy accurately label himself as a boy, or a girl label herself as a girl? What about labeling others? Does the toddler know which children in a peer group are boys and which are girls? Suppose that the objects to be labeled are more distinct from the self, perhaps adults rather than other children. Does the young child realize that Daddy is a boy and Mommy is a girl?

The most ambitious examination of these issues is found in a study by Thompson (1975). The subjects for Thompson's research were drawn from three age groups: 24-month-olds, 30-month-olds, and 36-month-olds. The procedure included a variety of simple, age-appropriate methods for assessing the child's understanding of gender and gender differences. In one test, for example, the child was asked to sort pictures into two boxes, one box for pictures of boys and one box for pictures of girls. The pictures included photographs of the child; hence the test provided a measure of the child's ability to recognize his or her own sex. Self-labeling was also probed verbally through a series of questions such as "Are you a boy [or girl]?" and "Are you going to be a daddy [or mommy]?" The ability to label others was examined through a simple operant-conditioning

procedure. The child first learned to touch the member of a pair of pictures labeled by the experimenter; such touches paid off in reinforcement (a toy bunny's face lit up upon each correct touch). Ability to apply gender labels was then assessed through presentation of pairs such as boy/girl, man/woman, brother/sister, and he/she. Finally, the sorting procedure was used to examine not only labeling but also sex-role stereotypes. In this case there were nine pictures of stereotypically masculine objects and nine of stereotypically feminine objects. The child's task was to sort the objects into either the masculine or feminine box.

Thompson found that 24-month-olds showed a rudimentary understanding of some but not all of the concepts studied. By 36 months performance had improved markedly but was still less than perfect for some questions. A sampling of Thompson's results, corresponding to the sampling of questions described in the preceding paragraph, is shown in Table 8–4.

Once we know that a child can label the sexes appropriately, a next question follows naturally: What criteria does the child use in making such distinctions? For adults, of course, the defining criteria are anatomical differences, although in most situations other cues (e.g., hair length, voice, dress) are both more available and quite sufficient. That young children may not possess the same criteria as adults is suggested by the following anecdote from Stone and Church (1973):

We have the account of a four-year-old girl reporting that a new family had moved in across the way, and that the newcomers had a baby. Asked whether the baby was a boy or a girl, she replied, "I don't know. It's so hard to tell at that age, especially with their clothes off." (p. 297)

Research confirms that this little girl's preference for dress over anatomy is by no means atypical. Thompson and Bentler (1971) examined the relative importance allocated to various cues for sex discrimination by samples of four ages: 4-year-olds, 5-year-olds, 6-year-olds, and adults. The stimuli were nude dolls that varied along three dimensions: type of genitals

TABLE 8–4 Percentage of Correct Responses to the Various Tests in Thompson's Study of Gender Understanding

	AVERAGE SCORES			
Test	*24 Months*	*30 Months*	*36 Months*	*Across Ages*
Self-sorting	55	75	95	75
Self-labeling	44	70	76	63
Gender labeling—nouns (e.g., boy/girl)	76	83	90	83
Gender labeling—pronouns (e.g., he/she)	50	75	88	71
Sex-role stereotypes	61	78	86	75

Note. Adapted from "Gender Labels and Early Sex Role Development" by S. K. Thompson, 1975, *Child Development, 46,* p. 343. Copyright 1975 by the Society for Research in Child Development. Adapted by permission.

(male or female), body build (a masculine build described as "muscular and sinewy" or a feminine build described as "well proportioned in the breasts and hips"), and hair length (long or short). All possible combinations of each value from each dimension were used, producing eight dolls in all. This meant, of course, that some dolls had congruent features (e.g., male genitals, masculine build, and short hair) whereas others had decidedly incongruent features (e.g., male genitals, feminine build, and long hair). Each subject was shown only one doll and was asked to indicate its sex. Three measures of sex selection were used: naming the doll as male or female, and dressing the doll in sex-appropriate clothes twice, once for a party and once for the beach.

Thompson and Bentler found that only the adults in their sample treated the genital cue as primary in cases of conflict. Although children could make some use of all the cues, they tended to weight hair length most heavily, followed by body build. Thus, the doll with male genitals but feminine body and long hair was judged as female by the great majority of children; conversely, the dolls with female genitals but short hair elicited a substantial number of masculine choices.

The studies of labeling and of the criteria for labeling suggest that the young child's cognitive grasp of gender is less than perfectly formed. This conclusion emerges even more dramati-cally from reseach directed to a final aspect of gender understanding: the realization that one's gender is a permanent attribute. Indeed, it was some theorizing by Kohlberg (1966) concerning such "gender constancy" that sparked the contemporary interest in the cognitive side of sex typing. In his 1966 paper Kohlberg argued for two general propositions. The first was that children only gradually come to realize that gender is a permanent quality, immutable in the face of changes in age, volition, or immediate circumstance (e.g., clothing or hair style). Kohlberg likened this gradual recognition of the invariance of gender to similar progressions in the child's understanding of constancies in the physical world, most notably the famous Piagetian conservation concepts. The second Kohlbergian claim was that the child's cognitive realization of gender constancy plays a causal role in the development of sex typing and sex differences. It is only when the little boy (for example) realizes that he is a male and will always remain a male that he identifies with the father (who is also male) and takes on masculine preferences and attributes.

Since Kohlberg's original paper dozens of studies have examined developmental changes in gender constancy. A study by Marcus and Overton (1978) can serve as an example. The subjects for this research were 5-, 6-, and 7-year-old children, all of whom received three sorts of tests: for gender constancy, for conservation, and for sex-role preferences. Here we concentrate on the gender-constancy measures. Figure 8–2 shows two of the stimuli used by Marcus and Overton (these stimuli were originally developed by Emmerich & Goldman, 1972). These schematic drawings of a girl and a boy were bound together in a booklet, with one drawing on top of the other. Because the top drawing was cut horizontally across the neck, transformations could be effected by simply turning the top or bottom segment of the top picture. A flip of the bottom part of the girl picture, for example, produced a girl's head perched on a masculinely dressed bottom. A flip of the top part resulted in a boy's head with a skirt beneath.

Five questions were asked of each child. Starting with the picture that was the same sex as the child, the experimenter produced successive transformations in the figure's hair style, clothing, and both hair style and clothing. Following each change the child was asked whether the figure was still a girl (or boy) or whether the sex had changed. The child was also asked whether the figure would change sex if she (or he) adopted different play interests or "really wanted" to be the other sex.

The procedure just described is a typical method of studying gender constancy. As in a Piagetian conservation task, the child must recognize invariance in the fact of irrelevant perceptual changes. And as with conservation, there are definite developmental changes in such recognition. Marcus and Overton found that kindergarten children showed only moderate levels of gender constancy, and that even by second grade performance was less than perfect. Studies that include preschool children (e.g., DeVries, 1969) have documented even more striking deficits in the child's understanding.

The Marcus and Overton study also illustrates a number of the procedural variations that have been explored in research on gender constancy. For half of the children the stimuli were the drawings illustrated in Figure 8–2. For half, however, the face portion of the same-sex picture was replaced by a Polaroid photograph of the child's own face. This manipulation allowed a comparison between constancy for the self and constancy for others. As predicted by Kohlberg (1966), responses were more mature when the child him- or herself was the target of the changes than when another child was the locus. Marcus and Overton also included a pictorial versus live comparison. Half of the children responded to the pictures (either drawings or photographs) just described. For half, however, the live drawings were replaced by carnival-like, life-size cardboard figures, sectioned (like the pictures) to allow various combinations of top half and bottom half. In this case one of the halves was provided by the head or torso of a real child. Contrary to Marcus and Overton's expectation, performance proved to be worse in the live than in the pictorial condition. Finally, as noted, Marcus and Overton included measures of both conservation and sex-role preference. They found a positive relation between gender constancy and conservation, a result

FIGURE 8–2. Drawings used to assess children's understanding of gender constancy. From "Boy-Girl Identity Task" by W. Emmerich and K. S. Goldman, 1972. In V. Shipman (Ed.), *Disadvantaged Children and Their First School Experiences* (ETS PR 72–20), Princeton, NJ: Educational Testing Service. Copyright 1972 by the Educational Testing Service. Reprinted by permission.

compatible with Kohlberg's theory of the cognitive bases of gender constancy. They found no relation between gender constancy and sex-role preference, a result inconsistent with Kohlberg's theory that gender constancy is one of the determinants of sex-role preference. Other researchers have examined both issues and results have been mixed: Sometimes cognition-constancy links emerge and sometimes they do not, and sometimes preference relates to constancy and sometimes it does not (see Huston, 1983, for a review).

TEMPERAMENT

The pioneering work on childhood temperament was carried out by Thomas, Chess, and Birch as part of the New York Longitudinal Study (Thomas, Birch, Chess, Hertzig, & Korn, 1963; Thomas & Chess, 1977; Thomas, Chess, & Birch, 1968). We begin, therefore, with a passage from these authors that summarizes their use of the term "temperament."

Temperament may best be viewed as a general term referring to the *how* of behavior. It differs from ability, which is concerned with the *what* and *how well* of behaving, and from motivation, which accounts for *why* a person does what he is doing. Temperament, by contrast, concerns the *way* in which an individual behaves . . . . Temperament can be equated to the term *behavioral style*. (Thomas & Chess, 1977, p. 9)

Temperament is a fairly recent subject for explicit scientific study. Many of the ideas behind such study are not new, however, for they reflect beliefs that have long been held by many parents. Children—even children within the same family—often seem to have distinctly different ways of approaching the world. Some children are bursting with energy and always on the go; other children are more placid and happier with quiet activities. Some children maintain attention for lengthy periods and persist in activities until they are completed; other children are more easily distracted and more likely to flit from one thing to another. These behavioral styles may generalize across a variety of situations and behaviors. They may also persist across time, appearing first in infancy and remaining characteristic of the child as he or she grows older. And they may appear so early in infancy that they appear to be at least partly biological, and not environmental, in origin.

The preceding paragraph summarizes many of the major issues in the study of temperament. A primary question is that of definition and measurement: What are the different behavioral styles that children show, and how can we gather evidence with respect to these styles? A further question, of both theoretical and practical importance, concerns stability: Do temperamental styles persist over time, so that the irritable infant, for example, is also the irritable 6-year-old, or does temperament change as the child develops? A related, and also important, question is that of origins: To what extent are temperamental differences biological in origin and to what extent are they shaped and modified by experience?

As noted, Thomas, Chess, and Birch initiated the systematic study of temperament, and their work has served as a mold for later research and theory. Thomas et al. identified nine "dimensions of temperament." These nine dimensions are listed and briefly described in Box 8–8. Each dimension is scored on a 3-point scale, although the definition of the three points varies to some extent across categories. Activity Level, for example, is rated as High, Medium, or Low. Intensity of Reaction is scored as Positive, Variable, or Negative.

In addition to the nine dimensions, Thomas et al. identified three "temperamental constellations." These constellations reflect distinctive patterns that emerge when all nine dimensions are simultaneously considered. The Easy Child is characterized by "regularity, positive approach responses to new stimuli, high adaptability to change and mild or moderately intense mood which is preponderantly positive" (Thomas & Chess, 1977, p. 22). For the Difficult Child the picture is quite different: "irregularity in biological functions, negative withdrawal responses to new stimuli, non-adaptability or slow adaptability to change, and

Leur article

BOX 8-8 Dimensions of temperament identified in the New York Longitudinal Study

1) *Activity Level:* the motor component present in a given child's functioning and the diurnal proportion of active and inactive periods. Protocol data on motility during bathing, eating, playing, dressing and handling, as well as information concerning the sleep-wake cycle, reaching, crawling and walking, are used in scoring this category.

2) *Rhythmicity (Regularity):* the predictability and/or unpredictability in time of any function. It can be analyzed in relation to the sleep-wake cycle, hunger, feeding pattern and elimination schedule.

3) *Approach or Withdrawal:* the nature of the initial response to a new stimulus, be it a new food, new toy or new person. Approach responses are positive, whether displayed by mood expression (smiling, verbalizations, etc.) or motor activity (swallowing a new food, reaching for a new toy, active play, etc.). Withdrawal reactions are negative, whether displayed by mood expression (crying, fussing, grimacing, verbalizations, etc.) or motor activity (moving away, spitting new food out, pushing new toy away, etc.).

Note. From *Temperament and Behavior* (pp. 21–22) by A. Thomas and S. Chess. New York: Brunner/Mazel, 1977. Copyright 1977 by Brunner/Mazel, Inc. Reprinted by permission.

4) *Adaptability:* responses to new or altered situations. One is not concerned with the nature of the initial responses, but with the ease with which they are modified in desired directions.

5) *Threshold of Responsiveness:* the intensity level of stimulation that is necessary to evoke a discernible response, irrespective of the specific form that the response may take, or the sensory modality affected. The behaviors utilized are those concerning reactions to sensory stimuli, environmental objects, and social contacts.

6) *Intensity of Reaction:* the energy level of response, irrespective of its quality or direction.

7) *Quality of Mood:* the amount of pleasant, joyful and friendly behavior, as contrasted with unpleasant, crying and unfriendly behavior.

8) *Distractiblity:* the effectiveness of extraneous environmental stimuli in interfering with or in altering the direction of the ongoing behavior.

9) *Attention Span and Persistence:* two categories which are related. Attention span concerns the length of time a particular activity is pursued by the child. Persistence refers to the continuation of an activity in the face of obstacles to the maintenance of the activity direction.

---

intense mood expressions which are frequently negative'' (p. 23). In between is the constellation labeled the Slow-To-Warm-Up Child, a pattern "marked by a combination of negative responses of mild intensity to new stimuli with slow adaptability after repeated contact. In contrast to the difficult children, these youngsters are characterized by mild intensity of reactions, whether positive or negative, and by less tendency to show irregularity of biological functions'' (p. 23). In the New York Longitudinal Study 40% of the children were classified as Easy, 10% as Difficult, and 15% as Slow-To-

Warm-Up. As these percentages reveal, a substantial number of children do not fit clearly into any of three groups.

Our discussion so far has focused more on conclusions than on methodology. How do Thomas et al. obtain their evidence about temperament? The answer—not only for Thomas et al. but for the great majority of temperament studies—is that researchers learn about child temperament by asking the parents about the child's temperament. In the New York Longitudinal Study the main data came from interviews with the children's parents. The initial interviews were carried out when the subjects (141 infants from predominantly middle- and upper middle-class families) were between 2 and 6 months of age. Subsequent interviews occurred at 3-month intervals during the first year and at 6-month intervals during the second. The interviews concerned a variety of common situations in which infant temperament might become apparent. The parents were asked, for example, about the baby's sleeping and eating patterns, about typical behavior when meeting a new person or being taken to the doctor, about responses to being washed, changed, or dressed. To increase the accuracy of the reports, an attempt was made to tie the questions to concrete situations and recent behaviors. An attempt was also made to elicit a description of the child's behavior, as opposed to the parent's interpretation of the behavior (e.g., "He spit the cereal out." rather than "He hated it."). The first 22 interviews were subjected to a content analysis, and from this analysis the nine dimensions of temperament described in Box 8–8 were derived.

Interviews are one method of eliciting parental reports. The other general approach is to administer a questionnaire. A questionnaire may cover the same ground as an interview; indeed, many of the questionnaires for measuring childhood temperament were derived from the Thomas et al. interviews and resulting dimensions. With a questionnaire, however, the oral response of the interview is replaced by a written response. This written response may take different forms; simplest and most common is for the subject to indicate his or her extent of agreement with some statement by marking a point along an ordered scale. Table 8–5 shows examples of items from a questionnaire directed to infancy and the Thomas et al. dimensions. In light of their greater simplicity and economy, it is not surprising that questionnaires have become much more common than interviews in the study of temperament. A review by Hubert, Wachs, Peters-Martin, and Gandour (1982) summarizes 29 instruments for measuring temperament, 22 of which use a questionnaire format.

Whether the format is interview or question-

naire, the data from the measures we have been discussing remain verbal reports about behavior rather than direct observations of behavior. The validity of parental reports has been perhaps the most hotly debated issue in the study of childhood temperament. On the one hand, it has been argued that the data from such measures are more properly labeled as "parental perceptions of the child" than as "child temperament." Such perceptions may still be interesting and informative; indeed, what the parent thinks about the child may be a better predictor of parental behavior than are the child's actual characteristics. Nevertheless, it is important to be clear about what has and has not been measured in such research. In support of such a perception-temperament distinction is the finding that parental reports of child temperament show only modest correlations with direct observations of the child's behavior (e.g., Bates, Freeland, & Lounsbury, 1979). Also supportive is the fact that independent ratings of temperament by the two parents typically correlate only moderately at best (e.g., Field & Greenberg, 1982), a finding that suggests that at least one parent is departing from accuracy. (See Bates, 1980, 1983, and Hubert et al., 1982, for further discussion).

Although the criticisms just noted are serious, counterarguments do exist. The studies that report low correlations between ratings and observations or between mother and father are themselves subject to criticism, and other studies have obtained more impressive correlations (e.g., Dunn & Kendrick, 1980). Furthermore, in cases in which parental ratings and direct observations do diverge, it is not immediately clear that the observations are more valid. Observations, after all, are always relatively short-term and situation-specific when compared to the range of situations from which parents can draw in describing their child. This point was made earlier in comparing ratings versus observations, but it may apply with special force to the measurement of temperament. With temperament, our interest is in the child's *characteristic* ways of approaching the world—in dimensions such as rhythmicity or adaptability that may become evident only across a number

TABLE 8–5 Examples of Items from the Infant Temperament Questionnaire

		Variable usually does not	Variable usually does	Frequently	Almost always
Almost never 1	Rarely 2	3	4	5	6

1. The infant eats about the same amount of solid food (within 1 oz.) from day to day.	almost never	1 2 3 4 5 6	almost always
2. The infant is fussy on waking up and going to sleep (frowns, cries).	almost never	1 2 3 4 5 6	almost always
3. The infant plays with a toy for under a minute and then looks for another toy or activity.	almost never	1 2 3 4 5 6	almost always
4. The infant sits still while watching TV or other nearby activity.	almost never	1 2 3 4 5 6	almost always
5. The infant accepts right away any change in place or position of feeding or person giving it.	almost never	1 2 3 4 5 6	almost always
6. The infant accepts nail cutting without protest.	almost never	1 2 3 4 5 6	almost always
7. The infant's hunger cry can be stopped for over a minute by picking up, pacifier, putting on bib, etc.	almost never	1 2 3 4 5 6	almost always
. . .			
. . .			
89. The infant is calm in the bath. Like or dislike is mildly expressed (smiles or frowns).	almost never	1 2 3 4 5 6	almost always
90. The infant requires introduction of a new food on 3 or more occasions before he/she will accept (swallow) it.	almost never	1 2 3 4 5 6	almost always
91. The infant's first reaction to any new procedure (first haircut, new medicine, etc.) is objection.	almost never	1 2 3 4 5 6	almost always
92. The infant acts the same when the diaper is wet as when it is dry. (no reaction)	almost never	1 2 3 4 5 6	almost always
93. The infant is fussy or cries during the physical examination by the doctor.	almost never	1 2 3 4 5 6	almost always
94. The infant accepts changes in solid food feedings (type, amount, timing) within 1 or 2 tries.	almost never	1 2 3 4 5 6	almost always
95. The infant moves much and for several minutes or more when playing by self (kicking, waving arms and bouncing).	almost never	1 2 3 4 5 6	almost always

Note. From "Revision of the Infant Temperament Questionnaire" by W. B. Carey and S. C. McDevitt, 1978, *Pediatrics, 61,* 735–739. Reproduced by permission of Pediatrics. Questionnaire available from William B. Carey, M. D., 319 W. Front Street, Media, PA, 19063.

of different situations and behaviors. Although existing measures could undoubtedly be improved, it may be unrealistic to think that temperament can ever be assessed without some use of parental reports.

We turn now to some central issues in the study of temperament. One issue is stability. How consistent are children's temperaments as they develop? Answering this question requires a longitudinal approach, in which the same children are studied repeatedly over time. As the title of the Thomas et al. project reveals, longitudinal analysis has been a part of temperament research from its inception. In the

New York Longitudinal Study the initial interview procedure covered the span of infancy; through various other methods—parent and teacher questionnaires, observations, interviews with the subjects themselves—many of the subjects were eventually followed until adolescence. The most general conclusion to emerge—a conclusion that also holds for other longitudinal studies of temperament—was that temperament shows some, but far from perfect, stability as children develop. Thomas et al. found that the degree of apparent stability varied across temperamental dimensions; activity level, for example, showed relatively good stability, whereas approach/withdrawal showed very little stability. They also found that stability decreased as the time span between the measures increased. Recall that this same (quite expectable) finding emerges in longitudinal studies of IQ.

The difficulties in doing longitudinal research have been discussed at several points. An especially salient problem in the case of longitudinal studies of temperament is that of *measurement equivalence*. Consider a dimension like "intensity of reaction" from the New York Longitudinal Study. At age 2 months the questions from which intensity is scored concern matters such as reactions to a wet diaper and response to new foods, and answers indicative of high intensity might include "screams when wet" and "spits out any new food." By 2 years these questions and corresponding responses are less clearly relevant, and by 7 years they are not appropriate at all. If intensity of reaction (or, for that matter, any of the dimensions from the Thomas et al. typology) is to be measured at 7 years, many of the specific behaviors that are asked about must be quite different from those that are measured in infancy. An apparent lack of stability might then reflect either genuine change in children as they develop or failure to establish equivalent measures at the different ages.

A second major issue in the study of temperament concerns the origin of individual differences. Much of the interest in measures of temperament has stemmed from the possibility that such measures might be tapping genetically based differences among children, differences that predate parental socialization efforts but also have a definite impact on eventual socialization. Indeed, the existence of a genetic component is an explicit criterion in some theories and definitions of temperament (e.g, Buss & Plomin, 1975).

Various lines of evidence suggest that temperament is in part genetically based. The fact that individual differences emerge so early, prior to much chance for socialization to operate, is one source of evidence. In the New York Longitudinal Study differences were apparent by 2 months, the youngest age sampled.

Other research has documented individual differences, including differences in temperament-like qualities, during the neonatal period, most notably on a test called the Brazelton Neonatal Behavioral Assessment Scale (Brazelton, 1973). The earlier in development a difference emerges, the more plausible a genetic contribution becomes.

The relation between genes and temperament can also be examined with the same research designs that were described in chapter 7 in the discussion of differences in IQ. Although adopted child studies are still rare in the temperament literature, twin studies have proliferated in recent years. The logic behind such studies is the same as that described for IQ: If genes contribute to the differences being measured, then identical twins should be more similar than fraternal twins. Greater similarity for identicals than for fraternals is in fact the common finding in twin studies of temperament. Beyond this general statement it is difficult to say much at all briefly, for complexities and contradictions abound. The importance of genetic factors may be greater for some temperamental dimensions than for others, may vary depending on the developmental level of the child, and may vary depending on the method used for assessing temperament (Goldsmith, 1983; Plomin, 1981). Note, however, that the greater similarity for identicals does *not* come about simply because parents have a response bias to describe identical twins as more similar than fraternal twins. Identical-fraternal differences emerge even when parents do not know the twins' zygosity, they emerge regardless of the degree of physical similarity between the twins, and they emerge on direct observations of the children's behavior and not only on parental ratings. There seems little doubt, therefore, that genes *do* contribute to individual differences in temperament.

A final point is that there is also little doubt that genes are not the sole explanation for differences in temperament. The ultimate effect of a child's genetic endowment depends very much on the environment in which the child develops. This point emerges clearly from longitudinal studies of the stability of temperament. As noted, Thomas and Chess (1977) found only moderate stability, at best, for individual dimensions of temperament. "Moderate stability" was also an accurate conclusion for the more global constellations, such as Easy Child or Difficult Child. Children classified in infancy as Difficult did have a heightened probability of later behavioral problems, a finding of considerable clinical as well as theoretical interest. The predictive power of early Difficult temperament was far from perfect, however, and much still depended on the later environment to which the child was exposed. In some cases the parents seemed to aggravate the child's early problems by their responses to them; in other cases the parents adapted more readily, the resulting "fit" between child and environment was more appropriate, and development proceeded more smoothly. As Thomas and Chess (1977) emphasize, "In no case did a given pattern of temperament, as such, result in behavioral disturbance. Deviant development was always the result of the *interaction* between a child's individual makeup and significant features of the environment" (p.38). It is the promise of insight into this interaction of biology and experience that explains much of the contemporary interest in the study of temperament.

In addition to the sources already cited, further discussions and reviews of temperament can be found in Porter and Collins (1982) and Campos et al. (1983). For examples of conceptions of temperament that deviate some from the Thomas et al. approach stressed here, see Buss and Plomin (1975) and Rothbart and Derryberry (1981).

SOCIALIZATION

We turn now to our second general issue: the question of determinants. Where do the child's social behaviors, both those we have been discussing and others, come from? Our approach to this question focuses on processes of socialization—ways in which other people (parents, teachers, siblings, peers) influence the child's

social development. We consider three approaches to the study of socialization: laboratory studies, observational measures, and self-report or rating measures. This is, of course, the same general division that we saw in the first part of the chapter.

A caveat is in order before we start. Although the socialization experiences that we consider are important, they do not provide a full explanation of the child's social development. Biological factors, for example, undoubtedly contribute. As we have just seen, temperament is generally believed to have a biological basis. Sex differences may also be in part (although only in part) biologically caused. Cognition also plays a role. As the discussion of both morality and sex typing suggested, cognitive factors have assumed increasing prominence in explanations for social development. Developmental changes in the child's cognitive abilities are only partly explained by the kinds of socialization processes that we discuss. The message, in short, is again one of selectivity: This section considers *some* of the explanations for social development.

Laboratory Studies

The goal in a laboratory study of socialization is to create an experimental analogue to the real-life socialization experiences of interest. It is never possible, of course, to duplicate exactly the complexities of the natural environment in a laboratory setting. It may be possible, however, to abstract critical *processes*—to reproduce certain experiences in a way that is similar enough to their natural occurrence to permit generalization. If so, then the control and precision of laboratory study may allow us to determine cause-and-effect relations.

We consider two examples. It seems clear even without formal study that one important contributor to the child's social development consists of the various *models* to whom the child is exposed. Children learn behaviors from first observing them in others; they also are influenced in their performance of already existing behaviors by what they see others do. Modeling has come to be stressed especially in contemporary social learning accounts of social development (Bandura, 1977).

How might the variable of modeling be studied in a laboratory setting? Let us take aggression as our content area. Aggression has undoubtedly been *the* most popular topic for experimental studies of modeling; hence there is no shortage of examples from which to choose. Our example is an experiment by Hicks (1968; see also chapter 5 in which other studies of modeling are briefly described). In Hicks's study the subjects (5- to 8-year-olds) were taken individually from their classrooms by a female experimenter to play with some toys. En route to the playroom, the experimenter remembered that she had some work to do in the library, and suggested that the child watch a short film while he or she waited. The film, which was shown on a TV screen in a room near the library, depicted an adult male performing various aggressive actions toward a Bobo doll. Following the completion of the film, the child was taken on to the playroom and left to play for 15 minutes. The room contained both toys that could be used for either imitative or nonimitative aggression (including a Bobo doll) and toys that lent themselves to nonaggressive play. The child's behavior was observed through a one-way screen, and all instances of aggression (which were frequent) were recorded.

The Hicks study is a typical modeling experiment in several respects. First, the presentation of the model involves what might be called an "exposure technique." The child is not explicitly instructed to watch the model, let alone to learn the model's behaviors; rather, the child is simply exposed to the behaviors. Similarly, the imitation test involves an opportunity to imitate but no instructions to do so; the child decides whether or not to copy the model. It could be argued that this procedure parallels most of the real-life situations in which we are interested, situations in which children observe behaviors in others but are not forced to imitate those behaviors. Finally, the Hicks experiment is also typical in allowing for both imitative and nonimitative effects of the model. Children in

Hick's study pound the Bobo doll with a hammer in the same way as the model; they also perform a number of aggressive actions that were not shown by the model at all. The study thus demonstrates the two ways in which models affect behavior: via exact imitation and via elicitation of related behaviors that are already part of the child's repertoire.

As we stressed earlier, one strength of the laboratory approach is that it permits systematic manipulation of a wide range of potentially important independent variables. Many such variables have been explored in modeling research. We can ask, for example, about the characteristics of the model that might influence imitation. In Hicks's study the model was an adult male; other studies have examined a male-female contrast (e.g., Perry & Perry, 1975) or an adult-child contrast (e.g., Bandura, Grusec, & Menlove, 1967). In Hicks's study the model was presented on film; many studies use live models, and some have included a filmed versus live contrast (e.g., McCall, Parke, & Kavanaugh, 1977). The relation between the model and child can also be manipulated. In some studies, like Hicks's, the model is a stranger to the child. In other studies the effects of various kinds of model-child relation (e.g., warm and supportive, cold and distant) have been explored, either through using a model who is already known to the child (e.g., Hetherington & Frankie, 1967) or by including a premodeling period of interaction between model and child (e.g., Jeffrey, Hartmann, & Gelfand, 1972). The consequences to the model following his or her behavior have also been of interest. We can ask, for example, whether children are most likely to imitate behaviors that they see reinforced and least likely to imitate behaviors that they see punished (e.g., Bandura, Ross, & Ross, 1963b; the answer, by the way, is in general yes). Finally, all sorts of situational aspects of either the modeling phase or the imitation phase can be experimentally manipulated. Hicks's study, for example, included a condition in which an adult male viewed the aggressive film with the subject and offered evaluative comments about the model's behaviors. For half the children the adult remained present during the imitation phase; for the other half the adult did not.

We have been discussing various manipulations that are possible at the independent-variable end in modeling research. The modeling paradigm also lends itself to a wide range of different outcome or dependent variables. Laboratory studies of modeling have demonstrated effects of models on dozens of different behaviors. Apart from aggression, perhaps the most often studied outcomes have been various behaviors under the heading of moral development. Modeling effects have been shown for all of the behaviors discussed in the first part of the chapter—cheating, resistance to temptation, sharing, help giving, and so forth. The effects, moreover, have been demonstrated in both the "prescribed" and the "proscribed" directions. A child who sees a model share, for example, becomes more likely to share later on; a child who sees a model refuse to share becomes less likely to share. Similarly, a child who sees a model resist temptation becomes better able to resist; a child who sees a model fail to resist becomes more likely to give in to the temptation (see Perry and Bussey, 1984, and Rushton, 1980, for reviews).

Let us summarize the virtues of the laboratory approach to the study of modeling. Such studies focus on a process that is of undeniable importance in the child's socialization: the impact of other people's behavior on related behaviors in the child. The control that is possible in the laboratory—control not only over the exact form of the modeling but over other aspects of the situation—permits a clear demonstration of cause-and-effect relations between modeling and subsequent behavior. This control also allows the examination of a wide range of independent variables.

Given the discussions in chapter 5 and the first part of this chapter, it is unnecessary to dwell on the limitations of laboratory studies. As always, the major concern has to do with external validity. What most lab studies of modeling show most clearly is that models presented in a very delimited situation can affect behavior immediately afterward in another very

delimited situation. In the natural environment it is often the more deferred, long-term effects of modeling that are of interest; except by inference, most lab studies tell us nothing about such long-term effects. In the natural environment models are often embedded in a wealth of other stimuli, and the child must somehow attend to them and transfer their effects to another, perhaps very different situation. In most lab studies both the presentation and the performance phases are greatly simplified, thus bypassing many of the questions of attention, selection, and transfer that apply in the more complex natural environment. Finally, in most lab studies the model is a stranger or relative stranger to the child. It remains debatable just how generalizable effects demonstrated in such studies are to the home setting, in which children are exposed countless times across many years to models with whom they have intense emotional relationships.

The second socialization process that we consider is *punishment*. Like modeling, punishment is an experience of undeniable salience in the lives of most children. All children receive punishments of some form, and all parents must make decisions about whether, when, and how to administer punishment. What can laboratory research tell us about this important issue?

The most common laboratory paradigm for studying punishment is exemplified in some research by Ross Parke (1969; Parke & Walters, 1967). The subjects for most of Parke's studies have been first and second graders; other researchers have used similar procedures with preschoolers (e.g., Aronfreed & Reber, 1965). The procedure begins with experimenter and child alone together in the experimental room and with the following instructions:

The *S* was seated at table B and instructed as follows: "What I'm going to do is put some toys out here on the table. Each time I'm going to put down two toys, and here is what I want you to do. I want you to choose the toy that you would like to play with. I want you to pick it up, hold it, and think about it, and if I ask you, I want you to tell me what it is or what it is used for. Do you understand?" After the *S* had indicated that he understood the nature of the task, the *E* continued, "Now some of these toys are for another boy, and you are not supposed to touch them. So if you touch a toy that is for the other boy, I'll tell you, and you will hear a noise like this. . . . O.K.?" (Parke & Walters, 1967, p. 8)

Pairs of toys are in fact then presented, and on certain predetermined trials the child's choice of a toy is punished. In most of Parke's studies the punishment has consisted of a loud buzzer coupled with a verbal rebuke (e.g., "No, that's for the other boy."). Other researchers have sometimes used withdrawal of candy as a punishment. In any case, the goal of the first phase of the study is to give children a history of being punished for attempting to play with certain toys.

The second phase of the study was described earlier in the section on Moral Development. It consists of a *resistance-to-temptation test*. The child is left alone with the toys, and his or her ability to resist the temptation to play with them is measured. The question is whether the children who have been punished for playing with the toys are better able to resist the temptation than a control group of children who have not been punished. The answer, on the average, is yes; thus punishment, at least in this situation, does work in producing later suppression of the punished response.

As with lab studies of modeling, the procedure just described lends itself to systematic manipulation of numerous potentially important variables. Experimental studies have identified a number of variables that can influence the effectiveness of punishment. One is the *timing* of the punishment. At least in the particular situation utilized by Parke, punishment that is delivered early in the response sequence is more effective in suppressing behavior than punishment delivered late in the response sequence. The *intensity* of the punishment can also be important. Within the narrow range of intensities examined in the lab research (moderate vs. high decibel levels for the buzzer), intense punishments work better than less intense ones. This conclusion depends, however, on the complexity of the behavior being punished. When the child must learn a new response, as opposed to

simply inhibiting an existing behavior, then intense punishments are generally not effective (Aronfreed & Leff, 1963). The *relation to the punishing agent* plays a role. Punishment works best when the punishing agent has previously established a warm, nurturant relation with the child. Finally, the *cognitive structuring* that accompanies the prohibition is one of the most important variables. Punishment works best when accompanied by a reason for the prohibition—for example, an indication that the toys belong to another child, or that they might break if the subject plays with them. Reasoning adds to the effectiveness of punishment; furthermore, reasoning alone, at least in this situation, is more effective than punishment alone.

Laboratory studies of punishment share some of the limitations discussed earlier with respect to lab studies of modeling. In most cases the adult delivering the punishment is a stranger or at least relative stranger to the child. Generalization to the home setting and to the issue of parental punishments must therefore be made with caution. The time span between the delivery of punishment and the test for its effects is generally very brief in a laboratory study. In the natural environment our interest is often in more long-term effects of punishment—the question whether the behavioral control instilled by punishment is still in effect some time after the punishment occurs. Finally, the punishment used in most laboratory studies—a loud, unpleasant buzzer—bears only a distant resemblance to the real-life punishments that children receive. In addition to the general challenges of laboratory study, researchers of punishment face an obvious ethical problem in designing punishments that can be delivered ethically to children. The punishments that have been used are, necessarily, rather different from those that are found in many homes, and caution in generalizing is therefore again necessary.

Naturalistic Observation

The first part of the chapter discussed naturalistic studies of important socialization outcomes such as moral behavior and sex typing.

The studies we consider next include such measures as part of their scope. They add to them, however, an attempt to measure naturally occurring socialization experiences as well. The goal is to establish a cause-and-effect relation between particular experience and particular outcome.

Again we consider two examples. The previous section focused on the models and punishments that adults provide to children. Adults are not the only socialization agents that children encounter, however; other children may also be important. And modeling and punishments are hardly the only socialization processes that affect a child's development. One does not have to be Skinnerian to believe that a third important contributor to socialization is the *reinforcement* that children receive for various behaviors. Our first example, therefore, concerns the variable of peer reinforcement.

Peers can and do reinforce a wide variety of behaviors. Michael Lamb and colleagues (Lamb, Easterbrooks, & Holden, 1980; Lamb & Roopnarine, 1979) examined possible contributions of peer reinforcement to the development of sex differences. Their subjects were nursery-school children, and their procedure involved naturalistic observation across a span of several weeks in the nursery school. A time-sampling procedure was used, with each child observed for three to six 10-minute periods. Two general classes of event were recorded. One was sex-typed behaviors. The male-typed activities (as defined from both previous research and adult consensus) included playing with vehicles, climbing, chasing, and wearing male costumes; the female-typed activities included playing with kitchen utensils, art work, doll play, and wearing female costumes. The second set of measurements focused on peer responses to the occurrence of sex-typed behaviors. Both reinforcing and punishing responses were of interest. Seven general categories of response were classified as reinforcers; examples include "praise," "approve," and "comply." Five types of punishing consequence were scored, including "criticize" and "disapprove."

Several findings emerged. Peer responses were definitely affected by the sex-appropriateness of the behavior. Both boys and girls were more likely to receive reinforcement from other children when they engaged in sex-appropriate behavior than when their behavior fit a pattern more typical of the opposite sex. Other researchers (e.g., Fagot, 1977) have also observed such differential response to sex-typed behaviors in the nursery school. Lamb and colleagues also reported evidence that the responses classified as reinforcers or punishers did in fact affect subsequent behavior. The mean latency to terminate a behavior was significantly longer when the behavior resulted in a reinforcer than when it resulted in a punisher, and the overall duration of behavior was greater for reinforced behaviors than for those that were either punished or received no response. Lamb et al. also found, however, that the effects of reinforcers or punishers were in part dependent on the sex-appropriateness of the behavior. Reinforced behaviors persisted longer when they were sex-appropriate; similarly, punished behaviors terminated more quickly when they were sex-inappropriate. Lamb et al. offer a cognitive interpretation of this finding. They suggest that even by age 3 children are aware of sex-role standards and are motivated to conform to them; reinforcement or punishment from peers then serves primarily as a reminder of these standards.

For our second example of a naturalistic study of socialization we move from peers in the nursery school to parents and siblings in the home. Across a series of articles Patterson (1979, 1982; Patterson & Cobb, 1971) has reported analyses from a long-term investigation of the determinants of coercive behavior in the home. The primary sample for the research has consisted of families who were referred to the Oregon "Social Learning Project" because at least one child in the family displayed high rates of aggressive behavior. The goal of the research has been to identify the social processes within the home that contribute to coercive behaviors, not only with regard to the target child but for family members in general. The strategy adopted has been naturalistic observation—

many hours of observation, within the natural home setting, of aggressive behaviors and their antecedents and consequences.

We focus here on one specific report from the Patterson project (Patterson & Cobb, 1971). The subjects for this analysis were 24 families with at least one hyperaggressive boy between the ages of 6 and 13. Each family was observed for a total of 10 hours—5 days a week, 1 hour a day, for 2 weeks. The observations were carried out in the kitchen or adjoining room, and all family members were required to remain in one or the other room during the data collection. Observations were made both of the subject's behavior (each family member in turn, for 5-minute periods at a time) and of the response of other family members to the behavior. The coding system occupied an intermediate position on the molecular-molar dimension discussed earlier. It consisted of 30 categories intended to capture aspects of social interaction: Approval, Attention, Command, Command Negative, Comply, Cry, Dependency, Destructiveness, Disapproval, High Rate (hyperactive), Hit, Humiliate, Ignore, Indulge, Laugh, Negativism, No Response, Noncomply, Normative, Physical Positive, Play, Proximity, Receive, Self-Stimulation, Talk, Tease, Touch, Whine, Work, and Yell. The category on which the Patterson and Cobb report focused was Hit, and the major interest was in the instigators and reinforcers for Hit.

The analysis utilized by Patterson and Cobb involved the calculation of *conditional probabilities*. The starting point for such calculations is the determination of the base rate for some behavior, such as Hit. The base rate is the overall rate of occurrence of the behavior—that is, the total number of occurrences of the targeted behavior divided by the total number of behaviors recorded. If, for example, 10,000 behaviors were recorded and 80 of those behaviors were Hits, then the base rate for Hit would be .008. Once the base rate is known, changes in the probability of the behavior can be examined as a function of various antecedent stimuli, and changes in the probability that an ongoing behavior will continue or be repeated can be ex-

amined as a function of various consequences. Here we focus on antecedents. Patterson and Cobb analyzed the probability of Hits as a function of the immediate presence of each other member of the family. They found, not surprisingly, that the presence of either the mother or the father was associated with a significant reduction in the probability of Hits relative to the baseline level—a sixfold reduction in the case of the father. In contrast, the presence of a younger sister or an older brother was associated with a significant increase in the probability of Hit. Presumably, these effects come about because parents and siblings offer different instigators for aggression and respond differently when aggression occurs. The specific behaviors that affected aggression were examined through a further set of conditional probabilities. This analysis revealed both *facilitating stimuli* that were associated with increased probabilities of Hit and *inhibitory stimuli* that were associated with decreased probabilities. In general, the facilitating stimuli were most likely to be delivered by siblings and the inhibitory stimuli by parents. Examples of inhibitory stimuli included both positive responses such as Approve and Physical Positive, responses that apparently encouraged alternative prosocial behavior, and negative, punishing responses such as Command Negative and Yell. Examples of facilitating stimuli included Cry, Laugh, and Hit. Hit was the most effective facilitating stimulus, a finding indicative of the cyclical, self-perpetuating nature of aggression in the home.

The strategy adopted by Patterson and Cobb is a form of *sequential analysis*. The goal of a sequential analysis is to capture cause-and-effect relations in the stream of ongoing social behavior. Such analyses always involve a focus on at least two individuals who are engaged in some form of social interaction. Both participants are observed and their behaviors recorded; in some cases the same observational system is used for both (as in the Patterson and Cobb study) and in some cases different systems are used (as in studies of mother-infant interaction). Whatever the specific coding system, the recordings always include information about not only the occurrence of both participants' behaviors but also the *temporal sequencing* of the behaviors. Suppose that our interest is in mothers and infants and the relation between maternal touching and infant smiling. By noting the sequence of behaviors we might find that maternal touches increase following infant smiles—that is, that the conditional probability of touch given a preceding smile is greater than the base rate for touch. This finding would suggest that the direction of cause and effect is from infant to mother, with infant smiles causing maternal touches. Alternatively, the analysis might reveal that infant smiles increase following maternal touches, which would suggest that the mother is playing the causal role and that touches promote smiling. The logic of such sequential analyses is the same as that described earlier for cross-lagged correlations in longitudinal research: Causes precede effects, and the causal relation between two variables can therefore be inferred from the degree to which variations in one variable at time 1 are associated with variations in the other variable at time 2.

Both the virtues and the limitations of naturalistic observation have been discussed at several points and need be only briefly reiterated here. Laboratory measures of socialization are often artificial and hence lacking in external validity. Rating measures of socialization (the subject of our next section) are verbal reports that may or may not reflect actual behavior. Naturalistic observations overcome both of these limitations: They focus on behaviors, not statements about behaviors, and they focus on naturally occurring behavior in the natural setting. Such studies may be the only way to answer the "does" question posed by McCall (1977): Not only *can* a particular socialization experience produce some effect, but *does* it in fact do so in the child's natural environment? With the development of techniques of sequential analysis, naturalistic observation now offers the possibility of moving beyond description of behavior to get closer to the underlying cause and effect.

The Patterson project provides a good context for talking about the challenges in naturalistic study. A basic problem is that of obtaining accurate observations. This problem is likely to be especially great when the attempt (as in the Patterson research) is to record a wide range of behaviors and to do so in the uncontrolled natural setting. A further problem, also related to the lack of control over the setting, is the possible infrequency of certain behaviors. Without the possibility of experimentally eliciting the responses of interest, the investigator may find that some behaviors occur too infrequently during the observation period to be usable. The possible effects of the observer on the behavior being observed are a major concern. Again, the Patterson project provides an obvious example: Not only are strangers introduced into the home, but the goal is to record such negative behaviors as hitting or yelling, precisely the sort of behaviors that seem most likely to be inhibited in the presence of an observer. Finally, the technique of sequential analysis, though enormously promising, is by no means as easy to apply or interpret as our brief discussion may have suggested. There are in fact many complexities and unresolved issues in the use of sequential analysis (Kraemer & Jacklin, 1979; Maccoby & Martin, 1983; Sackett, 1979). In addition, the approach, no matter how expertly executed, remains correlational and not experimental, and as such cannot yield the certainty about cause-and-effect relations that is possible with experimental manipulation.

Self-Report Measures

We have considered two general methods of obtaining evidence about socialization: laboratory studies and naturalistic observation. The third general approach is to elicit self-reports of socialization practices. In this case we learn how parents treat their children by asking the parents how they treat their children. As with any rating or verbal-report measure, the asking can take the form of either an interview or a questionnaire. The example on which we focus involves interviews with mothers.

A classic study of childrearing is Sears, Maccoby, and Levin's (1957) *Patterns of Childrearing.*

The Sears et al. project was one of the first really systematic attempts to assess parental child-rearing practices and their effects on children. It also remains one of the most ambitious and comprehensive such attempts.

The subjects for the Sears et al. study were 379 mothers of 5-year-old children. Each mother was interviewed regarding both her childrearing practices and aspects of development in her child. The interviews (which averaged 2 hours in length) were directed to a wide range of socialization issues. Mothers were asked about the techniques that they had used for feeding and toilet training when their child was younger. They were asked about their typical methods for handling aggression, sex play, or bids for dependency. Some of the questions concerned specific practices, such as breast versus bottle feeding or frequency of spanking; others were more general, directed to matters such as enjoyment of the baby or expectations with regard to obedience. Some questions concerned contemporary issues in the child's socialization; others were retrospective, directed to practices (such as method of infant feeding) from the past. A few asked about the father's behavior rather than the mother's. And several concerned characteristics of the child and not methods of parental socialization.

The Sears et al. interview included 72 questions in all. A sampling of items is shown in Box 8-9. In addition to giving some idea of the content of the interview, the examples illustrate the general format that was used. The questions were open-ended—that is, the mother was free to respond in any way and at any length that she wished, as opposed to simply agreeing or disagreeing with some statement or circling a point on a rating scale. Many of the 72 questions also had follow-up probes. Although the probes were semistandardized, exactly what was asked and how it was worded necessarily varied to some extent depending on the mother's initial response.

A procedure like Sears et al.'s generates a huge quantity of data. What is to be done with all this material? In *Patterns of Childrearing* the first step was to *quantify* the mother's responses along a set of common dimensions. Two raters read each of the interviews and assigned a value for each of 188 rating scales. The scales varied in the number of points that they contained. Some were limited to three or four points—for example, a rating of which parent was more strict about obedience, or of whether the father had ever shown a tendency to reject the child. Most of the scales were more differentiated, ranging from five to eight or nine distinct points. Both "severity of weaning" and "extent of use of reasoning," for example, were rated on 9-point scales. The scales also differed in how readily the scoring judgments could be made. Some were simply a transcription of information given directly in the interview and therefore required little judgment on the rater's part. One scale, for example, measured age at completion of weaning, and another coded age at which bowel training was begun. Other scales required considerably more interpretation in moving from interview response to scale rating. Examples here included scales such as "affectional bond of mother to infant" and "mother's sex anxiety." Not surprisingly, interrater reliability was greater for the first than for the second kind of scale.

The various scales for summarizing socialization attitudes and practices provided the basis for answering one of the major questions that motivated the *Patterns* book: How do parents in fact rear their children? The researchers were also interested, however, in a second major question: What effects do these patterns of childrearing have on the child's development? Answering this second question required data about the children as well as the parents. For the most part, the information about children that was utilized in the *Patterns* book came from the same source as the information about parents: the interviews with the mothers. As noted, a number of the interview questions were directed not to parental socialization but to the child's development; examples in Box 8-9 are questions 44, 44a, and 44b. The general strategy was then to look for relations between parental practices on the one hand and child outcomes on the other.

The findings from *Patterns of Childrearing* are far too extensive and complex to be summa-

BOX 8–9 Examples of questions from the Sears, Maccoby, and Levin childrearing interview

5. All babies cry, of course. Some mothers feel that if you pick up a baby every time it cries, you will spoil it. Others think you should never let a baby cry for long. How do you feel about this?

    5a. What did you do about this with X?

    5b. How about in the middle of the night?

6. Did you have time to spend with the baby besides the time that was necessary for feeding him, changing him, and just regular care like that?

    6a. [If yes] Tell me about what you did in this time. How much did you cuddle him and sing to him and that sort of thing?

7. Do you think that babies are fun to take care of when they're very little, or do you think they're more interesting when they're older?

    . . .

    . . .

16. Now we'd like to consider toilet training. When did you start bowel training with X?

    16a. How did it go?

    16b. How did you go about it?

    16c. How long did it take till he was pretty well trained?

    16d. What did you do about it when he had accidents after he was mostly trained?

17. Now would you tell me what you have done with X about bed-wetting?

    17a. How do you feel about it when he wets his bed?

    17b. How do you handle the situation when you find his bed is wet? (Or how did you the last time it happened?)

    . . .

    . . .

40. Now how about when X is playing with one of the other children in the neighborhood and there is a quarrel or a fight—how do you handle this?

41. Some people feel it is very important for a child to learn not to fight with other children, and other people feel there are times when a child has to learn to fight. How do you feel about this?

    41a. Have you ever encouraged your child to fight back?

42. Sometimes a child will get angry at his parents and hit them or kick them or shout angry things at them. How much of this sort of thing do you think parents ought to allow in a child of X's age?

    42a. How do you handle it when X acts like this? Give me an example.

    42b. [If this doesn't happen] How did you teach him not to do this?

    42c. How much of a problem have you had with X about shows of temper and angry shouting and that sort of thing around the house?

    . . .

    . . .

44. We'd like to get some idea of how X acts when he's naughty. (I know we've been talking about naughty behavior a lot, and we don't mean to imply that he's naughty all the time or anything, but most children do act up once in a while, and we're interested in knowing about it.) For instance, when he has deliberately done something he knows you don't want him to do, when your back is turned, how does he act?

    44a. Does he ever come and tell you about it without your having to ask him?

    44b. When you ask him about something he has done that he knows he's not supposed to do, does he usually admit it or deny it?

    44c. What do you do about it if he denies something you are pretty sure he has done?

Note. From *Patterns of Childrearing* (pp. 491–493, 496–497) by R. R. Sears, E. E. Maccoby, and H. Levin, 1957, Stanford: Stanford University Press. Copyright 1957 by Stanford University Press. Reprinted by permission.

rized here. A couple examples can be mentioned, however, just to give a flavor of the conclusions. Sears et al. reported that use of love-withdrawal techniques of discipline by the mother was associated with relatively strong development of conscience in the child. This relation held true, however, only for mothers who also had generally warm relations with their children. With regard to aggression, Sears et al. concluded that two aspects of the mother's behavior seemed to be especially important in promoting aggression: relatively high permissiveness for aggression, and relatively high use of physical punishment. Note that the latter finding is compatible with the idea, discussed both earlier in this chapter and in chapter 5, that aggressive models lead to aggression in children.

We turn now to an evaluation of the self-report approach. As always, the strengths and weaknesses of one approach are clearest when contrasted with the strengths and weaknesses of other approaches. We saw that laboratory studies have the virtue of experimental control but at the possible cost of artificiality and lack of generalizability. Furthermore, laboratory studies, even if they incorporate the parent as part of the experimental procedure, tell us only about possibilities; they cannot tell us what parents actually do. Observational studies *do* tell us what parents actually do, but with an important qualifier: They tell us what parents do when the parents know that they are being watched. In addition, observational measures are dependent on the ability of human observers to form accurate interpretations of complex streams of social behavior. And both laboratory measures and observational measures are limited in the range of situations and behaviors that they encompass.

It is this final variable of breadth of scope that constitutes perhaps the most obvious strength of the self-report approach. This strength is especially evident in *Patterns of Child-rearing*. Within a space of 2 hours Sears et al. were able to gather evidence regarding a wide range of socialization practices, a far wider range—in terms of time periods, environmental settings, and specific behaviors—than could

ever be captured in naturalistic observation or laboratory study. This evidence, moreover, concerned the mother's naturally occurring behavior in the natural setting, behavior unaffected by the presence of observers or by the artifices of the lab. Although the direct evidence consisted of verbal report rather than behavior, this report was provided by the person with by far the most knowledge—and in some cases unique knowledge—about maternal behavior: the mother herself.

The strengths of the self-report approach must be set against one obvious and all-important question: Do parents accurately report their own behavior? The general answer to this question is "sometimes yes and sometimes no." Various kinds of evidence tell us that parental self-reports are not always accurate. Correlations between parents' reports of their socialization practices and direct observations of parental behavior are often modest at best (e.g., Yarrow, Campbell, & Burton, 1968). Studies that solicit information about the same socialization agent from different informants (e.g., ask mother, father, and child about the mother's behavior) also typically report modest correlations (e.g., Kohn & Carroll, 1960; note that these are the same kinds of evidence that call into question parental ratings of child temperament). Parents may be inaccurate for a number of reasons. In some cases parents may distort their answers, either consciously or unconsciously, to make themselves look better. Such "prideful subject" behavior (see chapter 4) is always a special concern with self-report measures. Parents may misinterpret questions or use terms in their answers in ways different from the way that the researcher uses the terms. Different parents may have different referent systems or "anchor points." Two mothers, for example, may both describe themselves as "strict" with regard to disobedience; for one mother, however, "strict" may mean occasional admonishments whereas for the other it may mean invariable physical punishment. Parents may simply forget what it is that they do or used to do with their child. Memory problems are especially likely when the measures are retrospective—that is, concern socialization practices from some earlier period in the child's life. Research has shown that self-reports that extend back over several years are of very doubtful accuracy (Yarrow, Campbell, & Burton, 1970).

Methods of increasing the accuracy of self-report data follow from this list of sources of bias. Accurate reports are more likely if the questions concern contemporary socialization practices than if they concern events from the past. Accuracy is also more likely if the questions are directed to concrete situations and specific behaviors, thus minimizing the need for the parent to decipher exactly what it is that the researcher is asking. The value of specificity applies not only to the questions asked but also to the form in which the parent is expected to answer. If the questions elicit descriptions of specific behaviors, as opposed to the parent's interpretation of the behaviors, then the problem of anchor points is minimized and the researcher has the necessary information to make the desired interpretations (e.g., "love withdrawal," "permissive"). Finally, the inevitable tendency toward positive self-presentation can at least be reduced by couching the interview or questionnaire in as nonevaluative a framework as possible ("no right or wrong answers," "just want to know what parents do," etc.). Note in Box 8-9 the consistent attempt by Sears et al. to be reassuring and nonevaluative. Given the gaps in our knowledge of childrearing, such wording is in fact reasonably accurate.

Accuracy is one major issue in self-report studies of childrearing. The other major issue is the determination of causality. Studies like *Patterns of Childrearing* are inherently *correlational*. What they demonstrate is that some childrearing practice (such as love withdrawal) covaries with some developmental outcome in the child (such as measures of conscience). As we saw in chapter 5, however, a correlational design cannot tell us why the covariation occurs. In childrearing research there are always a number of possible explanations for a parent-child correlation. One is that the parent's behavior causes the child's behavior—in this case, that love withdrawal promotes moral development. This,

of course, is generally the explanation of greatest interest to the researcher. A second is that the child's behavior causes the parent's behavior. Ever since Bell's (1968) influential paper, the idea that children influence their parents has assumed increasing prominence in socialization research. A third possibility is that causal effects flow in both directions; perhaps over time the parent's behavior influences the child and the child's behavior influences the parent in a complex, reciprocal fashion. A final possibility is that there is no causal relation at all between the particular parental behavior and particular child outcome that we have decided to focus on. Love withdrawal and moral development may both result from some third factor or set of factors, and the relation between the two may therefore be merely statistical and not causal.

Chapter 5 considered not only the various alternative explanations for a correlation but also techniques for zeroing in on a particular causal interpretation. The point to note for now is that two of the techniques discussed there are in fact found in the first two approaches considered in the present Socialization section: experimental manipulation of the presumed causal variable, and determination of the sequential relation between the two variables. This observation leads to one last reiteration of the general point about the value of converging operations. Whenever specific methods for studying some topic are imperfect—and "imperfect" is certainly a safe description for methods in the knotty area of socialization—the only possible solution is a convergence of as many different methods as possible.

SUMMARY

This chapter is divided into two major sections. The first section discusses methods of studying important outcomes in the child's social development. The second section considers some of the socialization processes that contribute to these outcomes.

One important set of outcomes consists of the various behaviors, emotions, and cognitions that are grouped under the heading of "moral development.'' The behavioral aspect of morality includes both the production of positive, prosocial behaviors, such as sharing, and the avoidance of negative, prohibited behaviors, such as cheating. Moral behaviors—and indeed any topic in social development—can be studied in three general ways. With naturalistic observation the attempt is to measure the natural occurrence of behaviors in the natural setting. A laboratory study, in contrast, sets up a structured situation from which the behaviors of interest can be experimentally elicited. The third general approach is to collect ratings of moral behaviors from someone who knows the child well, such as a parent or teacher. Examples are discussed for each of these approaches, followed by a consideration of the strengths and weaknesses of the different methods of study. This discussion of strengths and weaknesses leads to a general point that recurs for each topic considered in the chapter: the importance of converging operations in studying methodologically challenging issues.

Studies of the emotional aspect of morality have examined both the negative emotion of guilt and the more positive, prosocial emotion of empathy. Guilt has occasionally been measured from the child's response to experimentally contrived deviations, such as the disappearing hamster test. A more common procedure, however, has been to infer the child's emotions from the endings that he or she provides for stories involving transgression, the assumption being that the child ''projects'' his or her own feelings onto the story character. Verbal measures have also been common in the assessment of empathy. Two tests for measuring empathy in childhood are described, both of which elicit the child's verbally reported emotion to a variety of potentially affect-arousing situations.

Research on the cognitive aspect of morality began with the pioneering work of Piaget. Like his research on cognitive development, Piaget's studies of morality stress the flexible clinical method of testing and the identification of qualitatively distinct stages of reasoning as the child matures. Another similarity between the two bodies of work lies in their ability to elicit crit-

icism and subsequent follow-up study, one subset of which (directed to the issue of intentions versus consequences in judging the morality of an action) is briefly described. In addition to stimulating follow-up study, Piaget's work is important as the forerunner of the major contemporary approach to moral reasoning, that of Kohlberg. Like Piaget, Kohlberg derives stages from children's responses to moral dilemmas; the dilemmas and corresponding stages, however, are a good deal more complex than those found in Piaget. The complexity of the scoring system and stage assignment has in fact always been one issue in evaluating Kohlberg's work. Another issue, central to the theory, concerns the claim that the stages emerge in an invariant sequence. Various methods of testing this claim are discussed.

The second major set of outcomes that the chapter considers fall under the heading of sex typing and sex differences. Findings regarding sex differences are often incidental to the main purpose of a study, a fact that complicates the interpretation of published sex differences and raises the possibility of biases in what information does get published. Biases may also occur at the point of data collection, perhaps especially as a result of the different expectancies that adults hold for boys and girls. The child's knowledge of the adult's sex may also have an effect. Children may respond differently to male testers and female testers, and there may occasionally be interactions between sex of child and sex of tester.

The discussion of general points is followed by a consideration of instruments explicitly designed for the study of sex differences and sex typing. Traditional tests of sex typing, such as the It Test, attempt to measure the child's adoption of stereotypically masculine or feminine behaviors and preferences. A criticism of such tests is that they treat ''masculine'' and ''feminine'' as polar opposites. Measures such as the CPAQ, therefore, incorporate separate masculinity and femininity scales, thus allowing for an ''androgynous'' mixture of traits. Finally, much recent attention has been directed to the cognitive side of sex typing and the child's understanding of gender and gender differences. Of interest here are the child's ability to label the sexes appropriately, the criteria that are used in applying labels, and the realization that gender is a permanent attribute.

The first section of the chapter concludes with a discussion of temperament. "Temperament" refers to behavioral style—to individual differences along dimensions such as activity level, approach/withdrawal, and distractibility. Temperament has typically been inferred from parents' responses to interviews or questionnaires concerning their child, a practice that has led to much debate about the validity of parental reports. Issues of interest in the temperament literature include the stability of temperament over time and the origin of individual differences. Longitudinal studies indicate that temperament has some, but far from perfect, stability across childhood. Various kinds of evidence (including twin studies) suggest that differences in temperament are in part biologically based.

The second major section of the chapter is directed to processes of socialization. Three general approaches to the study of socialization are discussed, approaches that parallel divisions drawn in the first part of the chapter. *Laboratory studies* attempt to reproduce important socialization experiences within the controlled environment of the laboratory. Examples are discussed for two much-studied issues in social development: the effects of *models* on the child's behavior, and the efficacy of *punishment* in suppressing behavior. The strengths of laboratory research lie in the experimental control and the consequent ability to specify cause-and-effect relations. A further strength is the possibility for experimental manipulation of a large number of potentially important variables. On the negative side, laboratory manipulations are always somewhat different from their real-life counterparts, and hence external validity must always be a concern.

A second general approach is *naturalistic observation*. The attempt in this case is to measure both socialization experiences and their effects within the natural setting. Again two examples are described, one concerned with peer responses to sex-typed behaviors in the nursery school and the other with the effects of parents and siblings on aggression in the home. Naturalistic studies escape the artificiality of the lab and provide the only direct measure of behaviors as they actually occur in the natural setting. Problems in such research include the difficulty of obtaining accurate observational measures, the possible effects of the observer on the behavior being observed, and the difficulty of establishing cause-and-effect relations in the stream of uncontrolled behavior. The technique of *sequential analysis* provides a promising approach to the last of these issues.

The final method is the *ratings or self-report* approach. In this case the measure of parental behavior is derived from the parent's responses to an interview or questionnaire concerning childrearing practices. The ambitious *Patterns of Childrearing* study is described as an example. The greatest strength of the self-report approach is the breadth of information that it provides about parental behavior. The greatest weakness is the possibility that such verbal reports do not accurately reflect behavior. Various methods for heightening the accuracy of self-reports are discussed. Also discussed is the second major challenge in childrearing research: determining the causal basis for parent-child correlations.

chapter 9

AGING

Until recently, the term "developmental psychology" was often merely a synonym for "child psychology." Most psychologists who labeled themselves as "developmental" were really researchers of childhood, and most texts in "developmental" were really texts about children. This state of affairs no longer holds true. Life-span treatments of development, both in general texts (e.g., Newman & Newman, 1984) and in more advanced treatises (e.g., Baltes & Brim, 1983), have proliferated. Within this general broadening of scope there has been special interest in the last part of the life span and the changes and challenges of old age. It is to the topic of the elderly years and the psychology of aging that the present chapter is devoted.

A number of reasons can be advanced for an interest in aging. One very simple reason is the increase in both the number and the proportion of elderly people. In 1900 approximately 4% of the population of the United States was aged 65 or older. Today approximately 11% of the population falls into this category, and it is estimated that by the year 2020 the figure will have risen to about 20% (Kausler, 1982). Both increases in life expectancy and fluctuations in birth rate have contributed to this trend. The greatest proportional increase, by the way, has come in the age group 80 and older (Myers & Soldo, 1977).

A second reason for an interest in aging is similar to one of the reasons for an interest in childhood. Childhood is in many respects a period of vulnerability, a time during which the growing organism is "at risk" for various problems. One reason to study children is to learn how to prevent these problems. Old age has also been considered a period of vulnerability and risk, a time when abilities decline and losses of various sorts (of health, job, spouse) occur. As we will see, a central question in the study of aging is how accurate this stereotypically negative picture is. Nevertheless, the problems are

211

clearly real for at least some elderly people, and the need to minimize their impact provides a further reason to study aging.

A third reason is more theoretical. "Development" is presumably a life-long process, and any model of development that stops with adolescence must therefore be incomplete. Within the long stretch from conception to death, it can be argued that special attention should be paid to those parts of the life span that are the locus for definite and major change. Childhood is clearly such a period—a time of frequent, inevitable, and monumental change. Many of the changes, moreover, are directional—a matter of upward movement, of adding on, of growth. Old age, it has been argued, may also be a period of major and at least somewhat inevitable change, but with an important difference: In this case the natural direction of change is negative rather than positive, a matter of losing rather than gaining. Again, the validity of such a negative characterization is very much a matter of dispute. The theoretical importance of the issue is clear, however, and hence the need for empirical study.

A final reason for an interest in aging is perhaps implied by the references in the preceding paragraphs to controversies and uncertainties. Such controversies and uncertainties arise, at least in part, because of the methodological challenges of studying development in old age and of comparing performance across different parts of the life span. Indeed, the psychology of aging illustrates with special clarity the challenges both of doing good research in general and of doing developmental research in particular. It thus constitutes an interesting and informative topic in scientific methodology, even for those who do not have any special professional or personal investment in its study.

It is, of course, the methodological aspects of research on aging that concern us here. This chapter follows the same general organization as chapter 6 on Infancy. We begin by considering general issues in the study of aging. As was true for infancy, these issues are for the most part not unique to the study of any one age group; as just suggested, however, many of

them apply with special force to research on aging. In the second part of the chapter we then consider some specific research topics in the psychology of aging.

The discussion of general issues will be clearest in the context of a specific example. The example that we use is the study of IQ. IQ is a good example, not only because IQ has probably been the most popular dependent variable in studies of aging but also because many of the methodological issues that we consider have been most fully explored in the context of IQ. The first part of the chapter, therefore, serves both as an overview of issues and as coverage of one important substantive topic.

GENERAL ISSUES (AS ILLUSTRATED BY THE STUDY OF IQ)

Sampling

We begin with the same question that was asked with regard to infancy: How do researchers find samples of elderly subjects to study? The answer is the same as for infancy: In a variety of ways, few of which fit a textbook model of random sampling. Unlike the researcher of childhood or young adulthood, the researcher of aging does not have an institutional setting such as a school or college to draw subjects from. Identifying and then randomly sampling from some representative pool of elderly people is therefore difficult. Probably the most common practice has been to solicit subjects from various groups or organizations to which elderly people belong, such as religious groups, senior citizens centers, or associations of retired people. Such an initial pool is obviously somewhat biased, because only relatively active and healthy older people are likely to belong to such groups. The sample may then become further biased because only volunteers can be included as subjects, and again only relatively competent older people are likely to volunteer for research. The result is that studies of aging have tended to employ somewhat nonrepresentative, positively biased samples of elderly people.

Obtaining a representative sample of the elderly is one goal of research on aging. The second goal is to obtain a sample of older people that is *comparable* to the younger sample to whom the elderly are being compared. Many studies of aging are not concerned simply with documenting levels of performance in older samples; their aim, rather, is to compare performance at older ages with that at younger ages. Because age is the independent variable in such research, it is important that the groups being compared be as similar as possible in every respect except age. As explained in chapter 2, this stricture does not mean that researchers should attempt to rule out all the ways in which 20-year-olds, say, differ from 70-year-olds. But it does mean that they should attempt to rule out any differences that are not naturally associated with age.

Deviations from representativeness in sampling subjects at any one age may bias the comparison of different age groups. The preceding discussion suggested that samples of elderly subjects may often be an above-average subset of the elderly population. If no comparable selectivity is exercised in sampling younger age groups, then the age comparison will be biased in favor of the elderly. On the other hand, if the "young adult" group consists of college students (a common practice), or if the elderly subjects are drawn from a nursing home, then the bias will go in the opposite direction. And even if the same selection procedures are used at each age, differences in volunteer rate (a seldom reported statistic in articles on aging) may still lead to noncomparable samples.

Two kinds of confound have been of particular concern in comparisons of young adults and elderly adults. One stems from differences in educational level. Imagine a study whose purpose is to compare mean levels of IQ at age 25 and at age 75. We will assume that the researcher solves the sampling problems discussed earlier and is able to obtain representative samples at each age. If the samples are truly representative of their age groups, then they are certain to differ not only in age but also in educational level: On the average, the young

adults will be better educated than the older adults. We will have, then, a confounding of age and education. Note the paradox here: Achieving one of the goals in sampling subjects, namely representative samples at each age, ensures some degree of failure with regard to the other goal, comparable samples at the different ages.

The general issue of age by cohort confounds in cross-sectional research was discussed in chapter 3. As noted then, the confounding is a problem only if the variable that is confounded with age bears some plausible relation to the dependent variable being examined. Is it plausible that educational level could relate to IQ? The answer is clearly yes. Indeed, not only is such a relation plausible; it has been clearly demonstrated in a number of studies. The standardization data for the WAIS, for example, showed a correlation of .68 between educational level and IQ (Wechsler, 1958). A subsequent analysis (Birren & Morrison, 1961) revealed that the relation between IQ and education was substantially stronger than the relation between IQ and age.

What is to be done about this confounding? As suggested in chapter 3, there is no really good solution. It is possible to match mean education level for different age groups through careful selection of subjects—for example, by tilting the selection toward unusually well-educated older adults and unusually poorly educated younger adults (e.g., Green, 1969). Such matching typically reduces but does not completely eliminate age differences in IQ. The obvious problem with this procedure is that it creates biased samples that are not representative of the general population. It is also possible to adjust statistically for the differences in education, in particular through a technique called analysis of covariance. Like other forms of statistical adjustment, however, analysis of covariance has a number of limitations, and its application to the age-education confound has been criticized (Storandt & Hudson, 1975; for general discussions of covariance see Reichardt, 1979, and Huitema, 1980). In addition, matching or statistical adjustment can at best equate subjects for *quantity* of education, as defined by years of schooling completed. There is no way to control either for *recency* of education or for possible changes in the *quality* of education over time.

The issue of education differences is part of the larger issue of cohort effects in cross-sectional designs, a topic that will be returned to shortly when we discuss questions of design. For now, one final point can be made. Whether the age-education confound is worrisome depends on exactly what we want to conclude from research. If our interest is limited to differences between young adults and elderly adults then there is no problem; it is simply a fact, consistently verified by a large number of studies, that there *is* an average age difference in IQ. The problem comes when we attempt to move beyond differences to talk about *changes* with age. Cross-sectional studies cannot provide direct evidence that IQ declines with age. Plausible alternative explanations for the superiority of young adults exist, including the possibility of cohort differences in educational opportunity. Indeed, the research we have been discussing demonstrates that the educational explanation is not merely plausible; differences in education *do* account for at least part of the age difference in IQ.

The second major kind of confound in cross-sectional studies of aging concerns differences in health status. Again, the confound follows naturally from the goal of representative sampling. As people get older, their health, on the average, gets worse. If we achieve representative sampling, therefore, we ensure ourselves of another confound: Our groups will differ not only in age but also in health.

Does health status relate to IQ? A variety of kinds of evidence tell us that it does. As with education, it is possible to produce a rough matching of groups for health status through careful selection of subjects. What has been done in particular is to include only exceptionally healthy individuals in samples at the oldest ages (e.g., Botwinick & Birren, 1963). This procedure typically reduces (but again does not eliminate) age differences in IQ. Note, of course, that such matching is subject to the

same criticism as matching for education: We are creating an atypical, positively biased sample of the elderly. It is also possible to examine IQ as a function of variations in health status within samples of the elderly. The typical finding here is of a clear relation: Relatively healthy older subjects outperform less healthy older subjects. A number of aspects of health can affect performance on IQ tests. Among the factors that have been identified as important are hearing loss (Granick, Kleben, & Weiss, 1976), hypertension (Wilkie & Eisdorfer, 1971), cardiovascular disease (Hertzog, Schaie, & Gribbin, 1978), and cerebrovascular disease (Spieth, 1965).

In several respects health status is a more complicated issue than is education. First, health status poses a measurement problem that is not present in the case of educational level. How can we know how healthy an elderly subject is? Ideally, what we would like is a physician's assessment based on a broad battery of medical tests. Although some studies do use physicians' reports (e.g., Palmore, 1971, 1974), most studies fall well short of this ideal. The most common practice is to base the assessment of health upon the subject's own report of his or her health. Such self-report measures range from quite simple (e.g., "all subjects reported themselves in good health") to considerably more detailed and ambitious. Table 9–1 shows a sampling of items from one of the more detailed self-report measures.

As we have seen, self-report measures are always somewhat suspect. It is important to note, therefore, that at least some self-report measures of health status do correlate with physicians' ratings and therefore do appear to have some validity (e.g., LaRue, Bank, Jarvik, & Hetland, 1979). Clearly, however, the fact that some self-reports are valid does not guarantee that all such measures are trustworthy. Furthermore, many studies of the elderly fail even to mention any attempt to measure or control for health (Abrahams, Hoyer, Elias, & Bradigan, 1975).

Health status is a more complicated variable than education from a conceptual as well as a methodological point of view. It is easy to imag-

TABLE 9-1 Examples of Items from the Physical Health Section of the OARS Multidimensional Functional Assessment

Item Number	Question
37[a]	About how many times have you seen a doctor during the past six months other than as an inpatient in a hospital? (exclude psychiatrists)
38	During the past six months how many days were you so sick that you were unable to carry on your usual activities—such as going to work or working around your house? 0 None 1 A week or less 2 More than a week but less than a month 3 1–3 months 4 4–6 months — Not answered
39	How many days in the past six months were you in a hospital for physical health problems?
..	
..	
42	I have a list of common medicines that people take. Would you please tell me if you've taken any of the following *in the past month?* [Eighteen medicines are listed—e.g., arthritis medication, prescription pain killer, high blood pressure medicine]
..	
..	
44	Do you have any of the following illnesses at the present time? [Twenty-six illnesses are listed—e.g., arthritis, glaucoma, asthma. For each, the subject rates both presence or absence and degree.]
..	
..	
53	How would you rate your overall health at the present time—excellent, good, fair, or poor? 3 Excellent 2 Good 1 Fair 0 Poor — Not answered
54	Is your health now better, about the same or worse than it was five years ago? 3 Better 2 About the same 0 Worse — Not answered
55	How much do your health troubles stand in the way of your doing the things you want to do—not at all, a little (some), or a great deal? 3 Not at all 2 A little (some) 0 A great deal — Not answered

Note. From *Multidimensional Functional Assessment: The OARS Methodology* (pp. 91, 92, 93, 96) by E. Pfeiffer (Ed.), 1975, Durham, NC: Center for the Study of Aging and Human Development. Copyright 1975 by Center for the Study of Aging and Human Development. Reprinted by permission.

[a]The Physical Health section begins with item 37.

ine—or for that matter to find—cultures or historical periods in which education does not vary with age. This separability of age and education tells us that differences in education are not an intrinsic part of aging—that is, that their covariation in our time and culture *is* a confound-ing. With health, however, the separability from age is much less clear. Should changes in health, and associated changes in mental performance, be regarded as distinct from aging itself, as "secondary" rather than "primary," as "disease" rather than "normal aging"? Or are declines in health an intrinsic part of the aging process?

How best to conceptualize the relation between health and aging is a complex and much-debated issue that can hardly be resolved here (for discussion, see Siegler, Nowlin, & Blumenthal, 1980). We can note, however, that whatever the ultimate resolution of the issue, there is little warrant in dismissing health-related declines in IQ as irrelevant or "artifactual." Health *does* vary with age, and IQ *does* vary with health. And even if all declines in IQ turn out to be health-related (which has not been demonstrated so far), the declines would remain just as genuine and important.

A final difference between the education variable and the health variable concerns their role in different designs. Both apply to cross-sectional designs, as the examples we have been discussing illustrate. Differences in education are generally not a concern in longitudinal designs, as long as the earliest age tested is beyond the age at which formal schooling is completed. Differences in health, in contrast, *are* a concern in longitudinal designs, for health, unlike formal education, does change as people age. Thus health, unlike education, contributes to age differences in both cross-sectional and longitudinal designs.

Let us return for a moment to the general issue of sampling, in this case with regard to longitudinal designs. We noted in chapter 3 that samples for longitudinal studies tend to be somewhat select, given the demands that longitudinal research places upon its subjects. We noted also that samples for longitudinal studies tend to be limited to members of a single cohort. Both of these factors may affect the conclusions that are drawn about stability or change in IQ with increased age. In addition to possible biases in initial selection of subjects, longitudinal research may also suffer from selective drop-out of subjects in the course of the project. In longitudinal studies of IQ it is quite clear that selective drop-out occurs: On the average, subjects with relatively low IQs are most likely to be lost from the study. This drop-out creates an obvious bias in favor of older age groups: The

older we go, the more select the sample becomes.

A dramatic illustration of the phenomenon of selective drop-out is provided by Siegler and Botwinick (1979). Siegler and Botwinick's subjects were tested first when they were between 65 and 74 years old, and they were then retested up to 10 additional times, depending on availability, over the next 10 years. Some subjects dropped out after the first test, some after the first two tests, and so on, so that only a small number of subjects (8 out of 130) were present for all 11 tests. Figure 9–1 shows the mean scores on the *initial* test plotted as a function of the number of test sessions for which the subject appeared. Note that scores are almost 30 points lower for subjects who dropped out after one test than for subjects who remained available throughout the project. The message is clear: The more test sessions that we attempt in a longitudinal study, the more positively biased our sample becomes.

Why does this pattern occur? There are two general reasons for selective drop-out. One is

FIGURE 9–1. Mean IQ scores at initial assessment as a function of the number of longitudinal assessments in which the subject participated. From *Experimental Psychology and Human Aging* (p. 84) by D. H. Kausler, 1982, New York: John Wiley & Sons. Copyright 1982 by John Wiley and Sons. Reprinted by permission. Kausler's figure is adapted from Siegler and Botwinick (1979).

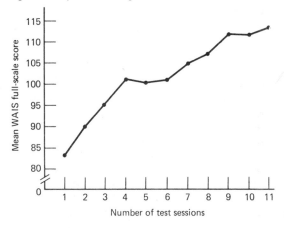

voluntary, having to do with the unwillingness of some subjects to continue to be tested. On the average, subjects with relatively low scores on an initial test are less willing to continue to participate than subjects with relatively high scores. A longitudinal study by Owens (1966) illustrates this point. The starting point for Owens' study was the administration in 1919 of the Army Alpha test (an early test of adult intelligence) to 363 freshmen at Iowa State University. In 1950 Owens sought to locate and retest as many of the 363 subjects as possible. He was able to locate 201 potential subjects, 138 of whom were classified as cooperative—that is, willing to be tested again—and 63 of whom were classified as noncooperative. An examination of the original, 1919 test scores revealed a mean of 5.63 for the cooperative subjects and 5.20 for the noncooperative subjects, a statistically significant difference (this difference would be comparable to a difference of about 7 IQ points on a standard IQ scale with a mean of 100). Thus, it was the higher IQ subjects who were most willing to be retested. Other studies (including the Siegler and Botwinick research discussed earlier) have documented similar selective drop-out over much shorter retest intervals than the 31 years examined by Owens.

The second basis for selective drop-out is death. In longitudinal research with elderly subjects some subjects die between one test session and the next. On the average, subjects with relatively low test scores are less likely to survive than subjects with relatively high test scores (e.g., Botwinick, West, & Storandt, 1978). Thus low IQ turns out to be predictive, in a very rough and imperfect way, of impending death.

A particularly interesting illustration of the relation between IQ and survival is provided by the phenomenon of *terminal drop*. Terminal drop refers to a fairly sharp and abrupt decline in mental abilities in the months or years immediately preceding death. It is associated, presumably, with a general deterioration of functioning that presages death. Terminal drop can be examined in any longitudinal study that

includes at least three testing occasions. Imagine a longitudinal study that tests IQ at age 65, again at age 70, and again at age 75. Such a study will have three groups of subjects: those who are available for all three tests, those who are available for the first two tests but die before the third, and those who are available for the first test but die before the second. It is the second group that is of interest now. On the average, IQ scores for these subjects show a marked decline from the first test to the second. This pattern is pictured in Figure 9–2. It is this deterioration in performance shortly before death that constitutes terminal drop. (Note that the phenomenon is not always as clear-cut as the figure suggests, and that its generality and importance remain controversial. See Siegler, 1975, for a review and discussion.)

It may be helpful to summarize the points that this section has made regarding the relation between health and IQ. There *is* a relation between health and IQ. On the average, healthy people perform better on IQ tests than less healthy people. There is also a relation between health and age. On the average, health problems become more common as people get older. The relation between health and age has implications for the samples that are examined in aging research. In both cross-sectional and lon-

FIGURE 9–2. Declines in IQ reflective of terminal drop (hypothetical data).

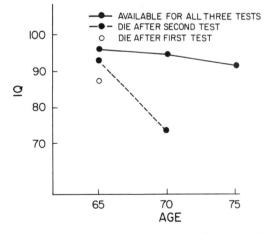

gitudinal designs, samples at the oldest ages are tilted toward relatively healthy individuals, a factor that reduces age differences in IQ. Even with this sampling bias, however, there are still differences in health between samples of different ages, and these differences in health clearly account for at least part of the age difference in IQ.

Measurement

So far we have been discussing findings with regard to IQ and aging without addressing a basic question: How is IQ measured in such research? The present section is directed to this question, as well as to more general issues of measurement in the study of aging.

As is true in the study of any age group, a variety of different IQ tests have been used in research on aging. Two tests, however, have been most common and most influential. One is the Wechsler Adult Intelligence Scale, or WAIS (Wechsler, 1981). The WAIS was briefly introduced in chapter 7 in the general discussion of IQ, primarily in the form of a sampling of items from the test (Table 7-6). The WAIS, like other Wechsler tests, is an individually administered test that yields an overall estimate of general intelligence. Because the test is divided into a Verbal scale and a Performance scale, it can also yield more differentiated information in the form of separate Verbal and Performance IQs. The Verbal scale and Performance scale are composed of six and five subtests respectively; thus at the most specific level age differences on the WAIS can be examined by subtest.

The other commonly used measure in studies of IQ and aging is the Primary Mental Abilities Test, or PMA (Thurstone & Thurstone, 1962). The PMA, unlike the WAIS, can be administered to groups of subjects at the same time. Like the WAIS, it is divided into subtests. The five PMA subtests are Verbal Meaning, Space, Reasoning, Number, and Word Fluency. Examples of the types of items found on several of the subtests are shown in Table 9-2.

What are the general measurement issues that are raised by the study of IQ and aging? One basic issue is *measurement equivalence*. To compare IQ at different ages, whether cross-sectionally or longitudinally, we must have equivalent measures of IQ at the different ages. It is, of course, easy enough to achieve a kind of literal or "formal" equivalence of measures: All we need do is use the same IQ test at the

TABLE 9-2   Types of Items Included on the Primary Mental Abilities Test (PMA)

VERBAL MEANING

Instructions: Find the word that means the same as the first word in the row.

ANCIENT	A. dry	B. long	C. happy	D. old	E. sloppy
QUIET	A. blue	B. still	C. tense	D. watery	E. exact
SAFE	A. secure	B. loyal	C. passive	D. young	E. deft

NUMBER

How do you write in numbers: Eleven thousand and eleven? A. 111 B. 1,111 C. 11,011 D. 110,001 E. 111, 011

| $\frac{1}{2} + \frac{1}{2} =$ | A. $\frac{1}{8}$ | B. $\frac{1}{4}$ | C. $\frac{1}{2}$ | D. 1 | E. 2 |
| $16 \times 99 =$ | A. 154 | B. 1,584 | C. 1,614 | D. 15,084 | E. 150,084 |

REASONING

Instructions: Find the letter that follows the last letter in the row.

c d c d c d	1. c	2. d	3. e	4. f	5. g
a b c a b d a b e a b	1. b	2. c	3. d	4. e	5. f
a m b a n b a o b a p b a	1. m	2. o	3. p	4. q	5. r

Note. From *SRA Primary Mental Abilities* (pp. 1,6,11) by L. L. Thurstone and T. G. Thurstone, 1962, Chicago: Science Research Associates. Copyright 1962 by Science Research Associates, Inc. Reprinted by permission.

different ages. The question is whether our test is actually measuring the same thing at different ages, whether we have achieved not only formal but also "functional" equivalence (Labouvie, 1980). If the test is less appropriate or valid for one age group than another, then age comparisons are of doubtful significance.

To a good extent, measures that are used in the study of elderly people—not only IQ tests but psychological measures in general—were first developed for the study of younger samples. IQ tests, as we saw, were originally devised to predict school performance in children, and their content was thus oriented to the kinds of academic-verbal skills that are important in school. IQ tests for adults have always had similar academic-pragmatic goals and content. The PMA was developed on samples of college students, and the Army Alpha test was devised to predict the success of young adults in the military. The WAIS, it is true, was standardized on samples that ranged in age from 16 to 74. Even here, however, the content often seems more appropriate for young adults, and the validation data have always centered on prediction to academic or occupational contexts that are characteristic of young adulthood. The result, in the words of Willis and Bates (1980), is that

we know how to compare the older person with the young in youth-oriented tasks and settings. But we have relatively few instruments that can tell us much about the unique nature of intellectual behavior and its predictive validity in the older adult. (p. 264)

Within the domain of intelligence testing there *have* been a few attempts to develop tests that are more appropriate for middle-aged or elderly subjects. Perhaps the earliest such attempt was that of Demming and Pressey (1957). Focusing on the informational component of intelligence, these authors devised a battery of questions that were intended to tap kinds of knowledge (e.g., use of the yellow pages, preparation of wills) that would be both familiar and important to older adults. More recently, Gardner and Monge (1977) reported a similar but somewhat more ambitious effort to develop age-appropriate measures for older subjects. Table

9–3 shows some sample items from their test. In both studies, it is worth noting, age differences in performance tended to favor older rather than younger subjects.

There are two problems with the kinds of measures just described. One has to do with the determination of validity. How can we demonstrate that differences on such tests are valid indices of general differences in adult competence? With children or young adults there are external criteria, such as academic or occupational performance, against which IQ measures can be validated. With elderly adults there are no such obvious external criteria. The second problem concerns age comparisons. If all we wish to do is construct an age-appropriate test for older adults, then this second issue is not a concern. If, however, we wish to compare young and old then the original problem returns: A test that is valid for only one age group cannot be used to compare two different age groups. It may, of course, still be instructive to demonstrate that there are measures on which the elderly perform well—perhaps even outperform younger adults. But the problem of making valid age comparisons still remains.

Note that the issue of measurement equivalence is not limited to the selection of the specific items that go into a test. The issue is a much broader one, for it extends in general to the kinds of settings and contexts within which we assess intellectual performance. To date, these settings have consisted almost exclusively of structured lab environments and highly standardized tests. Such an approach, it can be argued, is biased against the elderly subject, who is many years away from academic contexts and who may therefore be less familiar with and less motivated to respond to such measures than a younger adult. Perhaps the elderly person's competence would appear more impressive if it could be examined in more natural and familiar settings, such as when carrying out his or her job, shopping for the week's groceries, or explaining the operation of a toy to a grandchild. (For further discussion of ecological validity, see Labouvie-Vief & Chandler, 1978, and Scheidt & Schaie, 1978.)

Two general points emerge from this dis-

TABLE 9-3 Examples of Items from the Gardner and Monge Test of Adult Intelligence

Subtest	Items

Transportation	1. The part of a bridle that is inserted in a horse's mouth is the
	    1) tether 2) bit 3) chomp 4) spur 5) crop
	2. A hack is a
	    1) hotrod 2) vendor 3) subway 4) taxi 5) heap
	3. A wagon used to carry food is called a
	    1) chuck wagon 2) mess wagon 3) water wagon 4) track wagon 5) trek wagon
	. .
	22. A two-door electrically driven sedan is a
	    1) brougham 2) herdic 3) tourister 4) gibson 5) jaunting car
	23. "Haw" is a command to a horse which means
	    1) turn right 2) slow down 3) stop 4) turn left 5) move ahead

Death and Disease	1. The removal and examination of tissue from the living body is a (an)
	    1) paregoric 2) internal 3) dissection 4) biopsy 5) autopsy
	2. An inscription on a grave or a tomb is a (an)
	    1) epitaph 2) eulogy 3) idyll 4) thesis 5) epithet
	3. Arteriosceloris is arterial
	    1) bleeding 2) tearing 3) spasm 4) softening 5) hardening
	. .
	19. One who makes false teeth is a
	    1) pseudophile 2) paradontist 3) polydontist 4) periodontist 5) prosthodontist
	20. Loose flesh hanging from the jaw is called
	    1) steotopygia 2) hackles 3) wattles 4) jawls 5) dermatome

Finance	1. The person who is appointed to see that a will is carried out is the
	    1) probationer 2) legatee 3) executor 4) contestant 5) testator
	2. Revenue means
	    1) security 2) subsidy 3) rebate 4) audit 5) income
	3. A word relating to financial matters is
	    1) ventral 2) dorsal 3) fiscal 4) apical 5) montage
	. .
	19. A piece of paper used as evidence that the holder is entitled to receive something of financial value is called
	    1) scrip 2) bail 3) graft 4) script 5) gratis
	20. The word "condominium" has to do with
	    1) life insurance 2) real estate 3) income tax 4) wills 5) stocks

Note. From *A Program of Research in Adult Differences in Cognitive Performance and Learning: Backgrounds for Adult Education and Vocational Retraining* (Grant No. OEG 1-7-06-1963-0149, pp. 87, 88, 89, 90, 93, and 94) by R. H. Monge and E. F. Gardner, 1972. Washington, DC: Office of Education. Reprinted by permission.

cussion of measurement equivalence. One is that it is difficult to devise measurement procedures—both specific items and general context—that are equally appropriate for subjects of different ages. The other is that the procedures that have typically been used in the study of aging often seem to be biased against the oldest subjects.

Studies of IQ raise a second measurement issue that is in a sense even more basic. Intelligence, like any general construct, can be defined and measured in a variety of ways. IQ tests constitute one operational definition of intelligence—hardly the only one and hardly a completely satisfactory one. There are a number of other possible approaches to intelligence, some of which we consider in the second part of the chapter. In addition, "IQ" itself is not a single entity but a diverse conglomeration of different abilities. What we conclude about stability or change in IQ might well depend on the particular aspect of IQ on which we have decided to focus.

Let us briefly consider some data on this latter point. It is worth doing so, for the specific aspect of IQ that is studied turns out to be a very important determinant of conclusions about age differences in IQ. Perhaps the best-established finding in this regard concerns the Verbal-Performance distinction on the WAIS. Age differences are much more marked on the Performance scale than on the Verbal scale. Verbal IQ, in fact, often holds up quite well even into fairly advanced old age. Performance IQ, in contrast, is likely to show both earlier and larger decrements. This pattern has been labeled the "classic pattern of aging" (Botwinick, 1984). A typical example of the pattern is shown in Figure 9-3. Note that these data are derived from cross-sectional comparisons of different age groups. The same general Verbal-Performance contrast emerges in longitudinal research, but both the timing and the magnitude of age decrements differ from those observed in cross-sectional studies. We return to this point in the section on Design.

As we saw, both the WAIS and the PMA lend themselves to more differentiated analyses than simply "Verbal" versus "Performance." Both scales are divided into a number of subtests, and age differences can therefore be examined subtest by subtest. Different subtests do, in fact, show different patterns of aging. Within the WAIS Verbal scale, for example, Digit Span shows a more marked decline with age than does Vocabulary. On the PMA the Space and Reasoning tests are more likely to show age differences than are Number and Verbal Meaning. Reviews of this research can be found in Botwinick (1977) and Salthouse (1982). For our purposes the specific findings are less important than the general point: Whether "intelligence" declines with age depends on what kind of intelligence we are considering. Sweeping generalizations—about intelligence or any other important attribute—should therefore be avoided.

One more finding with regard to differential decline is of enough general interest to merit mention. Items on IQ tests can be divided into "speeded" items and "nonspeeded" items. Speeded items are those for which speed of response is important; the answer must be found within a particular time limit, and bonus points

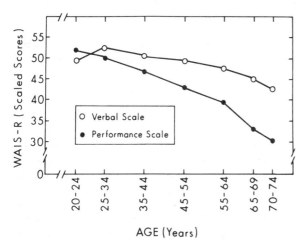

FIGURE 9-3. WAIS Verbal and Performance scores as a function of age. (Verbal scores multiplied by 5/6 to develop a common base with Performance scores). From *Aging and Behavior* (3rd ed., p. 255) by J. Botwinick, 1984, New York: Springer. Copyright 1984 by Springer Publishing Company, Inc. Reprinted by permission.

may be awarded for an especially quick response. Picture Completion on the WAIS (see Table 7–6) is an example of a speeded item. Nonspeeded items are those for which speed of response is not important; subjects have as long as they need to arrive at the answer, and quality of response, not speed, is all that is scored. Vocabulary on the WAIS is an example of a nonspeeded item. In general, age differences between young adults and elderly adults are greater on speeded items than on nonspeeded items. Thus, older people seem to have special difficulty in situations that require quick response.

Most of the data concerning the role of speed in IQ performance come from the WAIS, and this presents a problem: All of the five Performance items on the WAIS are speeded, whereas only one of the six Verbal items is speeded. There is, then, a confounding between content (Verbal versus Performance) and speed. Given this confound, it is important to note that conclusions about the relation between speed and aging are not limited to the WAIS subtests. Slowing of response with increased age is a general phenomenon that cuts across a wide variety of measures. Indeed, Birren, Woods, and Williams (1980) conclude that "perhaps the most ubiquitous and significant change observed in the older organism is slowness of behavior" (p. 293). It appears, moreover, that this slowing is not purely peripheral in origin—a matter, for example, of decreased sensory acuity or loss of manual dexterity. Evidence indicates, rather, that at least part of the slowing is central in origin, a reflection of general slowing in central nervous sytem processing (Botwinick, 1984; Salthouse, in press).

This last conclusion deserves a bit more comment, for the way in which it is established illustrates some general methodological points. How can we determine whether behavioral slowing with age is peripheral or central in origin? There are in fact a variety of kinds of evidence, discussions of which can be found in the sources just cited. It is this conjunction of evidence, rather than any single kind of research, that is critical. As an example, however, we focus on what is perhaps the most straightforward

line of argument: data from studies of reaction time. Two kinds of reaction time can be examined. One is *simple reaction time*. In a study of simple reaction time there is a single stimulus and a single response to it—for example, a light comes on and the subject must move a lever. Tasks of this sort can be contrasted with *choice reaction time*, in which there are two or more stimuli and two or more corresponding responses—for example, move the lever to the left if a blue light comes on and to the right if a yellow light comes on. Note that the sensory and motoric demands are essentially the same in the two tasks; what differs is the degree of decision making necessary before responding.

Several findings emerge from comparisons of different forms of reaction time. Young adults tend to be faster than elderly adults whatever the task. Choice reaction time, not surprisingly, is generally greater than simple reaction time, and this finding holds for both young and old. The difference between simple and choice, however, is greater for older subjects—that is, there is an *interaction* of age and experimental condition. Elderly people, therefore, seem to be especially affected by the additional cognitive demands of the choice paradigm. Further studies reveal that the interaction of age and complexity is quite general: The more complex the task, the greater the age difference in speed of response (Cerella, Poon, & Williams, 1980). This finding suggests that the slowing of behavior has a central rather than peripheral locus.

The studies of reaction time illustrate several methodological points. One is the value of experimental manipulations within an age group. The fact that response speed slows with age is an interesting phenomenon that can be easily demonstrated simply by administering the appropriate tasks. Determining *why* the slowing occurs, however, requires an experimental design that goes beyond demonstration to get at potentially important causal variables. The comparison of different forms of reaction time is just one example of such experimental manipulation. The second point concerns the value of experimental manipulation not just within but *across* age. As we saw in chapter 2, such age by condition designs may be especially inform- ative when they result in a significant interac- tion, for the interaction can suggest reasons for a main effect of age. This is exactly the outcome in studies of reaction time: Older and younger subjects are differentially affected by the de- mands of the choice paradigm, and this finding tells us that factors other than sensory or mo- toric problems contribute to age differences in response speed. A final point may not be evi- dent from our brief discussion but is clear in more extended reviews. Research on speed of response illustrates again the value of *converging operations*. Studies of simple versus choice re- action time suggest a central determinant of re- sponse speed; they do not prove it, however, nor do they indicate what its nature is. It is only when we add in other kinds of evidence—for example, examinations of task complexity in general, studies of physiological correlates of speed—that the conclusion becomes more cer- tain.

One final point about measurement remains to be made. Thus far our focus has been on dif- ferences between age groups in mean level of response—specifically, in possible differences in mean IQ across the life span. Although the mean is generally the statistic of greatest inter- est, it is not the only possible dependent vari- able. It is quite possible that there are interesting differences—or similarities—be- tween age groups that are not captured by a comparison of means. There may, for example, be age differences in the *variability* in response— that is, the extent to which responses cluster around or depart from the group mean. One stereotype of aging, in fact, is that individual differences lessen and people become more ho- mogeneous as they grow older. This stereotype implies that variability should be greater in younger samples than in older samples. In fact, just the reverse is often the case: When age dif- ferences in variability do emerge, they gener- ally reflect greater variability at the older ages. This conclusion holds not only for IQ but for a number of other dependent variables as well (Maddox & Douglas, 1974.) An exclusive con- centration on group means, therefore, might cause us to miss an interesting difference be-

tween ages. Note, in addition, the message that can be taken away from this particular finding. It again concerns the danger of broad gener- alization. Statements about declines in IQ (or, indeed, anything else) in old age are statements about group averages. The existence of marked individual differences among the elderly tells us that there are always plenty of exceptions to these group averages.

Studies of variability are just one alternative to a focus on mean levels of response. Another interesting question concerns the interrelation of different abilities, or what is sometimes called (after the statistical procedure of factor analy- sis) the "factor structure" of abilities. The issue here is how different skills fit together, or cor- relate, at different ages. The correlational pat- tern might vary in interesting ways across age, quite apart from similarities or differences in mean level of response. One theory of aging, for example, is that distinctions among differ- ent cognitive abilities weaken and skills become more interdependent as people get older. This "dedifferentiation" is contrasted with the "dif- ferentiation" of abilities that supposedly char- acterizes much of cognitive development throughout childhood and young adulthood. What the dedifferentiation hypothesis predicts is that correlations among abilities should in- crease in old age. In fact, most of the evidence seems to go against the notion of dedifferentia- tion (Reinert, 1970). Whatever the fate of the dedifferentiation hypothesis, however, the gen- eral issue of the structure of intelligence re- mains important, and possible similarities or differences across age in the factor structure of intellectual abilities are the focus of a number of ongoing research programs (e.g., Cun- ningham, 1980).

Design

We begin this section with a consideration of the two most common designs in the study of IQ and aging, the cross-sectional and the lon- gitudinal. We then move on to discuss some al- ternative approaches to the study of changes with age.

As Botwinick (1977) has argued, conclusions

from cross-sectional studies of IQ and longitudinal studies of IQ are in many respects similar. With both designs, the predominant age effect is a negative one; older subjects perform more poorly than younger subjects. With both designs, the same kinds of variables—health status, verbal versus performance content, speed—tend to affect performance. There are, however, also some differences. The major difference is that apparent declines in IQ are much less marked in longitudinal research than in cross-sectional research. Typically, the age at which decrements in IQ first appear is later in longitudinal studies than in cross-sectional studies, and the magnitude of decrements when they do appear is less. Thus, longitudinal research presents a more positive picture of aging than does cross-sectional research.

Why this difference between cross-sectional and longitudinal? The two most obvious explanations have already been discussed, both earlier in this chapter and in chapter 3's general treatment of developmental designs. In cross-sectional studies there is a confounding of age and cohort. Young adults and elderly adults differ not only in age but in generation, and the generational differences (in educational opportunities, for example) seem for the most part to favor the young. Such generational differences might well lead to differences in IQ quite apart from any contribution of age. In longitudinal studies, in contrast, the bias seems to work mainly in the opposite direction. Drop-out occurs in longitudinal research, and the drop-out tends to be selective, with low-IQ subjects becoming progressively less available as the study continues. The result is a positive bias in favor of older age groups.

In addition to selective drop-out, a second aspect of longitudinal designs works against decline with age. Subjects in a longitudinal study of IQ undergo repeated administrations of the same IQ test. Even though explicit feedback about performance is not provided, the repeated exposure to the same materials might well lead to a positive practice effect. Evidence indicates that such practice effects do occur: Subjects who have already taken an IQ test tend to do better on later administrations of the same

test (Nesselroade & Baltes, 1974). This factor, too, acts to minimize decline with age in longitudinal research.

What other methods of study are possible? Chapter 3 introduced a third "simple" design: the time-lag design. In a time-lag design age is held constant and cohort and time of measurement are varied (see Figure 3–1). The purpose of such a design is to determine whether factors that are normally confounded with age—cohort in a cross-sectional study and time of measurement in a longitudinal study—do in fact affect the dependent variable being studied.

The Owens (1966) study discussed earlier provides an example of a time-lag comparison. We noted that Owens compared IQ scores obtained in 1919 (when the subjects were approximately 19 years old) with scores obtained on a retest of the same people 31 years later. We can add now that there was actually a *third* testing occasion as well: a final follow-up in 1961, when the subjects were 61 years old. This final testing included not only the longitudinal retest but also administration of the same IQ test to a separate sample of 19-year-olds. The comparison of the original 1919 scores with those from this new, 1961 sample constitutes the time-lag dimension of the study: a comparison of two groups of the same age but belonging to different generations and tested at different times. Owens found that the new sample of 19-year-olds scored significantly higher than had the original sample when they were 19. This finding tells us that either time of measurement or cohort can affect performance on IQ tests. It is quite possible, of course, that both factors contribute.

The major alternative to a cross-sectional or longitudinal design is one or more of the *sequential* designs that were introduced in chapter 3. As we saw then, the various sequential designs involve combinations of the simpler cross-sectional, longitudinal, and time-lag approaches. Such designs provide more information than do the simpler approaches, but at the cost of considerably more time and resources. Their use to date has therefore been limited. Here we concentrate on one major sequential study that has been very influential—the research by Schaie and associates on IQ

(Schaie, Labouvie, & Buech, 1973; Schaie & Labouvie-Vief, 1974; Schaie & Parham, 1977; Schaie & Strother, 1968).

The Schaie et al. project began in 1956 with testing of 500 adults between the ages of 21 and 70. For purposes of data analysis, the sample (which we will call Sample 1) was organized into seven age groups with age intervals of 7 years. The mean age for the youngest group at the time of initial testing was 25; that for the oldest group was 67. Although several measures were administered, the principal dependent variable was the PMA, with a focus on both individual subtests and composite IQ.

The 1956 testing constituted a cross-sectional study, the results of which were reported by Schaie (1958). Like other cross-sectional research, it painted a negative picture of IQ and aging, with apparent declines in IQ beginning as people reached their 50s. These cross-sectional data, however, were just the starting point for the Schaie research. In 1963 a second testing took place utilizing two distinct samples. One sample was the original one; it consisted of the 301 subjects, from the initial 500, who could be located and retested in 1963. The age range for this sample was, of course, now 28 to 77. The second sample (Sample 2) was new: a second independent cross-sectional sample, spanning an age range of 21 to 74. There were 960 subjects in this new sample. With the 1963 data, therefore, Schaie and associates had a number of analyses and comparisons available to them. There were three sets of cross-sectional comparisons spanning most of the adult life span: Sample 1 in 1956 and again, with everyone 7 years older, in 1963, and Sample 2 in

1963. There was a longitudinal comparison, extending 7 years, for Sample 1 in the contrast of 1956 scores with 1963 scores. And there were time-lag comparisons available in the contrast between a particular age group in 1956 and the same age group in 1963.

A third testing occurred in 1970. Again, there was a longitudinal dimension: retests of as many of both the Sample 1 and the Sample 2 subjects as possible. Of the 301 Sample 1 subjects who had been retested in 1963 161 were available for a third testing. Their age range now was 35 to 84. Of the original 960 Sample 2 subjects 409 were successfully retested. In addition to the longitudinal comparisons, these samples, comprising as they did different cohorts, also permitted a variety of cross-sectional comparisons. Finally, still a third independent sample (Sample 3) was added in 1970: 701 new subjects, spanning an age range of 21 to 84.

A schematic summary may help to sort out the details of this very complex study. Table 9–4 provides such a summary. The various cross-sectional, longitudinal, and time-lag comparisons should be derivable from the table. Comparison with Figure 3–2 may help distinguish the particular sequential analyses that are embedded within the overall design. The top row of the table, for example, constitutes the design that was labeled in chapter 3 as a *longitudinal-sequential design*. The diagonal of the table—that is, the combination of Sample 1 in 1956, Sample 2 in 1963, and Sample 3 in 1970—yields a *cross-sectional-sequential design*.

What were the results from all this prodigious effort? The main conclusion reached by Schaie et al. (a conclusion which, as we will see,

TABLE 9–4 Summary of the Schaie et al. Sequential Studies: Ages and Sample Sizes at Each Testing Occasion

	TIME OF TESTING		
	1956	*1963*	*1970*
Sample 1	21–70 ($N = 500$) First Test	28–77 ($N = 301$) Second Test	35–84 ($N = 161$) Third Test
Sample 2		21–74 ($N = 960$) First Test	28–81 ($N = 409$) Second Test
Sample 3			21–84 ($N = 701$) First Test

has not been universally accepted) was that the extent of IQ decline with age has been grossly overstated. The bases for this conclusion are not easy to summarize, for they are spread across a dozen or so separate publications and scores of analyses. The general strategy adopted by the Schaie group has been to perform statistical analyses in which two of the three potentially important factors (age, cohort, and time of measurement) are treated as independent variables and the third factor is left uncontrolled. With the longitudinal-sequential design, for example, it is possible to analyze the contribution of year of birth (which ranges from 1886 to 1935) and age (which ranges from 21 to 84) while ignoring, for the moment, possible effects of time of measurement. Note that the same variables can be examined in the cross-sectional-sequential design, but this time with independent samples rather than repeated measures at each testing occasion. These analyses have revealed some decrements in performance as a function of age, especially at the most advanced ages and especially on speeded measures of ability. For the most part, however, the contribution of the age variable appears modest in comparison with the other two factors. Cohort, in particular, consistently emerges as an important factor in the Schaie et al. analyses. Part of the basis for this conclusion lies in their replication of the common finding that age decrements in IQ are much more marked in cross-sectional comparisons than in longitudinal comparisons.

From both an empirical and a methodological point of view the contribution of the Schaie et al. research is beyond dispute. As suggested earlier, however, some of their specific conclusions *have* been disputed, at least in the strong form in which Schaie et al. typically offer them. The essence of the critics' position is that Schaie et al. make assumptions that go beyond what their methodology can clearly demonstrate, assumptions, moreover, that tend consistently to maximize the cohort effect and minimize the age effect. Specific criticisms include the following points. Although Schaie et al. emphasize the similarities between their longitudinal data and

their independent-samples data, there are also differences. Apparent declines in IQ with age are greater with independent samples, a finding that suggests that either selective drop-out or practice effects are inflating performance at the oldest ages in the longitudinal analyses. The basic cross-sectional-longitudinal comparison is difficult to interpret because the time spans are so much greater for the cross-sectional analyses (up to 60 years) than for the longitudinal analyses (maximum of 14 years). Finally and most critically, the sequential approach cannot totally undo the confounds that are intrinsic to age comparisons, for only two of the three potentially important factors can ever be varied independently. As soon as decisions are made about two factors (say age and cohort) the levels of the third factor (time of measurement) follow automatically, and this third factor will always be to some extent confounded with the first two. Depending on how the data work out, the results may be more or less clearly interpretable; some uncertainty, however, will always remain.

The points just made are developed more fully in a number of sources, including Botwinick and Arenberg (1976), Kausler (1982), and Botwinick (1984). More generally, the Schaie et al. studies have been the focal point for a spirited and much-cited exchange concerning the "myth of intellectual decline" in adulthood (Baltes & Schaie, 1974, 1976; Horn & Donaldson, 1976, 1977; Schaie & Baltes, 1977). This exchange stands as a graphic example of our earlier point about methodological difficulties and resulting controversies in the study of aging.

SPECIFIC TOPICS

With the discussion of general issues as background, we turn now to some specific topics that have been of interest in the study of aging. IQ, of course, is one such topic. We consider next another major approach to the study of intelligence in old age, after which we turn to methods of studying personality and social development.

Memory

We noted earlier that IQ has "probably" been the most popular topic for psychological studies of aging. The "probably" was necessitated by the explosion of research on memory in recent years. In the 1983 volume of the *Journal of Gerontology*, for example, fully 43% of the studies in the "Psychological Sciences" section dealt in some way with memory.

As with IQ, there is a common stereotype about memory and old age. The stereotype is again one of decline: Old people can no longer remember things as well as they could when they were younger. As with IQ, there is some truth to the stereotype but also many qualifications and exceptions. The goal of much of the research on memory in the elderly has been to discover the conditions under which memory problems do or do not occur.

We have already considered one example of memory research with the elderly. Recall that one of the illustrative studies used in chapters 2 and 3, the experiment by Schonfield and Robertson (1966), compared memory in young (aged 20 to 29) and elderly (aged 60 to 75) adults. Two kinds of memory were examined: recall of a list of 24 unrelated words and recognition of a comparable list of words. Performance was better on recognition than on recall, a common and unsurprising finding. The recognition-recall difference, however, was greater for older than for younger subjects. The difference was greater because recognition memory showed no apparent decline with age; recall, however, was much better at the younger age. There was, then, an interaction of age and experimental condition (see Table 2-1).

The Schonfield and Robertson study is often cited, probably both because it was one of the earliest examinations of the recognition-recall issue and because its results were so clear-cut. Since this work, numerous other investigators have also compared recognition and recall in adults of different ages. Similar age by condition interactions are a frequent enough finding to justify the conclusion that difficulties in recall are a more likely accompaniment of old age than are difficulties in recognition. On the other hand, the flat age function for recognition reported by Schonfield and Robertson is by no means always obtained. In a number of studies age differences in favor of young adults emerge for recognition as well as recall (e.g., McCormack, 1981).

Why might recall and recognition show the developmental pattern illustrated in Table 2-1? A prior question is why recall and recognition might ever be expected to differ in difficulty. One obvious difference between the two kinds of memory concerns the storage-retrieval distinction. Both kinds of memory require storage of material over time; recall, however, presumably requires a more active effort at retrieval of the stored material than does recognition, in which the correct answer is present at the time of response. The fact that recognition is relatively impervious to developmental decline suggests, therefore, that the storage component of memory holds up fairly well with age; developmental changes result largely from decrements in retrieval as people get older. Like all generalizations about age differences in memory, this particular generalization has limitations and exceptions (such as the fact that age differences can occur in recognition as well). Nevertheless, it does appear to have some validity as a partial account of age differences in memory.

How else might the distinction between storage and retrieval be studied? Another common approach is the *cued-recall paradigm*. In studies of cued recall a contrast is drawn between a standard recall test and a recall test on which a hint, or "cue," is provided. Laurence (1967), for example, tested for recall in both young (mean age 20 years) and elderly (mean age 75 years) adults. The stimuli were 36 words drawn from six categories: flowers, trees, birds, formations of nature, vegetables, and countries. The list was presented just once, with the words randomly ordered—that is, *not* divided by category. Prior to the recall test, however, half of the subjects were given cue cards containing the six category names and were told that every word belonged to one of the six categories; the remaining subjects received no such hint. The results of this manipulation are shown in Figure 9–4. As can be seen, there was an interaction of age and condition: Older subjects benefited much more from the hint than did younger subjects. Indeed, under the cued-recall condition the two age groups did not differ in the number of words recalled.

As with the Schonfield and Robertson study, the early work by Laurence has met a mixed fate in more recent studies. Age by condition interactions of the sort found by Laurence are sometimes but by no means always obtained in research on cued recall; there are some studies in which young and old adults benefit equally from a cue (e.g., Hultsch, 1975) and some in which young adults actually benefit more than old adults (e.g., Simon, 1979). It has become clear that the exact effects of cuing may vary across procedures and across samples. The general conclusion seems the same as that in the recognition-recall literature. The fact that retrieval cues can be especially helpful for the elderly suggests that older people often learn and store material successfully but have difficulty in

later retrieving the material. The fact that retrieval cues do not always remove young-old differences suggests that there are other factors, in addition to difficulties in retrieval, that contribute to age differences in memory.

The argument about the need to be active in retrieving material is part of a more general hypothesis about age differences in memory. The general hypothesis is that elderly people are most likely to have difficulty in situations that require some sort of active processing in order to remember—situations that require *doing* something in order to acquire information in the first place, to maintain information over time, or to retrieve information when it is needed. This argument should have a familiar sound, for it is the same hypothesis that was offered as a partial explanation for age differences in memory across childhood. The emphasis again is on the *strategies* that can be used as aids to memory, and on possible age differences in the use of these strategies.

Research on mnemonic strategies in adulthood has followed the same general methodological lines as the research on strategies in

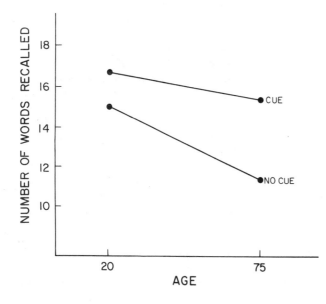

FIGURE 9–4. Interaction of age and experimental condition in the Laurence study of cued recall. Adapted from "Memory Loss with Age: A Test of Two Strategies for its Retardation" by M. W. Laurence, 1967, *Psychonomic Science, 9*, pp. 209–210.

childhood that we discussed in chapter 7. In some studies the use or nonuse of strategies is *inferred* from the overall pattern of memory performance. One adaptive mnemonic strategy, for example, is to utilize whatever organization there may be among the stimulus items that one is attempting to remember (see Table 7–10). Various studies have contrasted the performance of young adults and elderly adults on two types of stimulus materials: lists of related items that lend themselves to organization and lists of unrelated items. Usually, young-old differences are greater for lists of related items, an outcome compatible with the hypothesis that young adults are more likely to organize material as an aid to memory (e.g., Heron & Craik, 1964; Taub, 1974). Also supportive of this hypothesis is the finding that "clustering" of related items during recall (the specific organizational strategy shown in Table 7–10) is more common in young or middle-aged adults than in elderly adults (Denney, 1974).

Strategies can also be *experimentally elicited*. In a study similar to the Ornstein, Naus, and Liberty (1975) research discussed in chapter 7, Sanders, Murphy, Schmitt, and Walsh (1980) tested the effects of induced strategy use on young (mean age 24) and elderly (mean age 74) adults. The task was free recall, with lists of common words as the stimuli. Half of the subjects were assigned to an "overt rehearsal" condition, with instructions to "verbalize about everything they thought as they studied a list." The rehearsal was thus experimentally elicited, but its form was left up to the subject. The remaining subjects received no instructions regarding rehearsal.

A number of findings emerged. The young subjects recalled more words than the elderly subjects under both experimental conditions. They also engaged in more verbal rehearsal, especially for the early items in a list. Most interesting, however, were differences not just in the amount but in the *type* of rehearsal. The rehearsal efforts of the elderly subjects were limited largely to single repetitions of the words. The younger subjects, in contrast, were more likely to engage in cumulative rehearsal, and

also more likely to cluster words from the same category when rehearsing. At both ages the quality of the rehearsal was positively related to the number of words recalled. Thus the strategy "worked," whatever the age of the subject. Younger subjects, however, were more likely to generate an adaptive strategy than were older subjects.

As noted in chapter 7, mnemonic strategies can take a variety of forms. Numerous studies have demonstrated that young adults are more likely to use strategies of just about any sort than are elderly adults. It seems clear, therefore, that age differences in recall do stem at least in part from differences in both the tendency to generate strategies and the complexity and appropriateness of the strategies used. This conclusion is supported by demonstrations that strategy use correlates with recall (as in Sanders et al., 1980) and that experimental induction of a strategy can improve the performance of the elderly (as in Laurence, 1967). The occasional (but by no means inevitable) finding that strategy induction is especially helpful for the elderly—that is, that age and experimental condition interact—also supports the idea that older people have special difficulty in spontaneously employing strategies.

In addition to strategies, the other main content area considered in chapter 7 was constructive memory. As noted then, constructive memory concerns the effects of the general knowledge system upon memory—the tendency to fit material in, draw inferences, go beyond the information given, all in an attempt to *understand* what one has experienced. Research on mnemonic strategies has concentrated largely on arbitrary material and on explicit techniques for memorizing the material. Research on constructive memory is more likely to deal with meaningful material and with the effects of very general, often unconscious cognitive activities on what is remembered.

Constructive memory has been a very active research topic in the recent adult-memory literature. A variety of paradigms have been used in this research, only some of which were described in chapter 7's coverage of constructive memory in childhood. A basic finding concerns similarity in memory across the adult life span. Adults of any age, including the elderly, show constructive memory of various sorts, and the qualitative nature of the phenomena often seems identical whatever the age of the subject (Salthouse, 1982). Nevertheless, there *are* still reports of age differences in some studies of constructive memory. And when differences do occur they are in the same direction as the other differences discussed in this section: poorer performance by elderly subjects.

We consider two examples of this point. One concerns memory for stories and is thus similar to some of the research discussed in chapter 7. Across a series of experiments, Cohen (1979, 1981) has compared young adults' and elderly adults' memory for prose passages of various sorts. Examples of two of the passages used are shown in Box 9-1. Whatever the exact nature of the stimuli, the interest has been in two kinds of memory. One is verbatim recall for information explicitly presented in the story. The first question following each passage taps such verbatim recall. The other is for information that is implicit in the story and hence must be inferred. The second question after each story taps implicit recall. Cohen's basic finding has been that age differences are more marked for implicit recall than for explicit recall. Elderly subjects do well at understanding and retaining the explicit content of a passage, but appear to have difficulty in going beyond the explicit content to infer underlying meanings. And it is, of course, this going beyond what is immediately given that constitutes constructive memory.

Our second example involves a variant of the cued-recall paradigm. Till and Walsh (1980) tested young and old adults for memory of individually presented sentences. Each sentence carried with it an implication that could be inferred from its content. For example, one sentence was "The youngster watched the program"; the implication was that a television was involved. Another sentence was "The chauffeur drove on the left side"; the implication was that the action took place in England. During the subsequent recall test half of the subjects received the implied information (e.g., "television," "England") as a retrieval cue; half did not. Such retrieval cues proved quite helpful for the younger subjects; the older subjects however, for the most part showed no benefit. Once again, therefore, it appears that the elderly are less likely than the young to draw constructive inferences that go beyond the immediate input.

BOX 9-1　Examples of passages and questions from Cohen's research on constructive memory

Mrs. Brown goes to the park every afternoon if the weather is fine. She likes to watch the children playing, and she feeds the ducks with bread crusts. She enjoys the walk there and back. For the last three days it has been raining all the time although it's the middle of the summer and the town is still full of people on holiday.

1. What does Mrs. Brown give the ducks to eat?
2. Did Mrs. Brown go to the park yesterday?

Note. From "Language Comprehension in Old Age" by G. Cohen, 1979, *Cognitive Psychology, 11,* p. 416. Copyright 1979 by Academic Press, Inc. Reprinted by permission.

Downstairs there are three rooms; the kitchen, the dining-room, and the sitting-room. The sitting-room is in the front of the house and the kitchen and dining-room face onto the vegetable garden at the back of the house. The noise of the traffic is very disturbing in the front rooms. Mother is in the kitchen cooking and Grandfather is reading the paper in the sitting-room. The children are at school and won't be home till tea-time.

1. What is Mother doing?
2. Who is being disturbed by the traffic?

Why should there be such age differences in constructive memory? In childhood at least part of the explanation has to do with differences in the knowledge base: Older childen know more than younger children, and so of course the kinds of inferences that they can show will differ. In adulthood, however, such differential knowledge seems a less plausible explanation; adults of any age, for example, are certainly capable of linking "watched the program" with "television." The difference here seems to lie in the tendency to do such linking—to use one's knowledge spontaneously to draw inferences. It is this tendency that apparently decreases in old age. One explanation of why there should be an age decrement in spontaneous inference implicates speed of processing. It has been argued (e.g., Cohen, 1979, 1981; Salthouse, 1982) that the elderly are slower in taking in new information, and that their slower rate of processing makes it difficult for them both to attend to new material and to relate the new material to old, stored material. Since it is the relation between new and old on which inference depends, the result is a decline in constructive memory. Although the speed-of-processing explanation is not without problems (see Hartley, Harker, & Walsh, 1980, for a critique), it does appear valid as another partial explanation for age differences in memory. And it does show a nice compatibility with—and indeed is supported by—other research that demonstrates that slowing of response has negative effects on a variety of kinds of performance in old age.

We noted at the outset of this section that the stereotype of memory in old age is one of decline. This stereotype is sometimes qualified, however, by the assertion that really long-term memory may remain remarkably intact in old age, even in the face of declines in memory for recent events. The prototypical example of this modified stereotype is the elderly person who can recall events from his or her childhood in vivid detail yet is unable to remember what he or she had for breakfast that morning. Loss of memory is thus selective, or at least so the argument goes, and selective in surprising ways.

How much truth is there to this notion of the relative intactness of long-term or "remote" memory? The answer is, probably some, but the issue has proved difficult to study, and much of the evidence remains anecdotal. Here we briefly consider several examples of research on really long-term memory, along with some of the methodological difficulties in doing such research.

Bahrick, Bahrick, and Wittlinger (1975) tested high-school graduates ranging in age from 17 to 74 years. The criterion of high-school graduate was important in selecting subjects, because the memory examined was memory for one's high-school classmates. Six different memory tests were used, two of recall and four of recognition. The recall tests were to list the names of as many classmates as possible and to indicate the name when presented with a picture of a classmate. The recognition tests were to pick the picture of a classmate from a group of five pictures, to pick the name of a classmate from a group of five names, to match a name with one or several pictures, and to match a picture with one of several names. Obviously, the age of the memory (i.e., time since last exposure to high-school classmates) varies with the age of the subject in this study, varying from extremes of about 3 to 4 months for the youngest subjects to better than 50 years for the oldest subjects.

Not surprisingly, Bahrick et al. found that young subjects were more successful at remembering high-school classmates than were older subjects. The age differences were especially striking on the two measures of recall. For example, the youngest subjects averaged better than 50 names on the first recall task, as compared to only about 20 names for the oldest subjects. The recognition measures, in contrast, showed both higher overall levels of performance and more similarity in performance across age. Recognition of faces, in particular, was remarkably good even 30 to 40 years after graduation. The strong performance on recognition fits with data discussed earlier regarding the power of recognition memory. The greater decline in recall than in recognition with age fits with other demonstrations of age by type-of-memory interactions. And the fact that some forms of memory are so resilient across such a long period of time provides support for the claim that long-term memory can be surprisingly intact in the elderly.

The yearbook study is just one example of research by Bahrick and colleagues on long-term retention of real-world knowledge. Other topics examined include memory for street names and locations (Bahrick, 1983) and memory for Spanish learned in high school or college (Bahrick, 1984). The latter study is especially interesting for several reasons. First, because its focus is on retention of material learned in school, the work has a clear academic relevance that is lacking in most research on memory. Furthermore, the study incorporates a number of methodological refinements (e.g., measures of degree of original learning, measures of the amount of rehearsal in the interim between original learning and test) that seem likely to serve as models for future research on remote memory. Finally, the results of the study are perhaps even more intriguing than those in Bahrick et al. (1975). Again, substantial amounts of material are retained after even 50 years, in this case even though opportunities to rehearse (i.e., use Spanish) are generally low. What is especially striking, however, is the curve of retention over time: some forgetting in the first 5 or 6 years after original learning and some further forgetting after about 30 years, but essentially no forgetting in the 25 years in between! Bahrick's conclusion is that some especially well-learned material may achieve a "permastore" status that is resistant to loss across even very long periods of time.

The most obvious limitation of the Bahrick studies, at least with regard to issues of aging, was noted earlier: Age of memory varies with—that is, is *confounded* with—age of subject. Thus, if we find that older people perform more poorly than younger, we do not know whether to attribute the age difference to a weakening of memory in old age or to the greater difficulty of recapturing a 50-year-old memory than a 5-year-old memory. Probably both factors contribute, but they cannot be disentangled in the research performed to date.

An alternative approach to the study of remote memory is illustrated in some research by Botwinick and Storandt (1974). Adults ranging in age from 20 to 79 were given a variety of memory tests, including questions that dealt with memory for sociohistorical facts. Examples of the questions asked are shown in Box 9-2. (For those who wish to test themselves, the answers are included in the Appendix at the end of this chapter.) Because the questions covered events drawn from four different historical time periods, it was possible to examine memory as a function of age of subject, recency of event asked about, and age of subject at the time that the event occurred. Botwinick and Storandt found no overall age differences in performance on such questions. Thus 70-year-olds were just as good as 20-year-olds at this kind of remote memory. There was, however, an interesting interaction between age of subject and time period asked about. The interaction reflected the fact that subjects of any age were most likely to remember events that occurred when they were 15- to 25-years-old. Thus, subjects in their fifties did best on questions dealing with events from the 1930s and 1940s; subjects in their thirties were best on events from the 1950s and 1960s.[1] (See Perlmutter, 1978, for a similar measure with partly congruent and partly discrepant results.)

The Botwinick and Storandt methodology escapes some of the limitations in the Bahrick studies but runs into some difficulties of its own. When high-school classmates are the stimuli we can be reasonably certain that the information being asked about *was* once learned; hence any failures on the recall or recognition tests can be attributed to deficits in memory and not to problems in initial learning. With the kinds of sociohistorical facts examined by Botwinick and Storandt this equivalence in initial learning is less certain. Perhaps some adults never learned the real name of "The Red Baron." If so, failures to answer correctly can hardly be attributed to failures of memory. In addition, the label "memory" might seem debatable when the subject is being asked about events that oc-

---

[1] Actually, this conclusion was specific to the males in Botwinick and Storandt's sample. Female subjects did not show the age by time period interaction.

BOX 9-2   Items from the Botwinick and Storandt test of long-term memory

Period: 1950–1969

1. What was the name of the first man to set foot on the moon?
2. What was the name of the man who assassinated Dr. Martin Luther King?
3. In what city was President John F. Kennedy assassinated?
4. In what year did the Russians orbit the first satellite?
5. What was the name of the man who ran against Dwight Eisenhower for President in 1952 and again in 1956?
6. What was the name of the Senator from Wisconsin whose name is associated with congressional investigations of communism in the early 1950's?

Period: 1930–1949

7. What was the name of the man who was elected vice-president in 1948 when Harry Truman was elected president?
8. What was the name of the World War II German general nicknamed "The Desert Fox"?
9. What was the name of the commander of the famous Flying Tigers of World War II?
10. On what date (day, month, year) did the Japanese bomb Pearl Harbor?
11. What was the name of the only president

of the United States to be elected to four terms of office?

12. Where (in what state) did the German dirigible, the Von Hindenberg, burn and crash?

Period: 1910–1929

13. What was the name of the ship which hit an iceberg and sank on its maiden voyage in 1912?
14. What was the name of the man whose death set off World War I?
15. What was the name of the World War I German flying ace nicknamed "The Red Baron"?
16. What do the initials WCTU stand for?
17. What was the name of the man tried in the famous Monkey Trial of 1925?
18. What was the name of the plane in which Lindbergh flew the Atlantic?

Period: 1890–1909

19. What was the name of the man who discovered the North Pole?
20. In what state did the first legal electrocution for murder in the United States occur?
21. What was the name of the man who became president when President McKinley was assassinated in 1900?
22. Where did the Wright brothers make their first successful flight?
23. What was the name of the boxer who was nicknamed "Gentleman Jim"?
24. In what year did Henry Ford introduce the Model T?

Note. From *Memory, Related Functions, and Age* (pp. 189–191) by J. Botwinick and M. Storandt, 1974, Springfield, IL: Charles C Thomas. Copyright 1974 by Charles C Thomas. Reprinted by permission.

curred before his or her birth. The Botwinick and Storandt questions do not tap the kinds of specific, personal-experience memories that are the focus in the Bahrick et al. study. Instead, they deal more with general information about the world, information that may have been accumulated in a variety of ways.

Whatever its limitations, the Botwinick and Storandt study does illustrate some important points about adult memory. Most generally, it provides another demonstration that memory is not necessarily inferior in old age. For some types of questions the elderly may do as well as or even better than young adults. The finding that memory in the general knowledge-about-the-world sense holds up well with age is compatible with a good deal of other research in the aging literature. The same conclusion emerges, for example, from age comparisons on the Information subtest of the WAIS (see Table 7-6). Finally, the Botwinick and Storandt study—as well as much other research that we do not have the space to include—suggests that conclusions about memory in the elderly are likely to be more positive when the focus is on meaningful, real-world material, as opposed to arbitrary and unfamiliar laboratory tasks. The same issues of measurement equivalence and age-appropriateness that were discussed with regard to IQ apply to research on memory. At least part of the negative picture of memory in old age may stem from the heavy emphasis on measures that are more geared to young adults than to the elderly.

Personality and Social Development

We turn now from intelligence to the domain of personality and social functioning. We begin with two examples of often used tests of social adjustment in the elderly. We then move on to a critical evaluation of these and similar measures.

One popular topic in the psychology of aging is variously labeled "morale," "subjective well-being," "life satisfaction," or simply "happiness." The question is a basic and very important one: How satisfied is the person with his or her life? A variety of measuring instruments have been devised in an attempt to assess life satisfaction. Our example is drawn from one of the earliest and most influential of these instruments, the Life Satisfaction Index (LSI) of Neugarten, Havighurst, and Tobin (1961). Other tests for the measurement of morale, along with a review of results from such measures, can be found in Larson (1978).

The Life Satisfaction Index was developed as part of one of the major early studies of aging, the Kansas City Study of Adult Life. The original sample (some of whom eventually dropped out) consisted of 177 men and women between the ages of 50 and 90. As is often the case in aging research, the sample was a somewhat above average one, especially in the older half of the age range. Each subject in the study participated in a series of in-depth interviews,

spaced longitudinally across a period of about 2½ years. As the following description (Neugarten et al., 1961) suggests, the interviews were quite extensive, surveying a number of aspects of life in middle and old age.

Included was information on the daily round and the usual weekend-round of activity; other household members; relatives, friends, and neighbors; income and work; religion; voluntary organizations; estimates of the amount of social interaction as compared with the amount at age 45; attitudes toward old age, illness, death, and immortality; questions about loneliness, boredom, anger; and questions regarding the respondent's role models and his self-image. (p. 136)

The purpose of the interviews was to elicit responses from which various dimensions of life satisfaction might be scored. Eventually, five dimensions proved to be scorable: Zest versus Apathy, Resolution and Fortitude, Congruence between Desired and Achieved Goals, Self-Concept, and Mood Tone. For each dimension, scoring was on a 5-point scale; 5 represented the positive end of the dimension and 1 the negative end. The scales for two of the dimensions, Zest versus Apathy and Self-Concept, are described in Box 9-3.

The interview method, while perhaps necessary for the initial delineation of dimensions, is obviously a very time-consuming approach to individual assessment. Neugarten et al.'s next step, therefore, was to attempt to develop a briefer technique for eliciting the same information. The result was the LSI: a self-report questionnaire which requires subjects simply to agree or disagree with a series of 20 statements. The 20 items are shown in Table 9-5, along with an indication of the choice that would result in the most positive score on the various dimensions. According to Neugarten et al., scores on the LSI correlate .55 with judges' ratings derived from interviews—thus, moderately well but hardly perfectly.

What has the LSI revealed about life satisfaction in old age? In answering this question, we draw not only from the LSI but also from other measures of morale in the elderly, most

BOX 9–3 Examples of dimensions from the life satisfaction rating scales

Zest vs. apathy.

To be rated here are enthusiasm of response and degree of ego-involvement—in any of various activities, persons, or ideas, whether or not these are activities which involve R with other people, are "good" or "socially approved" or "status-giving." Thus, R who "just loves to sit home and knit" rates as high as R who "loves to get out and meet people." Although a low rating is given for listlessness and apathy, physical energy *per se* is not to be involved in this rating. Low ratings are given for being "bored with most things"; for " I have to force myself to do things"; and also for meaningless (and unenjoyed) hyper-activity.

5..... Speaks of several activities and relationships with enthusiasm. Feels that "now" is the best time of life. Loves to do things, even sitting at home. Takes up new activities; makes new friends readily, seeks self-improvement. Shows zest in several areas of life.

4..... Shows zest, but it is limited to one or two special interests, or limited to certain periods of time. May show disappointment or anger when things go wrong, if they keep him from active enjoyment of life. Plans ahead, even though in small time units.

3..... Has a bland approach to life. Does not seem to get much pleasure out of the things he does. Seeks relaxation and a limited degree of involvement. May be quite detached (aloof) from many activities, things, or people.

2..... Thinks life is monotonous for the most part. May complain of fatigue. Feels bored with many things. If active, finds little meaning or enjoyment in the activity.

Note. From "The Measurement of Life Satisfaction" by B. L. Neugarten, R. J. Havighurst, and S. S. Tobin, 1961, *Journal of Gerontology, 16*, pp. 137–138. Copyright 1961 by the Gerontological Society of America. Reprinted by permission.

1..... Lives on the basis of routine. Doesn't think anything worth doing.

Self-concept.

R's concept of self—physical as well as psychological and social attributes. High ratings go to R who is concerned with grooming and appearance; who thinks of himself as wise, mellow (and thus is comfortable in giving advice to others); who feels proud of his accomplishments; who feels he deserves whatever good breaks he has had; who feels he is important to someone else. Low ratings are given to R who feels "old," weak, sick, incompetent; who feels himself a burden to others; who speaks disparagingly of self or of old people.

5..... Feels at his best. "I do better work now than ever before." "There was never any better time." Thinks of self as wise, mellow; physically able; attractive; feels important to others. Feels he has the right to indulge himself.

4..... Feels more fortunate than the average. Is sure that he can meet the exigencies of life. "When I retire, I'll just substitute other activities." Compensates well for any difficulty of health. Feels worthy of being indulged. "Things I want to do I can do, but I'll not overexert myself." Feels in control of self in relation to the situation.

3..... Sees self as competent in at least one area, e.g., work; but has doubts about self in other areas. Acknowledges loss of youthful vigor, but accepts it in a realistic way. Feels relatively unimportant, but doesn't mind. Feels he takes, but also gives. Senses a general, but not extreme, loss of status as he grows older. Reports health better than average.

2..... Feels that other people look down on him. Tends to speak disparagingly of older people. Is defensive about what the years are doing to him.

1..... Feels old. Feels in the way, or worthless. Makes self-disparaging remarks. "I'm endured by others."

TABLE 9-5   Life Satisfaction Index

Here are some statements about life in general that people feel differently about. Would you read each statement on the list, and if you agree with it, put a check mark in the space under "AGREE." If you do not agree with a statement, put a check mark in the space under "DISAGREE." If you are not sure one way or the other, put a check mark in the space under "?." PLEASE BE SURE TO ANSWER EVERY QUESTION ON THE LIST.

(*Key: score 1 point for each response marked X.*)

	Agree	Disagree	?
1. As I grow older, things seem better than I thought they would be.	x		
2. I have gotten more of the breaks in life than most of the people I know.	x		
3. This is the dreariest time of my life.		x	
4. I am just as happy as when I was younger.	x		
5. My life could be happier than it is now.		x	
6. These are the best years of my life.	x		
7. Most of the things I do are boring or monotonous.		x	
8. I expect some interesting and pleasant things to happen to me in the future.	x		
9. The things I do are as interesting to me as they ever were.	x		
10. I feel old and somewhat tired.		x	
11. I feel my age, but it does not bother me.	x		
12. As I look back on my life, I am fairly well satisfied.	x		
13. I would not change my past life even if I could.	x		
14. Compared to other people my age, I've made a lot of foolish decisions in my life.		x	
15. Compared to other people my age, I make a good appearance.	x		
16. I have made plans for things I'll be doing a month or a year from now.	x		
17. When I think back over my life, I didn't get most of the important things I wanted.		x	
18. Compared to other people, I get down in the dumps too often.		x	
19. I've gotten pretty much what I expected out of life.	x		
20. In spite of what people say, the lot of the average man is getting worse, not better.		x	

Note. From "The Measurement of Life Satisfaction" by B. L. Neugarten, R. J. Havighurst, and S. S. Tobin, 1961, *Journal of Gerontology, 16,* p. 141. Copyright 1961 by the Gerontological Society of America. Reprinted by permission.

of which, it turns out, both correlate well with the LSI and lead to similar conclusions (Larson, 1978). We can ask first the major developmental question: Are there changes with age in life satisfaction? Answering this question is complicated by the fact that the great majority of studies are cross-sectional; hence apparent changes with age may reflect cohort differences rather than actual change as people get older. In any case, there *is* an on-the-average negative relation between age and life satisfaction, at least for individuals 60 or older. Edwards and Klemmack (1973), for example, reported a correlation of −.14 between age and LSI scores in a sample of 507 middle-aged and elderly adults. In this study and others, however, the relation between age and morale is modest at best.

Thus, the presence of substantial individual differences among the elderly is again a noteworthy point. There are plenty of elderly people who feel quite satisfied with their lives.

The results just discussed lead to a natural next question: What are the determinants of developmental or individual differences in life satisfaction? Much of the research with the LSI or similar instruments has been directed to this issue. A number of correlates have been identified, most of which are quite predictable. Health, for example, is positively related to life satisfaction; on the average, relatively healthy people report greater satisfaction than less healthy people. Marital status is also related; life satisfaction scores are higher for married people than for individuals who have been either widowed or divorced. Perhaps the most interesting finding concerns the relation between activity and life satisfaction. A number of studies have demonstrated that the relation is a positive one—that is, that elderly people who remain active report greater life satisfaction than those whose activity level has decreased. This finding has been seen as relevant to the clash between two major theories of aging: Disengagement Theory (Cumming & Henry, 1961), which posits that optimal aging is characterized by some degree of withdrawal from earlier activities and commitments, and Activity Theory (e.g., Maddox, 1965), which argues that successful aging is most likely if the elderly person remains active (see Kausler, 1982, and Botwinick, 1984, for fuller discussions).

Our second example of a personality measure is also related to the general question of the quality of life in old age. The focus now is on stress and response to stress. This, too, has been a popular research topic in the psychology of aging. There is little doubt that old age can be a period of great stress, a time during which problems of numerous sorts arise and the resources for coping with the problems may no longer be adequate. A number of tests have been devised in an attempt to assess stressful events and their impact on individuals of different ages. Here, we concentrate on one of the most influential of these tests, the Schedule of Recent Events (Holmes & Rahe, 1967). For critiques of the Holmes and Rahe test, along with discussion of some alternative approaches to the measurement of stress, see Chiriboga and Cutler, 1980, and Horowitz and Wilner, 1980.

The Holmes and Rahe research program actually involves two related tests: the Schedule of Recent Events, or SRE, and the Social Readjustment Rating Questionnaire, or SRRQ. The SRRQ asks subjects to rate a series of life events in terms of the degree of social readjustment that the event would require. Social readjustment is defined as "the amount and duration of change in one's accustomed pattern of life resulting from various life events . . . the intensity and length of time necessary to accommodate to a life event, *regardless of the desirability of this event*" (Holmes & Rahe, 1967, p. 213). Table 9-6 shows the 43 events included in the questionnaire. One of the events, Marriage, is taken as an anchor point and is assigned an arbitrary value of 500. Other events are then rated in terms of the degree to which they would require more or less readjustment than marriage. Subjects can assign whatever numbers they like to an event relative to the anchor point of 500; thus the measure yields not only a relative ordering of life events but also a quantitative estimate of the varying degrees of readjustment required by different kinds of experience.

The basic purpose of the SRRQ is to provide this quantitative scaling of the stressfulness of different life events. There is, of course, no single "correct" scaling; responses may vary across samples, and the particular statistical method used to translate the assigned numbers into a scale can affect the conclusions drawn. Nevertheless, there does seem to be at least some consistency in the ordering of life events across different subjects and different methods of scaling (Holmes & Rahe, 1967; Masuda & Holmes, 1967). A typical set of results, drawn from the original Holmes and Rahe (1967) sample, is shown in the righthand column of Table 9-6. The values in the column are obtained by dividing the mean of the assigned number by 10. The label "LCU" refers to "Life Change Units," which is Holmes and Rahe's term for the degree of readjustment required by a life event.

The SRRQ provides a metric for potential stressful events. The next question is an obvious one: How frequently do these events occur and what effects do they have? It is here that the SRE enters in. The purpose of the SRE is to measure the frequency of occurrence for the different life events included in the SRRQ. The format is again questionnaire, with the same 43 life events as the items. In this case subjects are asked to indicate how frequently they experienced each event during the preceding 10-year period. For some events (e.g., change in financial state) subjects mark presence or absence for each year; for others (e.g.,

TABLE 9–6 Items and Typical Ratings (in Life Change Units) from the Social Readjustment Rating Questionnaire

Event	LCU
1. Marriage	50
2. Troubles with the boss	23
3. Detention in jail or other institution	63
4. Death of spouse	100
5. Major change in sleeping habits (a lot more or a lot less sleep, or change in part of day when asleep)	16
6. Death of a close family member	63
7. Major change in eating habits (a lot more or a lot less food intake, or very different meal hours or surroundings)	15
8. Foreclosure on a mortgage or loan	30
9. Revision of personal habits (dress, manners, associations, etc.)	24
10. Death of a close friend	37
11. Minor violations of the law (e.g. traffic tickets, jay walking, disturbing the peace, etc.)	11
12. Outstanding personal achievement	28
13. Pregnancy	40
14. Major change in the health or behavior of a family member	44
15. Sexual difficulties	39
16. In-law troubles	29
17. Major change in number of family get-togethers (e.g. a lot more or a lot less than usual)	15
18. Major change in financial state (e.g. a lot worse off or a lot better off than usual)	38
19. Gaining a new family member (e.g. through birth, adoption, oldster moving in, etc.)	39
20. Change in residence	20
21. Son or daughter leaving home (e.g. marriage, attending college, etc.)	29
22. Marital separation from mate	65
23. Major change in church activities (e.g. a lot more or a lot less than usual)	19
24. Marital reconciliation with mate	45
25. Being fired from work	47
26. Divorce	73
27. Changing to a different line of work	36
28. Major change in the number of arguments with spouse (e.g. either a lot more or a lot less than usual regarding childrearing, personal habits, etc.)	35
29. Major change in responsibilities at work (e.g. promotion, demotion, lateral transfer)	29
30. Wife beginning or ceasing work outside the home	26
31. Major change in working hours or conditions	20
32. Major change in usual type and/or amount of recreation	19
33. Taking on a mortgage greater than $10,000 (e.g. purchasing a home, business, etc.)	31
34. Taking on a mortgage or loan less than $10,000 (e.g. purchasing a car, TV, freezer, etc.)	17
35. Major personal injury or illness	53
36. Major business readjustment (e.g. merger, reorganization, bankruptcy, etc.)	39
37. Major change in social activities (e.g. clubs, dancing, movies, visiting, etc.)	18
38. Major change in living conditions (e.g. building a new home, remodeling, deterioration of home or neighborhood)	25
39. Retirement from work	45
40. Vacation	13
41. Christmas	12
42. Changing to a new school	20
43. Beginning or ceasing formal schooling	26

Note. From ''The Social Readjustment Rating Scale'' by T. H. Holmes and R. H Rahe, 1967, *Journal of Psychosomatic Research, 11,* p. 214. Copyright 1967 by Pergamon Press. Reprinted by permission.

being fired) they mark number of occurrences per year. The obtained frequency for an event is then multiplied by the LCU for that event, and the sum across all events constitutes the magnitude of stressful life experiences.

The SRE has been put to a number of research uses. Probably the most often-studied question is the one that motivated the original development of the instrument: the relation between stress and illness. Many studies have confirmed that the relation is a positive one, both for physical illness and for mental illness (see Rahe, 1979, for a review). There is some evidence that the stress-health relation may be greater for young adults than for elderly adults, perhaps because negative stressors (e.g., health problems, widowhood) are more expectable and thus more prepared for as one gets older. It has also been argued, however, that detrimental effects of stress may be more likely in old age, when stressful experiences cumulate and coping resources are diminished. This issue, therefore, remains unresolved (Eisdorfer & Wilkie, 1977).

Let us look more generally at the relation between stress and age. Are there changes with age in response to the SRRQ and SRE? The answer is in part yes and in part no. When subjects of different ages rate the 43 events of the SRRQ the correlations in rank order are remarkably high, often in the .90s (e.g., Holmes & Rahe, 1967). Thus, there is little change with age in peoples' perception of the relative stressfulness of different life events. Even though the ordering remains constant, however, the magnitude of perceived stress—that is, the specific LCU assigned to a given event—might vary with age. The magnitudes for many life events do vary with age, and the variations show a consistent pattern: Older subjects assign lower values than do younger subjects. Thus, older people apparently perceive many life events as less stressful than do their younger counterparts. Older people also experience many life events less frequently than do younger people. Data from the SRE confirm what an inspection of the events sampled in the SRRQ suggests would be the case: The probability of experiencing many potentially stressful life events decreases in old age. Taken together, these two

findings—lower stress ratings and lower probability of experiencing life events—suggest that for many people old age might actually be less stressful than younger adulthood. It must be added, however (in anticipation of the coming discussion), that this conclusion obviously depends on the validity and age-appropriateness of the SRRQ and SRE. Some critics have argued, for example, that the lumping of positive and negative stressors on the SRE may obscure an important distinction. There is some evidence that the main decline in old age may be in the experience of *positive* life events (e.g., personal achievements, improvements in job status); *negative* stressors, however (e.g., declines in health), may still be quite important (Chiriboga & Cutler, 1980).

Let us turn now to some of the general methodological issues that are raised by our brief sampling of personality measures. A first point to be made is that this is a sampling, a very small subset of the many measuring instruments available for the study of adulthood and aging. "Personality" is no more reducible to a single test than is "intelligence," and even more specific constructs such as "life satisfaction" or "stress" lend themselves to a variety of interpretations and corresponding tests. There are, in fact, criticisms and alternatives for both of the instruments that we have considered. As we have just seen, the SRE has been criticized for failing to distinguish between positive and negative life events. It has also been criticized for not including enough items that are relevant to the experiences of older people. Both criticisms have led to the development of alternative tests for assessing stress in the elderly. One criticism of the LSI has been that it is essentially a unidimensional measure of morale—that is, the five dimensions (Zest vs. Apathy, etc.) are not really independent aspects of life satisfaction but are simply added together to give one overall value. One major direction for alternative approaches, therefore, has been an attempt to develop multidimensional measures that distinguish among different, statistically independent components of life satisfaction (e.g., Lawton, 1975).

The point of the preceding paragraph is that

any measure has its limitations. Some of the criticisms, however, are of general importance, for they reflect issues that apply to a broad range of different tasks. One of these issues, certainly, is measurement equivalence. Conclusions about age differences or age changes are valid only if the measures used are equally appropriate for the age groups being compared. As is true in the study of intelligence, many of the personality tests that are employed with the elderly were originally developed with younger samples. Even measures that were devised with life-span research in mind (such as the SRE) often seem to have content that is more appropriate for younger subjects. Conversely, a test that is too exclusively oriented to the concerns of old age may be informative with elderly subjects but inappropriate for younger adults, and the goal of making valid age comparisons will again be frustrated. Problems of measurement equivalence arise whenever the particular behaviors and contexts through which some psychological attribute is expressed change from one age to another. If anything, such changes seem even more likely for personality and social relations than for intelligence.

A second issue concerns the general approach that is taken to the assessment of personality. Throughout this book we have identified three general approaches that can be taken in the study of any behavioral domain: direct observation of the behaviors of interest in the natural setting, experimental elicitation of the behaviors in some structured laboratory setting, and ratings or verbal reports about typical behavior from someone who knows the subject. The measures that we have considered in this section clearly fall under this third heading of ratings or verbal reports. The rating approach has been by far the most common in the assessment of adult personality. Exceptions do exist. Experimental lab approaches have occasionally been used in the study of some topics; examples include conformity (e.g., Klein, 1972), rigidity (e.g., Brinley, 1965), and cautiousness (e.g., Okun & Elias, 1977). Observational data, although rare in the study of the elderly, do exist for some topics—for example, observational assessment of the experiences and behaviors of elderly people in a nursing home (Gottesman & Bourestom, 1974). Nevertheless, the bulk of what we know about personality and aging is derived from rating measures. Our earlier discussions of the pluses and minuses of such measures should therefore be kept in mind when evaluating this literature.

There is a further point. The measures that we have reviewed are not only verbal reports; they are *self*-reports. The source for information about the subject is the subject him- or herself. All of the problems and biases that can accompany self-report measures are therefore applicable to these tests. A review by Lawton, Whelinan, and Belsky (1980) provides a helpful discussion both of test-taking biases and of ways to minimize the biases when doing personality assessment with the elderly. As Lawton et al. make clear, such biases (e.g., evaluation apprehension, response sets, misunderstanding of instructions, fatigue) can affect not only conclusions about the elderly but also conclusions about age differences in personality. An apparent difference in depression, for example, might reflect an age-related difference in the willingness to admit negative emotions rather than a genuine personality difference between young and old. The same point applies, by the way, to an interesting topic that we have not had space to include—sex differences in the elderly (e.g., Turner, 1982). Most conclusions about apparent sex differences in old age are based on self-report data and therefore must be viewed with caution.[2]

Two issues remain to be discussed. This chapter has divided the psychology of aging into

---

[2]Another topic omitted for reasons of space can be noted here. The tests that we have reviewed are all "objective" measures, in the sense that the questions are focused fairly directly on the content of interest and the scoring is straightforward and requires little or no clinical judgment (Costa & McCrae, 1978). One way to try to minimize the biases of self-report measures is to employ "projective" tests, in which the purpose of the test is disguised and the subject is assumed to project deep and perhaps unconscious feelings through apparently trivial responses. Probably the most commonly used projective measures with adults have been the Rorschach Ink Blots Test and the Thematic Apperception Test or TAT. Kahana (1978) provides a review of the use of these and other projective tests with elderly adults.

a cognitive side and a social or personality side. But people, of course, show no such clear division; there is only a single, uncompartmentalized organism, and any aspect of functioning may influence any other aspect. It is quite possible, therefore, that personality and social relations in old age may be affected by the cognitive deficits that we have discussed, such as slowness in decision making or loss of memory. It is also possible—and it is this prospect that is worrisome from a methodological point of view—that response to personality *tests* may be biased by cognitive or perceptual problems, such as forgetting instructions or difficulty seeing or hearing the stimuli. In this case the effect of cognition is more artifactual than real, and we may easily draw false conclusions about the elderly subject's personality. Finally, as Kausler (1982) has noted, the influence can also go in the other direction, from personality characteristics to cognitive performance. Increases with age in attributes such as cautiousness or rigidity might well hamper the elderly subject's performance on a number of different cognitive tasks.

The final issue concerns the correlational nature of most of the data that we have been considering. The core relation of interest, that between personality and age, is, of course, correlational. Beyond this, many of the research programs that we have discussed are based upon the establishment of correlations. Does stress contribute to the onset of illness? The answer to this question lies in determining whether stress correlates with illness. Does a relatively high level of activity contribute to life satisfaction in old age? Again, the answer is based upon correlations. What we are interested in are cause-and-effect relations (stress as a cause of illness, activity as a cause of satisfaction), yet what we are working with are nonexperimental designs that do not permit the establishment of causality.

Both the limitations of correlational research and ways to overcome these limitations were discussed in chapter 5. As we saw then, there is no point in bemoaning the correlational nature of many research domains, for correlations are sometimes the best that we can do. Consider the issue of stress and health. We can hardly carry out an experimental study in which we induce stress in an elderly sample in order to determine the effects on their subsequent health. We *can*, however, do several things that can move us closer to causality. One is to use various statistical methods (such as the partial correlation technique discussed in chapter 5) to control for potential confounding factors and specify more exactly the relation between the variables of interest. We might ask, for example, what happens to the relation between activity and morale if we control for socioeconomic status. Such statistical controls are common for the topics that we have been considering. Another possibility is to trace the patterns of correlation over time, making use of the fact that causes must precede their effects. A demonstration, for example, that stressful events typically occur shortly before the onset of illness suggests a more certain causal relation than a simple one-point-in-time correlation. We can see here once again the value of longitudinal research for the study of central issues in developmental psychology.

SUMMARY

The first part of this chapter is devoted to general issues in the study of aging. It also provides an overview of research on one very extensively studied topic: stability or change in IQ as people age.

Research on aging faces the same methodological challenges as does developmental research in general, but often in heightened form. *Sampling* of subjects has two general goals: achieving representative samples at each age and achieving comparable samples across different ages. Neither goal is easy to achieve, and the two goals may sometimes conflict. Two kinds of confounds in particular have been of concern in comparisons of young adults and elderly adults. One is a confounding of age and education: On the average, young adults are better educated than are elderly adults. The other is a confounding of age and health: On the average, young adults are healthier than are elderly adults. Both factors contribute to the average IQ decrement in old age.

The discussion of the health variable leads to a general consideration of sampling problems in longitudinal research. *Selective drop-out* of subjects is a major problem in longitudinal study. In studies of IQ the relatively low IQ subjects are most likely to be lost from the study. Such drop-out has two bases: voluntary withdrawals from the study and involuntary withdrawals for reasons of health, including the extreme case of death. The result is a positive bias in favor of the elderly.

The discussion turns next to issues of *measurement*. Like any broad construct, IQ can be measured in a variety of ways. The two most commonly used instruments in the study of aging have been the WAIS and the PMA. Both tests are divided into subscales, and the probability of age differences varies across different subscales. One generalization, which extends to a variety of contexts in addition to IQ test performance, is that elderly subjects are especially handicapped on tasks that require quick response. Evidence is discussed that indicates that this slowing with age is central rather than peripheral in origin. Also discussed is an issue that is critical not only for IQ research but for any comparison of young and old: the problem of *measurement equivalence*. The tests and contexts used to assess the elderly often seem more appropriate for young adults, and this factor is another probable contributor to age differences in performance.

The first section of the chapter concludes with a consideration of issues of *design*. *Cross-sectional* designs involve a confounding of age and cohort; *longitudinal* designs involve a confounding of age and time of measurement. The importance of the variables of cohort and historical time is confirmed by a third "simple" design, the *time-lag* approach. These various confounds, together with the previously mentioned selective drop-out in longitudinal studies, provide an explanation for the often-reported finding that age decrements are greater in cross-sectional research than in longitudinal research. An attempt to overcome the limitations of simpler designs is found in the *sequential*

studies of Schaie and associates. Sequential designs involve combinations of the simpler designs and hence provide more opportunity to disentangle the contributions of age, time, and cohort. The major conclusion that Schaie et al. draw from their research is that cohort effects are much more important than age effects in the study of IQ. Even sequential designs have their limitations, however, and this conclusion has therefore remained controversial.

The second part of the chapter addresses selected research topics in the psychology of aging. Memory has been one popular topic. As with IQ, the probability of age differences in memory depends on a number of factors. Although exceptions exist, memory decrements in old age are less likely on *recognition* than on *recall*, and they are less likely on tasks of *cued-recall* than on noncued measures. Both of these findings suggest that elderly adults may have special difficulty in retrieving information from storage. More generally, it has been suggested that elderly adults have difficulty in situations that require the use of *mnemonic strategies*. Evidence from a variety of paradigms provides some, although not perfect, support for this notion. It has also been suggested that *constructive memory* may decline in old age, perhaps because of a general slowdown in information processing. Again, a variety of kinds of evidence provide some support for an age-related decline. Finally, a more positive picture of memory and aging is found in the belief that really long-term or *"remote" memory* may remain remarkably intact in old age. This hypothesis has proved difficult to study, but it does appear to have some validity.

This chapter concludes with a consideration of methods for studying personality and social relations in the elderly. Two sample tests are described, along with illustrative findings from their use. The LSI is one of many instruments developed to assess *life satisfaction* or morale in adulthood. Perhaps the most interesting finding from its use concerns the relation between activity and life satisfaction in the elderly. The SRRQ and SRE are related tests whose function is to assess perceptions and frequency of *stress* in adulthood. The major research question to which they have been applied concerns the effects of stress on both physical and mental health.

The presentation of specific tests is followed by a discussion of general issues in the study of personality in the elderly. One issue is measurement equivalence: Are the tests equally appropriate for the different age groups being compared? Another issue is validity: Does the test in fact measure what it claims to measure? A particular concern with regard to validity is the self-report nature of many measures, a factor that raises the possibility of various biases. The final issue considered is the correlational nature of many research programs in the study of aging. Such correlational designs cannot conclusively establish the cause-and-effect links (e.g., between activity and morale) that have been of interest in such research.

APPENDIX

Answers to the Botwinick and Storandt Questions.

1. Neil Armstrong
2. James Earl Ray
3. Dallas
4. 1957
5. Adlai Stevenson
6. Joseph McCarthy
7. Alvin Barkley
8. Erwin Rommel
9. Claire Chenault
10. December 7, 1941
11. Franklin Roosevelt
12. New Jersey
13. Titanic
14. Archduke Ferdinand
15. Baron Manfred Van Richtohfen
16. Women's Christian Temperance Union
17. John T. Scopes
18. Spirit of St. Louis
19. Robert E. Peary
20. New York
21. Theodore Roosevelt
22. Kitty Hawk
23. James Corbett
24. 1908

chapter 10
STATISTICS

All research in psychology involves statistics. No one can be a researcher in psychology without some basic competence in statistical analysis. And no one can hope to understand and evaluate the research of others without some grasp of how statistics works.

Any student who has penetrated very far in the study of psychology is familiar with the points just made. Any such student also knows that mastery of statistics is not a rapid process but typically requires several courses and several depressingly thick textbooks. There will be no attempt here to compress books' worth of information into a single chapter. The goal is more modest: to present some of the basic ideas and principles behind statistical tests, as a complement to much fuller discussions of the tests themselves. The chapter can serve as a preview of, accompaniment to, or reminder of course work in statistics.

The general direction of movement in the chapter is from the relatively simple to the more complex. We begin with some reminders about uses of statistics, after which the familiar t test is introduced as an example of statistical reasoning. To a good extent much of the rest of the chapter consists of complications of the simple case presented by the t—various situations in which we need other kinds of statistics, along with the possibilities available and bases for choosing among them. Because the discussion in every case remains brief and general, further sources are noted for each of the topics touched on.

USES OF STATISTICS

Psychologists use statistics for two purposes: to describe data and to draw inferences about the meaning of data. The first of these uses is relatively straightforward and familiar; the second is both more complicated and more challenging.

Descriptive Statistics

Let us return to one of our earlier examples. Imagine an observational study of aggression in a nursery-school setting. The researcher collects the (hypothetical) data shown in Table 10-1. As can be seen, there are clearly individual differences in frequency of aggression; there might also be differences associated with sex and age. But how can we move beyond this welter of numbers to determine what we really have?

The first step is to summarize the data by means of various *descriptive statistics*. Most descriptive statistics are concerned with identifying the *central tendency*, or dominant pattern of response in the sample. The most common measure of central tendency is the familiar arithmetical average or *mean*. Table 10-2 shows that the various groups in our hypothetical study do in fact show different mean levels of aggression.

In most cases the mean is the most informative descriptive statistic. It is not the only descriptive measure that can be derived, however, and in some cases the mean alone may give an incomplete picture of the results. Consider a comparison between the 3-year-old boys and the 4-year-old boys. We saw in Table 10-2 that the mean level of aggression was higher in the older boys. An examination of the raw data in Table 10-1, however, suggests that most of the aggression scores were in fact quite similar in the two groups. The higher mean for the older children resulted largely from a few very high values. Or consider a comparison between the 3-year-old boys and the 3-year-old girls. From the means in Table 10-2 we might conclude that these two groups responded in the same way. Yet the raw scores in Table 10-1 tell us that the similar means had somewhat different underlying bases.

These examples suggest the need for some further descriptive statistics beyond the mean. Two other measures of central tendency are available. One is the *median*. The median is the midpoint of the distribution, the point above which half of the scores fall and below which the remaining half fall. Consider again the comparison between 3-year-old boys and 4-year-old boys. We can see in Table 10-2 that both groups had a median score of 4. This finding suggests a basic similarity between the two distributions, a similarity that was obscured by the differences in means. In general, the median is a useful statistic whenever a distribution is *skewed*— that is, contains a few unusually large or a few unusually small values. In such cases, the mean may not give a representative picture of the typical level of response.

The third measure of central tendency is the

TABLE 10-1 Number of Aggressive Responses in a Sample of Nursery-School Children (Hypothetical Data)

3-Year-Old Boys	3-Year-Old Girls	4-Year-Old Boys	4-Year-Old Girls
5	0	2	3
4	0	27	3
0	10	3	0
14	3	34	10
5	0	3	1
15	18	38	4
0	2	0	3
2	0	4	0
9	5	19	4
5	15	35	3
3	0	3	5
2	6	2	11
1	0	3	0
16	10	18	1
3	6	10	3

TABLE 10–2 Descriptive Statistics for the Aggressive Responses Reported in Table 10–1

	Mean	*Median*	*Mode*	*Standard Deviation*
3-Year-Old Boys	5.6	4	5	5.38
3-Year-Old Girls	5.0	3	0	5.88
4-Year-Old Boys	13.4	4	3	13.90
4-Year-Old Girls	3.4	3	3	3.29
Boys Combined	9.5	4	3	11.09
Girls Combined	4.2	3	0	4.75
3-Year-Olds Combined	5.3	3.5	0	5.55
4-Year-Olds Combined	8.4	3	3	11.15

mode. The mode is the most common score in a particular group. It is not an often-used statistic, but in certain circumstances it can be informative. Look, for example, at the scores for the 3-year-old girls in Table 10-1. We saw earlier that this group averaged 5.0 aggressive responses, essentially the same as the 3-year-old boys. The modal response for the 3-year-old girls, however, was 0 aggressive acts, which was not true for the boys. This fact might well be worth reporting.

In addition to measures of central tendency, descriptive statistics are also used to summarize the *variability* of a distribution. We need to know not only what the central tendency is but also something about the extent to which scores either cluster around or depart from this central value. The most commonly calculated measure of variability is the *variance*. To find the variance we begin by calculating the mean for the sample. We then determine the difference between this mean and each individual score in the group. These difference, or "deviation," scores are then squared, the squares are summed, and the total is divided by $N - 1$, at which point we have the variance. The variance is thus essentially the average of the squared deviation scores—"essentially" because the denominator is $N - 1$ rather than N. The greater the differences between individual scores and the mean, the larger the variance will be.

Most journal articles do not report the variance but rather the *standard deviation* as the measure of variability. The standard deviation is simply the square root of the variance. This value is presented in Table 10-2 for each of the groups in our hypothetical study. These standard deviations confirm our earlier intuitions about the degree of spread in the various groups. Note, in particular, the relatively large standard deviation for the 4-year-old boys, the group with several extremely high scores.

Inferential Statistics

Suppose that we have found the means reported in Table 10-2. It appears that aggression may vary as a function of both age and sex. But how can we decide with any certainty whether the differences we have found are genuine and not simply chance fluctuations? This is an issue in *inferential statistics*.

To explain the need for inferential statistics, we need to return to a number of (partially overlapping) distinctions that were introduced in chapter 2. One is the distinction between true scores and errors of measurement. Any score always consists of two components: the subject's actual value on the dimension being measured and whatever errors of measurement have occurred in attempting to determine this true score. A second distinction is between primary variance and secondary or error variance. Primary variance is variance associated with the independent variables being examined; secondary variance and error variance refer to all other sources of variation in the study—that is, all the other reasons, apart from the independent variables, that scores might differ. A final distinction is between populations and samples. A population is the entire universe of observations in which the researcher is interested; a sample is the particular subset of observations actually included in the study.

What we are interested in when we compare two samples (two age groups, two sexes, two experimental conditions, etc.) is whether there is a genuine difference between the populations from which the samples were drawn. If we could somehow collect the entire population of relevant observations, rather than just a sample, and if we could somehow rule out all errors of measurement, then we would have our answer: The scores that we obtain *would* be the population values of interest. But of course we cannot do these things; samples are always partial, measurement is always imperfect, and many sources of unwanted variance always exist. It is for this reason that we need techniques for estimating, or "inferring," the likelihood that an obtained difference between samples is indicative of a true difference between populations.

Let us apply the argument to our aggression study and the issue of sex differences in aggression. We already know that there *was* a sex difference in our study, in the sense that boys' scores and girls' scores were not identical. We also know, however, that various errors of measurement and extraneous sources of variation have entered into this difference. Furthermore, we have observed only a minute sample of the population in which we are interested—only 60 children out of the millions of 3- and 4-year-olds attending nursery school in the United States, and only a few hours of these 60 children's behavior. Perhaps if we observed these same 60 children again we would obtain somewhat different results. Perhaps if we observed a second sample of 60 we would obtain still different results. And perhaps if we could somehow observe the entire population of interest we would obtain yet another set of results. It is to determine the probability of these various "perhapses" that we need inferential statistics.

The preceding paragraph expresses the two typical ways of thinking about the purpose of inferential statistics. One is in terms of replicability or reliability: If we performed the same experiment over and over again would we obtain the same results? The second (which is really the same thing) is in terms of moving from sample to population: Is the difference found in the sample sufficiently large to warrant the conclusion that there is a difference in the population? However we frame the question, we must decide between two possibilities: Our results are genuinely reflective of what is true in the population or our results have occurred because of chance factors operating in our particular study. And however we frame the question, inferential statistics cannot tell us with certainty which of these possibilities is correct; all that statistics can do is to establish a *probability* for the two alternatives. This, in fact, is a basic point to realize about statistical inference: Conclusions are always probabilistic, not certain.

Let us consider a specific example of how statistical inference works. We focus again on the apparent sex difference in aggression. We want to decide whether the difference we have found reflects a genuine population difference or whether it could have occurred by chance in our study. As noted, we will use the *t* test as our initial illustration of how statistical inference proceeds.

The formula for calculating a *t* test is shown in Figure 10–1. The logic behind the test is quite straightforward. The size of the *t* statistic—and therefore the probability that our results deviate from chance—depends on three things. One is the size of the difference between the means. The larger the difference, the larger the *t* will be. A second is the variability within each of the two groups being compared. It is the variability that is represented in the complicated-looking denominator. The smaller the variability, the larger the *t*. Finally, the third factor is the *n*, or sample size for each group. Sample size contributes to the calculation in two ways. First, as some thought about Figure 10–1 should reveal, sample size affects variability; the larger the *n*, the smaller the denominator in the *t* formula. Second, once we have obtained a *t* we still need to determine the probability that a *t* of such magnitude could have occurred by chance. This probability depends on both the size of the *t* and the size of the sample: The larger the *n*, the lower the probability that a particular-sized *t* could have resulted from chance variations alone.

Let us now apply the *t* test to the male-female

$$t = \frac{M_1 - M_2}{\sqrt{\dfrac{\Sigma X_1^2 - \dfrac{(\Sigma X_1)^2}{n_1} + \Sigma X_2^2 - \dfrac{(\Sigma X_2)^2}{n_2}}{(n_1 + n_2 - 2)}} \quad \dfrac{n_1 + n_2}{(n_1)(n_2)}}$$

Note : M_1 = mean for Group 1

M_2 = mean for Group 2

n_1 = sample size for Group 1

n_2 = sample size for Group 2

X_1 = each individual score in Group 1

X_2 = each individual score in Group 2

FIGURE 10-1. Formula for calculating a *t* test.

difference in our hypothetical study. Doing so yields a *t* of 2.41. If we now consult a *t* table (available in any statistics textbook), we find that a *t* of this size or greater could occur by chance fewer than 5 times in 100. This calculation of chance probability is based upon what is known as the *null hypothesis*—that is, an assumption that there really is no difference between the groups. By convention, outcomes whose probability of occurrence through chance alone is less than 5% are regarded as *statistically significant*. We can therefore reject the null hypothesis of no difference between the sexes and conclude that boys really are more aggressive than girls.

We return shortly to the notion of statistical significance. First, however, it is worth reiterating the reasoning behind the *t* test, for the same general rationale applies to a number of different inferential tests. As noted, this reasoning is really quite straightforward, embodying three commonsensical rules:

1. Large differences between groups are less likely to occur by chance than are small differences. Thus, many of the other mean differences summarized in Table 10-2 (e.g., 3-year-old girls vs. 3-year-old boys) are too small to yield a significant *t*, and are therefore best attributed to chance.

2. Differences based on chance alone are less likely when the within-group variability in response is small than when the variability is large. If few subjects deviate very much from the group mean, there is simply less opportunity for chance

deviations in a particular direction to affect the mean. This factor is relevant to the comparison between the 3-year-old boys and the 4-year-old boys. Despite a fairly large mean difference, a *t* test comparing these groups falls short of significance, largely because of the large variability shown by the 4-year-olds.

3. Finally, a difference found with large samples is less likely to be attributable to chance than is the same-sized difference found with small samples. When only a few subjects are involved, one or two extreme scores may have a disproportionate effect on the mean; with larger samples such chance fluctuations are more likely to even out. This factor too is relevant to the comparison between 3-year-old boys and 4-year-old boys. Had the sample size for this comparison been 30 per group rather than 15, then the particular *t* obtained *would* have been significant.

It should be clear from the preceding that the purpose of inferential tests is to establish statistical significance. It is important to be clear about exactly what is meant—and also what is *not* meant—by the term "statistically significant."

Recall first that conclusions from inferential statistics are always probabilistic. A statement that a particular mean difference is statistically significant means that a difference of this size *probably* did not occur by chance, assuming the null hypothesis of no population difference. There is, however, always the possibility of error. Two kinds of errors can occur. One consists of falsely rejecting the null hypothesis—that is, concluding that an effect exists when in fact none does. This type of error is called a *Type 1 error*. In our aggression study we would be making a Type 1 error if we concluded that boys and girls differ in aggression when in fact there is no such difference in the general population. The probability of a Type 1 error is determined by the probability level at which we reject the null hypothesis. If the probability level is .05 then we have 5 chances in 100 of making a Type 1 error. If the probability level is lower—say .01 or .001—then clearly our chances of being wrong are greatly reduced.

The second type of error consists of failing to reject the null hypothesis when there is in fact a genuine effect. This type of error is labeled a *Type 2 error*. In the aggression study we would be making a Type 2 error if 3-year-olds and 4-year-olds really do differ in aggression but we falsely conclude that they do not. The probability of a Type 2 error is more difficult to calculate than that of a Type 1 error, and no attempt is made to explain the calculation here. We can note, however, that the probabilities for the two error types vary inversely, that is, as one type of error gets less likely, the other type gets more likely. A researcher could, for example, reduce his chances of making a Type 1 error by insisting on a probability level of .001; at the same time, however, he would be greatly increasing his chances of making a Type 2 error. We can note too that psychologists have generally opted for minimizing Type 1 errors. This conservativeness in drawing positive conclusions is reflected in the general convention that only results whose chance probability is less than 5% merit the label "significant."

A finding of statistical significance, then, allows us to say that our results are probably not due to chance. It is important to realize that the significance test is directed *only* to the possibility of chance variations. The significance test cannot rule out other possible threats to validity. It can tell us that two groups differ, but it cannot tell us why they differ.

Consider the male-female difference in our aggression study. We are interested in the possibility that this is a genuine sex difference in behavior (a difference whose origins, of course,

would still need to be explained). But a significant difference could easily come about for other reasons. Perhaps our observers expect boys to be more aggressive than girls and slant their observations accordingly—hence a difference based on observer bias. Perhaps girls are more affected by the presence of the observer and more likely to inhibit aggression while being watched—hence a difference based on differential reactivity. Perhaps we observe the girls early in the school year and the boys only later in the year when aggression has become common—hence a difference based on a confounding of group and time of measurement. The point is that any of the various threats to validity that we have discussed throughout this book could still be operating to bias our results. A finding of statistical significance is no guarantee of overall validity. It is merely the starting point, a necessary but not sufficient basis for concluding that we really have found something.

A final point is that a finding of significance is no guarantee of the meaningfulness of the results. "Significance" in the sense that we have been using it refers only to statistical probability, not to theoretical or practical importance. A sex difference in aggression may be genuine, in the sense that it did not occur by chance or because of some invalidity in the study. Whether the difference is large enough to mean anything, however—with respect, for example, to how nursery-school teachers should treat boys and girls—is a separate question. It is important to remember that the statistical significance of a difference depends not only on the size of the difference but also on the size of the sample. With a large enough sample even a tiny difference may achieve significance. We return to this point later in the chapter when we discuss the notion of effect size.

CHOOSING A STATISTIC

To many students "statistics" connotes memorization of formulas and endless hours of painful calculations. In fact, most professional researchers remember few if any formulas, and most spend little time in calculations. There is simply no need; the formulas can be looked up in texts or programmed into a computer, and the calculations can be performed on a calculator or a computer (or by a student assistant!). What is much more important is to know which kinds of statistical analysis are appropriate and informative for which kinds of data. Many factors go into determining which statistic is best to use. In this section we discuss three such factors: the level of measurement at which the dependent variable has been assessed, the distribution of scores shown by the dependent variable, and the design of the study.

Level of Measurement

The topic of measurement was first introduced in chapter 2 and has been added to at various points since. In this section we add another important concept. Stevens (e.g., 1968) has distinguished among four different levels or "scales" of measurement. Each level fulfills the basic functions of any system of measurement; that is, a value is assigned to each observation, and the values serve to differentiate among the observations. The kinds of values that are assigned, however, vary across the different scales of measurement. The kinds of inferential statistics that are appropriate to use vary accordingly.

The simplest form of measurement is referred to as *nominal*. Nominal means naming: assigning some qualitative label to each observation in the sample. Imagine a study of toy preferences among preschool children. We present four different toys and allow each child to pick the one with which he or she would most like to play. Our measurement consists of recording which toy is selected. The measurement in this case would be nominal, for all we are doing is assigning a label to each response. The distinguishing thing about a nominal scale is that no numbers or magnitudes are involved. We could, of course, assign numbers—for example, write down a 1 each time the truck is selected, a 2 each time the teddy bear is picked, and so forth. Such numbers, however, would be merely substitute labels. They would not have any quantitative significance.

We can return to aggression for an example of the second level of measurement. Suppose that we have the nursery-school teacher rate how aggressive the different children in the classroom are. We use a 5-point rating scale ranging from "very aggressive" through "moderately aggressive" to "very unaggressive." The level of measurement in such a study would be *ordinal*, for what we are doing is ordering the observations in terms of magnitude. In this case, in contrast to a nominal scale, there *is* a quantitative dimension to our observations, and the measurement serves to place each observation along this dimension. Thus, we can say that the "very aggressive" child is more aggressive than the "moderately aggressive" one who is in turn more aggressive than the "very unaggressive" one—or that category 5 is indeed greater than 3 which is in turn greater than 1. Note, however, that we still cannot talk about the size of the differences. We do not know, for example, whether the difference between a rating of 5 and a rating of 3 is the same as that between a rating of 3 and a rating of 1. Nor, of course, do we have any warrant for saying that a child who earns a rating of 5 is five times as aggressive as the child whose rating is 1. All that we can talk about is the ordering.

This restriction is lifted in the third scale of measurement, the *interval* scale. In an interval scale the points of the scale are not only ordered but also equidistant. A common (albeit nonpsychological) example is a thermometer. Measurements of temperature are clearly ordered: 40° is hotter than 30° is hotter than 20°. Furthermore, the points of the thermometer are equally spaced. Thus, we can say that the difference between 40° and 30° is precisely the same as the difference between 30° and 20° (in a physical, if not a psychological, sense). As we saw, this sort of quantitative precision is impossible with an ordinal scale.

There is still one limitation to an interval scale: There is no true zero point. Thermometers do, of course, include a zero, but the zero on the thermometer is simply an arbitrary point with values on both sides, not a true bottom to the scale. It does not signify a total absence of the characteristic being measured. Scales of measurement that meet all of the criteria for an interval scale and also contain a true zero point are called *ratio* scales. A common example of a ratio scale concerns the measurement of physical characteristics such as height or weight. A balance scale comprises not only equal intervals of weight but also a true zero—that is, the absence of any weight on the balance. Because of the zero point, a ratio scale permits proportional statements that are not possible with an interval scale. We can say, for example, that 40 pounds is twice as heavy as 20 pounds. We cannot say that 40° is twice as hot as 20°.

The level of measurement is one factor that determines which inferential test is appropriate to use. Some tests, including the *t* test, require that the measurements constitute either an interval or a ratio scale. One reason for this requirement should be evident from a consideration of the formula in Figure 10-1. To calculate a *t* test we must perform various arithmetical operations on the numbers that we have obtained—adding them together and then dividing to get the mean, subtracting each number from the mean to get a deviation score, and so forth. These operations make sense only if we can assume that the numbers we are dealing with are accurate reflections of the quantities involved and not merely labels or ordinal rankings. The frequency scores in Table 10-1 meet this criterion, and the *t* test is therefore appropriate for these data. A *t* test would not

be appropriate, however, if our data came from the kind of rating scale described earlier. We could not, for example, add together a rating of 5 ("very aggressive") and a rating of 1 ("very unaggressive") to get an average of 3 ("moderately aggressive"). (We note some qualifications to this statement shortly.)

Distribution of Scores

Some inferential tests make assumptions about the distribution of scores that go into the test. In particular, so-called *parametric tests* are dependent on certain assumptions about how the data are distributed. This, in fact, is the meaning of "parametric": that the test depends on the validity of certain assumptions about "parameters" of the population from which the sample is drawn. The *t* test discussed earlier is one example of a parametric test; the analysis of variance (ANOVA) that we consider in the next section is another example.

More specifically, two assumptions about distribution underlie the use of most parametric tests. One is that the scores are normally distributed. The second is that the variances of the groups being compared are equal. The second assumption is less pervasive than the first, but it does apply to many often-used parametric tests, including the *t* test and the ANOVA.

We have already discussed the concept of variance. Let us consider for a moment the requirement of a normal distribution. The *a* portion of Figure 10-2 illustrates a normal distribution. "Normal" refers to the classic

FIGURE 10-2. Examples of normal and nonnormal distributions.

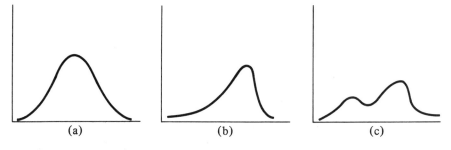

| (a) | (b) | (c) |

bellshaped curve, a distribution in which the mean, median, and mode are synonymous, and in which the scores slope gradually away from this center point on each side. The curves in parts *b* and *c*, in contrast, represent distinctly nonnormal distributions.

There is a relation between level of measurement and distribution. Scores obtained from a nominal or ordinal scale cannot be normally distributed. With a nominal scale there is no quantitative significance to the measures and thus no question of their distribution along some quantitative dimension; all that is possible is a frequency count of the number of cases in each category. With an ordinal scale there is no way to know the distance between scores and hence no way to determine their true distribution. Furthermore, in a perfectly ordered scale (i.e., one with no ties) there can be just one instance at each level of the scale; thus theoretically the distribution from an ordinal scale must always be a flat one. A ratio or interval scale, therefore, is a necessary basis for a normal distribution. It is not a sufficient basis, because the scores might still look like those in Figures 10–2*b* or *c*. But it is only if the scores are from the right sort of scale that the possibility of a normal distribution even arises.

We have been discussing assumptions that underlie the use of parametric tests such as the *t* test and ANOVA. Let us consider for a mo-

ment the alternative to such parametric tests, after which several further points can be made concerning choice of statistic.

As might be guessed, the alternatives to parametric tests are called *nonparametric tests*. Figure 10–3 illustrates a widely used nonparametric test, the chi square. The hypothetical data in the figure came from the toy-preference study sketched earlier; the hypothetical finding is that toy preference varies significantly as a function of sex.[1] The chi square is intended for nominal data such as those in the figure, data for which the *t* test would not be appropriate. Nonparametric tests exist for data at each of the four levels of measurement: nominal, ordinal, interval, and ratio. The approach is thus more generally applicable than is the parametric approach. Furthermore, nonparametric statistics do not depend on the assumptions about distribution that underlie parametric statistics; thus nonparametric tests may be applicable to interval or ratio data that fail to satisfy parametric assumptions. (Among the texts devoted to nonparametric statistics are Hollander &

----

[1] The formula given in the figure is called the "definitional formula" for chi square. There is also a "calculational formula": a mathematically equivalent but computationally simpler method of calculating the value. Many other statistics show a comparable division between definitional and calculational forms.

FIGURE 10–3.   Illustration of the chi square test.

Logic of the chi square test: Determine the extent to which the observed frequency in each cell deviates from the expected frequency assuming no difference between groups.

Observed Frequencies:	*Cars and Trucks*	*Construction Toys*	*Dolls and Furniture*	*Art Supplies*
Boys	12	10	1	5
Girls	1	4	12	11

E. ected Frequencies:				
Boys	6.5	7	6.5	8
Girls	6.5	7	6.5	8

$$\text{Formula: } \chi^2 = \Sigma \frac{(\text{observed frequency} - \text{expected frequency})^2}{\text{expected frequency}}$$

$$\chi^2 = 23.42, \text{ probability} < .01$$

Conclusion: There is a significant difference in toy preference between boys and girls.

Wolfe, 1973; Marascuilo & McSweeney, 1977; and Siegel, 1956.)

How do researchers decide between parametric tests and nonparametric tests? As just indicated, in some cases there is no decision to make, for the only possible test is a nonparametric one. In other cases a decision *is* necessary, and here several concepts become relevant. We discuss two: power and robustness.

The term *power* refers to the probability that an inferential test will reject the null hypothesis when the null hypothesis should in fact be rejected. The more powerful the test, the more likely it is to detect a genuine difference and thus lead to a correct rejection of the null hypothesis. This concept should sound familiar, for power is simply another way of talking about the probability of Type 2 error. The more powerful a test, the lower the probability of making a Type 2 error.

In some cases, parametric tests are more powerful than comparable nonparametric tests. Essentially, this greater power comes about because a parametric test uses more information about the data than does a comparable nonparametric test. Many nonparametric tests, for example, are limited to ordinal properties of the data—in particular, the relative rank orders of scores in the samples being compared. A *t* test, in contrast, is able to make use of the actual scores and the absolute differences between them; it can therefore sometimes reveal differences not revealed by a nonparametric test. It should be added that the difference in power is often small, and that it is found primarily when the samples are large. Furthermore, the difference is not inevitable. There are many situations in which parametric and nonparametric statistics are equally powerful. If the assumptions that underlie the parametric test are seriously violated, then the nonparametric alternative may actually be more powerful (see, for example, Blair & Higgins, 1980).

The point about assumptions leads to the concept of robustness. *Robustness* refers to the impunity with which the assumptions that underlie a test can be violated. A robust test is relatively insensitive to the violation of its assumptions—that is, it tends to yield accurate conclusions about significance even when the assumptions are not met. It turns out that both the *t* test and the ANOVA are fairly robust tests. It is for this reason that such tests are so common in the literature even for data that do not fit the criteria that we have been discussing—data that come from rating scales, for example, or that depart markedly from a normal distribution, or that reflect unequal variances in the groups being compared. This robustness does *not* mean that the researcher can automatically apply a parametric test to any sort of data. But it does mean that the possibility of a parametric test should not be too quickly abandoned just because some assumption of the test is violated. It may be worthwhile, rather, to seek some expert advice with respect to whether parametric statistics might nevertheless be applicable to the data.

Design of the Study

We have discussed two determinants of the choice of statistic: level of measurement and distribution of scores. A third important consideration is the design of the study.

Various aspects of the design are relevant. One factor is the number of levels of the independent variable. In our aggression-in-the-nursery-school example this factor was kept simple: two different ages and two different sexes. It was easy enough then to run *t* tests comparing the two levels of each variable. Suppose, however, that we complicate matters by adding more levels. Because it is a bit difficult to imagine doing so for sex, we will make the additions for age. Suppose that instead of two age groups we have six. What happens then to our *t* test?

The most obvious thing that happens is that we need many more tests. With six different age groups there are 15 possible pairwise comparisons. We therefore need to run 15 separate *t* tests to determine what we have found. Running, and reporting, 15 *t* tests is obviously rather unwieldy. The more important objection, however, concerns the level of significance for the tests. We want this level to remain fixed at whatever cut-off point for significance we have decided upon—for example, the traditional .05 level. With multiple tests, however, the interpretation of significance becomes very difficult. If we run 15 tests, each at a .05 level, then we have a .54 probability that at least one of these tests will be significant by chance alone.[2] How then can we interpret any statistically significant result?

The problem is actually more complicated still. The .54 probability rests on the assumption that the 15 t tests are independent of each other. Often, however, multiple t tests in the same study are not independent; rather they are related, in the sense that the same data enter into a number of different comparisons. This, in fact, would be the case in the age comparisons sketched earlier; each of the six age groups would contribute data—in fact exactly the same data—to 5 of the 15 tests. When this sort of interdependency among tests exists, it becomes impossible to determine the exact probability level for any one test. The researcher may calculate a t and report significance at the .05 level; the actual probability level, however, might be quite different from .05.

There is a further problem with multiple t tests that should be noted before we turn to the solution. Suppose now that we complicate our study not by adding more levels of an independent variable but by adding more independent variables. In addition to studying age and sex as determinants of aggression, we might examine possible effects of classroom structure, of indoor versus outdoor locus for the observations, of presentation of a violent cartoon to half the children prior to the observation period, and so forth. Clearly, the more independent variables we add, the more possible t tests there will be. But there is another problem beyond simply proliferation of tests. Whenever multiple independent variables are studied it is possible that the effects of one variable will depend on the level of the other variables. It is possible, in short, that there will be an *interaction* of variables. Such interaction effects are important to identify, but they can be difficult to uncover through t tests alone.

The most popular alternative to multiple t tests is the analysis of variance or ANOVA. The ANOVA is essentially an extension of the t test to situations involving more than two means. The method of calculation is different from, and more complicated than, that of the t, and we do not attempt to describe the calculation here. The underlying logic, however, is identical: We test for significance by determining the extent to which the primary variance associated with the groups being compared exceeds the secondary and error variance within groups. The statistic that the test yields is called an F, and the F, like the t, can be checked for significance in standard tables found in any statistics textbook.

Let us consider how the ANOVA would be applied to the aggression study. We have two independent variables: age and sex. To make the superiority of ANOVA to t clearer, we will assume that there are in fact six levels of the age variable, rather than just the two represented in Table 10-1. Application of the ANOVA will then yield Fs for each of the independent variables, or *main effects,* of the study. If the F for sex is significant then our work with regard to this variable is complete; since there are only two levels of sex, we can simply look at the means to determine where the effect comes from. A significant main effect for age would be more complicated. In this case the F would be based upon a simultaneous comparison of all six age groups, and significance would mean that at least one of the possible pairwise comparisons among these groups is significant. We would then need follow-up tests to determine which specific comparison or comparisons are significant. These follow-up tests are similar to a t test but more conservative, and they are run

---

[2] Perhaps the simplest way to see where this probability comes from is to ask what the chances are of *not* obtaining a significant result by chance alone. With a single test the probability of avoiding such an error is .95. With two independent tests the probability is the product of the two individual probabilities, or $.95^2$. With 15 independent tests the probability is $.95^{15}$, or .46. The probability that we *will* obtain at least one significant result by chance is therefore $1 - .46$.

only after the overall F has indicated significance.

The ANOVA will also yield a third F: that for the interaction between age and sex. In general, an ANOVA will yield interaction Fs for all of the possible combinations of independent variables in a study. If there are three independent variables, for example, then the ANOVA will give four interaction Fs: one for each of the three two-way combinations of variables and one for the three-way combination. As with a significant main effect, significant interactions can be followed up by specific tests to determine the exact basis for the effect.

It is worth noting that this ability to handle multifactor experiments and their consequent interactions has always been one further reason to prefer ANOVA to nonparametric alternatives. Most early nonparametric tests were designed to compare levels of a single factor, and hence were not really suited to more complex designs. In recent years, however, this particular gap between parametric and nonparametric has narrowed as the complexity of nonparametric statistics has increased. Marascuilo and McSweeney (1977) provide an extended discussion of nonparametric forms of analysis of variance.

One final aspect of design is relevant to the choice of statistic. Thus far we have been considering between-subject designs—that is, cases in which each subject contributes data to only one of the conditions or groups being compared. But we saw in chapter 3 that many independent variables can be examined via within-subject designs, in which each subject contributes data to each experimental condition. What happens to our statistics when each subject is represented in each condition?

The answer is simple enough: We merely switch from the between-subject tests that we have been discussing to comparable within-subject tests. There are, in fact, analogous within-subject tests for each of the procedures that we have considered thus far. There is a within-subject t test, for example, as well as a within-subject or repeated-measures analysis of variance. There are also nonparametric tests that are ap-

propriate for within-subject data (for example, a test called the McNemar test of change, which constitutes a kind of repeated-measures chi square). The logic of such tests is similar to that of between-subject tests; in most within-subject tests, however, actual difference scores (e.g., a subject's performance in Condition 1 minus his or her performance in Condition 2) are the grist for the analyses. Because difference scores are the focus, the tests are appropriate not only for literal repeated-measures designs but also for cases in which each subject in one condition has been matched with a comparable subject in another condition.

One further point can be made concerning within-subject statistics. It is a reiteration of a point made in chapter 3 when we discussed the relative merits of within-subject and between-subject designs. As we saw then, within-subject tests are often more powerful than comparable between-subject tests. This greater power comes about because of the reduction in secondary variance associated with subjects. If the same subjects appear in each condition, then there is less possibility for preexisting differences among subjects to contribute unwanted variance to the group comparisons. This greater power provides one possible basis for deciding between a within-subject approach and a between-subject approach.

ALTERNATIVES TO AND EXTENSIONS OF ANOVA

It seems safe to say that analysis of variance has been the most widely used statistical technique in psychological research for at least the past 50 years. Despite its popularity, however, ANOVA is not always the best statistical choice, even in cases in which the assumptions behind the test can be met. There are some situations in which other forms of analysis may provide either better or further insight into the results than does ANOVA. In this section we briefly consider several such situations and corresponding statistical tests. Even more than in earlier parts of the chapter there is no attempt at completeness;

the goal is simply to make the reader aware, or reaware, of various possibilities, and of further sources for more detailed treatments.

Planned Comparisons

We noted earlier the problems of multiple *t* tests and the consequent superiority of analysis of variance as an overall test for the presence or absence of significant effects. Overall tests are not always superior, however. ANOVA is most clearly appropriate when the investigator does not have clear-cut hypotheses to test but is interested instead in identifying any interesting results that may emerge from the research. In such cases a composite test like ANOVA is preferable to multiple individual tests. In some studies, however, there *are* definite hypotheses, and the main goal of the statistical analysis is to provide a clear answer with respect to each hypothesis. In these cases ANOVA may be an inefficient form of analysis, for it will include comparisons that are not of interest and yield less power for the comparisons that the researcher cares about.

Consider an example (adapted from an example in Hays, 1981). We are interested in the effects of training on response to Kohlberg's moral dilemmas (see chapter 8). We decide to examine two forms of training in children: exposure to an adult model who demonstrates advanced forms of moral reasoning and peer group discussions in which moral issues can be debated. We are also curious about the possible combined effects of these two experiences, and hence we include a third training condition in which children receive both modeling and peer group interaction. We know that to evaluate the effects of our training we will need a control group; thus a fourth condition consists of just the pretest and posttest with no experimental intervention. We have some concern, however, that mere exposure to a model or a peer group may affect response, quite apart from the moral content on which we wish to focus. Hence we include two more control conditions: one in which children see an adult model talk about something other than morality and one in which

children engage in peer discussions of some topic other than morality.

In a study like this we are not really interested in a main effect of condition, an effect that could result from a significant difference between *any* of the possible pairs of means. Our interests, rather, are both more specific and more limited, in that we know in advance that there are only certain comparisons between means that are important to examine. We will probably want to know, for example, whether each experimental condition differs significantly from its appropriate control condition, as well as whether the three experimental conditions differ among themselves. These comparisons make sense. Other comparisons make considerably less sense—for example, the peer group experimental condition versus the adult control condition. An overall *F* test lumps all of these comparisons together. We could, of course, begin with the *F* and then go on to specific follow-up tests of the comparisons of interest. There is always the danger, however, that the main effect *F* will not be significant, in which case we really have no warrant for follow-ups. Furthermore, the tests that follow a significant ANOVA are conservative and hence low in power, which means that we run the risk of failing to detect some genuine and important effect.

An alternative to ANOVA in such a situation is to use *planned comparisons*. With planned comparisons we specify in advance which means will be compared and *only* these comparisons are carried out. In our hypothetical training study, for example, we could draw the comparisons between treatments that we wish to draw while ignoring other comparisons of less interest. The techniques for making such specific, in-advance comparisons are beyond our scope here; descriptions can be found in most statistics textbooks (e.g., Hays, 1981). There is, of course, some potential loss of information entailed in such a selective approach. If we really know what we want to look for, however, the loss may be minimal. And because in-advance tests are more powerful than post-hoc tests, we have a better chance of gaining clear answers to the questions of interest.

It is important to stress that planned comparisons do imply planning and selectivity; that is, we cannot look at *every* possible contrast. How many contrasts can be examined has been a subject of dispute among statisticians. Some experts recommend that planned comparisons be limited to statistically independent or "orthogonal" contrasts. The number of such independent contrasts is one less than the number of means; thus in our training study there would be five possible independent contrasts (the Hays, 1981, source cited previously explains how to determine the independence of contrasts). Other experts advocate a somewhat more liberal approach that allows theoretically interesting contrasts to be tested even if they are not completely independent. Keppel (1982) provides a helpful discussion of the different viewpoints, as well as a set of techniques for adjusting the probability level in cases in which multiple and overlapping comparisons are made.

Trend Analysis

The existence of a significant main effect in an analysis of variance tells us that there is some functional relation between the independent variable and the dependent variable. The main effect, however, does not necessarily tell us exactly what the nature of this relation is. Do scores on the dependent variable rise steadily as the level of the independent variable increases (as in Figure 10-4a)? Do scores rise to a certain

point and then level off or drop (as in Figure 10-4b)? Or do scores perhaps rise, drop, and then rise again (as in Figure 10-4c)? The goal of *trend analysis* is to identify the shape of the relation between independent variable and dependent variable.

Trend analysis is a possibility when two criteria are met. One is that there are at least three levels of the independent variable. The reason for this requirement should be obvious: We can hardly fit a curve to our data points if there are only two points. The other is that the levels of the independent variable represent quantitative increments and not merely qualitative differences. Trend analysis makes sense only if we can specify both the ordering of levels and the spacing between them. With a quantitative variable (e.g., number of training trials, degree of drug dosage) such specification may be possible. With a qualitative variable (e.g., variations in teaching style, type of reinforcement) it is not.

Techniques for performing trend analysis, as well as the complexities involved in doing and interpreting such analyses, can be found in a number of sources (e.g., Hays, 1981; Winer, 1971). Here we make just a few quick points. One concerns frequency. In any study a number of logically possible trends might be discerned, including some quite complex "higher-order" trends. As Keppel (1982) notes, however, most studies in psychology generate trends of two sorts. One is the *linear* trend, in which scores on the dependent variable rise or fall in

FIGURE 10-4. Examples of different trends.

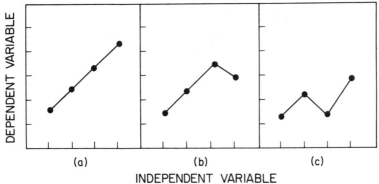

a regular, straight-line relation across levels of the independent variable. The curve in Figure 10–4a is an example of a linear trend. The other is a *quadratic* trend, in which scores on the dependent variable show a single reversal of direction across levels of the independent variable, either rising and then falling or the reverse. The curve in Figure 10–4b shows a quadratic trend. Unless they have been predicted from theory (or can be replicated in further research), more complicated trends are seldom interpretable.

The second point concerns the subject matter of the preceding section, the distinction between planned, in-advance tests and post-hoc, follow-up tests. Trend analysis can be used in either way. It is possible to bypass the overall ANOVA and move immediately to a planned analysis of trend. It is also possible to run an ANOVA, obtain a significant *F*, and then use trend analysis as a follow-up to specify the nature of the effect.

The final point is especially relevant to the developmental researcher. We noted earlier that trend analysis requires a quantitative independent variable for which we can specify the ordering and spacing of levels. Age is such a variable. If we do a study, for example, with 6-, 8-, 10-, and 12-year-olds, then we have a quantitative variable with clearly ordered and exactly spaced levels, and thus a candidate for trend analysis. There are situations, especially when several age levels are being compared, when planned trend analysis may be superior to ANOVA as a measure of changes with age. Not only does trend analysis provide information about the shape of the developmental function that is not given by ANOVA, but trend analysis can sometimes reveal significant effects that are obscured with ANOVA. Hale (1977) provides an easy-to-read discussion of this issue.

Effect Size

A very general similarity exists between this section and the preceding one. In both cases the goal is to move beyond the information provided by a significant *F* in an analysis of variance. With trend analysis the attempt is to specify the shape of the relation between independent variable and dependent variable. Our concern in this section is with the size of the relation—that is, how much effect does the independent variable have upon the dependent variable?

To understand the issue here we need to recall some points made earlier in the discussion of statistical significance. A finding of statistical significance indicates that there is *some* greater-than-chance relation between variables. The finding of significance does not tell us how great this relation is. It is possible, of course, to get some idea of the magnitude of an effect simply by looking at the means; a large difference between means obviously reflects a greater effect than a small difference. But is it possible to derive more rigorous measures of effect size?

The answer is that a number of techniques now exist for calculating effect size. Among the primary sources for descriptions of these techniques are Dodd and Schultz (1970), Dwyer (1974), and Cohen (1977). Here we describe the simplest of the various procedures, developed by Cohen (1977).[3] With this approach effect size, or *d*, is defined as the difference between two means divided by the standard deviation of the groups being compared. The approach thus takes into account the mean difference but weights it in terms of the variability in the scores. The smaller the variability, the more impressive any mean difference is.

Seitz (1984) provides an example. The standard deviation for most IQ tests is 15 points. A mean IQ difference between groups of 12 points (as is reported to exist, for example, between college freshmen and people with Ph.D.s) would therefore yield an effect size of .8. If the mean difference were 7½ points the effect size would be .5; if the difference were 3 points the effect

---

[3]Cohen's use of *d* is somewhat different from that discussed here. In Cohen's work *d* refers to a predicted effect in some population, as opposed to an observed effect in some sample. Given expectations about effect size, it is possible to make various calculations concerning both necessary sample size and power for different statistical tests. Cohen's book, in fact, is called *Statistical Power Analysis for the Behavioral Sciences*.

size would be .2. One way to interpret what these various values mean is to plot the extent to which scores for the two populations overlap. Curves for the three situations just described are shown in Figure 10–5. Note that the degree of overlap decreases as the effect size increases. As Seitz notes, the middle pair of curves may be especially informative. A mean difference of 7 ½ points—or, more generally, a difference of one-half standard deviation—may not seem very large. What such a difference means, however, is that 70% of one population will score above the mean of the other population.

Measures of effect size can provide useful information that is not directly given by most inferential tests. Thus far, however, estimates of effect size are rare in developmental research.

A survey of any developmental journal will reveal dozens of significant Fs and ts but few attempts to calculate formal measures of the size of the various effects.

Multivariate Analysis of Variance

The distinction between univariate statistics and multivariate statistics is a somewhat hazy one, and different statisticians draw the boundary at different points. One common criterion, however, concerns the number of dependent variables. If the analysis involves a single dependent variable, then the statistic is univariate. Both the t and the ANOVA are thus univariate tests. If the analysis involves more than one dependent variable, then the statistic

FIGURE 10–5. Population differences corresponding to different effect sizes.

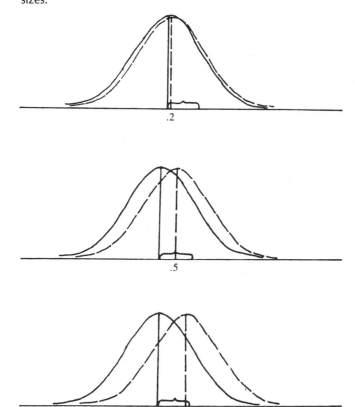

is multivariate. There are a number of multivariate statistical procedures, including a multivariate analysis of variance or MANOVA.

The widespread use of multivariate statistics is a fairly recent phenomenon in psychological research. As Seitz (1980) points out, the statistical bases for such procedures were worked out long ago; the problem came in application. The calculations required for multivariate statistics are often *exceedingly* complex and time-consuming, and the use of such procedures therefore had to wait for the development of computers and appropriate computer programs. Access to and expertise with the computer can be very helpful in any form of statistical analysis. With multivariate statistics, however, the computer is absolutely essential.

The calculations are not the only complicated part of multivariate statistics. In a sense, in fact, the calculations are the easy part, since the computer does the work. The real challenge for the researcher is to know both when multivariate analyses are appropriate and how to interpret the results of such analyses. Books are written and courses taught to answer such questions; among the detailed treatments are Bock (1975), Harris (1975) and Green (1978). Here we draw just a few points from a briefer discussion, oriented to the developmental researcher, by Applebaum and McCall (1983).

Suppose that a researcher has carried out a study with two or more dependent variables. How does he or she decide whether to perform separate ANOVAs for the different variables (which is always an option) or to combine them into one MANOVA? Applebaum and McCall suggest two general advantages that MANOVA has over ANOVA. One is similar to an advantage of F tests over separately calculated t tests. The more separate ANOVAs that we run, the greater the chance that some effects will achieve statistical significance purely by chance. MANOVA, in contrast, holds the probability level constant for all comparisons. The other advantage concerns MANOVA's ability to utilize information about relations among dependent variables, information that is ignored with ANOVA, which treats each variable separately. Among other virtues, this simultaneous consideration of variables means that MANOVA can sometimes detect significant effects that are not revealed by ANOVA.

As this last point may suggest, MANOVA is appropriate only when there is some reason to expect interesting relations among the dependent variables. In Applebaum and McCall's (1983) words, "You do not throw every available variable into a MANOVA to see what comes out. Dependent variables need to be picked deliberately. They must form a logical set that can be interpreted *as a set*" (p. 435; italics in original). Applebaum and McCall go on to give the example of a study of infant habituation in which the dependent variables consist of length of fixation on the first trial, trial of longest fixation, number of trials from longest fixation to criterion, and average fixation per trial. These variables form a cohesive (but not redundant) set of measures of infant habituation, and thus might be more profitably analyzed with MANOVA than with four separate ANOVAs. More generally, one natural situation for MANOVA is the case in which a study includes several somewhat different measures of the same underlying construct (as in the habituation example).

Brief though this discussion of MANOVA has been, a general point about statistics can be taken away from it. The existence of a powerful statistical procedure—and of computer procedures to execute that procedure—does not mean that the procedure can be blithely applied to any sort of data. Knowing what statistics are appropriate for what data, and planning research to get an optimal fit between statistics and data, remain the essence of good statistical practice.

Multiple Regression

Like MANOVA, multiple regression is a complicated statistical procedure—complicated both to do and to describe. As was true for MANOVA, there is little point in attempting to describe the how of multiple regression in a one- or two-page summary. Regression has become such a widely used statistical procedure, however, that a brief discussion of the general approach appears warranted.

In Kerlinger's (1986) words, multiple regression "is a method for studying the effects and the magnitudes of the effects of more than one independent variable on one dependent variable using principles of correlation and regression" (p. 527). In slightly different words, what multiple regression does is to tell us how two or more independent variables, or "predictors," relate to a single dependent variable, or "criterion." We might do a study, for example, in which we examine performance on a laboratory problem-solving task as a function of IQ, SES, nature of the task instructions, and time allowed to reach a solution. Applying multiple regression to our data will give us an estimate of the contribution, both singly and in combination, of each of these four predictor variables to variations in the criterion variable.

There is a close relation between regression and the correlation statistic discussed in the next section. In both cases, we use knowledge of a subject's values on one variable to predict scores on another variable. As the inclusion of IQ and SES in our example suggests, a further similarity is that regression is applicable to variables that, from a design point of view, are correlational, in that they are merely measured rather than experimentally manipulated.

There is also a close similarity between regression and analysis of variance. Both procedures have the same goals: to determine the effects, both singly and in interaction, of a set of independent variables upon some dependent variable. The study sketched earlier as an example of multiple regression could also be analyzed via a four-way ANOVA, with four main effect *F*s and a large number of interaction *F*s as well. This conclusion is, in fact, a quite general one: Most problems that lend themselves to multiple regression could also be analyzed with analysis of variance. As many authors have pointed out, however, regression is the more general of the two concepts, because ANOVA constitutes a special case under the general heading of techniques of regression. Thus, *any* problem that can be analyzed as a multifactor ANOVA can also be analyzed with multiple regression.

Given the wide applicability of multiple regression, what factors might lead us to prefer regression to ANOVA as a method of analyzing some data set? We can note first that such decisions are often a matter of personal preference, for in many cases the two approaches are equally appropriate and informative. There are some ways, however, in which multiple regression does have advantages. We note here two of the arguments in favor of regression.

1. Regression is especially appropriate when an independent variable is continuous—that is, encompasses a large number of different values rather than just a few discrete levels. IQ is an example of a continuous variable. If we included IQ in our problem-solving study, we would probably obtain a range of scores spanning some 60 or 70 IQ points. There is no way with ANOVA to capture all this variation; the best that we are likely to do is a gross classification system such as "high," "medium," and "low." With regression, however, there is no loss of information, for the variable is treated continuously and every distinct score enters into the analysis.

2. Regression is especially well suited to the issues discussed earlier in this general section, determining the magnitude and the nature of the effects that the independent variables have upon the dependent variable. The basic statistic that multiple regression yields is R^2: the proportion of variance in the dependent variable that is accounted for by the set of independent variables under study. R^2, then, tells us how well our "predictors" work—how well we can predict variations in the criterion given the particular set of independent variables that we have selected. Although doing so is by no means simple or straightforward, it is also possible with regression to derive separate estimates of the contribution of each of the individual predictor variables to the criterion, both the size of the contribution and the form of the relation between predictor and criterion.

Among the textbooks devoted to multiple regression are Cohen and Cohen (1983), Draper and Smith (1981), and Pedhazur (1982). The Kerlinger (1986) book referred to earlier provides a highly readable introduction; it is also a superb general text on methodology, well worth study by anyone interested in research in psychology.

CORRELATIONS

Thus far our emphasis has been on tests whose purpose is to identify differences between groups. Not all statistical tests fit this model. Imagine a study in which we collect the data shown in Table 10-3. We are interested in determining whether there is a relation between IQ and performance on standardized achievement tests. How can we proceed?

The statistic that is appropriate for the data in Table 10-3 is the *correlation statistic*. A correlation statistic is a measure of the relation between two variables. As we saw in chapter 5, correlations have a possible range of +1 to −1. A correlation of +1 indicates a perfect positive relation between variables, a correlation of 0 indicates no relation at all, and a correlation of −1 indicates a perfect negative relation. These possibilities are shown pictorially in the "scatterplots" in Figure 10-6. Correlations between 0 and 1 indicate varying degrees of positive or negative relation, with the strength of the relation increasing as the value approaches 1.

What about the data in Table 10-3? To determine the correlation for these data we must first decide which correlation statistic to use, for there are in fact several different methods of calculating correlations. Just as with inferential tests, which method is appropriate depends on certain assumptions about the nature of the data. The two most often-used tests are the Pearson product-moment correlation and the Spearman rank-order correlation. The Pearson is a parametric test that shares assumptions common to all parametric tests—namely, that the measures come from an interval or ratio scale and that the scores are normally distributed.[4] The Spearman is a nonparametric test that is based solely on the ordinal properties of the data and hence is more widely applicable than the Pearson. Both tests, it should be noted, are dependent on another important assumption: that the relation between variables is a *linear* one. If the relation is something other than linear (for example, a curvilinear relation in which scores on one variable first rise and then fall in conjunction with scores on the other), then a standard correlation test would not be appropriate.

Because it is the simpler of the two tests to illustrate, we will apply the Spearman to the data in Table 10-3. The formula for the Spearman, as well as its application to our illustrative data, is shown in Figure 10-7. As can be seen from a consideration of the formula, the Spearman is a measure of the extent to which the paired scores in the two distributions share the same rank order. If the agreement in rank is perfect, then there will be no deviation scores, the numerator and hence the solution on the right side of the equation will be 0, and the correlation will be +1. The more frequent and marked the deviations in rank, the further the correlation will depart from +1. In our sample data the correlation between IQ and achievement scores is .70, indicating a fairly strong but far from perfect positive relation. It is worth noting that application of the Pearson product-moment correlation to these data yields a very similar value: .71. For most data sets, in fact, the Spearman and the Pearson give quite similar values.

TABLE 10-3 IQ and Achievement Test Scores for a Sample of Fifth-Grade Children

Subject	IQ	Achievement Test
1	82	22
2	85	18
3	90	43
4	92	28
5	95	23
6	99	24
7	101	48
8	102	30
9	104	56
10	107	35
11	108	38
12	112	46
13	114	27
14	116	54
15	124	50
16	140	60

---

[4]Actually, *r* itself, as a descriptive statistic, is not parametric; determination of its statistical significance, however, depends on parametric assumptions.

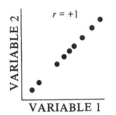
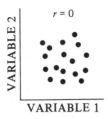
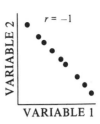

FIGURE 10-6. Scatterplots illustrating different degrees of correlation.

What do we know when we have established the correlation between two variables? A correlation, like a mean or median, is a descriptive statistic, a description in this case not of central tendency but of the association between variables. Before it can be interpreted, it must be tested for statistical significance. The null hypothesis for such tests is that of a 0 correlation between variables; the question then is whether the obtained correlation deviates significantly from 0. Answering this question is easy enough, for statistics texts provide tables in which the probability level for correlations of any magnitude can be checked directly. Both the size of the correlation and the size of the sample affect the determination of significance; as either increases, the probability of significance also increases. Reference to such a table tells us that a correlation of .70 with a sample size of 16 (i.e.,

16 *pairs* of scores) is significant at the .01 level; thus there *is* a relation between IQ and achievement.

Significance is important, but it is only part of the story. Recall that we are interested not just in the existence of a relation but also in the strength of the relation. The usual way to interpret the strength of a correlation is in terms of goodness of prediction: Given that we know the subject's score on one variable, how well can we predict the score on the other variable? If the correlation is 0, then the relation between the variables is random, and knowing one score adds nothing to our ability to predict the other. As the correlation departs from 0 its predictive power increases, the extremes being the perfect correlations of $+1$ or -1.

Another (equivalent) way to think about correlations is in terms of variance accounted for.

FIGURE 10-7. Illustration of the Spearman rank-order correlation.

Logic of the Spearman rank-order correlation: Determine the extent to which the paired scores in the two distributions share the same rank order.

RANK ORDER

IQ	Achievement Test		IQ	Achievement Test
1	2		9	15
2	1		10	8
3	10		11	9
4	6		12	11
5	3		13	5
6	4		14	14
7	12		15	13
8	7		16	16

Formula: $\text{rho} = 1 - \dfrac{6\Sigma D^2}{N(N^2 - 1)}$

$\text{rho} = .70$, probability $< .01$

Note: D = deviation score, i.e., the absolute difference between ranks

N = number of pairs

Conclusion: There is a significant positive correlation between IQ and achievement test score.

When we use scores on one measure to predict scores on a second measure we are "accounting," in a statistical-predictive sense, for a certain proportion of the variance on the second measure. This notion was discussed earlier with regard to regression, and it applies also to correlations. The higher a correlation, the more variance accounted for. We can be more precise than this, however. When the correlation statistic is the Pearson r then the proportion of variance accounted for is equivalent to r^2. Thus, the correlation of .71 between IQ and achievement means that variations in one measure account for 50% of the variations in the other.

This last statement should have a rather sobering sound. A correlation of .71 seems high, yet it still leaves half of the variance unaccounted for. As the correlation drops toward 0 the proportion of variance accounted for also drops, and quite rapidly. A correlation of .5 accounts for 25% of the variance. A correlation of .3 accounts for only 9% of the variance.

This discussion raises again the distinction between significance and meaningfulness. A correlation may be statistically significant but also so small that it has little theoretical or practical meaning. Such statistically significant but trivial correlations are especially likely when the sample size is large. With a sample of 50 a correlation of .27 achieves significance at the .05 level. With a sample of 100 a correlation of .19 is significant.

In addition to sample size, another important variable to consider in evaluating correlations is the range of scores on the two measures. Two sorts of problems with range can arise. Probably the more common is restriction of range: selection of scores on one variable that are so close together that the differences among them do not relate to variations on other measures. Suppose that we decided to limit the sample for our IQ-achievement comparison to children attending "gifted" or "enrichment" classes. There is typically an IQ cut-off for such classes; let us say in this case that the criterion is an IQ of 130 or above. The decision to focus only on the very high IQs means that we have greatly restricted the range of variation for one of our measures; instead of a range of perhaps 60 to 70 IQ points, our actual range might be about 20 points. When all the IQ scores are so closely bunched, it is unlikely that the small differences among them will show much relation to anything else, including differences in achievement.

It is also possible to have a range that is too broad rather than too narrow. Suppose now that we sample IQ in 20-point jumps, beginning with a child whose IQ is 40, moving next to one whose IQ is 60, and continuing until we reach an eighth child whose IQ is 180. With such enormous variability it is likely that IQ will correlate significantly and substantially with almost any other psychological measure that we might collect from our sample. It is doubtful, however, that the size of such correlations would mean very much.

Whether the problem is too little range or too much range, the underlying issue is one of external validity. For a correlation to mean anything, it must be generalizable beyond the immediate sample on which it was calculated to some broader population of interest. The sample must therefore be representative—in both central tendency and range of variation—of the larger population. If the sample is not representative, then correlations obtained with it cannot have much external validity.

META-ANALYSIS

Our discussion thus far has focused on the kinds of statistics that researchers use when analyzing the results of individual research projects. Such statistics are by far the most commonly encountered ones in psychology. Not all psychology articles are reports of original studies, however. Another major category consists of review articles that summarize the results of large numbers of studies. In recent years there has been a growing interest in the possibility of applying statistical techniques to such reviews and to the analysis of groups of studies. Such techniques fall under the general heading of *meta-analysis*.

The discussion of sex differences in chapter 8 touched on the problem of drawing reliable conclusions from large bodies of research. The influential Maccoby and Jacklin (1974) source cited there used a form of analysis that is sometimes called the "box score approach." In Maccoby and Jacklin's review, studies on various aspects of sex differences were tabulated under three headings: boys greater, girls greater, or no differences between the sexes. Conclusions about the presence or absence of reliable sex differences were then based on the distribution of studies across these three categories.

The box score approach is an attempt to bring some objectivity and quantitative precision to the often subjective task of reviewing research. As such, it can be regarded as a simple form of meta-analysis. It *is* a simple form, however. Among its limitations is the same limitation that we saw applies to most inferential tests within individual studies. The box score can give us some idea of whether a significant effect is or is not present. But it does not tell us anything for certain about how large the effect is.

Most contemporary applications of meta-analysis have at least two goals. One is to determine whether significant effects exist for the topic being reviewed. The other is to estimate the magnitude of the effects. Many analyses also add a third goal, which is to relate the existence and magnitude of effects to variations in design and procedure across studies. We might ask, for example, whether effects vary as a function of sample size, or whether they differ for between-subject designs compared to within-subject designs. These three goals are, of course, the same goals that are found in individual studies: to determine whether the independent variable affects the dependent variable, to determine how strong the relation is, and to explore the effects of variations in potentially important factors. The obvious stength of meta-analysis is the increase in the quantity of information. With meta-analysis we can base our conclusions on perhaps 100 studies rather than 1, and on thousands of subjects rather than a few dozen.

The example that we use is a study by Hyde (1981). Hyde's work was inspired by and builds upon the portion of the Maccoby and Jacklin (1974) book dealing with sex differences in cognitive abilities. Based on a tabulation of 169 studies, Maccoby and Jacklin concluded that three such sex differences are "well established": greater verbal ability for girls and greater visual-spatial and mathematical ability for boys. Their analysis constitutes the first step in a meta-analysis, in that it identifies relevant studies and calculates the consistency with which significant effects are found. Hyde's work takes their identification of studies and general conclusion regarding the existence of differences as a starting point. What she adds is an attempt to determine the size of the effects. Given that males and females differ, by how much do they differ?

Hyde uses two different methods of calculating effect size. One is the Cohen (1977) d statistic described in the section on Effect Size. With this statistic effect size is defined as the difference between two means divided by the standard deviation of the two samples. It is thus appropriate for any two-group comparison (which, of course, analyses of sex differences are), and it can be calculated whenever information about both means and variability is presented. The other statistic is labeled ω^2. This statistic can be calculated whenever information about a t or F test has been presented. In the case of a t test, for example, ω^2 is calculated from the following formula: $\omega^2 = (t^2 - 1)/(t^2 + n1 + n2 - 1)$. The interpretation of ω^2 is the same as that for r^2 in the case of correlations: It gives the proportion of variance accounted for by the variable in question (in this case sex). The larger ω^2, the more important the variable.

Hyde's major conclusion was that the magnitude of sex differences in cognitive abilities is quite small. In the case of verbal ability, for example, the median ω^2 was .01—that is, only 1% of the variance accounted for by the variable of sex. The median d was .24, indicating an average difference between males and females of about one-fourth standard deviation (which would mean, for example, a difference of about 2½ points on a test with a standard deviation of 10). In the case of visual-spatial ability the median ω^2 was .043; the median d was .45. These analyses make an important point: An effect can be well established, in the sense of appearing fairly consistently across studies, but also small.

Calculation of either ω^2 or d is possible only if authors of Results sections provide sufficient information about their data. One continuing frustration for those who attempt meta-analysis is that many authors fail to report such information. In Hyde's study, for example, 34% of the articles did not give enough information for ω^2 or d to be calculated. Letters to the authors elicited the necessary data in only 11% of the cases. The sample, therefore, was less complete than one would wish.

Another obstacle to meta-analysis stems from possible publication biases. Most meta-analyses (including Hyde's) are limited to published studies. For many topics, however, there is also a considerable body of relevant research that has never been published. As anyone in the field knows, a number of factors in addition to quality can affect publishability. It seems possible that studies with positive results are more likely to be accepted for publication than other studies, perhaps equally good, whose results are negative or unclear. There is evidence, in fact, to support this hunch: A survey of 11 meta-analyses found consistently larger effect sizes in published than in unpublished work (Glass, McGaw, & Smith, 1981). This issue is not unique to meta-analysis, of course; it applies to any literature review. Nevertheless, the possibility of publication bias means that conclusions from many meta-analyses must be evaluated cautiously.

Undoubtedly the most common criticism of meta-analysis is the criticism noted in the discussion of sex differences. It is the argument that meta-analysis lumps together disparate studies in a way that obscures important distinctions and therefore leads to dubious results. Of particular concern is what is seen as a kind of uncritical egalitarianism, a tendency to weight bad studies equally with good in drawing conclusions. Proponents of meta-analysis are aware of such criticisms and offer a sensible reply. Their argument is that variations among studies, including variations in quality, can themselves be coded and incorporated within the meta-analysis. It is then an empirical question whether particular variations do or do not affect the results. If better studies lead to different conclusions than poorer studies a properly conducted meta-analysis will reveal this fact. Although this argument is logically impeccable, questions can still arise with regard to how satisfactorily the interstudy variations have been identified and evaluated. Coding of quality, in particular, is a difficult and controversial enterprise.

Meta-analysis has become a much-discussed topic in recent years. Fuller presentations can be found in Glass et al. (1981), Hunter, Schmidt, and Jackson (1982), and Green and Hall (1984).

SOME GENERAL POINTS

We conclude the chapter with a few general pieces of advice about how to approach the statistical part of a study.

The first piece of advice was offered originally in chapter 1: Plan ahead. It should be clear from our discussion that there may sometimes be aspects of the data analysis that could not have been completely anticipated. The researcher may not know, for example, what the distribution of scores will be until he or she has actually collected the data. Unanticipated but interesting findings may emerge that require statistical tests that could not have been foreseen at the start. As far as possible, however, such after-the-fact statistical decisions should be minimized. The researcher should know at the outset both the major questions that the analyses will address and the particular statistical tests that will be used to address them. Such planning can help to guard against the tendency to engage in post-hoc "data snooping," in which multiple tests are run in an attempt to ferret out whatever looks as though it might be significant in the data. Such planning can also help to ensure that there will in fact be appropriate tests for the data and issues of interest. And it can help to ensure that the most powerful and informative of the potentially available tests will in fact be utilized.

A second piece of advice is to be careful. The conclusions that can be drawn from a study are completely dependent on the accuracy of the statistical calculations. An error in calculation can lead to an error in conclusions, in some cases a major error. Calculation errors, moreover, tend to be less detectable than other mistakes that a researcher might make; readers of a report may be able to spot other methodological flaws, but they generally have to take the calculations on faith. It is critical, therefore, that every calculation be checked very carefully. Ideally, each calculation should be done independently by at least two people. It may also be useful to compare two or more methods of performing the same calculation (e.g., hand calculator vs. computer).

In addition to the general need for care, there may sometimes be statistical outcomes that are so unlikely that they cry out for rechecking. In particular, suspicions should arise whenever there is a marked discrepancy between the descriptive statistics of the study and the inferential conclusions about significance. Descriptive and inferential are based on exactly the same data, and they should always show a reasonable correspondence. Finding that a tiny difference is statistically significant, or that a very large difference is not significant, should be a stimulus for rechecking the calculations.

One more point can be made about checking. Investigators should guard against the tendency to engage in differential checking, in which outcomes that contradict their expectations receive close scrutiny while those that are supportive go unchecked. Natural though this tendency is, it provides another opening for possible experimenter bias effects: If only the negative errors get corrected, the result may be a pseudo-confirmation of the researcher's hypotheses. Better practice, obviously, is to check and correct everything.

A last piece of advice is to seek help. So many sources of help are available—textbooks, computer programs, statistical experts—that it is foolhardy for the nonexpert to attempt to navigate through tricky statistical waters on his or her own. Expert help can be sought at any point in the research process, beginning with the initial planning of measurements and design and continuing through the write-up for publication.

It may be helpful to say a bit more about written sources of help. We have already cited some of the best general textbooks in psychological statistics, as well as more specialized sources for particular topics. There are also some statistical issues and corresponding procedures that are especially prominent in certain kinds of developmental psychology research. This chapter has not attempted to talk about statistics that are specific to developmental, for two reasons: Most of the statistical issues with which developmental psychologists grapple are not in fact specific to their field but are common to psychology as a whole, and those issues that *are* at all specific are too complex to go into here. We can note, however, that there are several helpful (although sometimes difficult) sources for discussions that are oriented specifically to statistics in developmental research. These sources include Achenbach (1978), Applebaum and McCall (1983), Nunnally (1982), Seitz (1980), and Wohlwill (1973).

SUMMARY

Psychologists use statistics for two related purposes. *Descriptive statistics* summarize data; they provide a kind of first-level description of what a study has found. Of interest are both the *central tendency* of response, typically indexed by the arithmetical *mean*, and the *variability* in response, typically measured by the *variance* or *standard deviation*.

Inferential statistics go beyond description to the determination of *statistical significance*. At issue is whether the obtained results deviate significantly from what could have occurred by chance, with chance based upon the *null hypothesis* of no difference between the groups being compared. The *t* test is described as a specific example of an inferential test, one that is appropriate for comparing the mean level of response in two groups. As in most inferential tests, significance in the *t* test depends on three factors: the size of the difference between the groups, the amount of variability within each group, and the size of the sample. It is stressed that conclusions from inferential tests are always probabilistic rather than certain, and that two kinds of errors can occur: *Type 1 errors,* in which there is an incorrect rejection of a true null hypothesis, and *Type 2 errors,* in which there is a failure to reject a false null hypothesis. It is also stressed that statistical significance is concerned only with ruling out chance variations as an explanation for the results, and that a finding of significance does not guarantee either the validity of the study or the meaningfulness of the results.

The discussion turns next to the issue of which kinds of statistical analysis are appropriate for which kinds of data—in other words, how to select an inferential test. Three factors are important to the choice of test. One is the level of measurement: whether the measurements are made on a *nominal, ordinal, interval,* or *ratio* scale. A second is the distribution of scores—in particular, whether the scores are normally distributed. So-called *parametric tests,* such as the ANOVA or *t* test, are dependent on certain assumptions about how the data are distributed. They are sometimes more powerful than *nonparametric tests*—that is, more likely to detect a true effect. At the same time, parametric tests are dependent on more assumptions than are nonparametric tests, and are therefore less widely applicable. The third factor is the design of the study: how many different independent variables are included, how many different levels of each variable there are, and whether the comparisons are made within- or between-subject.

Flexible and informative though ANOVA is, there are some situations in which other statistics may be more appropriate. In studies with clear hypotheses *planned comparisons* may be preferable to an overall ANOVA. Such planned, in-advance tests can provide greater power for specific comparisons of interest. With quanti-

tative independent variables *trend analysis* can be used to identify the shape of the relation between independent variable and dependent variable. Trend analysis can be used either instead of or as a follow-up to ANOVA. In addition to the shape of the relation, researchers are often interested in the magnitude of effect associated with an independent variable. Various measures of *effect size* exist, the simplest of which is *d*: the difference between two means divided by the standard deviation for the groups being compared. In studies with two or more dependent variables multivariate analysis of variance, or *MANOVA,* is a possible alternative to ANOVA. MANOVA is appropriate when the dependent variables form a cohesive set, in which case MANOVA may provide a more sensitive test of effects than independent ANOVAs. Finally, the most general alternative to a multifactor ANOVA is *multiple regression,* a broad system of analysis which in fact encompasses ANOVA as a special case. Although the two analyses are often interchangeable, there are situations in which regression may be preferable to ANOVA—most notably, when the independent variables are continuous rather than discrete.

In addition to inferential tests of group differences, another major use of statistics is to establish the correlation between variables. *Correlation statistics* measure the degree of linear relation between variables. The statistical significance of a correlation depends on both the size of the correlation and the size of the sample. The meaningfulness of a correlation depends on its size: The closer the value to 1, the better our ability to predict one score from knowledge of the other. Correlations are affected by the range of variation in the two sets of scores; for a correlation to be generalizable, this range should be representative of that in the population of interest.

Most statistics are designed to assess effects within a single study. *Meta-analysis,* in contrast, involves the application of statistical techniques to groups of studies. Most meta-analyses have three goals: to determine whether significant effects are present, to estimate the size of the effects, and to examine the contribution of cross-study variations to outcomes. As an illustration, a meta-analysis of sex differences in cognitive abilities is discussed. Also discussed are some of the problems that can arise in doing meta-analyses.

The chapter concludes with several general points about statistics. These points include three general pieces of advice: to plan ahead, to be careful in one's calculations, and to seek expert help whenever necessary.

chapter 11

ETHICS

We stressed in chapter 10 that questions of statistics should not be left until the concluding phase of a study. The same point applies even more strongly to questions of ethics. Research must always meet two criteria: scientific merit and ethical soundness. If there are serious doubts about either criterion then the research should not be done.

Twenty or thirty years ago decisions about ethics were left largely to the conscience of the individual investigator. This is no longer the case. Recent years have seen the development of multiple sets of guidelines concerning ethical principles in research with human subjects. There are also multiple layers of protection afforded the subject in research today. When the subjects are children the guidelines and the layers of protection become even more extensive.

We begin this chapter by reviewing the various guidelines under which researchers in developmental psychology operate. This introductory section outlines the steps that must be followed in determining whether a research project is ethical, as well as the issues that must be considered in this determination. We then move on to a fuller consideration of the basic rights possessed by every person who participates as a subject in research. We discuss three such rights: the right to informed consent prior to participating in research, the right to freedom from harm as a result of research, and the right to confidentiality with regard to the information obtained in research.

A cautionary point is in order before we begin our review of guidelines and procedures. Adherence to established rules is a necessary step in determining the ethics of a research project. It is not a sufficient step, however. Guidelines are of necessity always somewhat general, and the researcher must still think carefully about how the guidelines apply to his or her special case. Codes of ethics exist to aid the decision-making process, not to replace it. Furthermore, no matter how many levels of approval have been obtained in the course of a project, it is still the researcher who retains final responsibility for the ethics of the research.

GUIDELINES AND PROCEDURES

Imagine a researcher who has devised a study that she plans to carry out with grade-school children as subjects. She is comfortable with her proposed research from a scientific point of view, but wishes also to be sure that all of her projected procedures are ethically acceptable. In this section we consider two questions: To what sources can a researcher turn for guidance about ethics? And through what channels *must* a researcher work before he or she can begin testing subjects?

Guidelines for ethical conduct in research are available from a variety of sources. (Fuller accounts of the historical development of these standards can be found in Cooke, 1982, and Rheingold, 1982). At the most general level, both the Nuremberg Code (*Trials of War Criminals . . . ,* 1949) and the Declaration of Helsinki (World Medical Association, 1964) set forth international standards for the involvement and treatment of human subjects in research. The United States government also provides detailed standards for the use of human subjects, primarily in the form of rules propagated by the various agencies that dispense federal research grants. Finally, various professional societies whose members carry out research with human subjects have developed their own sets of ethical standards. The American Psychological Association, for example, has published *Ethical Principles in the Conduct of Research with Human Participants* (1973), and the Division of Developmental Psychology of the APA has added to this some special guidelines for work with children (1968). The Society for Research in Child Development, the major interdisciplinary organization for researchers of child development, has also published guidelines for research with children (1973).

The various publications just described are not, of course, independent of each other. The points made are similar and frequently identi-

cal, and the authors of one document often draw explicitly from the content of another. Because its guidelines are probably the most relevant for the developmental researcher, the ethical code of the Society for Research in Child Development is reprinted in Box 11-1.

Let us return now to our hypothetical researcher. We assume that she is familiar—as she certainly should be—with the principles set forth in the documents just listed. At the local level these principles are embodied in the form of an organization called an *institutional review board.* It is this board through which the researcher will work.

Institutional review boards are a reflection of one of the basic principles of research ethics: the principle of *independent review.* The idea behind independent review is that the researcher who designs a study has too great a personal investment in the research to be a trustworthy judge of its ethical soundness. What is needed is an independent evaluation of ethics by competent people who are not themselves directly involved in the research. To this end, every university at which research with human subjects is conducted maintains an institutional review board whose purpose is to judge the ethics of proposed research projects. Such boards consist of a number of members drawn from diverse backgrounds. Among the conditions set forth in the federal regulation that established such boards were the following: "The members could not have a direct interest in the research under review, could not all be employees or agents of the institution, and could not be members of a single professional group" (Cooke, 1982, p. 167).

Each institutional review board publishes its own set of ethical guidelines, guidelines that are drawn closely from the various federal and professional sources described previously. Each board also provides standard forms on which researchers can submit proposed research projects. Typically, these forms begin by asking for a general statement of the purposes of the research and of the procedures to be followed. If the board deems it necessary, copies of experimental protocols, questionnaires, and so forth may also be requested. In addition to such gen-

IMP.

BOX 11–1   Ethical standards for research with children (Society for Research in Child Development, 1973)

Children as research subjects present ethical problems for the investigator different from those presented by adult subjects. Not only are children often viewed as more vulnerable to stress but, having less knowledge and experience, they are less able to evaluate what participation in research may mean. Consent of the parent for the study of his child, moreover, must be obtained in addition to the child's consent. These are some of the major differences between research with children and research with adults.

1. No matter how young the child, he has rights that supersede the rights of the investigator. The investigator should measure each operation he proposes in terms of the child's rights, and before proceeding he should obtain the approval of a committee of peers. Institutional peer review committees should be established in any setting where children are the subjects of the study.

2. The final responsibility to establish and maintain ethical practices in research remains with the individual investigator. He is also responsible for the ethical practices of collaborators, assistants, students, and employees, all of whom, however, incur parallel obligations.

3. Any deviation from the following principles demands that the investigator seek consultation on the ethical issues in order to protect the rights of the research participants.

4. The investigator should inform the child of all features of the research that may affect his willingness to participate and he should answer the child's questions in terms appropriate to the child's comprehension.

5. The investigator should respect the child's freedom to choose to participate in research or not, as well as to discontinue participation at any time. The greater the power of the investigator with respect to the

Note. From "Ethical Standards for Research with Children," Society for Research in Child Development, 1973, *Newsletter,* 3–5. Reprinted by permission.

participant, the greater is the obligation to protect the child's freedom.

6. The informed consent of parents or of those who act in *loco parentis* (e.g., teachers, superintendents of institutions) similarly should be obtained, preferably in writing. Informed consent requires that the parent or other responsible adult be told all features of the research that may affect his willingness to allow the child to participate. This information should include the profession and institutional affiliation of the investigator. Not only should the right of the responsible adult to refuse consent be respected, but he should be given the opportunity to refuse without penalty.

7. The informed consent of any person whose interaction with the child is the subject of the study should also be obtained. As with the child and responsible adult, informed consent requires that the person be informed of all features of the research that may affect his willingness to participate; his questions should be answered; and he should be free to choose to participate or not, and to discontinue participation at any time.

8. From the beginning of each research investigation, there should be a clear agreement between the investigator and the research participant that defines the responsibilities of each. The investigator has the obligation to honor all promises and commitments of the agreement.

9. The investigator uses no research operation that may harm the child either physically or psychologically. Psychological harm, to be sure, is difficult to define; nevertheless, its definition remains the responsibility of the investigator. When the investigator is in doubt about the possible harmful effects of the research operations, he seeks consultation from others. When harm seems possible, he is obligated to find other means of obtaining the information or to abandon the research.

10. Although we accept the ethical ideal of full disclosure of information, a particular study may necessitate concealment or decep-

tion. Whenever concealment or deception is thought to be essential to the conduct of the study, the investigator should satisfy a committee of his peers that his judgment is correct. If concealment or deception is practiced, adequate measures should be taken after the study to ensure the participant's understanding of the reasons for the concealment or deception.

11. The investigator should keep in confidence all information obtained about research participants. The participant's identity should be concealed in written and verbal reports of the results, as well as in informal discussions with students and colleagues. When a possibility exists that others may gain access to such information, this possibility, together with the plans for protecting confidentiality, should be explained to the participants as a part of the procedure for obtaining informed consent.

12. To gain access to institutional records the investigator should obtain permission from responsible individuals or authorities in charge of records. He should preserve the anonymity of the information and extract no information other than that for which permission was obtained. It is the investigator's responsibility to insure that these authorities do, in fact, have the confidence of the subject and that they bear some degree of responsibility in giving such permission.

13. Immediately after the data are collected, the investigator should clarify for the research participant any misconceptions that may have arisen. The investigator also recognizes a duty to report general findings to participants in terms appropriate to their understanding. Where scientific or humane values may justify withholding information, every effort should be made so that withholding the information has no damaging consequences for the participant.

14. Because the investigator's words may carry unintended weight with parents and children, caution should be exercised in reporting results, making evaluative statements, or giving advice.

15. When in the course of research, informa-

tion comes to the investigator's attention that may seriously affect the child's well-being, the investigator has a responsibility to discuss the information with those expert in the field in order that the parents may arrange the necessary assistance for their child.

16. When research procedures may result in undesirable consequences for the participant that were previously unforeseen, the investigator should employ appropriate measures to correct these consequences, and should consider redesigning the procedures.

17. The investigator should be mindful of the social, political, and human implications of his research and should be especially careful in the presentation of his findings. This standard, however, in no way denies the investigator the right to pursue any area of research or the right to observe proper standards of scientific reporting.

18. When an experimental treatment under investigation is believed to be of benefit to children, control groups should be offered other beneficial alternative treatments, if available, instead of no treatment.

19. Teachers of courses related to children should demonstrate their concern for the rights of research participants by presenting these ethical standards to their students so that from the outset of training the participants' rights are regarded as important as substantive findings and experimental design.

20. Every investigator has a responsibility to maintain not only his own ethical standards but also those of his colleagues.

21. Editors of journals reporting investigations of children have certain responsibilities to the authors of studies they review: they should provide space where necessary for the investigator to justify his procedures and to report the precautions he has taken. When the procedures seem questionable, editors should ask for such information.

22. The Society and its members have a continuing responsibility to question, amend, and revise these standards.

eral information, the form also solicits information about a number of specific points of ethical concern. These points (which we discuss more fully shortly) include the following: What are the risks, if any, to the subject from participating in the research? What are the benefits, if any? How will subjects be recruited for the study, and what inducements, if any, will be used to secure their cooperation? What exactly will subjects be told about the research before agreeing to participate? Will it be clear to the subjects that participation in the study is voluntary and that they can withdraw at any time? Where appropriate, will subjects be debriefed with regard to any deception and told the true purpose of the study at the conclusion of testing? And how will the confidentiality of the results be preserved?

Approval from an institutional review board allows the researcher to submit a grant for funding or, if the research is unfunded, to seek out subjects and begin testing. In the case of our hypothetical grade-school study, the researcher will probably need to work through a public-school system. The exact procedure for doing so varies from one community to another, although there are some common elements. In some school districts there is a central office through which all research proposals must be channeled, and a proposal can be forwarded to a school only after it has been approved at this initial level. Once the proposal reaches the school it will need to gain the approval of the principal. In some schools the principal is the sole arbiter; in other schools the principal consults with the teachers whose classrooms are involved and grants approval only if the teachers agree. Once the proposal reaches the classroom it will need to be conveyed to the parents, usually via a letter describing the study and requesting permission to include their children. Only children whose parents return a signed permission form may be tested. Finally, the child must be given some idea of what the research involves and must be offered the choice of whether or not to participate.

As this description should make clear, there are numerous layers of protection between the researcher's initial idea for a study and the eventual testing of children. The primary purpose of these layers is, of course, to ensure that the rights of the child are safeguarded. From the researcher's point of view, the multiple safeguards have a couple other implications as well. First, it is important not only to think carefully about ethics when planning a study but also to communicate persuasively about the ethical soundness of one's ideas when presenting the research to others. Research can proceed only after many people have been convinced of the value and the ethical propriety of the project. Second, it is important to allow sufficient time for the various layers of approval to be obtained. Depending on the ease with which the different channels can be negotiated, weeks or even months may intervene between the planning of a study and the eventual work with subjects.

One last point should be reiterated here. Our emphasis in this section has been on the many sources of protection for child participants in research today. The fact that so many people have a chance to safeguard the children, however, does not exempt the researcher from personal responsibility. As was stressed earlier, ultimate responsibility for maintaining ethical standards in research always rests with the person carrying out the research.

RIGHTS OF THE SUBJECT

Informed Consent

Participation in research must be voluntary. No one can be studied without his or her knowledge, no one can be forced to be a subject in a study, and no one can be forced to continue in a study. These statements sum up the doctrine of informed consent: Subjects must know in advance what a research project involves, and they must give their explicit agreement to be included.[1]

---

[1]One exception to this statement is provided by some forms of observational research, especially those that occur in the natural setting. Imagine an observational study of purchase decisions in a supermarket, or of traffic patterns

The principle of informed consent is easy enough to state, but implementing it can give rise to a host of complexities. It is these complexities on which we concentrate here. We begin by considering more fully the two components of the phrase, "informed" and "consent." We then move on to some special issues that arise when the subjects are children.

As "informed" implies, simple agreement to participate is not sufficient; rather, the agreement must come after the subject has been fairly informed about what the research will entail. The principal way that prospective subjects learn about research is via an "informed consent form"; it is also this form that the subject signs to indicate willingness to participate. All institutional review boards pay close attention to the consent form that the researcher plans to use, and all review boards have definite criteria for what should be included on the form. As an example, the criteria set forth by the University of Florida Institutional Review Board are quoted in Box 11–2. Note that the guidelines, though quite definite concerning what should be included, leave considerable leeway as to exactly how the form should be worded. Note also that it is quite permissible, and usually desirable, to supplement the written information with oral comments, including answers to any questions the subject may have.

With such explicit guidelines to work from, how could an informed consent form ever fail to inform? Various problems can arise. Researchers may have difficulty meeting the criterion of "language appropriate to the level of understanding of the subject." Most psychologists have limited experience in writing for nonpsychologists, and many are not very successful when they have to attempt the task. A survey of institutional review boards (Tannenbaum & Cooke, 1977) included an analysis of the readability of informed consent forms. Seven levels of readability were established, ranging from "very easy" (the level found in comics) to "very difficult" (the level found in scientific and professional writing). The survey found that 55% of the consent forms fell in the category of "difficult," the category typical of scholarly and academic prose. Fully 85% fell in the three most advanced categories of "fairly difficult," "difficult," and "very difficult"; correspondingly, only 2% were classified in the first three categories of "very easy," "easy," and "fairly easy." The point that these data make is obvious: Consent forms cannot do a very good job of informing if they are written at levels that are not appropriate for many of the people reading them.

Consent forms also cannot do a full job of informing if some information about the research is deliberately withheld. In some projects the nature of the research requires that subjects not know in advance about some of the purposes or some of the procedures of the study. We encountered a number of examples in the middle chapters of this book. As we saw in both chapter 7 and chapter 9, many measures of constructive memory are intended to tap spontaneous processing of material in the absence of any intent to memorize the material. In such cases we can hardly tell the subjects that a memory test is coming, or we may destroy the phenomenon that we wish to study. Similarly, we cannot use surprise to diagnose cognitive level (chapters 6 and 7) if subjects know that they are to be tricked; by definition, surprise involves the unexpected. Nor can we look for instances of cheating in studies of moral development (chapter 8) if we tell subjects that cheating is being studied or that their behavior will be closely monitored. These are just a few examples of cases in which research is possible only if some information is withheld from the subject. In such cases the consent form can still convey much pertinent information about purposes and procedures, but it cannot convey everything.

---

at a busy intersection, or of spacing or crowding in a movie theater. It is unlikely that any review board would insist on informed consent from the persons who contribute data in such instances. Several justifications can be offered for the absence of consent: The behaviors are naturally occurring ones that are unaffected by the decision to study them; the behaviors are innocuous and in no way revealing or embarrassing; and the subjects are anonymous and certain always to remain anonymous. The APA's *Ethical Principles in the Conduct of Research with Human Participants* (1973) discusses such situations in detail.

BOX 11–2   Guidelines for informed consent (University of Florida Institutional Review Board)

The Principal Investigator must prepare in language appropriate to the level of understanding of the subject a narrative description of the planned procedure or treatment. This must be submitted as part of the protocol. The Informed Consent shall include the following elements of information:

1. A fair explanation of the *procedures* to be followed, and their *purposes,* including identification of any procedures which are experimental.

2. A description of any attendant *discomforts* and *risks* reasonably to be expected. Any benefits to the subject or knowledge reasonably to be expected; or a statement that there are no immediate benefits expected. Any appropriate *alternative procedures* that might be advantageous for the subject.

3. An offer to answer any inquiries concerning the procedures.

4. Instruction that the person is *free to withdraw* his/her consent and to discontinue participation in the project or activity at any time without prejudice.

5. A statement whether *monetary compensation* will be *awarded or not;* and if so, the amount.

6. Include the following statement *only* if there is a possibility of physical injury: "I under-

stand that if I am physically injured during this study, and if the investigator is at fault, the University of Florida and the Board of Regents of the State of Florida shall be liable only as provided by law. I understand that I may seek appropriate compensation for injury by contacting the Insurance Coordinator at 107 Tigert Hall, University of Florida, telephone number 392–1325."

7. A concluding sentence which reads, "I have read and I understand the procedure described above. I agree to participate in the procedure and I have received a copy of this description."

8. Signatures: _____ _____

     Subject   Date

_____ _____

     Witness   Date

_____ _____

     Relationship if   Date
     other than subject

_____ _____

     Principal Investigator's Date
     name

A copy of Informed Consent, signed by the subject and witnessed, is to be retained by the experimenter and a duplicate copy is to be given to the subject.

There is an important distinction to be made between two ways in which researchers can deliberately disguise aspects of their research. One is through *incomplete disclosure*: simply not telling subjects about some aspect of the study. In research on constructive memory, for example, we would simply not inform subjects that the test for memory is coming, nor would we make explicit the fact that one purpose of the research is to study this kind of memory. The second method is through *deception*: deliberately misinforming subjects about some aspect of the study. In research on cheating, for example, we would be practicing deception if we explicitly

told the subjects that they would not be observed and then nevertheless watched them through a one-way mirror. The deception may or may not occur on the informed consent form itself; the important point is that if deception is part of the study, then consent cannot be fully informed.

As might be expected, incomplete disclosure is considerably more common in developmental psychology research than is deception. As would also be expected, incomplete disclosure is generally regarded as less problematical from an ethical point of view than is active deception of subjects. Nevertheless, not all instances of incomplete disclosure are as benign-looking as the memory example. And both incomplete disclosure and deception involve some violation of the principle of informed consent. The use of either, therefore, requires close scrutiny.

When is incomplete disclosure or deception justified? From the various guidelines on ethics cited earlier a number of rules can be abstracted. Such practices should be used only if the topic is an important one and there is no other way to gather the necessary information. They should be used only after the researcher has convinced an independent review board that such procedures are in fact justified in his or her study. Although subjects cannot be told everything in advance about the research, they should be told as much as possible, short, of course, of anything that might bias their later responses. Among the facts that *must* be conveyed to subjects is any information about potential risks from participating in the research. Once the testing is completed, subjects should be fully informed about any purposes or experimental procedures that have hitherto been disguised. Finally and most critically, both the review board and the researcher must be convinced that the use of incomplete disclosure or deception will not result in any harm to the subject.

As always, it is easier to state general principles than to handle every specific application. We return to these matters, especially deception, in the next section when we discuss various kinds of research that may be harmful to subjects.

Let us turn now to the second component in the phrase "informed consent," the concept of consent. To be meaningful, consent must involve more than simply signing a consent form; consent must be *voluntary*. The notion of voluntary does not mean that subjects must seek out researchers simply for the chance to be studied, nor does it mean that researchers must foreswear all attempts at persuading subjects to take part. It does mean, however, that subjects should not be lured into a study through unfair inducements or coerced into participating through the greater power of the experimenter. It means also that subjects should not be forced

to continue in a study if they indicate clearly that they wish to withdraw.

Issues of coercion are generally greatest when there is a clear imbalance of power between subject and experimenter. Such is the case, of course, when children are the subjects. It may also be the case for the relation between the experimenter and the children's parents, especially if the experimenter is associated with (or perceived to be associated with) some institution that has control over the child, such as a hospital or school. In such cases parents may not realize that they have the right to refuse permission for their child's participation. Whatever the specific situation, researchers must strike a careful balance between the goal of eliciting maximum participation and the goal of ensuring that the participation is truly voluntary. Researchers are generally convinced of the scientific importance and ethical propriety of what they do; they may also be convinced that their research will yield social benefits, either directly to the subjects involved or more generally to people who are like the subjects. Under these circumstances, it is perfectly proper for the researcher to make a concerted effort to recruit and maintain a sufficiently large and representative sample. It is important, however, that this effort stop well short of misrepresentation or coercion, either in recruiting subjects in the first place or in persuading them to continue once the study is under way.

It is time now to consider how informed consent works when the subjects are children. Children are not competent, from either a legal or a psychological point of view, to give informed consent for their own participation in research. Consequently, permission must be sought elsewhere. In the great majority of cases it is the child's parent or parents who give the permission. Typically, permission from one parent is sufficient, although a review board may occasionally require that both parents give their agreement. In rare cases a review board may decide that parental permission is not necessary, just as it may occasionally decide that informed consent is not necessary in research with mature subjects. Even here, however, the researcher may be required to obtain permission from the child's school; indeed, such permission may be a condition for waiving parental approval. There are also cases in which the child's parents are not available—for example, when the child is institutionalized or living with a legal guardian. The principle, however, remains the same: Permission must be obtained from someone who is legally responsible for the child and who is competent to evaluate what the research will require of the child.

The requirement that parental permission be obtained in almost all research with children is a fairly recent development. Another recent development is a greatly increased concern with the child's right to decide whether he or she will participate. There has been much debate in recent years about whether written consent should be obtained from children as well as parents and, if so, at what age the child is competent to give such consent. Various minimum ages have been proposed for written consent from children, with some review boards setting cutoffs as young as age 7. It seems doubtful that having a 7-year-old sign a consent form accomplishes much. But then any age cut-off, short of the legal age for such consent, is going to be largely arbitrary. The important point is not to get something in writing; the important point is to ensure that the child is first given a fair idea of what the research involves and then voluntarily agrees to participate. Such agreement, whether written or oral, is referred to as "assent," to distinguish it from the legally effective "consent" that an adult can give.

Securing assent from child subjects can be a delicate business. The approach that is appropriate depends on both the age of the child and the nature of the study. Although systematic data do not exist, it seems safe to conclude that researchers typically tell their child subjects considerably less in advance than they do their adult subjects. This discrepancy can be justified in terms of the child's lowered capacity to understand the purpose of research; the fact that various adults have already agreed to a particular project is a further justification. Nevertheless, if the assent is to mean anything the child must be given *some* basis for deciding whether or not to come with the experimenter. Except

with very young subjects, it probably makes sense to attempt to convey the following pieces of information: a general idea of what will be done ("play some remembering games"), where the research will take place ("in Mrs. Smith's office"), how many people will be involved ("just you and me"), how long the session will be ("take about 20 minutes"), whether other children have done or will do the same thing ("lots of kids from the class will be doing it"), whether a reward will be offered ("get a little prize at the end"), and finally, an opportunity to say yes or no ("Would you like to come?"). As the age of the sample increases, the description can be moved closer and closer to the kind of informed consent that would be used with adults.

Freedom from Harm

Undoubtedly the most basic right that subjects possess is the right not to be harmed in research. Correspondingly, the greatest responsibility that the researcher has is to ensure that no harm comes to any subject.

How might a subject be harmed in research? In medically oriented projects the possibility of physical harm may sometimes arise. A new medical treatment, for example, may carry risks as well as expected benefits, and there may be no way to rule out all such risks before the research is conducted. It is in just such cases that informed consent is especially important, as is prior review by an independent review board. Indeed, it was to monitor medical research that institutional review boards were first set up. Their application to psychological research came later.

In psychological research there is generally not the slightest chance of physical harm to the subjects. The concern in this case lies in the possibility of psychological harm. Psychological harm is a more nebulous concept than physical harm, and as such has been the subject of numerous debates, both in general discussions of research ethics and in evaluations of specific research projects. We begin with a few general points, and then discuss kinds of research that could conceivably result in psychological harm.

The notion of psychological harm does *not* mean that nothing unpleasant can happen to the subject in the course of the study. Subjects may be bored by a repetitive task and wish they were elsewhere, may find parts of the procedure frustrating or confusing, may fail on some task on which they would very much like to succeed, and so forth. It is, of course, desirable to minimize such experiences, especially if boredom, frustration, or whatever is not the focus of the study. But the mere fact that the subject wishes things were otherwise does not make a study harmful. Two questions must be asked. Does the research expose the subject to experiences that are significantly different from those that he or she routinely encounters anyway? And is there any possibility that the effects will be permanent and not just transitory?

Consider a study of problem solving in grade-school children. The children are given a variety of problems to solve, some children are more successful than others, and all children fail on at least some problems. As described, the research experience sounds quite similar to what children routinely encounter every day in school, and there is no reason to think that any negative effects from the failures will persist beyond the study. Suppose, however, that one goal of the research is to determine the effects of anxiety on problem solving. To heighten anxiety, the experimenter tells half the subjects that the problem-solving battery is a test of their ability to succeed in school during the coming year. In this case failures on the tasks may well lead to strong negative reactions. And in this case the negative reactions may well persist beyond the study itself.

This example suggests one class of experimental manipulations that may result in psychological harm: manipulations that create negative feelings or a negative self-image in the subject. Induced failure experiences, especially on tasks that are labeled as important, fall under this heading. So do the paradigms for studying punishment discussed in chapter 8. And so do manipulations that induce the subject to engage in some unethical or forbidden behavior. Cheating is an obvious example. In a cheating study subjects (or at least *some* sub-

jects) are enticed into doing something that they know is against the rules and will lead to censure if discovered. Even if the child is left to believe that cheating was undetected, feelings of anxiety or guilt may result. If the child is not somehow reassured, these feelings may well persist.

The last sentence suggests a possible solution to the problem. Why not use the poststudy period to dispel whatever negative feelings may have arisen in the course of the study? In the problem-solving study, for example, the experimenter could explain to the child that the test does not really predict school performance and that all children get some problems wrong. In the cheating study the experimenter could emphasize that no harm was done by the cheating and that many other children behaved in the same way. Such after-the-fact clarification of the true nature of a study is referred to as *debriefing*. The goals of such debriefing efforts are two: to make clear the actual purpose of the experimental manipulations, and to leave the subject feeling as positive as possible about his or her behavior.

Debriefing is a recommended procedure whenever important information is initially withheld from the subject. If negative feelings are induced, then debriefing becomes even more important. With children, however, debriefing can be difficult, and may sometimes create more problems than it solves. Consider the cheating example again. It is not clear that the child will really feel better about him- or herself if the experimenter ends the study by explaining that cheating was being studied and that the child's cheating was in fact known about all along. After all, the child *has* misbehaved, and now he or she no longer even has the solace of having gotten away with it. Nor is it clear how fully young children can understand and benefit from explanations of the true purpose of research. The experimenter who attempts to explain the rationale behind a cheating study to a 5-year-old may succeed only in confusing and possibly alarming the child. Perhaps adults can see through *any* mirror! Under such circumstances, it may be better to forego the debriefing altogether.

Debriefing has another possible unwanted outcome. By definition, debriefing occurs only after the experimenter has somehow misled the subject. In many cases "misled" is a euphemism, for what has happened is that the experimenter has lied to the subject. The debriefing then spells out exactly what the lie was. It may be that the main message that the subject takes away from the debriefing is that researchers (or psychologists or adults in general) are not to be trusted. Children in particular may be susceptible to negative reactions when they learn that an adult has deceived them.

The preceding paragraph has a kind of shoot-the-messenger quality to it. Clearly, the prime culprit here is not the debriefing but the original act of deception. The obvious way to avoid problems attendant on lying to subjects is not to lie to subjects in the first place. Some issues, however—such as cheating—are very difficult to study without the use of deception. If all the criteria discussed in the preceding section can be met, then most researchers would agree that use of deception can sometimes be justified (not all researchers, however; cf. Baumrind, 1985). It is in these cases that the researcher—and the institutional review board—must decide whether debriefing would mitigate or add to the problems posed by the deception.

The example of cheating research can serve to illustrate another possible kind of psychological harm. We have discussed two possible negative effects from being a subject in cheating research: feelings of guilt at having misbehaved and feelings of mistrust upon learning of the deception. But there is a third possible effect that is in a sense more direct. Suppose that the subject does *not* feel guilty about his or her behavior but is instead delighted to have hit upon a new way to trick adults. Suppose, in short, that the subject learns to cheat from participating in a cheating study. Presumably, the ultimate purpose in doing cheating research is to discover things about cheating that will enable us to reduce its occurrence. Yet the immediate effect of our research may be to promote the behavior that we wish to reduce.

This argument may be more plausible in the context of another example. In chapter 5 we discussed various ways to study TV violence and aggression. All of the experimental approaches discussed there involved deliberately exposing the subject to violent TV material in the expectation that such violence might increase aggression. Often the exposure did increase aggression, including genuine interpersonal aggression toward other children. The research thus promoted a socially undesirable behavior, a behavior, moreover, that was directed toward an innocent class of victims. How can such research be justified?

To the extent that such research *can* be justified, the justification would draw upon a number of points made earlier in this chapter. Aggression is a very important topic, from both a scientific and a societal point of view. Understanding its causes, including the contribution of TV violence, is especially important. A clear determination of causality requires an experimental approach, as we have seen repeatedly throughout this book. The experiences embodied in such research—a few hours of watching violent TV, a scuffle on the playground—are not significantly different from children's everyday experiences. Considering the brevity of the experimental experience and the multiple determinants of aggression, any lasting effects of our manipulation are quite unlikely. There is, in short, a very slight risk and a potentially large benefit from such research.

Although this kind of justification may sometimes be warranted, researchers must be cautious in resorting to it. Experimental procedures that deliberately induce undesirable behavior should be used only when absolutely necessary. The general principle remains: We should not encourage subjects to engage in behaviors that we (and perhaps they) regard as undesirable.

The final ethically problematical area that we discuss is in a sense the converse of the problem just considered. We have been discussing cases in which a researcher deliberately brings about some sort of undesirable outcome in the subject, such as a heightened level of aggression. There are also cases in which a researcher may deliberately *fail* to bring about some desirable outcome. This issue is usually discussed under the heading of *withholding treatment*—that is, failing to make available some potentially beneficial experimental treatment.

Issues of withholding treatment first arose in medical research. Suppose that we have developed a new drug therapy that we expect to be effective in combatting a particular form of cancer. To test our hypothesis we need to apply our therapy to a sample of subjects who are suffering from the disease. We also need some sort of untreated control group against which to evaluate the effects of the treatment. In some cases already existing data about the natural, non-treated course of the illness may be sufficient for a control. In some cases, however, the only way to get a clear comparison may be by testing two initially equivalent groups: an experimental group to whom we apply the treatment and a control group from whom we withhold the treatment. We then would have a clear test of the effects of our treatment. But how can we justify withholding a potentially beneficial treatment from people who need it?

Consider a somewhat analogous psychological example. The last 20 years have seen the development of numerous preschool intervention programs designed to enhance young children's ability to succeed in school. Typically, these programs are oriented to children who for various reasons (e.g., low socioeconomic status) are perceived as being "at risk" for school failure. Determining how well any particular program works requires two groups of subjects: an experimental group who receive the program and a comparable control group who do not receive the program. We already know, however, that without some intervention many of the control subjects will fail in school. How can we justify withholding our program from them?

There are various justifications that can be offered for the deliberate withholding of an experimental treatment. Note first that we do not *know* that our treatment will work; if we did, there would be no need to carry out an experimental test. It is only if we can test our ideas experimentally that we can verify our treatment's value, a verification that may then prove beneficial for much larger numbers of people in the future. Note also that researchers seldom

have the resources to offer a treatment to all people, or even a very large proportion of people, who might benefit from it. Given this limitation, the sensible course is to adopt an approach that can simultaneously benefit as many as possible while also providing a scientific test of the treatment's worth. In determining who receives the treatment and who does not, a basic ethical principle is that assignment to conditions should be random, with no contribution from factors such as SES, race, or prior acquaintance with the researcher. Whenever possible, nontreated controls should be offered the treatment, or at least some form of help, at the conclusion of the experimental phase of the project. As a little thought about our two examples will reveal, such supplementary help may often be difficult to provide, but the attempt should be made. Finally, it may sometimes be possible to draw a contrast not between an experimental group and untreated controls but between two or more different experimental treatments. In this way all subjects can potentially derive some benefit from the research.

Confidentiality

A final basic right of the subject is the right to *confidentiality*. Information obtained about a subject in research must be confined to certain well-defined scientific uses that should be clear to the subject at the time of informed consent. Such information must not be made generally available in a way that could ever embarrass or harm the subject.

Issues of confidentiality arise at two points in the research process. One is at the time of data collection and storage. Clearly, if subjects' names appear on the data sheets, there is always the possibility that unauthorized persons might see the sheets and thereby learn something that should not be divulged. The obvious solution to this possibility is to record and store data in terms of code numbers rather than names. If there might ever be a need to link data and name, a separate list of number-name translations can be stored somewhere apart from the data. Information might also be transmitted to unauthorized persons if researchers talk about their subjects by name or in ways that make a subject's identity apparent. The obvious solution to this possibility is for researchers not to indulge in such talk.

The second point at which the issue of confidentiality arises is at the time of publication. The goal of publication, of course, is to share what was done and found with the broadest possible audience. In this sharing, however, it is critical that the anonymity of individual subjects be preserved. In most psychology research reports there is no difficulty in preserving anonymity: Large samples of subjects are tested, and all analyses are in terms of group averages and group differences. Occasionally, however, cases arise in which individual subjects might be identifiable—in case-study reports, for example, or in studies with small and distinctive samples. In such cases various strategies (e.g., use of pseudonyms, omission of geograpical information) may be necessary to ensure confidentiality.

As this discussion may suggest, in most research projects there is no particular difficulty in maintaining confidentiality. All that the researcher need do is to avoid the carelessness of loose talk or indiscretely exposed data sheets. We turn next to two situations that pose somewhat more complex problems of confidentiality.

Researchers of child subjects are often asked to provide information about the performance of particular children. A teacher may wish to know how a particular child from his or her classroom responded to some cognitive test. A parent may want to know what the researcher's measures have revealed about the psychological development of his or her child. Such requests can pose a delicate problem. On the one hand, it is only through the good graces of the parent or teacher that the researcher has been allowed to test the child at all. Refusal to share information may seem unreasonable, and may lead to diminished cooperation in the future. On the other hand, the child is the subject of the research, and the child should presumably have the same right to confidentiality as any other subject. In some kinds of research (e.g., children's perceptions of their parents' childrear-

ing) it is essential that the child be certain that his or her responses will be held in confidence.

Several general rules can help guide response to teacher or parent requests for feedback. A first rule is to be clear from the start about what information will or will not be shared. If no specific information about the child's performance will be provided, then this fact should be explicit on the permission form that the parent signs. A second rule is that student testers should be especially careful about providing feedback; the teacher or parent who persists in asking for specific information should be referred to the more experienced principal investigator. A third rule is to be positive, within reasonable bounds of honesty, when making evaluative statements. It is generally possible to find something good to say about a child's performance, although it is of course important to avoid conveying a misleadingly positive picture. Negative statements should be made only with the greatest care. A final rule is to be clear about the diagnostic limitations of one's measures. Most studies in developmental psychology are not set up to diagnose individual children, and most research measures in developmental psychology do not provide information about specific children that is useful in any clear-cut diagnostic or predictive sense. If teachers or parents are clear about these limitations, then requests for specific feedback may not arise. Note that the child subjects themselves also have a right to be told something about what can and cannot be concluded from their responses.

Although most research measures do not yield deep insight into a particular child, exceptions do occur, and these exceptions provide a second possible threat to confidentiality. Suppose that the research uncovers evidence of some serious problem in the child's development, a problem that seems so serious that it should be called to the attention of those responsible for the child's welfare. A battery of cognitive tests may reveal an alarmingly low score, so low that the researcher feels that school authorities should be informed. A set of personality measures may elicit bizarre responses suggestive of some deep-seated personality disorder. A study may uncover, perhaps quite inadvertently, what seems to be evidence of child abuse. As in all research, the information in these cases has been gathered in confidence. What then is the researcher's responsibility?

The Society for Research in Child Development code of ethics, reprinted in Box 11-1, provides a general answer. Principle 15 of the code states that "the investigator has a responsibility to discuss the information with those expert in the field in order that the parents may arrange the necessary assistance for their child." This statement, general though it is, makes two important points. The first is that confidentiality is not an absolutely inviolable principle. The ultimate goal remains the welfare of the subject, and in some cases securing the subject's welfare may require a violation of confidentiality. The second point is that the researcher should not act alone in making the decision to violate confidentiality. It is perhaps unnecessary to note what a serious undertaking it is to tell parents that their child may be psychologically disturbed, or to inform legal authorities that parents may be abusing their child. The costs of being wrong—either in acting or in failing to act—are very great. The researcher should obtain as much expert advice as possible before deciding how to proceed.

SUMMARY

Research must always meet the twin criteria of scientific merit and ethical soundness. This chapter discusses the ethical principles that guide research in developmental psychology.

The chapter begins by reviewing the various sets of guidelines under which researchers in developmental psychology operate. In recent years numerous codes of ethical conduct have been developed to which researchers can turn when evaluating the ethics of their own research. Probably the most helpful source for the developmental researcher is the code of standards of the Society for Research in Child Development, and this code is consequently reprinted as part of the chapter.

At a local level ethical principles are embod-ied in an organization called the *institutional review board*. All research with human subjects must be approved in advance by the institutional review board. The requirement of such approval is a reflection of a basic ethical principle in human research: the need for *independent review* in determining the ethics of a project. In research with children further layers of protection are provided by the requirement that parents and in some cases school authorities give permission for the child's participation. The discussion stresses, however, that the approval of others is a necessary but not sufficient step in the determination of ethics. Researchers are always ultimately responsible for the ethical standards of their own research.

The review of guidelines and procedures is followed by a consideration of the basic rights of subjects in research. One right is to give *informed consent* prior to participating in a study. Subjects must be told in advance what a research project entails, and they must agree freely to take part in it. Various obstacles to fully informed consent are discussed. In some cases researchers may fail to convey the purposes and demands of their research in language that is appropriate for the subject. In some cases researchers may deliberately not reveal certain aspects of their research, either through *incomplete disclosure* of information or through active *deception* of the subject. Although some topics may require such secrecy, it is still important that subjects be told as much as possible, including a fair account of any risks involved. When children are the subjects special problems of consent arise. With child subjects the parent or some responsible adult must be informed of the study and must give permission for the child's participation. The child should also receive an age-appropriate description of the study and should give his or her assent before being tested.

A second basic right that subjects possess is *freedom from harm*. In psychology research the concern is generally with psychological harm, a difficult-to-define and much debated concept. Two questions are important when assessing the likelihood that an experimental manipulation will prove harmful: Are the experimental experiences significantly different from those that subjects routinely encounter anyway? Are the effects of the experiences likely to persist beyond the experiment itself? Among the kinds of manipulations that may prove harmful are those that induce a negative self-image in the subject, those that create unpleasant feelings (e.g., hostility, anxiety), and those that induce the subject to engage in undesirable behavior. Whenever such manipulations are used, a period of *debriefing* and reassurance is generally appropriate at the conclusion of testing. Another ethically problematical kind of research involves *withholding treatment*: Some desirable treatment is withheld from subjects who might benefit from it. Whenever possible in such research, the untreated control group should receive some benefit from participation, such as an alternative form of treatment or later administration of the experimental treatment.

The final right that the chapter discusses is the right to *confidentiality*. Data obtained in research are confidential and must never be made available in a way that could harm the subject. It is important, therefore, that the anonymity of individual subjects be safeguarded both at the time of data collection and at the time of publication. Requests from parents or teachers for information pose one threat to confidentiality, and suggestions for responding to such requests are therefore offered. A more difficult challenge arises when the research uncovers evidence of some serious problem in the subject's development (e.g., evidence of child abuse). Confidentiality is not an inviolable principle in such cases, for the well-being of the subject remains the most important consideration.

chapter 12
COMMUNICATION

Chapter 1 outlined eight steps involved in doing good research. We have now reached the last of these steps: communicating one's work to others.

Scientists communicate about research in two ways. One way is through oral presentation. This is the method of communication used at professional conventions; it is also, of course, the familiar medium of classroom instruction. No student who sits through a dozen lectures a week needs to be told that oral presentations can vary greatly in their clarity and success.

The second method is written communication, usually in the form of publication in one of the many specialized research journals in the field. It is this method on which we concentrate in this chapter. Our basic focus, therefore, is on how to write reports for publication in an APA (American Psychological Association) journal. Many of the points made, however, have a broader application as well. Thus, much that is said is also relevant to preparing oral presen-

tations, as well as to writing papers other than psychology research reports.

As always, there are a number of further sources that can be consulted. An indispensable source of information about writing in psychology is the *Publication Manual of the American Psychological Association* (APA, 1983). The *Manual* provides both general guidelines for effective writing and specific rules for how various parts of a manuscript (e.g., headings, footnotes, references) should be handled. We refer to the *Manual* frequently throughout this chapter. A book by Sternberg (1977) called *Writing the Psychology Paper* provides a concise and highly readable overview of how to write papers in psychology. Unlike the present chapter, Sternberg's book deals with literature review papers as well as research reports. Saslow (1982) considers not only research reports but also oral presentations and research proposals in her sections on how to communicate. Among the many good general books on how to write, Strunk and

White's (1979) *The Elements of Style* remains a classic. Finally, no reader with a sense of humor should miss Harlow's (1962) ''Fundamental Principles for Preparing Psychology Journal Articles.''

The organization of this chapter is as follows. We begin with some general suggestions of how to write effectively, both in psychology papers and elsewhere. We then consider the various sections of a psychology research report, moving in order through Introduction, Method, Results, and Discussion. The chapter concludes with a focus on common writing problems of two sorts: violations of APA conventions and violations of English grammar.

SOME GENERAL POINTS

There are two basic issues to be resolved in writing for publication in psychology. One is what to say. The other is how to say it.

We have already said quite a bit about what kinds of information should be included in psychology journal articles. We have talked, for example, about what readers should be told about subject groups, about testers, about methods of data collection. More generally, having a clear conception of the important components of research—the major goal of our first 11 chapters—is necessary for deciding what is important to say when reporting research. More will be said about questions of ''what'' when we discuss the different sections of a research report shortly.

Questions of ''how'' are divisible into two sorts. A number of points of style are essentially matters of convention—that is, agreed-upon rules for handling particular aspects of writing. Some examples were mentioned earlier. There is, for instance, no single ''right'' way to do footnotes or references, and any reader has undoubtedly encountered a number of different approaches across different books or articles. Precisely because various possibilities exist, however, it is important for members of a discipline to agree upon a common approach. Thus, in psychology there *is* a right way to handle footnotes, references, and dozens of other

stylistic conventions, and this way is spelled out in the APA *Manual*. In the words of the *Manual* (1983), such rules ''spare readers from a distracting variety of forms throughout a work and permit readers to give full attention to content'' (p. 11).

No attempt will be made in this chapter to summarize all of the stylistic rules presented in the *Manual*, rules that occupy the bulk of the *Manual's* 194 pages. What we can attempt are two things. One is to highlight a small set of rules that seem to give students special difficulty. The other is to emphasize the importance of having and working from the *Manual* when writing a paper in psychology. A good rule of thumb is to assume that *any* stylistic issue that might arise will be covered somewhere in the *Manual*. And indeed it probably will be, starting with what kinds of spacing to set the typewriter for and moving on from there.

Adhering to the APA stylistic conventions is the relatively easy part of the ''how'' question. The more difficult part is not unique to psychology: It is the general question of how to write clear and readable prose. Needless to say, this question will not be answered in a brief chapter like the present one (wouldst that things were so easy!). What we can attempt to achieve are some more modest goals. In this section several general points about writing are made. Later, a number of specific stylistic points that seem to give students special difficulty will be noted. This latter section is a counterpart to the discussion of specific APA conventions.

We can begin by emphasizing the importance of writing in a clear and grammatical fashion. That such a seemingly obvious point needs to be emphasized at all is a reflection of two natural but nevertheless mistaken beliefs. One is the belief that the really interesting and important work of the researcher is done when the study is completed and the reseacher knows what he or she has found. Communicating one's findings to others is merely a bothersome addendum to the real business of doing research. The second is the belief that all that really matters in this communication is that all the important content be included; ''style'' is a nicety that can be left to English classes.

What both of these beliefs ignore is the basic point stated in chapter 1: Science is a matter of shared information. For a research finding to mean anything it must be made accessible to the scientific community as a whole. Furthermore, it must be made accessible in a way that heightens the probability that it will be attended to and assimilated. The written presentation must therefore be interesting, or the busy scientist may quickly turn elsewhere. It must be understandable, with all important details presented in a coherent fashion, or the reader will have no basis for evaluating the contribution. And it must be persuasive, with well-motivated arguments offered for the importance of the problem, the soundness of the methods, and the validity of the conclusions. It must, in short, be well written. The better the writer, the more likely it is that his or her work will have an impact on the field.

An even more obviously pragmatic justification can be offered for the importance of writing well. Before an article can be made available to the scientific community, it must be accepted for publication in a professional journal. Most journals are selective in what they publish, and the best journals have rejection rates of up to 90%. A poorly written article is simply much less likely ever to see the light of day than a well-written one. Busy editors and reviewers may be unwilling to make the effort to penetrate the poor writing to get to underlying content, and may be unable to find the content if they do make the effort. Furthermore, because the purpose of a research report is to communicate, the quality of the writing is a quite legitimate part of the evaluation process. It is an illusion to think that style and content can, or should, be separated in the evaluation of a written work.

Recognizing the importance of good writing is easy enough; achieving good writing is much harder. As noted, we settle in this chapter for offering a few general suggestions.

One suggestion is to read psychology before writing psychology. A basic difficulty that many students have in writing psychology research reports is simply that they have read few such reports themselves. Writing in psychology is not fundamentally different from other sorts of writing, as will be stressed shortly. Nevertheless, there is a kind of feeling for what is appropriate in a research report—for how things are said, for what should be included and what left out—that can be gained only by exposure to a number of real-life examples. Such exposure is not sufficient to ensure success, but it may well be necessary. There is no reason, of course, to seek models indiscriminately—there are plenty of bad examples in even the best journals. What makes more sense is to enlist some guidance in finding especially good examples and then learn from them.

The second suggestion is to seek simplicity in writing. The danger in a paragraph like the preceding one is that it may reinforce the notion that scientific writing is an abstruse business that is somehow basically different from other kinds of writing. In particular, scientific writing is *difficult*, packed with arcane technical terms, long and complex sentences, densely reasoned arguments, and so forth. It is true that scientific writing requires a kind of formality of discourse that may not be necessary in other kinds of writing. It is true too that technical terms exist in any science and are often preferable to less precise everyday language. It is not true, however, that scientific writing should *aim* for difficulty; rather just the reverse is true. There will be difficulties aplenty in the content being conveyed; the goal of the writing should be to help the reader surmount the difficulties and arrive at understanding. Thus in general the short, simple word is preferable to the long, complex one, the familiar word to the obscure one, and the short, simple sentence to the long, convoluted one. The aim, after all, is to communicate, not to impress the reader with one's sophistication.

The third suggestion is to seek variety in writing. Simple sentences may be desirable, but an unbroken string of simple sentences quickly begins to pall. The shorter word is not always the best one, and in any case an occasional long word or long sentence can impart a kind of rhythm to the prose that enhances readability. Recall that one goal of effective writing is to interest the reader. The writer who consistently uses the same vocabulary, the same sentence structure, and the same paragraph structure may succeed in being clear, but he or she is unlikely to be very interesting. Clarity of expression and grace of style are not incompatible, and both should be sought.

The fourth suggestion is to seek economy in writing. All readers have limits on their time and patience, and all journals have definite limits on their available space. Articles whose length is out of proportion to their content are responded to negatively. If submitted to a journal they may be rejected outright; at the least, reviewers are likely to demand substantial reductions in length. As they write, authors should continually ask themselves two questions: Is this information necessary to include? Have I expressed it in the most efficient manner possible? Or as Sternberg (1977) puts it, authors must always be ready "to recognize redundancy, repetition, reiteration, rehashing, restating, and duplication!" (p. 81).

The advice to be economical does not mean that scientific writing should be telegraphic. Brevity achieves nothing if important content is lost or if the terseness of the writing makes the paper unreadable. The primary goal remains communication, not space saving. A good rule is: When in doubt, include. It is generally easier, for both author and reader, to pare down an unnecessarily long draft than to try to make sense of a bewilderingly short one.

The final suggestion is to be careful in writing. All of us at times write less well than we might, simply because we do not take the time to think sufficiently before writing or to reread after writing. At a basic level, there is absolutely no excuse for not *proofreading* a paper before submitting it. A paper replete with typographical errors is not only an insult to the reader but also a sure stimulus for negative reactions. At a higher level, it is important to reread papers for ideas as well as for grammar and spelling. Many papers contain blatant misstatements, contradictions, inconsistencies, and so forth, that obviously would never have survived if their authors had simply taken the time to reread what they had written. Not everyone can be a master stylist; everyone, however, can

be careful, and thereby can avoid the most obvious mistakes in writing.

SECTIONS OF AN ARTICLE

In this section we consider the major parts into which psychology research reports are typically divided. Our discussion is meant as a highlighting of important issues rather than as an exhaustive consideration of every question that might arise. Both the APA *Manual* and Sternberg (1977) provide further discussion. Although it is directed to reviewers rather than authors, an article by Wellman and Cialdini (1980) is also helpful.

Introduction

The Introduction serves to orient the reader to the study. The kind of orientation that is appropriate depends to some extent on the particular study, and rigid guidelines about what should be said when should therefore not be taken too seriously. In general, however, the Introduction should attempt to answer several questions. What is the problem under investigation? Why is this an interesting problem to study? What has previous research on this problem shown? What are the limitations in previous research that make further study necessary? What exactly is the gain in knowledge that the new study is intended to produce? And how (in a general sense) will this gain in knowledge be achieved?

The typical direction of movement in the Introduction is from the general to the specific. Thus, an Introduction might start with a statement of the general area of study (e.g., Piagetian training studies) and move from there to the specific question being examined in the new research (e.g., Can preschool children be trained with an instrumental conditioning approach?). The first part of the Introduction is usually devoted to a review of relevant past research; the last part is more likely to point specifically to the new study. As noted, however, there are no fixed rules about sequence; the important point is to answer the questions sketched in the preceding paragraph, and to do so in a clear, readable, and persuasive fashion.

In reviewing past studies the key word is "relevant." An exhaustive literature review is not appropriate for a research report. Not only is there inadequate space for such a review, but the readers to whom the report is directed can be assumed to be professionals who are already familiar with the general background for the research. In the case of a Piagetian training study, for example, there is no need to spend paragraphs detailing the conservation phenomenon or citing sources that document its validity; this material can be assumed to be familiar to anyone who would seek out such a report. Nor is there any need to try to review every past attempt to train conservation; there are by now far too many such studies, and most will be only tangentially related to any new effort. What does make sense, if possible, is to cite one or a few good review articles that summarize what past research has shown. And what is absolutely essential is to discuss any previous studies that have direct bearing on one's own research. Thus in the training study example, any previous work with instrumental conditioning would have to be discussed; so too would any studies with preschool children. Only in the context of a full and accurate consideration of what has gone before can the potential contribution of a new study be evaluated.

The concluding paragraphs of the Introduction typically constitute a bridge between the background material with which the article opens and the new research that occupies the remaining pages. It is here that any important new aspects of the research can be spelled out for the reader. Here too is the place to present specific hypotheses, if the study in fact fits the hypothesis-testing mode. Even if the author does not want to pose specific hypotheses, it is usually helpful to summarize the major questions (e.g., "Can 3-year-olds be successfully trained?") with which the study is concerned. Finally, the Introduction often concludes with an overview of the design and procedures that will be used to examine the questions under study. Details of procedure are the province of the Method and therefore not appropriate; some orientation to what is to come, however, is often helpful.

Method

The Method section tells what was done in the study. The overall Method is usually divided into several subsections. At the least, divisions into *Subjects* and *Procedure* are typical. Depending on the study, separate sections for *Materials, Apparatus, Design,* and *Scoring* may also be appropriate. Alternatively, information relevant to these matters may be incorporated under a general *Procedure* section. The decision as to how many subsections to include depends on both the complexity of the study (e.g., was complicated apparatus used?) and the preferences of the researcher.

We have already said quite a bit about the kinds of information that should be conveyed under the heading of *Subjects*. Recall that this information should include not only obvious demographic data about the sample (e.g., number, age, sex) but also details about methods of selection, proportion agreeing to participate, and proportion remaining in the study to its completion. In the remainder of this section we concentrate on the other parts of the Method.

It is often said (in the APA *Manual*, for instance) that a Method section should be detailed enough to permit an experienced investigator to replicate the study. The validity of this statement depends on what is meant by "replicate." If the term is taken to mean "perform exactly the same study in every detail," then few Method sections would suffice; except perhaps in the simplest of studies, there is simply not space to spell out every aspect of the procedure. If the term is taken instead to mean "perform the same *kind* of study, with all *important* aspects of the procedure kept the same," then the goal of replicability becomes much more reasonable. The challenge then is to determine which aspects of the procedure are important, and therefore require description in the Method.

There are various bases for deciding that a procedural detail is *not* important enough to warrant inclusion. In any study there are a number of procedural minutiae (e.g., Did the subject sit to the left or the right of the experimenter?) that are so unlikely to affect the results that they can safely be omitted. In studies with verbal instructions it is seldom necessary to reproduce the instructions verbatim; paraphrasing what was said is usually sufficient. In studies with multiple tasks of a similar nature it is sometimes sufficient to describe one or two tasks which can then serve as examples of the rest. And just as in the Introduction, some kinds of information can be assumed to be already available to any professional reader. If a standard piece of apparatus was used, for example, then the name and perhaps the model number should be sufficient; readers who are not already familiar with the apparatus can easily look it up. Similarly, an often-used test need not be described in detail; a published source, coupled perhaps with a brief indication of contents, should be enough.

The important details of the Method are those that the reader must have in order to understand and to evaluate the study. The information about subjects discussed earlier falls in this category. So do various aspects of the experimental procedure, aspects that should be derivable from our discussion throughout this book of the important components of research. How were subjects assigned to experimental conditions? What exactly did the conditions consist of, and how were they conveyed to the subjects? (Note that verbatim quotation *may* sometimes be justified here.) What were the dependent variables, and how were they measured? In what order were the various events of the study presented to the subject? How many testers and how many observers were involved? Were the testers and observers blinded? Was reliability assessed, and if so, what was it? The particular information that needs to be conveyed will vary to some extent across studies. The replicability criterion is a helpful guide in thinking about what needs to be said. The really critical criterion, however, is the *evaluation* one: Has the reader been given enough information to evaluate the validity of the method?

Results

The Results section tells what was found in the study. It includes both descriptive statistics—for example, mean levels of performance in the different experimental conditions—and inferential statistics—for example, tests of significance for the differences between the means. It is essential that both kinds of statistics be provided. As we saw in chapter 10, descriptive statistics are hard to interpret without corresponding inferential tests. By the same token, an F test or a p level is of limited value without information about the means on which it is based. The reader needs to know both the statistical tests and the data that went into the tests.

Just as with the Introduction and the Method, the researcher must decide what information is important to include in the Results and what information can be omitted. If the earlier sections of the paper have done their job, they will have set up definite expectations with regard to exactly what questions are to be examined in the Results. Some answer should be given to each of these questions, even if in some cases the answer consists of a single sentence indicating that no significant effects were found. Furthermore, there is no law stating that every analysis in the Results must be clearly anticipated by what has gone before; unexpected or incidental findings of interest may emerge, and if so they should be included. On the other hand, there is also no law stating that *every* conceivable analysis of the data must find its way into the Results. Researchers should beware of cluttering their Results section with peripheral analyses that add little to the study.

The Results section is usually the hardest part of an article to read. Authors can do various things to make their readers' task easier. One is to adopt a logical order of presentation. A common practice is to begin with the major analyses and move only later to more secondary findings. If specific hypotheses were presented in the Introduction, then the results can be organized in terms of the hypotheses, with outcomes relevant to each hypothesis discussed in turn. If several dependent variables were assessed, then it may make sense to present results for each dependent variable separately. Again, the particular approach that will work best depends on the particular study. The important point is to adopt a logical order, and to be sure that the logic is evident to the reader.

Authors should also provide summary statements that help the reader make sense of the data. A common misconception is that a Results section must consist solely of numbers and statistical tests. It is true that the purpose of the Results section is to present data, whereas the purpose of the Discussion section is to interpret data. It is *not* true, however, that statements about the meaning of the data are forbidden in the Results. Indeed, quite the reverse is the case. An unbroken string of *t*s, *F*s, and correlations can be both difficult to decipher and extremely frustrating to read. Much better practice is to spend a sentence or two, either in preview before the tests or in summary afterward, to say in plain English what the numbers mean.[1]

It is important to be clear about what is meant here. What is permissible in the Results is a kind of first-order, close-to-the-data interpretation. Thus a passage like the following might be appropriate: "There was a significant interaction of age and experimental condition, $F(1,96) = 8.95$, $p < .01$ (see Table 1 for relevant means). The training did produce significant effects, but only at age 5; 3-year-olds showed essentially no progress." It would *not* be appropriate to go on to say "The greater susceptibility of the older children is compatible with Piaget's emphasis on the importance of operational structures. . . . " This sort of second-order interpretive statement should be saved for the Discussion.

Authors can also help their readers through judicious use of tables and figures. The word "judicious" is important: Tables and figures are expensive to set in print, and journal editors tend therefore to frown upon their overuse.

Whether a table or figure is justified depends on how easily the information in question could be conveyed in the text. If only a small number of means must be presented, then there is no need for a table, since the numbers can be easily given in the text. If 15 or 20 means are involved, however, then a table is much easier for the reader to process than a string of numbers in the text. In general, tables are preferable to figures for conveying exact values and for handling large sets of data (such as 15 or 20 means). Figures are especially useful for illustrating trends or interactions.

Several further rules govern the use of tables and figures. A table or figure should not repeat data given in the text or in another table or figure. If the same information appears in two places, one of the sources should be dropped. A table or figure should be largely self-explanatory—that is, comprehensible without reference to a detailed explanation in the text. Finally, although the table or figure may be self-explanatory, discussion of what it shows is still quite appropriate. Tables and figures supplement the text; they do not replace it.

Discussion

The Discussion section is the author's opportunity to draw everything together and to state the conclusions that he or she wishes the reader to take away. This section should have close links to both the Introduction and the Results. The Introduction lays out the questions that the research is intended to answer; the Discussion summarizes the answers that the researcher believes have emerged. The Results presents the data that the study has generated; the Discussion interprets these data and works always within their constraints. Whatever the author may have expected or hoped would occur, the data are the ultimate determinants of what the Discussion has to say.

For many authors, the Discussion is the hardest part of the paper to write (especially when the results are not all that was hoped!). We offer here a few "don'ts"—practices to

---

[1]Devereux (1970) provides an excellent discussion of how to interweave statistics with readable prose.

avoid when writing a Discussion section (and to watch for when reading one).

The Discussion should not simply reiterate the results already presented in the Results section. Some summarizing of findings is fine as a prelude to their interpretation. It is the job of the Results section, however, to make clear what the basic data are. The job of the Discussion is to explain the data.

With very rare exceptions, findings not previously presented should not be introduced in the Discussion. The place to introduce new data is the Results.

As with other sections of the article, the Discussion should follow a clear and logical sequence. Some students write Discussions in what has been called a "striptease" manner, beginning with peripheral points and only gradually working up to their main conclusions. Usually, it is most helpful to the reader if the major conclusions are stated early in the Discussion. Elaborations, qualifications, and subsidiary points can be worked in later.

The Discussion need not devote equal space to every hypothesis or every finding. Some weighting in terms of importance is one of the author's responsibilities. Too much selectivity, however, can result in a distortion of the study's results. It may be misleading, for example, to focus on the one finding that supported a particular hypothesis, while ignoring three others that failed to support it.

It is quite appropriate for a Discussion section to venture beyond the immediate data into various speculations about the more far-reaching implications of the research. Some authors, however, venture so far afield that they lose sight of the study that they are supposedly discussing. Such wandering may sometimes be a method of compensating for results that were not as strong as had been hoped. In any case, every point made in the Discussion should have a clear link to the research being reported.

One common method of concluding a Discussion section is with suggestions for future research. This practice is fine, as long as the suggestions are (1) specific; (2) sensible; and (3) concisely stated. Merely saying that more research is needed, however, does not tell the reader anything.

Another common method of concluding a Discussion is with a consideration of any weaknesses in the study that the author believes may have affected the results. This practice too is fine; indeed, some discussion of possible shortcomings can be seen as a basic form of honesty that the author owes the reader. It is important, however, not to dwell on the shortcomings or to become overly defensive or overly apologetic. For if the Discussion section is devoted mainly to negatives, the obvious question in the reader's mind will be "Why should I take this research seriously?" And the obvious question in an editor's mind will be "Why should this research be published?"

Other Sections

Although the Introduction, Method, Results, and Discussion constitute the main body, they do not exhaust the distinct parts of a research report. Table 12–1 provides a more comprehensive account of the different sections into which research reports are divided. The sections are listed in the order in which they would be typed in a submission to a journal. Again, a fuller discussion of what is appropriate for each section can be found in the APA *Manual*.

SOME SPECIFIC STYLISTIC POINTS

APA Conventions

As noted, our discussion here is quite selective, focusing on a few rules that are often violated in student papers.

Headings. APA style permits five levels of heading. These levels are shown in Table 12–2. When only one heading is needed (usually in very short articles), Level 2, the centered uppercase and lowercase heading, is used. When two headings are needed, Levels 2 and 4 are used. When three levels of heading are needed, the indented paragraph heading is added. Use of four or five headings is rare, being confined

TABLE 12-1 Sections of a Research Report

Section	Description
Title	Should be brief (maximum length: 12 to 15 words), clear, and informative. Avoid unnecessary phrases like "A Study of."
Abstract	Summarizes the study in 100 to 150 words (depending on the journal). Should include information about the problem being studied, method of study, major results, and major conclusions.
Introduction	Conveys to the reader the problem under investigation, the reasons for interest in this problem, and the status of current knowledge based on a review of relevant past research. Concludes with an overview of the present study, including specific goals and specific hypotheses.
Method	Summarizes how the study was carried out, including information about subject groups, apparatus or materials, and experimental procedures. Should be detailed enough to permit evaluation.
Results	Presents the major data obtained in the research, as well as the statistical analyses of the data.
Discussion	Interprets the results of the study. Should place the data in the theoretical context provided by the Introduction and should attempt to answer the specific questions or evaluate the specific hypotheses presented in the Introduction.
References	Present the sources for any references that were cited in the text. References are listed in alphabetical order.
Appendix	Presents relatively lengthy material (e.g., mathematical proofs, lists of stimulus materials) that would be difficult or inappropriate to convey in the text. Use should be minimized.
Footnotes	Present relatively brief material that would be difficult or inappropriate to convey in the body of the text. Use should be minimized.
Tables	Summarize bodies of data that can be more efficiently conveyed in a table than in the text.
Figure Captions	Describe the contents of each figure included in the article.
Figures	Summarize bodies of data for which a figural presentation is efficient and informative.

mainly to reports of multiple studies or to lengthy reviews or theoretical articles.

Measurements. APA policy is to express measurements in metric units—thus millimeters rather than inches, meters rather than yards, and so forth. Measurements expressed in nonmetric units are acceptable if accompanied by the metric equivalent—for example, "The rod was 3 ft (.91 m) in length."

Numbers in the text. For the most part, the numbers zero through nine are expressed in words, whereas numbers of two digits or more

are expressed in figures. Thus, "There were eight experimenters and 120 subjects." One exception to this rule is that a figure is never used to start a sentence (thus, "One hundred and twenty subjects participated in the study."). Other exceptions are given in the APA *Manual*.

Statistics in the text. The author must always make clear which statistical tests were used on which aspects of the data. Thus, "Correct responses on the posttest were analyzed via a two-way analysis of variance, with age and condition as the independent variables." Sources

TABLE 12-2 Levels of Heading in APA Journals

Type of Heading	Example
CENTERED UPPERCASE HEADING (Level 1)	EXPERIMENT 1: AN INTERVIEW VALIDATION STUDY
Centered Uppercase and Lowercase Heading (Level 2)	External Validation
Centered, Underlined, Uppercase and Lowercase Heading (Level 3)	Method
Flush Left, Underlined, Uppercase and Lowercase Side Heading (Level 4)	Subjects
Indented, underlined, lowercase, paragraph heading ending with a period. (Level 5)	The nonclinical group.

do not need to be given for statistical tests, unless the test is an unusual one or its use is in some way controversial. Summaries of the results of statistical tests should include the name of the statistic, the degrees of freedom, the value of the statistic, and the probability level—for example, "There was a significant effect of age, $F(1,96) = 7.90$, $p < .01$." Note that the statistical summary is set off from the text with commas, not parentheses.

References in the text. The APA form for references in the text is the one used throughout this book: the name of the author and the date of publication, enclosed in parentheses—for example, "(Smith, 1982)." When the author's name is part of the text only the date appears in parentheses—for example, "Smith (1982) reported. . . . " When a work has two authors, both names are always cited; in the text they are connected by "and," and within parentheses they are connected by an ampersand (&). When a work has three to five authors all names are cited on first mention; on subsequent mentions the citation consists of the name of the first author followed by "et al." When a work has six or more authors the "et al." is used even on first citation. When a parenthesis contains multiple citations by the same author the references are listed chronologically; when a parenthesis contains multiple citations by *different* authors the references are listed *alphabetically*. Thus, "(Smith, 1974, 1979, 1982)" and "(Brown, 1979; Jones, 1974; Smith, 1982)."

Reference list. The reference for every source cited in the text must be given in the References at the end of the article. *Only* sources cited in the text are included in the References. Authors must be certain that information provided in the References is accurate, so that interested readers can track down sources if they wish. Authors must also follow APA rules for References, rules that occupy a full 23 pages in the *Manual*!

General Matters of English

Our discussion here is even more selective (and idiosyncratic). What follows is a potpourri of points of English usage that are frequently violated in student papers (and elsewhere).

Affect–effect. Both "affect" and "effect" can be used as either nouns or verbs. In their most common uses, however, "affect" is a verb meaning influence, and "effect" is a noun meaning outcome or result. Thus, "Did the manipulation affect performance? The posttest showed a clear effect."

Contractions. Don't (i.e., do not) use contractions.

Data. "Data" is a plural noun. Thus, "The data were clear." not "The data was clear." Similarly, "criteria" and "phenomena" are plural nouns and require plural verbs. The singular forms are "datum" (rarely used), "criterion," and "phenomenon."

e.g.–i.e. The abbreviation "e.g." means for example; the abbreviation "i.e." means that is. Thus, "Numerous theorists (e.g., Brown, 1979; Smith, 1982) have claimed that. . . . " and "What seemed critical was the experimental manipulation (i.e., the presence or absence of reward)." The common mistake is to use "i.e." where "e.g." is appropriate. (Note that APA policy is to restrict the use of "e.g." and "i.e." to material within parentheses.)

Fewer–less. "Fewer" refers to number when countable objects are involved; "less" refers to amount or degree along some continuous, noncountable dimension. Thus, "The control subjects gave fewer correct responses." and "The control subjects showed less success." The common mistake is to use "less" in place of "fewer," as in "The control subjects gave less correct responses."

It's–its. "It's" is a contraction meaning it is or it has; "its" is a possessive meaning belonging to it. The mistake here is to use "it's" as a possessive, apparently out of the belief that possessives should have apostrophes in them.

Only. Although exceptions exist, the word "only" should usually come immediately before the word that it modifies. Thus, "The failure manipulation produced visible distress in only two children." not "The failure manipulation only produced visible distress in two children."

Pronouns. Various issues related to the use of pronouns can be problematic. The APA *Manual* indicates that use of the first person singular pronoun is now acceptable in scientific writing, and is even preferable to an exclusive reliance on the third person and passive voice. Students should be aware, however, that use of "I" is still rare, being confined mainly to senior (or perhaps very confident) researchers and theoretically oriented papers. Use of "I" in a routine research report is likely to be jarring to many readers. (For an interesting discussion of the first person versus third person issue, see Polyson, Levinson, and Miller, 1982.)

The *Manual* also encourages the use of nonsexist terms, including nonsexist pronouns; indeed, one of the additions to the newest version of the *Manual* is entitled "Guidelines for Nonsexist Language in APA Journals." Students should read this section carefully and refer to it when writing. It is important, however, that the search for nonsexist language does not impair the grammaticality or readability of the paper. Thus sentences of the following sort should be avoided: "The child was told to push his or her button as soon as he or she saw the flash appear on his or her screen." Arbitrary changes in sex of pronoun should also be avoided. Thus if the generic child starts the article as "she," then "she" should be used throughout (although in longer works, such as the present book, some switching is allowable as an alternative to the exclusive use either of one gender or of the sometimes awkward "he or she"). Finally, "it" should never be used in referring to a child, even a very young infant.

A final point is a matter of basic English: Pronouns should agree in number with their antecedents. Thus, "Each subject filled out his or her response sheet." not "Each subject filled out their response sheet."

Tense. A journal article reports events that have already occurred. For the most part,

therefore, past tense is appropriate—thus, "Smith reported," "Subjects were told," "The analysis revealed." Present tense can be used when discussing results that are literally there before the reader—for example, "The table shows." Present tense is also appropriate when making statements that are essentially timeless—"The theory states," "Young children are often impulsive," "Conservation is an important ability."

SUMMARY

The final step in a research project is communicating one's work to others. This chapter discusses how to write research reports in psychology.

The chapter begins by emphasizing the importance of writing well, noting that the clarity and persuasiveness with which research is presented have a direct bearing on the impact that the research is likely to have. A well-written article is more likely to be published than is a poorly written one, and is more likely to be attended to and assimilated after publication. A number of suggestions are offered for improving the effectiveness of one's writing. A first suggestion is to read good examples of writing in psychology, drawing from such models ideas about both what to say and how to say it. A second suggestion is to seek simplicity in writing, for jargonese and needless complexity are obstacles to clear communication. A third suggestion is to aim for variety in writing, the goal being to produce prose that is not only clear but also interesting and readable. A fourth suggestion is to be economical in writing, because both journal space and reader patience can be quickly exhausted by irrelevant detail or unnecessary wordiness. The final suggestion is to be careful when writing, because many obvious errors can be avoided if the author takes the time to be sure that every part of the manuscript is exactly what he or she intends.

The middle part of the chapter discusses the major sections into which psychology research reports are divided. Two general issues are considered for each section: what material should be included, and how this material should be conveyed. The Introduction presents the issues and goals that underlie the study. It sets the research in the context of relevant past work and prepares the reader for the specific study to follow. The Method describes the subject groups included in the study and the procedures used to collect the data. It should be detailed enough to permit critical evaluation of the research. The Results section summarizes the data produced by the study. It presents both descriptive statistics (e.g., mean levels of response) and inferential statistics (e.g., tests of significance for the differences between means), along with summary statements of what the statistics mean.

The Discussion interprets the results of the study. It answers questions posed in the Introduction, evaluates any specific hypotheses that were offered, and summarizes the author's assessment of what the research has and has not accomplished.

The concluding section of the chapter discusses specific stylistic points that often prove troublesome for students. Included are both matters of APA style (e.g., rules for headings and references) and matters of English grammar—i.e., don't write passages like this one, which would be likely, even if they contained less errors (and there are five here), to effect the reader negatively.

REFERENCES

ABRAHAMS, J. P., HOYER, W. J., ELIAS, M. F., & BRADIGAN, B. (1975). Gerontological research in psychology published in the *Journal of Gerontology,* 1963–1974: Perspectives and progress. *Journal of Gerontology, 30,* 668–673.

ACHENBACH, T. M. (1978). *Research in developmental psychology: Concepts, strategies, methods.* New York: The Free Press.

ACREDOLO, L. P., & HAKE, J. L. (1982). Infant perception. In B. B. Wolman (Ed.), *Handbook of developmental psychology* (pp. 244–283). Englewood Cliffs, NJ: Prentice-Hall.

AINSWORTH, M. D. S. (1967). *Infancy in Uganda: Infant care and the growth of love.* Baltimore: Johns Hopkins University Press.

AINSWORTH, M. D. S., BELL, S. M., & STAYTON, D. J. (1974). Infant mother attachment and social development: "Socialization" as a product of reciprocal responsiveness to signals. In M. P. M. Richards (Ed.), *The integration of a child into a social world* (pp. 99–135). Cambridge, Eng.: Cambridge University Press.

AINSWORTH, M. D. S., BLEHAR, M. C., WATERS, E., & WALL, S. (1978). *Patterns of attachment: A psychological study of the strange situation.* Hillsdale, NJ: Lawrence Erlbaum Associates.

ALS, H., TRONICK, E., & BRAZELTON, T. B. (1979). Analysis of face-to-face interaction in infant-adult dyads. In M. E. Lamb, S. J. Suomi, & G. R. Stephenson (Eds.), *Social interaction analysis: Methodological issues* (pp. 33–76). Madison: The University of Wisconsin Press.

American Psychological Association. (1973). *Ethical principles in the conduct of research with human participants.* Washington, DC: Author.

American Psychological Association. (1983). *Publication manual of the American Psychological Association* (3rd ed.). Washington, DC: Author.

ANDERS, T. F., & ROFFWARG, H. P. (1973). The effects of selective interruption and deprivation of sleep on the human newborn. *Developmental Psychobiology, 6,* 77–89.

APPLEBAUM, M. I., & McCALL, R. B. (1983). Design and analysis in developmental psychology. In P. H. Mussen (Ed.), *Handbook of child psychology: Volume 1. History, theory, and methods* (4th ed., pp. 415–476). New York: Wiley.

ARONFREED, J., & LEFF, R. (1963). *The effects of intensity of punishment and complexity of discrimination upon the generalization of an internalized inhibition.* Unpublished manuscript, University of Pennsylvania.

ARONFREED, J., & REBER, A. (1965). Internalized behavioral suppression and the timing of social punishment. *Journal of Personality and Social Psychology, 1,* 3–16.

ASHMEAD, D. H., & PERLMUTTER, M. (1980). Infant memory in everyday life. In M. Perlmutter (Ed.), *New directions for child development: Volume 10. Children's memory* (pp. 1–16). San Francisco: Jossey-Bass.

ASLIN, R. N., PISONI, D. B., & JUSCZYK, P. W. (1983). Auditory development and speech perception in infancy. In P. H. Mussen (Ed.), *Handbook of child psychology: Volume 2. Infancy and developmental psychobiology* (4th ed., pp. 573–687). New York: Wiley.

BAHRICK, H. P. (1983). The cognitive map of a city—50 years of learning and memory. In G. Bower (Ed.), *The psychology of learn-*

ing and motivation: Advances in research and theory (Volume 17, pp. 125–163). New York: Academic Press.

BAHRICK, H. P. (1984). Semantic memory content in permastore: Fifty years of memory for Spanish learned in school. *Journal of Experimental Psychology: General, 113,* 1–26.

BAHRICK, H. P., BAHRICK, P. O., & WITTLINGER, R. P. (1975). Fifty years of memory for names and faces: A cross-sectional approach. *Journal of Experimental Psychology: General, 104,* 54–75.

BALTES, P. B., & BRIM, O. G., Jr. (Eds.). (1983). *Life-span development and behavior* (Vol. 5). New York: Academic Press.

BALTES, P. B., REESE, H. W., & NESSELROADE, J. R. (1977). *Life-span developmental psychology: Introduction to research methods.* Monterey, CA: Brooks/Cole.

BALTES, P. B., & SCHAIE, K. W. (1974). Aging and IQ: The myth of the twilight years. *Psychology Today, 7,* 35–40.

BALTES, P. B., & SCHAIE, K. W. (1976). On the plasticity of intelligence in adulthood and old age: Where Horn and Donaldson fail. *American Psychologist, 31,* 720–725.

BANDURA, A. (1977). *Social learning theory.* Englewood Cliffs, NJ: Prentice-Hall.

BANDURA, A., GRUSEC, J. E., & MENLOVE, F. L. (1967). Some social determinants of self-monitoring reinforcement systems *Journal of Personality and Social Psychology, 5,* 449–455.

BANDURA, A., ROSS, D., & ROSS, S. A. (1963a). Imitation of film-mediated aggressive models. *Journal of Abnormal and Social Psychology, 66,* 3–11.

BANDURA, A., ROSS, D., & ROSS, S. A. (1963b). Vicarious reinforcement and imitative learning. *Journal of Abnormal and Social Psychology, 67,* 601–607.

BANKS, M. S., & SALAPATEK, P. (1983). Infant visual perception. In P. H. Mussen (Ed.), *Handbook of child psychology: Volume 2. Infancy and developmental psychobiology* (4th ed., pp. 435–571). New York: Wiley.

BARBER, T. X. (1976). *Pitfalls in human research: Ten pivotal points.* New York: Pergamon Press.

BARBER, T. X., & SILVER, M. J. (1968). Fact, fiction, and the experimenter bias effect. *Psychological Bulletin Monograph Supplement, 70,* 1–29.

BARKER, R. G., & WRIGHT, H. F. (1951). *One boy's day.* New York: Harper & Row.

BARNETT, M. A., KING, L. M., & HOWARD, J. A. (1979). Inducing affect about self or other: Effects on generosity in children. *Developmental Psychology, 15,* 164–167.

BARON, J., & TREIMAN, R. (1980). Some problems in the study of differences in cognitive processes. *Memory and Cognition, 4,* 313–321.

BARRETT, D. E., & YARROW, M. R. (1977). Prosocial behavior, social inferential ability, and assertiveness in children. *Child Development, 48,* 475–481.

BATES, J. E. (1980). The concept of difficult temperament. *Merrill-Palmer Quarterly, 26,* 299–319.

BATES, J. E. (1983). Issues in the assessment of difficult temperament: A reply to Thomas, Chess, and Korn. *Merrill-Palmer Quarterly, 29,* 89–97.

BATES, J. E., FREELAND, C. A. B., & LOUNSBURY, M. L. (1979). Measurement of infant difficultness. *Child Development, 50,* 794–803.

BAUMRIND, D. (1985). Research using intentional deception: Ethical issues revisited. *American Psychologist, 40,* 165–174.

BAYLEY, N. (1969). *Bayley Scales of Infant Development: Birth to Two Years.* New York: The Psychological Corporation.

BAYLEY, N. (1970). Development of mental abilities. In P. H. Mussen (Ed.), *Carmichael's manual of child psychology* (3rd ed., Vol. 1, pp. 1163–1209). New York: Wiley.

BAYLOR, G. W., GASCON, J., LEMOYNE, G., & POTHIER, N. (1973). An information processing model of some seriation tasks. *Canadian Psychologist, 14,* 167–196.

BEILIN, H. (1965). Learning and operational convergence in logical thought development. *Journal of Experimental Child Psychology, 2,* 317–339.

BELL, R. Q. (1968). A reinterpretation of the direction of effects of socialization. *Psychological Review, 75,* 81–95.

BEM, S. L. (1974). The measurement of psychological androgyny. *Journal of Consulting and Clinical Psychology, 42,* 155–162.

BERG, K. M., BERG, W. K., & GRAHAM, F. K. (1971). Infant heart rate response as a function of stimulus and state. *Psychophysiology, 8,* 30–44.

BERG, W. K., ADKINSON, C. D., & STROCK, B. D. (1973). Duration and frequency of periods of alertness in neonates. *Developmental Psychology, 9,* 434.

BERG, W. K., & BERG, K. M. (1979). Psychophysiological development in infancy: State, sensory function, and attention. In J. D. Osofsky (Ed.), *The handbook of infant development* (pp. 283–343). New York: Wiley.

BERG-CROSS, L. G. (1975). Intentionality, degree of damage, and moral judgments. *Child Development, 46,* 970–974.

BIRREN, J. E., & MORRISON, D. F. (1961). Analysis of the WAIS subtests in relation to age and education. *Journal of Gerontology, 16,* 363–369.

BIRREN, J. E., WOODS, A. M., & WILLIAMS, M. V. (1980). Behavioral slowing with age: Causes, organization, and consequences. In L. W. Poon (Ed.), *Aging in the 1980s: Psychological issues* (pp. 293–308). Washington, DC: American Psychological Association.

BLAIR, R. C., & HIGGINS, J. J. (1980). A comparison of the power of Wilcoxon's rank sum statistic to that of student's *t* statistic under various nonnormal distributions. *Journal of Educational Statistics, 5,* 309–335.

BLASI, A. (1980). Bridging moral cognition and moral action. *Psychological Bulletin, 88,* 593–637.

BLOCK, J. H. (1976). Issues, problems, and pitfalls in assessing sex differences: A critical review of *The psychology of sex differences. Merrill-Palmer Quarterly, 22,* 285–308.

BOCK, R. D. (1975). *Multivariate statistical methods in behavioral research.* New York: McGraw-Hill.

BORNSTEIN, M. H. (1978). Chromatic vision in infancy. In H. W. Reese & L. P. Lipsitt (Eds.), *Advances in child development and behavior* (Vol. 12, pp. 117–182). New York: Academic Press.

BOTWINICK, J. (1977). Intellectual abilities. In J. E. Birren & K. W. Schaie (Eds.), *Handbook of the psychology of aging* (pp. 580–605). New York: Van Nostrand Reinhold.

BOTWINICK, J. (1984). *Aging and behavior* (3rd ed.). New York: Springer.

BOTWINICK, J., & ARENBERG, D. (1976). Disparate time spans in sequential studies of aging. *Experimental Aging Research, 1,* 55–61.

BOTWINICK, J., & BIRREN, J. E. (1963). Cognitive processes: Mental abilities and psychomotor responses in healthy aged men. In J. E. Birren, R. N. Butler, S. W. Greenhouse, L. Sokoloff, & M. R. Yarrow (Eds.), *Human aging* (pp. 97–108). Washington, DC: U.S. Government Printing Office.

BOTWINICK, J., & STORANDT, M. (1974). *Memory, related functions, and age.* Springfield, IL: Charles C. Thomas.

BOTWINICK, J., WEST, R., & STORANDT, M. (1978). Predicting death from behavioral test performance. *Journal of Gerontology, 33,* 755–762.

BOWER, T. G. R. (1966). The visual world of infants. *Scientific American, 215,* 90–92.

BOWER, T. G. R. (1982). *Development in infancy* (2nd ed.). San Francisco: W. H. Freeman.

BOWLBY, J. (1952). *Maternal care and mental health* (2nd ed.). Geneva: World Health Organization.

BRANSFORD, J. D., BARCLAY, J. R., & FRANKS, J. J. (1972). Sentence memory: A constructive vs. interpretive approach. *Cognitive Psychology, 3,* 193–209.

BRAZELTON, T. B. (1973). *Neonatal Behavioral Assessment Scale.* London: Spastics International Medical Publications.

BRINLEY, J. F. (1965). *Rigidity and the control of cognitive sets in relation to speed and accuracy of performance in the elderly.* Unpublished doctoral dissertation, Catholic University of America.

BROADBENT, D. E. (1958). *Perception and communication.* London: Pergamon Press.

BRONFENBRENNER, U. (1977). Toward an experimental ecology of human development. *American Psychologist, 32,* 513–531.

BRONFENBRENNER, U. (1979). *The ecology of human development.* Cambridge, MA: Harvard University Press.

BROOKS, P. H., & KENDALL, E. D. (1982). Working with children. In R. Vasta (Ed.), *Strategies and techniques of child study* (pp. 325–343). New York: Academic Press.

BROWN, A. L. (1982). Learning to learn how to read. In J. Langer & T. Smith-Burke (Eds.), *Reader meets author, bridging the gap: A psycholinguistic perspective* (pp. 26–54). Newark, NJ: Dell.

BROWN, A. L., SMILEY, S. S., DAY, J. D., TOWNSEND, M. A. R., & LAWTON, S. C. (1977). Intrusion of a thematic idea in children's comprehension and retention of stories. *Child Development, 48,* 1454–1466.

BROWN, D. G. (1956). Sex role preference in young children. *Psychological Monographs, 70* (14, Whole No. 421).

BROWN, D. G. (1962). Sex-role preference in children: Methodological problems. *Psychological Reports, 11,* 477–478.

BROWN, R. (1973). *A first language: The early stages.* Cambridge, MA: Harvard University Press.

BRYANT, B. K. (1982). An index of empathy for children and adolescents. *Child Development, 53,* 412–425.

BRYANT, P. E., & TRABASSO, T. (1971). Transitive inferences and memory in young children. *Nature, 232,* 456–458.

BUCHANAN, J. P., & THOMPSON, S. K. (1973). A quantitative methodology to examine the development of moral judgment. *Child Development, 44,* 186–189.

BUCHER, B., & SCHNEIDER, R. E. (1973). Acquisition and generalization of conservation by pre-schoolers, using operant training. *Journal of Experimental Child Psychology, 16,* 187–204.

BURT, C. (1966). The genetic determination of differences in intelligence: A study of monozygotic twins reared together and apart. *British Journal of Psychology, 57,* 137–153.

BURT, C. (1972). Inheritance of general intelligence. *American Psychologist, 27,* 175–190.

BUSS, A. H., & PLOMIN, R. (1975). *A temperament theory of personality development.* New York: Wiley.

CAIRNS, R. B., & GREEN, J. A. (1979). How to assess personality and social patterns: Observations or ratings? In R. B. Cairns (Ed.), *The analysis of social interactions: Methods, issues, and illustrations* (pp. 209–226). Hillsdale, NJ: Lawrence Erlbaum Associates.

CAMPBELL, D. T., & STANLEY, J. C. (1966). *Experimental and quasi-experimental designs for research.* Chicago: Rand McNally.

CAMPOS, J. J., BARRETT, K. C., LAMB, M. E., GOLDSMITH, H. H., & STENBERG, C. (1983). Socioemotional development. In P. H. Mussen (Ed.), *Handbook of child psychology: Volume 2. Infancy and developmental psychobiology* (4th ed., pp. 793–915). New York: Wiley.

CAMPOS, J. J., LANGER, A., & KROWITZ, A. (1970). Cardiac responses on the visual cliff in prelocomotor human infants. *Science, 170,* 196–197.

CAREY, W. B., & McDEVITT, S. C. (1978). Revision of the infant temperament questionnaire. *Pediatrics, 61,* 735–739.

CASLER, L. (1961). Maternal deprivation: A critical review of the literature. *Monographs of the Society for Research in Child Development, 26* (2, Serial No. 80).

CERELLA, J., POON, L. W., & WILLIAMS, D. M. (1980). Age and the complexity hypothesis. In L. W. Poon (Ed.), *Aging in the 1980s* (pp. 332–340). Washington, DC: American Psychological Association.

CHANDLER, M. J., GREENSPAN, M., & BARENBOIM, C. (1973). Judgments of intentionality in response to videotaped and verbally presented moral dilemmas: The medium is the message. *Child Development, 44,* 315–320.

CHARLESWORTH, W. R. (1966, September). *Development of the object concept: A methodological study.* Paper presented at the meeting of the American Psychological Association, New York.

CHIRIBOGA, D. A., & CUTLER, L. (1980). Stress and adaptation: Life span perspectives. In L. W. Poon (Ed.), *Aging in the 1980s: Psychological issues* (pp. 347–362). Washington, DC: American Psychological Association.

CLARKE-STEWART, K. A. (1973). Interactions between mothers and their young children: Characteristics and consequences. *Monographs of the Society for Research in Child Development, 38,* (6–7, Serial No. 153).

COHEN, G. (1979). Language comprehension in old age. *Cognitive Psychology, 11,* 412–429.

COHEN, G. (1981). Inferential reasoning in old age. *Cognition, 9,* 59–72.

COHEN, J. (1977). *Statistical power analysis for the behavioral sciences* (rev. ed.). New York: Academic Press.

COHEN, J., & COHEN, P. (1983). *Applied multiple regression/correlation analysis for the behavioral sciences* (2nd ed.). Hillsdale, NJ: Lawrence Erlbaum Associates.

COLBY, A. (1978). Evaluation of a moral-developmental theory. In W. Damon (Ed.), *New directions for child development: Volume 2. Moral development* (pp. 89–104). San Francisco: Jossey-Bass.

COLBY, A., KOHLBERG, L., GIBBS, J., CANDEE, D., HEWER, A., POWER, C., & SPEICHER-DUBIN, B. (in press). *Measurement of moral judgment: Standard issue scoring manual.* New York: Cambridge University Press.

COLBY, A., KOHLBERG, L., GIBBS, J., & LIEBERMAN, M. (1983). A longitudinal study of moral judgment. *Monographs of the Society for Research in Child Development, 48* (1–2, Serial No. 200).

COLE, M., FRANKEL, F., & SHARP, D. (1971). Development of free recall learning in children. *Developmental Psychology, 4,* 109–123.

CONDRY, J., & CONDRY, S. (1976). Sex differences: A study of the eye of the beholder. *Child Development, 47,* 812–819.

COOK, T. D., & CAMPBELL, D. T. (1979). *Quasi-Experimentation.* Boston: Houghton Mifflin.

COOKE, R. A. (1982). The ethics and regulation of research involving children. In B. B. Wolman (Ed.), *Handbook of develop-*

mental psychology (pp. 149–172). Englewood Cliffs, NJ: Prentice-Hall.

COSTA, P. T., JR., & McCRAE, R. R. (1978). Objective personality assessment. In M. Storandt, I. C. Siegler, & M. F. Elias (Eds.), *The clinical psychology of aging* (pp. 119–143). New York: Plenum.

CUMMING, E., & HENRY, W. E. (1961). *Growing old: The process of disengagement.* New York: Basic Books.

CUNNINGHAM, W. R. (1980). Speed, age, and qualitative differences in cognitive functioning. In L. W. Poon (Ed.), *Aging in the 1980s: Psychological issues* (pp. 327–331). Washington, DC: American Psychological Association.

DAMON, W. (1977). *The social world of the child.* San Francisco: Jossey-Bass.

DARWIN, C. (1877). Biographical sketch of an infant. *Mind, 2,* 285–294.

DAWE, H. C. (1934). An analysis of two hundred quarrels of preschool children. *Child Development, 5,* 139–157.

DeLOACHE, J. S. (1980). Naturalistic studies of memory for object location in very young children. In M. Perlmutter (Ed.), *New directions for child development: Volume 10. Children's memory* (pp. 17–32). San Francisco: Jossey-Bass.

DEMMING, J. A., & PRESSEY, S. L. (1957). Tests "indigenous" to the adult and older years. *Journal of Counseling Psychology, 2,* 144–148.

DENNEY, N. W. (1974). Clustering in middle and old age. *Developmental Psychology, 10,* 471–475.

DEUR, J. L., & PARKE, R. D. (1970). Effects of inconsistent punishment on aggression in children. *Developmental Psychology, 2,* 403–411.

DEVEREUX, E. C. (1970). Some reflections on research reporting in psychology: An editorial. *Child Development, 41,* 901–907.

DeVRIES, R. (1969). Constancy of generic identity in the years three to six. *Monographs of the Society for Research in Child Development, 34* (3, Serial No. 127).

Division of Developmental Psychology of the American Psychological Association (1968, Spring). Ethical standards in psychological research. *Newsletter,* 1–3.

DODD, D. H., & SCHULTZ, R. F. (1970). Computational procedures for estimating magnitude of effect for some analysis of variance designs. *Psychological Bulletin, 79,* 391–395.

DONALDSON, M. (1982). Conservation: What is the question? *British Journal of Psychology, 73,* 199–207.

DRAPER, N. R., & SMITH, H. (1981). *Applied regression analyses* (2nd ed.). New York: Wiley.

DUNN, J., & KENDRICK, C. (1980). Studying temperament and parent-child interaction: Comparison of interview and direct observation. *Developmental Medicine and Child Neurology, 22,* 484–496.

DUNN, L. M., & DUNN, L. M. (1981). *Peabody Picture Vocabulary Test—Revised.* Circle Pines, MN: American Guidance Service.

DWYER, J. H. (1974). Analysis of variance and the magnitude of effects: A general approach. *Psychological Bulletin, 81,* 731–737.

EDELBROCK, C., & SUGAWARA, A. I. (1978). Acquisition of sex-typed preferences in preschool-aged children. *Developmental Psychology, 14,* 614–623.

EDWARDS, C. P. (1980). The comparative study of the development of moral judgment and reasoning. In R. L. Munroe, R. Munroe, & B. B. Whiting (Eds.), *Handbook of cross-cultural human development* (pp. 501–528). New York: Garland.

EDWARDS, J., & KLEMMACK, D. (1973). Correlates of life satisfaction: A reexamination. *Journal of Gerontology, 28,* 497–502.

EISDORFER, C., & WILKIE, F. (1977). Stress, disease, aging, and behavior. In J. E. Birren & K. W. Schaie (Eds.), *Handbook of the psychology of aging* (pp. 251–275). New York: Van Nostrand Reinhold.

EISENBERG, N. (1982). The development of reasoning regarding prosocial behavior. In N. Eisenberg (Ed.), *The development of prosocial behavior* (pp. 219–249). New York: Academic Press.

EISENBERG-BERG, N. (1979). Development of children's prosocial moral judgment. *Developmental Psychology, 15,* 128–137.

ELLIS, G. T., & SEKYRA, F. (1972). The effect of aggressive cartoons on the behavior of first grade children. *Journal of Psychology, 81,* 37–43.

EMMERICH, W., & GOLDMAN, K. S. (1972). Boy-girl identity task. In V. Shipman (Ed.), *Disadvantaged children and their first school experiences* (ETS PR-72-20). Princeton, NJ: Educational Testing Service.

ENGEN, T., LIPSITT, L. P., & KAYE, H. (1963). Olfactory responses and adaptation in the human neonate. *Journal of Comparative and Physiological Psychology, 56,* 73–77.

FAGAN, J. (1973). Infants' delayed recognition memory and forgetting. *Journal of Experimental Child Psychology, 16,* 424–450.

FAGOT, B. I. (1977). Consequences of moderate cross-gender behavior in preschool children. *Child Development, 48,* 902–907.

FAGOT, B. I. (1982). Sex role development. In R. Vasta (Ed.), *Strategies and techniques of child study* (pp. 273–303). New York: Academic Press.

FANTZ, R. L. (1961). The origin of form perception. *Scientific American, 204,* 66–72.

FARBER, S. L. (1981). *Identical twins reared apart: A reanalysis.* New York: Basic Books.

FERGUSON, R. P., & BRAY, N. W. (1976). Component processes of an overt rehearsal strategy in young children. *Journal of Experimental Child Psychology, 21,* 490–506.

FESHBACH, N. D., & ROE, K. (1968). Empathy in six- and seven-year-olds. *Child Development, 39,* 133–145.

FESHBACH, S., & SINGER, R. D. (1971). *Television and aggression: An experimental field study.* San Francisco: Jossey-Bass.

FIELD, J. (1977). Coordination of vision and prehension in young infants. *Child Development, 48,* 97–103.

FIELD, T. (1982). Infancy. In R. Vasta (Ed.), *Strategies and techniques of child study* (pp. 13–48). New York: Academic Press.

FIELD, T., & GREENBERG, R. (1982). Temperament ratings by parents and teachers of infants, toddlers, and preschool children. *Child Development, 53,* 160–163.

FLAVELL, J. H. (1963). *The developmental psychology of Jean Piaget.* Princeton, NJ: Van Nostrand.

FLAVELL, J. H. (1974). The development of inferences about others. In T. Mischel (Ed.), *Understanding other persons* (pp. 66–116). Oxford, Eng.: Blackwell, Basil, and Mott.

FLAVELL, J. H. (1978). The development of knowledge about visual perception. In C. B. Keasey (Ed.), *Nebraska symposium on motivation* (Vol. 25, pp. 43–76). Lincoln: University of Nebraska Press.

FLAVELL, J. H. (1982). Structures, stages, and sequences in cognitive development. In W. A. Collins (Ed.), *Minnesota symposia on child psychology* (Vol. 15, pp. 1–28). Hillsdale, NJ: Lawrence Erlbaum Associates.

FLAVELL, J. H. (1985). *Cognitive development* (2nd ed.). Englewood Cliffs, NJ: Prentice Hall.

FLAVELL, J. H., BEACH, D. H., & CHINSKY, J. M. (1966). Spontaneous verbal rehearsal in memory tasks as a function of age. *Child Development, 37,* 283–299.

FLAVELL, J. H., BOTKIN, P. T., FRY, C. L., Jr., WRIGHT, J. W., & JARVIS, P. E. (1968). *The development of role-taking and communication skills in children.* New York: Wiley.

FLING, S., & MANOSEVITZ, M. (1972). Sex typing in nursery school children's play interests. *Developmental Psychology, 7,* 146–152.

FREEDMAN, J. L. (1984). Effect of television violence on aggressiveness. *Psychological Bulletin, 96,* 227–246.

FURBY, L. (1973). Interpreting regression toward the mean in developmental research. *Developmental Psychology, 8,* 172–179.

FURTH, H. G., BAUR, M., & SMITH, J. E. (1976). Children's conception of social institutions: A Piagetian framework. *Human Development, 19,* 351–374.

GARDNER, E. F., & MONGE, R. H. (1977). Adult age differences in cognitive abilities and educational background. *Experimental Aging Research, 3,* 337–383.

GELMAN, R. (1969). Conservation acquisition: A problem of learning to attend to relevant attributes. *Journal of Experimental Child Psychology, 7,* 167–187.

GELMAN, R. (1972a). Logical capacity of very young children: Number invariance rules. *Child Development, 43,* 75–90.

GELMAN, R. (1972b). The nature and development of early number concepts. In H. W. Reese (Ed.), *Advances in child development and behavior* (Vol. 7, pp. 115–167). New York: Academic Press.

GELMAN, R., & GALLISTEL, C. R. (1978). *The child's understanding of number.* Cambridge, MA: Harvard University Press.

GIBBS, J. C., WIDAMAN, K. F., & COLBY, A. (1982). Construction and validation of a simplified, group-administerable equivalent to the moral judgment interview. *Child Development, 53,* 895–910.

GINSBURG, H., & OPPER, S. (1979). *Piaget's theory of intellectual development: An introduction* (2nd ed.). Englewood Cliffs, NJ: Prentice-Hall.

GLASS, G. V., McGAW, B., & SMITH, M. L. (1981). *Meta-Analysis in social research.* Beverly Hills, CA: Sage Publications.

GOLDBERG, S., & LEWIS, M. (1969). Play behavior in the year-old infant: Early sex differences. *Child Development, 40,* 21–31.

GOLDSMITH, H. H. (1983). Genetic influences on personality from infancy to adulthood. *Child Development, 54,* 331–355.

GOTTESMAN, L. E., & BOURESTOM, N. C. (1974). Why nursing homes do what they do. *The Gerontologist, 14,* 501–506.

GOTTLIEB, G., & KRASNEGOR, N. A. (Eds.). (1984). *Measurement of audition and vision in the first year of postnatal life: A methodological overview.* Norwood, NJ: Ablex.

GRANICK, S., KLEBAN, M. H., & WEISS, A. D. (1976). Relationships between hearing loss and cognition in normally hearing aged persons. *Journal of Gerontology, 4,* 434–440.

GREEN, B. F., & HALL, J. A. (1984). Quantitative methods for literature reviews. In M. R. Rosenzweig & L. W. Porter (Eds.), *Annual review of psychology* (Vol. 35, pp. 37–53). Palo Alto, CA: Annual Reviews.

GREEN, P. E. (1978). *Analyzing multivariate data.* Hinsdale, IL: Dryden Press.

GREEN, R. F. (1969). Age-intelligence relationship between ages sixteen and sixty-four: A rising trend. *Developmental Psychology, 1,* 618–627.

GROSSMANN, K. E., & GROSSMANN, K. (1982, March). *Maternal sensitivity to infants' signals during the first year as related to the year-old's behavior in Ainsworth's strange situation in a sample of northern German families.* Paper presented at the meeting of the International Conference on Infant Studies, Austin, TX.

GRUEN, G. E. (1965). Experiences affecting the development of number conservation. *Child Development, 36,* 963–979.

GRUSEC, J. E. (1982). Prosocial behavior and self-control. In R. Vasta (Ed.), *Strategies and techniques of child study* (pp. 245–272). New York: Academic Press.

HAGEN, J. W., & KINGSLEY, P. R. (1968). Labeling effects in short-term memory. *Child Development, 39,* 113–121.

HAINLINE, L., & LEMERISE, E. (1982). Infants' scanning of geometric forms varying in size. *Journal of Experimental Child Psychology, 33,* 235–256.

HALE, G. A. (1977). On use of ANOVA in developmental research. *Child Development, 48,* 1101–1106.

HALL, J. A., & HALBERSTADT, A. G. (1980). Masculinity and femininity in children: Development of the Children's Personal Attributes Questionnaire. *Developmental Psychology, 16,* 270–280.

HARLOW, H. F. (1958). The nature of love. *American Psychologist, 13,* 673–685.

HARLOW, H. F. (1962). Fundamental principles for preparing psychology journal articles. *Journal of Comparative and Physiological Psychology, 55,* 893–896.

HARRIS, R. J. (1975). *A primer of multivariate statistics.* New York: Academic Press.

HARTLEY, J. T., HARKER, J. O., & WALSH, D. A. (1980). Contemporary issues and new directions in adult development of learning and memory. In L. W. Poon (Ed.), *Aging in the 1980s: Psychological issues* (pp. 239–252). Washington, DC: American Psychological Association.

HARTSHORNE, H., & MAY, M. A. (1928). *Studies in the nature of character: Volume 1. Studies in deceit.* New York: Macmillan.

HAYS, W. L. (1981). *Statistics* (3rd ed.). New York: Holt, Rinehart & Winston.

HERON, A., & CRAIK, F. I. M. (1964). Age differences in cumulative learning of meaningful and meaningless material. *Scandinavian Journal of Psychology, 1964, 5,* 209–217.

HERRNSTEIN, R. J. (1973). *IQ in the meritocracy.* Boston: Little, Brown.

HERSCH, R., PAOLITTO, D., & REIMER, J. (1979). *Promoting moral growth from Piaget to Kohlberg.* New York: Longman.

HERTZOG, C., SCHAIE, K. W., & GRIBBIN, K. (1978). Cardiovascular disease and changes in intellectual functioning from middle to old age. *Journal of Gerontology, 33,* 872–883.

HETHERINGTON, E. M., & FRANKIE, G. (1967). Effects of parental dominance, warmth, and conflict on imitation in children. *Journal of Personality and Social Psychology, 6,* 119–125.

HICKS, D. J. (1968). Effects of co-observer's sanctions and adult presence on imitative aggression. *Child Development, 39,* 303–309.

HOFFMAN, M. L. (1970). Conscience, personality, and socialization techniques. *Human Development, 13,* 90–126.

HOFFMAN, M. L. (1975). Sex differences in moral internalization and values. *Journal of Personality and Social Psychology, 32,* 720–729.

HOFFMAN, M. L. (1982). The measurement of empathy. In C. E. Izard (Ed.), *Measuring emotions in infants and children* (pp. 279–296). Cambridge, Eng.: Cambridge University Press.

HOFFMAN, M. L., & SALTZSTEIN, H. D. (1967). Parent discipline and the child's moral development. *Journal of Personality and Social Psychology, 5,* 45–57.

HOLLANDER, M., & WOLFE, D. A. (1973). *Nonparametric statistical methods.* New York: Wiley.

HOLLENBECK, A. R. (1978). Problems of reliability in observational research. In G. P. Sackett (Ed.), *Observing behavior: Volume 2. Data collection and analysis methods* (pp. 79–98). Baltimore: University Park Press.

HOLMES, T. H., & RAHE, R. H. (1967). The social readjustment rating scale. *Journal of Psychosomatic Research, 11,* 213–218.

HORKA, S., & FARROW, B. (1970). A methodological note on intersubject communication as a contaminating factor in psychological experiments. *Journal of Experimental Child Psychology, 10,* 363–366.

HORN, J. L., & DONALDSON, G. (1976). On the myth of intellectual decline in adulthood. *American Psychologist, 31,* 701–709.

HORN, J. L., & DONALDSON, G. (1977). Faith is not enough: A reply to the Baltes-Schaie claim that intelligence does not wane. *American Psychologist, 32,* 369–373.

HOROWITZ, M. J., & WILNER, N. (1980). Life events, stress, and coping. In L. W. Poon (Ed.), *Aging in the 1980s: Psychological issues* (pp. 363–374). Washington, DC: American Psychological Association.

HUBERT, N. C., WACHS, T. D., PETERS-MARTIN, P., & GANDOUR, M. J. (1982). The study of early temperament: Measurement and conceptual issues. *Child Development, 53,* 571–600.

HUESMANN, L. R., LAGERSPETZ, K., & ERON, L. D. (1984). Intervening variables in the TV violence-aggression relation: Evidence from two countries. *Developmental Psychology, 20,* 746–775.

HUITEMA, B. E. (1980). *The analysis of covariance and alternatives.* New York: Wiley.

HULTSCH, D. F. (1975). Adult age differences in retrieval: Trace-dependent and cue-dependent forgetting. *Developmental Psychology, 11,* 197–201.

HUNT, T. D. (1975). Early number "conservation" and experimenter expectancy. *Child Development, 46,* 984–987.

HUNTER, J. E., SCHMIDT, F. L., & JACKSON, G. B. (1982). *Meta-Analysis: Cumulating findings across studies.* Beverly Hills, CA: Sage Publications.

HUSTON, A. C. (1983). Sex-typing. In P. H. Mussen (Ed.), *Handbook of child psychology: Volume 4. Socialization, personality, and social development* (4th ed., pp. 387–467). New York: Wiley.

HYDE, J. S. (1981). How large are cognitive gender differences? A meta-analysis using ω^2 and d. *American Psychologist, 36,* 892–901.

HYDE, J. S., & PHILLIS, D. E. (1979). Androgyny across the life span. *Developmental Psychology, 15,* 334–336.

IMAMOGLU, E. O. (1975). Children's awareness and usage of intention cues. *Child Development, 46,* 39–45.

INHELDER, B., & PIAGET, J. (1958). *The growth of logical thinking from childhood to adolescence.* New York: Basic Books.

INHELDER, B., & PIAGET, J. (1964). *The early growth of logic in the child.* London: Routledge & Kegan Paul.

IRWIN, D. M., & BUSHNELL, M. M. (1980). *Observational strategies for child study.* New York: Holt, Rinehart & Winston.

IZARD, C. E. (1979). *The Maximally Discriminative Facial Movement Coding System (Max.)* Newark: University of Delaware, Instructional Resources Center.

JACKLIN, C., MACCOBY, E. E., & DICK, A. (1973). Barrier behavior and toy preferences: Sex differences (and their absence) in the year-old child. *Child Development, 44,* 196–200.

JEFFREY, D. B., HARTMANN, D. P., & GELFAND, D. M. (1972). A comparison of the effects of contingent reinforcement, nurturance, and nonreinforcement on imitative learning. *Child Development, 43,* 1053–1059.

JENCKS, C. (1972). *Inequality.* New York: Basic Books.

JENSEN, A. R. (1981). *Straight talk about mental tests.* New York: Free Press.

KAGAN, J. (1964). American longitudinal research on psychological development. *Child Development, 35,* 1–32.

KAGAN, J., & MOSS, H. A. (1962). *Birth to maturity.* New York: Wiley.

KAHANA, B. (1978). The use of projective tests in personality assessment of the aged. In M. Storandt, I. C. Siegler, & M. F. Elias (Eds.), *The clinical psychology of aging* (pp. 145–180). New York: Plenum.

KAIL, R., & BISANZ, J. (1982). Cognitive development: An information-processing perspective. In R. Vasta (Ed.), *Strategies and techniques of child study* (pp. 209–243). New York: Academic Press.

KAMIN, L. J. (1974). *The science and politics of IQ.* Hillsdale, NJ: Lawrence Erlbaum Associates.

KAUSLER, D. H. (1982). *Experimental psychology and human aging.* New York: Wiley.

KEASEY, C. B. (1978). Children's developing awareness and usage of intentionality and motives. In H. H. Howe, Jr. & C. B. Keasey (Eds.), *1977 Nebraska symposium on motivation* (pp. 219–260). Lincoln: University of Nebraska Press.

KEENEY, T., CANNIZZO, S. R., & FLAVELL, J. H. (1967). Spontaneous and induced verbal rehearsal in a recall task. *Child Development, 38,* 953–966.

KENNY, D. A. (1975). Cross-lagged panel correlation: A test for spuriousness. *Psychological Bulletin, 82,* 887–903.

KENNY, D. A. (1979). *Correlation and causality.* New York: Wiley.

KENT, R. N., & FOSTER, S. L. (1977). Direct observational procedures: Methodological issues in naturalistic settings. In A. R. Ciminero, K. S. Calhoun, & H. E. Adams (Eds.), *Handbook of behavioral assessment* (pp. 279–328). New York: Wiley.

KENT, R. N., O'LEARY, K. D., DIAMENT, C., & DIETZ, A. (1974). Expectation biases in observational evaluation of therapeutic change. *Journal of Consulting and Clinical Psychology, 42,* 774–780.

KEPPEL, G. (1982). *Design and analysis: A researcher's handbook* (2nd ed.). Englewood Cliffs, NJ: Prentice-Hall.

KERLINGER, F. N. (1986). *Foundations of behavioral research* (3rd ed.). New York: Holt, Rinehart & Winston.

KLAHR, D., & WALLACE, J. G. (1976). *Cognitive development: An information-processing view.* Hillsdale, N.J.: Lawrence Erlbaum Associates.

KLEIN, R. L. (1972). Age, sex, and task difficulty as predictors of social conformity. *Journal of Gerontology, 27,* 229–236.

KOFSKY, E. (1966). A scalogram study of classificatory development. *Child Development, 37,* 191–204.

KOHLBERG, L. (1966). A cognitive-developmental analysis of children's sex-role concepts and attitudes. In E. Maccoby (Ed.), *The development of sex differences* (pp. 82–173). Stanford, CA: Stanford University Press.

KOHLBERG, L. (1969). Stage and sequence: The cognitive-developmental approach to socialization. In D. A. Goslin (Ed.), *Handbook of socialization theory and research* (pp. 347–480). Chicago: Rand McNally.

KOHN, M. L., & CARROLL, E. E. (1960). Social class and the allocation of parental responsibilities. *Sociometry, 23,* 372–392.

KORNER, A. F., & THOMAN, E. B. (1970). Visual alertness in neonates as evoked by maternal care. *Journal of Experimental Child Psychology, 10,* 67–78.

KORNER, A. F., & THOMAN, E. B. (1972). The relative efficacy of contact and vestibular-proprioceptive stimulation in soothing neonates. *Child Development, 43,* 443–453.

KRAEMER, H. C., & JACKLIN, C. N. (1979). Statistical analysis of dyadic social behavior. *Psychological Bulletin, 86,* 217–224.

KURTINES, W., & GREIF, E. B. (1974). The development of moral thought: Review and evaluation of Kohlberg's approach. *Psychological Bulletin, 81,* 453–470.

LABOUVIE, E. W. (1980). Identity vs. equivalence of psychological measures and constructs. In L. W. Poon (Ed.), *Aging in the 1980s: Psychological issues* (pp. 493–502). Washington, DC: American Psychological Association.

LABOUVIE-VIEF, G., & CHANDLER, M. (1978). Cognitive development and life-span development theory: Idealist versus contextual perspectives. In P. B. Baltes (Ed.), *Life-span development and behavior* (Vol. 1, pp. 181–210). New York: Academic Press.

LAMB, M. E. (1976). Twelve-month-olds and their parents: Interaction in a laboratory playroom. *Developmental Psychology, 12,* 237–244.

LAMB, M. E., EASTERBROOKS, M. A., & HOLDEN, G. W. (1980). Reinforcement and punishment among preschoolers: Characteristics, effects, and correlates. *Child Development, 51,* 1230–1236.

LAMB, M. E., & ROOPNARINE, J. L. (1979). Peer influences on sex-role development in preschoolers. *Child Development, 50,* 1219–1222.

LAMB, M. E., SUOMI, S. J., & STEPHENSON, G. R. (Eds.). (1979). *Social interaction analysis.* Madison: University of Wisconsin Press.

LAMB, M. E., THOMPSON, R. A., & FRODI, A. M. (1982). Early social development. In R. Vasta (Ed.), *Strategies and techniques of child study* (pp. 49–81). New York: Academic Press.

LARSON, R. (1978). Thirty years of research on the subjective well-being of older Americans. *Journal of Gerontology, 33,* 109–125.

LARUE, A., BANK, L., JARVIK, L., & HETLAND, M. (1979). Health in old age: How do physicians' ratings and self-ratings compare? *Journal of Gerontology, 34,* 687–691.

LAURENCE, M. W. (1967). Memory loss with age: A test of two strategies for its retardation. *Psychonomic Science, 9,* 209–210.

LAWTON, M. P. (1975). The Philadelphia Geriatric Center Morale Scale: A revision. *Journal of Gerontology, 30,* 85–89.

LAWTON, M. P., WHELIHAN, W. M., & BELSKY, J. K. (1980). Personality tests and their uses with older adults. In J. E. Birren & R. B. Sloane (Eds.), *Handbook of mental health and aging* (pp. 537–553). Englewood Cliffs, NJ: Prentice-Hall.

LEFKOWITZ, M. M., ERON, L. D., WALDER, L. O., & HUESMANN, L. R. (1972). Television violence and child aggression: A followup study. In G. A. Comstock & E. A. Rubinstein (Eds.), *Television and social behavior: Volume 3. Television and adolescent aggressiveness* (pp. 35–135). Washington, DC: U.S. Government Printing Office.

LEWIS, M., & JOHNSON, N. (1971). What's thrown out with the bath water: A baby? *Child Development, 42,* 1053–1055.

LIBEN, L. S. (1977a). Memory from a cognitive-developmental perspective: A theoretical and empirical review. In W. Overton & J. Gallagher (Eds.), *Knowledge and development* (Vol. 1, pp. 149–203). New York: Plenum.

LIBEN, L. S. (1977b). Memory in the context of cognitive development: The Piagetian approach. In R. V. Kail & J. W. Hagen (Eds.), *Perspectives on the development of memory and cognition* (pp. 297–331). Hillsdale, NJ: Lawrence Erlbaum Associates.

LIBEN, L. S., & POSNANSKY, C. J. (1977). Inferences on inference: The effects of age, transitive ability, memory load, and lexical factors. *Child Development, 48,* 1490–1497.

LIEBERT, R. M., & BARON, R. A. (1972). Some immediate effects of televised violence on children's behavior. *Developmental Psychology, 6,* 469–475.

LIGHT, P. H., BUCKINGHAM, N., & ROBBINS, A. H. (1979). The conservation task as an interactional setting. *British Journal of Educational Psychology, 49,* 304–310.

LOEHLIN, J. C., LINDZEY, G., & SPUHLER, J. N. (1975). *Race differences in intelligence.* San Francisco: W. H. Freeman.

LOO, C., & WENAR, C. (1971). Activity level and motor inhibition: Their relationship to intelligence-test performance in normal children. *Child Development, 42,* 967–971.

MACCOBY, E. E., & JACKLIN, C. N. (1974). *The psychology of sex differences.* Stanford, CA: Stanford University Press.

MACCOBY, E. E., & MARTIN, J. A. (1983). Socialization in the context of the family: Parent-child interaction. In P. H. Mussen (Ed.), *Handbook of child psychology: Volume 4. Socialization, personality, and social development* (4th ed., pp. 1–101). New York: Wiley.

MADDOX, G. L. (1965). Fact and artifact: Evidence bearing on disengagement theory from the Duke Geriatrics Project. *Human Development, 8,* 117–130.

MADDOX, G. L., & DOUGLASS, E. B. (1974). Aging and individual differences: A longitudinal analysis of social, psychological, and physiological indicators. *Journal of Gerontology, 29,* 555–563.

MARASCUILO, L. A., & McSWEENEY, M. (1977). *Nonparametric and distribution free methods for the social sciences.* Monterey, CA: Brooks/Cole.

MARCUS, D. E., & OVERTON, W. F. (1978). The development of cognitive gender constancy and sex role preferences. *Child Development, 49,* 434–444.

MASUDA, M., & HOLMES, T. H. (1967). The social readjustment rating scale: A cross-cultural study of Japanese and Americans. *Journal of Psychosomatic Research, 11,* 227–237.

MATAS, L., AREND, R., & SROUFE, L. A. (1978). Continuity of adaptation in the second year: The relationship between quality of attachment and later competence. *Child Development, 49,* 547–556.

McCALL, R. B. (1977). Challenges to a science of developmental psychology. *Child Development, 48,* 333–344.

McCALL, R. B., PARKE, R. D., & KAVANAUGH, R. D. (1977). Imitation of live and televised models by children one to three years of age. *Monographs of the Society for Research in Child Development, 42* (5, Serial No. 173).

McCORMACK, P. D. (1981). Temporal coding by young and elderly adults: A test of the Hasher-Zacks model. *Developmental Psychology, 17,* 509–515.

McGARRIGLE, J., & DONALDSON, M. (1974). Conservation accidents. *Cognition, 3,* 341–350.

McLEOD, J. M., ATKIN, C. K., & CHAFFEE, S. H. (1972). Adolescents, parents, and television use: Adolescent self-report measures from Maryland and Wisconsin samples. In G. A. Comstock & E. A. Rubinstein (Eds.), *Television and social behavior: Volume 3. Television and adolescent aggressiveness* (pp. 173–238). Washington, DC: U.S. Government Printing Office.

MEHLER, J., & BEVER, T. G. (1967). Cognitive capacity of very young children. *Science, 158,* 141–142.

MEHRABIAN, A., & EPSTEIN, N. (1972). A measure of emotional empathy. *Journal of Personality, 40,* 525–543.

MILLER, D. T., WEINSTEIN, S. M., & KARNIOL, R. (1978). Effects of age and self-verbalization on children's ability to delay gratification. *Developmental Psychology, 14,* 569–570.

MILLER, P. H. (1983). *Theories of developmental psychology.* San Francisco: W. H. Freeman.

MILLER, S. A. (1976a). Nonverbal assessment of conservation of number. *Child Development, 47,* 722–728.

MILLER, S. A. (1976b). Nonverbal assessment of Piagetian concepts. *Psychological Bulletin, 83,* 405–430.

MILLER, S. A. (1977). A disconfirmation of the quantitative identity-quantitative equivalence sequence. *Journal of Experimental Child Psychology, 24,* 180–189.

MILLER, S. A. (1982). Cognitive development: A Piagetian perspective. In R. Vasta (Ed.), *Strategies and techniques of child study* (pp. 161–207). New York: Academic Press.

MITCHELL, S. K. (1979). Interobserver agreement, reliability, and generalizability of data collected in observational studies. *Psychological Bulletin, 86,* 376–390.

MOELY, B. E., OLSON, F. A., HAWLES, T. G., & FLAVELL, J. H. (1969). Production deficiency in young children's clustered recall. *Developmental Psychology, 1,* 26–34.

MONGE, R. H., & GARDNER, E. F. (1972). *A program of research in adult differences in cognitive performance and learning: Backgrounds for adult education and vocational retraining* (Grant No. OEG 1-7-06-1963-0149). Washington, DC: Office of Education.

MUSSEN, P., & EISENBERG-BERG, N. (1977). *Roots of caring, sharing, and helping: The development of prosocial behavior in children.* San Francisco: W. H. Freeman.

MYERS, G. C., & SOLDO, B. J. (1977). Older Americans: Who are they? In R. A. Kalish (Ed.), *The later years: Social applications of gerontology* (pp. 14–23). Monterey, CA: Brooks/Cole.

NEALE, J. M., & LIEBERT, R. M. (1980). *Science and behavior: An introduction to methods of research* (2nd ed.). Englewood Cliffs, NJ: Prentice-Hall.

NESSELROADE, J. R., & BALTES, P. B. (1974). Adolescent personality development and historical change: 1970–1972. *Monographs of the Society for Research in Child Development, 39,* (1, Whole No. 154).

NEUGARTEN, B. L., HAVIGHURST, R. J., & TOBIN, S. S. (1961). The measurement of life satisfaction. *Journal of Gerontology, 16,* 134–143.

NEWELL, A., & SIMON, H. A. (1972). *Human problem solving.* Englewood Cliffs, NJ: Prentice-Hall.

NEWMAN, B. M., & NEWMAN, P. R. (1984). *Development through life: A psychosocial approach.* Homewood, IL: Dorsey Press.

NICHOLS, R. C. (1976, September). *Heredity and environment: Major findings from twin studies of ability, personality, and interests.* Paper presented at the meeting of the American Psychological Association, Washington, DC.

NUMMEDAL, S. G., & BASS, S. C. (1976). Effects of the salience of intention and consequence on children's moral judgments. *Developmental Psychology, 12,* 475–476.

NUNNALLY, J. C. (1978). *Psychometric theory* (2nd ed.). New York: McGraw-Hill.

NUNNALLY, J. C. (1982). The study of human change: Measurement, research strategies, and methods of analysis. In B. B. Wolman (Ed.), *Handbook of developmental psychology* (pp. 133–148). Englewood Cliffs, NJ: Prentice-Hall.

OKUN, M. A., & ELIAS, C. S. (1977). Cautiousness in adulthood as a function of age and payoff structure. *Journal of Gerontology, 32,* 451–455.

ORNE, M. T. (1962). On the social psychology of the psychological experiment: With particular reference to demand characteristics and their implications. *American Psychologist, 17,* 776–783.

ORNSTEIN, P. A., NAUS, M. J., & LIBERTY, C. (1975). Rehearsal and organization processes in children's memory. *Child Development, 46,* 818–830.

OWENS, W. A., Jr. (1966). Age and mental ability: A second follow-up. *Journal of Educational Psychology, 57,* 311–325.

PACHELLA, R. (1974). The interpretation of reaction time in information processing research. In B. Kantowitz (Ed.), *Human information processing: Tutorials in performance and cognition* (pp. 41–82). Hillsdale, NJ: Lawrence Erlbaum Associates.

PALMORE, E. (Ed.). (1971). *Normal aging I: Reports of the Duke longitudinal studies, 1955–1969.* Durham, NC: Duke University Press.

PALMORE, E. (Ed.). (1974). *Normal aging II: Reports from the Duke longitudinal studies, 1970–73.* Durham, NC: Duke University Press.

PALUDI, M. A. (1981). Sex role discrimination among girls: Effect on IT Scale for Children scores. *Developmental Psychology, 17,* 851–852.

PARIS, S. G. (1975). Integration and inference in children's comprehension and memory. In F. Restle, R. Shiffrin, J. Castellan, H. Lindman, & D. Pisoni (Eds.), *Cognitive theory* (Vol. 1, pp. 223–246). Hillsdale, NJ: Lawrence Erlbaum Associates.

PARIS, S. G., & CARTER, A. Y. (1973). Semantic and constructive aspects of sentence memory in children. *Developmental Psychology, 9,* 109–113.

PARIS, S. G., & MAHONEY, G. J. (1974). Cognitive integration in children's memory for sentences and pictures. *Child Development, 45,* 633–642.

PARIS, S. G., & UPTON, L. R. (1976). Children's memory for inferential relationships in prose. *Child Development, 47,* 660–668.

PARKE, R. D. (1967). Nurturance, nurturance withdrawal, and resistance to deviation. *Child Development, 38,* 1101–1110.

PARKE, R. D. (1969). Effectiveness of punishment as an interaction of intensity, timing, agent nurturance, and cognitive structuring. *Child Development, 40,* 213–236.

PARKE, R. D. (1979). Interactional designs. In R. B. Cairns (Ed.), *The analysis of social interactions: Methods, issues, and illustrations* (pp. 15–35). Hillsdale, NJ: Lawrence Erlbaum Associates.

PARKE, R. D., BERKOWITZ, L., LEYENS, J. P., WEST, S. G., & SEBASTIAN, R. J. (1977). Some effects of violent and nonviolent movies on the behavior of juvenile delinquents. In L. Berkowitz, (Ed.), *Advances in experimental social psychology* (Vol. 10, pp. 135–172). New York: Academic Press.

PARKE, R. D., & WALTERS, R. H. (1967). Some factors determining the efficacy of punishment for inducing response inhibition. *Monographs of the Society for Research in Child Development, 32,* (1, Serial No. 109).

PARMELEE, A. H., WENNER, W. H., & SCHULZ, H. R. (1964). Infant sleep patterns from birth to 16 weeks of age. *Journal of Pediatrics, 65,* 576–582.

PATTERSON, C. J., & CARTER, D. B. (1979). Attentional determinants of children's self-control in waiting and working situations. *Child Development, 50,* 272–275.

PATTERSON, G. R. (1979). A performance theory for coercive family interaction. In R. B. Cairns (Ed.), *The analysis of social interactions: Methods, issues, and illustrations* (pp. 119–162). Hillsdale, NJ: Lawrence Erlbaum Associates.

PATTERSON, G. R. (1982). *Coercive family process.* Eugene, OR: Castalia Press.

PATTERSON, G. R., & COBB, J. A. (1971). A dyadic analysis of "aggressive" behaviors. In J. P. Hill (Ed.), *Minnesota symposia on child psychology* (Vol. 5, pp. 72–129). Minneapolis: University of Minnesota Press.

PEDHAZUR, E. J. (1982). *Multiple regression in behavioral research* (2nd ed.). New York: Holt, Rinehart & Winston.

PERLMUTTER, M. (1978). What is memory aging the aging of? *Developmental Psychology, 14,* 330–345.

PERRY, D. G., & BUSSEY, K. (1984). *Social development.* Englewood Cliffs, NJ: Prentice-Hall.

PERRY, D. G., & PERRY, L. C. (1975). Observational learning in children: Effects of sex of model and subject's sex role behavior. *Journal of Personality and Social Psychology, 31*, 1083–1088.

PFEIFFER, E. (Ed.). (1975). *Multidimensional Functional Assessment: The OARS methodology*. Durham, NC: Center for the Study of Aging and Human Development.

PIAGET, J. (1926). *The language and thought of the child*. New York: Harcourt Brace.

PIAGET, J. (1929). *The child's conception of the world*. London: Routledge & Kegan Paul.

PIAGET, J. (1932). *The moral judgment of the child*. London: Routledge & Kegan Paul.

PIAGET, J. (1951). *Play, dreams, and imitation in childhood*. New York: Norton.

PIAGET, J. (1952). *The origins of intelligence in children*. New York: International Universities Press.

PIAGET, J. (1954). *The construction of reality in the child*. New York: Basic Books.

PIAGET, J., & INHELDER, B. (1956). *The child's conception of space*. London: Routledge & Kegan Paul.

PIAGET, J., & INHELDER, B. (1973). *Memory and intelligence*. New York: Basic Books.

PIAGET, J., & INHELDER, B. (1974). *The child's construction of quantities*. London: Routledge & Kegan Paul.

PIAGET, J., & SZEMINSKA, A. (1952). *The child's conception of number*. Atlantic Highlands, NJ: Humanities.

PLOMIN, R. (1981). Heredity and temperament: A comparison of twin data for self-report questionnaires, parental ratings, and objectively assessed behavior. In L. Gedda, P. Parisi, & W. Nance (Eds.), *Twin research 3: Intelligence, personality, and development* (pp. 269–278). New York: Liss.

POLYSON, J., LEVINSON, M., & MILLER, H. (1982). Writing styles: A survey of psychology journal editors. *American Psychologist, 37*, 335–338.

PORGES, S. W. (1979). Developmental designs for infancy research. In J. D. Osofsky (Ed.), *Handbook of infant development* (pp. 742–765). New York: Wiley.

PORTER, R., & COLLINS, G. (Eds.). (1982). *Temperamental differences in infants and young children*. London: Pitman Books.

PRESSLEY, M., LEVIN, J. R., & BRYANT, S. L. (1983). Memory strategy instruction during adolescence: When is explicit instruction needed? In M. Pressley & J. R. Levin (Eds.), *Cognitive strategy research: Psychological foundations* (pp. 25–49). New York: Springer-Verlag.

RAHE, R. H. (1979). Life change events and mental illness: An overview. *Journal of Human Stress, 5*, 2–10

REICHARDT, C. S. (1979). The statistical analysis of data from nonequivalent group designs. In T. D. Cook & D. T. Campbell (Eds.), *Quasi-Experimentation* (pp. 147–205). Boston: Houghton Mifflin.

REID, J. B. (1970). Reliability assessment of observation data: A possible methodological problem. *Child Development, 41*, 1143–1150.

REINERT, G. (1970). Comparative factor analytic studies of intelligence throughout the human life-span. In L. R. Goulet & P. B. Baltes (Eds.), *Life-span developmental psychology: Research and theory* (pp. 467–484). New York: Academic Press.

REST, J. R. (1979). *Development in judging moral issues*. Minneapolis: University of Minnesota Press.

REST, J. R. (1983). Morality. In P. H. Mussen (Ed.), *Handbook of child psychology: Volume 3. Cognitive development* (4th ed., pp. 556–629). New York: Wiley.

RHEINGOLD, H. L. (1982). Ethics as an integral part of research in child development. In R. Vasta (Ed.), *Strategies and techniques of child study* (pp. 305–325). New York: Academic Press.

RICHARDSON, G. A., & McCLUSKEY, K. A. (1983). Subject loss in infancy research: How biasing is it? *Infant Behavior and Development, 6*, 235–239.

ROGOSA, D. (1980). A critique of cross-lagged correlation. *Psychological Bulletin, 88*, 245–258.

ROSE, S. A., & BLANK, M. (1974). The potency of context in children's cognition: An illustration through conservation. *Child Development, 45*, 499–502.

ROSE, S. A., SCHMIDT, K., & BRIDGER, W. H. (1978). Changes in tactile responsivity during sleep in the human newborn infant. *Developmental Psychology, 14*, 163–172.

ROSENBERG, M. J. (1965). When dissonance fails: On eliminating evaluation apprehension from attitude measurement. *Journal of Personality and Social Psychology, 1*, 28–42.

ROSENTHAL, R. (1968). Experimenter expectancy and the reassuring nature of the null hypothesis decision procedure. *Psychological Bulletin Monograph Supplement, 70*, 30–47.

ROSENTHAL, R. (1976). *Experimenter effects in behavioral research* (enl. ed.). New York: Halsted Press.

ROSS, J. B., & McLAUGHLIN, M. M. (Eds.). (1949). *The portable medieval reader*. New York: Viking Press.

ROTHBART, M. K., & DERRYBERRY, D. (1981). Development of individual differences in temperament. In M. E. Lamb & A. L. Brown (Eds.), *Advances in developmental psychology* (Vol. 1, pp. 37–86). Hillsdale, NJ: Lawrence Erlbaum Associates.

RUBIN, K. H. (1978). Role taking in childhood: Some methodological considerations. *Child Development, 49*, 428–433.

RUBIN, R. A., & BALOW, B. (1979). Measures of infant development and socioeconomic status as predictors of later intelligence and school achievement. *Developmental Psychology, 15*, 225–227.

RUSHTON, J. P. (1980). *Altruism, socialization, and society*. Englewood Cliffs, NJ: Prentice-Hall.

RUSHTON, J. P., BRAINERD, C. J., & PRESSLEY, M. (1983). Behavioral development and construct validity. The principle of aggregation. *Psychological Bulletin, 94*, 18–38.

RUTHERFORD, E., & MUSSEN, P. (1968). Generosity in nursery school boys. *Child Development, 39*, 755–765.

SACKETT, G. P. (Ed.). (1978). *Observing behavior: Volume 2. Data collection and analysis methods*. Baltimore: University Park Press.

SACKETT, G. P. (1979). The lag sequential analysis of contingency and cyclicity in behavioral interaction research. In J. D. Osofsky (Ed.), *Handbook of infant development* (pp. 623–649). New York: Wiley.

SACKETT, G. P., RUPPENTHAL, G. C., & GLUCK, J. (1978). Introduction: An overview of methodological and statistical problems in observational research. In G. P. Sackett (Ed.), *Observing behavior: Volume 2. Data collection and analysis methods* (pp. 1–14). Baltimore: University Park Press.

SALTHOUSE, T. A. (1982). *Adult cognition: An experimental psychology of human aging*. New York: Springer-Verlag.

SALTHOUSE, T. A. (in press). Speed of behavior and its implications for cognition. In J. E. Birren & K. W. Schaie (Eds.), *Handbook of the psychology of aging* (2nd ed.). New York: Van Nostrand Reinhold.

SANDERS, R. E., MURPHY, M. D., SCHMITT, F. A., & WALSH, K. K. (1980). Age differences in free recall rehearsal strategies. *Journal of Gerontology, 35*, 550–558.

SASLOW, C. A. (1982). *Basic research methods*. Reading, MA: Addison-Wesley.

SAWIN, D. B. (1979, March). *Assessing empathy in children: A search for an elusive construct.* Paper presented at the meeting of the Society for Research in Child Development, San Francisco, CA.

SAWIN, D. B. (1980). *A field study of children's reactions to distress in their peers.* Unpublished manuscript, University of Texas, Austin, TX.

SCARR, S. (1977). *Genetic effects on human behavior: Recent family studies.* Washington, DC: American Psychological Association.

SCARR, S. (1981). *Race, social class, and individual differences in IQ: New studies of old problems.* Hillsdale, NJ: Lawrence Erlbaum Associates.

SCHAFFER, H. R., & EMERSON, P. (1964). The development of social attachments in infancy. *Monographs of the Society for Research in Child Development, 29* (3, Serial No. 94).

SCHAIE, K. W. (1958). Rigidity-flexibility and intelligence: A cross-sectional study of the adult life-span from 20 to 70. *Psychological Monographs, 72* (9, Whole No. 462).

SCHAIE, K. W., & BALTES, P. B. (1977). Some faith helps to see the forest. A final comment on the Horn and Donaldson myth of the Baltes-Schaie position on adult intelligence. *American Psychologist, 32,* 1118–1120.

SCHAIE, K. W., LABOUVIE, G. V., & BARRETT, T. J. (1973). Selective attrition effects in a fourteen-year study of adult intelligence. *Journal of Gerontology, 28,* 328–334.

SCHAIE, K. W., LABOUVIE, G., & BUECH, B. (1973). Generational and cohort-specific differences in adult cognitive functioning: A fourteen year study of independent samples. *Developmental Psychology, 9,* 151–166.

SCHAIE, K. W., & LABOUVIE-VIEF, G. (1974). Generational vs. ontogenetic components of change in adult cognitive behavior: A fourteen-year cross-sequential study. *Developmental Psychology, 10,* 305–320.

SCHAIE, K. W., & PARHAM, I. A. (1977). Cohort-sequential analyses of adult intellectual development. *Developmental Psychology, 13,* 649–653.

SCHAIE, K. W., & STROTHER, C. R. (1968). A cross-sequential study of age changes in cognitive behavior. *Psychological Bulletin, 70,* 671–680.

SCHEIDT, R. J., & SCHAIE, K. W. (1978). A taxonomy of situations for the elderly population: Generating situational criteria. *Journal of Gerontology, 33,* 848–857.

SCHNEIDER, B. A., TREHUB, S. E., & BULL, D. (1980). High-frequency sensitivity in infants. *Science, 207,* 1003–1004.

SCHONFIELD, D., & ROBERTSON, E. A. (1966). Memory storage and aging. *Canadian Journal of Psychology, 20,* 228–236.

SEARS, R. R., MACCOBY, E. E., & LEVIN, H. (1957). *Patterns of childrearing.* Stanford, CA: Stanford University Press.

SEARS, R. R., RAU, L. R., & ALPERT, R. (1965). *Identification and child rearing.* Stanford, CA: Stanford University Press.

SEITZ, V. (1980). Statistical issues and comparative methods. In M. H. Bornstein (Ed.), *Comparative methods in psychology* (pp. 149–182). Hillsdale, NJ: Lawrence Erlbaum Associates.

SEITZ, V. (1984). Methodology. In M. H. Bornstein & M. E. Lamb (Eds.), *Developmental psychology: An advanced textbook* (pp. 37–79). Hillsdale, NJ: Lawrence Erlbaum Associates.

SERBIN, L. A., CONNOR, J. M., & CITRON, C. C. (1981). Sex-differentiated free play behavior: Effects of teacher modeling, location, and gender. *Developmental Psychology, 17,* 640–646.

SHANTZ, C. U. (1975, April). *Communication skills and social-cognitive development.* Paper presented at the meeting of the Society for Research in Child Development, Denver, CO.

SHIFFRIN, R. M., & ATKINSON, R. C. (1969). Storage and retrieval processes in long-term memory. *Psychological Review, 76,* 179–193.

SIEGEL, L. S. (1978). The relationship of language and thought in the preoperational child: A reconsideration of non-verbal alternatives to Piagetian tasks. In L. S. Siegel & C. J. Brainerd (Eds.), *Alternatives to Piaget: Critical essays on the theory* (pp. 43–67). New York: Academic Press.

SIEGEL, L. S., MCCABE, A. E., BRAND, J., & MATTHEWS, J. (1978). Evidence for the understanding of class inclusion in preschool children: Linguistic factors and training effects. *Child Development, 49,* 688–693.

SIEGEL, S. (1956). *Nonparametric statistics for the behavioral sciences.* New York: McGraw-Hill.

SIEGLER, I. C. (1975). The terminal drop hypothesis: Fact or artifact? *Experimental Aging Research, 1,* 169–185.

SIEGLER, I. C., & BOTWINICK, J. (1979). A long-term longitudinal study of intellectual ability of older adults: The matter of selective subject attrition. *Journal of Gerontology, 34,* 242–245.

SIEGLER, I. C., NOWLIN, J. B., & BLUMENTHAL, J. A. (1980). Health and behavior: Methodological considerations for adult development and aging (1980). In L. W. Poon (Ed.), *Aging in the 1980s: Psychological issues* (pp. 599–612). Washington, DC: American Psychological Association.

SIEGLER, R. S. (1978). The origins of scientific reasoning. In R. S. Siegler (Ed.), *Children's thinking: What develops?* (pp. 109–149). Hillsdale, NJ: Lawrence Erlbaum Associates.

SIEGLER, R. S. (1981). Developmental sequences within and between concepts. *Monographs of the Society for Research in Child Development, 46,* (2, Serial No. 189).

SIEGLER, R. S. (1983). Information processing approaches to development. In P. H. Mussen (Ed.), *Handbook of child psychology: Volume 1. History, theory, and methods* (4th ed., pp. 129–211). New York: Wiley.

SILVERMAN, I. (1977). *The human subject in the psychological laboratory.* New York: Pergamon.

SILVERMAN, I., & SCHNEIDER, D. S. (1968). A study of the development of conservation by a nonverbal method. *Journal of Genetic Psychology, 112,* 287–291.

SIMON, E. (1979). Depth and elaboration of processing in relation to age. *Journal of Experimental Psychology: Human Learning and Memory, 5,* 115–124.

SIMON, H. A. (1972). On the development of the processor. In S. Farnham-Diggory (Ed.), *Information processing in children* (pp. 3–22). New York: Academic Press.

SMITH, C., & LLOYD, B. (1978). Maternal behavior and perceived sex of infant: Revisited. *Child Development, 49,* 1263–1266.

SMITH, I. D. (1968). The effects of training procedures upon the acquisition of conservation of weight. *Child Development, 39,* 515–526.

Society for Research in Child Development (1973, Winter). Ethical standards for research with children. *Newsletter,* 3–5.

SOPHIAN, C. (1980). Habituation is not enough: Novelty preferences, search, and memory in infancy. *Merrill-Palmer Quarterly, 26,* 239–257.

SPENCE, J. T., & HELMREICH, R. L. (1978). *Masculinity and femininity: Their psychological dimensions, correlates, and antecedents.* Austin: University of Texas Press.

SPIETH, W. (1965). Slowness of task performance and cardiovascular disease. In A. T. Welford & J. E. Birren (Eds.), *Behavior, aging, and the nervous system* (pp. 366–400). Springfield, IL: Charles C. Thomas.

SROUFE, L. A., WATERS, E., & MATAS, L. (1974). Contextual determinants of infant affective response. In M. Lewis & L. A. Rosenblum (Eds.), *The origins of fear* (pp. 49–72). New York: Wiley.

STANOVICH, K. E. (1976). Note on the interpretation of interactions in comparative research. *American Journal of Mental Deficiency, 81,* 394–396.

STEIN, A. H., & SMITHELLS, J. (1969). Age and sex differences in children's sex-role standards about achievement. *Developmental Psychology, 1,* 252–259.

STERNBERG, R. J. (1977). *Writing the psychology paper.* Woodbury, NY: Barron's Educational Series.

STEVENS, S. S. (1968). Measurement, statistics, and the schemapiric view. *Science, 161,* 849–856.

STEVENSON, H. W. (1965). Social reinforcement of children's behavior. In L. P. Lipsitt & C. C. Spiker (Eds.), *Advances in child development and behavior* (Vol. 2, pp. 97–126). New York: Academic Press.

STONE, L. J., & CHURCH, J. (1973). *Childhood and adolescence* (3rd ed.). New York: Random House.

STORANDT, M., & HUDSON, W. (1975). Misuse of analysis of covariance in aging research and some partial solutions. *Experimental Aging Research, 1,* 121–125.

STRAUSS, M., & COHEN, L. B. (1980, April). *Infant immediate and delayed memory for perceptual dimensions.* Paper presented at the meeting of the International Conference on Infant Studies, New Haven, CT.

STRAUSS, S., & LEVIN, I. (1981). Commentary. *Monographs of the Society for Research in Child Development, 46,* (2, Serial No. 189).

STRUNK, W., Jr., & WHITE, E. B. (1979). *The elements of style* (3rd ed.). New York: Macmillan.

TANNENBAUM, A. S., & COOKE, R. A. (1977). Research involving children. In National Commission for the Protection of Human Subjects of Biomedical and Behavioral Research (Eds.), *Appendix to report and recommendations on research involving children* (pp. 1-1-1-129). Washington, DC: U.S. Government Printing Office.

TAPLIN, P. S., & REID, J. B. (1973). Effects of instructional set and experimenter influence on observer reliability. *Child Development, 44,* 547–554.

TAUB, H. A. (1974). Coding for short-term memory as a function of age. *Journal of Genetic Psychology, 125,* 309–314.

TERMAN, L. M., & MERRILL, M. A. (1973). *Stanford-Binet Intelligence Scale.* Boston: Houghton Mifflin.

THOMAS, A., BIRCH, H. G., CHESS, S., HERTZIG, M., & KORN, S. (1963). *Behavioral individuality in early childhood.* New York: New York University Press.

THOMAS, A., & CHESS, S. (1977). *Temperament and development.* New York: Brunner/Mazel.

THOMAS, A., CHESS, S., & BIRCH, H. (1968). *Temperament and behavior disorders in children.* New York: New York University Press.

THOMPSON, N. L., & MCCANDLESS, B. R. (1970). It score variations by instructional style. *Child Development, 41,* 425–436.

THOMPSON, R. A., & HOFFMAN, M. L. (1980). Empathy and the development of guilt in children. *Developmental Psychology, 16,* 155–156.

THOMPSON, R. A., LAMB, M. E., & ESTES, D. (1982). Stability of infant-mother attachment and its relationship to changing life circumstances in an unselected middle class sample. *Child Development, 53,* 144–148.

THOMPSON, S. K. (1975). Gender labels and early sex-role development. *Child Development, 46,* 339–347.

THOMPSON, S. K., & BENTLER, P. M. (1971). The priority of cues in sex discriminations by children and adults. *Developmental Psychology, 5,* 181–185.

THORNDIKE, R. L. (1933). The effect of the interval between test and retest on the constancy of IQ. *Journal of Educational Psychology, 24,* 543–549.

THURSTONE, L. L., & THURSTONE, T. G. (1962). *SRA Primary Mental Abilities.* Chicago: Science Research Associates.

TILL, R. E., & WALSH, D. A. (1980). Encoding and retrieval factors in adult memory for implicational sentences. *Journal of Verbal Learning and Verbal Behavior, 19,* 1–16.

TOUSSAINT, N. A. (1974). An analysis of synchrony between concrete-operational tasks in terms of structure and performance demands. *Child Development, 45,* 992–1001.

TRABASSO, T. (1975). Representation, memory, and reasoning: How do we make transitive inferences? In A. D. Pick (Ed.), *Minnesota symposia on child psychology* (Vol. 9, pp. 135–172). Minneapolis: University of Minnesota Press.

TRABASSO, T., & NICHOLAS, D. W. (1980). Memory and inferences in the comprehension of narratives. In F. Wilkening, J. Becker, & T. Trabasso (Eds.), *Information integration by children* (pp. 215–242). Hillsdale, NJ: Lawrence Erlbaum Associates.

TRABASSO, T., RILEY, C. A., & WILSON, E. G. (1975). The representation of linear order and spatial strategies in reasoning: A developmental study. In R. Falmagne (Ed.), *Reasoning: Representation and process* (pp. 201–229). Hillsdale, NJ: Lawrence Erlbaum Associates.

Trials of war criminals before the Nuremberg military tribunals, U. S. vs. Karl Brandt (Volume 2) (1949). Washington, DC: U. S. Government Printing Office.

TURNER, B. F. (1982). Sex-related differences in aging. In B. B. Wolman (Ed.), *Handbook of developmental psychology* (pp. 912–936). Englewood Cliffs, NJ: Prentice-Hall.

UNDERWOOD, B. J., & SHAUGHNESSY, J. J. (1975). *Experimentation in psychology.* New York: Wiley.

VOYAT, G. E. (1982). *Piaget systematized.* Hillsdale, NJ: Lawrence Erlbaum Associates.

WADE, N. (1976). IQ and heredity: Suspicion of fraud beclouds classic experiment. *Science, 194,* 916–919.

WALK, R. D. (1981). *Perceptual development.* Belmont, CA: Brooks/Cole.

WALK, R. D., & GIBSON, E. J. (1961). A comparative and analytical study of visual depth perception. *Psychological Monographs, 75* (15, Whole No. 519).

WALLACH, L., WALL, A. J., & ANDERSON, L. (1967). Number conservation: The role of reversibility, addition-subtraction, and misleading perceptual cues. *Child Development, 38,* 425–442.

WATERS, E., WIPPMAN, J., & SROUFE, L. A. (1979). Attachment, positive affect, and competence in the peer group: Two studies in construct validation. *Child Development, 50,* 821–829.

WEBB, E. J., CAMPBELL, D. T., SCHWARTZ, R. D., & SECHREST, L. (1966). *Unobtrusive measures: Nonreactive research in the social sciences.* Chicago: Rand McNally.

WECHSLER, D. (1958). *The measurement and appraisal of adult intelligence* (4th ed.). Baltimore: Williams & Wilkins.

WECHSLER, D. (1967). *Wechsler Preschool and Primary Scale of Intelligence.* New York: The Psychological Corporation.

WECHSLER, D. (1974). *Wechsler Intelligence Scale for Children—Revised.* New York: The Psychological Corporation.

WECHSLER, D. (1981). *Wechsler Adult Intelligence Scale—Revised.* New York: The Psychological Corporation.

WEIZMANN, F., COHEN, L. B., & PRATT, R. J. (1971). Novelty, familiarity, and the development of infant attention. *Developmental Psychology, 4,* 149–154.

WELLMAN, H. M., & CIALDINI, R. (1980, Fall). Guidelines for reviewing research in developmental psychology. *Newsletter of the American Psychological Association Division on Developmental Psychology,* pp. 50–64.

WELLMAN, H. M., RITTER, K., & FLAVELL, J. H. (1975). Deliberate memory behavior in the delayed reactions of very young children. *Developmental Psychology, 11,* 780–787.

WETHERFORD, M. J., & COHEN, L. B. (1973). Developmental changes in infant visual preferences for novelty and familiarity. *Child Development, 44,* 416–424.

WHITE, M. A., & DUKER, J. (1973). Suggested standards for children's samples. *American Psychologist, 28,* 700–703.

WILKIE, F., & EISDORFER, C. (1971). Intelligence and blood pressure. *Science, 172,* 959–962.

WILKINSON, A. C. (1980). Children's understanding in reading and listening. *Journal of Educational Psychology, 72,* 561–574.

WILLEMSEN, E. (1979). *Understanding infancy.* San Francisco: W. H. Freeman.

WILLERMAN, L. (1979). Effects of families on intellectual development. *American Psychologist, 34,* 923–929.

WILLIS, S. L., & BALTES, P. B. (1980). Intelligence in adulthood and aging. In L. W. Poon (Ed.), *Aging in the 1980s: Psychological issues* (pp. 260–272). Washington, DC: American Psychological Association.

WINER, B. J. (1971). *Statistical principles in experimental design* (2nd ed.). New York: McGraw-Hill.

WOHLWILL, J. F. (1973). *The study of behavioral development.* New York: Academic Press.

WOLFF, P. H. (1966). The causes, controls, and organization of behavior in the neonate. *Psychological Issues, 5,* 7–11.

WOODS, W. S., RESNICK, L. B., & GROEN, G. J. (1975). An experimental test of five process models for subtraction. *Journal of Educational Psychology, 67,* 17–21.

World Medical Association (1964). Declaration of Helsinki. In H. K. Beecher (Ed.), *Research and the individual: Human studies* (pp. 277–278). Boston: Little, Brown.

YARROW, M. R., CAMPBELL, J. D., & BURTON, R. V. (1968). *Child rearing: An inquiry into research and methods.* San Francisco: Jossey-Bass.

YARROW, M. R., CAMPBELL, J. D., & BURTON, R. V. (1970). Recollections of childhood: A study of the retrospective method. *Monographs of the Society for Research in Child Development, 35,* (5, Serial No. 138).

YARROW, M. R., & WAXLER, C. Z. (1976). Dimensions and correlates of prosocial behavior in young children. *Child Development, 47,* 118–125.

YARROW, M. R., & WAXLER, C. Z. (1979). Observing interaction: A confrontation with methodology. In R. B. Cairns (Ed.), *The analysis of social interactions: Methods, issues, and illustrations* (pp. 37–65). Hillsdale, NJ: Lawrence Erlbaum Associates.

YONAS, A., BECHTOLD, A. G., FRANKEL, D., GORDON, F. R., McROBERTS, G., NORCIA, A., & STERNFELS, S. (1977). Development of sensitivity to information for impending collision. *Perception and Psychophysics, 21,* 97–104.

YOUNISS, J. (1980). *Parents and peers in social development.* Chicago: University of Chicago Press.

ZAHN-WAXLER, C., RADKE-YARROW, M., & KING, R. A. (1979). Child rearing and children's prosocial initiations toward victims of distress. *Child Development, 50,* 319–330.

ZELNICKER, T., OPPENHEIMER, L., & RENAN, A. (1975). Effect of dimensional salience and salience of variability on problem solving: A developmental study. *Developmental Psychology, 11,* 334–341.

ZIMMERMAN, B. J., & ROSENTHAL, T. L. (1974). Conserving and retaining equalities and inequalities through observation and correction. *Developmental Psychology, 10,* 260–268.

INDEXES

Name Index

Subject Index

Activity Theory, 237
Adopted child studies, 144
Affective Situation Test for Empathy, 172-73
Age:
   designs for comparing, 35-44
   as a variable, 18-19, 32, 39, 213
Aggregate, 83
Aggression:
   in home setting, 202-4
   measurement of, 13-14, 71, 72, 74
   and television violence, 70-81, 199-200, 280
Aging, 211-243
   designs for studying, 223-26
   and intelligence test performance, 212-26
   measurement issues, 218-23
   and memory, 11, 227-34
   and personality and social development, 234-41
   sampling issues, 212-18
Analysis of covariance, 213-14
Analysis of variance, 254-61
APA style, 292-94
   headings, 292-93
   measurements, 293
   numbers, 293
   references, 294
   statistics, 293-94
Attachment, 114-21

Baby biography, 107
Bayley Scales of Infant Development, 137, 141
Bem Sex-Role Inventory, 187, 188
Between-subject design, 31-32, 44-49, 96, 255
Blinding, 65-66, 89, 184, 185
Brazelton Neonatal Behavioral Assessment Scale, 197

Carry-over effects, 46-47
Causality:
   Piaget's studies of, 108-9
Ceiling effect, 5
Central tendency, 245-46
Cheating, 165, 169, 275, 276, 279, 280
Childrearing, 2, 120, 204-8
Children's Personal Attributes Questionnaire, 189-90
Chi square test, 252
Classification variables (*see* Subject variables)
Class inclusion, 125-26, 130
Clinical method, 128-29, 174